Kursstufe Sek. II

Pathway
Advanced

Lese- und Arbeitsbuch für die gymnasiale Oberstufe

Herausgegeben und erarbeitet von:
Iris Edelbrock

Unter beratender Mitwirkung von:
Katharina Einhoff
Alexandra Peschel
Dagmar Rothenberger

Sprachliche Betreuung:
Elin Arbin

Schöningh
westermann

Begleitmaterialien zum Lehrwerk für Schülerinnen und Schüler

Pathway Advanced Audio-CDs
3 CDs mit Hörtexten und Songs, Transkripte im Booklet
Best.-Nr. 062761-0

Pathway Advanced Abi *kompakt*
Thematic Vocabulary – Important Facts – Relevant Skills
Best.-Nr. 040184-5

westermann GRUPPE

Druck A^3/ Jahr 2018
Alle Drucke der Serie A sind im Unterricht parallel verwendbar.

Umschlaggestaltung: Nora Krull, Bielefeld; Fotos: © John R. Rogers Photography (vorn); stock.adobe.com/VladBrik (hinten)
Druck und Bindung: Westermann Druck GmbH, Braunschweig

ISBN 978-3-14-**040183**-8

Contents

Level of difficulty:
●○○ basic ●●○ intermediate ●●● advanced

M Mediation between German and English
Listening comprehension
☒ Comprehension tasks available (copies)
Listening comprehension (text supported)

Shaken, Not Stirred?! – The U.K. Between Tradition and Modernity

Once There Was ... An Empire ...

The Commonwealth – Common Sense? – Post-Colonial Tasks & Challenges

Ethnic Communities in the U.K.

Splendid Isolation? – The U.K.'s Position in the 21st Century

India: Democracy, Diversity and Determination

Start-up Activities

The Raj – Britain's Dreams and India's Nightmares

21st Century India: Booms, Boons and Burdens

The American Dream – Reveries and Realities

Start-up Activities

America and Americans: Insights and Outlooks

Founding and Shaping a Nation ... Political and Historical Visions and Challenges

"Separate But Equal" ... The African-American Struggle for Civil Rights

Africa – Between Exploitation and Expectation

The World Going Global: Opportunities and Options

Democracy Going Global: Peace, Stability and Human Rights

Science and Technology: Man Between Molecules and Machines

Communication or Confusion? – English Around the World

Start-up Activities

It's English, Stupid! – English as a Changing Language

Varieties of English

Key word/ terminology	Example	Definition	What you are expected to do
Level II: Analysis and re-structuring of texts			
analyse/examine *analysieren/ untersuchen*	Analyse the opposing views on immigration presented in the text. Examine the author's use of language.	describe and explain in detail certain aspects and/or features of a text	• focus on the structure of the text and pay attention to details • formulate a connecting sentence (contents → analysis) at the beginning • be as precise as possible by using the correct terms and expressions • use quotations/direct references to lines in the text to prove the accuracy of your analysis → FoS, Analysis of a Fictional Text, p. 374 → FoS, Analysis of a Non-Fictional Text, p. 377 → FoL, Vocabulary and Phrases for Text Analysis, p. 412 → FoL, Connectives and Adverbs, p. 404
characterize/write a characterization *charakterisieren/im Detail beschreiben und erklären*	Characterize/Write a characterization of the main character in the play.	analyse the typical features of sb., then describe, explain and interpret the way in which the character(s) is/are presented	• highlight/underline important details about the character and take notes in the margin, using different colours for specific devices • pay attention to details: do not cover everything but focus on the most striking devices/details • use quotations/direct references to lines in the text to prove the accuracy of your analysis → FoS, Characterization of a Figure in Literature, p. 383
explain *erklären*	Explain the protagonist's obsession with money.	describe and define in detail	• highlight/underline important details in the text and take notes in the margin, using different colours for specific devices • pay attention to details: do not cover everything but focus on the most striking devices/details • refer directly to certain lines/arguments etc. and use quotations and/or refer to lines in the text • be as precise as possible by using the correct terms and expressions → FoS, Analysis of a Fictional Text, p. 374 → FoS, Analysis of a Non-Fictional Text, p. 377
illustrate *veranschaulichen*	Illustrate the author's use of metaphorical language.	use examples to explain or make clear	• pay attention to details: do not cover everything but focus on the most striking devices/details • choose the most relevant/significant examples from the text for your explanation • use quotations/direct references to lines in the text to prove the accuracy of your analysis
interpret *interpretieren*	Interpret the message the author wishes to convey.	make clear the meaning of sth.	• try to read "between the lines" and use your background knowledge • do not give wordy explanations and opinions but be as specific and precise as possible • refer directly to certain lines/arguments etc. and use quotations and/or refer to lines in the text

Key word/ terminology	Example	Definition	What you are expected to do
compare *vergleichen*	Compare the view of the two writers on recycling. Compare the behaviour of the women.	point out similarities and/or differences of things/characters/ situations	• before writing your comparison, underline the most relevant differences/similarities in the text using different colours • make a table in two columns and compare/ juxtapose the different aspects and details • refer directly to certain lines/arguments etc. and use quotations and/or refer to lines in the text
Level III: Discussion/evaluation/text production			
comment (on) *Stellung nehmen*	Comment on the statement that the American Dream is over.	state clearly your opinions/views on a topic and support your views with evidence/arguments/reference to the text(s)	• before writing your text, make a table in two columns and juxtapose views/arguments/ evidence that refer to the argument <u>and</u> the counterargument of the matter • give your opinion on the topic/matter but do not be personal – your judgment should be based on evidence and facts • connect aspects/arguments given in the text with your background knowledge and further references • be careful not to just reproduce something that you have learned by heart but paraphrase and refer to the most specific/exemplary aspects • finish your text with a concluding sentence → FoF, Basic Types of Non-Fictional Texts, p. 368 → FoL, Conversation and Discussion, p. 385
evaluate *einschätzen/ einordnen/ bewerten*	Evaluate the author's view on the impact of global migration.	form an opinion after carefully considering a topic/question and presenting advantages and disadvantages	
assess *beurteilen*	Assess the importance of standards in education.	make a judgement after thinking carefully about the points for and against sth.	
discuss * *erörtern*	Discuss the consequences of consumerism as referred to in the text.	investigate or examine by argument; give reasons/examples for and against	• weigh different arguments and counter-arguments of a matter • try to take different positions on an issue • collect ideas/arguments and structure them before writing your text • finish your text with a conclusion that summarizes the most important aspects • do not express your own opinion but refer to aspects dealt with in the text → FoL, Conversation and Discussion, p. 385
justify *rechtfertigen/ begründen*	You are a CEO of a company. Justify your decision to give a microcredit loan to a village in Nigeria.	show adequate grounds for decisions and conclusions	• before writing your text, collect reasons and examples that support your decision • consider the weight of your arguments/reasons and structure them • finish your text with a concluding and summarizing statement → FoL, Conversation and Discussion, p. 385

* The task "Discuss (in class)" focuses on an oral activity together with a group rather than a written evaluation of a topic.

Key word/ terminology	Example	Definition	What you are expected to do
contrast *gegenüberstellen*	Contrast the main characters' opposing views on the USA.	emphasize the difference between two or more things	• before writing your text, make a table in two columns and juxtapose views/arguments/ evidence that refer to the argument <u>and</u> the counterargument of the matter • refer directly to certain lines/arguments etc. and use quotations and/or refer to lines in the text • collect ideas/arguments and structure them before writing your text
prove *am Text belegen*	Prove the effects of Western values on developing countries.	give evidence to provide a clear and convincing argument	• before writing your text, collect ideas about the respective matter and structure them • give examples and refer to background information on relevant aspects/arguments • do not give wordy explanations and opinions; be as specific and precise as possible • refer directly to certain lines/arguments etc. and use quotations and/or refer to lines in the text → FoF, Basic Types of Non-Fictional Texts, p. 368
reflect on *reflektieren/ bedenken*	Reflect on how the author deals with the problem of exploiting workers in sweatshops.	express your thoughts in a carefully considered and balanced way	• before writing, underline/highlight key words and relevant aspects in the text • collect ideas on how you want to respond to the matter • weigh different aspects/arguments by juxtaposing them in a table • you may state your opinion on the issue but avoid being personal – be factual and precise • finish your text with a concluding and summarizing statement → FoL, Conversation and Discussion, p. 385

Task Marker

START-UP ACTIVITIES Reactivating knowledge, preparing the new topic, introducing the new unit

AWARENESS Introducing a new text, giving an impetus

COMPREHENSION Tasks for the understanding, comprehension and reproduction of texts

ANALYSIS Tasks for the analysis, examination and interpretation of texts

ACTIVITIES Tasks for further discussion, creative writing, presentation, etc.

GRAMMAR/LANGUAGE Reactivating grammar and language skills, grammar exercises in context. Basic grammatical rules and examples can be found on the webcode SNG-40183-047 under www.schoeningh-schulbuch.de/webcode. Solutions are provided under SNG-40183-048.

Shaken, Not Stirred?! – The U.K. Between Tradition and Modernity

The Queen's performance as a Bond girl with actor Daniel Craig during the opening ceremonies of the 2012 Summer Olympics in London

> "You have become, to many of us, a kaleidoscope Queen, of a kaleidoscope country, in a kaleidoscope Commonwealth."
>
> John Bercow, Speaker of the House of Commons, in his address to HM the Queen, on occasion of her Diamond Jubilee in June 2012

"Solar-powered Queen and Corgi": solar panels on top of the Queen's bag and the pedestal of the Corgi power the Queen's royal hand wave and the movement of the Corgi's head

Tips on vocab

a parachute ■ Union flag/Jack design ■ Welsh Corgi ■ solar-powered collectible/souvenir

Tips on vocab

warm/earthy colours ■ symmetrical arrangement of ornaments ■ graphic design ■ native people ■ feathered headdress ■ pineapple ■ wooden club ■ protective shield ■ muscular physique ■ golden/silver bracelets

START-UP ACTIVITIES

1. The opening ceremony of the Olympic Games is commonly used to present the host country's culture and tradition.
   a) What does the Queen's performance as a Bond girl convey about Great Britain – and the Queen – in general?

   Webcode SNG-40183-001 @

   b) Watch the video of the Queen's performance using the webcode, and exchange your impressions in a group. What elements do you consider to be most appealing and convincing?
   c) The "Solar Queen" and her "Solar Corgi" are highly popular collectibles in the U.K. and elsewhere. Do you think these are funny and witty promotional items or kitschy "junk"?

2. What does John Bercow's remark reflect about the self-image of the British nation and its Queen?

3. What is the first thing that comes to your mind when you think about Britain? In a group, compile a website (e.g. "www.kaleidoscope-britain.co.uk") based on John Bercow's remark. Your websites can be funny, provocative or critical.

4. Look at the historical British advert dating back to the time of the Empire. Which function did the African colonies have – and what does the advert indirectly reveal about Britain as an imperial power?

5. Compare John Bercow's perception of Britain's position today with the view taken in the historical advert. Which similarities and differences can you detect? Discuss in class.

Britishness? Englishness? – Being British Today

What Being British Means ...

AWARENESS

Look at the design of the www.webritish.com homepage below. Which image of "Being British"/"Britishness" does it convey?

In a group, collect further ideas of what

a) you associate with Britishness,

b) *commonly* is presented as "typically British".

Discuss your ideas in class.

1 Being British is about loving this country, remembering the past and honouring the people who fought from the battlefields of France, to the deserts of North Africa, into the sands of Arabia and jungles of Asia, but also looking to the future, learn from history and build upon past mistakes, be proud to be British as we are a happy race of man, these islands a testament of Nature's Beauty, we have inhabited these islands for Thousands of Years, we built a culture and identity that is uniquely British, we built an Empire, stood defiantly[1] against the Evils of Hitler Nazi German and Stalin's Soviet Union. Today I think the only way to describe Britain is from a poem by Alfred Tennyson[2], "Though we are not that strength which on old days moved Earth and Heaven, that which we are, we are, one equal temper[3] of heroic hearts made weak by time but not in will, to strive[4] to seek, but not to yield[5]". Remember We Are, We Can & We Will, go forward like a breath exhaled[6] from the Earth ...

Toby, Maidstone, England

2 Being British isn't about being a specific race or culture, Britain is made up of 4 different countries, England, Ireland, Scotland and Wales. Do Scottish people call themselves British? Or do they call themselves Scottish? I was born it Britain and educated in Britain, worked etc. ... Does that make me British? Both my parents are British and the family I know of also British, but who am I to call myself British if I'm unsure myself? Ancestors and people I do not know about may or may not be British, which makes me reevaluate[7] whether I'm British or not. Biased[8] opinions of having to be white and speak the English language are where most of the problems are at. Just because somebody is black or Muslim[9] – does that give us the right to judge on what identity they are? Being British is simply about loving the country we live in, being proud to call yourself British and doing anything possible to be a good British citizen. If you truly believe that you are British, you are citizen and you help ...

Loren, Salford, United Kingdom

[1] **defiant** [dɪˈfaɪənt] *trotzig* – [2] **Alfred Tennyson** (1809–1892) one of the most popular and famous British poets – [3] **temper** here: character – [4] **to strive** (strove, striven) to try very hard to achieve sth. – [5] **to yield** here: to surrender; *aufgeben, kapitulieren* – [6] **to exhale** *ausatmen* – [7] **to reevaluate sth.** to think about sth. again, esp. to form a new opinion about it – [8] **biased** [ˈbaɪəst] *voreingenommen sein* – [9] **Muslim** [ˈmʊzlɪm]

3 To be British is to be multicultural. The 4 nations that make up Britain, each with their own cultures, the many peoples that conquered us in our ancient history and the many we conquered in more recent times have all contributed to our multi-cultural culture and multi-lingual language.
James, United Kingdom

4 British characteristics are contradictory[10] – eccentricity with privacy, pride with self-effacement[11], pragmatism with tradition. We're a people of innovation, on a permanent nostalgia trip.
Tim Staddon, United Kingdom

5 I was born in Afghanistan and came to Britain (legally) as a child with my parents – I am a British Afghan. I am proud to be British and proud to be an Afghan. I value the cultural and religious diversity of the British society. Being a citizen is about making positive contribution to society and living in harmony with others. We Brits moan[12] too much instead of appreciating the good things that we have!!
Safia, London, United Kingdom

6 Red Post boxes. Red buses. Number 10[13]. The Queen. British Bull dogs. Sunday Roast. Black Cabs. The Beatles. Bowler hats[14]. Laurel and Hardy[15]. Stiff upper lip[16]. London. The Union Jack. Parliament. Guy Fawkes[17]. British Ale. Margaret Thatcher[18]. Charles Darwin. The internet. Britannia[19]. Fish and Chips. Seaside Holidays. Blackpool. The BBC. The Church of England. Churchill. Lord Sugar[20]. Sir Paul McCartney. Queen. The 80's. CHAVs[21]. Council Estates[22]. Patrony[23].
Mary, Colchester, UK

www.webritish.co.uk [17.12.2014]

COMPREHENSION

1. Divide the class into groups of 3 – 4 students each, with half of the groups dealing with the "red" statements (1, 3, 6) and the other half with the "blue" statements (2, 4, 5).

Step 1: In a **first reading, skim** the statements and try to understand the **gist** of what is said. Pay attention to the most relevant information (who – where – when – what – why).

Step 2: In your groups, prepare posters on which you finish these sentences, using key terms from the statements above:

- "Being British is about …"
- "Important British characteristics are …"
- "British culture is based on …"

Step 3: Now, the "blue" and "red" groups mix and exchange their findings, adding further statements on their respective poster.
When reporting to each other what the respective letter writer said, **use indirect speech** and be careful to backshift the tenses if necessary.

Step 4: Display your posters in class and discuss your results, making alterations and/or corrections if necessary.

[10] **contradictory** *widersprüchlich* – [11] **self-effacement** *Zurückhaltung* – [12] **to moan** *stöhnen; lamentieren* – [13] **Number 10** 10 Downing Street, the address of the British Prime Minister in London – [14] **Bowler hat** *die Melone* – [15] **Laurel and Hardy**, Stan Laurel (1890 – 1965), Oliver Hardy (1892 – 1957), *Dick und Doof*, a comedy double act during the early Hollywood era – [16] **a stiff upper lip** (*idm.*) to keep calm and hide your feelings when you are in pain or in a difficult situation – [17] **Guy Fawkes** (1570 – 1606) a member of a group of English Catholics who planned the Gunfire Plot of 1605 – [18] **Margaret Thatcher** (1925 – 2013) Prime Minister of the UK (1979 – 1990) and Leader of the Conservative Party – [19] **Britannia** personification of Great Britain – [20] **Lord Sugar** (*1947) an English business magnate – [21] **CHAV** [tʃæv](*sl., derogatory*) a young lower-class person who displays brash and loutish behaviour and wears real or imitation designer clothes – [22] **Council Estates** *Siedlung mit Sozialwohnungen* – [23] **patrony** here: the act of patronizing one's peers

ANALYSIS

2. After a **second reading**, examine and analyse the choice of words and the use of positive and/or negative emotive words. What do they reveal about each person's stance on Britain's culture and tradition?
→ Focus on Skills, Analysis of a Non-Fictional Text, p. 374

3. Compare your findings from tasks 1 and 2 to your results from the awareness task – which similarities and differences in explaining "Britishness/Being British" can you detect? Complete the grid below.

external view (*your* findings)	**internal view**
• … • …	• a happy race of man • …

4. Take a closer look at clichés or stereotypes that
a) the letter writers use themselves and
b) you associated with Britishness in the awareness task.
Discuss possible similarities and differences in class.

Info

cliché
a phrase or an idea that has been used so often that it no longer has much meaning and is not interesting

stereotype
an idea that many people have of a particular person or thing, but which is often not true in reality

The terms are often used as synonyms.

ACTIVITIES

5. Do you think that people see their home country more clearly when they are abroad – or are they blinded by nostalgic feelings? Give a comment.

6. For a long time, Germans were unable to express their national identity – "waving the flag" in particular was associated with Nazism and right-wing politics.
This changed in 2006, when Germany hosted the world football championship during the so-called *Sommermärchen* and showed itself to be a hospitable, open-minded and modern nation. And again, in 2014, the Germans celebrated the football championship as a "festival of black, red and gold" and have obviously become a more "relaxed nation" when it comes to showing national pride and cheering for their team.
Looking at the matter of "national pride" and "national identity" from a German perspective, do you think there is a German equivalent to "Britishness" – something like "Germanness"? Where do you consider the border to be between "healthy national pride" and a fascist way of thinking?
Discuss in class.

Tips on vocab

national pride ■ to be proud of one's nationality ■ national consciousness ■ national feeling/sentiment ■ national anthem (*Nationalhymne*) ■ nationality ■ patriot/patriotic/patriotism ■ patriotically-minded ■ to sound patriotic

Webcode SNG-40183-002

7. Do a project on the various facets and aspects of "Being British" using the links provided on the webcode. You might focus on British contributions to science, culture, economy, famous British inventions, etc. You can either prepare a presentation or compile a "Being British" homepage on the topic.
→ Focus on Skills, Presentations, p. 391
→ Focus on Facts, Landmarks in British History, p. 38

Webcode SNG-40183-002 @

8. Prepare a presentation on "Britishness" based on the two-part BBC documentary provided on the webcode. The documentary presents a variety of different people and perspectives on the disputed topic of Britishness and national pride. Additionally, compile a brief handout for your classmates in which you outline the most relevant information given in the documentary.
→ Focus on Skills, Presentations, p. 391
→ Focus on Skills, Writing a Handout, p. 397

Info

On 5 July 2005, four Islamist men detonated bombs in the London Underground and on a bus, killing 52 civilians and injuring more than 700 people, which reignited a heated national debate on the potential danger radical Muslims pose on British society.
Against that background, the Chancellor of the Exchequer (*Finanzminister*), Gordon Brown, gave a speech in 2006 in which he promoted a "modern patriotism" and the integration of diverse cultures into British society. Thus, he intended to fight Islamophobia (*Anti-Islamismus*) and to diminish the growing influence of right-wing parties in the U. K.
He suggested that Britain have a national day to celebrate its national identity and Britons should embrace the Union Flag as a symbol of unity, liberty, fairness and responsibility. Brown hoped to reclaim the flag from the right-wing British National Party (BNP), which in contrast used the flag as a symbol of racial division.

Stephen Castle

Sadiq Khan Elected in London, Becoming Its First Muslim Mayor

AWARENESS

Step 1: Pair up with a partner and research on the Internet what a mayor's duties, responsibilities and tasks are.

Step 2: Collect and exchange your ideas about the characteristics, professional qualifications and personal skills a mayor should have in order to

- address the needs of various social groups in the community/city,
- be a good contact person for (local) businesses and companies,
- manage the many areas of administrative work.

In a Europe struggling with a rise in Islamophobia, riven[1] by debates about the flood of Syrian migrants and on edge[2] over religious, ethnic and cultural disputes, London has elected its first Muslim mayor.
Sadiq Khan – Labour Party leader, a former human rights lawyer and a son of a bus driver from Pakistan – was declared the winner after a protracted[3] count that extended into Saturday. He will be the first Muslim to lead Britain's capital.
The victory also makes him one of the most prominent Muslim politicians in the West.
London is hardly representative of Britain: About a quarter of its residents are foreign-born, and one-eighth are Muslim. And Mr. Khan is not the first Muslim to hold prominent office in Europe: Rotterdam, in the Netherlands, has had a Muslim mayor since 2009,

and Sajid Javid is the British secretary of state for business.
Nonetheless, Mr. Khan, 45, won a striking victory after a campaign dominated by anxieties over religion and

[1] **riven** violently divided – [2] **to be on edge** to be nervous, excited or bad-tempered – [3] **protracted** lasting for a long time or made to last longer than necessary

ethnicity. Britain has not sustained[4] a large-scale terrorist attack since 2005, and its Muslim population, in contrast to France, is considered well integrated. But an estimated 800 people have left Britain to fight for or support the Islamic State. Dozens of assaults on British Muslims were reported after the Paris terrorist attacks in November.

The Conservative candidate, Zac Goldsmith, attacked Mr. Khan's past advocacy[5] for criminal defendants, including his opposition to the extradition[6] of a man who was later convicted in the United States of supporting terrorism. Mr. Goldsmith said Mr. Khan had given "oxygen and cover" to extremists. When the Conservative prime minister, David Cameron, repeated those assertions[7] in Parliament, he was accused of racism.

Mr. Khan defended his work as a human rights lawyer, and has said he hoped Donald J. Trump – the presumptive[8] Republican presidential candidate who has called for barring Muslims from entering the United States – "loses badly."

Mr. Khan's victory was also his party's biggest boost in a series of elections on Thursday in which Labour further lost its grip on Scotland, once a stronghold[9], and clung[10], in some cases just barely, to seats in England and Wales.

Mr. Khan won with 56.8 percent of the vote, versus 43.2 percent for Mr. Goldsmith, according to London's election body. The results were not final until Saturday morning because in London's electoral system voters are allowed a first and second preference, and Mr. Khan did not win an outright majority in the first round.

In his acceptance speech, Mr. Khan said that the mayoral election "was not without controversy" and added that he was "proud that London has today chosen hope over fear and unity over division."

"I hope that we will never be offered such a stark choice again. Fear does not make us safer, it only makes us weaker and the politics of fear is simply not welcome in our city."

Mr. Khan's campaign focused on bread-and-butter issues like the cost of housing and transportation. He drew strong support from labor unions and kept a careful distance from his party's leader, Jeremy Corbyn, a socialist who has an ardent[11] base among young voters but faces heavy resistance among fellow Labour lawmakers.

In the past week, the Labour Party was distracted[12] by a dispute over anti-Semitism that led to the suspension[13] of a lawmaker, Naseem Shah, and a former London mayor, Ken Livingstone.

Mr. Khan argued that, as an observant Muslim, he was well placed to tackle extremism. "I'm a Londoner, I'm European, I'm British, I'm English, I'm of Islamic faith, of Asian origin, of Pakistani heritage, a dad, a husband," he said in a recent interview with The New York Times.

The fifth of eight children, Mr. Khan was born in Tooting, South London, to recent immigrants from Pakistan, and grew up in a public-housing project. His father drove a bus, and his mother was a seamstress[14].

Elected to Parliament in 2005, Mr. Khan was appointed a junior minister for communities in 2008, and minister for transport in 2009 under the last Labour prime minister, Gordon Brown. Although he was not one of the highest-ranking ministers, he became the first Muslim to attend cabinet meetings regularly and was admitted to the Privy Council[15], a largely ceremonial body in which induction normally requires taking an oath to the queen.

"The palace called me and said, 'What type of Bible do you want to swear on?'" Mr. Khan told the magazine The New Statesman. "When I said the Quran, they said, 'We haven't got one.' So I took one with me."

As London's mayor, he will have significant power over transportation and planning – as well as responsibilities for the police, civil defense and fire services – in a city with an acute shortage of affordable homes and a creaking[16], overcrowded mass transit network.

Mr. Khan will succeed Boris Johnson, a Conservative who has held the post since 2008 and is a leading figure in the campaign for Britain's departure from the European Union. That vote will take place on June 23 [2016]. Mr. Johnson is seen as a possible successor to Mr. Cameron as leader of the Conservatives, particularly if Britain votes to leave; Mr. Cameron is campaigning for Britain to remain.

Within Britain, the news of the collapse of the Labour Party in Scotland was almost as big as Mr. Khan's victory.

[4] **to sustain sth.** *(fml.)* to experience something bad – [5] **advocacy** the act of publicly supporting an idea, development or way of doing sth. – [6] **extradition** the return of sb. accused of a crime to the country where the crime was committed – [7] **assertion** a statement that you strongly believe is true – [8] **presumptive** *mutmaßlich* – [9] **stronghold** *Festung, Bollwerk* – [10] **cling** (clung, clung) *sich an jdn./etw. klammern* – [11] **ardent** *leidenschaftlich, inbrünstig* – [12] **distracted** *abgelenkt* – [13] **suspension** a punishment in which a person is temporarily not allowed to work; *Suspendierung* – [14] **seamstress** *Näherin, Schneiderin* – [15] **Privy Council** [ˌprɪvi ˈkaʊnsəl] in the U.K., a group of people of high ranks in politics who sometimes advise the king or queen but who have little power – [16] **to creak** *quietschen*

The Scottish National Party won its third straight victory in the Scottish Parliament – a triumph that its leader, Nicola Sturgeon, called historic, even though the party narrowly lost its majority. The Labour Party fell to a humiliating third place, behind the Conservatives, who won seats in part by appealing to Scots opposed to independence. Scots rejected independence in a 2014 referendum, but there is speculation that a new referendum could be called, particularly if Britain leaves the European Union.

http://www.nytimes.com/2016/05/07/world/europe/britain-election-results.html?_r=0, 6 May 2016 [07.07.2016]

COMPREHENSION

1. Complete the following sentence with evidence from the text:
   Sadiq Khan, London's new mayor, has been a controversial mayoral candidate because …

2. Give examples from the text that
   - describe London's special/exceptional status,
   - reveal London's and Britain's ongoing controversy about Islamophobia and Muslims,
   - prove Mr Khan's suitability for the job,
   - refer to the difficult political situation Britain finds itself in.

3. Team up with a partner and, in a paired reading activity, do the assignments below. After each step, exchange and crosscheck your results and make corrections and additions if necessary.

Tips on vocab

to be humbled here: to be honoured ■ **council estate** an area with low-income houses built by a local council ■ **to thrive** to grow, develop or be successful ■ **commute** a regular journey between work and home ■ **to afford sth.** to be able to buy or do sth. because you have enough money or time ■ **stark** here: unpleasant

1 CD 1

Step 1: In a **first listening**, specify Khan's words and phrases that underline the inaugural and honorary character of the speech.
→ Focus on Skills, Listening Comprehension, p. 366

Webcode SNG-40183-003

Tip: In order to get a better impression of Khan's performance, use the links provided on the webcode and watch the speech.

Step 2: In a **second listening**, take notes on what Khan states about
- his personal/family background,
- his electorate/voters,
- the city of London,
- his understanding of politics,
- his future plans as Mayor of London.

ANALYSIS

4. Examine the style of the *New York Times* article and determine what kind of text it is.
   → Focus on Facts, Basic Types of Non-Fictional Texts, p. 368

5. **Listen** to Sadiq Khan's mayoral acceptance speech **again** and examine his abilities as a speaker. Which specific rhetorical devices does he use to appeal to his listeners?
   → Focus on Skills, Analysis of a Political Speech, p. 379

ACTIVITIES

6. Sadiq Khan made a promise throughout his campaign which he confirmed after his election: "I promise to always be a mayor for all Londoners".
Discuss whether or not this is a realistic promise, given the controversy during Khan's election campaign and the ongoing discussion about Islamophobia and religious and cultural conflict in connection with refugees.
→ Focus on Language, Conversation and Discussion, p. 385

Huge Survey[1] Reveals Seven Social Classes in UK

AWARENESS

Look at the cartoon below and describe the people's outward appearance and behaviour. What "social classes" do you think these people belong to? Give reasons for your assumptions.

Step 1: Previously, the traditional categories for distinguishing social groups were working, middle and upper class. Together with a partner, collect ideas about possible social, economic and cultural characteristics that go along with the three social classes.

Step 2: As the headline of the article suggests, in addition to the three previous social classes, four "new" social classes have been revealed in a recent survey conducted[2] by the BBC. Speculate about these "new" social classes and about social, economic and cultural markers that identify them.

Tips on vocab

first class: to wear a bowler (hat) ■ to look dolled up (*aufgedonnert*) ■ teased (*toupiert*) hair ■ fur collar (*Pelzkragen*) ■ to look snobby/snobbish/uppish (*hochnäsig*)

economy class: backpacker ■ (traveling) salesman ■ shirt-sleeved (*hemdsärmelig*)

no class: drops of sweat ■ to be petrified of sb./sth. (*panische Angst haben vor jdm./etw.*) ■ to pick one's nose ■ to fart (*furzen*) ■ (to suffer from) flatulence (*an Blähungen leiden*) ■ to belch/to burp (*rülpsen*) ■ in disgust (*angewidert*)

People in the UK now fit into seven social classes, a major survey conducted by the BBC suggests.
It says the traditional categories of working, middle and upper class are outdated[3], fitting 39 % of people.
It found a new model of seven social classes ranging from the elite at the top to a "precariat[4]" – the poor, precarious[5] proletariat – at the bottom.
More than 161,000 people took part in the Great British Class Survey, the largest study of class in the UK.

Class has traditionally been defined by occupation[6], wealth and education. But this research argues that this is too simplistic[7], suggesting that class has three dimensions – economic, social and cultural.

[1] **survey** *Umfrage, Erhebung* – [2] **to conduct sth.** *etw. durchführen* – [3] **outdated** no longer useful because of being old-fashioned – [4] **precariat** the poor – [5] **precarious** not safe or certain, dangerous – [6] **occupation** job or profession – [7] **simplistic** (*disapproving*) making a situation or problem seem less difficult or complicated than it really is

The BBC Lab UK study measured economic capital – income, savings, house value – and social capital – the number and status of people someone knows.

The study also measured cultural capital, defined as the extent and nature of cultural interests and activities.

The new classes are defined as:

- **Elite[8]:** the most privileged group in the UK, distinct from[9] the other six classes through its wealth. This group has the highest levels of all three capitals.
- **Established middle class:** the second wealthiest, scoring[10] highly on all three capitals. The largest and most gregarious[11] group, scoring second highest for cultural capital.
- **Technical middle class:** a small, distinctive[12] new class group which is prosperous[13] but scores low for social and cultural capital. Distinguished[14] by its social isolation and cultural apathy[15].
- **New affluent[16] workers:** a young class group which is socially and culturally active, with middling levels of economic capital.
- **Traditional working class:** scores low on all forms of capital, but is not completely deprived[17]. Its members have reasonably high house values, explained by this group having the oldest average age at 66.
- **Emergent[18] service workers:** a new, young, urban group which is relatively poor but has high social and cultural capital.
- **Precariat, or precarious proletariat:** the poorest, most deprived class, scoring low for social and cultural capital.

The researchers said while the elite group had been identified before, this is the first time it had been placed within a wider analysis of the class structure, as it was normally put together with professionals and managers.

At the opposite extreme they said the precariat, the poorest and most deprived grouping, made up 15 % of the population.

The sociologists[19] said these two groups at the extremes of the class system had been missed in conventional approaches[20] to class analysis, which have focused on the middle and working classes. [...]

The researchers also found the established middle class made up 25 % of the population and was the largest of all the class groups, with the traditional working class now only making up 14 % of the population.

They say the new affluent workers and emergent service workers appear to be the children of the "traditional working class," which they say has been fragmented by de-industrialisation, mass unemployment, immigration and the restructuring of urban space.

www.bbc.com/news/uk-22007058, 3 April 2013 [23.07.2014]

COMPREHENSION

1. In a **first reading**, **skim** the article and jot down five aspects that the researchers found that had changed over time.

2. **Scan** the text in a **second reading**, looking for information about
   - what has changed in the definition of a social class,
   - which social classes have been determined,
   - new elements in the ranking system of society,
   - possible reasons for these social changes.

ANALYSIS

3. Have a look at the diagrams on p. 27 and relate the markers and characteristics given there to the information revealed in the text. Which additional information is given?

[8] **elite** [eɪˈliːt] – [9] **distinct from** clearly different or of a different kind – [10] **to score** to get points – [11] **gregarious** [grɪˈgeəriəs] sociable; *gesellig* – [12] **distinctive** characteristic – [13] **prosperous** rich – [14] **distinguished** very successful and admired by other people – [15] **apathy** [ˈæpəθi] the feeling of not being interested in things in general – [16] **affluent** (*fml.*) wealthy – [17] **deprived** *sozial benachteiligt* – [18] **emergent** *aufsteigend* – [19] **sociologist** [ˌsəʊsiˈɒlədʒɪst] – [20] **approach** *Vorgehensweise, Denkansatz*

Webcode SNG-40183-004 @

4. Do further research on the BBC survey using the *Daily Mail* link provided on the webcode and compile a pie chart that gives an overview of the social classes and includes the relevant statistical information. Present your diagrams in class and discuss your various results.
→ Focus on Skills, Analysis of Statistical Data, p. 380

5. Examine the choice of words used to categorize each of the social classes and compare them to the older expressions. Explain the respective implications.

social group	choice of words	intended meaning
elite	• wealthiest, most privileged • …	→ superlatives; top rank in society
established middle class	• …	→ …
technical middle class	• …	→ …
new affluent workers	• …	
traditional working class	• traditional • low on capital • …	→ stagnation → …
emergent service workers	• …	
precariat (precarious proletariat)	• …	

ACTIVITIES

6. The text indicates that the elite group has traditionally been associated with "professionals and managers" and that the "traditional working class" has declined to only 14 % of the population.
Against the background of the information given on the seven social classes and their characteristics, which professions or jobs would you assign to the respective classes? How much annual income do you think the different social classes have? Discuss in class.

Info

- In Germany, somebody who earns less than 60 % of the average income (= less than 940 euros a month) is considered poor.
- About 15 % of the German population is close to being defined as poor.
- In Germany, about 5.5 % of the population is defined as "working poor", i. e. people who have an extremely low-paying job.
- Examples: 3 % of the German population earn more than 4,500 euros per month; 14 % earn 2,100 – 2,600 euros per month; 19 % earn 901 – 1,300 euros per month and 6 % earn less than 500 euros per month.
- In the US, being poor is defined as
  - single person: earning less than $11,490 per year,
  - a family of four: earning less than $23,550 per year.

GRAMMAR / LANGUAGE

7. Reactivate your knowledge and **vocabulary** and collect words, expressions and phrases in connection with the topics
- social class,
- income,
- work/profession,
- culture.

Collect relevant words from the text and use your dictionary for further help. Arrange your findings in clusters, then compare your results with a partner.

1

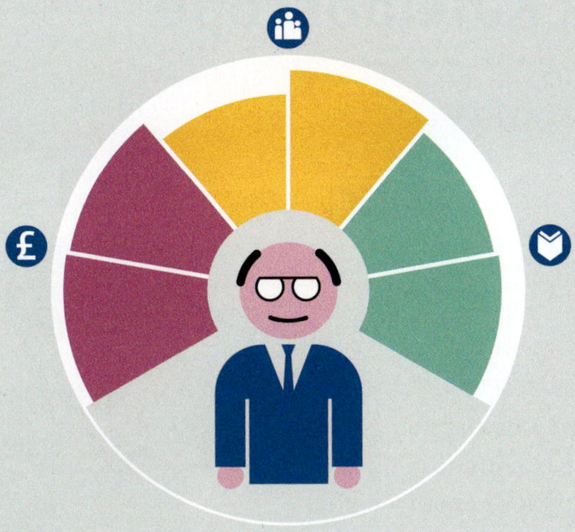

Elite

Percentage of population **6%**

Average age **57**

This is the wealthiest and most privileged group in the UK:

- They are the UK's biggest earners
- They score highest for social, cultural and economic factors
- Many went to private school and elite universities – 24% of people in this group were privately educated, far more than in any other class group
- This class is most likely to be found in London and the home counties
- This group is exclusive and very hard to join, most come from very privileged backgrounds
- 97% of people in this group own their own home

2

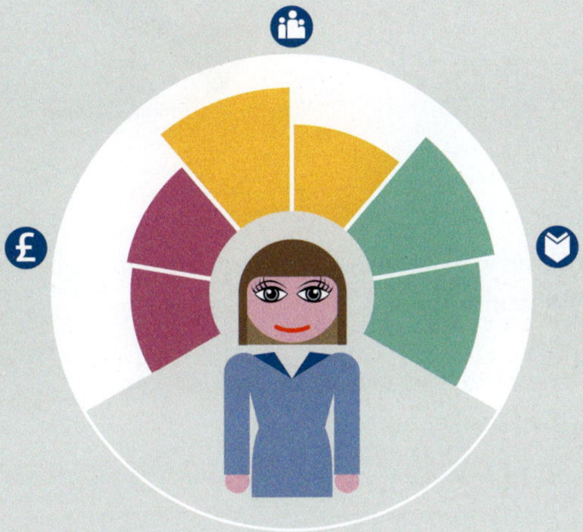

Technical middle class

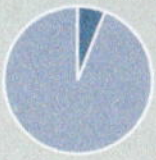

Percentage of population **6%**

Average age **52**

This is a small, distinctive and prosperous new class group:

- People in this group tend to mix socially with people similar to themselves
- They prefer emerging culture such as using social media to highbrow culture such as listening to classical music
- Many people in this group work in research science and technical occupations
- They tend to live in suburban locations, often in the south east of England
- They come from largely middle class backgrounds

3

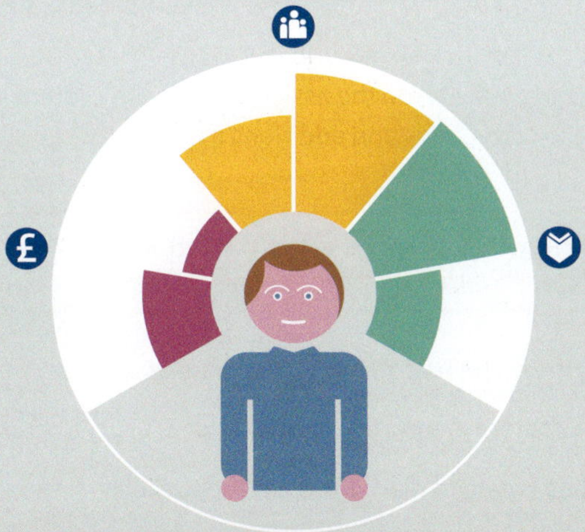

New affluent workers

Percentage of population **15%**

Average age **44**

This class group is sociable, has lots of cultural interests and sits in the middle of all the groups in terms of wealth:

- This youthful class group is economically secure without being well off
- These people have high scores for emerging culture, such as watching sport, going to gigs and using social media
- They do not tend to participate in highbrow culture, such as classical music and theatre
- People in this group are likely to come from a working class background
- Many people in this group live in old manufacturing centres of the UK in the Midlands and North West

Economic capital

The purple wedges show the economic "capital" score. The first wedge represents one's income and the second wedge shows the combination of one's savings and property value.

Social capital

The orange wedges show the social "capital" score, based on the professions of the people one knows socially. The first wedge indicates the average social status of the people one socialises with, while the second shows the number of different occupations within one's social group.

Cultural capital

The first green wedge shows the emerging cultural "capital" score and the second shows the "highbrow" cultural capital score. Emerging cultural activities include playing sport and going to gigs. Highbrow cultural activities include listening to classical music and going to the theatre.

A Kaleidoscope Queen in a Kaleidoscope Country?

The Queen's Diamond Jubilee 2012 – Ceremony at Westminster Hall

AWARENESS

In 2012, Queen Elizabeth II celebrated the 60th anniversary of her coronation on 6 February 1952. The only other British monarch who celebrated a Diamond Jubilee was Queen Victoria in 1897. Over the years, there have been discussions about whether the Queen should abdicate and hand over the throne to either her son, the Prince of Wales, or her grandson Prince William, the Duke of Cambridge.
In a 4-corners activity, reflect on whether the Queen should
a) abdicate, b) not abdicate, c) hand over the throne to Prince Charles,
d) hand over the throne to Prince William.

COMPREHENSION

Webcode SNG-40183-005 @

1. **Before reading:** Use the link provided on the webcode and watch the Queen's Diamond Jubilee ceremony at Westminster Hall and get an impression of the overall atmosphere.
   Pay particular attention to the ceremonial elements, e.g.
   - the function of the two maces[1],
   - the Lord Speaker's procession,
   - the various guards and their function,
   - the Speaker's procession.

   Take notes while watching the video clip and prepare a short presentation in class.
   → Focus on Skills, Presentations, p. 391

2. **While reading/listening:** You have a choice here between either **listening** to the audio version of the speeches or **reading** the texts provided here.

   Team up with a partner and, in a paired reading/listening activity, do the assignments below. After each step, exchange and crosscheck your findings and make corrections and additions if necessary.

   Tips on vocab

   plain ■ natural ■ precise ■ passionate ■ polished ■ elegant ■ poetic ■ stilted (*gestelzt*) ■ long-winded ■ solemn (*feierlich*) ■ colourful ■ humourous ■ playful

   2-4 CD 1

   Step 1: In a **first listening/reading**, pay attention to the manner of speaking and tone of
   a) Baroness D'Souza's,
   b) John Bercow's and
   c) Queen Elizabeth II's voices and the atmosphere they create to mark the special occasion.
   → Focus on Skills, Listening Comprehension, p. 366

   Step 2: In a **second listening/reading**, find out what each of the speakers emphasizes in particular in commemorating the sixty years of the Queen's reign.

[1] **mace** a decorative stick, carried as a sign of authority; here: the mace symbolically represents the monarch; *Amtsstab*

1 Baroness D'Souza: Honorary Address by the Speaker of the House of Lords

Most Gracious[1] Sovereign,

We, the Lords Spiritual and Temporal[2], are assembled here today to celebrate sixty years of Your reign. We record with warmth and affection our appreciation of Your dedicated service to Your people, and Your unequalled sense of public duty over the years – service and duty to which You have only recently, and so movingly, re-dedicated Yourself.

We celebrate too Your stewardship[3] of Your high office. You have personified continuity and stability while ensuring that Your role has evolved[4] imperceptibly[5], with the result that the Monarchy is as integral a part of our national life today as it was 60 years ago.

We rejoice[6] in this Jubilee and we give thanks for all that it represents.

At the same time, we record[7] our gratitude for the support which You have received throughout Your reign from His Royal Highness Prince Philip, for in this year of jubilee we celebrate his service too.

This is one of the first of many celebrations to be held up and down the land. In the coming months You and the Duke will travel widely throughout the Kingdom. But today You have come to Parliament, the constitutional heart of the nation, and granted us the privilege of being the first of Your people formally to honour Your Jubilee. And where better to begin the celebrations than here, in the splendor[8] of Westminster Hall – a hall of kings and queens for almost a millennium.

While this Hall has seen many historic events, few are permanently commemorated[9]. So we look forward with great anticipation to the unveiling of the stained glass[10] window which members of both Houses have commissioned[11] in honour of this day. When placed in the window above the great doors, Your Coat of Arms[12] and Royal Cypher[13] will bathe the Hall in colour and be seen daily by members and staff as they walk through to their offices – and by the many thousands of visitors we receive here weekly, from both home and abroad.

For we must remember that Your Jubilee will be celebrated with joy in Your other realms[14] and territories, and throughout the rest of the Commonwealth. The Commonwealth as we know it today is of course one of the great achievements of Your reign and under Your leadership continues to flourish, with a membership of 54 countries. It is still growing. It is a tremendous force for good in the world and we are aware of its special personal significance to You.

Many of us present here today take an active part in the work of the United Kingdom Branch of the Commonwealth Parliamentary Association. We work to share our experiences, to learn from one another, and to promote democracy. But our efforts are as nothing compared with those of Your Majesty in the service of Your beloved Commonwealth. Over the years You have visited all but two Commonwealth countries – some, many times – and attended all Heads of Government meetings since 1997. We look on with admiration and pride at the triumphs of some of Your recent tours and it is significant that members of the Royal Family are representing You this year at the Jubilee celebrations being held in all those lands in which You are Head of State.

Your Majesty, the Lords Spiritual and Temporal in Parliament Assembled give thanks for this Your Diamond Jubilee. We look forward to the years to come and we pray that You and Your realms may enjoy the peace, plenty and prosperity that have so distinguished Your reign.

www.parliament.uk/business/news/2012/march/lords-speaker-addresses-hm-the-queen, 22 March 2012 [18.12.2014]

2 John Bercow: Honorary Address by the Speaker of the House of Commons

Most Gracious Sovereign,

We Your faithful Commons are honoured to be here to commemorate and celebrate the sixty years of Your reign. We too are pleased to have contributed to the Jubilee Window to be revealed shortly and which will mark this occasion permanently. Time is better preserved in this historic place than in fallible[15] human memory.

Time also tells its own story. Sixty years ago, rationing[16] meant rather more than a short wait before the arrival of the latest electronic item. Sixty years ago, Britain had

[1] **gracious** (*BrE, formal*) used as a very polite word for royal people or their actions – [2] **Lords Spiritual and Temporal** Lords Spiritual: representatives of the Church of England; Lords Temporal: life peers appointed by the monarch – [3] **stewardship** the act of taking care of or managing sth. – [4] **to evolve** to develop gradually – [5] **imperceptibly** *unmerklich* – [6] **to rejoice** (*fml.*) to feel or show great happiness about sth. – [7] **to record** here: to make an official statement about sth. – [8] **splendour** great beauty – [9] **to commemorate** to remember officially and give respect to a great person – [10] **stained glass** *Glasmalerei* – [11] **to commission** *in Auftrag geben* – [12] **Coat of Arms** *Wappen* – [13] **Royal Cypher** *königliches Monogramm* – [14] **realm** [relm] *Reich* – [15] **fallible** able or likely to make mistakes – [16] **rationing** ['ræʃənɪŋ] *Rationierung*

just emerged from a war of an intensity never seen before or since and had slipped into the shadow of the Korean conflict. Sixty years ago, a new "Elizabethan Era" was awaited with enthusiasm tinged[17] with uncertainty about the challenges ahead for the country.
If, as Gandhi asserted[18], "the best way to find yourself is to lose yourself in the service of others", then Your Majesty must have found Yourself countless times over the past six decades. You have dedicated Your life to others. The daily example that You set, mirrored by our courageous armed forces of which You are Commander-in-Chief, is extraordinary. Yet perhaps Your Majesty's most profound[19] contribution has been to the continuity that has made change manageable.
For transformation is inevitably[20] turbulent. It has been Your singular accomplishment[21], Your unique capacity, to hold together that which could have been torn asunder[22]. You have moved with the times and allowed the times to move around the rest of society.
This is a different Britain from 1952 but not one detached from[23] then. We are in so many ways a much bigger, brighter and better United Kingdom. This is a land where men and women today are equal under the law and where Your people are respected, regardless of how they live, how they look or how they love. This is a nation of many races, faiths and customs, now beginning to be reflected in Parliament. All this progress has occurred during Your reign. You have become, to many of us, a kaleidoscope Queen of a kaleidoscope country in a kaleidoscope Commonwealth.
This gathering is one of many diverse events across these islands in tribute to You and this great anniversary. Our affection as a nation will rightly embrace the Duke of Edinburgh and other members of Your family. These will be moments striking for the sincerity[24] expressed as much as for the scenery encountered. Sixty years of stability. Sixty years of security. Sixty years of certainty. Sixty years of sacrifice. Sixty years of service. Gandhi also observed that "in a gentle way, you can shake the world". Your Majesty, in a gentle way You have shaken this United Kingdom and the world for six decades. On behalf of all the members of the House of Commons, may I thank You wholeheartedly for all that You have done, are doing and will do for the good of our country.

www.parliament.uk/business/news/2012/march/speaker-addresses-hm-the-queen, 22 March 2012 [18.12.2014]

3 Queen Elizabeth II: Address to Both Houses of Parliament

My Lords and Members of the House of Commons, I am most grateful for your Loyal Addresses and the generous words of the Lord Speaker and Mr Speaker.
This great institution has been at the heart of the country and the lives of our people throughout its history. As Parliamentarians, you share with your forebears[25] a fundamental role in the laws and decisions of your own age. Parliament has survived as an unshakeable cornerstone of our constitution and our way of life. History links monarchs and Parliament, a connecting thread[26] from one period to the next. So, in an era when the regular, worthy[27] rhythm of life is less eye-catching than doing something extraordinary, I am reassured that I am merely the second Sovereign to celebrate a Diamond Jubilee.
As today, it was my privilege to address you during my Silver and Golden Jubilees. Many of you were present ten years ago and some of you will recall the occasion in 1977. Since my Accession[28], I have been a regular visitor to the Palace of Westminster and, at the last count, have had the pleasurable duty of treating with twelve Prime Ministers.
Over such a period, one can observe that the experience of venerable[29] old age can be a mighty guide but not a prerequisite[30] for success in public office. I am therefore very pleased to be addressing many younger Parliamentarians and also those bringing such a wide range of background and experience to your vital, national work.
During these years as your Queen, the support of my family has, across the generations, been beyond measure. Prince Philip is, I believe, well-known for declining compliments[31] of any kind. But throughout he has been a constant strength and guide. He and I are very proud and grateful that The Prince of Wales and other members of our family are travelling on my behalf in this Diamond Jubilee year to visit all the Commonwealth Realms and a number of other Commonwealth countries.

[17] **to tinge** [tɪndʒ] *leicht einfärben* – [18] **to assert** (*fml.*) to say sth. is certainly true – [19] **profound** *tiefgründig* – [20] **inevitably** [ɪˈnevɪtəbli] *unvermeidbar* – [21] **accomplishment** *Errungenschaft* – [22] **to tear sth. asunder** *etw. auseinanderreißen* – [23] **detached from** separated from – [24] **sincerity** *Aufrichtigkeit* – [25] **forebear** (*fml.*) *Vorgänger* – [26] **thread** [θred] here: link, connection – [27] **worthy** (*fml.*) deserving respect, admiration, support – [28] **accession** *Thronbesteigung* – [29] **venerable** [ˈvenərəbl] deserving respect because of its importance – [30] **prerequisite** [ˌpriːˈrekwɪzɪt] (*fml.*) *Voraussetzung* – [31] **to decline a compliment** *ein Kompliment zurückweisen*

These overseas tours are a reminder of our close affinity[32] with the Commonwealth, encompassing about one-third of the world's population. My own association with the Commonwealth has taught me that the most important contact between nations is usually contact between its peoples. An organisation dedicated to certain values, the Commonwealth has flourished and grown by successfully promoting and protecting that contact.
At home, Prince Philip and I will be visiting towns and cities up and down the land. It is my sincere hope that the Diamond Jubilee will be an opportunity for people to come together in a spirit of neighbourliness and celebration of their own communities.
We also hope to celebrate the professional and voluntary service given by millions of people across the country who are working for the public good. They are a source of vital support to the welfare and well-being of others, often unseen or overlooked.
And as we reflect upon public service, let us again be mindful of the remarkable sacrifice and courage of our Armed Forces. Much may indeed have changed these past sixty years but the valour of those who risk their lives for the defence and freedom of us all remains undimmed[33].
The happy relationship I have enjoyed with Parliament has extended well beyond the more than three and a half thousand Bills[34] I have signed into law. I am therefore very touched by the magnificent gift before me, generously subscribed[35] by many of you. Should this beautiful window cause just a little extra colour to shine down upon this ancient place, I should gladly settle for[36] that.
We are reminded here of our past, of the continuity of our national story and the virtues[37] of resilience[38], ingenuity[39] and tolerance which created it. I have been privileged to witness some of that history and, with the support of my family, rededicate myself to the service of our great country and its people now and in the years to come.

www.bbc.com/news/uk-politics-17446804, 20 March 2012 [20.07.2014]

ANALYSIS

3. Although the overall tone of the speeches is highly official and rather "stiff", John Bercow and the Queen herself try to ease the atmosphere by employing some humorous remarks. Identify these remarks and explain what they hint at in particular.
→ Focus on Skills, Analysis of a Political Speech, p. 379

4. The three speeches are so-called "honorary speeches". Compare these speeches to political speeches that you know of (e. g. Sadiq Khan, Theresa May, pp. 23 ff., 88 ff.) and explain the differences in style and tone.

5. In 2013, the BBC commissioned an artwork called *The People's Monarch* that depicts the Queen at the time of her accession in 1952 and at her Diamond Jubilee in 2012 (see next page). It is a 38-square-metre canvas containing 5,000 photos of British people who contributed their private photos, snapshots, etc.

The People's Monarch Stories
Helen Marshall says: "Many people submitted family portraits, photos of their ancestors, snaps of important occasions in their lives and of times that made them laugh. Some viewers also used the opportunity to share precious memories of loved ones they had lost. Everyday family snapshots, scans of photos of ancestors or from an era gone by, times of celebration and ceremony or times of trouble and loss, all remind us of our century old love affair with the camera. But more important, this project proves that we do not need to be professional photographers or artists to be recognised or represented in an artwork, and that the photograph has a unique and simple ability to speak directly to all of us, no matter of our differences."
www.thepeoplespicture.com/helen-widget-test [20.07.2014]

[32] **affinity** a close relationship between two things – [33] **undimmed** here: *ungeschmälert* – [34] **bill** *Gesetzesvorlage* – [35] **to subscribe** *unterschreiben, abzeichnen* – [36] **to settle for sth.** (*phr. v.*) to accept or agree to sth. – [37] **virtue** *Tugend* – [38] **resilience** [rɪˈzɪliəns] (*fml.*) *Ausdauer* – [39] **ingenuity** [ˌɪndʒəˈnjuːɪti] *Genialität*

'The People's Monarch' by artist Helen Marshall was commissioned by BBC South East and depicts the Queen at the time of her coronation and at her Diamond Jubilee. It is 38 square metres containing 5.000 photos. It's current home after touring at Towner Gallery, Turner Contemporary and Rochester Cathedral is at Gatwick Airport.

a) Describe the artwork and state what effect it has on the viewer.

Webcode SNG-40183-005 @

b) Watch the video clips and examine further photos provided on the webcode and relate the message of *The People's Monarch* to John Bercow's remarks that Queen Elizabeth II is a "kaleidoscope Queen …" (ll. 39 f.). Explain the implications and allusions employed in the speech as well as in the artwork. Can the Queen really be considered a "people's monarch"?

→ Focus on Skills, Analysis of Visuals, p. 381

ACTIVITIES

6. John Bercow focused on the Queen's adaptability to change and her ability to "move with the time" – he calls her a "kaleidoscope Queen of a kaleidoscope country in a kaleidoscope Commonwealth" (ll. 39 f.). Assess John Bercow's observations and remarks and state whether or not you can subscribe to this view of the Queen, the UK and the Commonwealth.

Tip: Refer to texts and material from this unit you have already dealt with to underpin your assessment.

GRAMMAR / LANGUAGE

7. Choose one of the speeches and report it to a friend who has not watched the ceremony. Use **indirect speech** and be sure to use the correct **tenses** and to **backshift** if necessary. Do not forget to employ appropriate introductory verbs and sentences.

Examples:

- (ll. 11 f.) Baroness D'Souza said that the Queen's role had evolved imperceptibly.
- (ll. 15 f.) The Queen emphasized that it had been her privilege to address the Houses of Parliament during her Silver and Gold Jubilees.

The Stewarts

1642 – 45 **Civil War**

- ongoing quarrels between the kings and Parliament about rising debts; disputes and fights between Protestants and Catholics; (religious) rebellions in Ireland and Scotland

1649 – 60
- Britain: a republic under leadership of Oliver Cromwell who dissolves Parliament; he calls himself 'Lord Protector of England'

Revolution of thought

1688
- the 'Glorious Revolution' takes place; based on theories of thinkers like John Locke, Parliament has more power than the king; Britain becomes a constitutional monarchy; → Bill of Rights; Act of Settlement

1689/1701
- rising influence of Puritanism; revolution in scientific thinking, e. g. Francis Bacon, Isaac Newton and Christopher Wren

Oliver Cromwell

Isaac Newton

The 18th century

Beginning of Imperialism

1759
- British control over Canada (defeat of the French in Quebec); defeat of the French in India → control of most of India; rise of transatlantic trade
- growing radicalism leads to loss of the American colonies

1775 – 83
- war against the rebellious American colonies

Industrial Revolution

1769
- James Watt invents the steam engine which revolutionizes the (industrial) production of steel, cotton, etc.; rising numbers of factories and increasing production of goods

Watt's steam engine

The 19th century

The workshop of the world

- British factories produce more than any other country in the world; control of world traffic and world markets
- exploitation of workers and suffering farmers → rise of poverty and misery; Charles Dickens → descriptions of crime and poverty

1824/34
- first workers' unions are founded/workers' revolt in London

British Empire/Victorian Age

1837 – 1901
- reign of Queen Victoria; she is very popular – connects monarchy with Britain's 'glorious history'

Queen Victoria

The 20th century

1914 – 18 **World War I**

- after disastrous destruction and high number of casualties there is great hatred against Germany; Germany is severely punished
- demand of home rule for Ireland; riots and fighting; civil war

1939 – 45 **World War II**

- more than 360,000 Britons are killed; Britain, the USA, France and the Soviet Union become allies to fight Germany

1945
- the United Nations comes into existence

1945 – 65
- 500 million people in former colonies become self-governing

1973
- Britain joins the EU

1982
- in a war, Britain is able to recapture the Falkland Islands from Argentina

1980s
- black immigrants riot against bad housing and economic problems in London, Liverpool, Bristol

PM Winston Churchill

The 21st century

Wars on Iraq

1990 – 91
- Gulf War; invasion led by USA and UK

2003 – 10
- Iraq War; UK ends combat in 2009

2014
- Scottish independence referendum: the majority of Scots vote against independence (55.3 % vs. 44.7 %)

2016
- 23 June: referendum to leave the European Union (Brexit): 51.9 % of Britons vote in favour of leaving the EU
- 24 June: David Cameron announces resignation
- 13 July: Theresa May becomes new Prime Minister

PM Theresa May

Once There Was ... An Empire ...

Jeremy Paxman

Our Empire Was an Amazing Thing

AWARENESS

In groups of three students each, study the Focus on Facts pages *The British Empire* (pp. 49 f.) and reactivate your knowledge about

- the system of triangle trading and the slave trade,
- the origins of the British Empire in the 18th century,
- the rise of the British Empire in the 19th century and its peak around 1900.

Distribute the topics within your group and, in a first step, read the FoF texts individually and make notes on the most relevant information. Second, exchange your findings with your group members and add information on the other topics.

COMPREHENSION

1. **While reading** the text, finish the following statements using evidence and information from the text.
   a) The Empire was an amazing thing because ...
   b) The Empire has decisively influenced
      - British society today because ...
      - British politics today because ...
      - the way Britons see themselves today because ...
   c) The Empire was not entirely bad because ...
   d) The Empire was cruel and appalling (*entsetzlich*) because ...

The history of the British Empire is full of amazing stories of adventure, of war, of greed and plunder, cruelty and courage, heroism and low cunning[1]. It explains so much about who we are now, yet we increasingly pretend it never happened.

It's nothing short of a scandal that this history is not taught in schools. It may be unfashionable to say so, but building, securing and running an empire was the biggest international preoccupation[2] of this country for generations.

Imperial history explains both why Britain has a seat on the UN Security Council and the readiness[3] of British prime ministers to commit British troops to overseas wars.

But it goes much further, too. The empire reshaped our education system and redefined how we think of ourselves. It was the trigger for much post-war immigration, and anything that changes the very genetic make-up of the population can hardly be dismissed[4] as superficial.

The problem is that there seems to have been a set of ready-to-wear[5] prejudices handed out. According to the conventional view, there is only one way to look at the British Empire: it was A Thoroughly[6] Bad Thing. Sure, no one wants to be colonised and ruled by foreigners. But the picture is far more complicated than that. Of course there were many things that were bad. But there were others that were rather admirable.

The slave trade really was unforgivable. The 19th-century wars fought to force the Chinese to allow Scottish merchants to ship opium into the country were unconscionable[7] (if you want an example of cant[8], just look at the justifications given by the men who ran the trade).

[1] **cunning** (*disapproving*) able to get what you want in a clever way; *gerissen* – [2] **preoccupation** *Hauptbeschäftigung* – [3] **readiness** willingness – [4] **to dismiss** to decide that sb./sth. is not important and not worth thinking or talking about – [5] **ready-to-wear** here: sth. that is easily and generally accepted as true – [6] **thoroughly** completely – [7] **unconscionable** unscrupulous – [8] **cant** hypocrisy; *Heuchelei*

But are we also to condemn the campaign to abolish slavery? Once the British had become the first European nation to wake up to[9] its cruelties, they enforced an international ban on the trade. Hundreds of thousands of people were saved from slavery by the Royal Navy.

And what was so wrong with attempts to map Africa, to ban sati (the custom of burying widows when their husbands died) in India, to lay roads and railways, and drains[10], to make trade follow internationally agreed laws, to try to create a system of incorruptible[11] administration?

Of course, it is all undermined by distasteful assumptions about how the British were somehow superior to those they colonised ("Winning first prize in the lottery of life," as Cecil Rhodes[12] put it), which is probably why we prefer not to think about it. But we can take some consolation[13] from the fact that while the British Empire was motivated by self interest, it claimed to aspire[14] to nobler ambitions than many other empires. (The unluckiest Africans got colonised by Belgians.) And when the time came to leave, the British largely departed when asked to do so – unlike the French in places like Algeria.

Filming for our new BBC One series, Empire, took us all over the world in pursuit of astonishing stories – from India and Hong Kong to Malawi and Sudan, Canada and Jamaica. In many places we found imperial amnesia[15] to have less of a grip[16] than it has in Britain. One of the more astonishing conversations I had was with an elderly Kikuyu[17] lady who had been one of the leaders of the bloody Mau Mau uprising[18], which the British put down brutally. We were chatting outside her hut on the side of Mount Kenya when, to my astonishment, she suddenly started talking about how the British had created schools and hospitals and Kenya should accept and appreciate her colonial past.

From the black-gowned[19] lawyers bustling around[20] the courts in Calcutta to the old general watching Egyptians playing croquet at the old British military sports club in Cairo, there were plenty of others ready to embrace a more sophisticated recognition of what the empire was and did.

I suppose the greatest imperial spectacle in Britain was Queen Victoria's Diamond Jubilee. It's appropriate that we look at the empire again in the year of Queen Elizabeth's Jubilee. Victoria presided over more or less constant expansion, while our current queen has been there as the empire withered[21].

It now consists of a dozen-odd[22] (some of them very odd) specks[23] on the map, such as Pitcairn and Bermuda. In imperial terms, Queen Victoria was lucky, Elizabeth unlucky. The empire was always a monarchical thing, and our current queen is entitled[24] to some of the credit for largely peaceful decolonisation and the creation and survival of that worthy institution, the Commonwealth, an institution most of the British don't have the faintest idea about, but which countries like Mozambique and Rwanda – which weren't part of the empire – have clamoured[25] to join.

This empire we don't like to talk about explains so much. When so many places on the map – Lake Victoria, Mount Everest – carry British names, it changes the way we regard the rest of the world. The empire helps to explain our problems with Europe and the fact that Scotland will soon stage a referendum[26] on whether it wants to continue in a union with England [in September 2014]. Why the shock? Scotland only formally joined forces[27] with England when its own attempts to found an empire – a crackpot[28] scheme in central America – blew up[29] in the country's face and bankrupted it. Alex Salmond's[30] teenage years were spent watching countries tumbling[31] out of the empire like crowds leaving a football match. Is it any wonder that he seeks a similar destiny for his own folk?

Perhaps if we acknowledged the vital role the empire played in our development, we'd understand ourselves a little better.

www.telegraph.co.uk/culture/tvandradio/9085936/Jeremy-Paxman-Our-empire-was-an-amazing-thing.html, 16 February 2012 [16.12.2014]

[9] **to wake up to sth.** (*phr. v.*) to start to understand that a situation or problem exists – [10] **drain** *Kanalisation; Abwassersystem* – [11] **incorruptible** *unkorrumpierbar* – [12] **Cecil Rhodes** (1853–1902) British businessman, mining magnate and politician; empire builder of South Africa – [13] **consolation** *Trost* – [14] **to aspire** *emporstreben, aufstreben* – [15] **amnesia** [æmˈniːziə] *Amnesie; Gedächtnisverlust* – [16] **lose your grip** (*idm.*) to become unable to understand or control a situation – [17] **Kikuyu** largest ethnic group in Kenya – [18] **Mau Mau uprising** a military conflict (1952–1960) between Kikuyu groups and the British army – [19] **black-gowned** *schwarz gewandet* – [20] **to bustle around** to do things in a hurried and busy way – [21] **to wither** *verkümmern; allmählich verschwinden* – [22] **dozen-odd** about a dozen – [23] **speck** a very small spot – [24] **entitled** having the right to have or do sth. – [25] **to clamour** (*fml.*) to demand sth. loudly – [26] **referendum** *Volksentscheid* – [27] **to join forces** *sich zusammenschließen* – [28] **crackpot** (*infml.*) a person with strange and crazy ideas – [29] **to blow up in one's face** (*phr. v.*) to fail unexpectedly – [30] **Alex Salmond** (*1954) Scottish politician and first minister of Scotland – [31] **to tumble** *umfallen, stürzen*

COMPREHENSION

2. **After a second reading**, subdivide the text into paragraphs following the thematic units of the text. Find a suitable headline for each paragraph using your own words.

ANALYSIS

3. Analyse the author's stance on the Empire, taking into consideration
   a) the type of text, b) the stylistic devices*, c) the line of argument*.
   → Focus on Skills, Analysis of a Non-Fictional Text, p. 377
   → Focus on Facts, Basic Types of Non-Fictional Texts, p. 368

4. Using your findings from the awareness task, compare the information given there to Paxman's depiction of the Empire. Does he present a comprehensive picture or are there substantial parts missing?

ACTIVITIES

Webcode SNG-40183-007 @

5. Watch the video documentation about the British Empire provided on the webcode and prepare presentations on the many facets of the British Empire.
   → Focus on Skills, Presentations, p. 391

6. Evaluate Paxman's conclusions that
   a) "The Empire helps to explain our problems with Europe ..." (ll. 98 f.),
   b) "The Empire helps to explain ... the fact ... that Scotland will soon stage a referendum on whether it wants to continue in a union with England ..." (ll. 99 f.),
   c) "... if we acknowledged the vital role the Empire played in our development, we'd understand ourselves a little better" (ll. 110 f.).
   In order to give your evaluation a more solid foundation, you should refer to further texts you have dealt with so far (e. g. about "Britishness", the UK's position in the EU, etc.).

7. In 1940, Charlie Chaplin produced and starred in the political satirical comedy-drama *The Great Dictator*, a condemnation of Hitler, fascism and the Nazis. It was Chaplin's most successful film and one of the central scenes in it is the "globe scene" (cf. film still).
   Use the links provided on the webcode to get more information about the film and the means of parody/satire it employs.

Webcode SNG-40183-007 @

Info

A **satire** [ˈsætaɪə] is a fictional text that criticizes people or certain situations by making them appear ridiculous. This may involve exaggeration, (funny) comparison and puns. Some other satirical tools are: caricature, parody, irony, sarcasm and (black) humour.
Satire is aimed at ridiculing or criticizing the limitations of human perception, human shortcomings or failures, social values, bureaucracy, the military, political or societal scandals, etc. Its general aim is to "first make people laugh, and then make them think".

8. At some points, Paxman's article verges on the absurd, for example calling the slave trade "unforgivable" (l. 29) or asking "what was so wrong with attempts to map Africa … to try to create a system of incorruptible administration?" (ll. 41 ff.).
Together with a partner, transform the article into a satire (cf. info box, p. 42). Read out your satires on the British Empire in class and discuss the views taken.

Andrea Levy

Small Island – Prologue: Queenie

AWARENESS

Throughout the history of the British Empire, there have been five imperial exhibitions – the first one in 1815 and the last one in 1938. However, the largest exhibition ever staged anywhere in the world was the British Empire Exhibition of 1924/25 which was held at Wembley, London. Opened by King George V on St George's Day (23 April 1924), it attracted ca. 27 million visitors.
Based on your knowledge of the British Empire, collect ideas about the cultural, technical and industrial achievements and items that might have been presented and displayed at the Empire Exhibition of 1924. What would you organize and put on stage to impress the visitors? Discuss your various ideas.

1 I thought I'd been to Africa. Told all of my class I had. Early Bird, our teacher, stood[1] me in front of the British flag – she would let no one call it the common Union Jack: 'It's the flag of Empire not a musical turn.' And I stood there as bold as brass[2] and said, 'I went to Africa when it came to Wembley.' It was then that Early Bird informed me that Africa was a country. 'You're not usually a silly girl, Queenie Buxton,' she went on, 'but you did not go to Africa, you merely went to the British Empire Exhibition, as thousands of others did.'

2 It was a Butchers' Association trip. Every year there was an outing[3] organized for the butchers, the butchers' wives and children and even the butchers' favourite workers. A day out. Mother liked to go. 'It's like a holiday,' she would say to father.
'Bloody waste of time,' he'd grumble[4]. But he went all the same.
Some years nearly everyone from our farm went. The inside girls who helped Mother with the pies. The outside girls who fed the pigs and poultry[5]. Even the stupid boys, who helped Father in the shed, changed out of their splattered[6] aprons[7] and into their ill-fitting, fraying[8] best suits for the trip. We always got dressed in our best to paddle in the sea at Blackpool or ride a red bus round Piccadilly Circus or laugh at the monkeys in the zoo. Then it was time to go home again. The men would be dozing[9] from too much beer and the children would be sniveling[10] after being whacked[11] for dirtying their clothes or getting a piece of rock stuck in their hair. As often as not one of the farm girls would go missing with one of the farm boys only to turn up later, looking sheepish and disheveled[12].

3 The year we went to the Empire Exhibition, the Great War[13] was not long over but nearly forgotten. Even father agreed that the Empire Exhibition sounded like it was worth a look. The King had described it as 'the whole Empire in little'. Mother thought that meant it was a miniature, like a toy railway or model village. Until someone told her that they'd seen the real lifesize Stephenson's Rocket[14] on display. 'It must be as big as the whole world,' I said, which made everybody laugh. We had to leave my brothers Billy, Harry and Jim behind. They were too small and everyone agreed with Father when he told the grizzling[15] boys that they would get swallowed up by the crowd. 'I'm not scared of being eaten,' Billy whimpered[16]. They sobbed[17] and

[1] **to stand sb.** (*infml.*) to make sb. stand – [2] **as bold as brass** (*idm.*) with extreme confidence – [3] **outing** a short journey made by a group of people for fun – [4] **to grumble** *grummeln* – [5] **poultry** *Geflügel* – [6] **splattered** *bespritzt* – [7] **apron** *Schürze* – [8] **fraying** *abgenutzt, abgescheuert* – [9] **to doze** *dösen* – [10] **to snivel** (*infml.*) *plärren* – [11] **to whack sb.** (*infml.*) to hit sb. hard – [12] **dishevelled** *zerzaust* – [13] **Great War** World War I – [14] **Stephenson's Rocket** an early steam locomotive, built in 1829 – [15] **to grizzle** (*infml.*) to cry or complain in an annoying way; *nörgeln* – [16] **to whimper** *wimmern* – [17] **to sob** *schluchzen*

clung to Mother's coat. So she had to promise to bring each of them back something nice – a model engine or soldiers. She left them with the inside girl Molly, who stood at the window sulking[18], giving us all a look that could curdle[19] milk.

I was dressed in a white organza frock[20] with blue ribbons that trailed loose down the front and my hair was set in pigtails[21] adorned[22] with big white bows[23]. All the way there on the train Mother and Father chatted with other butchers and butchers' wives about, of all things, the bother of humane killing over the poleaxe[24]. Which left me sitting between two of our farm helpers, Emily and Graham, who spent the time giggling and flirting over my head.

Emily had been our outside girl for two months. She had a kindly foster-mother[25], who lived in Kent and made pictures from spring flowers, and a father and two uncles in London, who drank so much that they had not been awake long enough to take part in the war. Graham helped Father in the shed. He looked after the fire under the copper of pig swill, took the pork pies to the bakehouse when needed and generally ran round doing everything Father asked, only not quite quick enough. Father called Graham Jim. On Graham's first day he had said his name to Father who looked him up and down and said, 'I can't be bothered with a fancy name like that – I'll call you Jim.' Consequently some people called him Jim and others Graham – he'd learned to answer to both. But Graham's only ambition, as far as I could tell, was to get a feel of Emily's bust[26].

4 Hundreds and hundreds of people were tramping in[27] through the gates of the exhibition past the gardens and the lakes. Or milling about[28], chatting. Little kids being dragged to walk faster. Women pointing, old men wanting a seat. 'Over here! No, over here ... Over here's better.' The Empire in little. The palace of engineering, the palace of industry, and building after building that housed every country we British owned. Some of them were grand[29] like castles, some had funny pointed roofs[30] and one, I was sure, had half an onion on the top. Practically the whole world there to be looked at. 'Makes you proud,' Graham said to Father. At which Father looked his butcher's boy up and down for a minute and said, 'Will you listen to him?'

There was a lot of discussion about what we should see – the whole world and only one day to see it. Mother was not interested in the different woods of Burma or the big-game trophies[31] of Malaya. She said, 'Maybe later,' to the coffee of Jamaica. 'Ooh, no,' to the sugar of Barbados. 'What for?' to the chocolate of Grenada. And 'Where in heaven's name is that?' to Sarawak[32]. In Canada there was a lifesize model of the Prince of Wales made in yellow butter. I had to struggle to the front to get a good look. I pressed my face close to the glass and Mother came and dragged me back. 'You hold Emily's hand,' she told me. 'I don't want you getting lost.' Then she moaned[33] at Emily in front of the crowd, who strained[34] to look past my mother and her blushing outside girl, everyone muttering[35], 'Butter, really? Butter? Never.' Mother told Emily that she had only been brought along to look after me and that if she lost me then she would be in trouble – very big trouble indeed. So Emily attached herself to me like soot[36] to a miner. And where Emily went Graham followed.

Australia smelt of apples. Ripe, green, crisp apples. A smell so sharp and sweet it made my teeth tingle[37]. 'We'll have some of them,' Father said, as he joined the queue to buy a small brown bag of the fruit. Mother saved hers until later, but I ate mine and gave the core[38] to Emily. Graham then told us all that he was going to live in Australia. 'Australia – you? You draft beggar[39],' Father laughed.

I was promised that I would see a sheep being sheared in New Zealand but we only arrived in time to see the skinny shorn animal trotting round a pen with the fleece at the side. Hong Kong smelt of drains[40], and India was full of women brightly dressed in strange long colourful fabrics. And all these women had red dots in the middle of their forehead. No one could tell me what the red dots where for. 'Go and ask one of them,' Emily said to me. But Mother said I shouldn't in case the dots meant they were ill – in case they were contagious[41].

The smell of tea in Ceylon had Mother swallowing hard and saying, 'I'm dying for a cuppa[42] and a sit-down. My feet!' At which Father began grumbling that he hadn't

[18] **to sulk** *schmollen* – [19] **to curdle sth.** *etw. zum Gerinnen bringen* – [20] **frock** (*old fashioned*) dress – [21] **pigtails** *Zöpfe* – [22] **adorned** decorated – [23] **bow** [bəʊ] here: *Schleife* – [24] **poleaxe** *Axt* – [25] **foster-mother** *Pflegemutter* – [26] **bust** *Busen, Oberweite* – [27] **to tramp in** (*infml.*) *hereintrampeln* – [28] **to mill about** moving around without particular purpose – [29] **grand** impressive and large – [30] **pointed roof** *Spitzdach* – [31] **big-game trophy** *Großwildtrophäe* – [32] **Sarawak** one of the two Malaysian states on the island of Borneo – [33] **to moan at sb.** *stöhnen, wehklagen* – [34] **to strain** here: *sich anstrengen* – [35] **to mutter** *brummeln* – [36] **soot** *Ruß* – [37] **to tingle** *kribbeln* – [38] **core** *Kerngehäuse* – [39] **draft beggar** a person who illegally tries to avoid doing military service – [40] **drain** *Kanalisation* – [41] **contagious** [kənˈteɪdʒəs] *ansteckend* – [42] **cuppa** (*infml.*) a cup of tea

seen the biscuit-making or cigarette-packing machines yet. I cried because I wanted to see more countries. Emily called me a little madam and Mother told her to watch her mouth. So Father gave instructions to Graham – which he had to repeat twice to make sure he was understood – to meet him and Mother later in the rest lounge of the gas exhibit. Mother and Father then went off to find modern machinery and refrigeration, while me, Emily and, of course, the soppy[43] Graham carried on travelling the world alone.

5 That's when we got lost in Africa. We wandered in, following the syrupy-brown smell of chocolate. Emily trailed behind Graham only looking at me every so often to shout, 'Come on – hurry up.' I wanted one of the cups of cocoa that everyone was sipping but instead Emily pulled me by one of my pigtails and told me to keep up. Then we found ourselves in an African village with Graham looking around himself, scratching his head and telling Emily he was wanting the toilet.
We were in the jungle. Huts made out of mud[44] with pointy stick roofs[45] all around us. And in a hut sitting on a dirt floor was a woman with skin as black as the ink that filled the inkwell in my school desk. A shadow come to life. Sitting cross-legged, her hands weaving bright patterned cloth on a loom[46]. 'We've got machines that do all that now,' Graham said, as Emily nudged[47] him to be quiet. 'She can't understand what I'm saying,' Graham explained. 'They're not civilised. They only understand drums.' The woman just carried on like she'd heard no one speak – pushing her stick through the tangle of threads[48].

6 'Have you seen the toilet?' Graham asked her, but she didn't understand that either.
'I want to go,' I said, because there was nothing interesting to look at. But then suddenly there was a man. An African man. A black man who looked to be carved[49] from melting chocolate. I clung to Emily but she shooed me off[50]. He was right next to me, close enough so I could see him breathing. A monkey man sweating a smell of mothballs[51]. Blacker than when you smudge[52] your face with a sooty cork[53]. The droplets of sweat on his forehead glistened and shone like jewels. His lips were brown, not pink like they should be, and they bulged[54] with air like bicycle tyres[55]. His hair was woolly as a black shorn sheep. His nose, squashed flat, had two nostrils[56] big as train tunnels. And he was looking down at me.
'Would you like to kiss him?' Graham said. He nudged me, teasing, and pushed me forward – closer to this black man.
And Emily giggled. 'Go on Queenie, kiss him, kiss him.' This man was still looking down at me. I could feel the blood rising in my face, turning me crimson[57], as he smiled a perfect set of pure blinding white teeth. The inside of his mouth was pink and his face was coming closer and closer to mine. He could have swallowed me up, this big nigger man. But instead he said, in clear English, 'Perhaps we could shake hands instead?'
Graham's smile fell off his face. And I shook an African man's hand. It was warm and slightly sweaty like anyone else's. I shook his hand up and down for several seconds. And he bowed his head to me and said, 'It's nice to meet you.' Then he let my hand go and stepped out of our way so we could pass. Emily was still giggling, looking at Graham and rolling her eyes. She grabbed my arm and pulled me away while Graham mumbled again that he needed the toilet. And the African man must have understood because he pointed and said, 'Over there by the tree is a rest room where I think you will find what you need.'
But Graham never found the toilet. He had to wee[58] behind some bins[59] while me and Emily kept a look-out.
Father said later that this African man I was made to shake hands with would have been a chief or a prince in Africa. Evidently, when they speak English you know that they have learned to be civilised – taught English by the white man, missionaries probably. So Father told me not to worry about having shaken his hand because the African man was most likely a potentate[60].

7 To take my mind off the encounter Father promised me a trip on the scenic railway. 'Come on, we'll be able to see for miles up there,' he persuaded Mother. [...]
We went up and up into the heavens until people were just dots below us. As we hung right at the top – the twinkling electric lights below mingling with the stars – Father said something I will never forget. He said, 'See here, Queenie. Look around. You've got the whole world at your feet, lass[61].'

from *Small Island* by Andrea Levy. Headline Review, London, 2004, pp. 1 ff.

[43] **soppy** (*infml.*) silly and sentimental – [44] **mud** *Lehm* – [45] **pointy stick roof** *Spitzdach aus Stöcken* – [46] **loom** *Webstuhl* – [47] **to nudge sb.** *jdn. anschubsen* – [48] **thread** [θred] *Faden* – [49] **to carve** *schnitzen* – [50] **to shoo sb. off** to make sb. go away, esp. by saying 'shoo' and waving your arms and hands – [51] **mothball** *Mottenkugel* – [52] **to smudge** *schmieren* – [53] **sooty cork** *rußgeschwärzter Korken* – [54] **to bulge** *hervortreten* – [55] **tyre** *Reifen* – [56] **nostril** *Nasenloch* – [57] **crimson** dark red in colour – [58] **to wee** to urinate – [59] **bin** *Mülleimer* – [60] **potentate** a ruler who has a lot of power, esp. when it is not restricted by parliament etc.; *Machthaber* – [61] **lass** (*ScotE*) a girl or young woman

COMPREHENSION

1. The excerpt presents Queenie Buxton, the first-person narrator*, reporting on her impressions of the 1924/25 Empire Exhibition in Wembley, London. You can
a) improve your **listening skills** and just listen to the audio text,
b) just read the text to improve your **reading skills**,
c) **read and listen** to the text at the same time.

In a paired listening/reading activity, listen to/read the text on your own and take notes on the questions below. **After each paragraph**, you and your partner summarize the paragraph together, crosscheck the notes you have taken and make additions and/or corrections if necessary.

5 CD 1 **1**
- Point out the introductory situation in the classroom.
- What is Queenie's misunderstanding?

6 CD 1 **2**
- Present the various trips of the Butchers' Association.
- Who were/are the participants?

7 CD 1 **3**
- Describe the preparations the family makes for the trip to the Empire Exhibition.
- Briefly describe Emily and Graham and their relationship.

8 CD 1 **4**
- Give an outline of Queenie's impressions of
  – the Empire in little, – Canada, – Australia, – New Zealand, – Hong Kong, – India, – Ceylon.
- How do the different family members react to the attractions?
- What do Queenie's mother and father focus on?

9 CD 1 **5**
- Describe "Africa" and its "inhabitants".
- What is Graham's view of and reaction to African culture?

10 CD 1 **6**
- Give a description of the "African man".
- Outline Queenie's encounter with the "big nigger man".
- Point out Queenie's father's explanation for the African man's behaviour.

11 CD 1 **7**
- What are Queenie's observations during the trip on the scenic railway?
- What does her father tell her?

→ Focus on Skills, Listening Comprehension, p. 366

ANALYSIS

2. Examine the reaction of the different participants of the trip to the "Empire in little" and the sensational attractions that are presented.
Together with a partner, copy the grid and complete it.

participants	the Empire in little	various attractions	Africa	the African man
Queenie	• we British owned … • …	• …	• … • …	• melting chocolate … • …
Father	• …	• modern machinery …	• …	• …
Mother	• …	• …	• …	• …
Graham	• makes you proud … • …	• …	• toilet … • We've got …	• …
Emily	• …	• …	• …	• kiss him …

Explain how these reactions and attitudes
a) serve as markers of social and cultural identity and b) indicate the "clash of cultures".
→ Focus on Skills, Analysis of a Fictional Text, p. 374

3. Interpret the symbolic meaning of the setting.

4. Identify examples of direct and indirect characterization* and explain their function.
→ Focus on Skills, Characterization of a Figure in Literature, p. 383

	examples/lines	**function**
direct characterization	• I stood there as bold as brass … (l. 5) • You're not usually a silly girl … (ll. 7 f.) • …	→ making fun of herself → … → …
indirect characterization	• Mother liked to go. (l. 14) • Bloody waste of time … (l. 16) • …	→ sociable, outgoing … → straightforward, down-to-earth … → …

5. Illustrate the use of irony* and state how it contributes to the intention of the text.

6. "See the world and get paid for it" is the slogan on the historical advert (p. 48) that promotes joining the imperial civil services overseas.
a) Describe the advert in detail and examine the function and effect of its various visual elements and symbols.
→ Focus on Skills, Analysis of Visuals, p. 381
b) Compare the intended message of the advert to the way the "Empire" is presented in the excerpt, particularly its last sentence, "You've got the whole world at your feet …" (ll. 217 f.).

ACTIVITIES

7. Although the novel *Small Island* has been turned into a film, the scene of the visit to the Empire Exhibition has been omitted.
Now, for a remake of the 2009 film, you are asked to compile
a) a screenplay and
b) a storyboard of the "Prologue" to the novel, particularly the scene of the visit to the Empire Exhibition.
Divide the class into different groups, each group choosing one of the options mentioned above.
→ Focus on Facts, Screenplays and Storyboards, p. 369

Read out/act out your screenplay and display the storyboards in class and evaluate and discuss the various renderings of the scene(s).

8. Put yourself in the position of
a) the African woman in the village, weaving on a loom (ll. 153 ff.), or
b) the African man Queenie shakes hands with (ll. 166 ff.).
and tell the story of the Empire Exhibition from their point of view.
→ Focus on Skills, Continuation of a Fictional Text, p. 392

GRAMMAR / LANGUAGE

9. Imagine you are event managers whose job is to organize and promote the Empire Exhibition (of 1924/25).

Webcode SNG-40183-008 @

First, inform yourself about attractions and events of the exhibition, using the links provided on the webcode. Then, design posters like the ones on the historic "sandwich man" that inform about and promote the exhibition.

Think about appealing and informative headlines and slogans and employ **adjectives**, **adverbials** and **superlatives** to highlight the attractions.

Examples:

- Visit the sensational and unique attractions and breathtaking innovations …
- Get an impression of the 'Empire in little' and experience the spectacular and highly fascinating …

Present your posters in class and discuss and evaluate their content and message.

Sandwich Board Advertisers, 1920s

Tips on vocab

foreground:
proud Europeans ■ to strut (*stolzieren*) ■ topee (*Tropenhelm*) ■ khaki uniform ■ kilts ■ whip (*Gerte*) ■ distinctive jawline ■ self-esteem

background:
mosque ■ Arabian people ■ different headdresses: fez (cap); kufiya/pali (head scarf); turban ■ dresses: djeballah (hooded coat); caftan ■ open-air market ■ chicken coop ■ containers ■ earthware

The British Empire

The system of triangle trading

British involvement with the **triangular trade began with the colonization of America in 1607 and the West Indies in 1623**. The chief British ports were London, Liverpool, Bristol and Glasgow.
Triangular trade is a historical term that refers to trade among three ports or regions and countries. The best-known triangular trading system is the **transatlantic trade** that operated from the seventeenth until the early nineteenth century, carrying manufactured goods, raw materials, cash crops – and slaves – between West Africa, the Caribbean and American colonies and the European colonial powers.
The **use of African slaves was fundamental** to growing crops such as cotton and tobacco, which were then exported to Europe. In turn, European goods were used to buy slaves from traders in Africa or the Caribbean. The slaves were transported to the Americas on the sea lane, the so-called middle passage, which was a horrible journey during which many slaves died of diseases and maltreatment. **Slave trade was started in 1501** by Portuguese and Spanish traders; in 1807, the UK Parliament passed a bill that officially abolished the trading of slaves, but illegal slave trade across the Atlantic Ocean was still practiced until the second half of the nineteenth century. There are an estimated 27 million victims of slavery worldwide today.

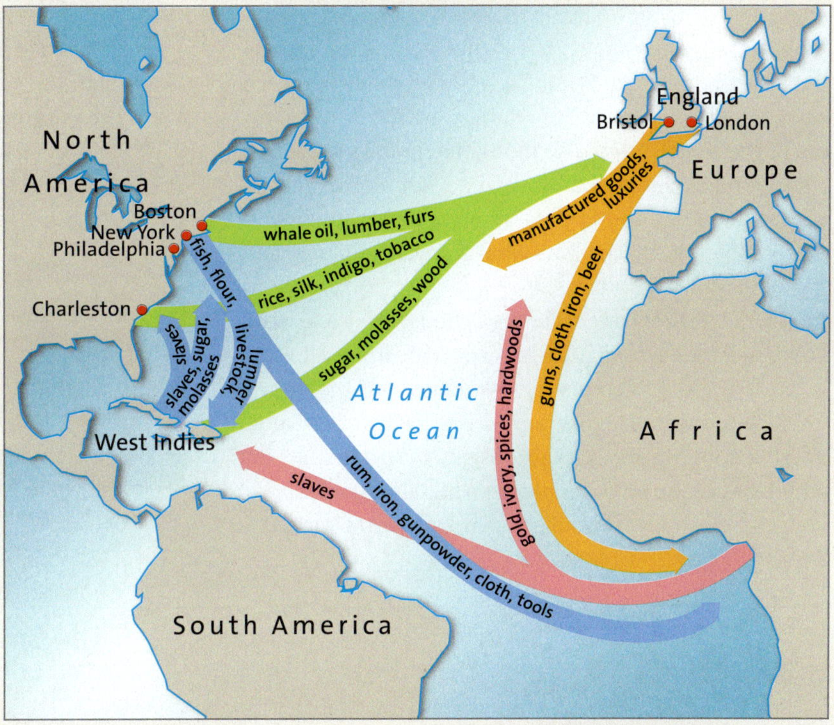

The British Empire in 1750

The British Empire in the 1750s (the blue shaded areas) traded goods worth £17 million – £8.7 million in exports and £8.3 million in imports. Britain's trade grew enormously as it gained control over many different parts of the world. The wish for expansion and the need for raw materials during the **Industrial Revolution** caused a series of overseas wars among several European countries such as France, Spain and Holland. However, one of the first British trading companies, the **East India Company**, founded in 1600 during the reign of Elizabeth I, and the **Virginia Company**, founded by her successor James I, which was the basis for the first North American colony, the **Jamestown Colony in 1607**, formed the foundations of the growth and rise of the British Empire. Many colonies began as trading centres or were founded to protect a trade route, and were run for the profit of the mother country. The wealthiest area in the early days of the Empire was the **West Indies** thanks to large profits from sugar cane and tobacco. Slaves were brought to the West Indies to work on the plantations.
The map shows the variety of goods that Britain imported from all over the world that greatly influenced the British economy and people's lives in the **mother country**.

The British Empire in 1900

Starting in 1801 the expanding empire was managed from London by the **Colonial Office**. District officers and civil servants were sent out to administer the colonies on behalf of Britain. Regular **imperial conferences** were held in Britain to discuss matters of general concern, such as trade, defence and foreign policy.

India was controlled for many years by the wealthy **East India Company**, roads and railroads were built to make trade easier, a **Governor-General** was put in charge, and British troops and civil servants were sent to the region. In 1858, following the Indian Mutiny, India was placed under the direct control of the British government and a **viceroy** replaced the Governor-General. British influence in India had expanded from a few trading stations into the **Raj** (= British rule). In 1876, **Queen Victoria** was proclaimed **Empress of India**. India brought Britain great wealth and strategic advantage, and was called the 'jewel in the crown of the Empire'. Local Indian rulers were allowed to remain in power provided they were loyal to the viceroy. Many British people spent years working in India as civil servants, engineers, police officers, etc. and took their families with them. The second period of empire-building took place in the late nineteenth century. The British Empire was at its largest and most powerful around 1920, when about 25 % of the world's population lived under British rule and over a quarter of the land in the world belonged to Britain. It was said that it was an empire **'on which the sun never sets'**, and the value of exports and imports was £970 million. At that time Britain was **one of the greatest economic and political powers in the world**. It was also thought by some people to be a moral obligation and destiny to govern poorer, less advanced countries and to pass on European culture to the native inhabitants. This was what Rudyard Kipling called the 'white man's burden'.

Britain did not only import foreign goods; there was also a great influence of foreign ideas, especially from India.

In the eighteenth century curry recipes and the famous 'mulligatawny soup' (the Tamil word for 'pepper-water') appeared in England. Indian designs influenced art and architecture, and polo, snooker and billiards, games which were played by British soldiers in India, were 'exported' to Britain.

The Brighton Pavillion was built in 'Hindoo' style in the early nineteenth century.

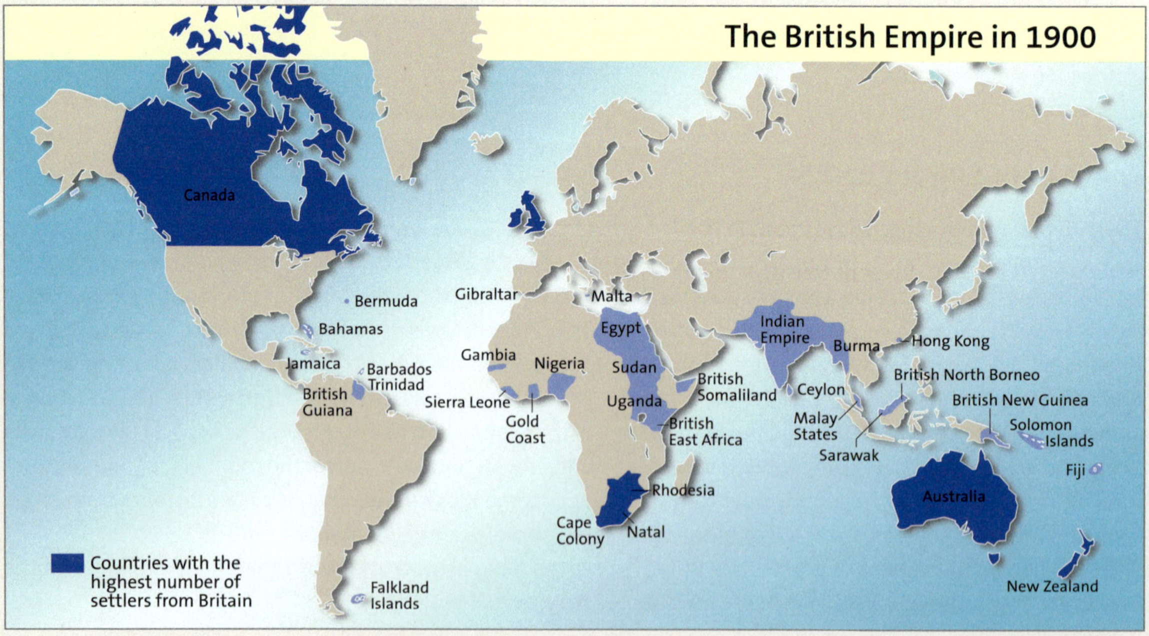

Nils Klawitter

Lizenz zum Plündern[1]

AWARENESS

What do you associate with the term "global player" and which "global players" do you know of?

Als sie das Elend nicht mehr übersehen konnten, als vor ihren Füßen in den Straßen Kalkuttas Menschen verreckten[2] und Eltern ihre Kinder für ein Stück Brot zum Verkauf anboten – in dieser Hungersnot[3] des Jahres 1770 stiegen die Händler der britischen East India Company in das Geschäft mit Nahrungsmitteln ein. Sie kauften Reis auf und lagerten[4] ihn in ihren zu Forts ausgebauten Faktoreien[5]. Dann warteten sie. Bis die Preise stiegen.

Allein im Juni 1770 erzielte ein junger Broker der Firma mit seinen Spekulationsgeschäften[6] 60 000 Pfund Profit. Doch viele konnten sich jetzt keine Nahrung mehr leisten. Mehrere Millionen Menschen starben damals im britisch beherrschten Bengalen an Unterernährung. Die Kolonialherren dagegen konnten 1770/71 über eine Million Pfund (heutiger Gegenwert: rund hundert Millionen Pfund) auf das Firmenkonto[7] nach London transferieren.

Den Ruf der East India Company konnten derartige Verbrechen kaum erschüttern[8]. Bis heute gilt die Firma, die im Dezember 1600 von 218 englischen Kaufleuten gegründet und von Königin Elizabeth I. mit einem Handelsmonopol für Asien auf den Weg geschickt wurde, Managern sogar als Vorbild: Rod Edington etwa, langjähriger Chef von British Airways, sah den Erfolg der Company als Ergebnis von „harter Arbeit, Scharfsinn[9] und Charme[10]". […]

Eine reine[11] Handelsgesellschaft, als die sie eigentlich 1600 von Elizabeth I. gegründet wurde, war die Company nie. Sie agierte wie eine Besatzungsarmee[12] mit der Lizenz zum Plündern, die von Beginn an auf „bewaffnete Stärke" setzte, wie es Nick Robins in seinem Buch „The Corporation that Changed the World" beschreibt. Um 1670 rüstete[13] König Charles II. die Firma in mehreren Erlassen[14] ganz offiziell auf: Er stattete sie mit dem Kriegs- und Gerichtsrecht[15] aus, und Münzen prägen[16] durfte sie nun auch. „Handle mit dem Schwert in der Hand" nannte das der Bombay-Statthalter der Kompanie 1677. […] In den 274 Jahren ihres Bestehens[17] [der East India Company] war der britische Anteil am Bruttoeinkommen[18] der Welt von 1,8 auf 9,1 Prozent gestiegen, der von Indien hingegen fiel von gut 22 auf 12,25 Prozent. 34 Hungerskatastrophen zählten Historiker während der britischen Herrschaft in Indien. Nur 17 jedoch in den zwei Jahrtausenden[19] zuvor. […] „Die Londoner", so [der amerikanische Soziologe] Davis, „aßen am Ende das Brot der Inder."

Spiegel Geschichte, *Das Britische Empire*, Hamburg 2013, pp. 68 ff.

COMPREHENSION

1. Subdivide the article into thematic units and find a suitable English headline for each.

2. Summarize each of the paragraphs in English. Leave out irrelevant data and numbers and use predominantly the present tense for your text.
   → Focus on Skills, Mediation, p. 384

ANALYSIS

3. Relate the key phrases and sentences from the text to Jeremy Paxman's article *The Empire Was an Amazing Thing* and explain where the texts focus on similar aspects and where they differ.
   → Focus on Skills, Analysis of a Non-Fictional Text, p. 377

[1] to plunder – [2] to die a miserable death – [3] famine – [4] to store sth. – [5] overseas trading establishment – [6] speculation – [7] company/business account – [8] to shatter – [9] astuteness – [10] charm – [11] solely – [12] occupying army – [13] to arm sth. – [14] decree/edict – [15] martial law; judicial power – [16] the right to mint coins – [17] existence – [18] gross income – [19] millennia

The Commonwealth – Common Sense? – Post-Colonial Tasks & Challenges

The Commonwealth – What Is It For?

AWARENESS

What does the name "Commonwealth" suggest about its function? Collect ideas in class.

Opening ceremony of the Commonwealth heads of government meeting (CHOGM) at the Mediterranean conference center in Valletta, 2005

The biggest achievement of the Commonwealth, its admirers say, is the fact of its unlikely[1] existence. That so many former British colonies and dominions should be content to co-exist in a club which has the queen as its head is remarkable. However, this is a low bar[2] to set for the success of an organisation nominally[3] committed to promoting democracy, human rights and the rule of law. Quite how nominally will be evident in Colombo[4] this weekend – at a gathering of Commonwealth leaders hosted by a nasty[5] and abusive[6] regime.

Be in no doubt of that. The most heinous[7] allegation[8] against Mahinda Rajapaksa's[9] family-based government – a battlefield slaughter of some 40,000 Tamil civilians – is complicated by the exigencies[10] of the appalling[11] civil war it helped end. It took ruthlessness[12] to defeat the Tamil Tigers, and Sri Lanka is better off as a result. Yet the war was also marked by reprisals[13] against journalists, human-rights activists and opposition politicians, and intimidation[14] continues today. Mr Rajapaksa has meanwhile dug in[15] for the long haul[16] – having used his popularity as a war victor to scrap[17] presidential-term limits. This amounts to a textbook transgression[18] of the Commonwealth Charter, which includes a commitment to freedom of expression, the separation of powers and the like[19], promulgated[20] by the queen in March. The meeting should never have been held in Sri Lanka.

[1] **unlikely** *unwahrscheinlich* – [2] **low bar** *niedrige Messlatte* – [3] **nominally** *dem Namen nach* – [4] **Colombo** capital of Sri Lanka – [5] **nasty** bad, very unpleasant – [6] **abusive** *misshandelnd* – [7] **heinous** ['heɪnəs] *abscheulich* – [8] **allegation** *Anschuldigung* – [9] **Mahinda Rajapaksa** President of Sri Lanka since 2005 – [10] **exigency** ['eksɪdʒənsi] (*fml.*) demand that you must deal with – [11] **appalling** *abstoßend* – [12] **ruthlessness** *Umbarmherzigkeit* – [13] **reprisal** *Vergeltungsmaßnahme* – [14] **intimidation** *Einschüchterung* – [15] **to dig in sth.** (*infml.*) *über etw. herfallen* – [16] **for the long haul** for a long period of time – [17] **to scrap** to get rid of sth. – [18] **transgression** *Überschreitung* – [19] **the like** *desgleichen* – [20] **to promulgate** to announce sth. publicly

The Commonwealth has too often failed to enforce its values. Nigeria was partially suspended[21] from the club after it hanged Ken Saro-Wiwa in 1995, as was Pakistan after its 1999 coup. But the club's overall record is timid[22]. With many more coups and killings left unsanctioned, membership is as likely to dignify[23] rights-abusers as to correct them.

What, then, is the point of the Commonwealth? Hardly any of its members' citizens can say; asked to name its head, a quarter of Jamaicans cited Barack Obama. Officials in the secretariat, housed in a splendid London mansion, toil away[24]. It is an open secret that many Commonwealth leaders attend the biennial[25] shindig[26] mainly for an opportunity to be photographed with the queen. Even that pleasure has been denied them in Colombo: for the first time in 40 years, perhaps because of her age, she is giving it a miss.

Despite these conspicuous[27] frailties[28], the Commonwealth has a few things going for it. It is cheap, costing only around £16m ($26m) a year. It runs a fine quadrennial[29] games, a respected annual literary prize and a decent scholarship programme. It could also help boost prosperity among a third of the world's population. Colonial ties, including a common law and language, boost trade; by one estimate, the cost of doing business within the Commonwealth is 20 % lower than the cost outside. By reforming its tangled[30] and ineffective bureaucracy, and using it to strengthen these advantages, the club could make more of them. That would make membership more valuable, and expulsion[31] more costly.

Come on, India

Yet bringing reform and toughness to the Commonwealth requires leadership, which it lacks. Britain, Australia and Canada would like to provide this, but cannot. Whenever they seek to improve the club – which they largely pay for – they mainly succeed in uniting its poorer members in resentful[32] opposition to their perceived post-colonial condescension[33]. The decision of Canada's prime minister, Stephen Harper, to boycott Mr Rajapaksa's fest has caused the regime little concern. His absence supports Sri Lanka's claim – with which many of its visitors sympathise – to be a victim of rich-world bullying.

The direction needs to come from the club's poor but powerful members: South Africa, Nigeria and, above all, India. Manmohan Singh, India's prime minister [until 2014], also refused to show up in Colombo – a decision he reached, ridiculously, this week. It looked like politics, not principle. A shrewder[34] India would have insisted earlier that the gathering not be held in Sri Lanka. Together with Nigeria and South Africa, Mr Singh should use the farce in Colombo as a pretext for change. Hold the members to high standards, deepen business ties – and this peculiar organisation could be a serious one.

www.economist.com/news/leaders/21589887-unreformed-commonwealth-deserves-die-improved-it-could-be-rather-useful-what-it, 16 November 2013 [23.07.2014]

COMPREHENSION

1. **Step 1:** Study the Focus on Facts (p. 55) and Focus on Documents (p. 56) pages.

   Webcode SNG-40183-009 @ **Step 2:** Watch the video clip about the Commonwealth provided on the webcode.

   Step 3: After gaining an overview of the Commonwealth, its member states and its goals, take notes on the questions below:
   - What is the status of the Commonwealth member states?
   - What are the basic criteria the member states have to meet?
   - Which aims and goals are promoted, and which principles are pursued by the Commonwealth?
   - What are the essential benefits for the member states?

2. Now read the magazine article and point out what information is given regarding the questions above.

3. What further aspects does the article refer to?

[21] **to suspend** *jdn. ausschließen* – [22] **timid** *zurückhaltend* – [23] **to dignify** *würdigen* – [24] **to toil away** to work hard – [25] **biennial** [baɪˈeniəl] every second year – [26] **shindig** (*infml.*) a noisy event; *Budenzauber* – [27] **conspicuous** very noticeable and attracting attention; *auffallend* – [28] **frailty** *Schwäche* – [29] **quadrennial** every fourth year – [30] **tangled** complicated, and not easy to understand – [31] **expulsion** *Ausschließung* – [32] **resentful** *aufgebracht* – [33] **condescension** *herablassende Haltung* – [34] **shrewd** *gewandt*

ANALYSIS

4. Examine the structural devices* employed in the article in order to express the author's critical view of the Commonwealth.
→ Focus on Skills, Analysis of a Non-Fictional Text, p. 368

5. Analyse the rhetorical devices* and explain how they create the overall tone of the article.

6. Now take another close look at the documents and examine the devices that are used to emphasize
a) aims and principles,
b) behaviour that should be opposed.

7. Interpret the cartoon and relate its message to the criticism expressed in the newspaper article.
→ Focus on Skills, Analysis of Visuals, p. 381

ACTIVITIES

8. Considering the author's harsh criticism, discuss whether it really makes sense to be a member of this organization.

The Commonwealth of Nations

The Commonwealth of Nations is an **intergovernmental organization** of 54 independent member states. All but three of these states were formerly part of the British Empire. **The cooperation of these states follows a set of values and goals outlined in the Singapore Declaration of 1971 and the Harare Declaration of 1991**. The Head of the Commonwealth is a ceremonial and representative position held by the English king or queen, currently Queen Elizabeth II.

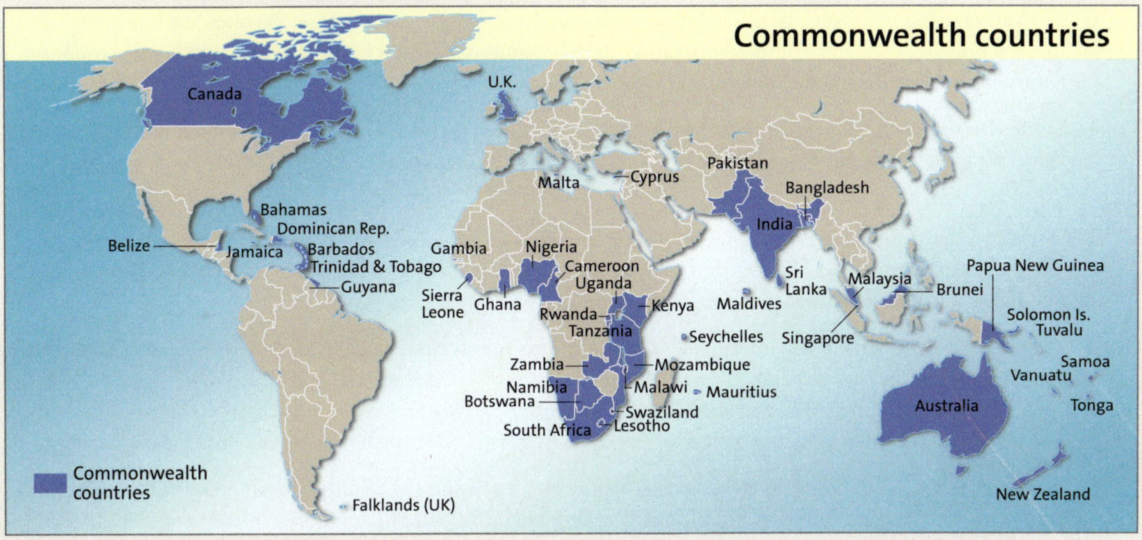

History

1926	in the **Balfour Declaration** at the Imperial Conference, Britain and its dominions agree they are equal in status, united by the common allegiance to the Crown and freely associated members of the **British Commonwealth of Nations**
1949	following the **London Declaration**, the word "British" is dropped from the title to reflect its changing nature (mostly politically independent member states)
1971	**Singapore Declaration**
1991	**Harare Declaration**
2003	**Aso Rock Declaration** states: "We are committed to democracy, good governance, gender equality, and a more equitable sharing of the benefits of globalisation."

Headquarters

The **Secretariat** was established in 1965 and is based in London; **headquarters** are in Marlborough House.

Members

The **54 current members** comprise all six inhabited continents, a population of 2.1 billion (= 1/3 of the world's population) and ca. 20 % of the world's trade. The three largest Commonwealth members are Canada, Australia and India.

Membership criteria include the promotion of (racial) equality, world peace, liberty, human rights and free trade.

Since 1939, every four years the **Commonwealth Games** are held, featuring the usual athletic disciplines as well as sports popular in the Commonwealth such as netball and rugby (2018: Gold Coast City, Queensland, Australia).

Singapore Declaration of Commonwealth Principles (1971)

This declaration was issued in Singapore on **22 January 1971** and set out the core political values that would form the main part of the Commonwealth's membership criteria. Along with the **Harare Declaration**, issued in 1991, it is considered one of the two most famous and important Commonwealth documents.

1. The Commonwealth of Nations is a voluntary association of independent sovereign states, each responsible for its own policies, consulting and co-operating in the common interests of their peoples and in the promotion of international understanding and world peace. [...]

4. Within this diversity, all members of the Commonwealth hold certain principles in common. It is by pursuing these principles that the Commonwealth can continue to influence international society for the benefit of mankind.

5. We believe that international peace and order are essential to the security and prosperity of mankind; we therefore support the United Nations and seek to strengthen its influence for peace in the world, and its efforts to remove the causes of tension between nations.

6. We believe in the liberty of the individual, in equal rights for all citizens regardless of race, colour, creed or political belief, and in their inalienable right to participate by means of free and democratic political processes in framing the society in which they live. We therefore strive to promote in each of our countries those representative institutions and guarantees for personal freedom under the law that are our common heritage.

7. We recognise racial prejudice as a dangerous sickness threatening the healthy development of the human race and racial discrimination as an unmitigated[1] evil of society. Each of us will vigorously[2] combat this evil within our own nation. No country will afford to regimes which practice racial discrimination assistance which in its own judgment directly contributes to the pursuit or consolidation of this evil policy.

8. We oppose all forms of colonial domination and racial oppression and are committed to the principles of human dignity and equality. We will therefore use all our efforts to foster human equality and dignity everywhere, and to further the principles of self-determination and non-racialism.

9. We believe that the wide disparities in wealth now existing between different sections of mankind are too great to be tolerated. They also create world tensions. Our aim is their progressive removal. We therefore seek to use our efforts to overcome poverty, ignorance and disease, in raising standards of life and achieving a more equitable international society.

10. To this end, our aim is to achieve the freest possible flow of international trade on terms fair and equitable to all, taking into account the special requirements of the developing countries, and to encourage the flow of adequate resources, including governmental and private resources, to the developing countries, bearing in mind the importance of doing this in a true spirit of partnership and of establishing for this purpose in the developing countries conditions which are conducive to sustained investment and growth.

11. We believe that international co-operation is essential to remove the causes of war, promote tolerance, combat injustice, and secure development among the peoples of the world. We are convinced that the Commonwealth is one of the most fruitful associations for these purposes. [...]

Note: In **1991, the Harare Commonwealth Declaration** reaffirmed and reinforced the Commonwealth's core principles and values, but additionally emphasized the equality of men and women, reducing debt burdens for developing countries as well as fighting environmental destruction.

[1] **unmitigated** *vollkommen* – [2] **vigorously** ['vɪgərəsli] using a lot of energy and determination

Ethnic Communities in the U.K.

Ethnic Minorities – Into the Melting Pot

AWARENESS

Take a look at the visual below and, in a Think! Pair! Share! activity, reflect on what it might express concerning the topics "multiethnic society" or "ethnic minorities".

The rapid rise of mixed-race Britain is changing neighbourhoods – and perplexing the authorities

Zadie Smith, a novelist born to a black Jamaican mother and a white British father, recently recalled that when she was growing up in Willesden Green, a London district with a large immigrant population, "nothing could be more normal than a mixed-race girl". The surprise, she said, was entering publishing and finding that people thought it unusual. Nobody could get that impression now: Britons are mixing at extraordinary speed.

The 2011 census revealed a country that is decreasingly white and British: England's ethnic-minority population grew from 9% of the total in 2001 to 14%. But the biggest single increase was in the number of people claiming a mixed-ethnic background. This almost doubled, to around 1.2 m. Among children under the age of five, 6% had a mixed background – more than belonged to any other minority group. Mixed-race children are now about as common in Britain as in America – a country with many more non-whites and a longer history of mass immigration.

As Britain's mixed-race population swells, another group appears destined to shrink. The Labour Force Survey reveals that 48% of black Caribbean men and 34% of black Caribbean women in couples are with partners of a different ethnic group – with higher proportions still among younger cohorts[1]. Black Caribbean children under ten years old are outnumbered[2] two-to-one by children who are a mixture of white and black Caribbean.

Rob Ford of Manchester University points out that Caribbean folk are following an Irish pattern of integration, in that their partners are often working-class. The Irish parallel also suggests they will eventually be fully absorbed into the British population. Polls[3] show that adults who are a mixture of white and black Caribbean tend to see themselves not so much as black, Caribbean or even as British, but rather as English – the identity of the comfortably assimilated.

Indians, who began arriving in large numbers in the 1960s, were slower to mix. They are now doing so – but along Jewish, rather than Irish, lines. For them, assimilation follows education: according to research by Raya Muttarak and Anthony Heath, Indians with degrees are far more likely to marry whites. Indians are not so much marrying into the white majority as into its suburban middle class, says Shamit Saggar at the University of Essex.

Their children are quietly transforming Britain's suburbs and commuter towns[4]. Whereas Asians are still concentrated in cities such as Leicester and in London boroughs like Tower Hamlets and Harrow, mixed Asian and white children are widespread. In Chiltern, an affluent commuter district in Buckinghamshire, 5% of children under five years old were mixed Asian and white in 2011 – more than in most of London. Their parents may have met at university or while working in the capital. Within Birmingham, too, mixed Asian and white chil-

[1] **cohort** a group of people who share a characteristic – [2] **to outnumber** to be greater in number than sb. else – [3] **poll** *Umfrage* – [4] **commuter town** a town with many inhabitants who regularly travel between work and home

dren are especially common in the largely middle-class white suburbs of Edgbaston, Moseley and Harborne.

Still warming up

Pakistanis and Bangladeshis mostly remain in cities, and are mixing more slowly. Just 8% of Pakistani men and 7% of Bangladeshi men in couples are with people of a different ethnic group, and the proportions for women are smaller. Oddly, older Pakistani men are more likely to have partners of another ethnicity, perhaps because many early migrants were single men. But even these groups are assimilating: another study finds that Pakistanis and Bangladeshis born in Britain are far likelier to socialise with whites than their parents were.

Britain's newer minorities are blending into[5] the larger population, too, but in ways that defy[6] easy categorisation. Mixed black-African and white children are particularly common in working-class suburbs and commuter towns such as Croydon and Southend-on-Sea, possibly because black Africans are rarely tied to city centres through social-housing tenancies[7]. They are also mixing with new immigrants from continental Europe. Most of the 21,000 children born to Polish mothers in 2012 had Polish fathers; but of the rest, 23% had African or Asian fathers.

Such esoteric[8] partnerships can confuse the authorities. Last November the Home Office invited journalists to accompany officers on a raid[9] of an apparent sham wedding[10] between an Italian man and a Chinese woman in north London. After interrogating the bride, groom[11] and guests, the officers emerged[12] sheepishly to admit that the union was probably real.

As race becomes less clear-cut, schools, hospitals and police forces, which record people's ethnic identity at almost every opportunity, will have to deal with more fragmented definitions. So too will researchers trying to measure racial injustices. Confusingly, police officers now record the ethnicity of the people they stop and search according to two separate systems: observed ethnic appearance (which does not include a mixed-race category) and self-identified ethnicity (which does).

Politicians in the habit of treating Britain's ethnic groups as distinct[13] "communities" will also have to adapt. The shrewder[14] black and Asian politicians have already built power bases that do not depend on ethnic block votes. Speeches such as the one made by Tony Blair in 2007 about the culture of black youth violence will look silly when so many black teenagers have white parents too. Crude[15] racist politics, thankfully now rare in Britain, ought to become almost impossible as more white families acquire[16] non-white members. Englishness, which has remained distinctly a white identity for many, may become less exclusive.

Most of all, the rise of mixed-race Britain shows that Britain is capable of absorbing even large numbers of newcomers. For the young, who are used to having people of all backgrounds in their midst, race already matters far less than it did for their parents. In a generation or two more of the melting pot, it may not matter at all.

www.economist.com/news/britain/21595908-rapid-rise-mixed-race-britain-changing-neighbourhoodsand-perplexing, 8 February 2014 [23.07.2014]

COMPREHENSION

1. Give an outline of what the 2011 census revealed about Britain's changing ethnicities.

2. Present Britain's mixed-raced population trends and people's assimilation and socializing habits focusing on:
   - Caribbeans
   - Indians
   - Asians
   - Pakistanis
   - Bangladeshis

ANALYSIS

3. Explain which "problems" multi-ethnicity poses on politicians and social researchers.
   → Focus on Skills, Analysis of a Non-Fictional Text, p. 377

4. Specify the positive "side effects" that growing numbers of mixed-race British newcomers have.

[5] **to blend into** (*phr. v.*) to look the same as surrounding people and therefore not easily noticeable – [6] **to defy** to refuse to obey a person, decision – [7] **social-housing tenancy** *Sozialwohnungsmietverhältnis* – [8] **esoteric** here: very unusual – [9] **raid** *Überfall* – [10] **sham wedding** *vorgetäuschte Heirat* – [11] **groom** *Bräutigam* – [12] **to emerge** *heraustreten* [13] **distinct** *eigen* – [14] **shrewd** *gewitzt* – [15] **crude** *roh, ungehobelt* – [16] **to acquire** to get sth.

Versi said better recording was the first step in the long process of reducing the occurrences of Islamophobic crimes. "Islamophobia and antisemitism are both serious crimes, but work to tackle antisemitism is well developed. Now we need to replicate[20] that fantastic work with Islamophobia. All forms of bigotry[21] need to be treated equally." Many Muslims were wary[22] of reporting attacks to the police, he said, believing they would be viewed "through the lens of counter-terrorism. We need a situation where the police are seen as allies against hate crimes".

http://www.theguardian.com/world/2015/oct/26/muslim-leaders-in-uk-warn-of-worrying-levels-of-islamophobia, 26 October 2015 [19.05.2016]

COMPREHENSION

2. In a **paired reading activity**, read the article from *The Guardian* and find a suitable headline for each of the thematic units 1–5.

3. After **reading** the article **a second time**, say whether the statements below are true or false or not mentioned in the text. Take notes on necessary corrections in your notebook.
- The British government has ordered police to treat crimes in connection with Islamophobia like antisemitism.
- Because London is very cosmopolitan, racially motivated crimes are rare.
- Most British Muslims have suffered from online, physical or verbal abuse.
- Videos showing anti-Muslim abuse have led to a significant rise in arrests and self-accusations.
- Statistics reveal that religiously motivated crime is very low in Britain.
- Muslims are by far the biggest group of victims of religiously motivated attacks.
- Muslim women are often victims of gender-motivated abuse and attacks.
- Online threats have been increasing after the Charlie Hebdo shootings in Paris in January 2015.
- David Cameron ordered police forces to record data on anti-Muslim hate crimes.
- Muslims all over the U.K. welcome the new anti-Islamophobia policy.

ANALYSIS

4. Examine the style of the newspaper article and explain how the author shows credibility and reliability. Pay particular attention to
- the choice of words,
- examples and references,
- citations,
- statistical data.

→ Focus on Skills, Analysis of a Non-Fictional Text, p. 377
→ Focus on Facts, The Press, p. 370

5. Compare the article from the renowned British quality newspaper *The Guardian* and the German TV documentary from *ARD Weltspiegel*. Which similarities and differences can you detect between the formats?

→ Focus on Facts, The Press, p. 370
→ Focus on Facts, The Media, p. 325

6. Analyse the line graphs on page 62 and explain the recent trends of hate crimes in England and Wales.

→ Focus on Skills, Analysis of Statistical Data, p. 380

[20] **to replicate** *(fml.)* to make or do sth. in exactly the same way – [21] **bigotry** [ˈbɪɡətri] *Borniertheit, Fanatismus* – [22] **wary** feeling or showing caution about possible dangers or problems

ACTIVITIES

7. Based on the information given in the German news documentary and the article from *The Guardian*, discuss the cartoon below. Is there some truth in the women's remarks or are they both wrong?

→ Focus on Skills, Analysis of Visuals, p. 381
→ Focus on Language, Conversation and Discussion, p. 385

Cruel Culture

Tips on vocab

left side: to wear a pony tail ■ sunglasses ■ bikini ■ high heels ■ to be dolled up ■ to strut (stolzieren)
right side: to wear a (black) Niqab (that covers the entire body, with a thin slit for the eyes)

8. Examine the statistical data on immigration and ethnic groups on the Focus on Facts page (p. 65) and relate them to the information in the article.
Do the statistical data justify the described Islamophobic fears and anxieties?
Discuss in class.

→ Focus on Facts, Great Britain – Immigration and Minorities, p. 65
→ Focus on Language, Conversation and Discussion, p. 385

Great Britain – Immigration and Minorities

Immigration, minorities and ethnic groups

After World War II, Britain needed more workers and admitted citizens of Commonwealth countries without restriction. Many came from the Caribbean and from India, Pakistan and Bangladesh. They found work in hospitals, the textile industry and the public transport system, for example. **Nearly 500,000 Commonwealth citizens came to Britain before 1962**, many of whom were later joined by their families. When there were no longer enough jobs, the **Commonwealth Immigrants Act (1962)** was passed to restrict the number of immigrants entering Britain. In the following years, several more acts were passed. **Immigration is now strictly controlled.** Normally, only people from the European Union and certain Commonwealth citizens can get permission to live in Britain. Until the Brexit of 2016, Britain accepted about 50,000 immigrants every year.

2011 Census Ethnicity

Ethnic groups, England and Wales, 2011

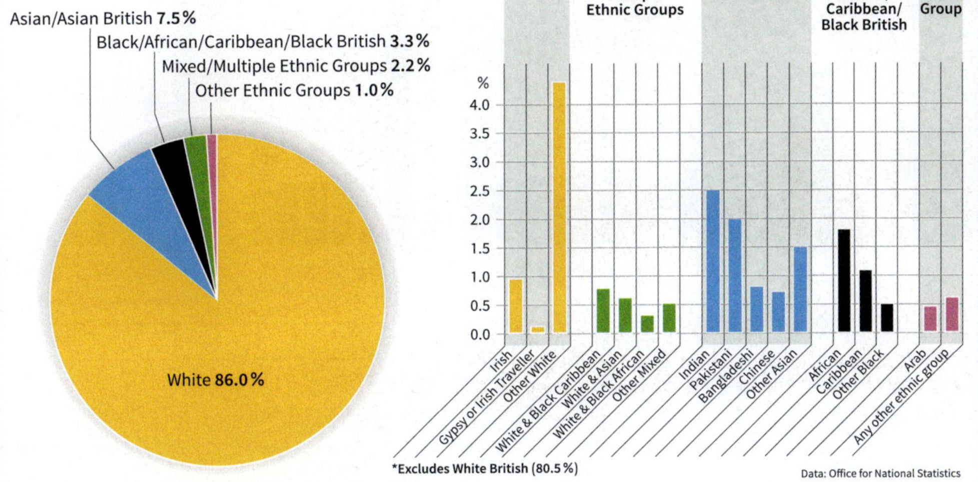

*Excludes White British (80.5 %)

Data: Office for National Statistics

2011 Census Religion

Religion in England and Wales, 2001 and 2011, all usual residents (000s)

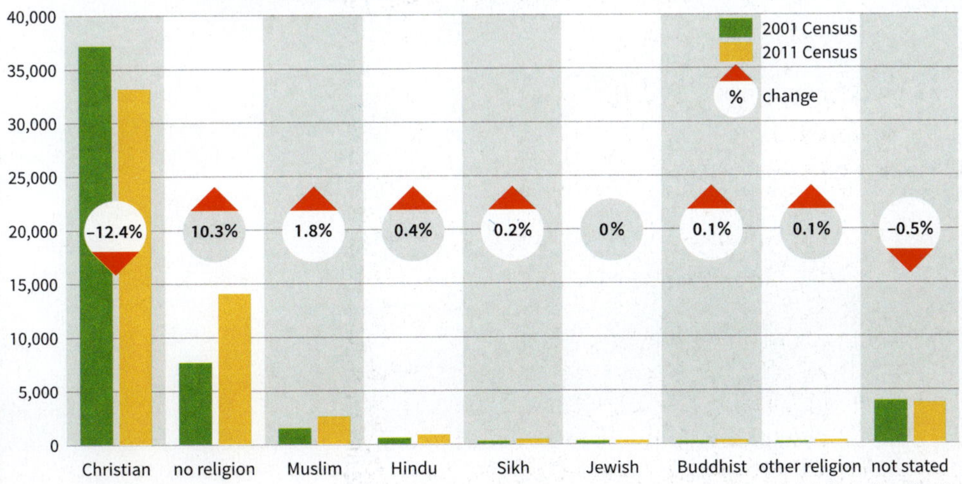

Data: Office for National Statistics

In order to control and systematize immigration, Britain introduced a **Points Based System (PBS)** in 2008, which categorizes non-EU citizens into five tiers according to their professional qualifications and background.

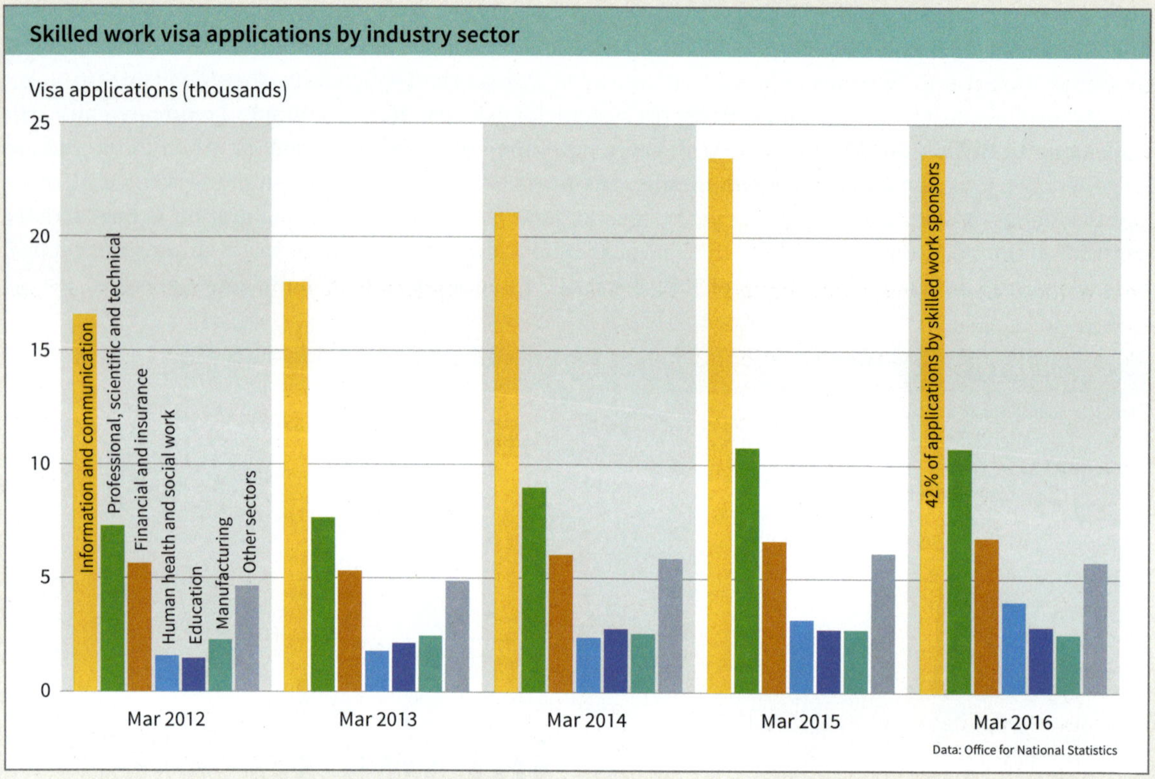

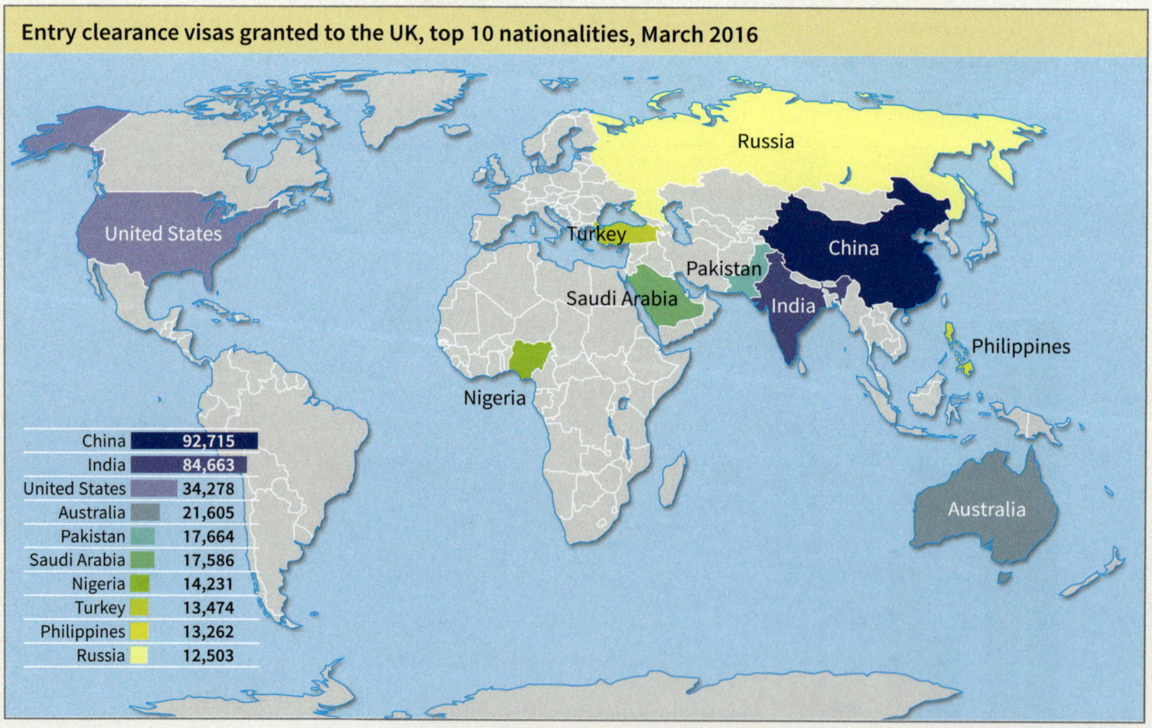

Splendid Isolation? – The U.K.'s Position in the 21st Century

Mark Mardell

Brexit: The Story of an Island Apart ☒

AWARENESS

Look at the cartoon below, which was published in a German newspaper four days after the EU referendum, and describe it in detail.
What kind of "before and after" situation is depicted and what gruesome scenario does the cartoon hint at?

Tips on vocab

left side: to walk off a cliff ■ blue skies ■ to live/walk around in cloud cuckoo land ■ to be a Johnny Head-in-the-Air *(Hans Guck-in-die-Luft)* ■ to wear a grey business suit/a bowler hat/a moustache ■ blindfold glasses ■ a sign with the EU flag/logo
right side: to suddenly fall ■ bulging eyes ■ to fly off sb.'s head ■ to tense up in fear ■ to be torn apart ■ to be torn in two ■ the English flag (St George's Cross) ■ the Scottish flag (St Andrew's Cross) ■ flock of birds

COMPREHENSION

1. **Before reading:**
In the run-up to the EU referendum, the German media covered the possible Brexit scenario in detail, speculating about the outcome of the referendum and possible consequences.
The German political TV magazine *ARD Weltspiegel* visited and interviewed people from Cornwall *before* the referendum and people from Stoke-on-Trent *afterwards* and tried to capture the atmosphere and people's thoughts.

Webcode SNG-40183-011

Step 1: In a group puzzle activity, divide the class into six groups. There are two documentaries provided on the webcode; three groups work with one documentary, three with the other.

Tip: Use the Tips on vocab boxes and/or your dictionary to mediate the statements and information into English. Keep your notes because you will need them later on (cf. task No. 7).

M **Step 2:** Watch the respective documentary and take notes in English on the aspects listed below.

Großbritannien: Das Referendum (19 June 2016)

- the social consequences of the Brexit campaign
- the position and problems of Cornwall's fishermen
- money and subsidization from Brussels
- people's stubbornness and (hurt) pride
- unforeseeable consequences for the younger generation

Tips on vocab

cheesy romantic films ■ hedge ■ outer tip ■ sb.'s nerves are on edge ■ to go down the drain ■ xenophobia ■ core English ■ in the heat of the battle ■ fleet ■ to blame sb. ■ fishing quota ■ to the highest bidder ■ non-seafaring people ■ domestic market ■ cooling system ■ boardwalk ■ to hold sway ■ pension ■ vocational school ■ to leave sb. behind ■ to put sb. down as a scapegoat ■ stubbornness ■ tin mine ■ downhill ■ structural fund ■ to beat the drum for sb./sth. ■ stupid fool ■ to be subsidized ■ uncertainty ■ to snatch sth. away from sb. ■ nostalgia ■ to keep one's fingers crossed for sb. ■ to shoulder sth. ■ ballot box

Großbritannien: Katerstimmung auf der Insel (3 July 2016)

- the economic situation of the citizens of Stoke-on-Trent
- reasons for Stoke-on-Trent's economic decline
- Sajid Hashni's situation
- Islamophobia in Stoke-on-Trent
- reasons why Stoke-on-Trent voted for Brexit
- Stoke-on-Trent and the government in London

Tips on vocab

hangover ■ pottery industry ■ decline ■ window cleaner ■ right-wing populist ■ to complain ■ to ruin sth. ■ barber ■ beauty salon ■ discrepancy ■ neglect ■ cross-off list ■ welfare organization ■ the necessity for saving money ■ public service ■ austerity ■ scapegoat ■ to serve as sth. ■ dilapidated ■ housing estate ■ mob, attackers ■ for sb.'s benefit ■ to rebel against sb./sth. ■ slogan ■ to become entangled ■ to teach sb. a lesson ■ to be based on lies ■ government leaders

Step 3: After completing your notes, remix the groups and exchange your results.

1 Our little archipelago[1] of isles on the outer edges of a huge land mass has often thought of itself as rather special, even before it was the centre of an empire that changed the world.

As so often, Shakespeare put it best: "This precious stone set in the silver sea/ Which serves it in the office of a wall/ Or as a moat[2] defensive to a house,/ Against the envy of less happier lands,/ This blessed plot, this earth, this realm, this England."

It is that silver sea that helps define our relationship with the rest of Europe.

These isles have very rarely been in isolation from it, whether splendid or otherwise. How could it be, as one historian recently argued, when the Magna Carta was signed by French nobles and the Bill of Rights designed for a Dutch prince?

But it has always kept a beady[3] eye on other powers across the water.

It has been often concerned with stopping other European powers dominating the continent, playing one off against another.

But from that physical separation flows a psychological distance too.

2 As the BBC's first Europe editor, I spent a lot of time thinking about our tricky relationship. After all, in my previous incarnation[4] as a political journalist based at Westminster I had seen how some politicians' pro-

[1] **archipelago** an extensive group of islands – [2] **moat** *Festungsgraben* – [3] **beady** bright and keenly observant; *wachsam* – [4] **incarnation** here: profession

found[5] distaste[6] for the evolving project of the European Union had blown back into British politics with profound and startling[7] consequences.
I had watched as Margaret Thatcher's[8] attitude towards the EU's nascent[9] plans for a single currency, summed up by "no, no, no", had her own side bringing her down. It was the defenestration[10] of a prime minister deeply beloved by most of her party.
I had reported for Newsnight as John Major's[11] government was harried[12] and hamstrung[13] by those who rebelled against the Maastricht treaty[14]. Europe meant it could do nothing. Blair's[15] government was much friendlier, with any tensions buried by his own project.
Now Europe has claimed another scalp, that of a man who told his party to stop banging on about it. It will be the thing that David Cameron is remembered for – banging on about Europe, and losing the argument.
Now I know the European Union is not Europe. But those who stress that are missing the point. No, it is not the same as European culture. No it is not a geographically exact expression. But there are only a couple of European countries who are "out", and firmly intend to stay out. All the others, or at least their leaders, want a share in this deeply political expression of a dream.

3 By the end of my time based in Brussels I was convinced that I had understood the key difference. To many in the UK being part of the EU was a hard-headed[16] economic relationship, about free markets, selling and buying stuff. It was a sort of second best, a consolation prize[17] after the loss of empire, but not one that had a similar place in patriots' hearts.
But for nearly all the other countries it was a refuge. It was a home they were constructing as a bulwark[18] against history, against horror.
Germany was fleeing its role in spreading death and destruction to every corner of the continent, fleeing its own political ambitions. France was running away from defeat and occupation, from humiliation and powerlessness.
So were many other countries. Greece, Portugal and Spain found refuge – in an imagined future – from the real past of right-wing dictatorships. The countries of the East were replacing communist tyranny with a new attempt to create peace and democracy.
The thought that war could once again ravage[19] a continent, so risible[20] to David Cameron's detractors[21], do not seem so funny to many on the continent.
For many Britons, World War Two was our finest hour, standing alone, and putting those Europeans to shame, withstanding Hitler and beating him. Some realised the Russians and the Americans helped a little bit too. But we were still better than the rest of the Quislings[22] and dictators.
The European Union, for all its bureaucracy, is a deeply romantic project, a desire to forge[23] something new, something different. A new relationship binding nation states in a way that will exorcise forever the ghosts of the inglorious past.

4 I sat in a cafe next to some fairly senior people who work in the commission in Brussels. They were despairing of Brexit, making desperate, rather hysterical jokes about it and the future in Britain. But then one by one they confessed when they got up on Friday morning, switched on the news, checked their phones, they cried. Few in the UK would say that if another country left the EU.
But the irritations of these dozen or so people of different nationalities, with the UK – comments about British pride, warm beer and arrogant politicians – underlined a more fundamental frustration with British attitudes.
These Spanish, and Swedes, a Belgian and a Hungarian, were all emoting[24] and swearing and arguing in English. One said (in French) "maybe we can all go back to speaking French now". She was shouted down – in English – "that will never happen. English is the language of the European Union now."
I remember Neil Kinnock[25] joking that the EU changed forever when the Swedes arrived and started saying "good morning" in the lift.
One might think that is trivial. But maybe it highlights something we rarely realise in our desire for hard power

[5] **profound** intense, very great – [6] **distaste** dislike, aversion – [7] **startling** surprising, astonishing, remarkable – [8] **Margaret Thatcher** (1925 – 2013) British politician, leader of the Conservative Party and prime minister (1979 – 1990) – [9] **nascent** ['næsnt] *aufkeimend* – [10] **defenestration** *(infml.)* the act of dismissing sb. from a position of power – [11] **John Major** (*1943) British politician, leader of the Conservative Party and prime minister (1990 – 1997) – [12] **harried** *bedrängt* – [13] **hamstrung** *handlungsunfähig gemacht* – [14] **Maastricht Treaty** (1992) treaty that created the European Union – [15] **Tony Blair** (*1953) British politician, leader of the Labour Party and prime minister (1997 – 2007) – [16] **hard-headed** *stur* – [17] **consolation prize** *Trostpreis* – [18] **bulwark** *Bollwerk* – [19] **to ravage** ['rævɪdʒ] to cause severe and extensive damage – [20] **risible** *lächerlich* – [21] **detractor** opponent, critic – [22] **Quisling** a person who collaborates with an enemy occupying force – [23] **to forge** *schmieden* – [24] **to emote** *dramatisieren* – [25] **Neil Kinnock** (*1942) British Labour Party politician

– the extent of our soft power. It also underscores a real frustration with the British that has been growing. Many in Europe think we've won. While readers of some British newspapers have been treated to stories of little Britain being bullied by the big commission, that is not how you see it if you are, say, Portuguese or Latvian. Then you would see, time after time, Britain being given a special deal, treated with kid gloves[26] and washed with buckets[27] of soft soap. [...]

They say we've won. We won and turned Europe on to a free-market, anti-statist, liberal economic agenda. We won on enlargement – the unlovely word for our insistence that the EU couldn't wait, and had to rapidly take in the countries of the former communist block.

Then there are those deals.

We are outside the Euro. Outside home affairs and justice rules. Outside the passport-free Schengen zone. David Cameron won a concession that we would be outside "ever closer union".

Now we want to be outside the whole shebang[28]. Don't be surprised if the instinct of some is to make sure that we feel some discomfort[29] on our way out.

5 I realised something else during my time based in Brussels. The old caricature of those who were opposed to the EU was less and less true. They didn't base their arguments on dislike of foreigners. They professed to love Europe's variety and embraced its language and culture. It was the organisation they disliked.

Many of the political elites were snobby about these opponents, and felt the questions they were raising were illegitimate[30]. They didn't engage with the argument but swept it under the carpet, turned a blind eye and hoped they wouldn't be heard.

The Dutch and French rejected the constitution in a referendum, but it was politicians from the UK who voiced the discontent some European voters felt.

What was once as rare in Europe as a dodo[31] riding on a unicorn is now commonplace. All over Europe there is deep suspicion of the European Union.

It took the financial crisis to turn these new Eurosceptics into an alternative to the mainstream. But the very heart of their objection will not go away for the European Union – and it is difficult to see how it is solved.

It is their old joke playing on the root of the word "democracy" – that the EU can't be a democracy as it has a "cracy" [rule] but not a "demos" [people].

6 Now, there is nothing either sacred or immutable[32] about the nation state or people's fellow feeling towards others. Roman citizens felt Roman, even while not being what we would call Italian, let alone from the Eternal City.

During the Depression, as recorded by John Steinbeck[33] in *The Grapes of Wrath*, people living in one US state, California, resented the poor from another American state, Oklahoma, moving there to work. Even though they were all Americans.

But it is undoubtedly true the UK's immigration debate and the Greek crisis are so heated because people don't feel the same connection, the same (often limited) desire to help people from other European nations, as they do those they define as their own.

That, not red tape[34] or some ill-defined responsiveness[35], is the EU's central problem. It will have to start recognising it and wrestling with it rather than resenting[36] it and ignoring it, if it wants to survive.

Indeed our exit leaves the European Union with multiple headaches. The threat of other countries following suit is perhaps the main one.

But it is what it does to Britain's old ambition that is perhaps more intriguing[37]. It changes the balance of power.

Germany will almost certainly end up paying more. They will no longer be able to rely on the UK joining them and the Finns and the Swedes and the Dutch to join their side in an economic argument.

A hefty[38] weight will soon be withdrawn from the balance. A straight North-South fight will become sharper.

Economic liberals may not like the result. But there is an even more central problem.

I thought it odd when Boris Johnson during the campaign was picked up for claiming that the EU wanted to fulfil Hitler's ambitions by other means. He was lam-

[26] **kid gloves** *Samthandschuhe* – [27] **bucket** *Eimer* – [28] **shebang** matter, operation – [29] **discomfort** worry – [30] **illegitimate** [ˌɪlə'dʒɪtəmət] illegal, unlawful – [31] **dodo** an extinct bird; *Dodo* – [32] **immutable** unchanging or unable to be changed – [33] **John Steinbeck** (1902–1968) American author; winner of the 1962 Nobel Prize in Literature – [34] **red tape** bureaucracy – [35] **responsiveness** the quality of reacting quickly and positively – [36] **to resent** to feel bitterness – [37] **intriguing** [ɪn'tri:gɪŋ] fascinating – [38] **hefty** large and heavy – [39] **to lambaste sb.** to criticize sb. harshly

basted[39] for the sin of mentioning Hitler, but not tackled on the central point he was making.

You could argue the very purpose of the EU is not to achieve continent-wide dictatorship from some Brussels bunker, but to prevent the domination of Europe by one power, namely Germany. Now modern Germany is sane and sober, cautious of military adventure and brutal power, to a degree rarely seen in other nations. There is perhaps little we need fear.

But the euro crisis and the refugee crisis shows that German political might is powerfully resented. As its past recedes[40] it will inevitably[41] act more openly in its own interests, less cloaked in an apparently altruistic[42] care for the whole continent. Britain may have to watch from the sidelines, across the Channel, powerless to intervene, or offer guidance, unless by megaphone.

We see ourselves as separate, and so we shall soon be cut out of councils and commission that are still shaping a continent. Some in Brussels may reflect smugly[43] on how John of Gaunt's[44] speech in Richard II[45] concludes: "That England that was wont[46] to conquer others/Hath made a shameful conquest of itself."

http://www.bbc.com/news/magazine-36620426, 25 June 2016 [14.09.2016]

COMPREHENSION

2. In the magazine article, the author reflects on Britain's complex, complicated and even contradictory relationship with the European continent.
In a **paired reading** activity, read the text on your own and take notes on the questions below. After each paragraph, you and your partner summarize the paragraph together, crosscheck the notes you have taken and make corrections and/or additions if necessary.

1
- Point out Britain's special place/position within Europe.
- What are the consequences of being an island nation?

2
- Present the different Prime Ministers' attitudes towards the EU.
- Describe the difference between the EU and Europe.

3
- What was the function of the EU to Britain?
- What did the EU mean to the other European nations?
- How did the Britons view themselves after WWII?

4
- Describe people's reactions to the British exit.
- Outline what makes Britain a soft power.
- What were the special deals that Britain enjoyed – much to the frustration of the other EU nations?

5
- Outline the process of more and more European nations becoming Eurosceptic.
- What did (most) European nations embrace and adopt from the EU as a whole?

6
- Point out the reasons that make people feel
  a) united,
  b) disconnected from others.
- Describe the consequences of the Brexit with regard to
  a) the (future) balance of power within the EU,
  b) Germany's position and power,
  c) Britain's exclusion from European politics.

[40] **to recede** to move further away – [41] **inevitable** [ɪn'evɪtəb(ə)l] certain to happen; unavoidable – [42] **altruistic** unselfish – [43] **smugly** *eingebildet, selbstgefällig* – [44] **John of Gaunt** (1340 – 1399) 1st Duke of Lancaster; member of the House of Plantagenet; ancestor of the House of Lancaster, incl. King Henry VI; Richard II's uncle – [45] **Richard II King of England** (1377 – 1399); history play by William Shakespeare (ca. 1595) – [46] **wont** *(lit.)* in the habit of doing sth.; accustomed to sth.

ANALYSIS

3. Examine the author's observations and remarks on Britain's relationship with the EU and illustrate how he juxtaposes the contradictions and controversies that have existed throughout British-European relationship.
   → Focus on Skills, Analysis of a Non-Fictional Text, p. 377

4. Analyse the author's choice of words and explain how it emphasizes the ambivalent relationship Britain has to continental Europe and the EU.
   → Focus on Skills, Analysis of a Non-Fictional Text, p. 377

5. **Step 1:** Take a look at the article from the German daily newspaper *Express* (p. 73) and extract further information on the negative consequences of the Brexit, in addition to the information given in the BBC article.
   → Focus on Skills, Mediation, p. 384

   Step 2: Explain to what extent the information in the article and the bar chart matches the impression conveyed in the German TV documentary *Großbritannien: Katerstimmung auf der Insel* (p. 67 f.).
   Use your notes from the before-reading task (Step 2, p. 68) and discuss the similarities and differences in class.

ACTIVITIES

Webcode SNG-40183-011

6. Do a project on the British referendum and subsequent Brexit using the weblinks provided on the webcode.

7. Based on the information you have collected in the previous tasks, prepare and act out a panel discussion in which you reflect on the different positions taken on the matter, e.g.
   - Eurosceptic Britons who feel deprived of their right to independently decide on national matters
   - Euro-friendly Britons who primarily consider themselves to be European and who are concerned about being isolated economically and politically
   - young Britons who do not want to lose touch with continental Europe
   - old Britons who fear being overrun by immigrants and being economically disadvantaged by the EU
   - etc.

   → Focus on Language, Conversation and Discussion, p. 385

GRAMMAR / LANGUAGE

8. Against the different views taken on the Brexit, formulate different types of conditional sentences to express people's feelings and concerns.
   Example:
   - If older Britons had had less nationalistic views, the referendum would have had a different result. (type III)
   - If politicians do not listen to people's concerns and fears more carefully, the societal division of Britain will grow even more. (type I)

Zerrissenes Land: Die Alten stimmten für den Brexit, die Jungen sind entsetzt[1]

„Ich bin am Boden zerstört[2]“, sagt die 51-jährige Londonerin Anne-Marie Williams angesichts[3] der Mehrheit für den Brexit. „Ich habe richtig Bauchschmerzen[4].“

Das Ergebnis der Volksabstimmung sei eine Katastophe. Abgesehen von den wirtschaftlichen Folgen tut es ihr vor allem um ihre Kinder leid. „Meine Kinder haben weniger Möglichkeiten in der Zukunft. Sie werden weniger frei reisen und studieren können. Und wofür eigentlich? Da haben alte Leute über die Zukunft junger Menschen entschieden, das ist nicht fair“, empört[5] sie sich.

In der Wählergruppe[6] er 65-Jährigen und Älteren stimmten 58 Prozent für den Austritt aus der EU, so viele wie in keiner anderen Altersgruppe. Bei den 18-24-Jährigen waren es dagegen nur 33 Prozent.

Pop-Sängerin Lily Allen (31) brachte die Stimmung in ihrer Generation drastisch auf den Punkt[7]: „Für uns ist die Sache richtig scheiße gelaufen[8].“

Es geht ein tiefer Riss[9] durch die britische Gesellschaft: Die jungen, gebildeten Menschen in den Städten hatten sich mit übergroßer[10] Mehrheit für die EU ausgesprochen.

Jetzt ist die Wut groß auf die Alten, eher Ungebildeten[11] auf dem Land, die für den Brexit waren. Schon 100,000 Menschen unterzeichneten gestern eine Petition. Darin wird angesichts des knappen[12] Siegs der Brexit-Befürworter[13] eine neue, zweite Volksabstimmung gefordert.

Express, 25 June 2016, p. 4

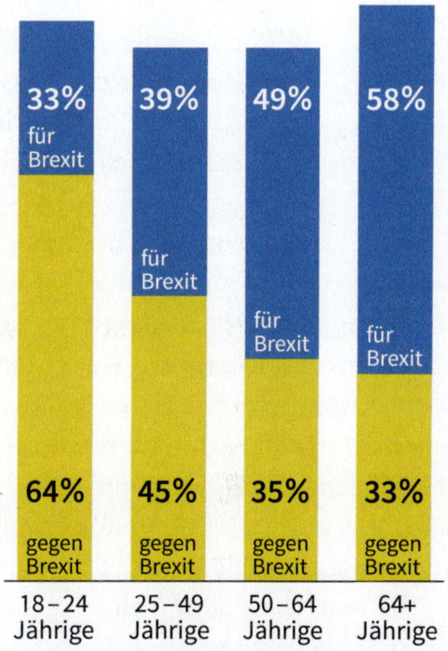

Je älter, desto Brexit-freundlicher: 58% der Gruppe 65+ waren für den Ausstieg

Daten: YouGov

Boris Johnson

I Cannot Stress Too Much That Britain Is Part of Europe – And Always Will Be

AWARENESS

Boris Johnson (*1964), a British politician and member of the Conservative Party, was Mayor of London from 2008 until 2016 and has been Secretary of State for Foreign and Commonwealth Affairs since July 2016. He is a controversial figure in British politics. On the one hand, he has been praised for his wit and humour; on the other hand, he has been criticized for being elitist, cynical, lazy, dishonest, racist, and using xenophobic and homophobic language. In February 2016, Johnson endorsed the *VoteLeave* campaign for the U.K.'s EU membership referendum and became one of the most prominent figures in the Brexit discussion. After Britain's Brexit vote, Johnson was criticized for tearing apart the Conservative Party and for his role in the U.K.'s constitutional crisis.

Reflect and speculate on the headline of Johnson's article, published three days after the Brexit vote. What might have been Johnson's reason for writing the article?

[1] shocked – [2] devastated – [3] in view of – [4] makes me sick to my stomach – [5] to be up in arms against sb./sth. – [6] voting bloc – [7] to put sth. in a nutshell – [8] things went terribly wrong – [9] rift – [10] gigantic – [11] uneducated – [12] tight – [13] proponent, advocate

COMPREHENSION

1. **While reading** the article, finish the following statements using information from the text.
   a) The EU referendum was divisive for the U.K. because …
   b) People voted *Leave* because …
   c) The negative consequences are greatly overdone because …
   d) Despite the Brexit, Britain and British people will be able to …
   e) There is big cause for optimism because …

This EU referendum has been the most extraordinary political event of our lifetime. Never in our history have so many people been asked to decide a big question about the nation's future. Never have so many thought so deeply, or wrestled so hard with their consciences, in an effort to come up with the right answer.

It has been a grueling[1] campaign in which we have seen divisions between family and friends and colleagues – sometimes entirely amicable[2], sometimes, alas[3], less so. In the end, there was a clear result. More than 17 million people voted to leave the EU – more than have ever assented[4] to any proposition[5] in our democratic history. Some now cast doubt on their motives, or even on their understanding of what was at stake[6].

It is said that those who voted Leave were mainly driven by anxieties about immigration. I do not believe that is so. After meeting thousands of people in the course of the campaign, I can tell you that the number one issue was control – a sense that British democracy was being undermined by the EU system, and that we should restore to the people that vital power: to kick out their rulers at elections, and to choose new ones.

I believe that millions of people who voted Leave were also inspired by the belief that Britain is a great country, and that outside the job-destroying coils[7] of EU bureaucracy we can survive and thrive[8] as never before. I think that they are right in their analysis, and right in their choice. And yet we who agreed with this majority verdict[9] must accept that it was not entirely overwhelming.

There were more than 16 million who wanted to remain. They are our neighbours, brothers and sisters who did what they passionately believe was right. In a democracy majorities may decide but everyone is of equal value. We who are part of this narrow majority must do everything we can to reassure the Remainers. We must reach out, we must heal, we must build bridges – because it is clear that some have feelings of dismay[10], and of loss, and confusion.

I believe that this climate of apprehension is understandable, given what people were told during the campaign, but based on a profound misunderstanding about what has really taken place. At home and abroad, the negative consequences are being wildly overdone, and the upside is being ignored. The stock market is way above its level of last autumn; the pound remains higher than it was in 2013 and 2014.

The economy is in good hands. Most sensible people can see that Bank of England governor Mark Carney has done a superb job – and now that the referendum is over, he will be able to continue his work without being in the political firing-line. Thanks in large part to the reforms put in place by David Cameron and George Osborne, the fundamentals of the UK economy are outstandingly strong – a dynamic and outward-looking economy with an ever-improving skills base, and with a big lead in some of the key growth sectors of the 21st century.

We should be incredibly proud and positive about the UK, and what it can now achieve. And we will achieve those things together, with all four nations united. We had one Scotland referendum in 2014, and I do not detect any real appetite to have another one soon; and it goes without saying that we are much better together in forging[11] a new and better relationship with the EU – based on free trade and partnership, rather than a federal system.

I cannot stress too much that Britain is part of Europe, and always will be. There will still be intense and intensifying European cooperation and partnership in a huge number of fields: the arts, the sciences, the universities, and on improving the environment. EU citizens living in this country will have their rights fully protected, and the same goes for British citizens living in the EU.

[1] **grueling** extremely tiring and difficult – [2] **amicable** ['æmɪkəbəl] *einvernehmlich* – [3] **alas** used to express sadness or feeling sorry about sth. – [4] **to assent to sth.** *(fml.)* to agree or give official approval to sth. – [5] **proposition** idea or opinion – [6] **to be at stake** *auf dem Spiel stehen* – [7] **coils** here: *Windungen; Hürden* – [8] **to thrive** to grow, develop or be successful – [9] **verdict** an opinion or decision made after judging the facts that are given – [10] **dismay** a feeling of unhappiness and disappointment – [11] **to forge** *schmieden*

Her intervention has also led to calls by Sinn Fein[2] for a vote on Irish unity because Northern Ireland also backed *Remain*.

While the UK as a whole voted to leave the European Union, Scots overwhelmingly opted to remain, with Ms Sturgeon declaring the result meant there had been a 'significant and material change in the circumstances in which Scotland voted against independence' in 2014.

Many Scots on social media who voted 'No' to the country breaking away from the UK in 2014 say they would change their vote if a new referendum was to be held.

Ms Sturgeon said: 'As things stand, Scotland faces the prospect of being taken out of the EU against our will. I regard that as democratically unacceptable.'

Speaking at her official residence, Bute House in Edinburgh, she said: 'I intend to take all possible steps and explore all possible options to give effect to how people in Scotland voted – in other words to secure our continuing place in the EU, and in the single market in particular.' […]

Ms Sturgeon said: 'It is, therefore, a statement of the obvious that a second referendum must be on the table, and it is on the table.'

And last night, a key ally[3] of German chancellor Angela Merkel told Scots that they would be welcome to remain in the EU if they left the United Kingdom.

Manfred Weber, leader of the biggest group in the European Parliament, said: 'On the Scottish level, to go the other way, it is up to them. Europe is open to new member states, that is totally clear. Those who want to stay are welcome in the European Union.'

The invitation is in stark[4] contrast to two years ago, when senior Brussels figures said they would not accept Scotland as a member because they did not want to reward secessionist[5] parts of member states.

All 32 local authority areas north of the border returned a majority for Remain in the EU referendum, with the country voting by 62 % to 38 % in favour of *Remain*.

Ms Sturgeon said: 'Unfortunately, of course, yesterday's result in Scotland was not echoed across the whole of the United Kingdom. The UK-wide vote to leave the EU is one that I deeply regret.

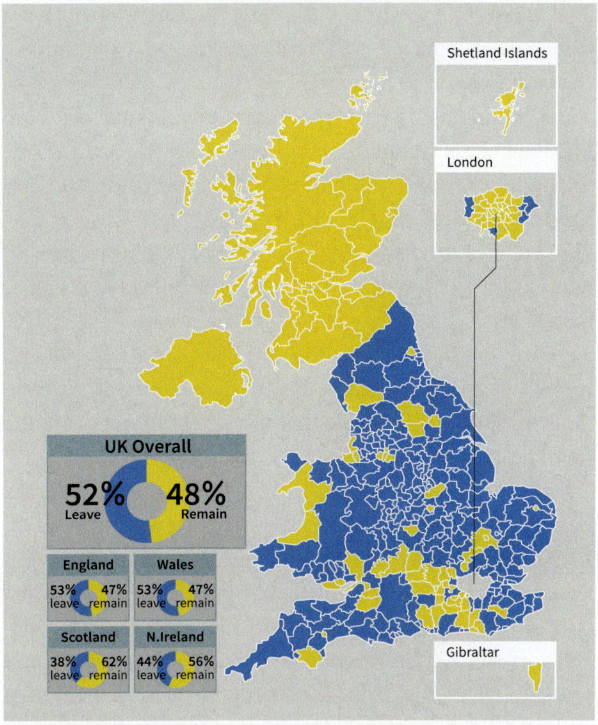

All 32 local authorities in Scotland delivered a vote for Remain

'The vote across England and Wales was a rejection of the EU and it was a sign of divergence[6] between Scotland and large parts of the rest of the UK and how we see our place in the rest of the world.'

Furious Scottish nationalists had already pounced[7] on today's historic vote to leave the EU by immediately demanding a second referendum on splitting from the UK. The SNP said the UK faces a 'constitutional crisis' after Scotland voted overwhelmingly in favour of staying in the EU but is on course to cut ties[8] with Brussels after the *Leave* won the overall UK vote.

All 32 authorities north of the border delivered majority wins for Remain and joined only London and Northern Ireland as areas that did not vote for Brexit. Irish republicans have already used the referendum result to call for the reunification of Ireland. […]

The passionate pro-union Harry Potter author JK Rowling angrily hit out at David Cameron, accusing him of putting the future of the UK in jeopardy[9] for calling the referendum in the first place.

[2] **Sinn Fein** [ˌʃɪn ˈfeɪn] an Irish political party that wants Northern Ireland to become part of the Republic of Ireland – [3] **ally** [ˈælaɪ] *Verbündeter, Alliierter* – [4] **stark** obvious – [5] **secessionist** *abtrünnig* – [6] **divergence** [ˌdaɪˈvɜːdʒəns] the situation in which two things become different – [7] **to pounce** to jump or move quickly in order to catch or get hold of sth. – [8] **to cut ties** *die Verbindungen abbrechen* – [9] **jeopardy** [ˈdʒepədi] in danger of being damaged or destroyed

She wrote: 'Scotland will seek independence now. Cameron's legacy[10] will be breaking up two unions. Neither needed to happen.'

This morning Ms Sturgeon's predecessor[11] as First Minister Alex Salmond said he was 'quite certain' Ms Sturgeon would 'implement the manifesto' because England is 'dragging us out the EU'.

He said a second referendum on splitting from the UK should be held within two years so Scotland is not forced out of the EU.

The process of withdrawing from Brussels will take up to two years from when the UK Government triggers Article 50 of the Lisbon treaty[12] – which sets out the formal arrangements for leaving.

'From when that starting gun is fired, it's a two-year period,' Mr Salmond said of the withdrawal process.

Insisting a second independence referendum was justified, he added: 'So whatever that period is – two years, two-and-a-half years, that would have to be the timescale of the next referendum because what you would want to do is remain in the European Union while the rest of the UK moved out.'

Holyrood[13] External Affairs Secretary Fiona Hylsop warned that a decision by the UK to quit Europe would have 'consequences'. [...]

To stage[14] a second vote on Scottish independence Nicola Sturgeon would have to secure agreement from the Westminster Government. This is because legislating for a referendum is a reserved power – not devolved to the Scottish Parliament. Without agreement from the UK Government, any vote held on Scottish independence would have no legal effect on the Union.

The Scottish Government could decide to hold an 'advisory[15] referendum on extending the powers of the Scottish Parliament' but the result could not be enforced. Lacking a majority, the SNP would need Green support to get a referendum through. But Ruth Davidson, the Scottish Tory leader, said a second vote would not be in Scotland's best interests.

If Mrs Sturgeon went ahead with an 'advisory' vote, she could use the results as proof of the overwhelming desire for independence and demand the UK Government grant her the right to hold a legally-binding second vote on Scottish independence.

In reality, despite Alex Salmond insisting the 2014 was a 'once in a lifetime' vote, Scottish voters will almost certainly be given another chance very soon in their lifetimes. The fact that all 32 authorities voted in favour of remaining in the EU means Scotland is being taken out of the EU against its will. This 'constitutional crisis' – as many have called it – is not going to go away anytime soon.

http://www.dailymail.co.uk/news/article-3657649/Now-Scotland-demands-independence-Nicola-Sturgeon-quite-certain-stage-second-referendum-raging-Scots-dragged-EU-against-says-furious-Alex-Salmond.html, 24 June 2016 [08.09.2016]

2 Nicola Sturgeon: Interview on the EU Referendum and Scotland's Position

Nicola Sturgeon (*1970) is a Scottish politician and current First Minister of Scotland and Leader of the Scotish National Party (SNP).

In a TV interview on 26 June 2016, she described the post-Brexit situation from the Scottish perspective and explained which political steps she planned to take.

Tips on vocab

to cast one's eyes to look at sb./sth. ■ **disarray** the state of being confused and having no organization ■ **shambolic** confused and badly organized ■ **to abdicate responsibility** to stop controlling or managing sth. that you are in charge of ■ **to let sb. down** *(phr. v.)* to disappoint sb. by failing to do what you agreed to or were expected to do ■ **to entail** to make sth. necessary, to involve sth. ■ **premise** an idea or theory on which a statement or action is based ■ **explicit** clear and exact ■ **uncharted** a situation that is completely new ■ **unprecedented** never having happened or existed before

[10] **legacy** ['legəsi] *Erbe* – [11] **predecessor** *Vorgänger* – [12] **Article 50** of the Lisbon treaty: the article that defines the procedure and timetable of the Brexit – [13] **Holyrood** seat of the Scottish Parliament – [14] **to stage** to arrange or organize sth. – [15] **advisory** [ədvaɪzəri] *beratend*

3 Angus Robertson: Scotland Is a European Country

Angus Robertson (*1969) is a Scottish National Party (SNP) politician and the SNP's Parliamentary Group Leader and spokesperson on the Constitution in the House of Commons of the U.K.

On 27 June 2016, he issued an insistent warning to the House of Commons, stating that taking Scotland out of the EU would be utterly undemocratic.

Tips on vocab

to cast one's vote to vote ■ **Single European Market** the EU as one territory without any internal borders or other regulatory obstacles to the free movement of goods and services ■ **safeguard** a means to protect sb./sth. from harm ■ **diminished** reduced in size and importance ■ **farce** here: joke ■ **share prices** *Aktienpreise* ■ **volatile** *unberechenbar* ■ **to suspend** to stop from being active ■ **Sterling** Pound Sterling; British currency ■ **to repudiate** to refuse to accept sb./sth. as true, good or reasonable ■ **despicable** very unpleasant and bad ■ **prosecuting authorities** *Strafverfolgungsbehörden* ■ **interest rates** *Zinsraten* ■ **austerity** *Sparpolitik* ■ **unprecedented** never having happened or existed before ■ **drift** general development ■ **to exacerbate** to make worse ■ **to take a firm grip** to get/have control over sb./sth.

4 Christoph Scheuermann: Zorn[1] und Leere

Wer in diesen Tagen auf die britische Demokratie schaut, sieht ein bröckelndes[2] Gebäude. Das ist nicht nur metaphorisch gemeint. Teile des Palastes von Westminster, Sitz des Ober- und Unterhauses, sind von Gerüsten[3] und Plastikplanen[4] umgeben. Die Fassade ist brüchig[5], durch das Dach dringt Wasser, Leitungen[6] und Abflüsse[7] sind undicht[8]. Die Renovierung wird Jahre dauern und Milliarden kosten. Am Montag musste die Sprecherin des Premierministers ihre wöchentliche Pressekonferenz immer wieder unterbrechen, weil das Gehämmer[9] der Arbeiter draußen zu laut war. Die Risse[10] zeigen sich im gesamten Königreich. Über dem Land liegt der Kater[11] einer Revolution, die niemand für möglich hielt. Seit dem Brexit-Votum wanken viele Gewissheiten[12], das Parlament als Herzkammer[13] der Demokratie etwa. Oder die Bindungskraft[14] der großen Parteien. Bei den Konservativen wird er Krieg um die Nachfolge David Camerons vor den gierigen[15] Blicken der Öffentlichkeit ausgetragen, inklusive Verrat[16] und Intrige[17]. Bei Labour kann die Abneigung zwischen der Fraktion und ihrem Vorsitzenden Jeremy Corbyn zu einer Spaltung der Partei führen.

Man verliert schnell den Überblick. Die Kurzfassung der vergangenen zwei Wochen: Der Premierminister tritt ab, weil er die Krise nicht bewältigen möchte, die er verursacht hat. Sein wahrscheinlicher Nachfolger wird vom Justizminister hintergangen[18], der selbst Premier werden will, damit aber kläglich scheitert. Während die Labour-Abgeordneten ihrem Chef die Schuld am Brexit geben, hoffen die Schotten auf eine zweite Chance zur Abspaltung. Und der Mann, der die ganze Sache losgetreten hat – Nigel Farage – , schlendert in den Ruhestand[19], bevor der Austritt überhaupt vollzogen ist.

Am Ende bleibt nun eine Frau, die aufräumen muss, was ihre Vorgänger angerichtet haben. Am Donnerstag wählten die Tory-Abgeordneten zwei Kandidatinnen für den Parteivorsitz; bis September können die Parteimitglieder zwischen den beiden entscheiden.

Theresa May, 59, bislang Innenministerin, hat die besten Chancen auf den Einzug in die Downing Street. Sie gilt als euroskeptische Technokratin, die hart gegen illegale Einwanderer vorging und kaum Verbündete in Westminster hat, eine Einzelgängerin. Nach der Jungsclique aus Eton und Oxford um Cameron herum wäre sie die erfrischendere Wahl für turbulente Zeiten. […]

Das EU-Referendum hat die Risse in der Gesellschaft nicht verursacht, sondern nur deutlicher hervortreten lassen. Die Kluft zwischen liberalen Großstädtern und Menschen auf dem Land, zwischen Jung und Alt, gebildet und weniger gebildet, zwischen Establishment und Unterschicht.

[1] anger – [2] to crumble – [3] scaffolding – [4] plastic tarpaulin – [5] crumbly, decayed – [6] plumbing – [7] drain – [8] to leak; leaky – [9] hammering – [10] crack – [11] a hangover – [12] certainty – [13] the heart – [14] cohesisive power – [15] greedy – [16] betrayal – [17] intrigue – [18] to deceive sb. – [19] retirement

Das Referendum hat die Grundlagen der repräsentativen Demokratie erschüttert[20]. Die Abgeordneten im Unterhaus stehen nun vor der Aufgabe, in den kommenden Jahren eine Trennung zu begleiten, die sie nie wollten. Sie müssen sich die Frage stellen, ob sie ihre Wähler noch vertreten. [...]

Eine Folge des 23. Juni ist, dass Großbritannien bis auf Weiteres mit sich selbst beschäftigt sein wird. Große Teile der Regierung werden in den Austrittsgesprächen gebunden sein. Eine kohärente Außenpolitik[21] wird sich unter diesen Bedingungen kaum entwickeln, zumal Brexit-Kämpfer wie Michael Gove immer wieder versprochen haben, schnellstmöglich Handelsverträge[22] mit Indien, China, Australien und dem Rest der Welt auf den Weg zu bringen. Daran wird die neue Regierung gemessen werden. Außenpolitich kann man die Briten für die nächsten Jahre abschreiben. [...]

Politisch war das EU-Referendum die teuerste Fehlspekulation[23] eines britischen Premierministers seit Jahrzehnten. Cameron wird in die Geschichte eingehen wie Lord North, der als Premier versehentlich die Kolonien in Amerika verlor, oder Blair, der seit dem Irakdesaster nur noch Tony „Bliar“ heißt – Lügner. Traurige Figuren, alle drei.

Die Kunst für die nächste Regierung wird darin bestehen, das gespaltene Königreich wieder zu vereinen. In etliche Gegenden Englands stellen die Bürger schon lange keine Ansprüche[24] mehr an die Politik, nach all den Spesenskandalen[25] im Parlament, den Milliarden zur Rettung von Banken. Viele Briten haben nur das Bedürfnis, die Frage nach Aufstieg und Wohlstand beantwortet zu bekommen: Wird mein Leben morgen besser sein als heute, wenn ich mich anstrenge? Oder ist ohnehin alles verloren, egal, was ich tue?

Zynismus ist eine zersetzende[26] Kraft in einer Gesellschaft. Die Mehrheit der Briten vertraut ihren Eliten nicht mehr. Der ökonomische Pragmatismus der Briten, auf den immer Verlass war, kam irgendwann abhanden. Das Volk ist längst nicht mehr so staatsgläubig und konformistisch wie in den Nachkriegsjahren. Die EU-Gegner haben das gespürt. Der Brexit wurde aus Trotz[27] geboren.

Lässt sich der Brexit jetzt abwenden? Die einfache Antwort lautet: nein. [...]

Über 17 Millionen Briten haben für den Austritt aus der EU gestimmt, 1,3 Millionen mehr als für den Verbleib. Selbst wenn viele Briten zu dem Schluss kommen sollten, dass sie den Brexit doch nicht wünschen, lässt sich das Referendum nicht zurückdrehen[28]. Europa tut gut daran, diese Realität zu akzeptieren, auch wenn das Triumphgeheul eines Populisten wie Nigel Farage nur schwer erträglich ist.

Farage war kaum mehr als ein polternder Zwischenrufer im großen Pub der britischen Politik. Sein Abgang zeigt, dass er nie Verantwortung übernehmen wollte. Aus seiner Sicht war es konsequent zu verschwinden. Der Fehler war, die Leute, für die er sprach, nicht ernst zu nehmen.

Was bleibt, sind Zorn und Leere. „Ich kann mich an keine Zeit erinnern, in der so viel Wut so nah an der Oberfläche war“, sagt der Historiker Garton Ash. [...]

Europa muss einen Weg finden, die Briten in den kommenden Jahren nicht ganz zu verlieren. Denn was auch noch bleibt, sind jene 48 Prozent auf der Insel, die für die EU gestimmt haben. Fast ein halbes Land, das enttäuscht von seiner anderen Hälfte ist und nun auf Europa blickt. Der größte Fehler wäre es, diesen Teil Britanniens im Stich zu lassen[29].

Der Spiegel, 28/2016, 9 July 2016, pp. 80ff.

[20] to shatter sth. – [21] foreign policy – [22] trade agreement/treaty – [23] bad speculation – [24] claims – [25] public expenses scandal – [26] corrosive – [27] defiance – [28] to undo sth./to make sth. undone – [29] to let sb. down

5 Jochen Wittmann: Jetzt droht[1] Kleinbritannien

Das Brexit-Votum befeuert von Neuem das schottische Streben[2] nach Unabhängigkeit. In Nordirland fürchtet man noch ernstere Folgen.

Eine bittere Ironie der Entscheidung für den Austritt aus der Europäischen Union könnte sein, was stolze Brexit-Wähler sich gewiss nicht wünschen: dass nämlich aus dem angeblich bald wieder unabhängigen Groß- ein Kleinbritannien wird. Die Fliehkräfte[3], die das Referendum um den britischen EU-Austritt freigesetzt hat, befeuern[4] jetzt in Schottland ein zweites Unabhängigkeitsreferendum, und in Nordirland führen sie zumindest zum Nachdenken über ein Zusammengehen mit der Republik Irland im Süden.

Denn die Brexit-Entscheidung war in erster Linie eine der Engländer, also im bevölkerungsreichsten[5] Landesteil des Vereinigten Königreichs. […]

In Schottland dagegen stimmten sämtliche 32 Bezirke[6] und insgesamt 62 Prozent der Bürger für den Verbleib, während es in Nordirland 55,8 Prozent waren. Jetzt ist die Situation eingetreten, dass Schottland gegen seinen Willen aus der Gemeinschaft mit der Europäischen Union gezerrt wird.

In Edinburgh, wo die EU-Abstimmung mit 74 Prozent am deutlichsten ausgefallen war, herrschte blankes Entsetzen[7]. […]

Die Ministerpräsidentin der schottischen Regionalregierung, Nicola Sturgeon, unterstrich das deutliche schottische Votum: „Wir haben klar gesagt, dass wir nicht die EU verlassen wollen. Ich als Ministerpräsidentin werde alles tun, damit der Wählerwille respektiert wird.“ Das Brexit-Ergebnis, sagte sie, sei für Schottland „demokratisch inakzeptabel“. Sturgeon steuert ein zweites Referendum über die Unabhängigkeit an, nachdem 2014 eine solche Abstimmung für die Nationalisten verloren gegangen war. […]

Die nordirische Ministerpräsidentin Arlene Foster begrüßte die Brexit-Entscheidung. Immerhin ist sie Chefin der rechten und pro-britischen Democratic Unionist Party, die für den EU-Austritt geworben hatte. Doch Foster stellt sich gegen die Volksmeinung. Die Nachfrage[8] unter Nordiren nach einem Pass der irischen Republik schnellte[9] nach dem Referendumsausgang steil nach oben. […] Der stellvertretende Ministerpräsident in der nordirischen Regionalregierung, Martin McGuinness von der Sinn-Fein-Partei, sagte: „Uns aus Europa zu zerren, ist zum Nachteil für alle unsere Bürger und wird schlecht für Handel, Investment und die Gesellschaft sein.“ McGuinness sieht jetzt einen „demokratischen Imperativ“ für ein nordirisches Referendum über das Zusammengehen mit Irland. Es ist aber unwahrscheinlich[10], dass die pro-britische und unionistische DUP diesem Ansinnen zustimmen würde.

In Nordirland könnte ein Brexit deshalb wirklich fatale Folgen haben – hier hatten sich pro-irische Katholiken und pro-britische Protestanten 30 Jahre lang einen Bürgerkrieg geliefert, der erst 1998 endete. Die beiden früheren britischen Premierminister Tony Blair und John Major haben erst kürzlich bei einem Besuch in der Provinz vor einem Wiederaufflammen[11] der Gewalt im Fall eines Brexit gewarnt.

Rheinische Post, 25 June 2016, p. A5

COMPREHENSION

1 Matt Dathan et al.

3. In a **first reading**, take notes on these aspects:

- the Scottish vote in the EU referendum
- the Scottish independence referendum of 2014
- immediate reactions to the Brexit vote (Irish and Scottish)
- political consequences and options resulting from Brexit
- reactions from other EU member states
- Nicola Sturgeon's plans for Scotland's future
- the process of exiting the EU and Scotland's consequences in reaction to the U.K.'s withdrawal from the EU

[1] to threaten – [2] pursuit of/quest for sth. – [3] centrifugal force – [4] to incite sth. – [5] most-populated – [6] district [7] horror – [8] demand for sth. – [9] to skyrocket – [10] unlikely – [11] resurgence

4. After a second reading, summarize the article in about 200 words.
→ Focus on Skills, Writing a Summary, p. 401

5. Take a look at the map (p. 81) and give an overview of the voting results.

Webcode SNG-40183-012 @ **Tip:** In order to get more detailed data, you can use the interactive maps provided on the webcode.

2 Nicola Sturgeon

Webcode SNG-40183-012 @ **6. Tip:** To get a better impression of the interview, you can watch the video clip provided on the webcode.

12 CD 1 **Listen to/watch** the interview with Nicola sturgeon **a first time** and take notes on what she states about:
- her view of the British government
- responsibility and political leadership with regard to Scotland
- protecting Scotland's interest
- possible options concerning another Scottish independence referendum and remaining in the EU
- the premises for Scotland's future

→ Focus on Skills, Listening Comprehension, p. 366

7. After a second listening/viewing, complete your notes.

3 Angus Robertson

Webcode SNG-40183-012 @ **8. Tip:** To get a better impression of the interview, you can watch the video clip provided on the webcode.

13 CD 1 **Step 1: While listening to/watching** Robertson's statement/speech **a first time**, extract information about:
- reasons for Scottish voters to vote for *Remain*
- EU citizenship vs. Little Britain
- Westminster's undemocratic demands
- the possibility of a new Scottish independence referendum
- the political and economic impact of Brexit
- demands on measures to be taken from Whitehall

→ Focus on Skills, Listening Comprehension, p. 366

Step 2: Now, **focus on David Cameron's response** to Robertson's statement and take notes on:
- his view of leaving the EU
- his comment concerning racist attacks on foreigners
- the economic dangers triggered by Brexit
- Scotland's specific economic position

Step 3: After listening to/watching the statement **a second time**, pay attention to the MPs' reactions to Robertson's statement and Cameron's response.
What is the overall atmosphere like at the House of Commons?

4 Christoph Scheuermann

M **9.** The German media reported comprehensively about the British EU referendum and, after the *Leave* vote, reacted with concern and deep regret to Britain's tight decision to leave the EU.
The German magazine *Der Spiegel* even published a bilingual (German-English) edition entitled *Bitte geht nicht! – Please don't go! ● Warum wir die Briten brauchen – Why Germany needs the British* (issue 24/2016, 11 June 2016). This article – published after Brexit – reflects the German view on the matter.

Step 1: Read the German magazine article, identify the key terms and put them in topical order.

Tip: Use the annotations to turn the relevant phrases into English. Be sure to use your own words whenever possible and do not translate word by word.
→ Focus on Skills, Mediation, p. 384

Step 2: Describe the *Spiegel* cover in detail and relate it to the statements made in the article.
→ Focus on Skills, Analysis of Visuals, p. 381

5 Jochen Wittmann

M **10.** The article taken from the daily newspaper *Rheinische Post* was published only two days after the Brexit vote. Find relevant passages concerning the aspects listed below and turn them into English.

- the Scottish and Northern Irish reaction to Brexit
- the Scottish vote
- consequences of the Brexit vote – for Scotland – for Northern Ireland
- the particularly complicated political situation in Northern Ireland

→ Focus on Skills, Mediation, p. 384

ANALYSIS

1 Matt Dathan et al.

11. By definition, the *Daily Mail* is a popular and rather sensationalist daily newspaper.

Step 1: Reactivate your knowledge of the characteristics of popular and quality newspapers and study the Focus on Facts page *The Press* (p. 370) in your Students' Book.

Step 2: Examine the article and determine its quality.
→ Focus on Skills, Analysis of a Non-Fictional Text, p. 377

12. Compare the article from the *Daily Mail* to Mark Mardell's article *Brexit: The Story of an Island Apart* published by the BBC (pp. 67 ff.). Which similarities and differences concerning journalistic quality can you detect?

2 Nicola Sturgeon

13. Examine Nicola Sturgeon's competence as a speaker in general and her persuasive strategies in particular. Which linguistic and rhetorical devices does she use to convey determination, responsible leadership and reliability to the viewer (and her electorate)?
→ Focus on Skills, Analysis of a Political Speech, p. 379

3 Angus Robertson

14. At first glance, Robertson does not appear to be a very skilled and charismatic speaker. However, the strong reaction of the other MPs reveals that his statements and views are shared and approved of. Analyse Robertson's line of argument and rhetorical strategy and explain how they convey his message.
→ Focus on Skills, Analysis of a Political Speech, p. 376

4 Christoph Scheuermann

15. Compare the *Spiegel* cover page *Jeder für sich* (p. 84) to the cartoon *Patriotische Europäer* by Gerhard Mester (p. 76). Explain
a) which visual you prefer and
b) which one you consider to be more effective.
→ Focus on Skills, Analysis of Visuals, p. 381

ACTIVITIES

16. In a role play, take on the positions of different politicians/citizens who are confronted with the post-Brexit situation, e.g. English, Scottish, Northern Irish, Republican Irish, members of the EU Parliament, etc. In groups:

a) compile a formal complaint/petition to Parliament that lists the problems, hardships and challenges and demand that action is taken to solve them.
or:

b) prepare short speeches which lay out the controversial topic/situation and call for immediate action.
→ Focus on Skills, Writing a Speech Script, p. 400 and Giving a Speech, p. 390
or:

c) prepare and act out a public hearing, presenting and discussing the various views on the matter with concerned citizens and politicians from different backgrounds. Prepare role cards and flesh out your line of argument with information and data from the articles and speeches.
→ Focus on Language, Conversation and Discussion, p. 385

17. Your English pen pal David is highly concerned about the situation of post-Brexit Britain. He and his friends have followed the political debates and British media reports. He wants to know how the German media have reported on Brexit and asks you to give him a short overview.

M Use your results from tasks 9 and 10 and write a letter of about 300 words in which you inform your friend about the German perspective. Be prepared to add background information on the matter if necessary.
→ Focus on Skills, Mediation, p. 384

Theresa May

First Speech as Prime Minister

AWARENESS

Look at the cartoon below. How does it present Britain's situation after Brexit and what is the new Prime Minister, Theresa May, expected to do?

Alles neu macht die May

Tips on vocab

the office of the Prime Minister / 10 Downing Street ■ cracked walls ■ a heap of rubble ■ files ■ to look like a cleaning lady ■ to carry a bucket/ broom ■ to wear an apron ■ to roll up one's sleeves

COMPREHENSION

14 CD 1

1. On 13 July 2016, Theresa May was appointed the new Prime Minister by the Queen. Shortly afterwards, she delivered her speech as PM. In **a first listening**, try to understand the gist of Theresa May's remarks. Exchange your first listening impressions with a partner and clarify any questions.

→ Focus on Skills, Listening Comprehension, p. 366

Tips on vocab

legacy ['legəsi] *Erbe* ■ **mortgage** ['mɔːɡɪdʒ] *Hypothek* ■ **just about** *gerade so, gerade eben* ■ **to take the big calls** here: to speak with people who have a lot of money or power ■ **prioritise** [praɪ'ɒrɪtaɪz] to decide which of a group of things are the most important so that you can deal with them first ■ **to entrench** to firmly establish something, especially an idea or a problem, so that it cannot be changed ■ **to forge** *schmieden* ■ **bold** brave and confident

2. After **listening a second time**, take notes on these questions:

- What does May appreciate and praise about Cameron's work as PM?
- What are the guiding principles for her work as the newly elected PM?
- How does she want to tackle injustices?
- Who does she particularly want to help and support?
- How does she define the government's mission for the post-Brexit U.K.?

ANALYSIS

Webcode SNG-40183-013

14 CD 1

3. In order to get a deeper understanding of the speech, you can listen to and watch a video of the speech, which is provided on the webcode.

Step 1: Divide the class into groups of four students each and **watch/listen** to the video clip. Each member of the group focuses on <u>one</u> of the devices listed below and takes notes on relevant aspects:

- **language** (choice of words, phrases, etc.)
- **grammar** (sentence structure, grammatical tenses, etc.)
- **rhetoric** (key symbols, use of grammatical persons, metaphors, etc.)
- **manner of speaking** (volume, tempo, stress, pauses, etc.)

→ Focus on Skills, Analysis of a Political Speech, p. 379

Step 2: Inform each other about your findings and make sure that everything has been understood.

4. A few days before May was appointed PM by the Queen, she gave a speech to the members of the Conservative Party to position herself and announce her candidacy to become the Leader of the Conservative Party and Prime Minister. In your groups, take a close look at the following excerpt from her speech:

[…] First, following last week's referendum, our country needs strong, proven leadership – to steer us through this period of economic and political uncertainty, and to negotiate the best possible terms as we leave the European Union.

Second, we need leadership that can unite our Party and our country. With the Labour Party tearing itself to pieces, and divisive nationalists in Scotland and Wales, it is nothing less than the patriotic duty of our Party to unite and govern in the best interests of the whole country.

And third, we need a bold, new, positive vision for the future of our country – a vision of a country that works not for a privileged few but for every one of us. […]

But beyond that, I want to use this opportunity to make several things clear.

First, Brexit means Brexit. The campaign was fought, the vote was held, turnout was high, and the public gave their verdict. There must be no attempts to remain inside the EU, no attempts to rejoin it through the back door, and no second referendum. The country voted to leave the European Union, and it is the duty of the Government and of Parliament to make sure we do just that.

Second, there should be no general election until 2020. There should be a normal Autumn Statement, held in the normal way at the normal time, and no emergency Budget. And there should be no decision to invoke Article Fifty until the British negotiating strategy is agreed and clear – which means Article Fifty should not be invoked before the end of this year.

Third, we should make clear that for the foreseeable future there is absolutely no change in Britain's trading relationships with the EU or other markets. And until a new legal agreement is reached with the EU, which will not happen for some time, the legal status of British nationals living or working in Europe will not change – and neither will the status of EU nationals in Britain.

And fourth, while it is absolutely vital that the Government continues with its intention to reduce public spending and cut the budget deficit, we should no longer seek to reach a budget surplus by the end of the Parliament. If before 2020 there is a choice between further spending cuts, more borrowing and tax rises, the priority must be to avoid tax increases since they would disrupt consumption, employment and investment.

These are all measures that will be taken by a Conservative Government I lead, and they offer stability and certainty to consumers, employers and investors for the foreseeable future. And I want to reassure foreign governments, international companies and foreign nationals living in Britain that we are the same outward-looking and globally-minded and big-thinking country we have always been – and we remain open for business and welcoming to foreign talent.

http://www.independent.co.uk/news/uk/politics/theresa-mays-tory-leadership-launch-statement-full-text-a7111026.html, 30 June 2016 [30.11.2016]

ACTIVITIES

5. Together with a partner, conduct an interview with Britain's new Prime Minister on her vision of Britain's post-Brexit future, with one of you playing Theresa May and the other playing the journalist. Prepare role cards and act out your interview in class.

→ Focus on Skills, Writing an Interview, p. 398

Tip: As a **journalist**, you want to challenge the PM in order to get as much information as possible – but be careful not to be offensive. You want to make your interviewee talk, not insult him.
As **Prime Minister**, you want to show your commitment and responsibility – but you must be careful not make promises that you cannot keep.

Tips on vocab

Journalist
- Is leaving the EU a means that is justified by the end … so to speak?
- Do you think that threatening the EU commission might …?
- Against the background of the UK's impressive history, shouldn't it …?
- Can you talk more about …?
- Has the UK not always taken pride in …?
- Speaking about "a better deal for Europe" – what do you consider to be …?
- Regarding globalisation, what urgent measures need to be taken …?

Tips on vocab

Prime Minister
- It is unavoidable that …
- Compared to other European nations …
- If we do not … we will/will not …
- Economically/Socially, it is irresponsible …
- With regard to globalisation, the EU …
- The UK and the Continent share …
- The EU cannot afford … without the UK …
- It is part of our British tradition to …

The European Union

The European Union (EU) is an **economic and political union** of 28 member states (ca. 505 million citizens) that has developed a single market **ensuring free movement of people, goods, services and capital**. The EU operates through supranational and intergovernmental negotiations and treaties between the member states. Economically the EU generates ca. 25 % of the gross world product.

History

1957	**Rome Treaty** creates the European Economic Community (EEC) as a customs union. Members: Belgium, France, Italy, Luxembourg, the Netherlands, West Germany
1979	first direct democratic elections to the **European Parliament**
1985	**Schengen Agreement** creates open borders without passport control between most member states
1986	the European flag is first used
1990	after German reunification, (former) East Germany joins the community
1993	in the **Maastricht Treaty**, the European Union is formally established
2002	the **Euro** is introduced as European currency and replaces national currencies in twelve of the member states
2016	23 June: 51.9 % of Britons vote in favour of leaving the European Union (→ Brexit)

Fundamental rights

- In 2009, the **Lisbon Treaty** gave legal effect to the **Charter of Fundamental Rights of the European Union** which is a catalogue of fundamental (human) rights which were derived from the constitutional traditions of the member states (e. g. **Article 1:** Human dignity is inviolable. It must be respected and protected; **Article 2:** Everyone has the right to live. No one shall be condemned to the death penalty, or executed).

Important EU institutions

- the **European Council** is the EU's supreme political authority; it defines the EU's political agenda and strategies
- the **European Commision** is the EU's executive branch and responsible for its legislation
- the **European Parliament** (in Strasbourg) forms half of the EU's legislature; the members of the European Parliament are directly elected by the EU citizens every five years
- the **Council of the European Union** is the other half of the EU's legislature; in addition to legislative functions it also has executive functions, e. g. the Common Foreign and Security Policy
- the **Court of Justice of the European Union** interprets and applies the treaties and the law of the EU
- the **European Central Bank** administers the monetary policy of the 18 member states taking part in the **Eurozone**; it is one of the world's most important central banks

The 28 EU member states

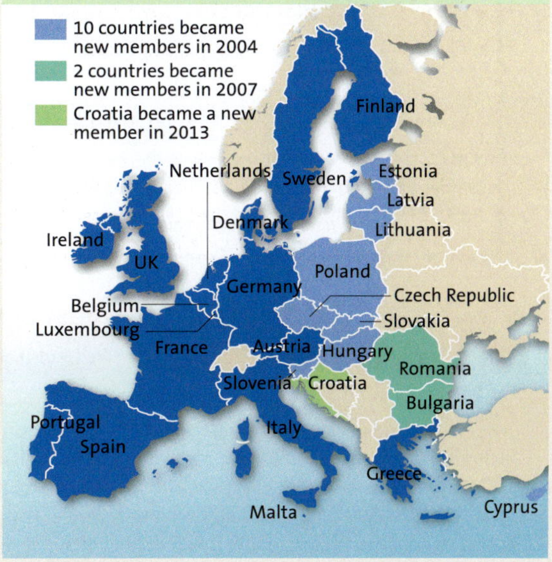

The Political System of the United Kingdom

The **United Kingdom** (of Great Britain and Northern Ireland) is **a constitutional monarchy**, in which the **monarch is the head of state** and **the Prime Minister is the head of government**. The UK has been a multi-party system since the 1920s, the two largest parties being the Conservative Party and the Labour Party.

Political parties

The Conservative Party	**Labouar Party**
• centre-right • conservatism • British Unionism (against Scottish and Welsh independence) • opposition to the Euro, strong defense of Pound Sterling • Eurosceptic position • free-market policy • criticism of Labour's state multiculturalism	• left to centre-left • democratic socialist party • supports government intervention in the economy • for redistribution of wealth • advocates increased rights for workers • favours an extended welfare state • support of multiculturalism

The U.K. system of government (separation of powers)

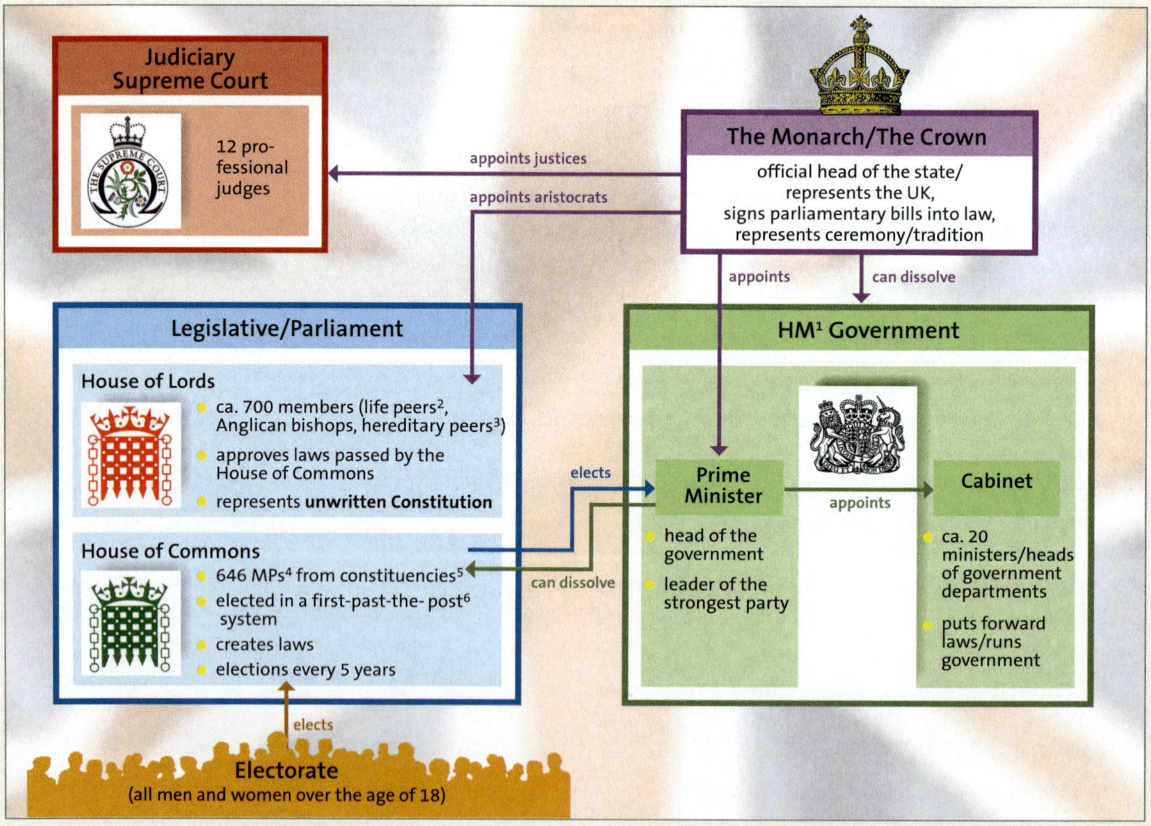

[1] **HM** (*abbr.*) Her/His Majesty's – [2] **peer** in Britain, a person who has a high social position and any of a range of titles, including baron, earl, and duke, or a life peer – [3] **hereditary peer** [həˈredɪtəri] someone who became a peer (= a high social rank) when a parent died, and who can pass it on to their oldest child; *Mitglied des Hochadels mit ererbtem Titel* – [4] **MP** (*abbr.*) Member of Parliament – [5] **constituency** [kənˈstɪtjuənsi] *Wahlbezirk* – [6] **first-past-the-post** system using a voting system in which a person is elected because they get more votes than anyone else in the area that they want to represent; *einfache Mehrheitswahl*

the Commonwealth		
allegiance to sb./sth. [ə'li:dʒəns]	loyalty to a leader	*Loyalität/Ergebenheit gegenüber jmd.*
ceremonial position	a position that gives no real power	*zeremonielle/ förmliche Position*
declaration	an official statement	*(öffentliche) Erklärung, Bekanntgabe*
geopolitics	ideas and activities relating to the way that a country's position, population, etc. affect its political development and its relationship with other countries	*politische Geografie*
head of state	a leader or a person in charge of a state	*Staatsoberhaupt*
to share a common heritage	to have the same traditional beliefs, values, customs, etc.	*ein gemeinsames Erbe/ Kultur haben*
intergovernmental	between different governments	*zwischenstaatlich, international*
legacy ['legəsi]	sth. that exists as a result of sth. that happened at an earlier time	*Erbe*
representative position	a position in which sb. represents a state, a community, an interest, etc.	*repräsentative Position*
self-determination	the right of the people to govern themselves	*Selbstbestimmung*
sovereign ['sɒvrɪn] **sovereignty** ['sɒvrənti]	independent; complete freedom and power to govern	*uneingeschränkt, unabhängig, souverän; Eigenstaatlichkeit*
multicultural Britain		
alien	foreigner; foreign	*Fremder; fremd*
asylum seeker [ə'saɪlem 'si:kə(r)]	sb. who leaves their own country because they are in danger and who asks the government of another country to allow them to live there	*Asylbewerber*
citizen; citizenship	a member of a state, subject; the legal right of belonging to a particular country	*Staatsbürger; Staatsbürgerschaft*
culture clash	a conflict arising from the interaction of people with different cultural values	*Zusammenprall der Kulturen*
(racial) discrimination	the practice of treating people in an unfair way because of their ethnicity	*(rassistische) Diskriminierung*
diversity [daɪ'vɜ:səti]	the fact of including many different types of people or things	*Vielfalt*
emigrant	sb. who leaves their own country to live in another	*Aussiedler, Emigrant*
to emigrate; emigration	to leave one's own country in order to live in another	*auswandern, emigrieren; Auswanderung, Emigration*
hospitable [hɒ'spɪtəbl] **hospitality**	friendly and welcoming to visitors	*gastfreundlich; Gastfreundschaft*
identity crisis, crisis of identity	a feeling of uncertainty of who you really are and what your purpose is	*Identitätskrise*
immigrant	sb. who enters another country to live there permanently	*Einwanderer, Immigrant*
to immigrate; immigration	to come into a country in order to live there permanently	*einwandern, immigrieren; Einwanderung*
immigration control, border control	the place at an airport, sea port, etc. where officials check the documents of everyone entering the country	*Grenzkontrolle*
to integrate (sb. into/with) integration	to become part of a group or society and be accepted by them, or to help someone do this	*integrieren; Integration*
interracial marriage	marriage between people of different races	*Ehe zwischen Angehörigen verschiedener Ethnien*
labour shortage	a situation in which there are not enough workers	*Mangel an Arbeitskräften*

the middle class	the social class that includes people who are educated and work in professional jobs, e.g. teachers or managers	*die Mittelklasse/Mittelschicht*
minority	a small group of people or things within a much larger group (= majority)	*Minderheit*
race relations	the relationship that exists between people from different countries, religions, etc. who are now living in the same place	*Beziehungen zwischen ethnischen Gruppen*
refugee [ˌrefjuˈdʒi]	sb. who has been forced to leave a country, especially during a war, or for political or religious reasons	*Flüchtling*
temporary stay	a stay continuing for a limited period of time	*befristeter Aufenthalt*
Western values	the beliefs, traditions, customs, etc. of the Western community	*westliche Werte*
	constitution/independence/treaties	
act	a law that has been officially accepted	*Gesetz*
bill	a written proposal for a new law that is brought to a parliament to be discussed	*Gesetzesentwurf*
charter/carta	a statement of the principles, duties and purposes of an organization	*Charta, Satzung*
constitutional document	an officially/legally accepted document	*Verfassungsurkunde*
constitutional monarchy, parliamentary monarchy	a country ruled by a king or queen whose power is limited by a constitution	*konstitutionelle Monarchie*
to deny sth. to sb., to deny sb. sth.	to refuse to allow sb. to have or do sth.	*jdm. etwas verweigern/ vorenthalten*
despot [ˈdespɒt]	tyrant	*Despot, Tyrann*
Dominion	a country belonging to the British Empire or Commonwealth	*Dominion (selbstständiges Land des Commonwealth)*
to grant sb. sth., to grant sth. to sb.	to give sb. sth. or allow them to have sth. that they have asked for	*jdm. etwas gewähren*
to negotiate; negotiation	to discuss sth. in order to reach an agreement, especially in business or politics	*verhandeln; Verhandlung*
petition	an official letter to a law court asking for a legal case to be considered	*Petition, Antrag*
referendum (on sth.)	when people vote to make a decision about a particular subject, rather than voting for a person	*Referendum, Volksentscheid*
	British Empire	
diplomacy [dɪˈpləʊməsi]	the job or quality of managing the relationships between countries	*Diplomatie, Verhandlungsgeschick*
emperor/empress	the man/woman who rules an empire	*Kaiser(in)*
to expand; expansion	to become larger in size or number; growth	*expandieren, sich vergrößern; Expansion, Wachstum*
fall	loss of power, failure	*Sturz, Umsturz*
foreign policy	involving or dealing with other countries	*Außenpolitik*
to found sth.; foundation	to start sth., to establish sth.	*etwas beginnen/gründen; Gründung*
to gain independence	to become independent	*(an) Unabhängigkeit gewinnen*
to grant sb. independence	to allow sb. to act on their own	*jmd. Unabhängigkeit bewilligen*
(policy of) imperialism	a political system in which one country rules a lot of other countries	*Imperialismus; imperialistische Politik*
indigenous [ɪnˈdɪdʒənəs]	native people who have always lived in a place	*einheimisch*
to be loyal to sb.	to support sb.	*jdm. treu sein*

maharaja [ˌmɑːhəˈrɑːdʒə]	an Indian prince or king	*Maharadscha*
overseas	to or in a foreign country that is across the sea	*Übersee*
to possess sth.	to own sth.	*etwas besitzen*
Raj [rɑːdʒ]	British rule in India	*Britische Kolonialzeit in Indien*
to reign	to rule a nation as their king, queen or emperor	*regieren*
rule	to have the official power to control a country	*Herrschaft*
self-government	a country or organization that is controlled by its own members	*Selbstverwaltung*
superiority over sth.	the quality of being better, more skilful, powerful, etc. than other people or things	*Überlegenheit*
viceroy [ˈvaɪsrɔɪ]	a man who was sent by a king or queen in the past to rule another country	*Vizekönig*
	colonization	
the acquisition of colonies	here: the act of getting land	*Aneignung von Land/Fläche*
to civilize sb.	to improve a society so that it is more organized and developed	*jdn. zivilisieren, jdm. Manieren beibringen*
to claim a territory	to conquer a territory	*ein Territorium erobern/ in Anspruch nehmen*
colonial power	when a powerful country rules many weaker ones, and establishes its own trade and society there	*Kolonialmacht*
to colonize; colonization [ˌkɒlənaɪˈzeɪʃn]	to establish political control over another country, and send your citizens there to settle	*kolonisieren, besiedeln; Kolonisierung, Besiedlung*
colony	a country/area that is under the political control of a more powerful country, usually one that is far away	*Kolonie*
colonist	sb. who settles in a new colony	*Kolonist, Siedler*
to conquer [ˈkɒŋkə(r)] **conquest**	to take control of a country by fighting	*erobern; Eroberung, Sieg*
conqueror	a person (often an army) who fights to take control of a country	*Eroberer*
to decolonize sb.	to make a former colony politically independent	*jdn. entkolonialisieren/in die Unabhängigkeit entlassen*
to discover; discovery	if sb. discovers a new place, they are the first person to find it	*entdecken; Entdeckung*
to divide sth. up	to separate sth. into parts and share them between people	*etwas aufteilen*
to establish	to start e. g. an organization, esp. one that exists for a long time; to set up	*etwas gründen*
to exploit; exploitation	to try to get as much as you can out of a situation, sometimes unfairly	*ausnutzen, ausbeuten; Ausbeutung*
to explore; exploration	to travel to or around a place in order to learn about it	*erforschen; Erforschung, Erkundung*
to gain control over sb.	to obtain or achieve control over sb. you want or need	*Kontrolle über jdn. erlangen*
to invade; invasion [ɪnˈveɪʒn]	to enter a country using military force in order to take control of it	*einmarschieren; Einmarsch*
mother country, mother-land, fatherland	the country where someone was born (implies a strong emotional connection)	*Herkunftsland, Vaterland*
native	someone who lives in a place all the time or has lived there a long time	*Ureinwohner*
negotiations	diplomatic talks to reach an agreement	*Verhandlungen*
postcolonial	later than or after colonialism	*postkolonial*
to settle; settlement	to go to a place where no people have lived permanent-ly before and start to live there	*(be-)siedeln; Besiedlung*

India: Democracy, Diversity and Determination

Indian students celebrating Holi, the Hindu festival of colours, which is celebrated across India. The festival takes place at the end of the winter season and marks the beginning of spring

START-UP ACTIVITIES

15 CD 1

1. Listen to the music taken from the soundtrack of the film *The Best Exotic Marigold Hotel* and imagine the atmosphere. In a round robin activity, exchange your listening impressions. What pictures, colours, smells, etc. does the music evoke in you?

2. First, describe the photo above and the atmosphere and mood it conveys. Then state whether your listening impressions match the photo. Does the photo match your ideas about India?

Tips on vocab

blotch of paint ■ multi-coloured ■ bright ■ flower garland ■ to grin ■ to smirk (*schmunzeln*) ■ to exchange telling (*viel-sagend*)/meaningful looks ■ to scream with laughter ■ horselaugh (*wieherndes Lachen/laute Lache*)

3. In groups, read the excerpt from the screenplay of *The Best Exotic Marigold Hotel* and take notes on what is said about a) the hotel itself, b) its manager and CEO Sonny and c) India in general.

4. In groups, work creatively with the film script and choose between these tasks:
   a) Based on the description of the hotel as well as Sonny's comments, design a homepage in which you promote the hotel to (British) pensioners.
   b) As there is almost no dialogue in the excerpt, you are asked to add either interior monologues* depicting the thoughts of the pensioners or dialogues* in which they talk to each other or to Sonny about the situation. In order to get further ideas, you can watch the film trailer provided on the webcode.

Webcode SNG-40183-014

Ol Parker

The Best Exotic Marigold Hotel

Seven British pensioners have decided to spend their old age at a retirement hotel called "The Best Exotic Marigold Hotel" in Jaipur, India. Based on pictures on the hotel's website the Britons expect to find a picturesque hotel, dating back to the time of the Raj[1], which offers luxurious accommodation[2] and services at affordable rates. The following excerpt from the screenplay depicts the last part of their long and exciting journey to the hotel.

32 EXT. BUS – DAWN 32

The sun rises. A beautiful, pearly dawn. The bus drives through the great gates of Jaipur. Below, the city shimmers in the heat. It's a magnificent sight.

EVELYN (O.S.) What exactly is a tuk-tuk[3]?

33 EXT. JAIPUR STREET – DAWN 33

Our heroes are squashed[4] into a pair of them, facing forwards and backwards, attempting not to swallow too much dust as they wheel crazily through the teeming[5] morning streets of the city. They stare in amazement at the world racing past them.
A scooter overtakes. A young man is driving, his girl-friend riding side-saddle on the back. Her sari billows out behind her. Douglas and Evelyn both watch her, struck by this image of beauty, youth and vitality.

34 EXT. STREET/GARDEN PATH. MARIGOLD HOTEL – MORNING 34
The tuk-tuks have pulled up, and our travelers emerge[6], exhausted and dirty, staring through some garden gates at the Marigold Hotel. Once a beautiful building, once possibly even luxurious, it is clearly in the process of being given at least half the face-lift it badly needs. Parts of the building are freshly painted, some of the ornate[7] balconies are crumbling[8], and one wall is clad[9] with crazily skewed[10] bamboo scaffolding[11]. A huge old tree towers over an untended[12] garden, its branches poking[13] into the windows of the building.

34A EXT. ROOFTOP. MARIGOLD HOTEL – MORNING 34A
A young man leans out from an upper balcony to see the arrival below: SONNY KAPOOR (early 20s). He deposits a paint pot and brush on a parapet[14], and races off across the rooftop.

34B EXT. GARDEN/PATH/COURTYARD. MARIGOLD HOTEL – MORNING 34B
Dazed[15] and horrified, the travelers wander up the pathway. A cow standing in front of them is pushed into the garden by a couple of young houseboys who then run to the tuk-tuks to collect their luggage.

23.
34C EXT. STAIRWAY/COURTYARD. MARIGOLD HOTEL – MORNING 34C
Sonny clatters[16] down the steep[17] steps, and comes tearing[18] out onto a verandah, as the travelers arrive in the courtyard below. He spreads his arms wide.

SONNY Welcome to India!!!
They stare up at him.

35 EXT/INT. COURTYARD/HALLWAY. BEDROOM. MARIGOLD HOTEL – DAY 35
The courtyard is not without charm, although somewhat dilapidated[19]. A fountain at the centre does not look as if it has seen water in years, and faded awnings are strung up haphazardly[20]. Sonny is leading Madge into the darkness of the building, towards her room.

SONNY This is a building of the utmost[21] character, which means that perhaps not everything will function in the way you expect it to. But as the manager and chief executive supervising officer of the Marigold Hotel, I can tell you with great pride that the building has stood for centuries, and will stand for many more, in 100 % shipshape[22] condition. Please follow me, carefully avoiding that naughty stone there round this corner, leading us most successfully all the way to – your bedroom!
The room is very small, comfortable, and tastefully decorated. But there's no door.

MADGE Where?

SONNY Here. In here.

MADGE My dear man. Rooms have doors. What you're showing me here is an alcove[23].

SONNY The door is coming soon, most definitely.

MADGE How soon?

24.
SONNY Let us not concern ourselves with details, Mrs Hardcastle. Rather than speaking of doors, we should instead take pleasure in the freedom to roam[24].

www.imsdb.com/scripts/Best-Exotic-Marigold-Hotel.-The.html [10.08.2014]

[1] **Raj** [rɑːdʒ] British rule in India – [2] **accommodation** *Unterbringung* – [3] **tuk-tuk** a motorized three-wheeled rickshaw – [4] **to squash sb./sth.** *quetschen* – [5] **teeming** *von Menschen wimmelnd* – [6] **to emerge** *heraustreten* – [7] **ornate** *verschnörkelt* – [8] **to crumble** *zerbröckeln* – [9] **clad** here: covered – [10] **skewed** *schräg* – [11] **scaffolding** *Gerüst* – [12] **untended** *ungepflegt* – [13] **to poke** *ausstrecken* – [14] **parapet** *Brüstung* – [15] **dazed** *benommen* – [16] **to clatter** *klappern* – [17] **steep** *steil* – [18] **to tear** to move somewhere very quickly or in an excited way – [19] **dilapidated** *baufällig* – [20] **haphazard** ['hæp'hæzəd] *willkürlich* – [21] **utmost** greatest – [22] **shipshape** clean and neat – [23] **alcove** *Wandnische* – [24] **to roam** to wander freely

The Raj – Britain's Dreams and India's Nightmares

Mahatma Gandhi

There Is No Salvation[1] for India (1916) ☒

AWARENESS

"Be the change that you want to see in the world."
"First they ignore you, then they laugh at you, then they fight you, then you win." *Mahatma Gandhi*

Discuss these Gandhi quotations in class.

The following speech from which this excerpt is taken was given on the occasion of the opening of the Banares Hindu University on 4 February 1916. The Viceroy, Lord Hardinge, as well as eminent persons from all over India attended.

Our language is the reflection of ourselves, and if you tell me that our languages are too poor to express the best thought, then I say that the sooner we are wiped out of existence the better for us. Is there a man who dreams that English can ever become the national language of India? (Cries of 'Never') Why this handicap on the nation? Just consider for one moment what an unequal race our lads have to run with every English lad. I had the privilege of a close conversation with some Poona[2] professors. They assured me that every Indian youth, because he reached his knowledge through the English language, lost at least six precious years of life. Multiply that by the number of students turned out by our schools and colleges, and find out for yourselves how many thousand years have been lost to the nation. The charge[3] against us is that we have no initiative. How can we have any if we are to devote the precious years of our life to the mastery of a foreign tongue? …

The only education we receive is English education. Surely we must show something for it. But suppose that we had been receiving during the past fifty years education through our vernaculars[4], what should we have today? We should have today a free India, we should have our educated men, not as if they were foreigners in their own land but speaking to the heart of the nation; they would be working amongst the poorest of the poor, and whatever they would have gained during the past fifty years would be a heritage for the nation. (Applause)

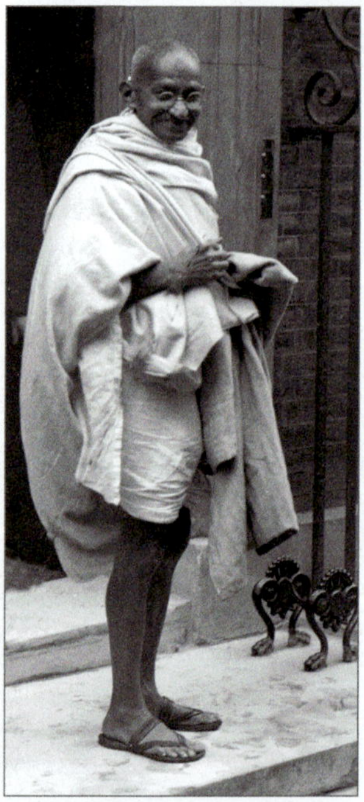

Gandhi at 10 Downing Street in 1931

His Highness the Maharajah who presided[5] yesterday over our deliberations[6] spoke about the poverty of India … But what did we witness in the great pandal[7] in which the foundation ceremony was performed by the Viceroy? Certainly a most gorgeous[8] show, an exhibition of jewellery which made a splendid feast for the eyes of the greatest jeweler who chose to come from Paris. I compare with the richly bedecked[9] noblemen the millions of the poor. And I feel like saying to these noblemen, 'There is no salvation for India unless you strip[10] yourselves of this jewellery and hold it in trust for your countrymen in India.' ('Hear, hear' and applause) […]

Look at the history of the British Empire and the British nation; freedom-loving as it is, it will not be a party to give freedom to a people who will not take it themselves.

www.mkgandhi.org/speeches/bhu.htm [17.12.2014]

[1] **salvation** *Erlösung, Errettung* – [2] **Poona** an important centre in the religious and social movements of the late 19th century in India – [3] **charge** *Anschuldigung* – [4] **vernacular** [vəˈnækjələ(r)] local language – [5] **to preside** [prɪˈzaɪd] *den Vorsitz haben* – [6] **deliberation** careful consideration or discussion – [7] **pandal** *provisorische Plattform* – [8] **gorgeous** extremely attractive – [9] **bedecked** decorated – [10] **to strip** to remove sth.

British Perspectives on the Raj

George Orwell: Reflections on Gandhi

At about the time when the [Gandhi's] autobiography first appeared I remember reading its opening chapters in the ill-printed[1] pages of some Indian newspaper. They made a good impression on me, which Gandhi himself, at that time, did not. The things that I associated with him – homespun cloth, 'soul forces' and vegetarianism – were unappealing, and his medieval[2] programme was obviously not viable[3] in a backward, starving, overpopulated country. It was also apparent that the British were making use of him, or thought they were making use of him. Strictly speaking, as a Nationalist, he was an enemy, but since in every crisis he would exert[4] himself to prevent violence – which, from the British point of view, meant preventing any effective action whatever – he could be regarded as 'our man'. In private this was sometimes cynically admitted. The attitude of the Indian millionaires was similar. Gandhi called upon them to repent[5], and naturally they preferred him to the Socialists and Communists who, given the chance, would actually have taken their money away. How reliable such calculations are in the long run is doubtful; as Gandhi himself says 'in the end deceivers deceive only themselves'; but at any rate the gentleness with which he was nearly always handled was due partly to the feeling that he was useful. The British Conservatives only became really angry with him when, as in 1942, he was in effect turning his non-violence against a different conqueror.
But I could see even then that the British officials who spoke of him with a mixture of amusement and disapproval also genuinely liked and admired him, after fashion.

from *Essays* by George Orwell. Penguin, London, 1984, pp. 459 f.

Viscount Rothermere (1861–1949), highly successful newspaper publisher (*Daily Mail, Daily Mirror*)

British rule in India is irreplaceable. It has been bought by British lives and built up by British capital. If we had not gone to India, she would still be in a state of semi-barbaric[6] anarchy[7]. Our duty there is not to argue with base agitators[8], but to govern.
India, 1930s

transcription from the DVD *The British Empire*, narrated by Art Malik, Lingua Video, Bonn

Marjorie Usher, an officer's wife

Entertaining in this country is very simple. You just tell the servants how many are coming and they see to[9] everything.
We have nine servants, including the ayah, the head servant, who acts as valet[10] to Colonel Sterling, the kitmugar, who waits at table and looks after the silver and the dhobi, or washerman, who does our clothes very well indeed.
Chakrata, 1930s

transcription from the DVD *The British Empire*, narrated by Art Malik, Lingua Video, Bonn

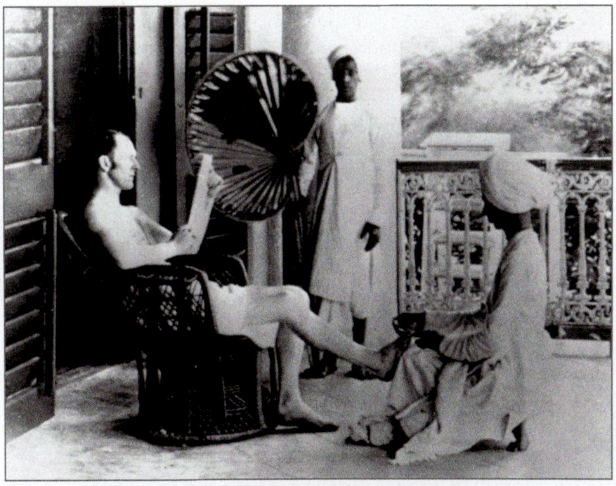

A sahib being pedicured and fanned by servants, early 1900s

[1] **ill-printed** of bad quality – [2] **medieval** [ˌmediˈiːvl] *mittelalterlich* – [3] **viable** [ˈvaɪəbl] realistic – [4] **to exert oneself** [ɪgˈzɜːt] to work very hard and use a lot of physical or mental energy – [5] **to repent** [rɪˈpent] (*fml.*) to be sorry for sth. and wish you had not done it – [6] **semi-barbaric** [ˌsemibɑˈbærɪk] half uncivilized – [7] **anarchy** [ˈænəki] a situation in which there is no effective government and no order – [8] **agitator** [ˈædʒɪteɪtə(r)] sb. who encourages people to change sth. in society – [9] **to see to sth.** to make sure or check that sth. is done, to take care of sth. – [10] **valet** [ˈvæleɪ] a male servant who looks after a man's clothes, serves his meals, etc.

COMPREHENSION

1. In a paired reading activity,
   a) subdivide the excerpt from Gandhi's speech into thematic units,
   b) summarize these units to each other and
   c) find an appropriate headline for each thematic unit.

2. State why Gandhi thinks that education is so important for the identity of the people.

3. Specify who in particular Gandhi is criticizing.

16 CD 1

4. Looking at George Orwell's reflections on Gandhi and Gandhi's second quote at the top of p. 98, say who the players and the winner were and give reasons for your answer.

17–18 CD 1

5. Listen to the statements of Viscount Rothermere and Marjorie Usher: How do they see their role in colonial India?

Info

Mahatma Gandhi (1869 – 1948) was the most important political, ideological and spiritual leader of India during the Indian independence movement. His idea and strategy was to resist British rule through mass civil disobedience and total non-violence. He inspired movements for civil rights and freedom across the world. In 1930, he and his followers protested the British-imposed salt tax with the non-cooperation movement and the famous salt march. In 1942, he launched the "Quit India" civil disobedience movement. On 30 January 1948 he was assassinated by a Hindu extremist.

Info

George Orwell (1903 – 1950) was an English author and journalist, known for his awareness of social justice and opposition to totalitarianism. His grandmother lived in Moulmein, and Orwell spent several years in Burma and Moulmein (1922 – 1927), where he first served as an Imperial Police Officer. Later he was promoted to Assistant District Superintendent. Based on these experiences he wrote numerous essays on politics, literature and culture. He is best known for the dystopian novel *Nineteen Eighty-Four* and the satirical novella *Animal Farm*.

ANALYSIS

6. Gandhi could not end his speech in 1916 because his audience was very upset. Analyse his arguments and his choice of words and try to find out what upset them most.
   → Focus on Skills, Analysis of a Political Speech, p. 379

7. Compare the photo showing Gandhi in front of 10 Downing Street in London to Orwell's impression and assessment of Gandhi. How does he interpret people's reaction to Gandhi?

8. Take a close look at Gandhi's concluding remarks (ll. 53 – 57): Which events in British history might Gandhi have had in mind?
   @ Study the Focus on Facts page *Landmarks in British History* (pp. 38 f.) and/or do research on the Internet and find examples that match Gandhi's assumption.

ACTIVITIES

9. Look at the photo below taken of a tea party. Choose one of the people in the picture and imagine what they might have been thinking. Write an interior monologue*.
In a role play, stage the photo and read out your monologues.

Sahibs being waited on by their Indian servants, early 1900s

GRAMMAR / LANGUAGE

10. Imagine you are a journalist who listened to Gandhi's speech. Write an editorial in which you outline the main aspects of his speech as well as the audience's reaction to it. Use **indirect speech** and think about appropriate **introductory verbs and phrases** to report what Gandhi said. Be careful to use the correct grammatical tenses.

Example: Mr Gandhi recalled a close conversation he had had with some Poona professors. They had assured him that …

Tips on vocab

to emphasize sth. ■ to criticize sb./sth. ■ to imply ■ to refer to sth. ■ to allude to ■ to mention ■ to state ■ to express (clearly) ■ to blame sb. for sth. ■ to address sb./sth. ■ to call sth. into question/to doubt sth.

Alice Perrin

The Rise of Ram Din

AWARENESS

The following excerpt is taken from a short story that was written during British rule in India. The daughter of a general serving in the Bengal Cavalry, Perrin wrote many novels and short stories based on her experiences. Do you think that the phrase "I was just following orders …" is an excuse for doing something bad or criminal? Discuss in class.

COMPREHENSION

1. **Before reading/listening:**
   Take a close look at the historical photo on page 103.
   a) What do you assume to be each servant's job/chore [tʃɔːr] (*Hausarbeit*) in the household?
   b) What do you consider to be the servants' hierarchy? Make a ranking and give reasons for your answer.
   c) Relate the historical photo to the title of the short story and speculate: How can a servant "rise", i.e. get promoted and reach a higher position in the household?
   → Focus on Skills, Analysis of Visuals, p. 381

1 It was in the year of the famine[1], when my father, Ram Bux of Kansrao in the Mathura district, bade me make ready to go with him to the city of Kings – which is two days' journey by road from the village – that I might there obtain[2] employment as dish-washer in the service of a sahib[3]; for there were many of us in my father's house, and his crops had failed for want[4] of rain, so that there was not enough food to fill our stomachs. In his youth my father, Ram Bux, had himself served the *Feringhees*[5], and having heard him speak much of those days I felt that I should learn my duties with the greater ease[6]; and as we journeyed through the dry, empty fields in the early morning time, he also told me many more things concerning the ways of the sahibs, which are not the ways of the dark people. I was but a stripling[7], and knew little of what happened beyond the village of my birth where I worked in the fields and tended the cattle until the day came of which I now speak; and I learned from my father that it is well to obey the orders of the master without thought or question, even when it might be hard to understand the reason of his wishes.

[…]

'And what if the sahib beats me for no fault, as thou[8] sayest[9] will happen on occasions?'

'Take thy[10] beating and say nothing. Above all things, do not run away. The *Feringhees* themselves are brave, though they are dogs and sons of dogs, and when they behold[11] courage in others do they respect it. A beating does little harm. I lived once with a colonel-sahib who gave medicine as a punishment, and that was bad. There are certain sahibs who neither drink, nor beat, nor swear, but it is hard for a newcomer without recommendations or experience to obtain service with such, and the sahibs whom I served in the old days have now all died or gone back across the black water many years since. Thou must be content at first with what thou canst[12] get; only remember this – obey orders without question, quarrel not with thy fellow-servants, and squander[13] not thy wages in the bazaar.' […]

2 My father told me that, though the native city was wide and full of people, there were now but few sahibs, and no regiments at all; whereas he remembered that before the Mutiny[14] there had been a large cantonment[15] and many sepoys[16].

[1] **famine** ['fæmɪn] *Hungersnot* – [2] **to obtain sth.** to get sth. – [3] **sahib** used when talking to a man in authority – [4] **for want of sth.** for lack of sth. – [5] **feringhee** European, lit. foreigner – [6] **with ease** easily – [7] **stripling** (*old-fashioned*) youth – [8] **thou** [ðaʊ] (*old use*) you – [9] **thou sayest** (*old use*) you say – [10] **thy** [ðaɪ] (old use) your – [11] **to behold** (*lit.*) to look at sth. – [12] **thou canst** (*old use*) you can – [13] **to squander sth.** ['skwɒndə(r)] here: to waste – [14] **Mutiny** Indian Mutiny against the British in 1857 – [15] **cantonment** a camp where soldiers live – [16] **sepoy** Indian soldier in the British army

There was no service to be had at the house of the magistrate-sahib, or with the colonel – sahib of police, nor with the doctor-sahib, so we went to the bungalow of the engineer-sahib who looked after the roads and buildings of the district. There we heard that a dishwasher was needed, and the *khansamah-jee*[17] said that if my father gave him a *backsheesh*[18], and I promised him a percentage of my pay, he could get me the place without any recommendation. He also said that the engineer-sahib was a good sahib, and the service to be desired, and that I should be well treated. So after some argument my father paid the *khansamah*, who was named Kullan, and I gave the promise. My father told me again to obey orders and answer not[19] to abuse, and then he left me and went back to his village. […]

3 Two days later, when the sahib was sitting at breakfast eating but little and drinking whisky, the *khansamah* spilt some sauce on the tablecloth, and my knees shook as the sahib rose slowly from his seat, and, looking at Kullan with eyes like those of a tiger, walked towards him just as the striped-one[20] approaches its victim. Kullan knelt and prayed for mercy, but the sahib dragged him over the floor till his coat came off in the sahib's hand, and he kicked the man along the ground like a game ball, driving him into the verandah. Kullan rose quickly, looking like a beast that is hunted, but before he could flee the sahib caught him and pushed him into the lamp-closet[21] that led from the verandah, and locked the door. He laughed as he put the padlock[22] key in his pocket, and heard Kullan crying and smiting[23] at the door from the darkness within the godown[24]. When he turned and saw me looking, he shook his fist at me, and told me to go to my work. Then the sahib went to his room and lay on the bed and slept, and I cleared away the breakfast and washed up everything; afterwards I went to the kitchen and found it empty, and none answered to my call. They had all fled in fear, having doubtless heard the noise of the sahib's rage, and there was no one left save I, Ram Din the dish-washer, and Kullan the *khansamah*, who was crying and calling in the lamp godown.

Towards sundown a telegram came for the sahib, and not without misgiving[25] in my heart I took it to his room. He awoke and read the telegram, and then arose in haste, speaking of trouble concerning a bridge in the district, and bidding me pack his bag with clothes sufficient for a day and night, and order his trap[26] to be got ready, and bring him whisky.

Domestic servants at Madras in 1870

I packed the bag and brought the whisky, and I said, 'Your highness, there is no syce[27] in the stables, they have all run away. But thy slave can harness[28] the horse.'

I went straightaway, and with trouble and patience I put the horse to the cart and brought it to the door. The sahib did not beat me, though from want[29] of knowledge I had done it badly, and when I told him there were no servants left at all he cursed[30] their souls to hell, and bade me stay and take care of everything till he should return.

I asked him, 'What are the orders concerning Kullan *khansamah* who is imprisoned with the lamp godown?' He laughed, and the sound was like the cry of a hyena[31] round the walls of the village at dusk[32]. 'The order is that he stay there till I return. Dost thou understand?'

I *salaamed*[33], and he drove away.

4 Then did my heart glow within me, for now had my time come, and the sahib should see that I was of use, and could obey. All that evening was I alone in the

[17] **khansamah-jee** cook, -jee: a term of respect – [18] **backsheesh** tip, present – [19] **to answer to sth.** (*phr. v.*) here: to object to sth. – [20] **striped-one** tiger – [21] **closet** *Vorratskammer, Abstellkammer* – [22] **padlock** a strong lock – [23] **to smite** [smaɪt] (smote, smitten) (*old use*) to hit sb./sth. very hard – [24] **godown** here: closet – [25] **misgiving** doubt – [26] **trap** here: a vehicle with two wheels, pulled by a horse – [27] **syce** [saɪs] a stable groom – [28] **to harness** *einem Pferd Zaumzeug anlegen* – [29] **want of sth.** (*idm.*) because of a lack of sth. – [30] **to curse sb.** *jdn. verfluchen* – [31] **hyena** [haɪ'iːnə] *Hyäne* – [32] **dusk** *Abenddämmerung* – [33] **to salaam** to greet sb. with a bow of the head and right palm raised to forehead

kitchen, and Kullan cried in the godown. I fed the horses and the fowls[34], and after locking up the house at night I took my bed and placed it in the verandah that I might guard against thieves. But I could not sleep by reason of the noise made by the *khansamah*, and I answered him not, for I feared he might persuade me to disobey orders and break open the padlock, and I remembered my father's words. Also did I rejoice[35] that Kullan was in trouble, for had he not deceived my father and taken money under false pretences[36], and did he not get exact percentage from my miserable pay as dish-washer? So I smiled when I heard him beating on the door and calling, and I only feared that when the sahib returned and let him out Kullan might kill me for heeding[37] not his entreaties[38].

But the sahib did not return the next evening nor the next, and I was forced to move my bed from the front verandah to back of the house on account of the howling of Kullan in the godown. I slept on the other side of the house, and I kept away from the front verandah, but still could I hear him wailing[39] and calling, and I refrained[40] from bursting open the padlock on the door because of the orders of the sahib.

On the fourth day the sahib had not returned; and the voice of Kullan was hoarse[41] and faint[42]. By the sixth day it was altogether silent, and I thought, 'Now shall I rise to be chief servant; also now will the household accounts be in my hands, and I shall amass[43] wealth.'

5 When the sahib came back on the morning of the seventh day he looked weary[44], and as though he had suffered much care and anxiety[45]; he took no notice of me nor did he ask me any questions. I led his horse and trap to the stables, I got his bath and laid out his clean clothes, and brought his breakfast. All the time he was deep in thought and was making figures with a pencil on a piece of paper. I wished to speak, and remind him about Kullan, but it was hard to attract his attention. I coughed[46] and walked about the room, and moved the plates on the breakfast-table, and I took a fly-trap[47] and killed flies with some noise.

At last, when the sahib began to light a big cheerot[48], I carved[49] permission to speak, and he told me to say what I had to say quickly and not to disturb him.

'Sahib,' I said, with humility[50], 'concerning the matter of Kullan *khansamah* who is in the godown, it is necessary to get out the lamp oil.'

He stared at me maybe for one minute, and then he dropped his cheerot, and his red face became white as my clean muslin[51] coat. He rose and pushed me aside, saying no word, and strode[52] into the verandah, I following him. He searched for the key of the padlock in his pockets, but found it not: so he wrenched[53] the chain from the woodwork of the door with great force, and the dead body of Kullan *khansamah* fell out of the godown face downwards on the verandah floor.

Then the sahib caught me by the shoulder and shook me backwards and forwards, shouting in mine[54] ear and calling me names, and his voice sounded as though his throat were filled with dust. He cried out that he had meant to return in a day and a night, but that the damage to the bridge had delayed him, and he had forgotten all about Kullan the *khansamah*. He cursed[55] me for a fool because I had not broken open the padlock.

'Sahib,' I said, and bowed my head before him, 'the order was that Kullan should stay in the godown until the day of thine honour's return. This slave did but[56] obey thy commands.'

Then the face of the sahib grew purple, and he choked[57] and gasped[58], and fell at my feet with foam on his lips; and with much effort I got him into the house, and laid him on his bed.

Afterwards he was ill for many days; but no one, not even the doctor-sahib, or the nurse-*mem*[59] who came to take care of him ever knew what had happened, for before I fetched the doctor-sahib I pushed the body of Kullan *khansamah* back into the godown and left it there till the night-time, when I buried it in a corner of the compound[60] with all precaution[61].

There were none to witness the burial or to ask any question, for he was a down-country man, and I said in the bazaar that he had departed to his home.

[34] **fowl** [faʊl] *Geflügel* – [35] **to rejoice** (*lit.*) to feel very happy – [36] **pretence** [prɪˈtens] *Vortäuschung* – [37] **to heed** (*fml.*) to pay attention to sb. – [38] **entreaty** [ɪnˈtriːti] (*fml.*) a serious request in which you ask sb. to do sth. for you – [39] **to wail** to cry – [40] **to refrain** (*fml.*) to not do sth. – [41] **hoarse** *heiser* – [42] **faint** here: difficult to hear – [43] **to amass sth.** to gradually collect a large amount of sth., e. g. money – [44] **weary** [ˈwɪəri] tired and exhausted – [45] **anxiety** [æŋˈzaɪəti] fear – [46] **to cough** [kɒf] *husten* – [47] **fly-trap** *Fliegenklatsche* – [48] **cheerot** a Burmese cigar – [49] **to carve** here: to ask for sth. very politely – [50] **humility** *Bescheidenheit* – [51] **muslin** [ˈmʌzlɪn] *Musselin (ein Gewebe)* – [52] **to stride** (strode, stridden) *durchschreiten* – [53] **to wrench sth.** to twist and pull sth. roughly from a place – [54] **mine** (*old use*) my – [55] **to curse sb.** *jdn. verfluchen* – [56] **but** here: only – [57] **to choke** to be unable to breathe properly – [58] **to gasp** *nach Luft schnappen* – [59] **(nurse-)mem** used when talking to a woman in authority; here: a white/British nurse – [60] **compound** an area that contains a group of buildings, *Anwesen* – [61] **precaution** *Vorsichtsmaßnahme*

6 While the sahib lay sick I made for him jelly, soup and custard[62], for I had learned from Kullan how to cook. I took my turn in watching by his bedside, and when his health returned I told him privately of what I had done.

For many years after this was I the sahib's head-servant on thirty rupees a month, and he was as wax in the hands of his slave, Ram Din. I it was who had charge of the sahib's keys and kept his money. It was I who appointed the other servants and exacted percentage from their wages. It was I who made payments and gave the orders, and the sahib ever settled my accounts[63] without argument. I had authority in the compound. I grew prosperous, and had a large stomach, and a watch and chain.

Now has the sahib retired from the service of the Government and has gone to England, and I, Ram Din, have bought land in mine own district and have married four wives and am a person of importance in the village.

So is it true what my father had told me: that by obeying orders and being fearless may a man rise in the service of the sahib-people, and gain wealth and honour.

from *The Oxford Anthology of Raj Stories* by Saros Cowasjee (ed.). Oxford University Press, Oxford 1998, pp. 161 ff.

COMPREHENSION

2. The material at hand can be dealt with in different ways:

- You can improve your **listening skills** and listen to the **audio version** of the short story.
- Alternatively, you can **read the print version**.
- Finally, you can **combine both text versions** and listen to the audio version while reading the short story in order to get a deeper understanding of details.

While reading or listening to the text, focus and take notes on these points:

19 CD 1 **1**
- Ram Din's familial situation
- Ram Din's father's pieces of advice and orders

20 CD 1 **2**
- the situation in the city
- the process of finding work for Ram Din

21 CD 1 **3**
- the incident at breakfast and its consequences
- the sahib's orders and Ram Din's new tasks

22 CD 1 **4**
- Ram Din's way of following the sahib's orders
- Ram Din's plans for making a career

23 CD 1 **5**
- the sahib's return
- the sahib's reaction to Kullan's death

24 CD 1 **6**
- Ram Din's new position in the sahib's household
- Ram Din's "rise" after the sahib's return to England

→ Focus on Skills, Listening Comprehension, p. 366

3. After completing the listening/reading tasks, team up with a partner and summarize the short story to each other.

4. Based on your results from the awareness task: What "lesson" does the story teach the reader?

[62] **custard** a sweet yellow sauce that is made with milk, sugar, eggs and flour – [63] **to settle sb.'s accounts** to pay money that is owed; to pay bills

ANALYSIS

5. Characterize the narrator, Ram Din, and his master and their relationship.
Pay attention to means of direct and indirect characterization* employed in the excerpt.

Examples:
- the sahib was sitting at breakfast ... drinking whisky
  → the sahib is an alcoholic/addicted to alcohol (→ indirect characterization)
- the sahib ... looking ... with eyes like those of a tiger
  → unpredictable, dangerous (→ direct characterization)

→ Focus on Skills, Characterization of a Figure in Literature, p. 383

6. Analyse the kind of language the father uses to prepare his son for his future life in the sahib's household.

Example:
It was in the year of the famine ... to the city of Kings (ll. 1 ff.) → fairy tale-like, long-ago past ...

7. Examine how the narrative devices* create the unique atmosphere of the short story.

8. Can the short story be interpreted as an allegory*? Give examples from the text that support your thesis.

Info

An **allegory** is a fictional text in which the characters are usually personifications of abstract ideas or qualities and the plot is sometimes related to e. g. a historical or political event.
A rather simple storyline conveys a great deal of meaning, thus allowing the reader to understand general concepts.

ACTIVITIES

9. Imagine: Ram Din does not bury the khansamah's body and the corpse is found. As the engineer's commanding officer you have to investigate the case of the dead servant.
a) Describe the scene of the crime.
b) Take notes on the statements of the Indian servant and the British engineer.
c) Write a closing statement and come to a conclusion about who is to blame and what should be done.

10. Imagine the investigations of the police finally lead to a trial at court.
Choose *one* of the following persons and write a statement. Be prepared to read it out loud in class:
a) a British prosecutor (*Ankläger*) accusing Ram Din of murdering Kullan
b) an Indian prosecutor accusing the British engineer of murdering Kullan
c) a British counsel for the defence (of the engineer)
d) an Indian counsel for the defence (of Ram Din)
e) the British engineer defending himself at court
f) Ram Din defending himself at court
In a role play, act out the trial and present the respective statements in class. Finally, the class should consider the evidence and announce a verdict.

Indian Independence Act (1947)

After months of negotiations, the Indian Independence Act was formulated by the British government when representatives of the Indian National Congress (led by Jawaharlal Nehru), the Muslim League (led by Muhammad Ali Jinnah), and the Sikh community came to an agreement with the Viceroy of India, Lord Mountbatten. It was signed on 18 July 1947, and its result **was the independence of the dominions India (Hindu) and Pakistan (Muslim) beginning on 15 August 1947**.

Be it enacted by the King's most Excellent Majesty, by and with the advice and consent of the Lords Spiritual and temporal[1], and Commons[2], in this present Parliament assembled, and by the authority of the same as follows:

1. (1) As from the fifteenth day of August, nineteen hundred and forty-seven, two independent Dominions[3] shall be set up in India, to be known respectively as India and Pakistan. [...]

6. (1) The Legislature[4] of each of the new Dominions shall have full power to make laws for that Dominion, including laws having extra-territorial operation. [...]
(3) The Governor-General of each of the new Dominions shall have full power to assent in His Majesty's name to any law of the Legislature of the Dominion ... [...]

7. (1) As from that appointed day –
(a) His Majesty's Government in the United Kingdom have no responsibility as respects the government of any of the territories which, immediately before that day, were included in British India;
(b) the suzerainty[5] of His Majesty over the Indian States lapses[6], and with it, all treaties and agreements in force at the date of the passing of this Act between His Majesty and the rulers of Indian States, all functions exercisable by His Majesty at that date with respect to Indian States, all obligations[7] of His majesty existing at that date towards Indian States or the rulers thereof, and all powers, rights, authority or jurisdiction to Indian States by treaty, grant[8], usage, sufferance[9] or otherwise; and
(c) there lapse also any treaties or agreements in force at the date of the passing of this Act between His Majesty and any persons having authority in the tribal areas, any obligations of His Majesty existing at that date to any such persons or with respect to the tribal areas, and all powers, rights authority or jurisdiction exercisable at that date by His Majesty in or in relation to the tribal areas by treaty, grant usage, sufferance or otherwise: [...]
(2) The assent[10] of the parliament of the United Kingdom is hereby given to the omission[11] from the Royal Style and Titles of the words "Indiae Imperator" and the words "Emperor of India" and to the issue by His Majesty for that Purpose of His Royal Proclamation under the Great Seal of the Realm[12].

[1] **Lord Spiritual and temporal** members of the House of Lords; spiritual refers to members who are bishops in the Church of England; temporal refers to life peers and members of the nobility – [2] **Commons** the House of Commons – [3] **Dominions** autonomous polities under British sovereignty – [4] **legislature** ['ledʒɪsleɪtʃə(r)] (*fml.*) *Legislative* – [5] **suzerainty** ['su:zərənti] the fight of a country to rule over another country – [6] **to lapse** to gradually come to an end or stop – [7] **obligation** *Verpflichtung* – [8] **grant** guarantee – [9] **sufferance** *Duldung* – [10] **assent** (*fml.*) approval or agreement from sb. who has authority – [11] **omission from sth.** (*fml.*) the act of not including sb./sth.; *Ausschluss von* – [12] **realm** [relm] empire; *Reich*

Jawaharlal Nehru

A Tryst[1] with Destiny – Independence Day Speech of 1947

AWARENESS

The following speech was given by India's first prime minister, Jawaharlal Nehru, after India gained its independence in 1947. It was held before the Constituent Assembly of India in New Delhi shortly before midnight on 14 August 1947. It is considered to be a masterpiece of oratory, and marks the triumph of the 100-year Indian struggle against the Raj, the British Empire in India.
Put yourself into Nehru's shoes: Finally, after decades of suffering, struggle and fighting, India's independence is about to become reality. Being the Prime Minister, what would you tell the people of India? In groups, collect ideas and sketch out short speeches. Afterwards, perform them in class.

Long years ago we made a tryst with destiny, and now the time comes when we shall redeem[2] our pledge, not wholly or in full measure, but very substantially.

At the stroke of the midnight hour, when the world sleeps, India will awake to life and freedom. A moment comes, which comes but rarely in history, when we step out from the old to the new, when an age ends, and when the soul of a nation, long suppressed, finds utterance[3].

It is fitting that at this solemn[4] moment we take the pledge of dedication to the service of India and her people and to the still larger cause of humanity.

At the dawn of history India started on her unending quest[5], and trackless[6] centuries are filled with her striving and the grandeur[7] of her success and failures. Through good and ill fortune alike she has never lost sight of that quest or forgotten the ideals which gave her strength. We end today a period of ill fortune[8] and India discovers herself again. [...]

Freedom and power bring responsibility. The responsibility rests upon this assembly, a sovereign body representing the sovereign people of India. Before the birth of freedom we have endured[9] all the pains of labour and our hearts are heavy with the memory of this sorrow. Some of those pains continue even now. Nevertheless, the past is over and it is the future that beckons[10] to us now.

That future is not one of ease or resting but of incessant[11] striving so that we may fulfill the pledges we have so often taken and the one we shall take today. The service of India means the service of the millions who suffer. It means the ending of poverty and ignorance and disease and inequality of opportunity.

Prime Minister Jawaharlal Nehru (left) discussing matters with Mahatma Gandhi

The ambition of the greatest man of our generation [Gandhi] has been to wipe every tear from every eye. That may be beyond us, but as long as there are tears and suffering, so long our work will not be over.

And so we have to labour and to work, and work hard, to give reality to our dreams. Those dreams are for India, but they are also for the world, for all the nations and the peoples are too closely knit together today for anyone of them to imagine that it can live apart.

[1] **tryst** [trɪst] (*lit., joc.*) a meeting between lovers in a secret place or at a secret time – [2] **to redeem** (*fml.*) to do what you promised to do – [3] **utterance** ['ʌtərəns] here: a voice – [4] **solemn** *feierlich* – [5] **quest** (*fml.*) a long search for sth. – [6] **trackless** here: uncountable, very many – [7] **grandeur** ['grændʒə(r)] impressive beauty, power or size – [8] **ill fortune** misery, hardship, suffering – [9] **to endure** to be in a difficult or painful situation for a long time without complaining – [10] **to beckon to sb.** *jdn. heranwinken* – [11] **incessant** [ɪn'sesnt] constant

Peace has been said to be indivisible[12]; so is freedom, so is prosperity now, and so also is disaster in this one world that can no longer be split into isolated fragments.

To the people of India, whose representatives we are, we make an appeal to join us with faith and confidence in this great adventure. This is no time for petty[13] and destructive criticism, no time for ill will or blaming others. We have to build the noble mansion[14] of free India where all her children may dwell[15]. [...]

The future beckons to us. Whither[16] do we go and what shall be our endeavour[17]? To bring freedom and opportunity to the common man, to the peasants[18] and workers of India; to fight and end poverty and ignorance and disease; to build up a prosperous, democratic and progressive nation, and to create social, economic and political institutions which will ensure justice and fullness of life to every man and woman.

[...] To all the nations and peoples of the world we send greetings and pledge ourselves to cooperate with them in furthering[19] peace, freedom and democracy.

And to India, our much-loved motherland, the ancient, the eternal and the ever-new, we pay our reverent[20] homage[21] and we bind ourselves afresh to her service. Jai Hind[22].

www.indianembassy.org/inews/aug15 [26.09.2010]

COMPREHENSION

25 CD1

1. **Step 1:** Listen to the historical audio document of Nehru's speech to get an impression of his voice and intonation.
   → Focus on Skills, Listening Comprehension, p. 366

   Step 2: Read the excerpt from the speech.
   a) Point out what Nehru states about the difficulties in the making of India.
   b) State what he wants India to be like in the future.

2. Point out what Nehru says about India's relevance in the world.

ANALYSIS

3. Examine the images as well as rhetorical and stylistic devices that are employed in the speech.
   → Focus on Skills, Analysis of a Political Speech, p. 379

4. Show how euphemistic language is used instead of naming problems directly.

   Example: ll. 12 ff.: ... her unending quest → India's never-ending struggle, fight, etc.

[12] **indivisible** that cannot be divided – [13] **petty** ['peti] small and unimportant, trivial – [14] **mansion** a very large house – [15] **to dwell** to live in a particular place – [16] **whither** ['wɪðə(r)] where – [17] **endeavour** [ɪn'devə(r)] (*fml.*) an attempt to do sth. new or difficult – [18] **peasant** ['peznt] a poor farmer who owns a small piece of land – [19] **to further** to help sth. progress or to be successful – [20] **reverent** (*fml.*) respectful – [21] **homage** ['hɑmɪdʒ] (*fml.*) showing respect – [22] **Jai Hind** salutation used in speeches, "Hail India" or "Long live India"

21st Century India: Booms, Boons and Burdens

Andrea Glaubacker

Gesellschaft im Wandel – Tata und Cola

AWARENESS

The German author and graphic designer Sebastian Löschner has documented his impressions of a journey to India in a sketch book from which the illustrations below are taken. Ruha, a 20-year-old Indian student he met in Bangalore, gives him a ride on her moped.
What do the sketches below tell you about “modern India” and “modern Indian women”?

Tips on vocab

neon signs ■ billboards ■ advertising ■ international companies ■ heavy traffic ■ traffic junction (*Verkehrsknotenpunkt*) ■ crowded streets ■ to speed forward/through sth. (*vorwärtsschießen/rasen*) ■ passenger seat ■ to hold on to sb. ■ rear view mirror (*Rückspiegel*) ■ (to have a) topknot (*Haarknoten*)

The German text below is taken from a travel journal which portrays India in 151 essays and photos.

"Tata", the name mentioned in the headline, is an Indian multinational conglomerate headquartered in Mumbai. It includes seven major business sectors: communications and information technology, engineering, materials, services, energy, consumer products and chemicals. More than 550,000 people work for the company worldwide. Speculate: How do Tata and Coca Cola change Indian society – as indicated in the headline?

Das *Monsoon* ist angesagt bei den Jugendlichen. Kareena und ihre Freundinnen haben es geschafft, einen Tisch zu ergattern, packen ihre Smartphones auf den Tisch und plaudern über die gestrige Party und harmlose[1] Jungsgeschichten.

Hier gibt's die beste Pizza und mit einer Cola dazu fühlen sich die Jugendlichen in ihren Jeans und engen Shirts vor allem eines: angesagt[2] und hip. Sie sind es vergleichsweise[3] auch. Das Mädchen vor der Türe, das Nüsse verkauft, hat allerdings mit Sicherheit anderes im Kopf, als angesagt zu sein.

Kareenas Eltern sind beide berufstätig. Der Vater programmiert Software, die Mutter ist Ärztin. Sie will in die USA, wie ihr Cousin, der in Los Angeles studiert. Die USA stehen hoch im Kurs[4]. Wessen Eltern es finanzieren können, der geht ins Land der unbegrenzten Möglichkeiten und will dort auch am liebsten bleiben.

Ein Drittel der Bevölkerung, um die 300 Millionen Menschen, wird der indischen Mittelschicht zugerechnet. Zusammen mit der sehr reichen Oberschicht verfügt diese über die Kaufkraft[5] der US-amerikanischen Mittelschicht. Das rief US-Konzerne auf den Plan[6], die in der großen Hoffnung auf Milliardengewinne[7] den indischen Markt enterten. Aber ganz entgegen der Einschätzung[8] der Konzerne blieben die meisten kaufkräftigen Inder bei indischen Produkten. Bata-Schuhe statt Nike, Idlis statt Kellogg's, Tata statt Mercedes Benz.

Bei einer Reise durchs Land fällt ins Auge, wie viele Häuser heutzutage massiv[9] statt aus Lehm[10] gebaut werden, wie viele Fernsehantennen und Satellitenschüsseln[11] aus den Dächern wachsen, wie viele Autos und Motorräder vor den Häusern stehen.

Doch wie sieht es im Innenleben aus? Werden Traditionen mit zunehmender Kaufkraft verworfen[12]? Ja und Nein. Die Gesellschafft ist zwar in einem Wandel begriffen, aber der geht langsam voran und ist momentan hauptsächlich in den Städten zu beobachten. Moderne Mädchen wie Kareena haben im Dorf keinen Platz. Und Traditionen spielen noch immer eine große Rolle. Ehen werden noch immer arrangiert, Kastengrenzen heben sich nur in den Städten auf, Frauen sind weit von der Gleichberechtigung entfernt. Jahrhunderte alte Traditionen sind einfach langlebiger[13] als ein Paar Nike-Schuhe.

Und auch Kareena weiß, dass sie sich ihren Zukünftigen nicht ganz alleine aussuchen[14] kann, aber sie hätte Mitspracherecht[15], sagt sie nicht ohne Stolz und nimmt erst mal einen Schluck Cola.

from *Indien 151, Porträt eines Landes mit vielen Gesichtern in 151 Momentaufnahmen* by Andrea Glaubacker. Conbook Medien, Meerbusch 2013, pp. 98 f.

COMPREHENSION

1. Subdivide the article into thematic units and find a suitable headline in English for each.

2. Your American pen pal is planning a gap year in India and collecting information on "modern India". Summarize each of the paragraphs in English, being sure to
- focus on the most relevant information,
- leave out irrelevant data and facts,
- use predominantly the present tense.

→ Focus on Skills, Mediation, p. 384

[1] harmless, naive – [2] hip, hot – [3] comparatively – [4] to be of great importance – [5] purchasing power – [6] to bring sb. to the scene – [7] profits in billions – [8] estimation – [9] solid – [10] mud – [11] satelite dish – [12] to neglect, to abandon – [13] durable, long-lasting – [14] to choose – [15] to have a say in sth.

ANALYSIS

3. Examine the cartoon on page 110 and pay attention to details. What do the neon signs, billboards and the advertising in general convey about
   - India's economy,
   - India's global role,
   - the influence of Western culture?

   → Focus on Skills, Analysis of Visuals, p. 381
   → Focus on Facts, India: From Raj to Modern Democracy, p. 117

ACTIVITIES

4. **Step 1:** Use the information given in the text and turn it into an interview (in English) with
   a) the German journalist Andrea Glaubacker about her travelling experiences or
   b) Kareena and her friends.
   Think up suitable questions that match the answers and information given in the text.
   - Ms Glaubacker, after having visited India – which of your encounters there do you remember best?
   - Kareena, your cousin is already studying in the US – what are your plans?

   Step 2: Together with a partner, think about further questions you would like to ask either of them about "modern India" and think up possible answers.

   Tip: Be careful not to ask questions that can simply be answered with "yes" or "no"; instead, ask open questions that make people talk.

   Act out your interviews in class and discuss the various results.
   → Focus on Skills, Writing an Interview, p. 398

GRAMMAR / LANGUAGE

5. After doing the interview (cf. no. 4), report the interview to each other using **indirect speech**, the right **tenses** and the appropriate **introductory verbs**.

   Example: Asked which of her encounters she remembered best, Ms Glaubacker said …

Manufacturing in India: The Masala[1] Mittelstand

AWARENESS

Together with a partner, take a close look at the visual on the following page and describe it in detail, using the words provided in the vocab box.
Tip: Pay particular attention to the dichotomy (*Zweiteilung, Gegensätzlichkeit*) of the different people, their body language and environments.

"traditional India"	**"manufacturing India"**
• elephant • jungle • …	• robots • modern building • …

[1] **masala** [mə'sɑːlə] (*Indian English*) a traditional South-Asian dish made with a sauce containing a mixture of spices

Tips on vocab

background: manufacturing robots ■ manufacturing belt/assembly line ■ to assemble sth. ■ to operate a dashboard ■ square building ■ German flag ■ company logo ■ blue/steely-grey colours ■ safety helmet ■ to wear (orange) overalls

foreground: jungle ■ palm trees ■ to watch sth. with interest ■ to wear traditional clothes (turban, sari, loincloth (*Lendenschurz*)) ■ to applaud sb./to clap one's hands ■ to sit in a semicircle ■ to rest on one's elbows ■ brown/sepia coloured

COMPREHENSION

1. Before reading:
Taking into consideration your findings from the awareness task and the headline of the article, speculate about its content. What might be said about a) manufacturing and b) the "Mittelstand" in India? Discuss and exchange your ideas in class.

Manufacturing is taking off[1] in India. But not in the way many hoped

If India is to become "the next China" – a manufacturing powerhouse – it is taking its time about it. "We have to industrialise India, and as rapidly as possible," said the country's first prime minister, Jawaharlal Nehru, in 1951. Politicians have tried everything since, including Soviet-style planning. But India seems to prefer growing crops and selling services to making things you can drop on your foot.

Manufacturing is still just 15% of output (see chart), far below Asian norms. India needs a big manufacturing base. No major country has grown rich without one and nothing else is likely to absorb the labour of the 250m youngsters set to reach working age in the next 15 years. But it can seem a remote[2] prospect[3]. In July power cuts[4] plunged[5] an area in which over 600m people live into darkness, reminding investors that India's infrastructure is not wholly[6] reliable. And workers boiled over[7] at a car factory run by Maruti Suzuki. Almost 100 people were injured and the plant was torched[8]. The charred[9] body of a human-resources chief was found in the ashes. Yet not all is farce[10] and tragedy. Take Pune in west India, a booming industrial hub[11] that has won the steely

[1] **to take off** to become successful or popular very quickly or suddenly – [2] **remote** here: *abwegig* – [3] **prospect** *Aussicht* – [4] **power cut** an interruption in the supply of electricity – [5] **to plunge into sth.** to experience sth. unpleasant – [6] **wholly** completely – [7] **to boil over** to become very angry – [8] **to torch sth.** to burn a building intentionally – [9] **charred** burned and black – [10] **farce** [fɑːs] a situation that is badly organized and/or unfair – [11] **hub** the central and main part of sth. which has the most activity

hearts of Germany's car firms. Inside a $700m Volkswagen plant on the city's outskirts[12], laser-wielding[13] robots test car frames' dimensions and a giant conveyor belt slips by, with sprung-wood[14] surfaces to protect workers' knees. It is "probably the cheapest factory we have worldwide," says John Chacko, VW's boss in India. In time it could become an export hub. Nearby, in the distance it takes a Polo to get to 60 mph, is a plant owned by Mercedes-Benz.

Both German firms were attracted by (fairly) reliable power and access to land but also Pune's engineering colleges and tradition of manufacturing. "It is a hub for auto-suppliers," says Peter Honegg, Mercedes's boss. Smaller firms are arriving too. Zubin Kabraji, of the Indo-German chamber of commerce, says Pune hosts[15] 262 German companies, up from 130-odd in 2008.

The foreign influx is not limited to Germans; and local suppliers benefit regardless. Three-quarters of VW's parts are bought locally. Some foreigners are not really manufacturing but rather assembling[16] imported parts to get around Indian customs duties. Still they use some Indian suppliers too – 30 – 40 % of Mercedes's components are local. Indian champions are also prospering. Tata, a conglomerate[17], has been in Pune for decades and has a new plant assembling Land Rover cars. Bharat Forge, with $1.3 billion of sales, makes car parts, with 70 % going abroad. Its boss, B. N. Kalyani, says local entrepreneurs are "doing a damn good job".

Industrial hotspots such as Pune, Chennai and the state of Gujarat are not the only evidence that manufacturing has momentum[18]. India's share of global merchandise exports has doubled to 1.5 % since 2000 (but is still far below China's 11 %).

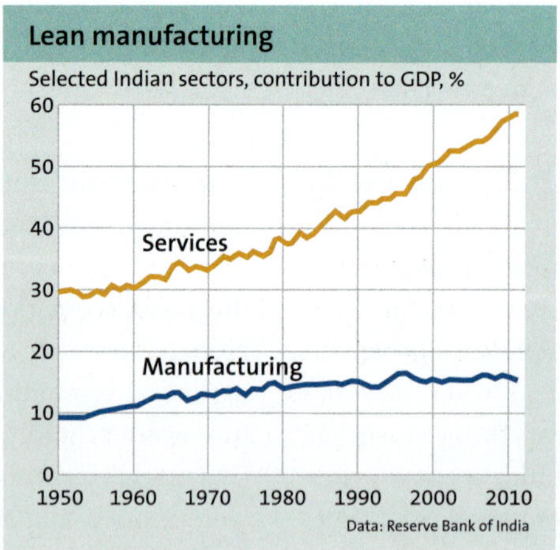

The next China, or more of the same?

Exports have shifted towards engineering products, which now make up a fifth of the total. Indian firms have become good at flogging[19] everything from motorbikes to spare parts[20], particularly to Africa and the Middle East. And most have got fighting fit. Anil Gupta, the boss of Havells, a Noida-headquartered firm which makes electrical equipment, recalls visiting a vast Chinese factory in 2002: "It was a shock." But now his firm has invested heavily and, he says, can hold its own.

Indian labour may even have grown relatively cheaper. A 2010 study by America's Bureau of Labour Statistics found that, at just under a dollar an hour, labour costs (including social-security costs and taxes) were similar to China's and just 3 % of American levels. Since the data were collected the rupee has fallen by a third against the renminbi[21] and a fifth against the dollar, making things even cheaper. And those data only included elite workers in the "official" sector – an unskilled labourer might get four dollars a day. Unadjusted for productivity, Indian labour is dirt cheap.

Of course scarce land, red tape[22], poor education and infrastructure, and onerous[23] labour laws partly offset this. But optimists can point to a government policy, in place since late 2011, to create giant new special economic zones (SEZs) that deal with these problems.

Japan, then South Korea, then China. Will India become the next workshop of the world? It is far too soon to crack open the champagne[24]. For one thing, the state seems incapable[25] of resolving[26] bottlenecks[27], even through SEZs. Some 300 km north-west of Pune lies Silvassa, part of an enclave[28] governed by Portugal until 1954. It has long been lavished[29] with tax breaks to attract industry and is controlled by the central government. Yet today it is notable for derelict[30] factories and its trade selling grog[31] to Gujarat, a dry state next door.

What is happening in Pune is more sophisticated than epic feats[32] of metal-bashing[33]. While VW's plant is more labour-intensive than its German equivalent, it still relies more on computers than humans. Local firms, such as Bharat Forge, have been shedding[34] unskilled labour, in-

[12] **outskirt** *Außenbezirk* – [13] **to wield** *handhaben* – [14] **sprung-wood** *Sperrholz* – [15] **to host sb.** *jdns. Gastgeber sein* – [16] **to assemble** *zusammenbauen* – [17] **conglomerate** *Großkonzern* – [18] **momentum** *Schwung* – [19] **to flog sb./sth.** (*BE, infml.*) to sell sth., esp. very quickly and cheaply – [20] **spare part** *Ersatzteil* – [21] **renminbi** the currency of the People's Republic of China – [22] **red tape** *Bürokratie* – [23] **onerous** difficult to do – [24] **to crack open the champagne** (*infml.*) *die Korken knallen lassen* – [25] **incapable** unable to do sth. – [26] **to resolve** to find an acceptable solution to a problem or difficulty – [27] **bottleneck** *Engpass* – [28] **enclave** [ˈeŋkleɪv] *Enklave; fremdstaatliches Gebiet im eigenen Staatsgebiet* – [29] **to lavish sb. with sth.** *jdn. mit etw. überhäufen* – [30] **derelict** *verfallen* – [31] **grog** *Grog* – [32] **feat** *Kunststück, Meisterleistung* – [33] **metal-bashing** *Metallverarbeitung* – [34] **to shed** to get rid of sth. you do not need or want

vesting in technology and building brands and distribution overseas. "Indian firms that are technology-focused are extremely successful," says Mr Kalyani. But "commodity[35] manufacturing is unsuccessful. It is the opposite of China ... We have archaic labour laws. Nobody in their right mind is going to set up a plant employing 10,000 people." His ambition is to make his firm another Siemens or General Electric.

This fits a pattern. Even as high-end engineering boomed, manufacturing jobs dropped slightly between 2004 and 2010, to 50 m. Basic industries that soak up[36] labour, such as textiles and leathers, are in relative decline. India is at last getting good at making things – but not in quite the way its founding fathers envisioned. Visitors to the country's industrial centres, such as Pune, can only marvel[37] at the great leaps[38] Indian firms and entrepreneurs are making. And worry about the consequences of another decade in which the country struggles to create jobs.

www.economist.com/node/21560263, 11 August 2012 [20.09.2014]

COMPREHENSION

2. In a **first reading**, try to get a general understanding of what is written.

3. While reading the magazine article **a second time**, find sentences that match the following statements. **Be careful:** There are more aspects listed than can be found in the text.

a) India has the potential to become a manufacturing powerhouse.
b) The only option India has in order to catch up to the rich countries is to develop major manufacturing industries.
c) India will face major unemployment of young people in the future.
d) India's infrastructure and technical development are backward and underdeveloped.
e) In contrast to other areas in India, Pune offers reliable infrastructure to VW and Mercedes.
f) Pune has a tradition of manufacturing and therefore is a reliable partner for foreign investors.
g) Germany is particularly interested in Pune.
h) Foreign investment supports the local industry and suppliers.
i) India's global exports have significantly risen in recent years.
j) Chinese companies are technologically far more advanced than Indian ones.
k) India's low wages attract foreign manufacturing investors.
l) India's ongoing problems with corruption are major obstacles to attracting foreign investors.
m) India is very successful at high-end engineering and IT but is struggling to manage its manufacturing capacities.

ANALYSIS

4. Together with a partner, compile a diagram that visualizes the various statistical data given in the article on
a) successes and failures in manufacturing, b) foreign investment,
c) India's economic position compared to Africa, China and the Middle East.

5. Step 1: Juxtapose the information given in the article about the opportunities India offers to the problems it is still struggling with.

possible opportunities/advantages	**problems/disadvantages**
• 250 m young people • low wages • ...	• bad infrastructure • ...

[35] **commodity** *Massenware, Verbrauchsartikel* – [36] **to soak up** here: to require a great number of people – [37] **to marvel** to show great surprise or admiration – [38] **leap** a big increase or improvement

Step 2: Analyse whether there are more advantages or disadvantages for foreign investors.
→ Focus on Skills, Analysis of a Non-Fictional Text, p. 377

6. Examine the author's choice of words* and explain how it emphasizes his/her line of argument* as well as the overall message of the text.

7. Compare the data given in the line graphs on p. 114 and below to the statements made in the text.
→ Focus on Skills, Analysis of Statistical Data, p. 380

ACTIVITIES

8. You are a local Indian businessman who thinks that he is "doing a damn good job" (l. 52) and you are upset and concerned about the negative image that the world and potential foreign investors might get of India. Write a critical letter to the editor in response to the many problems mentioned in the article and present India and its potential in a better light.

Tip: Use your previous results (cf. task no. 5) for your argumentation as well as the data given on the Focus on Facts page *India* (p. 117).
→ Focus on Skills, Writing a Letter to the Editor, p. 403

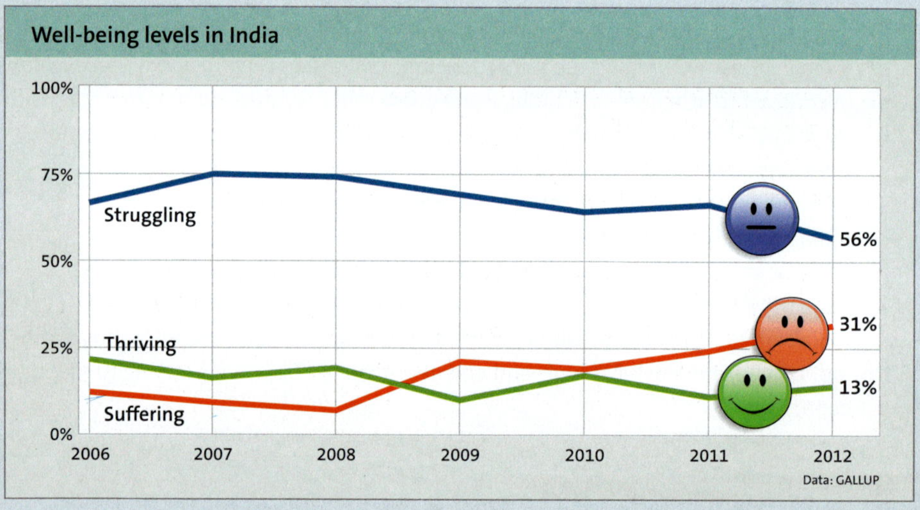

More than 3 out of every 10 Indians consider themselves to be "suffering", a worrying sign that long-standing social inequities[1] in the world's largest democracy are getting worse. Although the nation boasts[2] a booming, dynamic economy, Gallup[3] data – drawn from 5,000 people spread over 90 % of the country – suggest that success hasn't trickled down[4] to many of its citizens. Exacerbating[5] the misery is a lack of access to decent education, a problem India's sclerotic[6] government is struggling to address amid a host[7] of corruption scandals and political infighting[8].

Time, 14 May 2012, p. 9

[1] **inequity** [ɪˈnekwɪti] *Ungerechtigkeit* – [2] **to boast** to have sth. that is impressive and that you can be proud of – [3] **Gallup** American research- based global consulting company – [4] **to trickle down** *heruntertröpfeln* – [5] **to exacerbate** [ɪɡˈzæsəbeɪt] *etw. verschlimmern, verschärfen* – [6] **sclerotic** *erstarrt, verhärtet* – [7] **a host of sb./sth.** a large number of people or things – [8] **infighting** competition between people within a group

India: From Raj to Modern Democracy

With its 1.237 billion people (2012) **the Republic of India** is the second-most populous country in the world and the world's largest democracy.
Today India is a federal constitutional republic with a parliamentary democracy and consists of 28 states and 7 union territories. Head of State is the President of India, but the most executive power is exercised by the Prime Minister, who is also the head of government.
India is considered to be one of the fastest-growing economies in the world and is well known for its pluralistic, multilingual and multi-ethnic society and for its commercial and cultural wealth and diversity.

India's flag, the Tricolour, with the navy blue wheel with 24 spokes (= Ashoka's Dharma Chakra). Each spoke depicts one hour of the day and portrays the prevalence of righteousness all 24 hours.

India's national emblem, the Lion of Sarnath, third century B. C.

History

Third cent. B. C.	**Ashoka the Great** unites most of South Asia
320 – 550 A. D.	the **Gupta dynasty** is considered to be the **Golden Age of India**; extensive inventions and discoveries in science, technology, art, literature, religion and philosophy were the foundation of the **Hindu culture**
1526 – 1857	age of the **Mughal Empire**; Mughal Emperors control most of the Indian subcontinent by means of a highly centralized administration
16th cent.	European powers establish trading posts
1616	the **British East India Company** is founded
1856	the British East India Company controls most of India
1857	**Indian Mutiny:** native soldiers employed by the British Army rebel against racial injustice and inequities; as a consequence civilian rebellions follow → the East India Company is dissolved and India is directly governed by the Crown → **British Rule/Raj**
1885	the **Indian National Congress** is founded and developed into one of the largest democratic political parties in the world; it is a major force in the struggle against British rule in India
1920s	the Indian National Congress adopts **Gandhi's ideas of non-violent civil disobedience and resistance**, which later leads to the **Quit India Movement** which is also led by Gandhi
1947	the **Indian Independence Act** leads to the dissolution of the British Indian Empire
15 Aug. 1947	India gains independence; **Partition of India** into two independent states: the **Dominion of Pakistan** (later Islamic Republic of Pakistan and People's Republic of Bangladesh) and the **Union of India** (later Republic of India)
1948	**Mahatma Gandhi is assassinated** by a Hindu fanatic
1948/1965/ 1971/1999	**Indo-Pakistan wars** over disputed territory in Kashmir and Jammu
1974	first **nuclear test explosion** under the codename "Smiling Buddha" (five further tests in 1998)
1991	economic liberalization and major reforms initiated by Prime Minister Rajiv Gandhi
2005	the **Right to Information Act** ensures the right to information for citizens
2009	the **Right to Education Bill** provides free and compulsory education for children between 6 and 14; it requires all private schools to reserve 25 % of seats for children from poor families
2013	the **National Food Security Act** aims at providing subsidized food grains to ca. two thirds of India's population; beneficiaries can buy 5 kg per eligible person per month of cereals like rice, wheat or millet (*Hirse*); pregnant women, lactating (breastfeeding) mothers and certain categories of children are eligible for daily free meals

Facts and figures: Modern India

Name	Republic of India
Capital	New Delhi
Area	3,287,590 square km
Population	1.237 billion (2012)
Growth of population	1.58 % p. a. (2014) (Germany: -2.7 %; 2011)
Life expectancy	68.89 years (Germany: 80.89; 2012)
Child mortality	44 deaths (per 1,000) (Germany: 3.8)
Official languages	17 major languages (e. g. Hindi, English, Telugu, Assamese, Urdu, Santali, Punjabi, Bengali, Tamil, etc.) and 844 dialects
Literacy rate	74.04 % (men: 82.14 %; women: 65.46 %) (Germany: 99 %)
Religions	Hinduism 80.5 %, Islam 13.4 %, Christianity 2.3 %, Sikhism 1.9 %, Buddhism 0.7 %, Jainism 0.5 %
Government type	Sovereign Socialist Democratic Republic with a Parliamentary system of Government
National days	**26 January – Republic Day** 15 August – Independence Day 2 October – Mahatma Gandhi's birthday
GDP[1] by sector	service: 64.8 % agriculture: 13.7 % industry: 21.5 % (2013) Germany: service: 69.0 % agriculture: 0.8 % industry: 25.5 % (2013)
GDP per capita	$1,504 (2013) (Germany: $45,097; 2013)
GDP growth	4.7 % (2013) (Germany: 3.2 %; 2013)
Population below poverty line	22 % (data: Reserve Bank of India, 2012) 14.3 % (data: World Bank, 2014) (Germany: 15 %; OECD, 2014)
Main industries	telecommunications, information technology, textiles, chemicals, pharmaceuticals, food processing, steel, transportation equipment, cement, mining, petroleum, machinery
Natural resources	oil, natural gas, coal (ca. 10 % of world's coal reserve), iron, bauxite, titanium, chromite, etc.

Share of top eight investing countries in FDI[2] inflows in 2014

Rank	Country	Inflows (Million USD)	Inflows (%)
1	Mauritius	78,527	36 %
2	Singapore	25,445	12 %
3	U. K.	20,764	10 %
4	Japan	16,268	8 %
5	USA	11,927	6 %
6	Netherlands	11,236	5 %
7	Cyprus	7,446	3 %
8	Germany	6,519	3 %

dipp.nic.in/English/Publications/FDI_Statistics/2014/india_FDI_March2014.pdf

[1] **GDP** (*abbr.*) Gross Domestic Product; *Bruttoinlandsprodukt* – [2] **FDI** (*abbr.*) Foreign Direct Investment

Laxman Khumbi

Living in Dharavi, Mumbai (India)

AWARENESS

In 2008, for the first time in history, more people lived in cities than rural areas worldwide. One third of these urban dwellers[1] – more than one billion people – live in slums. Their number will double in the next twenty-five years, according to a United Nations forecast. Although the common perception of slums is that they are locations of poverty, danger and neglect[2], their people are ambitious and hard workers. Mumbai is one of India's richest and most densely populated cities with its approximately 18 million people, two-thirds of whom live in slums called "zopadpattis". Dharavi is Mumbai's best-known slum which is situated in its center, and is home to ca. one million people.
What do you think are the daily challenges that people living in slums have to deal with?

They will demolish this area, but we don't know when they'll give us notice. Some say it will be demolished within one month, some say within two, some say within three months. There are no guarantees. Whose house will be taken down first?

They say they'll give people new places to live after the demolitions, near Mankhurd. But over there, there's no water. It's also very far away, and there are no work or business opportunities. We'd had to come back here for work, and the transportation fares are expensive. But when they give us a room, we'll have to go. As the government solves this for everyone, it has to be good for everyone.

I have been living in this area since my childhood. We used to stay in a chawl building with my parents where we had our own room. But after I got married and my father and mother died, we had to sell that place and move here. We've been staying in this place for the last four years; no one lived here before that. This place was just a creek before; there was muck all around. This area is very fast, there are thousands of shanties here. For toilet purposes, we have to go outside – it's a problem – we have to go on the road.

The electricity is on for two days, then off two days, or not on at all. We don't have much space for the children to play in. They use the road to play, and accidents take place, again and again.

I've not studied at all and am illiterate.

For work, I stitch government jeans and pants. It's fine, but the workday ends late. I want to educate my kids. Until I die, I'll educate them – as long as I'm around, that's guaranteed.

from *The Places We Live* by Jonas Bendiksen. aperture foundation, New York 2008

1 Laxman Khumbi and his son

Tips on vocab

Laxman Khumbi and his son
tarpaulin (*Zeltplane*) ■ sackcloth ■ dampness (*Feuchtigkeit*) ■ windowless ■ dark ■ dismal (*trostlos*) ■ stone floor ■ camp bed/cot (*Feldbett*) ■ broken-down/skinny people ■ tinware (*Blechgeschirr*) ■ shabby ■ flimsy sheets (*fadenscheinige Laken*) ■ barefoot

[1] **dweller** inhabitant – [2] **neglect** *Verwahrlosung*

Walking on a water main **2**

Tips on vocab

Water main
corrugated iron shacks (*Wellblechhütten*) ■ sewage water (*Abwasser*) ■ waste water ■ cess-pool (*Jauchegrube*) ■ rags (*Lumpen*) ■ dilapi-dated (*verfallen*) huts/shacks ■ narrow street/lane ■ rusty sheet metal ■ cramped (*be-engt, überfüllt*) ■ card-board roofs ■ unsani-tary ■ sandbags to keep out water ■ plastic bags

COMPREHENSION

1. Describe the photos, paying attention to details, and say what they reveal about the living conditions of the people.
   → Focus on Skills, Analysis of Visuals, p. 381
2. Summarize what Laxman Khumbi says about Mumbai's largest slum area.

Info

The Indian Caste [kast] **System**
The Indian caste system involves four castes (= varnas) and one outcast social group:
1. Brahmins (teachers, scholars, priests)
2. Kshatriyas (kings, warriors)
3. Vaishyas (farmers, traders)
4. Shudras (service providers, laborers)

All those who do not match these norms, e.g. foreigners, tribals or nomads, were considered contagious (*ansteckend*) and untouchables (= Harijans). These people were segregated and had unpleasant or toxic jobs, often lived in extreme poverty and suffered from social discrimination. These barriers have mostly broken down in large cities, but still exist in rural areas. Since the Constitution of India (1950) outlawed the practice of untouchability, it has declined significantly – even allowing former untouchables to take up high political offices.

ANALYSIS

3. Explain the hierarchy of the Indian caste system and relate it to Laxman Khumbi's situation and his ambitions. Looking at his situation, what opportunities and perspectives do you realistically see for him and his children?

ACTIVITIES

4. Compare the seemingly archaic Indian caste system to modern social (class) barriers – what differences and similarities do you perceive? Discuss in class.

Webcode SNG-40183-015 @

5. Watch the video clips provided on the webcode and collect information about
   - the history and development of Dharavi,
   - the living conditions of the people,
   - opportunities and risks the inhabitants of Dharavi face (e.g. crime, health conditions, poverty, (un-) employment, etc.).

   Afterwards, prepare and give a short presentation (ca. 5 minutes) in class that depicts the most relevant information.
   → Focus on Skills, Presentations, p. 391

economy and trade		
to benefit from sth.; benefit	to get an advantage from sth.; advantage	*von etwas profitieren; Profit, Vorteil*
commerce ['kɒmɜːs]	trade	*Handel*
corruption	dishonest, illegal or immoral behaviour, especially from someone in power, often involving money	*Korruption, Bestechung*
demand	the need or desire people have for particular goods and services	*Nachfrage*
developing country	a poor country that is trying to increase its industry and trade and improve life for its people	*Entwicklungsland*
(the) digital age	a period in history that is characterized by the shift from traditional industry to an economy based on information technology	*das digitale Zeitalter, Computer-, Internet-Zeitalter*
economic growth	relating to a positive development of a country's economy	*Wirtschaftswachstum*
economic power	a country that is economically strong and important and can influence events	*Wirtschaftskraft, Wirtschafts-macht*
economy	the system by which a country's money and goods are produced and used, or a country considered in this way	*Wirtschaft*
emerging market	a country/an economy in an early stage of development, a country that does not (yet) meet the standards of a developed market	*Schwellenland, Wachstums-markt*
to export sth. [ɪk'spɔːt] **export**	to sell goods to another country	*etwas exportieren; Waren-export, Warenausfuhr*
foreign investment	business and investments of money involving other countries	*Auslandsinvestitionen*
goods (*pl.*)	things that are produced in order to be sold	*Waren*
living standard	the level of comfort and the amount of money people have; standard of living	*Lebensstandard*
low-wage country	a country where workers only earn very little money	*Niedriglohnland*
to import sth.; import of goods	to bring a product from one country into another so that it can be sold there	*etwas importieren; Waren-import, Wareneinfuhr*
to manufacture sth.; manufacturing	to produce sth.; the process or business of producing goods in factories; production	*etwas herstellen; Produktion, Fertigung*
(natural) resources [rɪ'sɔːsəz]	soil, minerals, forests, water and energy sources	*natürliche Ressourcen*
outsourcing	when a company uses workers from outside the company to do a job	*Ausgliederung von Produktion oder Dienstleistungen an Externe*
to provide sth.	to make sth. available	*zur Verfügung stellen*
raw [rɔː] **materials**	natural substances that are used in manufacturing goods	*Rohstoffe*
supply and demand	the relationship between the quantity of goods for sale and the quantity of goods that people want to buy, especially the way it influences prices	*Angebot und Nachfrage*
sweatshop	a small business, factory, etc. where people work hard in bad conditions for very little money	*ausbeuterischer Betrieb*
to trade	to buy and sell goods	*handeln; Handel treiben*
trade route [treɪd ruːt]	a way across land or sea used by traders	*Handelsweg*
trading company	business that buys and sells goods, esp. internationally	*Handelsgesellschaft*
waste imports	litter/rubbish that is brought from one country to another so that it can be sold to businesses that specialize in treating, dumping or burning it	*Einfuhr von Abfällen*

The American Dream – Reveries and Realities

Banksy: *Child disguised as Liberty*, New York

Tips on vocab

to pick one's nose ■ shawl (*Umhängetuch*) ■ a long train (*Schleppe*) ■ a crown with 6 rays ■ to stand on a crate (*Kasten*) ■ a sack dress ■ rough shoes ■ to look defiant (*trotzig*) ■ peeling/flaking paint ■ cracks in the wall

START-UP ACTIVITIES

1. The Statue of Liberty: a defiant child "from the streets"?
   a) Team up with a partner and describe the mural to each other, paying attention to details such as the child's facial expression, body language, the condition of the wall, etc.
   b) Speculate about the child's social background and what she might be thinking.

2. In class, speculate on the artist's intention to personify one of America's core symbols in this way.
→ Focus on Skills, Analysis of Visuals, p. 381

Bruce Springsteen

American Land

What is this land of America, so many travel there
I'm going now while I'm still young, my darling meet me there
Wish me luck my lovely, I'll send for you when I can
And we'll make our home in the American Land

Over there all the women wear silk and satin to their knees
And children dear, the sweets, I hear, are growing on the trees
Gold comes rushing out the rivers straight into your hands
When you make your home in the American Land

There's diamonds in the sidewalks, there's gutters[1] lined in song[2]
Dear, I hear that beer flows through the faucets[3] all night long
There's treasure for the taking[4], for any hard working man
Who will make his home in the American Land

I docked[5] at Ellis Island in a city of light and spire[6]
I wandered to the valley of red-hot steel and fire
We made the steel that built the cities with the sweat of our two hands
And I made my home in the American Land

There's diamonds in the sidewalk, there's gutters lined in song
Dear I hear that beer flows through the faucets all night long
There's treasure for the taking, for any hard working man
Who will make his home in the American Land

The McNicholas, the Posalskis, the Smiths, Zerillis too
The Blacks, the Irish, Italians, the Germans and the Jews
Come across the water a thousand miles from home
With nothing in their bellies but the fire down below

They died building the railroads, worked to bones and skin
They died in the fields and factories, names scattered[7] in the wind
They died to get here a hundred years ago, they're still dyin' now
The hands that built the country we're always trying to keep down[8]

There's diamonds in the sidewalk, there's gutters lined in song
Dear I hear that beer flows through the faucets all night long
There's treasure for the taking, for any hard working man
Who will make his home in the American Land ...

27 CD1

3. Listen to/read the song by Bruce Springsteen.
a) What dreams and hopes of America are expressed by the speaker?
b) Which ethnic groups try to "make a home" in the US?
c) What has become of people's dreams?

[1] **gutter** *Straßengraben; Gosse* – [2] **to be lined in sth.** here: to be covered in sth. – [3] **faucet** (*US*) *Wasserhahn, Fasshahn* – [4] **for the taking** easily available – [5] **to dock at** *andocken* – [6] **spire** *(Turm-)Spitze* – [7] **scattered** dispersed; *verteilt* – [8] **to keep sb. down** (*phr. v.*) to oppress sb.

America and Americans – Insights and Outlooks

David Lynch, Jason S., Austin Lynch

Interview Project

AWARENESS

From June 2009 until May 2010, the American film-makers Jason S. and Austin Lynch interviewed 121 Americans and created the online documentary series *Interview Project*. David Lynch, famous American film-maker and visual artist, helped produce the project and gave support. The interviews, each between three and five minutes, introduce ordinary people in contemporary America and are posted on the project's website. David Lynch explains: "People should watch *Interview Project* because they're going to meet hundreds of people. [...] *Interview Project* is a 20,000-mile road trip across and back the United States. [...] The people told their stories. It's so fascinating to look and listen to people. What I hope people will get out of *Interview Project* is a chance to meet these people. It's something that's human and you can't stay away."

What questions would you ask people that you meet along the road to make them talk about their life?

(109) Jenny Brown, 17, Bozeman, Montana

(83) Bernie, 74, Barneveld, Wisconsin

(60) Faulk, 84, Catskill, New York

(107) Asaph Adonai, Billings, Montana

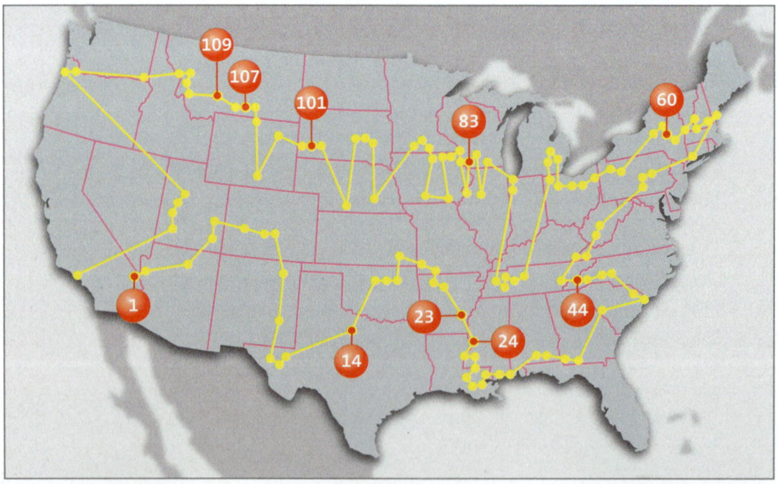

(44) Lauren Beach, 24, Asheville, North Carolina

(101) John Blackbear, 66, Pine Ridge Indian Reservation, South Dakota

(24) Mrs. Dennis, 92, Vicksburg, Mississippi

(1) Jess, 64, Needles, California

(14) Lynn, 42, Graham, Texas

(23) Anthony Dumas, Arkansas

COMPREHENSION

1. Form six groups, each focusing on a different US region as shown in the map below.
As this is a cultural-geographic-demographic project, you should get some background knowledge before watching the interviews.

Webcode NG-40183-017

Pre-viewing:
- Do research on the region and its people, using the links provided on the webcode.
- Focus on the most important cultural/historical information.
- Discuss in your group what questions you would ask the people if you were the interviewer.
- In a group puzzle, inform each other about the respective US regions in class.

Webcode NG-40183-017

While-viewing:
Choose 1 – 2 people from the *Interview Project* per group and watch the interviews provided on the webcode.
Take notes concerning the following aspects:

biographical data	historical references	cultural aspects	connection to USA
• Jess • 64 years old	• Vietnam • …	• …	• …

ANALYSIS

2. Determine how the personal lives of the people were/are influenced by historical, political or social events.

3. Characterize each person's stance on life and his/her personality as revealed by their outward appearance, language, body language and facial expression.

4. Explain how the camera presents the people and their living conditions. What do the "props" reveal about the person's life?

ACTIVITIES

5. After-viewing:
In class, design a poster in the shape of the USA that contains the different regions the interviewed people are from.
In your group, compile CVs of the interviewed people using your notes from above and attach them to the poster.
Finally, exchange your findings in class.

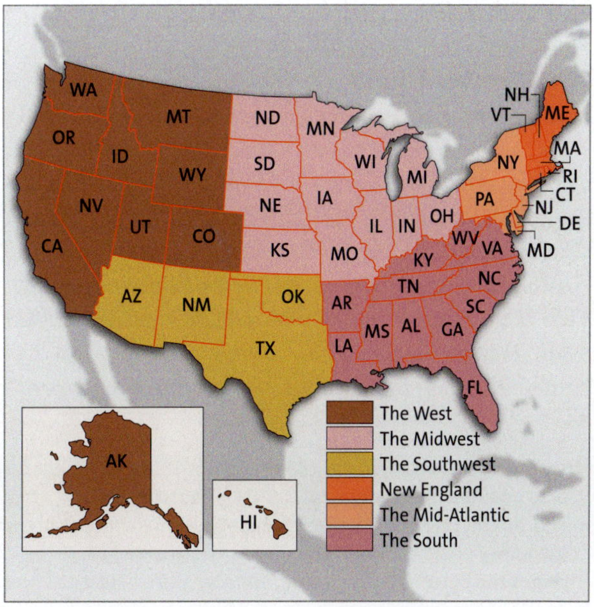

6. As a class, reflect on what insights you have gained about
a) the people and their lives,
b) the culture and diversity of the USA.

7. Collect and discuss questions about the USA and its inhabitants and culture that have come up while working on the *Interview Project*.

John Steinbeck

America and Americans

AWARENESS

For centuries, America has fascinated and inspired people all over the world. Whether they love it or hate it, there is hardly anyone who doesn't have an opinion about the United States of America and its people. Prepare two slips of paper, the first titled "America is ...", the second titled "Americans are ...". Write down three thoughts that come to your mind on each slip, then attach them to the board. In a next step, sort your slips according to topic and discuss your findings in class.

COMPREHENSION

1. Before reading:
Describe the cartoon and the clichés it conveys and compare it to your own thoughts about Americans.

1 This essay is not an attempt to answer or refute the sausage-like propaganda which is ground out[1] in our disfavor[2]. It cannot even pretend to be objective truth. Of course it is opinion, conjecture[3], and speculation. What else could it be? But at least it is informed by America, and inspired by curiosity, impatience, some anger, and a passionate love of America and the Americans. For I believe that out of the whole body of our past, out of our differences, our quarrels, our many interests and directions, something has emerged that is itself unique in the world: America – complicated, paradoxical, bullheaded, shy, cruel, boisterous[4], unspeakably dear, and very beautiful. [...]

2 E Pluribus Unum[5]

Our land is of every kind geologically and climatically – and our people are of every kind also – of every race, of every ethnic category – and yet our land is one nation, and our people are Americans. Mottoes have a way of being compounded of wishes and dreams. The motto of the United States, "*E Pluribus Unum,*" is a fact. This is the strange and almost unbelievable truth; and even stranger is the fact that the unit America has come into being in slightly over four hundred years – almost exactly the same amount of time as that during which England was occupied by the Roman legions.

It is customary[6] (indeed, at high-school graduations it is a requirement) for speakers to refer to America as a "precious inheritance[7]" – our heritage[8], a gift proffered[9] like a sandwich wrapped in plastic on a plastic tray. Our ancestors, so it is implied, gathered to the invitation of a golden land and accepted the sacrament of milk and honey. This is not so.

In the beginning, we crept, scuttled[10], escaped, were driven out of the safe and settled corners of the earth to the fringes[11] of a strange and hostile[12] wilderness, a nameless and hostile continent. Some rulers granted large sections of unmapped territory, in places they did not own or even know, as cheap gifts to favorites or to potential enemies for the purpose of getting rid of them. Many others were sent here as a punishment for penal[13] offenses. Far from welcoming us, this continent resisted us. The Indigenes[14] fought to the best of their ability to hold on to a land they thought was theirs. The rocky soils fought back, and the bewildering forests, and the deserts. Diseases, unknown and therefore incurable, decimated[15] the early comers, and in their energy of restlessness they fought one another. The land was no

[1] **to grind sth. out** to produce information, writing etc. in such large amounts that it becomes boring – [2] **disfavor** (*US*) the feeling that you do not like sth. – [3] **conjecture** guess – [4] **boisterous** *wild, ungestüm* – [5] **E Pluribus Unum** (Latin for "out of many, one") motto found in 1776 on the Seal of the United States suggesting that out of many colonies, states or ancestries emerges a single people and nation [6] **customary** usual – [7] **inheritance** *Erbe* – [8] **heritance** *Kulturerbe* – [9] **to proffer sth.** *anbieten* – [10] **to scuttle** to run with quick short steps – [11] **fringes** the outer edge of an area, *Randbereich* – [12] **hostile** [ˈhɒstaɪl] very unfriendly and aggressive – [13] **penal** [ˈpiːnl] connected with or used for punishment, esp. by law – [14] **Indigenes** [ˈɪndəˌdʒinz] native people – [15] **to decimate** to kill large numbers of animals, plants or people in a particular area

gift. The firstlings worked for it, fought for it, and died for it. They stole and cheated and double-crossed[16] for it, and when they had taken a little piece, the way a fierce-hearted man ropes a wild mustang, they had then to gentle it and smooth it and make it habitable at all. Once they had a foothold, they had to defend their holdings against new waves of the restless and ferocious[17] and hungry.

America did not exist. Four centuries of work, of bloodshed, of loneliness and fear created this land. We built America and the process made us Americans – a new breed, rooted in all races, stained and tinted[18] with all colors, a seeming ethnic anarchy. Then in a little, little time, we became more alike than we were different – a new society; not great, but fitted by our very faults for greatness, *E Pluribus Unum*. [...]

What happened is one of the strange quirks[19] of human nature – but perhaps it is a perfectly natural direction that was taken, since no child can long endure[20] his parents. It seemed to happen by instinct. In spite of all the pressure the old people could bring to bear, the children of each ethnic group denied their background and their ancestral language.

Despite the anger, the contempt, the jealousy, the self-imposed ghettos and segregation, something was loose[21] in this land called America. Its people were Americans. The new generations wanted to be Americans more than they wanted to be Poles or Germans or Hungarians or Italians or British. They wanted this and they did it. America was not planned; it became. [...]

3 Paradox and dream

One of the generalities[22] most often noted about Americans is that we are a restless, a dissatisfied, a searching people. We bridle and buck[23] under failure, and we go mad with dissatisfaction in the face of success. We spend our time searching for security, and hate it when we get it. For the most part we are intemperate[24] people: we eat too much when we can, drink too much, indulge[25] our senses too much. Even in our so-called virtues we are intemperate: a teetotaler[26] is not content not to drink – he must stop all the drinking in the world; a vegetarian among us would outlaw the eating of meat. We work too hard, and many die under the strain; and then to make up for that we play with a violence as suicidal.

The result is that we seem to be in a state of turmoil[27] all the time, both physically and mentally. We are able to believe that our government is weak, stupid, overbearing, dishonest, and inefficient, and at the same time we are deeply convinced that it is the best government in the world, and we would like to impose[28] it upon everyone else. We speak of the American Way of Life as though it involved the ground rules for the governance of heaven. A man hungry and unemployed through his own stupidity and that of others, a man beaten by a brutal policeman, a woman forced into prostitution by her own laziness, high prizes, availability, and despair – all bow[29] with reverence toward the American Way of Life, although each one would look puzzled and angry if he were asked to define it. We scramble[30] and scrabble[31] up the stony path toward the pot of gold we have taken to mean security. We trample friends, relatives, and strangers who get in the way of our achieving it; and once we get it we shower it on psychoanalysts to try to find out why we are unhappy, and finally – if we have enough of the gold – we contribute it back to the nation in the form of foundations and charities. [...]

4 Now there is a set of generalities for you, each one of them cancelled out by another generality. Americans seem to live and breathe and function by paradox; but in nothing are we so paradoxical as in our passionate belief in our own myths. We truly believe ourselves to be natural-born mechanics and do-it-yourself-ers. We spend our lives in motor cars, yet most of us – a great many of us at least – do not know enough about a car to look in the gas tank when the motor fails. Our lives as we live them would not function without electricity, but it is a rare man or woman who, when the power goes off, knows how to look for a burned-out fuse[32] and replace it. We believe implicitly[33] that we are the heirs[34] of the pioneers; that we have inherited self-sufficiency and the ability to take care of ourselves, particularly in relation to nature. There isn't a man among us in ten thousand who knows how to butcher a cow or a pig

[16] **to double-cross sb.** to cheat or trick sb. – [17] **ferocious** [fəˈrəʊʃəs] *wild, grausam* – [18] **tinted** [ˈtɪntəd] sth. that has a small amount of colour to it – [19] **quirk** *Eigenheit* – [20] **to endure** here: to bear – [21] **to be loose** here: not strictly organized or controlled – [22] **generality** *Verallgemeinerung* – [23] **to bridle and buck** (*lit.*) to show that you are annoyed at sth. – [24] **intemperate** (*fml.*) *unmäßig* – [25] **to indulge** *sich etw. hingeben* – [26] **teetotaler** a person who does not drink alcohol – [27] **turmoil** a state of confusion or anxiety – [28] **to impose sth. on/upon sb./sth.** to force sb./sth. to accept your ideas – [29] **to bow to sth.** here: to agree unwillingly to do sth. – [30] **to scramble** *klettern* – [31] **to scrabble** *herumwühlen* – [32] **fuse** *(elektrische) Sicherung* – [33] **implicitly** [ɪməplɪsɪtli] absolutely – [34] **heir** [eə(r)] *Erbe, Erbin*

and cut it up for eating, let alone a wild animal. By natural endowment[35], we are great rifle shots and great hunters – but when hunting season opens there is a slaughter of farm animals and humans by men and women who couldn't hit a real target if they could see it. Americans treasure the knowledge that they live close to nature, but fewer and fewer farmers feed more and more people; and as soon as we can afford to we eat out of cans, buy frozen TV dinners, and haunt[36] the delicatessens[37]. Affluence[38] means moving to the suburbs, but the American suburbanite[39] sees, if anything, less of the country than the city apartment dweller with his window boxes and his African violets carefully tended under lights. In no country are more seeds and plants and equipment purchased, and less vegetables and flowers raised. [...]

5 The pursuit of happiness

In nothing are the Americans so strange and set apart from the rest of the world as in their attitudes toward the treatment of their children. [...]

The great change seems to have set in toward the end of the last [19th] century; perhaps it came with the large numbers of poor and bewildered immigrants suddenly faced with hope of plenty and liberty of development beyond their dreams. Our child sickness has developed very rapidly in the last sixty years and it runs parallel, it would seem, with increasing material plenty and the medical conquest of child-killing diseases. No longer was it even acceptable that the child should be like his parents and live as they did; he must be better, live better, know more, dress more richly, and if possible change from his father's trade to a profession. This dream became touchingly national. Since it was demanded of the child that he or she be better than his parents, he must be gaited[40], guided, pushed, admired, disciplined, flattered, and forced. But since the parents were and are no better than they are, the rules they propounded[41] were based not on their experience but on their wishes and hopes. [...]

from *America and Americans* by John Steinbeck. Viking Press, New York 1966, pp. 7 ff.

COMPREHENSION

2. The material at hand can be dealt with in various ways:
   a) as a **text-supported listening comprehension** exercise to improve listening skills with textual support if necessary
   b) as **text only** to improve your reading skills
   c) as **audio text only** for an advanced listening comprehension exercise

Tip: Be prepared to listen to/read the essay at least two times, as it contains a lot of elaborated and metaphorical language.

Here are some **methodological instructions** first:

Step 1: Divide the class into four groups, each group working with one paragraph: However, **all** groups read the first introductory paragraph.

Step 2: First, **listen to/read the paragraph individually**, trying to get a general understanding of the text. Then, in your groups, ask each other questions about the paragraph to make sure you have understood everything correctly.

Step 3: While **listening to/reading the paragraph a second time**, take notes on the questions below. Crosscheck your findings with your group and make additions and/or corrections if necessary.

28 CD 1 | 1

- What is the author's reason for writing this essay?
- What – according to the author – makes America and the Americans unique?
- Which qualities define America?

[35] **endowment** [ɪnədaʊmənt] (*fml.*) here: a quality or an ability that you are born with – [36] **to haunt** [hɔːnt] here: continuously visit a place – [37] **delicatessen** a shop that sells cooked meats and cheeses and special or unusual foods that come from other countries – [38] **affluence** wealth – [39] **suburbanite** [səəbɜːbənaɪt] a person who lives in the suburbs of a city – [40] **gaited** *gegängelt* – [41] **to propound** to suggest an idea for people to consider

2
- Define America's motto, "E Pluribus Unum".
- What is said about America's diversity?
- Outline the reasons/examples given to prove that in the beginning America was not a "land of milk and honey".
- Present the different stages in the process of "becoming America/American".

3
- What is depicted about the Americans' character?
- What is the result of the "American way of life"?
- Point out the manifold contradictions of the "American character" and behaviour.

4
- Which "generalities" and "paradoxes" does the author exemplify?
- Which different areas of American life are presented?
- Which "myths" are mocked?

5
- Which "child sickness" does the author refer to?
- Which "cures" or "remedies" does he mention to treat it?
- State the author's view of the Americans' capacity to cure their "child sickness".

Finally, after finishing the various tasks, the groups remix and exchange their results.

3. In order to highlight the line of argument* in Steinbeck's essay, find further sub-headlines for each of the aspects mentioned in the text.

ANALYSIS

4. Show which stylistic devices* Steinbeck uses to juxtapose myth and reality.
→ Focus on Skills, Analysis of a Fictional Text, p. 374

Examples:
- Our ancestors ... gathered ... golden land (ll. 30 ff.) → myth (reference to Bible)
- This is not so. (l. 32) ... we crept, scuttled ... (l. 33) → reality

5. Examine the means of irony* Steinbeck employs to sketch and mock the typical traits of Americans.

Example: Of course it is opinion ... speculation. What else could it be? (ll. 4 ff.) → irony

6. Explain in detail what is meant by America's "precious inheritance ... a gift proffered like a sandwich wrapped in plastic and on a plastic tray." (ll. 28 ff.)

7. Compare what Steinbeck says about the Americans' "attitudes toward the treatment of [their] children" and "child sickness" (ll. 156 ff.) to the childlike Lady Liberty on p. 128.
What kind of "child sickness" does the author hint at?
→ Focus on Skills, Analysis of Visuals, p. 381
→ Focus on Skills, Analysis of a Fictional Text, p. 374

ACTIVITIES

8. Reflect on why Steinbeck deems it necessary to emphasize his deep love of America in the introductory part before he starts to criticize it.

American Beliefs and Values

Although there have been significant shifts in societal concepts and traditions, the following ideals, beliefs and values continue to be some of the most important in American culture.

Fundamental, inalienable and God-given rights

- **Liberty:** personal and religious freedom
- **Pursuit of happiness:**
  - (personal and material) success and wealth
  - optimism and belief in "anticipated success"
  - individuality/individual ways of pursuing one's dreams and realizing one's goals
- **Equality:** equal rights for men and women/equal rights for people from different ethnicities and social backgrounds
- **Life:** leading a secure life protected by the law, government and military

Patriotism

- importance of **national symbols** (e.g. the Statue of Liberty, the Declaration of Independence, the Constitution, the U.S. flag, the National Anthem, etc.)
- strong identification with one's nationality and **pride in being American**

Puritanism/Protestant work ethic

- the **Puritan belief that hard work, thrift, discipline, self-improvement and responsibility** lead to worldly success and prosperity and that this is a sign of God's benevolence and grace
- continuous and active participation in society and entrepreneurial endeavors
- believing that one is exceptional, **a member of "God's chosen people"**, following a divine providence (→ **Manifest Destiny**)
- belief in authority as a means of protecting the personal rights of the people

The American Dream

- the phrase "American Dream" was first expressed by the American historian and writer **James Truslow Adams in 1931**, describing a set of complex beliefs, promises of religious and personal freedom and opportunities for prosperity and success, as well as political and social expectations
- its basic underlying concept has roots in the **Declaration of Independence of 1776** which refers to basic human rights such as **"Life, Liberty and the Pursuit of Happiness"** which are **"inalienable"** and God-given and based on the assumption that "all [people] are created equal"

→ Focus on Documents, The American Dream, p. 139

An Uncle Sam wind wheel toy for children

An open and dynamic society

- being generally open to new ideas and inventions (→ progress)
- being generally open to immigrants of any nationality, provided they contribute positively to the country
- different concepts of how to integrate immigrants:
  a) the **melting pot** image: people are "melted together", i.e. they are expected to give up their original culture and identity and are "transformed" into a homogeneous "American culture"
  b) the **salad bowl** image: national, ethnic and cultural patterns/habits are kept distinct by the immigrants while they are rather loosely integrated into the "American culture"

→ Focus on Facts, The United States: Immigration and Minorities, p. 173

J. Hector St. John de Crèvecœur

The American Is a New Man (1782)

AWARENESS

John Hector de Crèvecœur was a French-American writer who immigrated to America in 1755, where he wrote about life in the American colonies and the emergence of an American society. In 1782, his observations were published in London under the title *Letters of an American Farmer*. The book was immediately successful and helped create an American identity in the minds of Europeans. Imagine what life was like for the colonists in the “new world”, and discuss what kind of personality and “pioneer spirit” a colonist might have had.

Archibald M. Willard (1836–1918): The Spirit of ’76 (1875)

What attachment[1] can a poor European emigrant have for a country where he had nothing? The knowledge of the language, the love of a few kindred[2] as poor as himself, were the only cords[3] that tied him: his country is now that which gives him land, bread, protection and consequence[4]. *Ubi panis ibi patria*[5], is the motto of all emigrants. What then is the American, this new man? He is either a European or the descendant of a European; hence that strange mixture of blood which you will find in no other country. I could point out to you a family whose grandfather was an Englishman, whose wife was Dutch, whose son married a French woman, and whose present four sons have now four wives of different nations. *He* is an American, who, leaving behind him all his ancient prejudices and manners, receives new ones from the new mode of life he has embraced, the new government he obeys, and the new rank he holds. He becomes an American by being received in the broad lap of our great *Alma Mater*[6]. Here individuals of all nations are melted into a new race of men, whose labors and posterity[7] will one day cause great changes in the world. Americans are the western pilgrims who are carrying along with them the great mass of arts, sciences, vigor[8], and industry which began long since in the east; they will finish the great circle. The Americans were once scattered all over Europe; here they are incorporated into one of the finest systems of population which has ever appeared, and which hereafter become distinct by the power of the different climates they inhabit. The American ought therefore to love this country much better than that wherein either he or his forefathers were born. Here the rewards of his industry[9] follow with equal steps the progress of his labor; his labor is founded on the basis of nature, *self-interest*; can it want a stronger allurement[10]? Wives and children, who before in vain demanded of him a morsel[11] of bread, now, fat and frolicsome[12], gladly help their father to clear those fields whence exuberant[13] crops are to arise to feed and to clothe them all, without any part being claimed, either by a despotic prince, a rich abbot, or a mighty lord. Here religion demands but little of him; a small voluntary salary to the minister[14], and gratitude to God; can he refuse these? The American is a new man, who acts upon new principles; he must therefore entertain new ideas, and form new opinions. From involuntary idleness[15], servile[16] dependence, penury[17], and useless labor, he has passed to toils[18] of a very different nature, rewarded by ample[19] subsistence[20]. This is an American.

from *Letters of an American Farmer* by J. Hector St. John de Crèvecœur. Philadelphia, Matthew Carey, 1793, pp. 46 f.

[1] **attachment** belief in and loyalty towards a particular idea, organization, etc. – [2] **kindred** [ˈkɪndrəd] relative by birth – [3] **cord** bond, relation – [4] **consequence** social importance – [5] **Ubi panis ibi patria** (*Latin*) where there is bread (livelihood), there is (my) fatherland – [6] **Alma Mater** (*Latin*) bountiful mother; the school, college, etc. that sb. used to attend, used figuratively here – [7] **posterity** (*fml.*) all the people in the future who will be alive after you are dead – [8] **vigor** [ˈvɪgə(r)] energy – [9] **industry** here: (*fml.*) the act of working hard – [10] **allurement** attraction – [11] **morsel** a very small amount of sth., esp. food – [12] **frolicsome** lively – [13] **exuberant** [ɪgˈzjuːbərənt] plentiful – [14] **minister** priest – [15] **idleness** [ˈaɪdlnəs] laziness – [16] **servile** [ˈsɜːvaɪl] slave-like – [17] **penury** [ˈpenjəri] (*fml.*) severe poverty – [18] **toil** hard work – [19] **ample** more than enough – [20] **subsistence** money or food

COMPREHENSION

1. Point out the qualities of “old Europe” and the reasons why some Europeans emigrated.
2. Describe what America has to offer to the immigrants.
3. Define who the “new American” is and describe the process of becoming American.

ANALYSIS

4. Analyse the stylistic devices* Crèvecœur uses
   a) to juxtapose the situation in Europe and in America,
   b) to depict the opportunities America has to offer.
   → Focus on Skills, Analysis of a Non-Fictional Text, p. 377

line(s)	Europe vs. America	line(s)	opportunities
1	… poor European immigrant … land, bread, protection … → contrast	22 f.	… new mode of life … new government … → repetition
21	… ancient prejudices … new mode of life … → …		…

5. Give evidence from the text that reveals the author’s view on America and its new inhabitants.
6. Explain how the cartoon views the immigrants’ qualities and intentions and relate it to the concept of the “melting pot” that Crèvecœur depicts.
   → Focus on Skills, Analysis of Visuals, p. 381
   → Focus on Facts, American Beliefs and Values, p. 136
7. Compare Crèvecœur’s statement “his labor is founded on the basis of nature” (p. 137, ll. 43 f.) with Steinbeck’s remarks on inheritance and reality (pp. 132 f., ll. 26 ff.).

"THEY SAY THEY'RE BUILDING A WALL BECAUSE TOO MANY OF US ENTER ILLEGALLY AND WON'T LEARN THEIR LANGUAGE OR ASSIMILATE INTO THEIR CULTURE..."

ACTIVITIES

8. Crèvecœur’s book was translated into several European languages. What do you think was so appealing about his views and descriptions to European readers at that time? Discuss in class.
9. Discuss in class whether the views expressed by Crèvecœur are still relevant. What would Crèvecœur write about America and the “American man” today?
10. Imagine it’s the year 1800. Based on the information given in the text and your knowledge of history, design an advert in which you promote America and the benefits of becoming an American to Europeans.

The American Dream

The phrase "American Dream" includes a wide range of hopes and beliefs that are commonly connected with the ideas expressed in the Declaration of Independence (1776), such as "Life, Liberty and the Pursuit of Happiness". The Founding Fathers themselves, in fact, never used this term.

How "the dream" came into existence

In the middle of the Great Depression, in **1931**, the American writer and historian **James Truslow Adams** (1878–1949) coined the term "the American Dream" in his book *The Epic of America*. In the preface to this book Adams expresses his attempts to paint a picture of "the beginnings at their several points of entry of such American concepts as '**bigger and better**,' and of our attitude toward business, of many characteristics which are generally considered as being 'typically American,' and, in special, of that **American dream of a better, richer, and happier life for all our citizens of every rank** which is the greatest contribution we have as yet made to the thought and welfare of the world. That dream or hope has been present from the start."

How the American settlers shaped "the dream"

"The settlers had come from a land with a strongly stratified social scale. They were not engaged in building a Utopia. Their hope was for a civilization which should be, as soon as might be, like that they had known, but in which they would each **be freer, richer, and more independent**."
"It was this **'land in the woods' as a possibility for almost every inhabitant** of America that was to prove one of the most powerful of the forces which worked toward **a democracy of feeling and outlook**, toward the shaping of our American Dream."

The "dream" in the twentieth century

"... there has been also the *American dream*, that dream of a land in **which life should be better and richer and fuller for every man**, with **opportunity for each according** to his ability or achievement. It is a difficult dream for the European upper classes to interpret adequately, and too many of us ourselves have grown weary and mistrustful of it. It is not a dream of motor cars and high wages merely, but **a dream of a social order** in which **each man and each woman shall be able to attain to the fullest stature** of which they are innately capable, and **be recognized by others for what they are**, regardless of the fortuitous circumstances of birth or position."
"... the American dream that has lured tens of millions of all nations to our shores in the past century has not been a dream of merely material plenty, though that has doubtless counted heavily. It has been much more than that. It has been **a dream of being able to grow to fullest development as man and woman**, unhampered by the barriers which had slowly been erected in older civilizations, unrepressed by social orders which had developed for the benefit of classes rather than for the simple human being of any and every class. And that dream has been realized more fully in actual life here than anywhere else, though very imperfectly even among ourselves. It has been a great epic and a great dream."
"If the American dream is to come true and to abide with us, it will, at bottom, depend on the people themselves. If we are to achieve a richer and fuller life for all, they have got to know what such an achievement implies. [...] If we are to make the dream come true we must all work together, **no longer to build bigger, but to build better. There is a time for quantity and a time for quality.**"

from *The Epic of America* by James Truslow Adams. Little, Brown & Co., Boston 1931

Barack Obama

Let's Dream – Commencement Address at Knox College

AWARENESS

In 2005, then newly-elected Senator Barack Obama delivered a speech to the graduates of Knox College in Galesburg, Illinois, in which he talked about American ideals and the various challenges the US faces because of its involvement in wars and the impact of globalisation.
In class, collect ideas about what the Senator might say on the occasion of a college graduation. What would you expect or want him to say?

COMPREHENSION

1. **Before listening:**
Here are some keywords and phrases taken from the excerpt:

- Talent is the 21st century wealth.
- the opportunity to upgrade
- everybody's got a shot at opportunity
- the winners in life's lottery
- new skills and a world-class education
- land of big dreams and big hopes
- ownership society
- collective responsibilities
- Social Darwinism
- life-long education
- biotechnology research lab
- national commitment
- brainpower
- individual initiative
- reform
- resources
- talent

Step 1: Together with a partner, get an overview of the keywords and phrases above and arrange them thematically.

Step 2: Speculate on the speech Barack Obama might have held and sketch out the potential structure of this speech using your previous notes.

Step 3: Deliver 2 – 3 minute off-the-cuff speeches (*Stegreifrede*) on the topic "Let's Dream" in class using your previous notes and ideas.
→ Focus on Skills, Writing a Speech Script, p. 400
→ Focus on Skills, Giving a Speech, p. 390

Tips on vocab

Part 1:
commencement the ceremony at which students officially receive their degree ■ **to divvy sth. up** (*phr. v.*) to share sth. between a number of people ■ **tax break** *Steuererlass* ■ **tempting** *verlockend* ■ **ingenuity** *Genialität* ■ **tuition** the money that you pay to be taught, especially in a college or university ■ **Maytag** an American home and commercial appliance company ■ **Donald Trump** American business magnate ■ **chump** a silly or stupid person ■ **decent** *anständig* ■ **to prosper** to be or become financially successful ■ **mutual** *gegenseitig*

Part 2:
to sustain to keep alive ■ **affordable** not expensive ■ **to cut budgets** *Budgets kürzen* ■ **to fuel sth.** to increase sth. or make it stronger ■ **refinery** *Raffinerie* ■ **cusp** the dividing line between two very different things; *Scheitel-punkt* ■ **to churn sth. out** (*phr. v., infml.*) to produce large amounts of sth. quickly; *etw. am laufenden Band produzieren* ■ **to hit the books** (*infml.*) to study hard

2. In a **first listening**, take notes on these questions:

1
- Point out the importance of talent and education for the 21st century.
- Define the terms “ownership society” and “Social Darwinism”.
- Present the reasons why “Social Darwinism” will not work in the US – according to Obama.
- What challenges does globalisation pose?

2
- Which “dreams” of America’s past does Obama refer to?
- What “dreams” does Obama have for the 21st century?
- Which skills and attitudes do these “21st century dreams” require?
- What are America’s resources for making future dreams come true?

→ Focus on Skills, Listening Comprehension, p. 366

After listening, team up with a partner and compare your results. Make sure that you have understood everything correctly and make additions or corrections if necessary.

3. **After a second listening**, complete your notes.

ANALYSIS

4. Before listening to the speech again, form groups of four students each, with each group focusing on one particular stylistic/rhetorical device*.
Examine and take notes on these aspects:
a) the use of **repetition** (e. g. anaphora, parallelism)
b) the use of **conditional sentences**
c) the use of **rhetorical questions**
d) the **choice of words** (e. g. keywords, key phrases, positive/negative emotive words)
In a group puzzle activity, compare and exchange your results with the other groups.

5. Explain how the use of various rhetorical devices affects the audience and motivates them to take action.
→ Focus on Skills, Analysis of a Political Speech, p. 379

6. **Step 1:** Describe Vik Muniz’ collage *Obama* on the following page which he created after Obama’s re-election in 2012, and explain its overall effect.
Does it convey elements of the “dream” that Barack Obama had as a young Senator back in 2005?

Step 2: Compare the collage *Obama* with the collage *The People’s Monarch* depicting Queen Elizabeth II (p. 32). Which similarities and disparities concerning the intention and message of the artworks can you detect?
→ Focus on Skills, Analysis of Visuals, p. 381

ACTIVITIES

7. Do research on Barack Obama’s presidency and compile a collage yourself.
Collect snippets from newspapers, magazines or printouts from Obama’s speeches and arrange them.
Be prepared to present and explain your collage and its message in a short presentation in class.
→ Focus on Skills, Presentations, p. 391

Vik Muniz, Obama (2012); photographs, digital print

Eric Bogosian

No Problems

AWARENESS

The monologue below is taken from a collection of rather experimental "monodramas" which usually portray one character. Everything the audience views on stage is portrayed from the mental state of the protagonist. In the scene at hand, the protagonist is the "typical" average American who is reflecting on his life and family.
What is the difference between "no problem", "it's not my problem" or "what's your problem?" Look this up in a dictionary first as to how the meaning changes with intonation. Then make a mind map of problems people might be confronted with in their everyday lives. In a final step link the expressions above to the problems laid out in the mind map. Which expression would you choose if confronted with one of the problems?

A man comes out to center stage and in a normal voice casually addresses the audience.

I have no problems. I'm happy with life. Things are fine as far as I'm concerned. I know some people have problems, some people have quite a few. I, fortunately[1], have none.

First of all, I'm in perfect health. I just got back from the doctor's office, he gave me a completely clean bill[2] of

[1] **fortunately** *glücklicherweise* – [2] **a clean bill** (*infml.*) no illness etc. was found in the checkup

health. He checked me from top to bottom. He couldn't believe what great shape[3] I'm in. I guess all that jogging and bran[4] paid off. He even checked my teeth ... no cavities[5] ... so I'm in perfect health.

I have a good job. It's a, uh ... I guess you would call it a "semi-creative" job, very little pressure to perform[6]. I put in about forty hours a week ... when I want to. I have the weekends off every week, three weeks' paid vacation in the summer. I get paid very well for what I do. It's a good job. I like it.

My wife and I have been married for fifteen years. We're very loving and have a very supportive relationship. My wife's very attractive, a very lovely lady. We have a great sex life, if you have to know. I don't fool around[7]. Wasn't it Paul Newman[8] who said, "Why go out for hamburger when you can have steak at home?" I subscribe[9] to that theory.

Our daughter's eleven and she's doing very well in school. She gets very high grades, has a lot of friends. Besides her school work she also uh ... she's also studying modern dance, violin. Next month she starts her Latin lessons. She's a very precocious[10], very pretty little girl. We like her very much.

Our parents are alive on both sides and uh ... we all like each other. None of this "mother-in law" stuff in our household. We all enjoy each other's company. They're all retired[11] now. They worked hard and saved during their active years and now they're enjoying a ... "golden harvest" so to speak. Certainly no burden on us, we're very proud of them.

Our friends are all happy and healthy as far as we know. We usually see them around once a week. We go over to their house and uh ... have dinner over at their house. Or at our house. I like to cook. I'm kind of a gourmet chef[12]. I like to cook things like uh ... I don't know ... uh, tortellini with sun-dried tomatoes or uh ... arugula[13] salad with endives[14], something you wouldn't think of ... that's my cooking style. Or we go out and see a movie ... something with Meryl Streep[15] in it or ... uh, a play, a Sam Shephard[16] play usually or one of those oneperson shows or magic juggling[17] plays. We like them, there's so many to choose from ... Or we go bowling. We all like to bowl. They're very nice people, we've had a lot of good times with them.

So, that's it, uh ... our neighborhood is safe and clean. We have an excellent town council[18], an activist school committee (and that's important!). Ummm ... fire department, police department, garbage disposal ... all top-rated.

The house is in good shape, just had a new boiler put in last year, there's nothing wrong with the house. The Volvo's running smoothly, nothing wrong with the car. So uh ...

I mean, there are times, when. Uh, I mean, I'll be honest ... there are times when I am concerned about all the, uh, you know, all the trouble there is in the world these days. You know, you turn on the news and uh ... it's disturbing, you know ... and nobody likes being disturbed. I make myself watch it because I know I should. For their sake[19].

And I worry about it all. But then I just think to myself, there's always been trouble, we didn't invent it, you know, and uh, I should just be thankful for all the good things I have in my life. Those people are doing their thing out there, whatever it is and uh, well anyway, I ... I guess this isn't really the point ...

The future looks good. We're going to have the house paid off in ten years. We're buying a little condo[20] down by the water, kind as an investment/vacation/retirement thing. We're really excited about that ...

Ummmm, we've got money in a pension fund, so we're cool there ... insurance ... some stock[21].

Like I said, I have no problems. None. I'm happy. I'm healthy. I love my wife, I love my kid ... good job ... no problems.

That's what it's all about ... I guess.

from *The Essential Bogosian* by Eric Bogosian. Theatre Communications Group, New York, 1994, pp. 119 ff.

[3] **shape** (*infml.*) condition – [4] **bran** cereal; *Frühstücksflocken* – [5] **cavities** *Karies* – [6] **to perform** here: to function, to do a good job – [7] **to fool around** (*infml.*) here: to have affairs – [8] **Paul Newman** (1925 – 2008) American actor – [9] **to subscribe to sth.** to agree with sb./sth.; *sich einer Meinung anschließen* – [10] **precocious** [prɪ'kəʊʃəs] *altklug* – [11] **to retire** *in den Ruhestand gehen* – [12] **gourmet chef** ['gʊəmeɪ ʃef] *Gourmetkoch* – [13] **arugula** [æ'ruːgjʊlə] *Rucola* – [14] **endives** ['endaɪvs] *Endiviensalat* – [15] **Meryl Streep** (*1949) American actress – [16] **Sam Shepard** (*1943) American playwright, actor, director – [17] **magic juggling** *magisches Jonglieren* – [18] **town council** *Stadtrat, Gemeinderat* – [19] **for sb.'s sake** (*idm.*) *um jds. Willen* – [20] **condo** (*infml., abbr.*) condominium, *Eigentumswohnung* – [21] **stock** *Aktie*

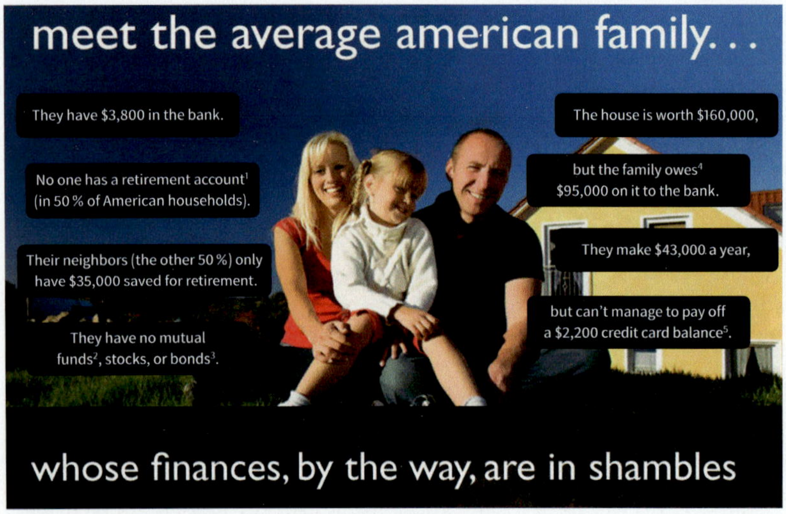

Info

- Average credit card debt[1] is $2,000.
- 40 % of working Americans are not saving for retirement.
- $117,951 is the average American household's debt.
- 25 % of households have no savings whatsoever.
- 24 % have postponed[2] retirement.
- Only 18 % are very confident about their retirement situation.
- $2 trillion is the combined amount of personal debt held by Americans.
- 7.7 % don't own a bank account[3].

Data: www.thedigeratilife.com/blog/average-american-family-finances-infographic [28.06.2013]

COMPREHENSION

1. Listen to Eric Bogosian's "No Problems". In a **first listening** take notes on the following aspects: What information does he provide about
   - himself,
   - his family,
   - his friends,
   - his environment?

2. In a **second listening**, focus on what the speaker is concerned about.

3. Describe the visual "Meet the Average American Family" and point out whether the figures match the impression the family makes on the onlooker.
   → Focus on Skills, Analysis of Visuals, p. 381

ANALYSIS

4. Examine the author's choice of adjectives and intensifying adverbs.
   → Focus on Skills, Analysis of a Fictional Text, p. 374
   Example: **intensifying adverbs:** completely, very → emphasis of perfection and extraordinariness
   adjectives: clean, attractive → positively connoted words

5. Analyse whether all the positive expressions are really meant positively and show what some of these expressions actually imply.
   Example: semi-creative job, very little pressure to perform (ll. 14 f.) → not very demanding, boring

6. Compare the figures from the infographic and the Info box above with the statements made in the monologue.
   → Focus on Skills, Analysis of Statistical Data, p. 380

7. Characterize the protagonist by analysing his choice of words and manner of speaking.
   → Focus on Skills, Characterization of a Figure in Literature, p. 383

Abb.: [1] **retirement account** *Pensionsrücklage* – [2] **mutual funds** *Investmentfonds* – [3] **bonds** *Wertpapiere* – [4] **to owe sth. to sb.** *jdm. etw. schulden* – [5] **credit card balance** *Kreditkartenguthaben* – [6] **to be in shambles** to be in a mess

Info: [1] **credit card debt** *Kreditkartenschulden* – [2] **to postpone sth.** *etw. aufschieben/hinauszögern* – [3] **bank account** *Bankkonto*

Founding and Shaping a Nation: Political and Historical Visions and Challenges

Presidents' Views on Democracy

AWARENESS

What do you know about the presidents who delivered the following speeches? Collect your ideas in class – if necessary, do research in your history book or on the Internet.

Thomas Jefferson (1743–1826)

Let us, then, fellow-citizens, unite with one heart and one mind. Let us restore[1] to social intercourse that harmony and affection without which liberty and even life itself are but dreary[2] things. And let us reflect that, having banished from our land that religious intolerance under which mankind so long bled and suffered, we have yet gained little if we countenance[3] a political intolerance as despotic, as wicked[4], and capable of as bitter and bloody persecutions[5]. [...] A wise and frugal[6] government, which shall restrain[7] men from injuring one another, shall leave them otherwise free to regulate their own pursuits of industry and improvement, and shall not take from the mouth of labour the bread it has earned. This is the sum of good government, and this is necessary to close the circle of our felicities[8]. [...] Equal and exact justice to all men, of whatever state or persuasion, religious or political; peace, commerce, and honest friendship with all nations, entangling[9] alliances with none; [...] encouragement of agriculture, and of commerce as its handmaid; the diffusion of information and arraignment of all abuses at the bar of the public reason; freedom of religion; freedom of the press and freedom of person under the protection of the habeas corpus[10] [...].

Inaugural Address, 4 March 1801

Abraham Lincoln (1809–1865)

Plainly the central idea of secession[11] is the essence of anarchy. A majority held in restraint[12] by constitutional checks and limitations, and always changing easily with deliberate changes of popular opinions and sentiments, is the only true sovereign of a free people. Whoever rejects it does of necessity fly to anarchy or despotism. Unanimity[13] is impossible. The rule of a minority, as a permanent arrangement, is wholly inadmissible[14]; so that, rejecting the majority principle, anarchy or despotism in some form is all that is left. [...] Physically speaking, we cannot separate. We cannot remove our respective sections from each other nor build an impassible[15] wall between them. A husband and wife may be divorced and go out of the presence and beyond the reach of each other, but the different parts of our country cannot do this.

First Inaugural Address, 4 March 1861

Franklin D. Roosevelt (1882–1945)

In the future days, which we seek to make secure, we look forward to a world founded upon four essential human freedoms. The first is the freedom of speech and expression – everywhere in the world. The second is freedom of every person to worship God in his own way – everywhere in the world. The third is freedom from want, which translated into world terms, means economic understandings which will secure to every nation a healthy peacetime life for its inhabitants – everywhere in the world. The fourth is freedom from fear, which, translated into world terms, means a world-wide reduction of armaments to such a point and in such a thorough fashion that no nation will be in a position to commit an act of physical aggression against any neighbor – anywhere in the world. That is no vision of a distant millennium. It is a definite basis for a kind of world attainable[16] in our own time and generation. That kind of work is the very antithesis of the so-called "new order" of tyranny which the dictators seek to create with the crash of a bomb. To that new order we oppose the greater conception – the moral order. A good society is able to face schemes of world domination and foreign revolutions alike without fear.

Franklin D. Roosevelt, The Four Freedoms, 6 January 1941

[1] **to restore** *wiederherstellen* – [2] **dreary** ['drɪəri] boring and making you feel unhappy – [3] **to countenance** ['kaʊntənəns] to permit sth. – [4] **wicked** *böse* – [5] **persecution** *Verfolgung* – [6] **frugal** *sparsam* – [7] **to restrain sb.** to control sb.'s actions or behaviour – [8] **felicity** (*lit.*) happiness – [9] **to entangle** *sich verfangen* – [10] **habeas corpus** ['heɪbiəs 'kɔːpəs] a law which says that a person can only be kept in prison following a court's decision – [11] **secession** the act of withdrawing from a country to start one's own country – [12] **restraint** *Beherrschung* – [13] **unanimity** [ˌjuːnə'nɪmɪti] (*fml.*) *Einmütigkeit, Einstimmigkeit* – [14] **inadmissible** *unakzeptabel* – [15] **impassible** *unpassierbar* – [16] **attainable** (*fml.*) possible to achieve

John F. Kennedy (1917 – 1963)

But I tell you the New Frontier[17] is here, whether we seek it or not. Beyond that frontier are the uncharted[18] areas of science and space, unsolved problems of peace and war, unconquered pockets of ignorance and prejudice, unanswered questions of poverty and surplus[19]. It would be easier to shrink back from that frontier, to the safe mediocrity[20] of the past, to be lulled[21] by good intentions and high rhetoric – and those who prefer that course should not cast their votes for me, regardless of party. [...] But I believe the times demand new invention, innovation, imagination, decision. I am asking each of you to be pioneers on that New Frontier. [...] All mankind waits upon our decision. A whole world looks to see what we will do. We cannot fail their trust, we cannot fail to try.

Address Accepting the Nomination for the Presidency of the United States, 15 July 1960

Bill Clinton (*1946)

The promise of America was born in the eighteenth century out of the bold conviction that we are all created equal. It was extended and preserved in the nineteenth century, when our nation spread across the continent, saved the Union, and abolished the awful scourge[22] of slavery. Then, in turmoil[23] and triumph, that promise exploded onto the world stage to make this the American century. What a century it has been! America has become the world's mightiest industrial power, saved the world from tyranny[24] in two world wars and a long cold war, and time and time again reached across the globe to millions who longed for the blessings of liberty.

Second Inaugural Address, 20 January 1997

COMPREHENSION

1. Divide the class into five groups, each group focusing on one president.
- First, collect detailed background information on the respective president (biographical information, historical data).
- In your group, devise a grid to collect and structure your findings and data.

President	biographical info	historical background	America's international position
Thomas Jefferson	• drafted the Declaration of Independence • third President	• fighting for independence • ...	• isolationist policy • ...
Abraham Lincoln	• ...	• ...	• ...

2. Now listen to the excerpts from the speeches and pay attention to key terms and phrases that refer to
a) responsibilities of the government,
b) the understanding of democracy,
c) America's international/global position,
d) future duties and responsibilities of the US.
→ Focus on Skills, Listening Comprehension, p. 366

ANALYSIS

3. Examine and analyse the rhetorical devices* the speakers employ to emphasize their views and requests.
→ Focus on Skills, Analysis of a Political Speech, p. 379

ACTIVITIES

4. Finally, each group displays its completed grid, then presents and explains its findings and results to the class.
→ Focus on Skills, Presentations, p. 391

[17] **frontier** ['frʌntɪə(r)] the limit of sth., esp. the limit of what is known of sth., e.g. of science – [18] **uncharted** (*lit.*) *unerforscht* – [19] **surplus** *Überfluss* – [20] **mediocrity** [ˌmi:di'ɒkrəti] *Mittelmäßigkeit* – [21] **to lull sb.** [lʌl] *jdn. einlullen, einschläfern* – [22] **scourge** [skɜ:dʒ] *Plage, Geißel* – [23] **turmoil** *Tumult, Aufruhr* – [24] **tyranny** ['tɪrəni]

Landmarks in United States History

The colonial period

- 1607 — the **first English settlement: Jamestown, Virginia** is financed by the Virginia Company in London
- 1620 — voyage of the **Pilgrim Fathers** with their ship **Mayflower**; founding of Plymouth Plantation at Cape Cod, Massachusetts; **Mayflower Compact** (cf. FoD, p. 122) is established; more and more **Puritans** leave England to escape religious persecution
- May 1626 — **Peter Minuit** (Dutch governor) "buys" Mannahatta from the Algonquin Indians for trade goods worth $24; settlement along the coast is called "**New Amsterdam**"; the colony is owned and run by the Dutch West India Company
- June 1626 — the **first eleven African slaves** arrive in New Amsterdam
- 1664 — English warships take the harbour of New Amsterdam; the Dutch surrender and the colony is officially renamed "**New York**"
- 1681 — **William Penn founds Pennsylvania**, a growing community of Quakers
- 1733 — **the British own thirteen separate colonies** along the Atlantic coast of America, largest city: Philadelphia (28,000 inhabitants)

Advert of a voyage to America, 1609

Fighting for independence

- 1751–65 — several **acts are passed by the British** government to control the economy of the American colonies (e. g. Navigation Act, **Stamp Act**); this leads to rising anger and opposition among the colonists
- 1770 — the **Boston Massacre**: in a riot five civilians are killed by the British troops, which helps spark the rebellion against the British
- 1773 — **the Boston Tea Party**: colonists object to the British Tea Act, board the ships of the British East India Company and destroy the tea by throwing it into the harbour; their slogan is "**No taxation without representation**" because the American colonists do not have a political voice in the British parliament
- 1774 — a group of political leaders form the **First Continental Congress**, the first American national government
- 1775 — begin of the **War of Independence**; leading American general is George Washington
- 4 July 1776 — the Continental Congress issues the **Declaration of Independence**, drafted by Thomas Jefferson
- 1783 — **Treaty of Paris**: Britain officially recognizes its former colonies as an independent nation, the **United States of America**

Etablishing a new nation

- 1789 — the Constitutional Convention works out a completely new system of government, the **Constitution of the United States,** a federal system in which the power to rule is shared and representatives are elected; **a system of "checks and balances"** is established
- 1791 — the **Bill of Rights** is issued; amendments ensure civil rights (e. g. freedom of religion, freedom of speech, a free press, the right to carry arms, the right to a fair trial by a jury)

Slave advert, South Carolina, 1787

The 19th century – westward expansion and politics of isolationism

- 1803 — **Louisiana Purchase**: a huge area west of the Mississippi is sold to the USA by Napoleon for $15 million (under President Thomas Jefferson)
- 1823 — **Monroe Doctrine**: President James Monroe warns European nations not to interfere with Latin American affairs; it is one of the most important ideas in American foreign policy
- 1830 — **Indian Removal Act**: all Native Americans living east of the Mississippi River are moved west
- until 1850s — **exploration of the West** – the frontier; the idea of "Manifest Destiny", making the US stretch from east to west coast, is born; Lewis and Clark explore the western plains
- 1848 — Mexico is annexed; westward expansion is completed – the **Manifest Destiny has come true**

1862	**Homestead Act** is passed by Congress, offering free farms in the West to settlers
1861 – 65	**Civil War** between the Confederate States of America (South) and the Union (North)
1863	**Emancipation Proclamation**: official abolition of slavery
1890	massacre of Sioux Indians in the **Battle of Wounded Knee**

The 20th century – politics of interventionism – "The American Century"

1913	**Henry Ford** invents assembly-line production to produce his most famous car, the **Model T**
1900 – 20	**peak years of immigration** to the USA (ca. 16 million immigrants)
1917	US declares **war on Germany**; President Wilson wants to defeat Germany "**to make the world safe for democracy ... and to end all wars**"
1918	"Wilson's Fourteen Points"; ideas for lasting peace and **a League of Nations**
1920s	**The Roaring Twenties**; first Immigration Acts are passed by Congress to reduce immigration
1929	**Wall Street Crash**
1930s	the **Great Depression** and **Roosevelt's New Deal** policy
1939 – 45	**World War II**; 1944 invasion of Normandy (D-Day, 6 June)
1945	6 August: American B29 bomber drops **atomic bomb on Hiroshima**; 9 August: second atomic bomb is dropped on the city of **Nagasaki**
1948 – 52	Marshall Plan: humanitarian aid for millions of suffering people in Europe; Berlin Airlift
1940s – 89	**Cold War**; communist versus capitalist nations; 1950s: "Balance of Terror": politics of deterrence, nuclear armament
1961 – 63	**John F. Kennedy**: first Catholic president; assassinated in Nov. 1963
1955 – 68	**Civil Rights Movement: Martin Luther King** is its most famous leader; he is assassinated in 1968
1964	**Civil Rights Act** outlaws racial discrimination and segregation
1950 – 53	**Korean War**
1962	**Cuban Missile Crisis**
1965 – 73	**Vietnam War**
1969	**Moon landing**; US astronauts are the first human beings on the moon
1987 – 89	**Mikhail Gorbachev** and Ronald Reagan **end the era of the Cold War**; destruction of nuclear missiles; German reunification
1990/91	President George Bush begins the **Gulf War**

Historical advert, 1921

Apollo 11 moon landing

The 21st century

2001	**9/11 attacks** on World Trade Center and Pentagon; invasion of Afghanistan → President declares "War on Terror" and the so-called "Axis of Evil"
2002	**Department of Homeland Security** is created; US Naval base in **Guantánamo**, Cuba is turned into a detainment camp for prisoners charged with terrorism
2003	invasion of **Iraq, begin of Iraq War**
2007	the **US "housing bubble" collapses** causing the crash of the real estate market and damaging financial institutions worldwide
2008	the bankruptcy of Lehman Brothers Holdings Inc. causes drastic losses on the stock market which lead to one of the most serious **global economic crises** since 1929
2009	**Barack Obama** is the first African-American President, re-elected in 2012
2010	gradual **withdrawal of the troops in Iraq**
	the **Patient Protection and Affordable Care Act ("Obamacare")** is signed into law
	Don't Ask, Don't Tell Repeal Act allows gays, lesbians and bisexuals to serve openly in the US Armed Forces
2013	**US Federal Government Shutdown** (Oct 1 – 16) due to lack of funds in the state budget
2014	as the **crisis in Iraq** worsens and ISIS (Islamic State of Iraq and Syria) attacks become more violent, the US sends military personnel to Iraq to protect Iranian citizens and the US embassy
2016	**Donald Trump** is elected President

Attack on World Trade Center, 9/11

Obama election poster

America's Cornerstone Documents

The Mayflower Compact

The Mayflower Compact was **the first political agreement for self-government in America**. It was signed on 21 November **1620**, aboard the ship **Mayflower** anchored off Cape Cod, Massachusetts. This course of action was deemed necessary because the Pilgrims were about to settle in an area outside the jurisdiction of their patent issued by the Virginia Company of London, and because several passengers threatened to make their own rules once ashore. The Pilgrim leaders persuaded forty-one of the male adults on board to sign the **Mayflower Compact** and set up a government in **Plymouth Colony**.

In the name of God, Amen. We, whose names are underwritten, the Loyal Subjects of our dread[1] Sovereign Lord King James, by the Grace of God, of Great Britain, France and Ireland, King, Defender of the Faith, &c. Having undertaken for the Glory of God, and Advancement of the Christian Faith, and the Honour of our King and Country, a Voyage to plant the first colony in the northern Parts of Virginia; Do by these presents, solemnly[2] and mutually[3] in the Presence of God and one another, covenant[4] and combine ourselves together into a civil Body Politick, for our better Ordering and Preservation, and Furtherance[5] of the Ends aforesaid; And by Virtue[6] hereof do enact[7], constitute, and frame, such just and equal Laws, Ordinances[8], Acts, Constitutions, and Offices, from time to time, as shall be thought most meet and convenient for the general Good of the Colony; unto which we promise all due Submission and Obedience. In WITNESS whereof we have hereunto subscribed our names at Cape Cod the eleventh of November, in the Reign of our Sovereign Lord King James of England, France, and Ireland, the eighteenth and of Scotland, the fifty-fourth. Anno Domini 1620

from *America's Freedom Documents*, Thomas Publications, Gettysburg, PA, USA, 1989

The Declaration of Independence

In the Declaration of Independence the thirteen American colonies announced their **freedom from British rule.** On 11 June 1776, Congress appointed a committee to draft a formal **Declaration of Independence**. **Thomas Jefferson**, one of the appointed members, was asked to write the draft, which he completed in about two weeks. The date of its adoption by the Second Continental Congress on **4 July 1776**, is celebrated as **the birthday of the United States**.

When, in the course of human events, it becomes necessary for one people to dissolve the political bands which have connected them with another, and to assume[9] among the powers of the earth, the separate and equal station[10] to which the Laws of Nature and of Nature's God entitle them, a decent respect to the opinions of mankind requires[11] that they should declare the causes which impel[12] them to the separation. – We hold these thruths to be self-evident, that all men are created equal; that they are endowed[13] by their Creator with certain unalienable[14] rights; that among these, are life, liberty, and the pursuit[15] of happiness. – That, to secure these rights, governments are instituted among men, deriving[16] their just powers from the consent[17] of the governed; – that, whenever any form of government becomes destructive of these ends, it is the right of the people to alter or to abolish it, and to institute a new government, laying its foundation on such principles, and organizing its powers in such form, as to them shall seem most likely to effect their Safety and Happiness.

from *America's Freedom Documents*, Thomas Publications, Gettysburg, PA, USA, 1989

[1] **dread** (*lit.*) [dred] making you feel afraid – [2] **solemnly** *feierlich* – [3] **mutual** *gegenseitig* – [4] **to covenant** to promise – [5] **furtherance** (*fml.*) the act of helping sth. progress – [6] **virtue** an attractive or useful quality – [7] **to enact** (*fml.*) to make a proposal into a law – [8] **ordinance** *Verordnung* – [9] **to assume** *etwas übernehmen* – [10] **station** (*fml.*) position, status – [11] **to require** to demand – [12] **to impel** [ɪmˈpel] (*fml.*) here: to force – [13] **to endow sb. with sth.** [ɪnˈdaʊ] (*phr. v., fml.*) to give sb. a particular quality – [14] **unalienable** cannot be taken away – [15] **pursuit** the act of trying to achieve sth. – [16] **to derive** to get sth. from sth. – [17] **consent** [kənˈsent] agreement about sth.

The Bill of Rights

The original Constitution had few guaranties for the protection of individual liberties, and most Americans felt that a clear statement of these rights was necessary in order to make the document complete. The Bill of Rights describes **the basic rights of the people** and forbids the government from denying these liberties. Included are the **freedoms of speech, religion, the press and the right to assemble**. By 15 December **1791**, a majority of the states had approved the ten amendments which became **a permanent addition to the Constitution** and are known as the Bill of Rights.

Amendment 1: Congress shall make no law respecting an establishment of religion, or prohibiting[18] the free exercise thereof; or abridging the freedom of speech, or the press; or the right of the people peacefully to assemble[19], and to petition the government for a redress[20] of grievances[21].

Amendment 2: A well-regulated militia, being necessary to the security of a free state, the right of the people to keep and bear arms shall not be infringed[22]. [...]

Amendment 4: The right of the people to be secure in their persons, houses, papers, and effects, against unreasonable searches and seizures[23], shall not be violated, and no warrants[24] shall issue, but upon probable cause, supported by oath or affirmation, and particularly describing the place to be searched, and the persons or things to be seized.

Amendment 5: No person shall be held to answer for a capital, or otherwise infamous crime, unless on a presentment or indictment[25] of a grand jury, except in cases arising in the land or naval forces, or in the militia, when in actual service in time of war or public danger; nor shall any person be subject for the same offense to be twice put in jeopardy[26] of life or limb[27]; nor shall be compelled[28] in any criminal case to be a witness against himself, nor be deprived[29] of life, liberty, or property, without the process of law; nor shall private property be taken for public use, without just compensation.

Amendment 6: In all criminal prosecutions[30], the accused shall enjoy the right to a speedy and public trial, by an impartial[31] jury of the state and district wherein the crime shall have been committed, which district shall have been previously ascertained[32] by law, and to be informed of the nature and cause of the accusation; to be confronted with the witnesses against him; to have compulsory process for obtaining[33] witnesses in his favor, and to have the assistance of a counsel for his defense.

Amendment 7: In suits of common law, where the value in controversy shall exceed[34] twenty dollars, the right of trial by jury shall be preserved, and no fact tried by jury, shall be otherwise re-examined in any court of the United States, than according to the rules of the common law.

Amendment 8: Excessive bail[35] shall not be required, nor excessive fines[36] imposed, nor cruel and unusual punishments inflicted[37]. [...]

from *America's Freedom Documents*, Thomas Publications, Gettysburg, PA, USA, 1989

[18] **to prohibit** to stop – [19] **to assemble** to come together as a group – [20] **redress** [rɪˈdres] (*fml.*) money that sb. pays you because they have caused you harm or damaged your property – [21] **grievance** [ˈgriːvəns] *Missstand* – [22] **to infringe** to break a law – [23] **seizure** [ˈsiːʒə(r)] *Festnahme, Beschlagnahme* – [24] **warrant** *Haftbefehl* – [25] **indictment** (*US) Anklage* – [26] **jeopardy** [ˈdʒepədi] the danger of being harmed – [27] **limb** serious injury – [28] **to compel** [kəmˈpel] to force sb. to do sth. – [29] **to deprive sb. of sth.** [dɪˈpraɪv] (*phr. v.)* to prevent sb. from having sth. – [30] **prosecution** *(Straf-)Verfolgung* – [31] **impartial** *unparteiisch* – [32] **to ascertain** (*fml.*) to find out sth. – [33] **to obtain** to get – [34] **to exceed** (*fml.*) *überschreiten* – [35] **bail** *Kaution* – [36] **fine** *Geldstrafe* – [37] **to inflict** to make sb. suffer

"Separate But Equal" ... The African-American Struggle for Civil Rights

African-American Encounters ...

AWARENESS

While hundreds of thousands of people from all over the world immigrated to the USA to gain freedom and prosperity, a large section of the population involuntarily "immigrated" to the USA – the enslaved people who were caught by slave hunters in Africa and transported to the American colonies via the West Indies.

a) In class, exchange your first impressions of the painting and speculate about its message.
b) Then, reactivate your knowledge of slavery and triangular trade.
→ Focus on Facts, The British Empire, p. 49
c) Now take a closer look at the painting and relate your background knowledge to the crowned figure. What might the artist's intention be?

Jean-Michel Basquiat: Untitled (1982)

Phillis Wheatley: On Being Brought from Africa to America

'Twas mercy brought me from my *Pagan*[1] land,
Taught my benighted[2] soul to understand
That there's a God, that there's a *Saviour* too:
Once I redemption[3] neither sought nor knew.
Some view our sable[4] race with scornful[5] eye,
"Their colour is a diabolic die[6]."
Remember *Christians*, *Negroes*, black as *Cain*[7],
May be refin'd[8], and join th' angelic[9] train.

from *Poems and Letters* by Phillis Wheatley. Ed. C. F. Heartman, New York 1916

Tips on vocab

Aztec god ■ skull (*Schädel, Totenkopf*) ■ crown ■ skeleton ■ skeletal hands ■ bone ■ demonic ■ distorted/twisted limbs (*deformiert, verdreht*) ■ archaic ■ grimace ■ grotesque face ■ square contours ■ colossal ■ over-sized ■ scepter ■ graphic colour patches ■ shadow ■ (to) scrawl (*kritzeln*) ■ strong contrasts

[1] **pagan** [ˈpeɪˈgən] *heidnisch* – [2] **benighted** (*lit.*) having no knowledge or understanding – [3] **redemption** *Erlösung* – [4] **sable** (*lit.*) black or very dark in colour – [5] **scornful** *verächtlich* – [6] **diabolic die** devilish colour – [7] **Cain** [keɪn] in the Bible Cain is the son of Adam and Eve and the older brother and murderer of Abel – [8] **refined** polite and well-educated – [9] **angelic** [ænˈdʒelɪk] heavenly

COMPREHENSION

1. Describe the highly symbolical painting by the American neo-expressionist artist Jean-Michel Basquiat, who was of mixed Haitian and Puerto Rican heritage, and try to find a suitable title for it.
   → Focus on Skills, Analysis of Visuals, p. 381
2. What was the speaker* of the poem taught on the journey to America?
3. State how "some" view the skin colour and race of the African people.
4. What thought does the speaker offer to the "Christians"?

ANALYSIS

5. Specify the topic of the poem.
6. Analyse the poet's use of contrast.
7. Explain the importance of "redemption" for the speaker. Why is this aspect emphasized throughout the poem?
8. Compare Basquiat's painting and Wheatley's poem. What do the "Pagan" (l. 1) and the crowned figure in the painting have in common?
   → Focus on Skills, Analysis of Poetry and Lyrics, p. 378
   → Focus on Skills, Analysis of Visuals, p. 381

Info

Phillis Wheatley (1753 – 1784) was kidnapped from Senegal as a child and sold as a slave to John Wheatley in Boston who discovered her talent and made her take lessons at his home. In 1767, she wrote her first poems which immediately attracted enormous interest. After the death of Wheatley and his wife, who had enfranchised[1] her, she married a free African-American, who left her after a short marriage. Shortly afterwards, she died in humble[2] circumstances.

ACTIVITIES

9. Do research on Jean-Michel Basquiat and his particular way of portraying the history of African-Americans and slavery, and prepare a presentation in class.
   → Focus on Skills, Presentations, p. 391

Historical African-American Views on Liberty and Slavery

AWARENESS

Reactivate your knowledge of slavery and the American Civil War and try to clarify the terms below in class (→ FoF The British Empire, p. 49; FoF Landmarks in United States History, p. 147).

Triangular Trade	Civil War	the Union	Confederate States
Underground Railroad	Emancipation Proclamation	Fugitive[1] Slave Law	

[1] **to enfranchise** to give sb./a group of people the right to vote – [2] **humble** here: of low social class or position

[1] **fugitive** ['fju:dʒɪtɪv] *Flüchtling*

COMPREHENSION

Before reading:

1. Together with a partner, write down what you associate with the "Fourth of July" (1776) and its importance for Americans.

2. Frederick Douglass (1818 – 1895) was an African-American social reformer, orator, writer and statesman who, after escaping slavery, became a leader of the abolitionist movement and fought for the emancipation of African-Americans in the U. S. In class, reflect on the title of Frederick Douglass' speech. What would a slave's answer have been to that question?
Collect possible answers and discuss them in class.

Frederick Douglass: What, to the Slave, Is the Fourth of July? (1852)

1 Fellow citizens, I am not wanting[2] in respect for the fathers of this republic. The signers of the Declaration of Independence were brave men. They were great men, too – great enough to give frame to a great age. [...] They loved their country better than their own private interests; and, though this is not the highest form of human excellence, all will concede[3] that it is a rare virtue, and that when it is exhibited, it ought to command respect. He who will intelligently lay down his life for his country is a man whom it is not in human nature to despise[4]. Your fathers staked[5] their lives, their fortunes and their sacred honor on the cause of their country. In their admiration of liberty, they lost sight of other interests.

They were peace men; but they preferred revolution to a peaceful submission[6] to bondage[7]. They were quiet men; but they did not shrink[8] from agitating[9] against oppression. They showed their forbearance[10], but that they knew its limits. They believed in order, but not in the order of tyranny[11]. With them, nothing was "settled" that was not right. With them, justice, liberty and humanity were "final", not slavery and oppression. You may well cherish[12] the memory of such men. They were great in their day and generation. Their solid manhood stands out the more as we contrast it with these degenerate times. [...]

2 Fellow citizens, pardon me, allow me to ask, why am I called upon to speak here today? What have I, or those I represent, to do with your national independence? [...] I am not included within the pale[13] of this glorious anniversary! Your high independence only reveals the immeasurable distance between us. The blessings in which you, this day, rejoice[14], are not enjoyed in common. The rich inheritance of justice, liberty, prosperity and independence, bequeathed[15] by your fathers, is shared by you, not by me. The sunlight that brought light and healing to you, has brought stripes[16] and death to me. This Fourth of July is *yours*, not *mine*. *You* may rejoice, *I* must mourn[17]. [...]

What, to the American slave, is your Fourth of July? I answer: a day that reveals to him more than all the other days in the year, the gross[18] injustice and cruelty to which he is a constant victim. To him, your celebration is a sham[19]; your boasted[20] liberty an unholy license; your national greatness swelling[21] vanity[22]; your sounds of rejoicing are empty and heartless; your denunciations of tyrants brass-fronted[23] impudence[24]; your shouts of liberty and equality hollow[25] mockery[26]; your prayers and hymns, your sermons and thanksgivings, with all your religious parade and solemnity[27], are to Him mere bombast, fraud[28], deception[29], impiety[30] and hypocrisy[31] – a thin veil[32] to cover up crimes which would dis-

[2] **to be wanting** *mangeln an* – [3] **to concede** to admit, often unwillingly, that sth. is true – [4] **to despise** *verachten* – [5] **to stake** here: to risk sth. – [6] **submission** *Unterwürfigkeit* – [7] **bondage** (*lit.*) the state of being another person's slave – [8] **to shrink** (shrank, shrunk) **from sth.** (*phr. v.*) to avoid doing sth. that is unpleasant or difficult – [9] **to agitate** *gegen etw. agitieren* – [10] **forbearance** (*fml.*) *Duldsamkeit* – [11] **tyranny** ['tɪrəni] – [12] **to cherish** *verehren* – [13] **within the pale** (*fig.*) *innerhalb der Genzen* – [14] **to rejoice** to feel great happiness about sth. – [15] **to bequeath** *vererben* – [16] **stripe** here: *Peitschenhieb* – [17] **to mourn** *trauern* – [18] **gross** unacceptable – [19] **sham** *Betrug, Augenwischerei* – [20] **to boast** *prahlen* – [21] **swelling** *aufgebläht* – [22] **vanity** *Eitelkeit* – [23] **brass-fronted** *mit einer Messingfront* – [24] **impudence** *Unverfrorenheit, Unverschämtheit* – [25] **hollow** *hohl* – [26] **mockery** *Verhöhnung* – [27] **solemnity** *Feierlichkeit* – [28] **fraud** *Betrug* – [29] **deception** *Betrug, Schwindel* – [30] **impiety** [ɪm'paɪəti] *Pietätlosigkeit* – [31] **hypocrisy** [hɪ'pɒkrɪsi] *Heuchelei* – [32] **veil** *Schleier*

grace[33] a nation of savages[34]. There is not a nation on the earth guilty of practices more shocking and bloody than the people of the United States at this very hour.
Go where you may, search where you will, roam[35] through all the monarchies and despotisms of the Old World, travel through South America, search out every abuse, and when you have found the last, lay your facts by the side of the everyday practices of this nation, and you will say with me, that, for revolting[36] barbarity and shameless hypocrisy, America reigns without a rival.

from *Great Speeches by African Americans* by James Daley (ed.). Dover Publications Inc., New York 2006, pp. 17 ff.

Frank Bell: When I Was a Slave

I was owned by Johnson Bell and born in New Orleans, in Louisiana. Accordin' to the bill of sale, I'm eighty-six years old, and my master was a Frenchman and was real mean to me. He run a saloon and kept bad women. I don't know nothing about my folks, if I even had any, 'cept Mama. They done tell me that she was a bad woman and a French Creole. I worked round master's saloon, kept everything cleaned up after they'd have all night drinkin' parties, men and women. I earned nickels to tip off where to go, so's they could sow wild oats[37]. I buried the nickels under rocks. If Master done cotch[38] me with money, he'd take it and beat me nearly to death. All I had to eat was old stuff those people left, all scraps[39] that was left. [...]
When war[40] was over he won't free me, says I'm valuable to him in his trade. He say, "Nigger, you's supposed to be free but I'll pay you a dollar a week and if you runs off I'll kill you." [...] After long time I marries Feline Graham. Then I has a home and we has a white preacher marry us. We has one boy and he farms and I lives with him. I worked at sawmill and farms all my life, but never could make much money.
You know, the nigger was wild till the white man made what he has out of the nigger. He done educate them real smart.

from *When I Was a Slave, Memoirs*, ed. by Norman Yetman. Dover Publications Inc., New York 2002 (republication from *The Slave Narrative Collection*, 1936 – 1938); pp. 9 ff.

Andrew Goodman: When I Was a Slave

I was born in slavery and I think them days was better for the niggers than the days we see now. One thing was, I never was cold and hungry when my old master lived, and I has been plenty hungry and cold a lot of times since he has gone. But sometimes I think Marse[41] Goodman was the bestest man God made in a long time.
[...]
Marse Bob didn't put his little niggers in the fields till they's big 'nough to work, and the mammies[42] was give time off from the fields to come back to the nursin' home to suck the babies. He didn't never put the niggers out in bad weather. He give us somethin' to do, in out of the weather, like shellin' corn[43], and the women could spin and knit. They made us plenty of good clothes. In summer we wore long shirts, split up the sides, made out of lowerings[44] – that's same as cotton sacks was made out of. In winter we had good jeans and knitted sweaters and knitted socks. [...]
We didn't know what the War was about but Master was gone four years. [...] When Marse Bob come home, he sent for all the slaves. [...] Then he said, "I got something to tell you. You is just as free as I is. You don't belong to nobody but yourselves. We went to the War and fought, but the Yankees[45] done whip[46] us, and they say the niggers is free. You can go where you wants to go, or you can stay here, just as you likes." He couldn't help but cry. The niggers cry and don't know much what Marse Bob means. They is sorry about the freedom, 'cause they don't know where to go, and they's always 'pend on Old Marse to look after them.

from *When I Was a Slave, Memoirs*, ed. by Norman Yetman. Dover Publications Inc., New York 2002 (republication from *The Slave Narrative Collection*, 1936 – 1938); pp. 52 ff.

[33] **to disgrace** *Schande bringen* – [34] **savage** ['sævɪdʒ] (*old-fashioned, taboo*) an offensive word for somebody who belongs to a people that is simple and not developed – [35] **to roam** to move about or travel – [36] **revolting** appalling, *abscheulich* – [37] **to sow your wild oats** *sich die Hörner abstoßen* – [38] **cotch** catch – [39] **scraps** food left after a meal – [40] **war** here: Civil War (1861 – 65) – [41] **Marse** Master – [42] **mammy** (*US, old use*) a black woman whose job is to take care of white children – [43] **to shell corn** *Getreide schälen* – [44] **lowering** *Abfall* – [45] **Yankee** (*infml.*) an American who comes from the northern US – [46] **to whip sb.** here: to defeat sb.

COMPREHENSION

3. The orator uses the first part of the speech to praise the American Founding Fathers and their outstanding political achievements and selfless service to the nation.

   In a paired reading activity, read **the first part** of the excerpt and find evidence in the text that matches the aspects mentioned in the statement above.

4. In the **second part**, the speaker's tone changes significantly.
   Together with a partner, detect examples in the excerpt in which Douglass
   a) refuses to celebrate the "blessings" of the nation's independence in general,
   b) specifically criticizes the Americans'
      - injustice,
      - arrogance/vanity,
      - hypocrisy,
      - savagery/brutality.

5. First, divide the class into **two groups**, each group working with one of the memoirs – **Frank Bell or Andrew Goodman**.
   Then, present the respective person's remarks on
   - how he was treated by his master,
   - what happened to him after the Civil War,
   - what kind of person his master was,
   - how he observed the lives of slaves in general.

ANALYSIS

6. Examine Frederick Douglass' abilities as a speaker and analyse
   - the line of argument*,
   - the choice of words*,
   - the use of rhetorical devices*

   he employs in his speech to bring across his message to the audience.
   → Focus on Skills, Analysis of a Political Speech, p. 379

7. Take a close look at the slave memoirs again and compare the language registers of Frederick Douglass and the other two former slaves and find out to what extent they differ.
   What does it reveal about their respective education and social status?
   → Focus on Skills, Analysis of a Non-Fictional Text, p. 377

ACTIVITIES

8. Based on your results from task no. 5, imagine how Frank Bell or Andrew Goodman would have responded to Frederick Douglass' question in the title of his speech.
   Work out short answers and statements and display and discuss them in class.

Martin Luther King

Letter from Birmingham Jail

AWARENESS

Martin Luther King wrote this open letter from the city jail in Birmingham, Alabama, on 16 April 1963, where he was confined for planning and taking part in the non-violent campaign against racial segregation by Birmingham's city government and downtown retailers.
In a group, explain and define the terms "extreme" and "extremism" and their implications.

But though I was initially disappointed at being categorized as an extremist, as I continued to think about the matter I gradually gained a measure of satisfaction from the label. Was not Jesus an extremist for love: "Love your enemies, bless them that curse you, do good to them that hate you, and pray for them which despitefully[1] use you, and persecute you." Was not Amos[2] an extremist for justice: "Let justice roll down like waters and righteousness like an everflowing stream." Was not Paul an extremist for the Christian gospel: "I bear in my body the marks of the Lord Jesus." Was not Martin Luther an extremist: "Here I stand; I cannot do otherwise, so help me God." And John Bunyan[3]: "I will stay in jail to the end of my days before I make a butchery of my conscience." And Abraham Lincoln: "This nation cannot survive half slave and half free." And Thomas Jefferson: "We hold these truths to be self-evident, that all men are created equal ..." So the question is not whether we will be extremists, but what kind of extremists we will be. Will we be extremists for hate or for love? Will we be extremists for the preservation of injustice or for the extension of justice? In that dramatic scene on Calvary's hill[4] three men were crucified for the same crime – the crime of extremism. Two were extremists for immorality, and thus fell below their environment. The other, Jesus Christ, was an extremist for love, truth, and goodness, and thereby rose above his environment. Perhaps the South, the nation, and the world are in dire[5] need of creative extremists.

from *Letter from Birmingham Jail* by Martin Luther King Jr. Perfection Learning Corporation, USA, 1990, pp. 24 f.

COMPREHENSION

1. Point out why King thinks that the world is in need of extremists.

2. What kind of extremism is he speaking of? Make a list.

[1] **despiteful** *boshaft, gemein* – [2] **Amos** 8th-century B. C. Hebrew prophet whose revolutionary ideas paved the way for cooperation among nations and the belief in one God – [3] **John Bunyan** 7th-century English preacher and author who was jailed for twelve years for preaching without a license – [4] **Calvary's hill** Golgotha, the hill on which Jesus was crucified – [5] **dire** ['daɪə(r)] extremely serious or terrible

ANALYSIS

3. Analyse King's strategy of self-persuasion and pay special attention to the conjunction "but".
→ Focus on Skills, Analysis of a Non-Fictional Text, p. 377

4. Compare the photo taken of King in jail and the cover from *The Economist* and speculate why America locks up too many people.
Webcode SNG-40183-018 @ Do research using the links provided on the webcode and find statistical data about who is in jail and for what reasons/offenses.
→ Focus on Skills, Analysis of Visuals, p. 381

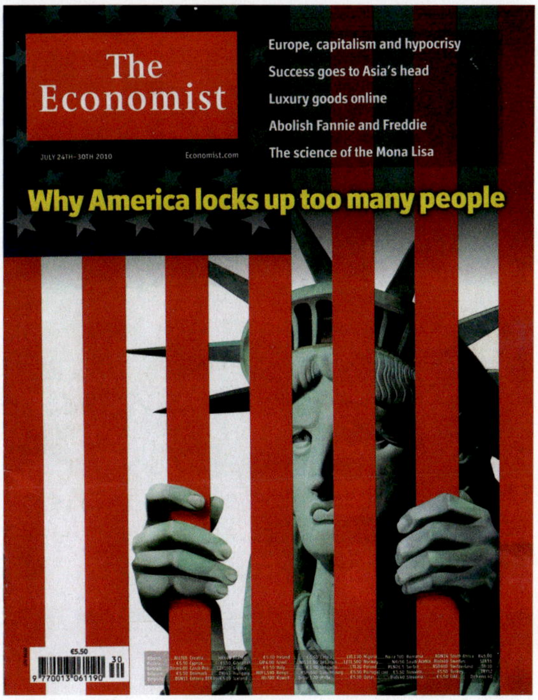

ACTIVITIES

5. Write a letter to Martin Luther King in answer to his letter.
What could you tell him that might encourage him to continue to fight for human rights?

Danny Strong

The Butler

AWARENESS

The 2013 historical drama film *The Butler* is based on the real-life memoirs of Eugene Allen (1926 – 2010), an African-American born on a cotton plantation in Georgia who worked his way up from being a hotel servant to serving as White House butler from 1952 to 1986.
During his time there, he worked for eight US Presidents, from Dwight D. Eisenhower to Ronald Reagan.
In class, reactivate your knowledge of United States history and find out which major historical events his time of service covered. Speculate on what he might have written about these events in his memoir.

COMPREHENSION

1. Before reading:
In the film version, the butler, Cecil Gaines, has a wife (Gloria) and two sons (Louis and Charlie). Louis, his older son, is a student and actively engaged in the Civil Rights and Freedom Riders[1] Movements. Together with his girlfriend Carol, Louis takes part in a non-violent sit-in at a segregated diner, where he is arrested.
Webcode SNG-40183-019 @ Before reading the excerpt from the screenplay, watch the video featurette provided on the webcode and get an overview of the plot and the historical and political background of the film.

[1] **Freedom Riders** groups of both black and white people from the northern US who in 1961 rode together in buses in the Deep South as a protest against segregation on public transport there

INT. FISK UNIVERSITY[2] MEETING ROOM – DAY – 1960

Carol and Louis walk into the room. The room is full of college students, black and white, getting ready to listen to JAMES LAWSON, 29, a very zen[3] black priest with glasses.
Lawson begins to speak to the group.

JAMES LAWSON ... You can't sustain[4] a movement like this in one week. Nor could you sustain it in over a month. This requires time, commitment[5], dedication, and discipline and focus. And we are measuring our accomplishments[6] in waves. Right? This is not a fly-by-night affair, this doesn't happen over a week, this requires a fierce[7] discipline, which is what we've been discussing. How do we measure these things? We go back and look at someone like Gandhi.

He points to a picture on the wall of MAHATMA GANDHI.

JAMES LAWSON (CONT'D) Together we are going to study and examine Gandhi's techniques. What has been so effective in South Africa, what has been so effective in India, for his own people and others, and we're gonna employ it right here, in Nashville. So we're gonna form an army, you and I. This army has one weapon, and this weapon is love. Now I am of the – Yes?

CAROL (raising her hand) If our only weapon is love and their weapons are ... weapons, isn't that dangerous?

JAMES LAWSON You can be killed. If anyone is uncomfortable with that, you know where the door is. I understand that sounds provocative, but it's true.

No one does.

JAMES LAWSON Alright kids. It's show time.

Masking his excitement to this new world, Louis tries to be cool, giving Carol an assured[8] nod[9].

INT. WHITE HOUSE – STATE DINING ROOM – DAY – 1960

Twenty butlers enter the State Dining room ready to serve.

EXT. DOWNTOWN NASHVILLE – DAY – 1960

Louis and Carol walk down the street with several other students. All nervous but determined[10]. Carol grabs Louis' hand as they walk toward a Woolworth department store.

JAMES LAWSON V.O.[11] Gandhi has demonstrated for us that a brown man, in his native land, or anywhere that he being oppressed, can pull himself out of segregation with patience, with persistence[12], with intelligence and thought.

INT. WOOLWORTHS LUNCH COUNTER – 2ND FLOOR – DAY – 1960

The five students walk up to the lunch counter. It is half filled with white patrons[13].

JAMES LAWSON V.O. With discipline and a bit of a sense of humor.

The black students sit down at the counter. The white patrons immediately look at them, stunned. A waitress drops her tray[14].

WAITRESS You know y'all can't sit here.

LOUIS We would like to be served.

JAMES LAWSON V.O. This is unprecedented[15] what we're talking about. But it needs a patience that none of us have ever seen.

WAITRESS You can order food in the colored section, but I'm not going to be serving you here.

The students stare forward. They aren't going to move.

INT. WHITE HOUSE STATE DINING ROOM – DAY – 1960

[2] **Fisk University** a historically black university founded in 1866 in Nashville, Tennessee – [3] **zen** (*infml.*) extremely relaxed and confident – [4] **to sustain** to make sth. continue; *aufrechterhalten* – [5] **commitment** *Engagement, Hingabe* – [6] **accomplishment** *Errungenschaft* – [7] **fierce** strong and powerful – [8] **assured** confident in yourself and your abilities – [9] **nod** *Kopfnicken* – [10] **determined** *entschlossen* – [11] **V. O.** (*abbr.*) voice over – [12] **persistence** *Beharrlichkeit, Hartnäckigkeit* – [13] **patron** (*fml.*) customer – [14] **tray** *Tablett* – [15] **unprecedented** *unerhört*

All the butlers prepare for an elaborate[16] state dinner.

INT. WOOLWORTHS LUNCH COUNTER – DAY – 1960

Patrons stare at the students. Everyone is giving them confused and dirty looks[17]. Black patrons sitting in the *colored section* look nervous. The students all look calm as they stare forward, waiting to be served.

JAMES LAWSON V. O. We are organized. We have a leader with every group. We have lookouts[18], with pocket change, and the local phone numbers for ambulances ready. And when one wave comes off that lunch counter, what follows?

A whole 'nother wave of negro students sitting right there at that lunch counter blowing their minds[19].

Louis turns to the waitress.

2

LOUIS We would like to be served, please.

She just stares back at him like he's crazy. [...]

An elderly patron, 70's, jumps to her feet, losing her patience and temper[20] with the students.

ELDERLY WOMAN PATRON You need to be sitting in the colored section! This is not for you! You cannot be served here! [...]
The Elderly Woman patron is getting even angrier, she starts yelling at the restaurant staff.

ELDERLY WOMAN PATRON If you want us to shop in this establishment, make them go!

She throws up her arms, has had enough.

ELDERLY WOMAN PATRON Come on, Robert. Let's go.

They exit. Louis watches her go and looks around to see if anyone else is going to start yelling. No one does. For now.

TIME LAPSE[21]: Hours go by. Day turns into night as the students sit patiently at the lunch counter. At the end of the lapse, several of the students are reading books, studying. Then –
A group of angry white teenagers walk towards the sit-in.
They enter the lunch counter area and begin to brutally yell at the students. They spit at them, throw food on them, until it turns into an all out beating!

INT. WHITE HOUSE – STATE DINING ROOM – NIGHT – 1960

The doors to the State Dining Room open revealing[22] dinner guests and the butlers upright at their stations dressed in tailed tuxedos[23].
The candle-lit tables are covered in the finest china[24], flatware[25] and crystal. A vision of pure opulence[26]. The butlers seat the President and First Lady.

3

4

INT. WOOLWORTH LUNCH COUNTER – NIGHT – 1960

A white student dumps[27] ketchup on a black girl's head. The black students stare forward calmly.

[16] **elaborate** containing a lot of careful detail; *kunstvoll, sorgfältig ausgeführt* – [17] **dirty look** (*infml.*) *böser Blick* – [18] **lookout** a person who watches for danger – [19] **to blow sb.'s mind** (*infml.*) to shock sb. – [20] **to lose one's temper** to fail to control one's anger – [21] **time lapse** *Zeitsprung* – [22] **to reveal sb./sth.** *etw. erkennen lassen* – [23] **tuxedo** *Smoking* – [24] **china** *Porzellan* – [25] **flatware** cutlery; *Besteck* – [26] **opulence** *Opulenz, Pracht* – [27] **to dump sth.** to drop sth. in a careless way

A white girl spits on Carol.
A white teenager throws coffee at Louis' face. He screams!

INT. WHITE HOUSE – STATE DINING ROOM – 1960

We continue to hear Louis' screams as Cecil stares forward standing at attention behind the President. He becomes invisible as the opulent dinner takes place around him. But Louis' screams won't go away.

INT. WHITE HOUSE – KITCHEN – NIGHT – 1960

All of the butlers are lounging in the kitchen. They are all exhausted as they hold up wine glasses for a toast.

FREDDIE To serving our country.

ALL To serving our country!

Cecil, genuinely proud, clinks[28] his glass with Freddie.

A TV plays in the background. News footage[29] of arrests begins to play. As we push in[30] on the TV we see that Louis is being arrested on the television.

www.pages.drexel.edu/~ina22/splaylib/Screenplay-Butler.pdf, TWC Films [31.08.2014]

COMPREHENSION

2. Read the **first part** of the excerpt describing the meeting at Fisk University (ll. 1–35). Point out what James Lawson tells the students about
- the attitude and strength that is required of the participants,
- Mahatma Gandhi and his techniques,
- the weapons the participants are allowed to use.

3. The following sequences of the excerpt intertwine (*verflechten*) two different storylines and James Lawson's voice-over instructions and comments.
Divide the class into groups of four students each and read the text.
Next, work out storyboards on wallpaper that visualize the development of the plot and the interconnections.

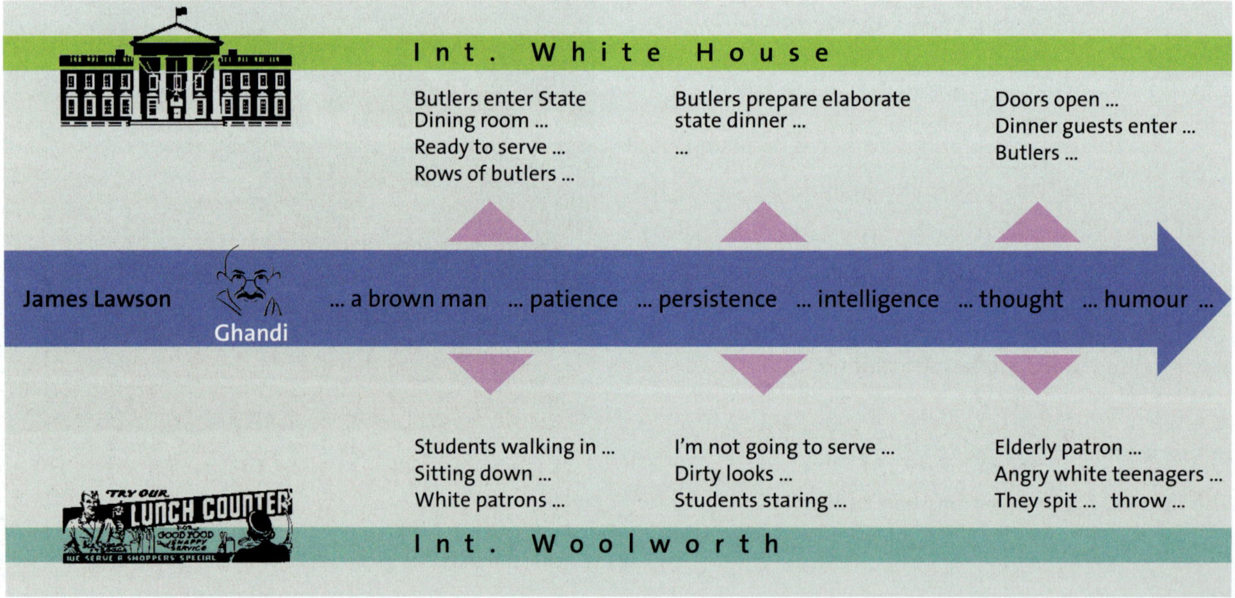

Display the storyboards in class and compare and discuss them.
→ Focus on Facts, Screenplays and Storyboards, p. 369

[28] **to clink one's glass with sb.** *mit jdm. anstoßen* – [29] **footage** a piece of film, esp. one showing an event – [30] **to push in** (*phr. v.*) *sich näher an etwas herandrängeln*

4. Summarize the scene in about 150 – 200 words, using your results from the storyboards.
→ Focus on Skills, Writing a Summary, p. 401

ANALYSIS

5. Closely examine the paragraphs depicting James Lawson's explanations concerning Gandhi's teachings and explain how they correspond with what is going on in the Woolworth lunch counter and the White House State Dining Room.
→ Focus on Skills, Analysis of a Screenplay, p. 376

6. Illustrate how the screenplay juxtaposes the two parallel events:
a) the sit-in at the lunch counter
b) the serving butlers at the White House state dinner.
Show how the roles are reversed and explain the effect this creates.

7. Analyse the symbolism of the last part of the excerpt which describes Cecil becoming "invisible" and Louis screaming (ll. 124 ff.).

8. Explain the pun* and the implied irony of the butlers' toast "To serving our country" (l. 131).

9. Take a close look at the film stills on the previous pages.
a) Describe them in detail (setting, persons, colours, body language, facial expressions).
b) Juxtapose and compare the film stills 1, 2, 3 and 4 and explain the use of cinematic devices and their function and effect.
→ Focus on Facts, Camera Operations, p. 372
→ Focus on Skills, Analysis of a Film Scene, p. 375

10. First, describe and analyse the film poster. Then
a) relate the visual symbols to the scene at hand and
b) correlate the plot of the film to the slogan "One quiet voice can ignite (*entzünden*) a revolution".
→ Focus on Skills, Analysis of Visuals, p. 381

Tips on vocab

to raise a gloved fist ■ allusion to the Black Power salute ■ white glove → serving/black fist → Black Power ■ to serve sth. on a tray ■ to stand upright ■ to look down ■ to wear a butler's uniform ■ to wear a bow tie (*Fliege*)

ACTIVITIES

11. Late that night, Cecil Gaines visits his son Louis in prison. Together with a partner, write a dialogue that reflects their opposing views, their thoughts and emotions. How might Cecil Gaines reproach his son (*jdm. Vorwürfe machen*) – what might Louis answer to explain his ideas and his fight for equal rights?

Tip: Pick up and continue the format and style of the screenplay, employing slug lines* and common abbreviations as well as descriptions of the setting and dialogue.

→ Focus on Facts, Screenplays and Storyboards, p. 369
→ Focus on Skills, Continuation of a Fictional Text, p. 392

Finally, act out your scenes in class and discuss the various perspectives taken.

12. Do a project on the film *The Butler* and the historical and political topics connected with it, for example the Civil Rights Movement, the Freedom Riders, the Black Power Movement, the protest of Tommie Smith and John Carlos during the 1968 Olympic Games, etc.
After doing background research, prepare presentations in class about your chosen topics.

→ Focus on Skills, Presentations, p. 391

13. Fighting for civil rights took place on many different levels and African-American women in particular courageously participated in this struggle. The historical photographs below show two famous African-American women who were forerunners of their time.

a) In a first step, describe the photos and the impression the women make on you.

Webcode SNG-40183-019

b) Do further research using the links provided on the webcode and explain which social taboos of their time the women broke.

→ Focus on Skills, Analysis of Visuals, p. 381

Elizabeth Eckford, 15, bullied by a mob at Little Rock Central High School on the first day of the school year, 4 September 1957

Josephine Baker's "banana dance" in the Folies Bergère production "Un Vent de Folie", 1927

The Civil Rights Movement: Fighting for Freedom and Equality

[illegible] **years of the American civil rights movement** were [illegible] and **1960s**, when African-Americans kept demon- [illegible] nd fighting for human and civil rights, thus forcing the U.S. government **to guarantee** them certain **constitutional rights**, e.g. the right to vote and to attend public facilities like schools, buses or restaurants together with white Americans.

However, African-Americans have been struggling to overcome slavery and racial injustice since the 17th century and famous leaders and activists like **Sojourner Truth** (1798 – 1883), **Booker T. Washington** (1856 – 1915), **W. E. B. Du Bois** (1868 – 1963) and **Frederick Douglass** (1817 – 1895) paved the way for "modern" activists like **Martin Luther King Jr.** (1929 – 1968) and **Malcolm X** (1925 – 1965).

June 1623	the **first eleven slaves** arrive in New Amsterdam (New York)
1863	President Abraham Lincoln signs **Emancipation Proclamation** that officially abolishes slavery
1865	• 15 April: **President Lincoln is assassinated** by a fanatical Confederate • the **Thirteenth Amendment** to the Constitution **abolishes slavery** by law; more than 4 mio slaves gain freedom *"Neither slavery nor involuntary servitude … shall exist within the United States, or any other place subject to their jurisdiction."*
1865/66	the **Black Codes**, a set of rules, are passed in the South to "restore all of slavery but its name"; southern blacks are • denied the right to vote, • restricted from moving freely, • denied the right to own land, • excluded from certain jobs, • subject to a separate and much more severe penal code, • prohibited from possessing firearms.
1866	the **Ku Klux Klan** is founded in Tennessee as a fraternal organization opposed to the emancipation of the blacks; white southern "aristocracy" fears "nigger domination" and aims at restoring white supremacy in the South; terrorist acts against blacks like lynching are carried out
1868	the **Fourteenth Amendment** affirms **black citizenship**
1870	the **Fifteenth Amendment** guarantees blacks **the right to vote**
1870s	**racial segregation** is gradually enforced in the **American South**
1890	Louisiana passes a law enforcing "**equal but separate**" access to colleges, trains, etc.
1880s – 1920s	peak years of black **lynchings**
1910	**NAACP** (National Association for the Advancement of Colored People) is founded; the U. S.'s oldest civil rights organization
1920s	the **Black Muslims**, later the Nation of Islam, promotes the separation of blacks from white Americans
WWI	**segregated regiments** of white and African-Americans fight for the U. S.
WWII	ca. 1 mio African-American soldiers fight for the U. S.
1955/56	• **Rosa Parks** is arrested in Montgomery, Alabama • **Montgomery bus boycott** • 26-year-old Baptist Reverend **Martin Luther King Jr.** begins active participation in the civil rights movement
1957	the **SCLL** (Southern Christian Leadership Conference) is founded to support the protest movement; leader: Martin Luther King Jr.
1960s	• **Malcolm X** becomes famous leader of **Black Muslims**; promotion of a separate black state and acceptance of violence as a means of self-defense

1960s	• **Freedom Riders**: black and white civil rights activists travel through the segregated South to peacefully protest against racial segregation → Gandhian philosophy of non-violent resistance • **sit-ins** at segregated lunch counters in southern towns
1961	January: **John F. Kennedy** is elected **President** of the U. S.
1963 – 1965	• Martin Luther King Jr. leads **marches from Selma to Montgomery**; civil rights activists march peacefully for the African-Americans' right to vote • 28 August: **March on Washington**; 250,000 people listen to **Martin Luther King's famous speech "I have a dream"**, delivered in front of the Lincoln Memorial in Washington D. C. • 22 November: **assassination of John F. Kennedy** in Dallas, Texas
1964	• President Lyndon B. Johnson signs **Civil Rights Act**, ensuring voting rights to African-Americans • **Freedom Summer**: a campaign to register as many African-American voters in the state of Mississippi as possible • **revival of the Ku Klux Klan** in Mississippi
1965	• 21 February: **assassination of Malcolm X** • President Lyndon B. Johnson signs **Voting Rights Act**; literacy tests required to be allowed to vote are suspended in order to allow many illiterate southern blacks to vote
1965 – 1968	• **Black Power Movement**; stronger political focus; urban protests • **Black Panthers**: culminating frustration; radicalization; guns; urban protests
1967	Martin Luther King launches **Poor People's Campaign**: economic protest and civil disobedience of rural and urban poor of all races
1968	• 3 April: **Martin Luther King is assassinated** in Memphis, Tennessee • eruption of violence in 125 cities nationwide
1992	April: **riots in Los Angeles** following the beating of African-American Rodney King by white policemen
1995	October: **Million Man March** to Washington D. C. organized by the Nation of Islam to promote "unity, atonement, and brotherhood"; more than 250,000 participants
2008/2012	**Barack Obama** becomes **first African-American President**
2012/2014	• public protests following the killing of unarmed African-American teenagers • 26 February 2012: 17-year-old African-American teenager **Trayvon Martin** is shot by a Hispanic security officer in Sanford, Florida • 9 August 2014: 18-year-old African-American student **Michael Brown** is shot by a white police officer in Ferguson, Missouri
2016	• 5 July: Alton Sterling, a 37-year-old black man, is shot by white police officers in Baton Rouge, Louisiana • 6 July: Philando Castile is shot by a St. Anthony, Minnesota police officer; his girlfriend livestreams a video of the shooting on Facebook • 7 July: at the end of a peaceful *Black Lives Matter* protest, African-American Army Reserve Afghan War veteran Micah Xavier Johnson, 25, shoots five police officers in Dallas, Texas • in response to these shootings, civil unrest and protests are held in New York, St. Paul, Minnesota and Baton Rouge, Louisiana; at least 261 people are arrested

Lincoln Memorial in Washington D. C. being cleaned by an African-American worker

Minorities in the USA: Trying to Get Their Share of the Pie

Mark Helprin

Ellis Island

Fresh off the boat, immigrants wait with their possessions at Ellis Island, 1907

AWARENESS

The following audio text is an excerpt from a short story that takes place at a time when Ellis Island was still used as a US immigration port (1892 – 1954). It depicts the situation of the protagonist as he goes through the immigration procedure. Reactivate your knowledge about Ellis Island and gather information in class.

COMPREHENSION

1. Look at the photo taken in 1907. What impression do you have of the newly-arrived immigrants and what might their hopes and expectations be?

10 CD 2

2. Now, **listen to the first part** of the excerpt and describe the journey across the Atlantic Ocean. How do the passengers try to adapt to the situation on board?
   → Focus on Skills, Listening Comprehension, p. 366

11 CD 2

3. Outline the narrator's observations on Ellis Island as depicted in **the second part** of the excerpt.

4. State the course of the "conversations" between the narrator and the immigration inspectors. What abilities are required of the immigrants?

ANALYSIS

5. Which words does the narrator use to characterize the strenuous (*anstrengend*) journey across the ocean?

6. Examine the stylistic devices* the author employs to underline the challenging and exhausting procedure on Ellis Island.

7. Find allusions to "the dream" in the text.

8. Why do you think the inspector is "very suspicious"?
   → Focus on Skills, Analysis of a Fictional Text, p. 374

9. The immigration procedure has always been a difficult and frightening barrier for immigrants, and inspectors have been trained to critically examine the immigrants' eligibility (*Eignung*) of becoming a U. S. citizen. What impression of the U. S. is conveyed in the cartoon on the following page?
   Compare: How has "Miss Liberty" (and what she represents) changed?
   → Focus on Skills, Analysis of Visuals, p. 381

ACTIVITIES

10. Imagine you work for the American immigration authority (today or in the past) and – in a group – compile a catalogue of questions that immigrants have to answer. You want to find out who is capable of becoming a "real American citizen". Act out this "interview" in class, one student playing the immigrant and one student playing the immigration inspector.

Pathway to U.S. Citizenship

AWARENESS

For an adult immigrant to become a U.S. citizen, he or she must go through the process of naturalization.
The following graphics explain the general requirements.
In a group, discuss what kinds of requirements you consider to be most important when somebody wants to obtain citizenship in their new country.

COMPREHENSION

1. Get an overview of the different steps leading to U.S. citizenship and categorize them according to the different fields they belong to.

residency	lawfulness	moral standards	knowledge	...
• ...	• lawfully admitted • ...	• ...	• basic English skills • ...	• ...

Webcode SNG-40183-020 @ **2.** Do further research on the process of naturalization in the USA by using the links provided on the webcode. Gather the information in class.

ANALYSIS

3. Compare the infographic "Pathway to U. S. Citizenship" (p. 172) to the cartoon on page 224. What further qualities and qualifications that immigrants are required to have after 9/11 does the cartoon hint at?

ACTIVITIES

4. Together with a partner, first describe the cartoons and explain how the "path to US Citizenship" is interpreted and mocked.
Then read the Focus on Facts page *The United States: Immigration and Minorities* (p. 173) and inform yourself about recent US immigration reforms. How do the cartoons view the political efforts?
→ Focus on Skills, Analysis of Visuals, p. 381

Tips on vocab

to follow a serpentine path ■ rows of plants ■ agricultural worker ■ to be stunned ■ Hispanic worker ■ to carry a bundle/bag ■ to be fooled

Tips on vocab

construction site (*Baustelle*) ■ concrete mixer/concrete lorry ■ to pour concrete ■ chute (*Schütte*) ■ concrete paving slab (*Betonbodenplatte*) ■ construction worker ■ donkey (symbol of the Democratic Party) ■ elephant (symbol of the Republican Party) ■ to wear working clothes/garment ■ out of the corner of one's eye ■ to steal a glance (*einen verstohlenen Blick werfen*) ■ bashful (*verschämt*) ■ to whistle (*pfeifen*) ■ to be stuck in sth. ■ to harden (*aushärten*) ■ to look desperate

Webcode SNG-40183-020 @ **5.** Do research on the requirements that immigrants to Germany have to meet by using the links provided on the webcode. Point out the differences and similarities to the U. S. system of naturalization and discuss the possible consequences for potential immigrants in class.

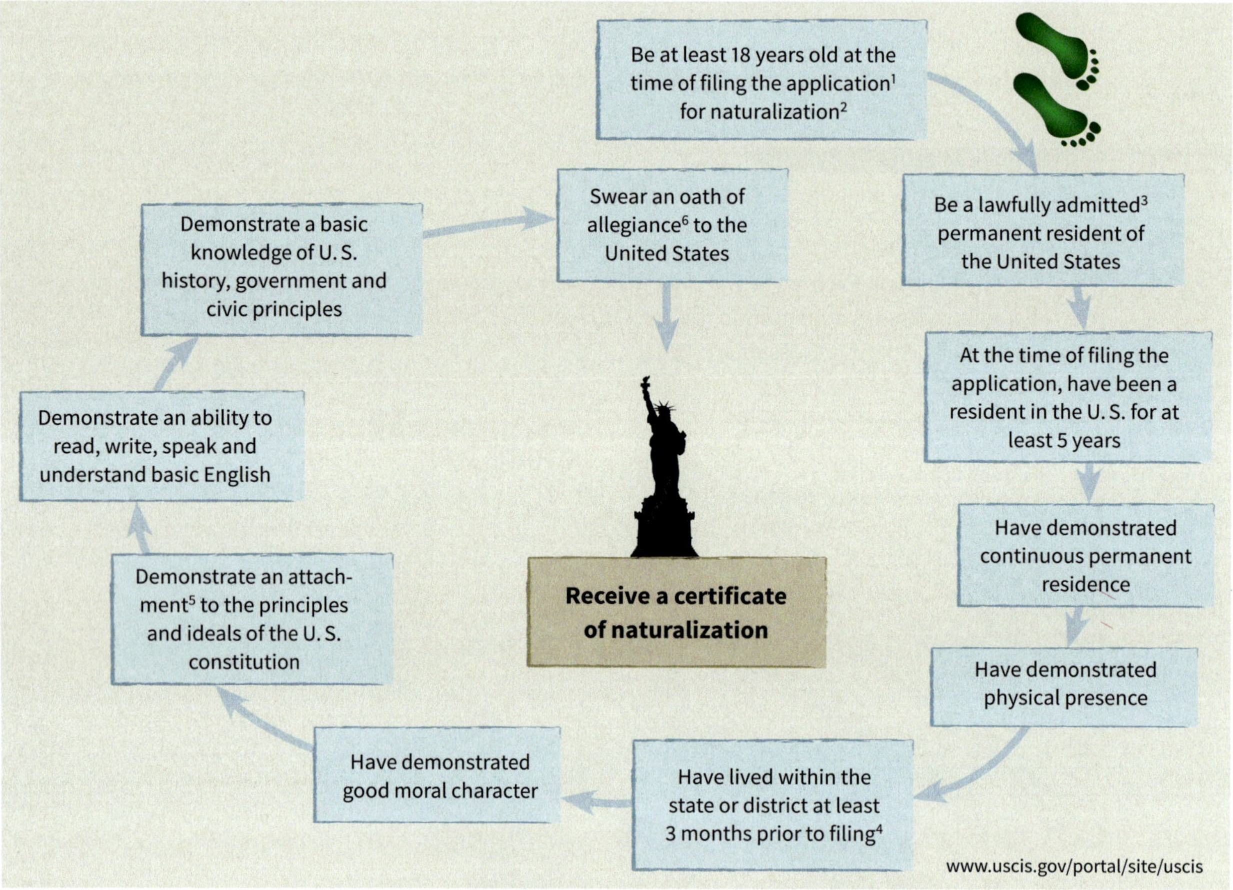

[1] **to file an application** (*fml.*) *einen offiziellen Antrag stellen* – [2] **naturalization** *Einbürgerung* – [3] **lawfully admitted** *rechtmäßig/legal zugelassen* – [4] **filing** *Einreichung* – [5] **attachment** a strong feeling for sb./sth. – [6] **oath of allegiance** [əʊθ əv ə'liːdʒəns] *Treueeid*

The United States: Immigration and Minorities

The English have been going to North America from the late 16th century on; Spain sent people to the southern part of the region and many Dutch and Germans also went over. When the U. S. became independent, it was written into the **Constitution** that there could be no limits on immigration until 1808. The main period of immigration was between 1800 and 1917. Early in this period, many immigrants arrived from Britain and Germany, and many Chinese went to California. Later, the main groups were Italians, Irish, Eastern Europeans and Scandinavians. Many Jews came from Germany and Eastern Europe. Just before World War I, there were nearly a million immigrants a year. Most Americans have a clear idea of what life was like for the immigrants: they left home because they were poor and thought they would have better opportunities in the U. S. Many immigrants came to New York and Boston, and **Ellis Island**, near New York, became famous as a receiving station. The **Immigration Act of 1917**, and other laws that followed it, limited the number of immigrants and the countries that they could come from. Since then, immigration has been limited to a few people who are selected for an **immigrant visa**, commonly called a **green card**. Hispanics and Asians now make up the largest groups of immigrants. **The Immigration and Naturalization Service** (INS) is responsible for issuing visas. It also tries to prevent people from crossing the borders and entering the U. S. illegally. In 2013, a bipartisan (*aus Mitgliedern beider Parteien bestehend*) group of eight Senators ("The Gang of Eight") announced four basic principles for a comprehensive immigration reform:

- a citizenship path for illegal immigrants already in the US
- business immigration system reforms
- an expanded and improved employment verification system
- improved work visa options for low-skill workers and an agricultural worker programme

On 27 June 2013, the U. S. Senate approved the "Border Security, Economic Opportunity, and Immigration Modernization Act of 2013" (short "S. 744"). However, so far the bill has ended in deadlock in the U. S. House of Representatives.

Ethnic minorities in the USA (US census of 2010)

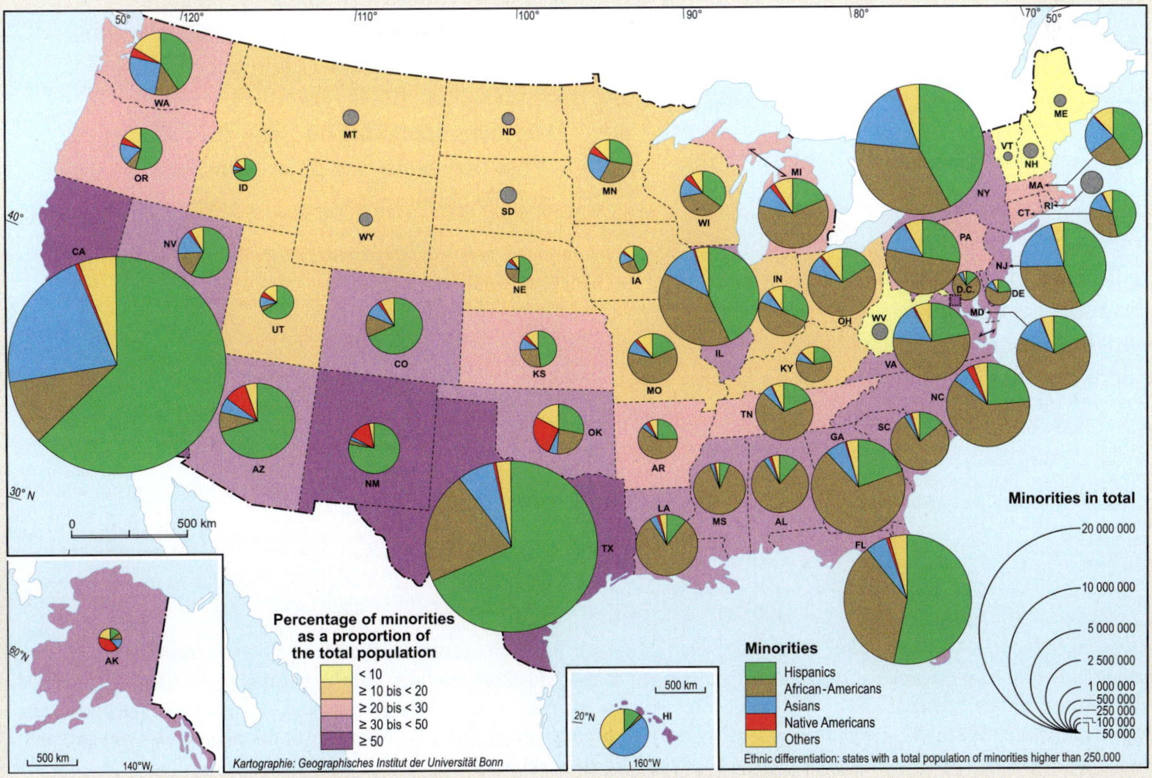

Jimmy Santiago Baca

So Mexicans Are Taking Jobs from Americans

AWARENESS

Look at the photos on p. 175 showing Mexican migrant workers on their way to work and pay attention to details. What do these photos tell you about the migrants, their lives and their work?

1 O Yes? Do they come on horses
with rifles, and say,
Ese[1], gringo[2], gimme your job?
And do you, gringo, take off your ring,
drop your wallet[3] into a blanket
spread over the ground, and walk away?

I hear Mexicans are taking your jobs away.
Do they sneak[4] into town at night,
and as you're walking home with a whore[5],
do they mug[6] you, a knife at your throat[7],
saying, I want your job?

Even on TV, an asthmatic leader
crawls[8] turtle heavy[9], leaning on an assistant,
and from a nest of wrinkles[10] on his face,
a tongue paddles through flashing waves
of lightbulbs, of cameramen, rasping[11],
"They're taking our jobs away."

Well, I've gone about trying to find them,
asking just where the hell are these fighters.

2 The rifles I hear sound in the night
are white farmers shooting blacks and browns
whose ribs I see jutting out[12]
and starving[13] children,
I see the poor marching for a little work,
I see small white farmers selling out[14]
to clean-suited farmers living in New York,
who've never been on a farm,
don't know the look of a hoof[15] or the smell
of a woman's body bending[16] all day long in fields.

I see this, and I hear only a few people
got all the money in this world, the rest
count their pennies to buy bread and butter.

3 Below that cool green sea of money,
millions and millions of people fight to live,
search for pearls in the darkest depths
of their dreams, hold their breath for years
trying to cross poverty to just having something.

The children are dead already. We are killing them,
that is what America should be saying;
on TV, in the streets, in offices, should be saying,
"We aren't giving the children a chance to live."

Mexicans are taking our jobs, they say instead.
What they really say is, let them die,
and the children, too.

from *Immigrants in Our Own Land and Selected Early Poems* by Jimmy Santiago Baca. New Directions Publishing, New York 1982

[1] **ese** (*Spanish*) that one, you – [2] **gringo** (*infml., disapproving*) used in Latin American countries to refer to a person from the US – [3] **wallet** (*US*) *Brieftasche, Portemonnaie* – [4] **to sneak into** *sich hineinschleichen* – [5] **whore** prostitute – [6] **to mug sb.** to attack sb. violently in order to steal their money – [7] **throat** *Kehle* – [8] **to crawl** *kriechen* – [9] **turtle heavy** (*infml.*) heavy and slow, like a turtle – [10] **wrinkle** *Falte (im Gesicht)* – [11] **to rasp** to say sth. in a rough unpleasant voice – [12] **to jut out** *hervorstehen* – [13] **to starve** to die of hunger – [14] **to sell out** to sell your business at a very low price – [15] **hoof** *Pferde-, Rinderhuf* – [16] **to bend** *sich vornüber beugen, bücken*

COMPREHENSION

12 CD 2

1. The poem can roughly be subdivided into three thematic units.
Step 1: While **listening** to (and reading) the poem for the **first time**, take notes and try to find suitable headlines for the three thematic units.
Step 2: Listen to and read the poem **a second time** and take notes on the following questions:

1
- How do Mexicans try to get jobs from the "gringos"?
- What kind of white people or "gringos" does the speaker describe?

2
- What observations does the speaker make about
  - white farmers,
  - poor "blacks and browns",
  - small white farmers,
  - rich farmers in New York?
- What is his conclusion from these observations?

3
- How do people try to forget poverty?
- What does America do to children?

→ Focus on Skills, Listening Comprehension, p. 366

ANALYSIS

2. Analyse the structure of the poem and the stylistic devices* that are used.
→ Focus on Skills, Analysis of Poetry and Lyrics, p. 378

3. Explain the influence and function of the media, particularly TV, in dealing with the situation.

4. Interestingly, the poet combines harsh sarcasm and rather offensive language with metaphorical and poetical phrases. Try to explain his intention and the effect of this unusual combination.

ACTIVITIES

5. Migrant workers are a common sight in many countries. In Germany, for example, thousands of seasonal workers from eastern European countries work on farms every year.
In groups, discuss whether you agree with the view that migrant workers are taking jobs away from the native inhabitants, e. g. in Germany.
→ Focus on Language, Conversation and Discussion, p. 385

1

2

Marike Frick

Tanz mit mir

AWARENESS

Look at the cartoon below and state which "multicultural problem" is depicted there. Discuss what the man could reply to ease the embarrassing situation.

Die Zeit: Was sind typische Fehler, wenn jemand zum ersten Mal mit Geschäftspartnern aus einer anderen Kultur zu tun hat?

Gary Thomas: Urteile wie: „Das ist doch nicht normal." Oder: „Das macht man doch nicht." Dann wird die eigene Normalität als Maßstab genommen[1], dabei ist Kultur wie ein Tanz: Man kann nicht mittanzen, wenn man die Schritte nicht kennt. Vor allem kann man nicht führen. Deshalb sollte man den anderen erst mal zuschauen und die Schritte beobachten.

Zeit: Was stört den Tanz zwischen den Kulturen ganz besonders[2]?

Thomas: Deutsche sind bekannt für ihre direkten Ansagen[3]. In den Niederlanden und Österreich mag das funktionieren, aber schon die Briten sind anders. Sie formulieren in E-Mails für gewöhnlich so: „Ich schlage vor[4], dass ihr die Idee überdenkt." Oder: „Ich denke, das bedarf[5] einer Nachbesserung[6]." Was würde ein Deutscher sagen? „Nein, so machen wir das nicht." Oder: „So geht das nicht." In anderen Kulturen wird mehr umschrieben, sind die Formulierungen blumiger[7]. Wenn Geschäftspartner sagen wollen: „Ihr Bericht ist voller Fehler", schreiben sie auf Englisch: *„There seem to be some issues in your report."* Und die Aussage[8] „Sie haben die Verkaufszahlen vergessen", klänge so: *„I can't seem to find the sales numbers."* Die Formulierung ist indirekt, mit dem Ziel, die Beziehung zu schützen. Die deutsche Kultur ist eine sehr sachorientierte[9] Kultur. Da gibt es wenige Bedenken[10], die Beziehung zum Empfänger zu gefährden[11]. [...]

Zeit: Was, wenn der Gesprächspartner blumig um den heißen Brei herumredet[12], und man hat das Gefühl, man kommt nicht weiter?

Thomas: Dann sollte man nachfassen[13]. Man kann sagen: „Hilf mir bitte, was genau meinst du?" Beziehungsorientierte[14] Kulturen reagieren in der Regel gut darauf: „Ich brauche deine Hilfe."

Zeit: Kann es auch passieren, dass man sein Gegenüber falsch versteht? Dass man meint, man habe eine Zusage[15] erhalten – und dann stellt sich heraus: Das war gar nicht als Zusage gemeint!

Thomas: Ja, zum Beispiel in Italien: Dort spielen Hierarchie[16] und *bella figura*[17] eine große Rolle. Man will gut vor den anderen dastehen. Dann versuchen Deutsche, jemanden auf eine Vereinbarung festzunageln[18] – und stellen hinterher fest, dass sie doch nicht eingehalten[19] wird. Etwa weil der italienische Verhandlungspartner[20] nicht zugegeben hat, dass er gar nicht entscheidungsbefugt[21] ist. Schon beim „Ja" gibt es häufig Missverständnisse. Für Deutsche bedeutet es eine eindeutige[22] Zustimmung. Hinter einem *„Yes, we will see"* oder *„Yes, we will try"* versteckt sich in Kulturen wie Indien aber der Hinweis: „Bitte merke, dass ich nicht Nein sagen kann, weil ich die Beziehung nicht gefährden möchte." Oder es wird *„Yes"* gesagt und dann das Thema gewechselt. Das ist ebenfalls eine Art, Nein zu sagen.

Die Zeit, 25. Oktober 2012, p. 79

[1] to be a measure of sth./to serve as a rule – [2] in particular – [3] frank statements – [4] to suggest sth. to sb. – [5] to require – [6] rectification – [7] metaphorical/wrote – [8] assertion/statement – [9] topic-oriented/prosaic – [10] concern – [11] to jeopardize ['dʒepədaɪz]/to put sth. at risk – [12] to beat around the bush – [13] to follow up on sth. – [14] relationship-oriented – [15] approval – [16] hierarchy ['haɪrɑ:ki] – [17] to be well-received – [18] to pin sb. down to sth. – [19] to comply with sth. – [20] negotiating partner – [21] authorized – [22] distinct

Sandra Cisneros

No Speak English

AWARENESS

Which image of a “Latina”, i. e. a Latin American or Hispanic woman, do the covers convey? You can use the vocab box for help.

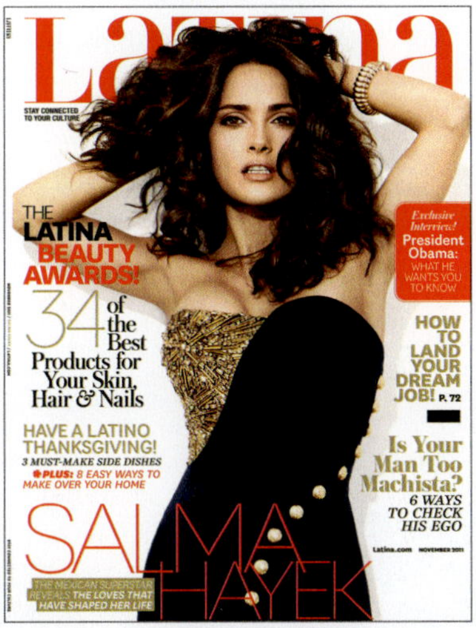

Tips on vocab

to pose/to have a sexy posture ▪ to directly look at the viewer/into the viewer’s eyes ▪ a deep neckline/cleavage (*Ausschnitt*) ▪ wrap dress (*Wickelkleid*) ▪ silky shimmering satin ▪ sleeveless (*ärmellos*) ▪ to highlight the female shape ▪ draped around the body ▪ a crimping of the cloth (*eine Kräuselung des Stoffes*)

Mamacita[1] is the big mama of the man across the street, third-floor front. Rachel says her name ought to be *Mamasota*[2], but I think that’s mean.

The man saved his money to bring her here. He saved and saved because he was alone with the baby boy in that country. He worked two jobs. He came home late and he left early. Every day.

Then one day *Mamacita* and the baby boy arrived in a yellow taxi. The taxi door opened like a waiter’s arm. Out stepped a tiny pink show, a foot soft as a rabbit’s ear, then the thick ankle[3], a flutter[4] of hips, fuchsia[5] roses and green perfume. The man had to pull her, the taxicab driver had to push. Push, pull. Push, pull. Poof! All at once she bloomed[6]. Huge, enormous, beautiful to look at, from the salmon-pink[7] feather on the tip of her hat down to the little rosebuds of her toes. I couldn’t take my eyes off her tiny shoes.

Up, up, up the stairs she went with the baby boy in a blue blanket, the man carrying her suitcases, her lavender hatboxes, a dozen boxes of satin high heels. Then we didn’t see her.

Somebody said because she’s too fat, somebody because of the three flights[8] of stairs, but I believe she doesn’t come out because she is afraid to speak English, and maybe this is so since she only knows eight words. She knows to say: *He not here* when the landlord comes, *No speak English* if anybody else comes, and *Holy smokes*. I don’t know where she learned this, but I heard her say it one time and it surprised me.

My father says when he came to this country he ate ham-andeggs for three months. Breakfast, lunch and dinner. Hamandeggs. That was the only word he knew. He doesn’t eat hamandeggs anymore.

Whatever her reasons, whether she is fat, or can’t climb the stairs, or is afraid of English, she won’t come down. She sits all day by the window and plays the Spanish radio show and sings all the homesick songs about her country in a voice that sounds like a seagull[9].

Home. Home. Home is a house in a photograph, a pink house, pinks as hollyhocks[10] with lots of startled light[11]. The man paints the walls of the apartment

[1] **Mamacita** (*Spanish*) little mother – [2] **Mamasota** (*Spanish*) Big Mama – [3] **ankle** *Fußknöchel* – [4] **flutter** *Geflatter* – [5] **fuchsia** [ˈfjuːʃə] *Fuchsien* – [6] **to bloom** (*fig.*) *in voller Blüte stehen, erblühen* – [7] **salmon-pink** *lachsrosa* – [8] **flight of stairs** *Treppe* – [9] **seagull** *Möwe* – [10] **hollyhock** *Malve* – [11] **startled light** here: *flirrendes, schillerndes Licht*

pink, but it's not the same, you know. She still sighs for her pink house, and then I think she cries. I would.

Sometimes the man gets disgusted. He starts screaming and you can hear it all the way down the street.

Ay, she says, she is sad. Oh, he says. Not again.

¿Cuándo[12], *cuándo, cuándo?* She asks.

¡Ay, caray[13]*!* We are home. This is home. Here I am and here I stay. Speak English. Speak English. Christ!

¡A! Mamacita, who does not belong, every once in a while lets out a cry, hysterical, high, as if he had torn the only skinny[14] thread[15] that kept her alive, the only road out to that country.

And then to break her heart forever, the baby boy, who has begun to talk, starts to sing the Pepsi commercial he heard on T.V.

No speak English, she says to the child who is singing in the language that sounds like tin. No speak English, no speak English, and bubbles into tears. No, no, no, as if she can't believe her ears.

from *The House on Mango Street* by Sandra Cisneros. Vintage Books, New York 1984, pp. 76 ff.

COMPREHENSION

1. Describe the arrival of *Mamacita* in the USA.
2. How does *Mamacita* communicate?
3. Point out what her life is like in the new country.
4. What are the consequences of her isolation
   a) for herself,
   b) for the relationship with her husband,
   c) for the relationship with her little boy?

ANALYSIS

5. Identify the narrative perspective* and examine the narrator's stance on *Mamacita's* stay in the USA. Give evidence from the text that proves your findings.
   → Focus on Skills, Analysis of a Fictional Text, p. 374
6. How do you interpret *Mamacita's* repeatedly asking her husband *¿Cuándo*?
7. Analyse the stylistic devices* that create both the satirical/ironic and the melancholic/sentimental character of the excerpt from the episodic novel.
8. Interpret the ending of the excerpt:
   a) Why does the baby boy's singing the Pepsi commercial "break her heart forever" (l. 56?
   b) What does the baby boy's way of learning English demonstrate about the culture of the family's new "home"?

ACTIVITIES

9. *Mamacita's* husband does not know what to do about the desperate situation. Finally, he decides to write a letter to the "agony aunt" of a local American newspaper and asks for help.
   Together with a partner, first write the man's letter and in a second step, write the agony aunt's response. What kind of advice might she give to him?
   Afterwards, read out your letters in class.

[12] **¿Cuándo?** (*Spanish*) when – [13] **caray** Damn it! – [14] **skinny** very thin – [15] **thread** [θred] *Faden*

When Dreams Go Bust ...

Wanted: The Dream – Dead or Alive?

AWARENESS

Before reading the article about the "American Dream" on the following page, complete the following activity: Together with a partner, take a look at the cartoons below depicting views on income inequality and social mobility in the US. Describe the cartoons to each other using the vocab boxes and paying attention to details.

A

B

Tips on vocab

bunk bed ■ rope ladder ■ to fall off

top: golden ornaments ■ to loll (*sich lümmeln*) ■ to lounge ■ to drink champagne ■ to be dolled up

middle: different ethnicities ■ to sit cross-legged ■ to lean against sth. ■ reading lamp ■ duvet (*Federbett*)

bottom: to be cramped ■ to look sleepy ■ ragged blankets ■ metal springs ■ naked bulb (*Glühlampe*) ■ to look stunned

Tips on vocab

top: to wear evening dress ■ tuxedo/dinner jacket

bottom: to be crammed (*eingepfercht sein*) ■ squeezed (*gequetscht*) ■ to crawl (*herum-kriechen*) ■ to squat (*hocken, kauern*) ■ to crouch down (*sich zusammenkauern*)

COMPREHENSION

1. Now, what would happen if the American Dream did *not* go on?
In a 4-corners activity, reflect on and discuss the introductory question of the first article: "Could America survive the end of the American Dream?"
Before choosing "your" corner and collecting arguments, reactivate your knowledge of the American Dream and read the corresponding Focus on pages in your Students' Book (→ FoF American Beliefs and Values, p. 136; FoD The American Dream, p. 139).

1 The American Dream, RIP? ☒

Could America survive the end of the American Dream? The idea is unthinkable, say political leaders of right and left. Yet it is predicted in "Average is Over", a bracing[1] new book by Tyler Cowen, an economist. Mr Cowen is no stranger to controversy. In 2011 he galvanized[2] Washington with "The Great Stagnation", in which he argued that America has used up[3] the low-hanging fruit of free land, abundant[4] labour and new technologies. His new book suggests that the disruptive[5] effects of automation and ever-cheaper computer power have only just begun to be felt.

It described a future largely stripped[6] of middling jobs and broad prosperity. An elite 10–15 % of Americans will have the brains and self-discipline to master tomorrow's technology and extract profit from it, he speculates. They will enjoy great wealth and stimulating[7] lives. Others will endure[8] stagnant or even falling wages, as employers measure their output with "oppressive precision". Some will thrive as service-providers to the rich. A few will claw[9] their way into the elite (cheap online education will be a great leveler), bolstering[10] the idea of a "hyper-meritocracy[11]" at work: this "will make it easier to ignore those left behind".

Mr Cowen's vision is neither warm nor fuzzy[12]. In his future, mistakes and even mediocrity[13] will be hard to hide: e. g., an ever-expanding array[14] of ratings will expose so-so doctors and also patients who do not take their medicines or otherwise spell trouble. Young men will struggle in a labour market that rewards conscientiousness[15] over muscle. With incomes squeezed, many Americans will head to the sort of cheap, sun-baked sprawling[16] exurbs[17] that give the farmers'-market-and-bike-lanes set[18] heartburn[19]. [...] The left is sure that inequality is a recipe for riots. Mr Cowen doubts it. The have-nots will be too engrossed[20] in video games to light real petrol bombs. An ageing population will be rather conservative, he thinks. There will be lots of Tea-Party sorts[21] among the economically left-behind. Aid for the poor will be slashed[22] but benefits for the old preserved. He does not fear protectionism, as most jobs that can be sent overseas have already gone. He notes that the late 1960s, when society was in turmoil, was a golden age of income equality, while some highly unequal moments in history, including in medieval times, were rather stable. [...]

Inter-generational tensions fuelled 1960s unrest and would be back with a vengeance[23], this time in the form of economic competition for scarce resources. The Middle Ages were stable partly because peasants[24] could not vote; an unhappy modern electorate, by contrast, would be prey[25] to demagogues[26] peddling[27] simple solutions, from xenophobia[28] to soak-the-rich taxes[29], or harsh, self-defeating crime policies. Yet Mr Cowen's main point is plausible: gigantic shifts are under way, and they may be unstoppable. [...]

In short, both sides never tire of explaining how the other is destroying the American Dream. Alas, neither can explain, convincingly, how to revive it. [...]

Many voters remember a time when hard work was reliably rewarded with economic security. This was not really true in the 1950s and 60s if you were black or female, but the question still remains: what if Mr Cowen is right? What if the bottom 85 % today are mostly doomed[30] to stay there? In a country founded on hope, that would require something like a new social contract. Politicians cannot duck[31] Mr Cowen's conundrum[32] forever.

The Economist, 21 September 2013, p. 41

[1] **bracing** here: thought-provoking – [2] **to galvanize** *wachrütteln* – [3] **to use sth. up** *etw. aufbrauchen* – [4] **abundant** more than enough – [5] **disruptive** *Unruhe stiftend* – [6] **to strip sth.** to remove sth. – [7] **stimulating** interesting – [8] **to endure** to suffer sth. difficult or painful – [9] **to claw your way** (*idm.*) *sich durchkämpfen* – [10] **to bolster** to support sth. or make it stronger – [11] **hyper-meritocracy** [haɪpər-ˈmerɪˈtɒkrəsi] *Über-Leistungsgesellschaft* – [12] **warm and fuzzy** making you feel happy and comforted – [13] **mediocrity** [ˈmiːdiˈɒkrəti] *Mittelmaß* – [14] **array** here: a large number – [15] **conscientiousness** [ˈkɒnʃiˈenʃəsnəs] *Pflichtbewusstsein* – [16] **sprawling** spreading in an untidy way – [17] **exurb** a commuter town that lies beyond the suburbs, usually wealthy – [18] **farmers'-market-and-bike-lanes set** wealthy, privileged people who lead an alternative, environmentally conscious lifestyle – [19] **heartburn** *Sodbrennen* – [20] **to engross** *sich vertiefen* – [21] **Tea-Party sorts** (*disapprov.*) supporters of the Tea Party – [22] **to slash** *etw. drastisch kürzen* – [23] **with a vengeance** [ˈvendʒəns] (*infml.*) to a greater degree than is expected or usual – [24] **peasant** [ˈpezənt] *Landarbeiter* – [25] **prey** victim – [26] **demagogue** [ˈdeməgɒg] *Populist* – [27] **to peddle** *hausieren* – [28] **xenophobia** *Fremdenfeindlichkeit* – [29] **soak-the-rich taxes** tax laws that favour the wealthy – [30] **doomed** *verdammt* – [31] **to duck sth.** to avoid sth. – [32] **conundrum** a problem that is difficult to deal with

2 Class in America: Mobility, Measured

America is no less socially mobile than it was a generation ago

Americans are deeply divided as to whether widening inequality is a problem, let alone what the government should do about it. Some are appalled[1] that Bill Gates has so much money; others say good luck to him: But nearly everyone agrees that declining[2] social mobility is a bad thing. Barack Obama's state-of-the union speech on January 28th [2014] dwelt on[3] how America's "ladders of opportunity" were failing [...].

Paul Ryan and Marco Rubio, two leading Republicans, recently gave speeches decrying[4] social immobility and demanding more effort to ensure poor people who work hard can better their lot. Just as the two sides have found something to agree on, however, a new study suggests the conventional wisdom may be wrong. Despite huge increases in inequality, America may be no less mobile a society than it was 40 years ago.

The study, by a clutch[5] of economists at Harvard University and the University of California, Berkeley, is far bigger than any previous effort to measure social mobility. The economists crunch numbers[6] from over 40 m tax returns of people born between 1971 and 1993 (with all identifying information removed). They focus on mobility between generations and use several ways to measure it, including the correlation of parents' and children's income, and the odds that a child born into the bottom fifth of the income distribution will climb all the way up to the top fifth.

They find that none of the measures has changed much. In 1971, a child from these poorest fifth had an 8.4% chance of making it to the top quintile[7]. For a child born in 1986 the odds[8] were 9%. The study confirms previous findings that America's social mobility is low compared with many European countries. (In Denmark, a poor child has twice as much chance of making it to the top quintile as in America.) But it challenges several smaller recent studies that concluded that America had become less socially mobile. [...]

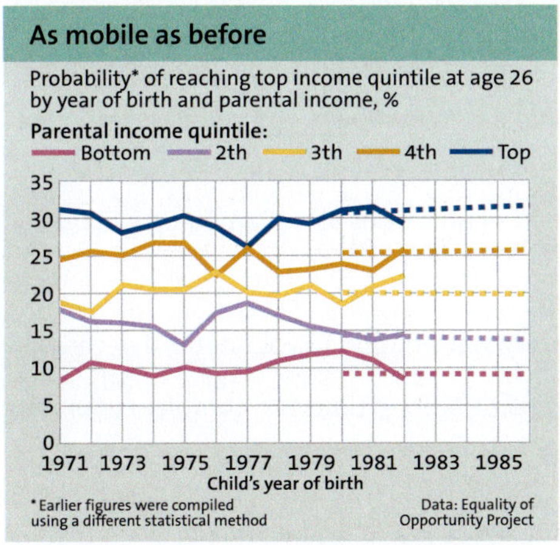

The result has caused a huge stir[9], not least because it runs counter[10] to public perceptions. A recent Gallup[11] poll found that only 52% of Americans think there is plenty of opportunity for the average Joe[12] to get ahead, down from 81% in 1998. It also jars[13] with other circumstantial evidence. Several studies point to widening gaps between rich and poor in the factors you would expect to influence mobility, such as the quality of schools or parents' investment of time and money in their children. Cross-country analyses also suggest there is an inverse[14] relationship between income inequality and social mobility – a phenomenon that has become known as the "Great Gatsby" curve[15]. [...]

Most likely, the answer lies in the nature of America's inequality, whose main characteristic is the soaring[16] share of overall income going to the top 1% (from 10% in 1980 to 22% 8n 2012). The correlation between vast wealth accruing[17] to a tiny elite and the ability of people to move between the rest of the rungs[18] of the income ladder may be small – at least for now.

Whatever the explanation, it would be unwise to take much comfort from this study. For a start, since the gap between top and bottom has widened, the consequences of an accident of birth have become bigger. Second, if the gains of growth are going mostly to those at the top, that bodes ill[19] for those whose skills are less in demand. Many economists worry that living standards for the non-elite will stagnate for a long time. [...]

The economists found five factors that were correlated with differences in social mobility in different parts of America: residential segregation (whether by

[1] **appalled** *entsetzt* – [2] **to decline** to gradually become less, worse or lower – [3] **to dwell on sth.** (*phr. v.*) to keep thinking or talking about sth., esp. sth. unpleasant – [4] **to decry** (*fml.*) to criticize sth. as bad, without value or unnecessary – [5] **clutch** a small group of people – [6] **to crunch numbers** *rechnen* – [7] **quintile** a fifth – [8] **the odds** *Wahrscheinlichkeit* – [9] **stir** (*infml.*) a lot of interest or excitement – [10] **to run counter sth.** *etw. entgegenlaufen* – [11] **Gallup** an American research-based consulting company – [12] **the average Joe** sb. who is just like everyone else; a normal person – [13] **to jar** to disagree – [14] **inverse** opposite in relation to sth. else – [15] **the Great Gatsby curve** a chart illustrating the relationship between inequality and intergenerational social immobility in several countries around the world – [16] **to soar** to rise very quickly to a high level – [17] **to accrue** (*fml.*) to increase in number over a period of time – [18] **rung** one of the bars that forms a step in a ladder – [19] **to bode ill** to be a sign that sth. bad will happen in the future

income or race); the quality of schooling; family structure (e.g. how many children live with only one parent); "social capital" (such as taking part in community groups); and inequality (particularly income gaps among those outside the top 1%). Social mobility is higher in integrated places with good schools, strong families, lots of community spirit and smaller income gaps within the broad middle class. Not a bad agenda[20], for politicians to push, if only they knew how.

The Economist, 1 February 2014, p. 35

3 Barack Obama: State of the Union Address, 28 January 2014

Tips on vocab

to rebound *zurückschnellen, sich erholen* ■ **grit** (*fig.*) *Entschlossenheit* ■ **to hinder** to limit the development of sth. ■ **rancorous** ['ræŋkərəs] (*fml.*) having a feeling of hate and continued anger about sth. in the past; *verbittert* ■ **stock price** *Aktienpreis* ■ **scope** extent or range ■ **CEO** (*abbr.*) chief executive officer; the person with the highest rank in a company ■ **to insource** to do work within a company rather than employing another organization to do it ■ **riddled with sth.** (*idm.*) full of sth., especially sth. bad ■ **loophole** *Schlupfloch* ■ **to flip sth.** to turn sth. over quickly ■ **equation** a difficult problem or complex situation

COMPREHENSION

2. The three texts above – two magazine articles and an excerpt from a political speech – take different views on the "well-being" of the American Dream and its promises. They were all published within four months, between September 2013 and February 2014.

Before reading/listening, divide the class into three groups, with each group working with one of the texts and doing the respective assignments.

Here are some **methodological tips** on how to work in your team:

Step 1:

- Read/listen to the text individually first.
- Take notes on words, phrases, references, etc. you do not understand.
- Take notes on information, facts, numbers, etc. you consider relevant.

Step 2:

- In your group, ask each other questions about anything you do not understand and clarify unknown vocabulary, etc.
- Use a dictionary for help.
- Correct and/or add relevant information to your notes if necessary.

Step 3: Read/listen to your text a second time and complete your notes.

While reading/listening, focus and take notes on these points:

1
- the effects of automation and cheap computer power
- the widening gap between the elite and "the rest"
- the effects of ratings on people and businesses
- the reaction of a growing group of have-nots
- the consequences of political and social instability

[20] **agenda** [ə'dʒendə] *Tagesordnung*

2
- the political disparity in America
- Harvard University's findings on social mobility
- the results of the Gallup poll and other studies
- America's income inequality
- the five factors of social mobility

3
- the positive results of the government's efforts
- the threat to the upward trend
- future opportunities
- current inequalities and stagnations
- factors affecting opportunity

→ Focus on Skills, Listening Comprehension, p. 366

Finally, the groups should present their results to the whole class in short presentations.
→ Focus on Skills, Presentations, p. 391

ANALYSIS

All groups:

3. Examine the line of argument* and train of thought* in your text and explain how the given examples and factual information emphasize the message of the text.
→ Focus on Skills, Analysis of a Non-Fictional Text, p. 377

4. Against the background of Barack Obama's State of the Union Address, describe and analyse cartoon No. 3.
→ Focus on Skills, Analysis of Visuals, p. 381

C

ACTIVITIES

5. a) Contrast the social and economic realities of 2013/14 as presented in the texts to Obama's "wishlist" of 2005 (cf. pp. 140 ff.). Which of his dreams have come true?

b) As a hard-working American citizen and long-standing supporter of Obama's politics, you are disappointed and annoyed about the social and economic state of the country. Write a letter to your president in which you express your frustration and demand the change that was promised.

Tip: Your letter should refer to the president's speech(es) as well as the information given in the articles.
→ Focus on Skills, Writing a Formal Letter, p. 396
→ Focus on Skills, Writing a Letter to the Editor, p. 403

GRAMMAR / LANGUAGE

6. Report the excerpt from Obama's State of the Union speech to a friend who has not had the opportunity of listening to it. Use **indirect speech** and pay attention to the **tenses** and **pronouns**. Do not forget to formulate an appropriate introductory sentence.
The vocab box provides you with some verbs to begin with.

Examples:
- The President emphasized the importance of the citizens to strengthen the state …
- He then presented the results of their efforts …

Tips on vocab

to highlight ■ to present ■ to focus on ■ to criticize ■ to doubt ■ to refer to ■ to ask for sth. ■ to accuse sb. of sth. ■ to demand ■ to question whether … ■ to underline

Broke[1] in the 'Burbs[2]

AWARENESS

Years ago, people moved from the cities to the suburbs in order to find a better quality of life. Collect ideas why
a) living in the suburbs was attractive for many people and families in the past,
b) suburban areas have become increasingly problematic with regard to poverty, crime and municipal services like schools, hospitals, sanitation and transportation.

Kim, who is 35 years old and has two children, left high school to look after her mother, a cocaine addict[3]. When Kim's marriage began to fail and her husband fell ill, she developed addictions of her own – to alcohol and pills, from which she has been free for eight months. She now works at a fast-food restaurant, making, she guesses, around $14,000 a year.

Melissa once had an event-planning company. She says it was doing well, but "when the economy went down it took my company with it". She is now jobless. She and her 16-month-old son live in an apartment provided by the Centre for Family Resources (CFR), a charity.

Kim and Melissa live in Cobb County, north-west of Atlanta. It ranks fifth out of Georgia's 159 counties in income per head, at $33,514 – well above the American median of $27,915 and nearly three times the poverty level of $11,484 for a single person. It is home to a big convention centre[4] and some smart malls[5] and hotels. But it is also home to many who are hard-up[6]. In 2000 6.5 % of the people in Cobb County were poor; in 2011, 12.6 % were. CFR saw requests for help with the rent rise from 207 in January 2010 to 577 in January this year. The number of people who came in asking for assistance of some kind rose from 754 in January 2009 to 1,326 in January 2013.

Americans tend to think of poverty as urban or rural – housing estates[7] or shacks[8] in the woods. And it is true that poverty rates tend to be higher in cities and the countryside. But the suburbs are where you will find America's biggest and fastest-growing poor population, as Elizabeth Kneebone and Alan Berube of the Brookings Institution explain in their book "Confronting Suburban Poverty in America". Between 2000 and 2010 the number of people living below the federal poverty line ($22,314 for a family of four in 2010) in the suburbs grew by 53 %, compared with just 23 % in cities. In 2010 roughly 15.3 m poor people lived in the suburbs, compared with 12.8 m in cities (see chart).

Of picket fences and poverty

Percentage of America's poor* living in:

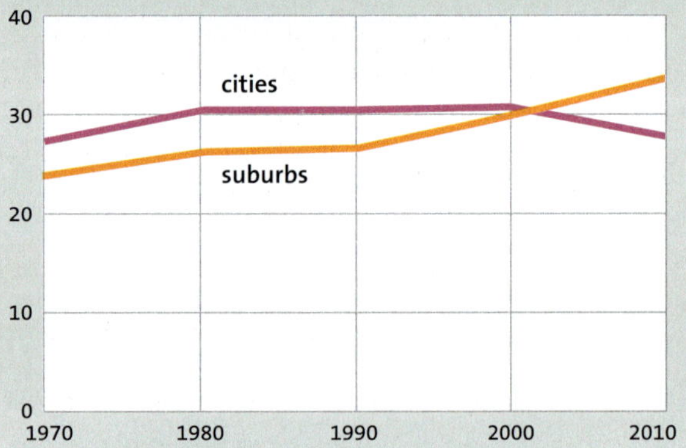

*People living below the federal poverty threshold[9]

Data: Brookings Institution

Suburban poverty began to rise before the recession. As American cities have grown safer and richer, homes there have become less affordable. During the subprime[10] bubble, many people with bad credit scores[11] got mortgages[12] and moved to the suburbs. A shift towards housing vouchers[13] and away from massive urban projects encouraged people in subsidized[14] housing to make the same move. Immigrants, too, chased the American dream of neat lawns and picket fences[15]. Now 51 % of immigrants (who are more likely than the native-born to be poor) live in suburbs, compared with just 33 % in cities.

When the bubble burst, the suburbs suffered. Construction and manufacturing, two of the most suburban industries, lost more jobs between 2007 and 2010 than any other sector.

[1] **broke** bankrupt – [2] **burb** (*abbr., infml.*) suburb – [3] **addict** *Süchtige(r)* – [4] **convention centre** *Messezentrum* – [5] **smart mall** shopping centre, especially for wealthy people – [6] **hard-up** (*infml.*) having very little money – [7] **estate** a large area of land owned by a family or business – [8] **shack** *Baracke* – [9] **threshold** *Schwelle* – [10] **subprime** the practice of lending money to people who may not be able to pay it back – [11] **score** *Bewertung* – [12] **mortgage** ['mɔːɡɪdʒ] *Hypothek* – [13] **voucher** coupon – [14] **to subsidize** *subventionieren* – [15] **picket fence** *Lattenzaun*

Nowhere is it easy to be poor, but the suburbs present particular difficulties. Consider Cobb County, where Kim and Melissa live. Atlanta's commuter-rail system, MARTA, does not run to Cobb. That leaves the carless, such as Kim, or those who have a car but worry about the cost of petrol, like Melissa, dependent on the bus. But Cobb's bus network bypasses much of the county and does not run on Sundays. During non-rush hours, service is spotty[16]; during rush hours, the traffic is awful. So relying on buses can easily add two or three hours to an eight-hour day. Rents have been rising, says Kate Tettamant, a CFR case manager; some of her clients spend half their income on rent. Flexible child care – essential if you are working odd[17] hours – is also hard to find.

One might wonder why the suburban poor do not simply pack up and move back to the cities. Many remain in the suburbs for the same reasons others do: safety, better schools and cheaper homes. And increasingly, suburbia is where the jobs are: between 2000 and 2010 the number of jobs within three miles of central business districts in America's 100 biggest cities fell by 10.4 %, while the number of jobs 10 – 35 miles away rose by 1.2 %.

But while suburban jobs and suburban poverty are both growing, America's anti-poverty infrastructure lags[18]. Suburban safety nets can be thin and patchy[19]; grant-making[20] organisations are often used to focusing on urban rather than suburban poverty. Just as many of the suburban poor have never experienced poverty before, so many of the organisations that help the poor have been overwhelmed by the rapid rise in numbers, says Lesley Grady, a vice-president of the Community Foundation for Greater Atlanta, a charity. Unlike cities, too, suburbs are not politically cohesive[21] entities[22]: they shift, expand and cut across[23] boundaries. Metropolitan Atlanta, for instance, comprises[24] nearly 30 counties, each with its own government, laws and regulations. To be effective, aid organisations must find a way to co-ordinate across those political boundaries. Doing so will not be easy: governments do not easily cede[25] or share power. But for the sake of Kim, Melissa and millions like them, America will have to try.

www.economist.com/news/united-states/21582019-poverty-has-moved-suburbs-broke-burbs, 20 July 2013 [20.08.2014]

COMPREHENSION

1. Give quotes from the text that refer to these topics:
- Cobb County faces increasing poverty rates
- American cities and suburban areas have undergone dramatic changes
- well-to-do people move back to the cities
- suburbs pose problems for low-income families
- many Americans stay in the suburbs
- America's anti-poverty measures are insufficient
- charity and aid organizations fail to help in suburban areas

2. Team up with a partner and summarize the main points of the text.

ANALYSIS

3. Categorize the magazine article after examining
- the topical order and structure of the text,
- the article's style (e. g. matter-of-fact, passionate, etc.),
- the use of rhetorical devices.

→ Focus on Skills, Analysis of a Non-Fictional Text, p. 377
→ Focus on Facts, Basic Types of Non-Fictional Texts, p. 368
→ Focus on Facts, The Press, p. 370

[16] **spotty** *lückenhaft* – [17] **odd** *ungewohnt, seltsam* – [18] **to lag** to move so slowly that you are behind other people or things – [19] **patchy** *lückenhaft* – [20] **grant-making** *spendend* – [21] **cohesive** [kəʊˈhiːsɪv] united and working together effectively – [22] **entity** *Einheit* – [23] **to cut across sth.** (*phr. v.*) *überqueren, kreuzen* – [24] **to comprise** (*fml.*) to have sb./sth. as parts and members – [25] **to cede** *aufgeben*

ACTIVITIES

4. You are members of a citizens' committee and demand changes and action from your local city council. In groups,

a) design placards and posters that depict the dilapidation of your suburb and force the local politicians to declare their positions.
or:

b) compile a formal complaint/petition to your local city council/MP that lists the problems, hardships and privations and demand their elimination.
or:

c) prepare short speeches which lay out the problematic and appalling situation and call for immediate action.
→ Focus on Skills, Writing a Speech Script, p. 400
→ Focus on Skills, Giving a Speech, p. 390
or:

d) prepare and act out a public hearing, presenting and discussing the various views on the matter with local authorities. Prepare role cards and flesh out your lines of argument with information and data from the article.
→ Focus on Language, Conversation and Discussion, p. 385

Tales from the Streets

AWARENESS

According to official numbers, there are about 610,000 homeless people in the US.
Discuss in class
a) possible reasons that might lead to homelessness,
b) what you imagine life is like being homeless.

Homelessness has fallen. But will it stay low?

Soon after Christy Respress started working with the homeless on the streets of Washington, DC, she became frustrated. "They were stuck on the street," she says, because in order to get housing her clients first had to bring their serious mental illnesses and addictions under control. It was a tall order.

That was in 1997. Ms Respress is less frustrated these days. She heads Pathways to Housing DC, a non-profit organisation that helps homeless people get an apartment first and then adds "wrap-around" help with treatment, food stamps, and managing personal finances. This model, known as permanent supportive housing, is one of the efforts that has kept homelessness in America at bay[1] through six years of economic woes[2].

There are 23% fewer vagrants[3] on America's streets than in 2007, according to figures recently released by the housing department. About a third of the 610,000 homeless found in this year's count were sleeping rough[4]. The rest were in shelters, where numbers have remained stable.

Government policy has done much to help. A bill passed in 2009, as the recession unfolded, helped more than 1.3m who were on the brink[5] of homelessness to keep their homes (paying rent arrears[6] and utility[7] bills for them) or to quickly find new ones. A $1.5 billion stimulus pot paid for this over three years, boosting[8] by a quarter the housing department's budget for the homeless. That saved money, says Nan Roman of the National Alliance to End Homelessness, because helping those in

[1] **to hold sb./sth. at bay** *jdn./etw. in Schach halten* – [2] **woe** [wəʊ] great problems and troubles – [3] **vagrants** (*fml.*) a person who is poor and does not have a home or job – [4] **to sleep rough** (*infml.*) to be homeless and have no place to stay or sleep – [5] **on the brink** *am Rande* – [6] **arrears** *rückständige Schuld* – [7] **utility** a service provided for the public, for example an electricity, water or gas supply – [8] **to boost** to improve or increase sth.

short-term financial straits[9] to stay in their homes is cheaper than keeping them in shelters until they can rent again.

About 300,000 are now housed through programmes like Pathways – a 50 % increase since 2007. Most of them need intensive care, from help getting identity documents ("A lot of detective work," says Ms Respress) to daily visits from social workers. But they cost taxpayers more when they are homeless – emergency-room visits, detox[10] treatment and stints[11] in jail. In 2008 homeless ex-servicemen (one in ten vagrants) got an earmarked[12] pot that now pays for housing 43,000 of them. And government agencies that help them are now better at working together. (Eric Shinseki, the 71-year-old secretary for veterans' affairs, and Shaun Donovan, his 47-year old colleague at the housing department, both hit[13] the cold streets of Washington with 180 other volunteers to do the annual homeless count last January.) Homelessness among ex-servicemen has fallen by a quarter since 2009.

Now there are fears that the tide may turn[14]. Although employment is recovering, the number of people at risk of becoming homeless is staggering[15]. In 2011 8.5 m households were spending over half their income on rent and earning less than half of their area's median wage. Since then, rents have gone up. But incomes have not, and the poverty rate is unchanged.

Poor households are one small financial crisis away from losing their homes. A common story in the shelters is that of the single mother who gets behind on the rent because her child falls ill and she has no savings to dip into[16] for treatment and time off work. Relatives or friends usually take in – for a time – those who lose their homes. The number of such shared households is

up from last year, according to the Census Bureau. But that is a worry, because three in ten people showing up at shelters come from other people's homes.

The safety net, too, now has big holes. The stimulus funding has expired[17]. And the sequester[18] – a sweeping[19] federal budget cut that kicked off[20] in March – is starting to hurt the programmes that tackle homelessness. A day after sharing the good news from the homeless count, the housing department announced budget cuts which, it reckons[21], would remove more than 100,000 people from shelters and homes such as those supported by Pathways.

Affordable-housing programmes are also closing waiting lists and rescinding[22] rent subsidies. These subsidies, coupled with other mainstream benefits for the poor such as food stamps and Medicaid (government-paid health insurance), are the exit from homelessness for most who fall into it, says Ms Roman. That exit seems to be closing.

The Economist, 7 December 2013, p. 46

COMPREHENSION

1. Describe the model of "permanent supportive housing" and its benefits.
2. Give an outline of how government policy and programmes like "Pathways" helped decrease the numbers of homeless people.
3. Point out the contradiction of recovering employment rates and a staggering number of people at risk of becoming homeless and its impact.

[9] **straits** a difficult situation because of financial problems – [10] **detox** *Entzug, Entgiftung* – [11] **stint** a period of time that you spend working somewhere or doing a particular activity – [12] **to earmark** *etw. für etw. vorsehen* – [13] **to hit the streets** (*infml.*) to go out to the streets – [14] **to turn the tide** to cause a great change – [15] **staggering** *überwältigend* – [16] **to dip into** (*phr. v.*) to take an amount from money that you have saved – [17] **to expire** to end – [18] **sequester** *automatische Einkommenskürzung* – [19] **sweeping** *durchschlagend* – [20] **to kick off** (*infml.*) to start – [21] **to reckon** (*infml.*) to think or believe – [22] **to rescind** *annullieren*

ANALYSIS

4. Explain the possible effects of budget cuts on
- public housing programmes,
- food stamps,
- programmes like "Pathways",
- health care.

How do these programmes and subsidies save people from homelessness?

@ **5.** Do research on the states of California, Texas, Florida and New York and try to find reasons for their peaking numbers of homeless people.
Examine the data given in the map and explain striking trends concerning certain regions in the US.
→ Focus on Skills, Analysis of Statistical Data, p. 380

EXHIBIT 1.4: Estimates of Homeless People
By State 2013

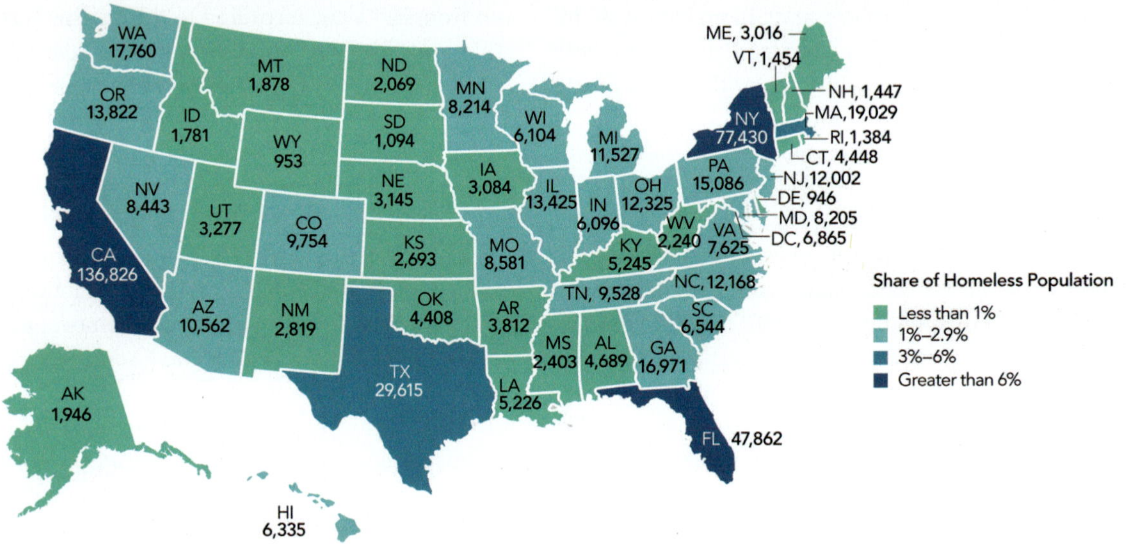

The 2013 Annual Homeless Assessment Report to Congress (AHAR)

ACTIVITIES

Webcode SNG-40183-021 @ **6.** As an additional project, find further information about the situation of homeless people in the US by reading the 2013 Annual Homeless Assessment Report (AHAR) to Congress, using the link on the webcode.
In a presentation to your class, give information about
- the reasons for homelessness,
- the situation of homeless families,
- homeless children and adolescents.

→ Focus on Skills, Presentations, p. 391

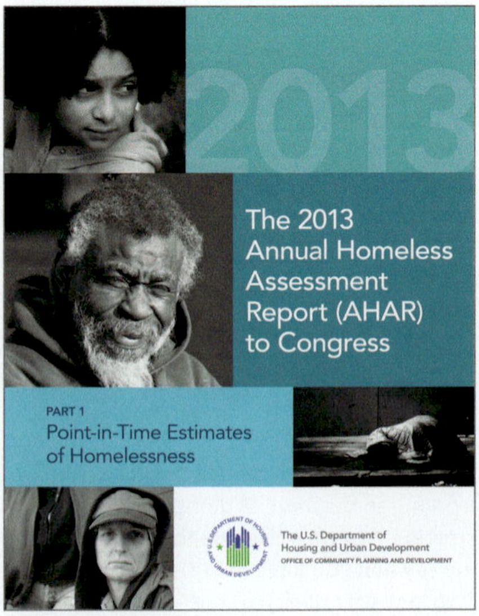

Moms Demand Action on Gun Laws

AWARENESS

"Moms Demand Action", a collective of mothers calling for gun law reform, has launched a print and television advertising campaign focused on children in school.
In a round robin activity, state your first impression of this idea/campaign.

1

2

3

COMPREHENSION

1. One day after the Sandy Hook massacre, on December 15, 2012, Shannon Watts, a 42-year-old mother of five children from Indianapolis, Indiana, founded "Moms Demand Action" (MDA) on Facebook. The initiative immediately gained tens of thousands of followers and has launched several anti-gun advertising campaigns since.
   Take a look at the adverts and describe them in detail taking into consideration
   a) pictorial and
   b) textual elements in order to identify the message of the adverts.
   → Focus on Skills, Analysis of Visuals, p. 381

Tips on vocab

(1) chocolate surprise egg ■ to hold sth. in one's hands ■ to carry a machine gun/assault weapon ■ to have bleak (*düster*) facial expressions ■ a dreary (*trostlos*) atmosphere ■ to stand upright

(2) a gym ■ dodgeball (*Völkerball*)

(3) a library ■ shelves with books ■ rocking chair ■ Little Red Riding Hood (*Rotkäppchen*) ■ fairy tale ■ to sit cross-legged

ANALYSIS

2. Relate the message of the adverts to the article "Kill Zone" by Christopher Dickey and explain what they have in common.
   Webcode SNG-40183-023 @ The links on the webcode provide you with further information on "Moms Demand Action" and their campaigns.

ACTIVITIES

3. Together with a partner, write an Internet blog in response to the advertising campaign "Moms Demand Action". State what you like or dislike about it and make suggestions for further/different campaigns.
→ Focus on Skills, Writing a Letter to the Editor, p. 403

4. In groups, think about other campaigns to reduce (gun) violence in schools, school buses, etc. Design and create posters, websites or blogs that demand action to be taken.
Afterwards, display your results in class and discuss their various messages.

The 2016 Election Campaign

AWARENESS

In early 2015, Hillary Clinton and Donald Trump launched their presidential election campaigns. In July 2016, they became the official candidates of the Democratic and Republican Party, respectively.

In groups, look at their campaign slogans and collect ideas about what each campaign might have focused on. Stepping into the candidates' shoes, what would you do to "make America great again" and be "stronger together"?

COMPREHENSION

1. **While reading/listening:** You can choose between either **listening** to the audio version of the speeches or **reading** the texts provided here.

Webcode NG-40183-024

Tip: To get a better impression of the speakers' rhetorical abilities and the overall atmosphere, watch the video clips provided on the webcode.

14 CD 2

Step 1: While reading/listening to Donald Trump's announcement speech, finish the following statements using evidence and information given in the text.

a) The U.S. has serious (economic) problems because …
b) Many Americans are unemployed because …
c) Politicians will *not* make America great again because …
d) The American people can make their country great again because …
e) The U.S. is like a third world country because …

Step 2: After **a second reading/listening**, subdivide the speech into thematic units and find a suitable headline for each unit that captures its message.
→ Focus on Skills, Listening Comprehension, p. 366

1 Donald Trump: Presidential Announcement Speech

Our country is in serious trouble. We don't have victories anymore. We used to have victories, but we don't have them. When was the last time anybody saw us beating, let's say, China in a trade deal? They kill us. I beat China all the time. All the time.

When did we beat Japan at anything? They send their cars over by the millions, and what do we do? When was the last time you saw a Chevrolet in Tokyo? It doesn't exist, folks. They beat us all the time.

When do we beat Mexico at the border? They're laughing at us, at our stupidity. And now they are beating us economically. They are not our friend, believe me. But they're killing us economically.

The U.S. has become a dumping ground[1] for everybody else's problems. [...]

And our real unemployment is anywhere from 18 to 20 percent. Don't believe the 5.6. Don't believe it.

That's right. A lot of people up there can't get jobs. They can't get jobs, because there are no jobs, because China has our jobs and Mexico has our jobs. They all have jobs. But the real number, the real number is anywhere from 18 to 19 and maybe even 21 percent, and nobody talks about it, because it's a statistic that's full of nonsense.

Our enemies are getting stronger and stronger by the day, and we as a country are getting weaker. Even our nuclear arsenal doesn't work. [...]

So I've watched the politicians. I've dealt with them all my life. If you can't make a good deal with a politician, then there's something wrong with you. You're certainly not very good. And that's what we have representing us. They will never make America great again. They don't even have a chance. They're controlled fully – they're controlled fully by the lobbyists[2], by the donors[3], and by the special interests, fully.

Yes, they control them. Hey, I have lobbyists. I have to tell you. I have lobbyists that can produce anything for me. They're great. But you know what? It won't happen. It won't happen. Because we have to stop doing things for some people, but for this country, it's destroying our country. We have to stop, and it has to stop now.

Now, our country needs – our country needs a truly great leader, and we need a truly great leader now. We need a leader that wrote "The Art of the Deal[4]." [...]

So ladies and gentlemen ... I am officially running ... for president of the United States, and we are going to make our country great again.

It can happen. Our country has tremendous potential. We have tremendous people.

We have people that aren't working. We have people that have no incentive to work. But they're going to have incentive to work, because the greatest social program is a job. And they'll be proud, and they'll love it, and they'll make much more than they would've ever made, and they'll be – they'll be doing so well, and we're going to be thriving as a country, thriving. It can happen.

I will be the greatest jobs president that God ever created. I tell you that.

I'll bring back our jobs from China, from Mexico, from Japan, from so many places. I'll bring back our jobs, and I'll bring back our money. [...]

So the reporter said to me the other day, "But, Mr. Trump, you're not a nice person. How can you get people to vote for you?"

I said, "I don't know." I said, "I think that number one, I am a nice person. I give a lot of money away to charities and other things. I think I'm actually a very nice person." But, I said, "This is going to be an election that's based on competence, because people are tired of these nice people. And they're tired of being ripped off[5] by everybody in the world. And they're tired of spending more money on education than any nation in the world per capita, than any nation in the world, and we are 26th in the world, 25 countries are better than us in education. And some of them are like third world countries. But we're becoming a third world country, because of our infrastructure, our airports, our roads, everything. So one of the things I did, and I said, you know what I'll do. I'll do it. Because a lot of people said, "He'll never run. Number one, he won't want to give up his lifestyle." They're right about that, but I'm doing it. [...]

Sadly, the American dream is dead.

But if I get elected president I will bring it back bigger and better and stronger than ever before, and we will make America great again.

Thank you. Thank you very much.

http://time.com/3923128/donald-trump-announcement-speech, 16 June 2016 [10.11.2016]

[1] **dumping ground** a place where sth. that is not wanted is left; *Müllhalde* – [2] **lobbyist** sb. who tries to persuade the government or an official group to do sth. – [3] **donor** sb. who gives money or goods to an organization; *Spender* – [4] **The Art of the Deal** a 1987 book written by Donald Trump and journalist Tony Schwartz; part memoir, part business advice book – [5] **to rip sb. off** *(infml.)* to cheat sb. by making them pay too much, by selling them something of poor quality, etc.

COMPREHENSION

2. **While reading/listening to Michelle Obama's speech** (pp. 203 f.), take notes on what she says about:
   - what makes Clinton a good presidential candidate
   - her personal experience as an African-American
   - her hopes and expectations for women in general and her two daughters in particular
   - what needs to be done to overcome frustration and cynicism

   → Focus on Skills, Listening Comprehension, p. 366

ANALYSIS

3. **Step 1:** Divide the class into two groups, with each group working on one of the speeches.

   Step 2: Analyse the persuasive techniques employed in the speeches, focusing on these aspects:
   - the line of argument*
   - the use of contrast/antithesis* with regard to
     a) personal and possessive pronouns and b) positive and negative emotive words.

   → Focus on Skills, Analysis of a Political Speech, p. 379

4. Identify and explain the speakers' references and allusions to American core beliefs and values.
   → Focus on Facts, American Beliefs and Values, p. 132
   → Focus on Documents, America's Cornerstone Documents, p. 149
   → Focus on Documents, The American Dream, p. 139

5. Compare the two speeches and their respective messages and outline the fundamental differences.

ACTIVITIES

6. Discuss the various aspects mentioned in Trump's announcement speech. What do you think convinced people to vote for him?
   → Focus on Language, Conversation and Discussion, p. 385

2 Michelle Obama: Speech at the Democratic Convention, July 2016

[...] [Our country needs] leaders like Hillary Clinton, who has the guts[1] and the grace to keep coming back and putting those cracks in that highest and hardest glass ceiling[2] until she finally breaks through, lifting all of us along with her.

(CHEERS, APPLAUSE)

That is the story of this country, the story that has brought me to this stage tonight, the story of generations of people who felt the lash[3] of bondage[4], the shame of servitude[5], the sting[6] of segregation[7], but who kept on striving and hoping and doing what needed to be done so that today I wake up every morning in a house that was built by slaves.

(CHEERS, APPLAUSE)

And I watch my daughters, two beautiful, intelligent, black young women playing with their dogs on the White House lawn.

(CHEERS, APPLAUSE)

And because of Hillary Clinton, my daughters and all our sons and daughters now take for granted that a woman can be president of the United States.

(CHEERS, APPLAUSE)

So, look, so don't let anyone ever tell you that this country isn't great, that somehow we need to make it great again. Because this right now is the greatest country on earth!

[1] **to have the guts** to be brave and determined – [2] **the glass ceiling** an invisible but real barrier through which the next stage or level of advancement can be seen but not be reached; here: the barrier to a woman becoming president of the U.S. – [3] **lash** *Peitsche* – [4] **bondage** the state of being another person's slave – [5] **servitude** the state of being under control of sb. and having no freedom – [6] **sting** here: *Schmerz* – [7] **segregation** *Rassentrennung*

(CHEERS, APPLAUSE) And as my daughters prepare to set out into the world, I want a leader who is worthy of that truth, a leader who is worthy of my girls' promise and all our kids' promise, a leader who will be guided every day by the love and hope and impossibly big dreams that we all have for our children.

So in this election, we cannot sit back and hope that everything works out for the best. We cannot afford to be tired or frustrated or cynical. No, hear me. Between now and November, we need to do what we did eight years ago and four years ago.

(CHEERS, APPLAUSE)

We need to knock on every door, we need to get out every vote, we need to pour every last ounce of our passion and our strength and our love for this country into electing Hillary Clinton as president of the United States of America!

(CHEERS, APPLAUSE)

So let's get to work. Thank you all and God bless.

(CHEERS, APPLAUSE)

http://time.com/4421538/democratic-convention-michelle-obama-transcript, 26 July 2016 [10.11.2016]

STRONGER TOGETHER

The Winner ... The Loser ...

AWARENESS

After winning or losing an election, it is customary for candidates to give a speech to their voters, campaign team, supporters and donors.
What important aspects do you think should be mentioned in these speeches, especially after a hard-fought campaign like this one?

COMPREHENSION

Webcode SNG-40183-024 @

1. **Before reading:** Use the link provided on the webcode and watch **Donald Trump's election night victory speech** which he delivered to his supporters at a hotel in New York City. Get an impression of the overall atmosphere.

2. **While reading/listening:** You can choose between either **listening** to the audio version of the speech or **reading** the text provided here.

   Step 1: Team up with a partner. In a paired reading/listening activity, complete the tasks below. After each step, exchange and crosscheck your findings and make corrections and additions if necessary.

   16 CD2

   Step 2: In **a first reading/listening**, take notes on these aspects:
   - Trump's remarks on Hillary Clinton
   - Trump's pledge to every citizen of the United States
   - the "movement" that his campaign incited

- the most urgent tasks for the future
- Trump's plans for reviving the economy
- foreign/international relationships
- the American Dream

→ Focus on Skills, Listening Comprehension, p. 366

Step 3: In a second reading/listening, complete your notes.

1 Donald Trump: Presidential Acceptance Speech

Thank you. Thank you very much, everybody. Sorry to keep you waiting. Complicated business. Complicated. Thank you very much.

I've just received a call from Secretary Clinton. She congratulated us. It's about us. On our victory, and I congratulated her and her family on a very, very hard-fought campaign.

I mean, she fought very hard. Hillary has worked very long and very hard over a long period of time, and we owe her a major debt of gratitude[1] for her service to our country. I mean that very sincerely.

Now it is time for America to bind the wounds of division, have to get together.

To all Republicans and Democrats and independents across this nation, I say it is time for us to come together as one united people. It is time. I pledge[2] to every citizen of our land that I will be President for all of Americans, and this is so important to me.

For those who have chosen not to support me in the past, of which there were a few people, I'm reaching out to you for your guidance[3] and your help so that we can work together and unify our great country.

As I've said from the beginning, ours was not a campaign but rather an incredible and great movement, made up of millions of hard-working men and women who love their country and want a better, brighter future for themselves and for their family.

It is a movement comprised of[4] Americans from all races, religions, backgrounds, and beliefs, who want and expect our government to serve the people – and serve the people it will.

Working together, we will begin the urgent[5] task of rebuilding our nation and renewing the American dream. I've spent my entire life in business, looking at the untapped[6] potential in projects and in people all over the world.

That is now what I want to do for our country. Tremendous potential. I've gotten to know our country so well. Tremendous potential. It is going to be a beautiful thing.

Every single American will have the opportunity to realize his or her fullest potential. The forgotten men and women of our country will be forgotten no longer.

We are going to fix our inner cities and rebuild our highways, bridges, tunnels, airports, schools, hospitals. We're going to rebuild our infrastructure, which will become, by the way, second to none. And we will put millions of our people to work as we rebuild it.

We will also finally take care of our great veterans who have been so loyal, and I've gotten to know so many over this 18-month journey. The time I've spent with them during this campaign has been among my greatest honors. Our veterans are incredible people.

We will embark upon[7] a project of national growth and renewal. I will harness[8] the creative talents of our people, and we will call upon the best and brightest to lev-

[1] **to owe sb. a debt of gratitude** *jdm. Dank schuldig sein* – [2] **to pledge** to formally promise to give or do sth. – [3] **guidance** ['gaɪdəns] help and advice – [4] **to comprise of sb./sth.** to have as members or parts – [5] **urgent** needing attention very soon; *dringend* – [6] **untapped** not yet used or taken advantage of – [7] **to embark upon sth.** to start sth. new or important – [8] **to harness sth.** to control and use the force or strength of sth. to produce power or to achieve sth.

erage[9] their tremendous talent for the benefit of all. It is going to happen.

We have a great economic plan. We will double our growth and have the strongest economy anywhere in the world. At the same time, we will get along with all other nations willing to get along with us. We will have great relationships.

We expect to have great, great relationships. No dream is too big, no challenge is too great. Nothing we want for our future is beyond our reach.

America will no longer settle for[10] anything less than the best. We must reclaim our country's destiny and dream big and bold[11] and daring[12]. We have to do that. We're going to dream of things for our country, and beautiful things and successful things once again.

I want to tell the world community that while we will always put America's interests first, we will deal fairly with everyone, with everyone. All people and all other nations. We will seek common ground, not hostility; partnership, not conflict.

http://www.telegraph.co.uk/news/2016/11/09/donald-trumps-victory-speech-in-full, 9 November 2016 [07.12.2016]

2 Hillary Clinton: Concession Speech

COMPREHENSION

3. In contrast to Donald Trump, who gave his victory speech immediately after winning the election, Hillary Clinton postponed her concession speech until the following afternoon.

17–18 CD 2

Step 1: In a **first listening**, try to understand the gist of Clinton's speech.
→ Focus on Skills, Listening Comprehension, p. 366

Tips on vocab

(Part 1) rowdy noisy ■ **unruly** difficult to control or manage ■ **to enshrine** *bewahren* ■ **to cherish** to love, protect and care for sb./sth. that is important to you ■ **participation** the act of taking part or being involved in sth. ■ **to advance sth.** to develop or improve sth. ■ **LGBT** *(abbr.)* lesbian, gay, bisexual and transgender ■ **(Part 2) Tim Kaine** the Democratic Party's nominee for Vice President ■ **Anne Holton** Tim Kaine's wife ■ **to owe sb. a debt of gratitude** *jdm. Dank schuldig sein* ■ **dedicated** believing that something is very important and giving a lot of time and energy to it ■ **to shatter the highest glass ceiling** here: a woman becoming the first U.S. president ■ **to pursue sth.** to try very hard to get or reach sth. ■ **blessing** *Segen* ■ **conviction** *Überzeugung* ■ **to regret** *bereuen* ■ **scripture** the holy writings of a religion, here: the Bible ■ **to reap** *ernten* ■ **to grow weary** [ˈwɪəri] to become very tired, esp. after long hard work ■ **consequential** important

Step 2: Exchange your first listening impressions with a partner and clarify any questions.

Step 3: Listen to Clinton's speech **a second time** and take notes on these details:

1
- her remarks on Donald Trump
- her personal impression of the campaign and being a candidate
- how she is coping with her defeat and how she wants her supporters to treat Trump
- Clinton's understanding of what a constitutional democracy demands from its citizens
- core American values and causes

2
- how she expresses her gratitude – and to whom
- pieces of advice given to young people
- her appeals to young women and girls
- her wishes and hopes for the future

Webcode SNG-40183-024 @

Tip: To get a better impression of the speech, watch the video clip provided on the webcode.

[9] **to leverage sth.** *(US)* [ˈlevərɪdʒ] to get as much advantage or profit as possible from sth. – [10] **to settle for sth.** *(phr. v.)* to accept or agree to sth. – [11] **bold** brave – [12] **daring** brave and taking risks

ANALYSIS

4. In a group puzzle activity, examine Trump and Clinton's abilities as speakers.

a) Examine the argumentative structure of their speeches.

b) Analyse the most relevant rhetorical devices that are used to convey the speakers' messages, e.g.:

- references to the American Dream and the Declaration of Independence
- metaphors*
- words that create a feeling of common identity and solidarity

→ Focus on Skills, Analysis of a Political Speech, p. 379
→ Focus on Documents, The American Dream, p. 139
→ Focus on Documents, America's Cornerstone Documents, p. 149

5. Compare the issues mentioned in Trump's acceptance speech to his presidential announcement speech of June 2015. What similarities and differences can you detect? How has Trump's overall tone changed?

6. Compare the message of the German cartoon on p. 205 to Donald Trump's speech and the "great" future he has promised to his supporters and voters.

→ Focus on Skills, Analysis of Visuals, p. 381

7. Immediately after Trump's victory, the cartoons below were published.

a) Describe them in detail.

b) Explain what the cartoonists are criticizing about Trump's campaign, his qualifications and personality.

→ Focus on Skills, Analysis of Visuals, p. 381

1

Tips on vocab

Cartoon No. 1
the Statue of Liberty ■ the upper part of the body ■ to have one's eyes blindfolded (with a toupee) ■ to wear a baseball cap (with an inscription) ■ to wear a cardboard nose

2

Tips on vocab

Cartoon No. 2
United States Capitol Rotunda (in the Capitol Building, Home of the US Congress) ■ balcony ■ presidential portraits (from left to right: George W. Bush, Barack Obama, Donald Trump, George Washington, John Adams, Thomas Jefferson) ■ *There goes the neighborhood* = a real estate term; it usually means poverty, noise, pollution and crime have taken over the neighborhood; the neighborhood is turning into a ghetto

The Aftermath ...

AWARENESS

In a round robin activity, share your first reactions to the news that Donald Trump won the election and will be the 45th president of the United States.

1

2

3

4

Tips on vocab

(1) to facepalm *(sich die Hände vors Gesicht schlagen)* ■ an approaching thunderstorm ■ threatening dark clouds ■ the end of the world **(2)** to be speechless ■ cartoon ■ **(3)** a fireball ■ a comet ■ to hurtle towards sth. ■ the end of the world/Armageddon ■ to attack sb./sth. **(4)** to be huddled over ■ to wrap oneself in sth. (the American flag) ■ to look distressed *(gequält)*

Political parties

In 1787, America's founders expected constitutional provisions such as the separation of power, checks and balances, federalism and indirect election of the president by an electoral college[1] would deter[2] the formation of parties. However, **in 1800 the US became the first nation to develop organized political parties** which had executive[3] power. Since the 1860s, the Republican and Democratic parties have dominated American politics. In a 2006 Gallup Poll, ca. 59 percent of Americans identified themselves as either Republicans or Democrats. Those people claiming to be independent normally have partisan[4] leanings[5].

Democratic Party	**Republican Party**
• evolved from the party of Thomas Jefferson, formed before 1800 • is considered to be more liberal • believes that government has an obligation to provide social and economic programs • favours a higher taxation of the rich • has a stronger obligation to environmental engagement	• was established in the 1850s by Abraham Lincoln and others who opposed slavery • is considered to be more conservative • tends to believe that social and economic programs are too costly to taxpayers • encourages private enterprise • believes that a strong private sector makes citizens less dependent on government

The election process

- the US Constitution stipulates[6] that **a presidential election is to be held once every four years**
- in February of the election year, the parties nominate candidates in so-called state primaries[7] and caucuses (*US, Gremium, Ausschuss*)
- at national party conventions, usually held in the summer, **state delegates vote for the party's presidential candidate**
- on election day (usually the first Tuesday following the first Monday in November) every citizen has an opportunity to vote in **a process of indirect popular election known as the electoral college**, in which the number of electors is based on the population of the state
- these electors assemble following election day, cast their ballots and officially select the next president
- the Constitution mandates[8] that **Senators be elected directly by the voters of their state** once every six years
- the **members of the House of Representatives are also elected directly by the voters** of their state every two years

"I ... do solemnly swear that I will faithfully execute the office of President of the United States, and will to the best of my ability, preserve, protect, and defend the Constitution of the United States."

The inauguration[9] of the president

- the president-elect and the vice president-elect **take the oath of office** and are inaugurated on 20 January
- over the years, the inauguration has been expanded to a day-long event, including the oath-taking[10] ceremony, parades, speeches and balls
- traditionally, the sworn-in president delivers a speech, the so-called **inaugural address**, in which he inspires hope for the future and outlines fundamental plans and objectives[11]

[1] **Electoral College** a group of people who come together to elect the President and Vice-President, based on the votes of people in each state – [2] **to deter sb.** [dɪˈtɜːr] *abschrecken* – [3] **executive** [ɪgˈzekjʊtɪv] the part of a government that is responsible for making certain that laws and decisions are put into action – [4] **partisan** strongly supporting a person, principle, political party – [5] **leaning** *Tendenz, Neigung* – [6] **to stipulate** (*fml.*) to state clearly and firmly that something must be done, or how it must be done; *schriftlich vereinbaren* – [7] **(state) primary** *Vorwahlen* – [8] **to mandate** to order sb. to do sth. – [9] **inauguration** [ɪˌnɔːgjʊˈreɪʃən] the ceremony in which sb. is put into an official position – [10] **oath-taking** *den Amtseid ablegen* – [11] **objective** *(politisches) Ziel*

Europe and America: Old Alliances – New Friendships?

The Special Relationship Between the United States and Great Britain

AWARENESS

In an address to parliament, delivered in Westminster Hall, London on 25 May 2011, President Obama discusses how the special relationship between the United States and the United Kingdom serves as a catalyst for global action. How do you think politicians greet one another when they meet on official state visits? Collect ideas and stereotypical expressions that might be used. Then, speculate about the headline and collect ideas about what makes the relationship between the United States and Great Britain so special.

1 John Bercow: Introductory Remarks by the Speaker of the House of Commons

Mr President, ladies and gentlemen.
History is more than the path left by the past. It influences the present and can shake the future.
We meet today in Westminster Hall, a building begun 900 years ago. When the Vikings[1] were visiting the shores of what would become the United States. Even if it was Columbus who would subsequently[2] demonstrate the politician's art of arriving late but claiming all the credit[3].
This hall has witnessed grim[4] trials and the sentencing to death of a king, coronation banquets, ceremonial addresses and the coffins[5] of those receiving the last respects of our people.
Few places reach so far into the heart of our nation. Yet, until today no American President has stood on these steps to address our country's parliament.
It is my honour, Mr President, to welcome you as our friend and as a statesman. Statesmanship is the cement which seals our shared idealism as nations. It makes meaningful the unity of ambition, passion for freedom and abhorrence[6] of injustice, that is the core of our close alliance.
It has fallen to you, to tackle economic turbulence at home, to protect the health of those without wealth, and to seek that precious balance between security, which is too often threatened, and human rights, which are too often denied. History is not the burden of any one man or woman alone, but some are called to meet a special share of its challenges.
It is a duty that you discharge[7] with a dignity, determination and distinction that are widely admired. Abraham Lincoln once observed that nearly all men can stand adversity[8], but if you want to test a man's character, give him power.
Ladies and gentlemen, the President of the United States of America, Barack Obama.

www.youtube.com/watch?v=fp85zRg2cwg [12.12.2012]
transcript by Iris Edelbrock

2 Barack Obama: Remarks by the President to Parliament (excerpt)

Thank you very much. Thank you. (Applause.)
My Lord Chancellor, Mr. Speaker, Mr. Prime Minister, my Lords, and Members of the House of Commons:
I have known few greater honors than the opportunity to address the Mother of Parliaments at Westminster Hall. I am told that the last three speakers here have been the Pope, Her Majesty the Queen,

[1] **Viking** ['vaɪkɪŋ] – [2] **subsequently** (*fml.*) after sth. else has happened, later – [3] **to claim all the credit** *das Lob für sich selbst beanspruchen* – [4] **grim** very serious – [5] **coffin** *Sarg* – [6] **abhorrence** [əb'hɒrəns] (*fml.*) a feeling of strong hatred – [7] **to discharge** here: to do everything that is necessary to perform and complete a particular duty; *seine Aufgaben erfüllen* – [8] **adversity** [əd'vɜ:səti] (*fml.*) *Missgeschick, Widrigkeit*

and Nelson Mandela – which is either a very high bar[1] or the beginning of a very funny joke. (Laughter.)

I've come here today to reaffirm one of the oldest, one of the strongest alliances the world has ever known. It's long been said that the United States and the United Kingdom share a special relationship. And since we also share an especially active press corps, that relationship is often analyzed and overanalyzed for the slightest hint of stress or strain[2].

Of course, all relationships have their ups and downs. Admittedly[3], ours got off on the wrong foot with a small scrape[4] about tea and taxes. (Laughter.) There may also have been some hurt feelings when the White House was set on fire during the War of 1812. (Laughter.) But fortunately, it's been smooth sailing[5] ever since.

The reason for this close friendship doesn't just have to do with our shared history, our shared heritage; our ties of language and culture; or even the strong partnership between our governments. Our relationship is special because of the values and beliefs that have united our people through the ages.

Centuries ago, when kings, emperors, and warlords reigned over much of the world, it was the English who first spelled out[6] the rights and liberties of man in the Magna Carta. It was here, in this very hall, where the rule of law first developed, courts were established, disputes were settled, and citizens came to petition their leaders.

Over time, the people of this nation waged[7] a long and sometimes bloody struggle to expand and secure their freedom from the crown. Propelled[8] by the ideals of the Enlightenment[9], they would ultimately forge[10] an English Bill of Rights, and invest the power to govern in an elected parliament that's gathered here today.

What began on this island would inspire millions throughout the continent of Europe and across the world. But perhaps no one drew greater inspiration from these notions[11] of freedom than your rabble-rousing[12] colonists on the other side of the Atlantic. As Winston Churchill said, the "... Magna Carta, the Bill of Rights, Habeas Corpus[21], trial by jury, and English common law find their most famous expression in the American Declaration of Independence." [...] (Applause)

www.youtube.com/watch?v=fp85zRg2cwg [12.12.2012]
transcript from www.whitehouse.gov/the-press-office/2011/05/25/remarks-president-parliament-london-united-kingdom [10.10.2012]

3 Baroness Helene Hayman: Closing Remarks by the Speaker of the House of Lords

3 CD3

Mr President,

I think that response describes far more eloquently[1] than any words of mine could do how much that very memorable and inspiring address was appreciated by everybody who heard it here today.

You spoke ... [Applause] ... you spoke with great warmth and great generosity about the British Parliament and the British people and about the links that bind us, the values and the traditions that we share, the history that we have experienced ... together.

But more than that, you spoke, too, not just of the relationship of the past, but the relationships of the future. And I think that was what made what you said so inspirational.

It was a distinguished[2] American governor of New York who remarked on the propensity[3] of politicians to campaign in poetry but to govern in prose. The world you described to us today was not just one that is prosaic[4], it is one where the challenges are difficult and sometimes dangerous. One that is fast moving, that is complex, sometimes contradic-

[1] **high bar** here: *hoher Anspruch, hohe Messlatte* – [2] **strain** worry, pressure on sb.– [3] **admittedly** *zugegebenermaßen* – [4] **scrape** (*old-fashioned*) *Schwierigkeit* – [5] **smooth sailing** here: a relationship without difficulties – [6] **to spell sth. out** (*phr. v.*) to explain sth. in a simple, clear way –[7] **to wage** to begin and continue a war, battle, etc. – [8] **to propel** [prəˈpel] *etw. vorantreiben* – [9] **Age of Enlightenment** *Epoche der Aufklärung, 18. Jahrhundert* – [10] **to forge** here: to create sth. – [11] **notion** an idea or an understanding of sth. – [12] **rabble-rousing** *aufwieglerisch* – [13] **Habeas Corpus** [ˈheɪbiəs ˈkɔːpəs] *Habeas-Corpus-Akte; Gesetz zum Schutz der persönl. Freiheit*

[1] **eloquent** *wortgewandt* – [2] **distinguished** *verehrte(r)* – [3] **propensity** [prəˈpensəti] *Neigung* – [4] **prosaic** [prəˈzeɪɪk] *(disapproving)* ordinary and not showing any imagination

tory[5] and that offers at least as many threats[6] as opportunities.
But in the eloquence of your address you reminded us of the importance of maintaining the poetry in government. Because to lead, that poetry is necessary. Necessary not only to articulate the challenges, as you did so masterfully, but also to bring others together to face those challenges with common principles and with shared purpose.
Mr President, it has been a privilege for all of us to hear you speak today.
It is a privilege for me to have the responsibility of thanking you on behalf of both Houses of Parliament for coming to Westminster, and to wish you and Mrs Obama a very happy and pleasant rest of your stay in the United Kingdom. Thank you so much.

www.youtube.com/watch?v=fp85zRg2cwg [12.12.2012]
transcript by Iris Edelbrock

COMPREHENSION

1-3 CD3

1. In a **first listening/reading**, pay attention to the tone of
   a) John Bercow's, b) President Obama's, c) Baroness Hayman's
   voices and the atmosphere that is created by all three speakers.
   → Focus on Skills, Listening Comprehension, p. 366
   Note: The audio text is longer than the printed excerpt in your Students' Book.

2. In a **second listening/reading**, find out what the speakers do to mark the occasion or the addressee as extraordinary.

3. In a **third listening/reading**, find out what historical events the speakers are alluding to.

ANALYSIS

4. Examine why the speakers use so many historical allusions.
   → Focus on Skills, Analysis of a Political Speech, p. 379

Webcode SNG-40183-025 @

5. Use the link provided on the webcode and watch the video of the three speeches. Pay attention to the speakers and the audience's reaction. Now, explain the effect of chosen words on the addressee and the audience.

6. Compare the photo of President Obama being escorted to the Houses of Parliament with the impression the speeches have on the audience.
   → Focus on Skills, Analysis of Visuals, p. 381

U.S. President Barack Obama is escorted to address both Houses of Parliament in London on Wednesday, 25 May 2011. Flanking Obama are Speaker of the House of Commons, John Bercow, left, and Speaker of the House of Lords, Baroness Helene Hayman

ACTIVITIES

7. Work in groups of three. Each one of you should imagine to be one of the persons in the photo above. Write an interior monologue*, compare your thoughts and then present them in class.

[5] **contradictory** *widersprüchlich* – [6] **threat** [θret] *(Be-)Drohung*

Germans in America

AWARENESS

Step 1: In a round robin activity, complete the following sentence:
Germany and the United States have a special relationship because …

Step 2: Write down your answers on slips of paper and display them on a wall/blackboard.

Step 3: Sort the slips of paper and assign them to certain keywords or topics, e. g.:
- history
- culture
- politics
- economy
- education
- private/familial relationships

Step 4: Discuss your statements in class and make a ranking. What do you consider to be the most/least important aspects of the German-American relationship?

COMPREHENSION

1. About seven million Germans have immigrated to the United States since the 18th century.

Step 1: Before reading the texts on the following pages, reactivate your knowledge about Germans who have played a vital role in American history, politics, science and society.

Team up with a partner and do research on the following names, using the links provided on the webcode.

Webcode SNG-40183-026

Hannah Arendt • Albert Einstein • Wernher von Braun • Kurt Weill • Fritz Lang • Henry John Heinz
Levi Strauss • Friedrich, Baron von Steuben • Peter Minuit • Ruth Westheimer • Herbert Marcuse
Mies van der Rohe • Joseph Pulitzer • Ottmar Mergenthaler • Francis Daniel Pastorius • Henry Steinway

Step 2: Discuss in class: What were these people's reasons for leaving Germany and immigrating to the United States?

1 Philip Oltermann: Spirit of "Forty-Eighters": Germany Eyes[1] a Special Relationship with US

German revolutionary Carl Schurz was an all-American hero. A teacher who climbed the barricades during the failed uprising against an autocratic Prussian state in 1848, he exported his democratic fervour[2] to America four years later: Schurz fought for the unionist cause[3] in the civil war, served as US secretary of the interior and introduced to his adopted homeland the concept of the kindergarten.

Yet most Americans, and even more Germans, would struggle to put a face to the name of the man whose memorial in Wisconsin identifies him as America's "greatest German American". The UK and the US may quarrel over of the precise location of Winston Church-

Carl Schurz

[1] **to eye** to look at sb./sth. with interest – [2] **fervour** (*fml.*) strong and sincere beliefs – [3] **unionist cause** during the American Civil War (1861 – 1865), the northeastern states of the USA, the Union, i. e. the states which fought against the "South", i. e. the states that had slavery

ill's bust[4] inside the White House, but at least they know who they are talking about.If the German foreign policy circles are to be believed, all that could change if the UK leaves the European Union. Since Barack Obama's visit to Europe last weekend, Germany's media has been alive with speculation that the country could take over the UK's role in a "special relationship" with the US after Brexit.

After the US president on Saturday warned Eurosceptics in the UK that Britain could find itself at the "back of the queue" if they had their way, he heaped praise on Angela Merkel on Sunday, describing their tie[5] as "as important a relationship as I've had during the course of my presidency".

"Over the last three to four years, Germany's importance for America has grown enormously," Marc Overhaus of German thinktank SWP[6] told *Der Spiegel*. While Britain's strategic importance for the US had fallen with its defence spending, Germany was considered "the only state in Europe capable of decisive action," he said.

If the UK was to leave the EU, "the Americans would increasingly rely on Berlin and Paris", said Christian Democrat MEP[7] Elmar Brok. "Britain would then only be a strategically insignificant island in the Atlantic."

The notion[8] that the US would invest all its diplomatic energy into one bilateral relationship rather than spreading its bets[9] across the continent is questionable. "America breaking off relations with Britain is just not on the cards when you look at military matters and the intelligence sharing that is going on between the two countries," said Derek Chollet, a former Obama security official and senior adviser at the German Marshall Fund.

Angela Merkel with Barack Obama during his state visit to Germany

On attitudes to data protection, the two states remain miles apart and scepticism towards the Transatlantic Trade and Investment Partnership (TTIP) is growing on both sides of the Atlantic.

"But in terms of geopolitics, if the UK continues to go down its existential path and move away from Europe, the US president will be more likely to pick up the phone to call to the German chancellor than the British prime minister," Chollet told the Guardian. "On Russia, it's already happening."

Efforts to rediscover America and Germany's joint[10] history, with a particular emphasis on the role of German emigres in US nation-building, are already happening, too.

In Berlin, there are plans for a memorial to Schurz and the other "Forty-Eighters" – German revolutionaries who fought against slavery during the US civil war. Erardo Cristoforo Rautenberg, the chief public prosecutor[11] of Brandenburg state who is driving the initiative, has suggested placing a statue on the site the reconstructed Berlin city palace, as a counterpoint to the neoprussian revival.

Germany's foreign minis-ter last week announced his support for the memorial "In many people's memory, it was the Americans, supported by the British and the French, who brought democracy to Germany in 1945," Frank-Walter Steinmeier told *Der Spiegel*.

"But many had experi-enced parliamentary democracy before 1933, fought for by the actors of 1848. That is why a memorial to the so-called Forty-Eighters are a great opportunity to evoke the memory of mutual influences during the foundation of stable democracies on both sides of the ocean."

Historians and publishers too are rediscovering America's German heritage. When US journalist and author Erica Wagner started researching a biography of Washington Roebling, a civil engineer best known for his work on the Brooklyn Bridge, she was startled[12] by the fact that the man behind one of America's most famous landmarks did not speak English until he was

[4] **bust** a model of the head and shoulders of the person; *Büste* – [5] **tie** special connections between people or places – [6] **SWP** (*abb.*) *Stifung Wissenschaft und Politik* – [7] **MEP** (*abbr.*) Member of the European Parliament – [8] **notion** a belief or idea – [9] **to spread one's bets** to reduce the risk of losing or making a mistake by supporting more than one side in a competition, an argument, etc., or by having several choices available to you – [10] **joint** belonging to or shared between two or more people (here: countries) – [11] **prosecutor** *Staatsanwalt* – [12] **startled** *überrascht*

10. He grew up in Saxonburg, Pennsylvania, a German immigrant town founded by his father, John who initially designed the bridge. Her book, The Chief Engineer, published by Bloomsbury next summer, tells the story of what she calls "a monument to German-American engineering."

It is a story that may resonate[13] more than British transatlanticists[14] assume. German Americans make up the largest ethnic group in the US, if you divide Hispanics into Mexican Americans, Cuban Americans etc. In the 2013 American Community Survey, 46 million Americans claimed German ancestry: more than the number who traced their roots to Ireland (33 million) or England (25 million).

http://www.theguardian.com/world/2016/apr/30/germany-special0-relationship-us-obama-carl-schurz-brexit, 30 April 2016 [20.05.2016]

COMPREHENSION

2. In a group puzzle activity, divide the class into two or four groups, with one or two groups working with one of the texts.

Step 1: Read the text individually first and try to get a general understanding.

Step 2: In your group, summarize the most relevant information and ask each other questions about anything that is unclear.

Step 3: Correct and/or add information that you consider to be important.

Step 4: Each group compiles a short abstract which contains the most relevant information of each text.

Following this, the groups remix and inform each other about their results.

ANALYSIS

3. Take a closer look at the second text (p. 220) and examine the various statistical data concerning the German-American relationship. Compare: On which issues/matters do Germans and Americans agree – which matters do their views differ on? Copy the grid below and complete it.

issue/matter/topic	**German view**	**American view**
Is the U.S./Germany a reliable ally?	• 62 % (68 % ♂; 56 % ♀) • 13 % Washington • 31 %	• 72 % • 24 % very
Is Britain a reliable ally?	• 55 % • 31 %	• 85 % • 54 % very • 60 % ♂; 49 % ♀
Prefers to focus on domestic tasks/ problems	…	…
TTIP	…	…

agreement   disagreement

[13] **to resonate** *mitschwingen, nachhallen* – [14] **transatlanticist** used to describe someone in Europe (here: Britons) with a special relationship with the US

4. The cartoon on p. 221 depicts another facet of the German-American relationship.
a) First, team up with a partner and describe the cartoon in detail to each other.
b) Second, explain the cartoon's message.
→ Focus on Skills, Analysis of Visuals, p. 381

ACTIVITIES

5. Germany's former minister of foreign affairs, Frank-Walter Steinmeier, stated that "[i]n many people's memory, it was the Americans, supported by the British and the French, who brought democracy to Germany in 1945" (p. 218, ll. 70 ff.).
In groups, reactivate your knowledge about how the United States "brought democracy to Germany in 1945". Do research on the Internet or at a library and collect information about the American presence in post-WW II Germany.

2 Pew Research Center[1]: Germany and the United States: Reliable Allies[2]

Seven decades after the end of World War II and a quarter-century after the end of the Cold War, roughly seven-in-ten Americans see Germany as a reliable ally, and about six-in-ten Germans trust the United States, according to a Pew Research Center survey. [...]
But Germans and Americans do not see eye-to-eye on salient[3] points in the history of the postwar alliance, nor about some of the key issues in its future. For Americans, the most important event in U.S.-German relations over the past 75 years remains World War II and the Holocaust. Germans are less unanimous[4] in their views of historical importance, but to the extent that one event stands out it is the 1989 fall of the Berlin Wall. In the eyes of most Americans, the "special relationship" with Britain is still stronger than that with Germany. Americans want Germany to play a more active military role in the world, but Germans emphatically[5] disagree. [...]

The U.S.-German relationship today

Economically and geopolitically, the U.S.-German alliance has become the linchpin[6] of the trans-Atlantic relationship in the 21st century. Despite their disagreements at the time over the Iraq War and U.S. National Security Agency spying, Americans and Germans view each other as reliable allies. But Germans are slightly more circumspect[7] than Americans about the alliance.
A widespread majority of Americans (72%) see Germany as a reliable ally, including nearly a quarter (24%) who thinks of Germany as very reliable. Older Americans (77%) have more faith in Germany than younger ones do (66%).
About six-in-ten Germans (62%) believe the United States is a reliable ally. But only 13% see Washington as very reliable. German men (68%) are more likely than women (56%) to see the U.S. as a dependable[8] strategic partner. Notably[9], 31% of Germans think the U.S. is not a reliable ally.
But Americans are more likely to see Britain as a reliable ally: 85% say Britain is dependable, including 54% who consider it very reliable. American men (60%) more than women (49%) are likely to voice the opinion that Britain is very dependable. Similarly, Americans 65 years of age and older (64%) are more likely than Americans ages 18 to 29 (39%) to express such strong confidence[10] in the "special relationship."
A majority of Germans (55%) also view Britain as a reliable ally. But they have less faith in their EU and NATO partner than do the Americans. Moreover, only 8% voice the view that London is very dependable.
And 32% of Germans see Britain as not too reliable or not at all reliable. Younger Germans, ages 18 to 29 (67%), are more likely to see Britain as reliable than are their elders, those ages 65 and older (44%). [...]

[1] **Pew Research Center** a nonpartisan American think tank based in Washington D.C. – [2] **ally** ['ælaɪ] *Verbündeter* – [3] **salient** ['seɪliənt] most important – [4] **unanimous** *einstimmig, einmütig* – [5] **emphatically** done or said in a strong way and without any doubt – [6] **linchpin** *der Dreh- und Angelpunkt* – [7] **circumspect** careful not to take risks – [8] **dependable** *zuverlässig* – [9] **notably** *bemerkenswert* – [10] **confidence** *Selbstvertrauen, Zuversicht*

In recent years, there has been much discussion among foreign policy elites and pundits[11] about resurgent[12] American isolationism and German reluctance[13] to take on greater global responsibilities. The public appetite to engage with the rest of the world can wax and wane[14] over time depending on circumstances. But by one broad measure – public willingness to assume greater international obligations – Germans and Americans see eye-to-eye: They would prefer to focus on domestic tasks.

Half of both the German and American public say their country should deal with its own problems and let other countries deal with their own challenges. Roughly comparable proportions of Germans (43 %) and Americans (39 %) believe that their nation should help other countries deal with their difficulties.

In particular, it is younger Germans and Americans who are more inward looking than their older counterparts. More than half of both Americans (57 %) and Germans (54 %) ages 18 to 29 hold the view that their country should deal with its own problems and let others deal with theirs. And only 36 % of that age group in Germany and 31 % in the United States believe that their country should help other nations deal with their difficulties. This stands in sharp contrast with the attitudes of their older countrymen: 46 % of both Americans and Germans ages 65 and older are of the opinion that their countries should do more to help others.

In addition, low-income Germans (61 %) are more likely than high-income Germans (40 %) to be inward-looking. There is no significant difference in attitudes on this issue between high- and low-income Americans. In Germany, those living in the East (60 %) are far more likely to want Berlin to focus on domestic problems than are people in the West (47 %), who are divided on the issue. […]

Germans are also divided over deepening economic ties with the U.S. Just 41 % think a U.S.-European Union free trade agreement called the Transatlantic Trade and Investment Partnership (TTIP), which is now under negotiation, would be good for Germany; 36 % say it would be a bad idea. That support is down 14 percentage points since a Pew Research Center survey in February-March 2014. High-income Germans (43 %) are more likely to hold the view that TTIP is a bad thing than are low-income Germans (32 %).

Half (50 %) of the American public backs TTIP, largely unchanged from 2014. And only about two-in-ten (21 %) think it would be bad for the United States. Democrats (59 %) are more supportive than Republicans (45 %). Nevertheless, as with Germans, much of the public is undecided. More than a quarter of Americans (28 %) have not heard enough about the negotiation, think it is neither good nor bad or have no view on the topic.

http://www.pewglobal.org/2015/05/07/germany-and-the-united-states-reliable-allies, 7 May 2015 [20.05.2016]

2

Tips on vocab

left: a beetle/Volkswagen ■ drops of sweat ■ bulging eyes ■ company logo

right: an oversize/giant spray can ■ EPA (Environmental Protection Agency) ■ insect repellent/spray ■ to impose a fine/penalty on sb. (*über jdn. eine Strafe verhängen*) ■ an oversize/giant hand ■ cuffs (*Manschetten*) in the national colours of the U.S. (symbolizing the United States)

[11] **pundit** expert, specialist – [12] **resurgent** increasing again, or becoming popular again – [13] **reluctance** an unwillingness to do sth. – [14] **to wax and wane** to grow stronger and then weaker again

US history		
to abolish sth. [ə'bɒlɪʃ] **abolition of sth.** ['æbə'lɪʃn]	to officially end a law, a system	*etwas abschaffen; Abschaffung*
to become independent of sb./sth.	to be one's own master	*von jdm./etw. unabhängig werden*
independence	freedom from political control by the government of another country	*Unabhängigkeit*
civil rights movement	citizens who fight for the rights that each person has in a society, whatever their race, sex or religion	*Bürgerrechtsbewegung*
discrimination	the practice of treating a person or group less fairly than others	*Diskriminierung*
to escape persecution	to get away from persecution	*Verfolgung entgehen; fliehen*
to found sth.	to start sth., e. g. an organization, a company, etc.	*etwas gründen*
Founding Fathers	sb. who begins sth., e. g. a new way of thinking (here: Thomas Jefferson, Benjamin Franklin, George Washington, etc.)	*Gründungsväter*
the Frontier ['frʌntɪə(r)]	the border between settled/civilized and unsettled/uncivilized country	*das Grenzland*
to gain independence	to become independent	*Unabhängigkeit erlangen*
interventionism	the policy of intervening in the affairs of another sovereign state	*Interventionismus*
isolationism	the policy of nonparticipation in international economic and political relations	*Isolation, Isolationismus*
native	a word used by white people to refer to the people who lived in America, etc. before Europeans arrived	*Ureinwohner*
pilgrim	a religious person who travels to a holy place	*Pilger*
plantation	a large piece of land where crops are grown	*Plantage*
prejudice ['predʒudɪs]	an unreasonable dislike of people who are different	*Vorurteil*
to be prejudiced	having an unreasonable dislike of sb. or sth., mostly because of foreignness	*voreingenommen sein, Vorurteile haben*
protest movement	a large group of people who come together to publicly express disapproval or opposition to sth.	*Protestbewegung*
purchase ['pɜːtʃəs]	sth. you buy	*Ankauf*
Puritan ['pjʊərɪtən]	a member of a Protestant religious sect in the 16th and 17th centuries, who wanted to make religion simpler	*Puritaner(in)*
racial segregation	when people of different races are kept apart so that they live, work or study separately	*Rassentrennung*
to rebel [rɪ'bel] **rebellion** [rɪ'beljən]	to oppose or fight against people in authority or against an idea or a situation which you do not agree with; an organized attempt to change the government or a leader of a country, using violence	*rebellieren; Rebellion, Aufstand*
subject (*fml.*)	here: citizen	*Staatsbürger*
trading post	a place where people can buy and exchange goods far away from town, esp. in the past	*Handelsstützpunkt*
politics/constitution		
administration	the government of a country	*Regierung, Verwaltung*
amendment	a change to a law that is still being discussed	*Zusatz (zur Verfassung)*
to amend [ə'mend] **a bill**	to make changes to a (draft) law	*eine Gesetzesvorlage/ein Gesetz ändern*
appointment	the act of choosing sb. for a position or job	*Ernennung*
article	paragraph (of a law)	*Paragraf, Artikel*

civil servant	sb. employed in the civil service	*Beamter*
Constitution	a set of basic laws and principles that a country or organization is governed by	*Verfassung*
to declare sth. unconstitutional	to say officially that sth. is not allowed by the constitution	*etwas für verfassungswidrig erklären*
domestic policy	the internal policy of a country without involving other countries	*Innenpolitik*
to ensure (a right)	to make certain that sth. will happen properly; to assure	*zusichern*
foreign policy	involving or dealing with other countries	*Außenpolitik*
to govern	to rule	*regieren*
grass roots (democracy)	the ordinary people rather than the rulers	*Basis, „Fußvolk"*
Head of State	the main representative of a country, e.g. a king	*Staatsoberhaupt*
to interfere with sth.	to prevent sth. from happening the way that it was planned	*sich in etwas einmischen*
policy	a set of ideas of what to do in certain situations that has been agreed on by a government or a party	*eine bestimmte Politik*
politician [ˈpɒləˈtɪʃn]	someone who works in politics, especially an elected member of the government	*Politiker*
political [pəˈlɪtɪkl]	relating to governmental actions or people	*politisch*
to be (politically) impartial	not supporting one person or group more than another	*unparteiisch sein*
to ratify a treaty	to make a treaty official by signing it	*einen Vertrag unterzeichnen*
reunification	to join the parts of sth. together again, especially a country that was divided	*Wiedervereinigung*
	beliefs/values	
achievement	sth. that you succeed in doing by your own efforts	*Errungenschaft*
authority [ɔːˈθɒrəti]	the power you have because of your official position	*Autorität, Amtsgewalt*
cultural patterns/habits	cultural ideas/behaviour	*kulturelle Gewohnheiten*
divine providence	what is thought to be God's intervention in the world	*göttliche Vorsehung*
to be equal; equality [iˈkwɒləti]	to have the same rights and opportunities as everyone else, no matter what your sex, race, age, religion, etc.	*gleichgestellt sein; Gleichheit, Gleichberechtigung*
God's chosen people	in 1630, the founding Puritans believed they were the chosen people of God and had the duty to build an ideal Christian community in the new World	*Gottes auserwähltes Volk*
heterogeneous society [ˈhetərəˈdʒiːniəs]	a very diverse society	*verschiedenartige, breit gefächerte Gesellschaft*
to identify with sb./sth.; identification [aɪˌdentɪfɪˈkeɪʃn]	to feel sympathy for sb./sth. or be able to share their feelings; a strong feeling of sympathy and similarity with someone	*sich mit jdm./etw. identifizieren; Identifikation*
inalienable/unalienable rights [ɪnˈeɪlɪənəbl]	rights that cannot be taken from you	*unveräußerliche Rechte*
individuality [ˌɪndɪˌvɪdʒuˈæləti]	the qualities that make sb. or sth. different from other people or things	*Individualität*
Manifest Destiny [ˈmænɪfest ˈdestəni]	the belief that the US people had the right and the duty to take land in North America from other people, because this was God's plan	*offensichtliche Bestimmung (amerik. Doktrin des 19. Jahrhunderts; göttlicher Auftrag zur Expansion)*
Melting Pot	the idea of a place where people's different races, cultures, etc. blend together into one nation	*Schmelztiegel (der Kulturen)*
national anthem	the official song of a nation	*Nationalhymne*
national pride	being proud of having a particular nationality	*Nationalstolz*
to offer an opportunity to sb.	to give sb. a chance to do sth.	*eine Gelegenheit bieten*

patriotism [ˈpeɪtriətɪzəm]	when you love your country and are proud of it; national pride	*Patriotismus*
(to be) patriotic	having or expressing a great love of your country	*patriotisch (sein)*
prosperity	wealth	*Reichtum, Wohlstand*
Pursuit of Happiness [pəˈsjuːt]	the act of trying to find happiness	*Streben nach Glück, existenzieller Sicherheit, Zufriedenheit*
rags-to-riches	the idea of becoming very rich after starting life very poor	*vom Tellerwäscher zum Millionär*
religious tolerance [rɪˈlɪdʒəs ˈtɒlərəns]	not discriminating against people from different religions	*religiöse Toleranz*
self-improvement	the process of trying to become a better person	*(selbstständige) Weiterbildung*
thrift	the habit of saving money and spending it carefully	*Wirtschaftlichkeit, Sparsamkeit*
unlimited possibilities	endless/limitless opportunities and possibilities	*unbegrenzte Möglichkeiten*
immigration/minorities		
alien	a person who is not a citizen of the country in which they live and work	*Fremde/r*
to assimilate; assimilation	to become a part of a country/community	*anpassen/Anpassung*
border control	measures taken to prevent illegal immigrants from entering a country; immigration control	*Grenzkontrolle*
citizen	a person who has the legal right to belong to a particular country	*Staatsbürger*
descendant	sb. who is related to a person that lived a long time ago	*Nachkomme*
to emigrate (from); emigration	to leave one's own country in order to live in another	*auswandern; Auswanderung*
ethnic; ethnicity	connected with a nation, race or people that shares certain cultural traditions	*ethnisch; Ethnizität, Volkszugehörigkeit*
illegal alien	an illegal immigrant	*illegaler Einwanderer*
Hispanic	a person whose first language is Spanish, esp. one who comes from a Latin American country	*Lateinamerikaner(in), Südamerikaner(in)*
to immigrate (to) [ˈɪmɪgreɪt]	to come into a country in order to live there	*immigrieren, einwandern*
immigration control	the place where the passports and other documents of people coming into the country are checked	*Einwanderungskontrolle*
(cultural) interaction	the act of communicating with sb. (from a different culture)	*(kulturelle) Interaktion*
multi-ethnic	involving or including different ethnicities	*Vielvölker-*
naturalization	to become a citizen of a particular country	*Einbürgerung*
to be processed through sth.	to be moved forward from one checkpoint to the next	*durchgereicht werden, weitergeschickt werden*
to take an oath of allegiance	a formal promise to be loyal to a country	*den Treueeid schwören*
economy		
to go bankrupt; bankruptcy	to become officially unable to pay your debts; to go bust; the state of being unable to pay your debts	*Pleite gehen; Pleite, Bankrott*
capitalism [ˈkæpɪtəlɪzəm]	an economic and political system in which businesses belong mostly to private owners, not to the government	*Kapitalismus*
capitalist [ˈkæpɪtəlɪst]	sb. who owns or controls a lot of money and lends it to businesses, banks, etc. to produce more wealth	*Kapitalist*
commerce	trade	*Handel*
to drop; drop	to fall to a lower level or amount; reduction	*fallen, einbrechen; Absturz, Abfall*
financial recession	a difficult time when there is less business activity, trade, etc. in a country	*finanzielle Rezession, Flaute*

hire and fire policy	to employ and dismiss people in quick succession	*Einstellen und Feuern von Beschäftigten*
homeowner(s)	people who own their home	*Hauseigentümer*
to be low-income	to be below an acceptable or usual level of income	*geringverdienend sein*
ownership society	a society in which personal responsibility, economic liberty, and the possession of property are very important	*von G. W. Bush vertretenes Gesellschaftsmodell, in dem die Bürger für sich und ihr Wohlergehen zuständig sind*
real estate ['ri:əl ɪ'steɪt] (*US*)	property in the form of land and houses	*Grundbesitz*
to regenerate [rɪ'dʒenəreɪt]	to make sth. develop and grow strong again	*erneuern, umgestalten*
to subsidize ['sʌbsɪdaɪz]	if a government subsidizes a company, activity, etc., it pays parts of its costs	*subventionieren*
subsidy ['sʌbsədi]	money that is paid by a government or organization to make prices lower and reduce the cost of producing goods	*Subvention*
to tax sb.	to pay an amount of money to the government according to your income, property, etc.	*jdn./etwas besteuern*
tax system	the system of charging taxes	*Steuersystem*
upward mobility	the act of moving up through the social classes and becoming richer	*sozialer Aufstieg*
to be wealthy; wealth [welθ]	to have a lot of property, money, etc.; a large amount of money, etc. that sb. owns	*wohlhabend sein; Wohlstand*
	crises/war/poverty	
to accomplish a mission	to succeed in doing sth.	*eine Mission erfüllen*
combat	fighting, esp. during a war	*Kampf, Gefecht*
civil war	a war in which opposing groups of people from the same country fight each other to gain political control	*Bürgerkrieg*
crisis (crises) ['kraɪsɪs]	situation(s) in which problems must be dealt with quickly	*Krise (Krisen)*
to declare war on sb.	to start a war against someone	*jdm. den Krieg erklären*
the (Great) Depression	the world economic crisis during the 1930s	*Weltwirtschaftskrise*
to fall into poverty	to become poor	*verarmen, in Armut stürzen*
to invade; invasion of a country	to enter a country using military force in order to control it	*eindringen, überfallen; Überfall, Einmarsch in ein Land*
occupant	member of the occupying force	*Besatzer*
to occupy ['ɒkjupaɪ] **occupation of** [,ɒkju'peɪʃn]	to enter a place in a large group and keep control of it, especially by military force	*belagern, besetzen; Besatzung*
pre-military training	training that people get before joining the army	*militärische Vorbereitung, Training*
to recruit sb. [rɪ'kru:t]	to hire sb.	*jdn. rekrutieren/einstellen*
retaliation	an action against sb. who has done sth. bad to you	*Vergeltung*
social benefits	money provided by the government to people who are not able to work	*Sozialhilfe*
social ranking	related to the social classes people belong to	*soziale Rangordnung*
tense (*adj.*)**; tension**	feeling worried, uncomfortable and unable to relax; the feeling that exists when people or countries do not trust each other and may suddenly attack each other	*(an)gespannt; Spannung*
welfare (state)	a system in which the government provides money, medical care, etc. for people who are unemployed or not able to work	*Wohlfahrtsstaat*
to withdraw; withdrawal	to stop taking part in an activity; to move away an army from the area where they were fighting	*sich zurückziehen; Rückzug*

Africa – Between Exploitation and Expectation

Commuting in Africa: workers from Niger on their long way home from working in Libya. There are only two wells to fill their water cans for the 1,000-kilometer ride through the Sahara.

Tips on vocab

to commute from/to/between ■ commuter ■ to travel long distances ■ construction worker ■ guest worker ■ pick-up truck ■ crammed with people ■ to be/become overloaded with sb./sth. ■ loads of luggage ■ bundles of things ■ to wear a scarf/to cover one's head/face ■ people and goods jutting out of the truck ■ exhausting ■ to travel to/beyond the point of exhaustion ■ to hold on to sth. ■ sandy/unsurfaced track

"When the missionaries came to Africa they had the Bible and we had the land. They said, 'Let us pray.' We closed our eyes. When we opened them again, we had the Bible and they had the land."

Bishop Desmond Tutu (*1931, African spiritual leader)

"I've heard an African leader tell me that, 'I like doing business with the Chinese because they come, they discuss business, they sign and give you the cheque – without a lecture on democracy and human rights."

Kofi Annan (*1938, Ghanaian diplomat, 7th Secretary General of the UN, 1987 – 2006)

Exodus of elephants, Kenya, 2013

In the Amboseli region of East Africa – an extra-ordinary 2 million acre ecosystem in the shadow of Mount Kilimanjaro, straddling[1] Kenya and Tanzania – this elephant was just one of many elephants killed in the last few years by poachers[2]. [...]

Since 2008, there has been a massively increased demand for ivory and other animal parts from China and the Far East. As a result, there is a continent-wide apocalypse[3] of animals going on.

Ivory prices have soared[4] from $200 a pound in 2004 to more than $2,000 today. Some experts estimate that as much as 35,000 elephants a year are being slaughtered, 10 % of Africa's elephant population each year alone. [...]

Because as the illegal demand for ivory, rhino horn and other wildlife parts continues to grow, there will be many who cannot resist the easy profits to be made out of killing these irreplaceable creatures.

Africa is Africa because of the animals there. The elephants, lions, giraffes, cheetah[5], rhinos – they are all iconic creatures that exert a powerful, deep emotional and mythical hold over our imaginations. But we can no longer take their presence for granted. At the current rate of destruction, by the next generation, they will be gone. Imagine a world where very soon you and future generations are only able to see elephants and lions in the sad, drab[6] confines[7] of a zoo.

Big Life Foundation is working hard, and so far successfully, to staunch[8] the flow of blood, and preserve these extraordinary animals in the hopes of a better future for both them, and us.

www.biglife.org

START-UP ACTIVITIES

1. Look at the photo and pay attention to details. What do these details tell you about people's lives? Then, as a staff member of the NGO World Social Forum, conduct an interview with the workers on the truck about:

- their work
- their working conditions
- their payment
- their living conditions

Act out these interviews in class.

2. What do the two statements reveal about international business relations with Africa in the past and today? Discuss in class.

3. In discussions about Africa, politicians today usually talk about resources, economic and/or agricultural development or emergency aid. The Big Life Foundation focuses on preserving Africa's animals in order to provide a better future for people as well.
Discuss why preserving and protecting a country's flora and fauna is ethically, culturally and economically as important as protecting its people/citizens.
→ Focus on Language, Conversation and Discussion, p. 385

[1] **to straddle** to be on either side of sth. – [2] **poacher** *Wilderer* – [3] **apocalypse** [əˈpɒkəlɪps] – [4] **to soar** to rise quickly to a high level – [5] **cheetah** *der Gepard* – [6] **drab** boring – [7] **confines** borders – [8] **to staunch** to stop sth. happening

Manufacturing – Not Making It

AWARENESS

Africa is the world's second largest and second most populous continent; its Gross National Income, GNI) of $2.3 billion is about 3.1 % of the global GNI (= ca. $78.3 billion).

a) Team up with a partner and describe the bar chart below which compares the WTO (World Trade Organization) members' shares of merchandise trade by region.
b) Discuss possible reasons for these striking differences.
c) Collect ideas about what kind of products and services Africa – as a continent – manufactures and trades.

→ Focus on Skills, Analysis of Statistical Data, p. 380

A successful manufacturing sector requires many things that Africa lacks

[...] Manufacturing in Africa is only for the brave. In Nigeria it makes up about 10 % of GDP[1], according to official statistics, which may not be reliable. In South Africa, a far more developed economy, it accounts for 13 % of GDP, down from a fifth in 1990. In Thailand the equivalent figure is 28 %. Between 1970 and 2013, says the Brookings Institution, an American think-tank, Africa's share of global manufacturing output fell from 3 % to 2 %; as a share of sub-Saharan Africa's GDP, manufacturing has shrunk from almost 20 % to about half that. Almost the entire output is for domestic consumption, not export.

Even though labour is generally cheap, making stuff can be more expensive than in parts of Europe because of poor infrastructure, powerful trade unions (in South Africa) and pervasive[2] corruption. There is almost nothing like China's electronics factories or Bangladesh's textile sweatshops. Everything from cornflakes to kettles[3] is imported from Europe or Asia.

Africa boosters[4] say that the fall in commodity[5] prices is a dose of nasty but necessary medicine. The way they see it, falling currencies will drive up the cost of imports, and governments will have to open up to investment and reduce regulation and corruption in order to increase tax revenue[6]. Yet this scenario is far too rosy. South Africa and Nigeria are not entirely representative of the rest of Africa, but together they make up roughly half of sub-Saharan Africa's GDP and give some idea of the challenges the region faces.

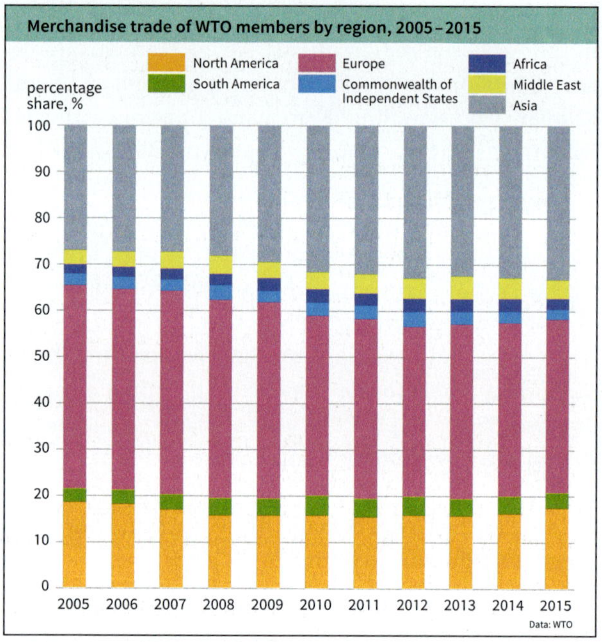

Powerless

The biggest immediate problem is power. [...] Most factories have to rely on diesel generators to keep going. A new tomato-processing[7] facility belonging to the Dangote Group, a huge Nigerian conglomerate[8] owned by Africa's richest man, has had to import two enormous generators which together produce about 2MW of electricity. "Every hour they use 400 litres of diesel," says Alhaji Keita, who manages the plant. "It's by far our biggest overhead[9]." Even the diesel is mostly imported: despite its oil wealth, Nigeria has very little refining[10] capacity.

[1] **GDP** *(abbr.)* Gross Domestic Product; the total value of goods and services produced by a country in a year – [2] **pervasive** present or noticeable – [3] **kettle** *Kessel* – [4] **booster** a person who gives their support to sb./sth., especially in politics – [5] **commodity** *Ware, Handelsartikel* – [6] **tax revenue** *Steuereinnahme* – [7] **to process** ['prəʊses] here: to prepare, change, or treat food or natural substances as a part of an industrial operation – [8] **conglomerate** *Großkonzern* – [9] **overhead** the regular and necessary costs, such as rent and heating, that are involved in operating a business – [10] **oil refining** *Erdölraffination*

World Bank figures show that the amount of power consumed per person in Africa has fallen in recent decades because generating capacity has not kept up with population growth. With 1.2 billion people, the continent has a sixth of the world's population but only 3 % of its generating capacity, which is heavily concentrated in just a few countries. In places like Zambia and Malawi, most of the existing capacity comes from hydroelectric plants[11] built in colonial times or shortly after independence, which often do not run in the dry season. South Africa has many crumbling[12] power stations from the 1960s that have not been upgraded or replaced, so people in its big cities suffer blackouts[13] and factories often come to a halt.

Poor roads are another problem. Suleiman Umar owns a factory in Kano that makes relief blankets[14] on ancient-looking looms[15]. But only ten of the 68 machines are currently working, and that is not bad for a textile business in Nigeria, he says. It costs him more to transport a container from coastal Lagos than it does to ship one all the way from China. Even in South Africa, where rail and road connections are generally good, the vast distances make it expensive to move anything across the country. [...]

But the main industry that thrives[16] thanks to Nigeria's trade barriers is corruption. In a Kano hotel, a gap-toothed[17] smuggler explains that his syndicate has spent a decade manoeuvring[18] fabric, rice, pasta and vegetable oil to huge warehouses in Kano via Benin and Niger. "The official process is tedious[19] and expensive. You have to deal with customs, immigration, security, and it takes so long," he says in the local Hausa language. "We organise the illegal route so the products come successfully." Up to 50 containers might cross the Jibia border post at once, he says, each yielding a profit[20] of up to 5 million naira ($15,000). [...]

South Africa's huge potential is being wasted by a toxic combination of power cuts and poor labour relations. At the Nissan factory, stickers plastered all over the machinery encourage workers to vote for "strong shop stewards[21] to confront the bosses." Last year a strike shut the plant down for two months. For historical reasons, managers in the car factories tend to be white and workers black. Disputes are politicised, confrontational and frequent. Relative to their productivity, South African industrial workers are some of the most expensive in the world. A cheap rand[22] should help, by lowering the cost of labour (although it may also raise inflation, which could induce more strikes). [...]

In the meantime, the best hope comes from locals, who know how the system works, and from products sold locally rather than across borders. At Wilson's Juice, a new factory at the edge of Lagos, lemonade is being bottled on an assembly line manned by 16 people. On the other side of the room workers chop up[23] pineapples. The business was started by Seun and Seyi Abolaji, two brothers who were raised and educated in America and returned to Nigeria, to the bemusement of their families. The margins[24] are good and the firm is expanding quickly. The only materials that have to be imported from outside Africa are for the bottles and the labels, so the shortage of foreign exchange has not hurt too much. "A lot of people are apprehensive[25], but we are super-excited. For people who source their own materials locally, now is a great time to grow," says Seyi.

http://www.economist.com/news/special-report/21696785-successful-manufacturing-sector-requires-many-things-africa-lacks-not-making-it, 16 April 2016 [19.05.2016]

COMPREHENSION

1. In a paired reading activity,
   a) **skim** the magazine article and get an overview of Africa's problems with manufacturing goods,
   b) exchange your first reading results with your partner,
   c) **scan** the text and find details about
   - Africa's potentials for manufacturing,
   - Africa's lacking performance with regard to using its resources efficiently.

[11] **hydroelectric plant** ['haɪdrəʊɪ'lektrɪk] *das Wasserkraftwerk* – [12] **to crumble** *zerfallen* – [13] **blackout** *Stromausfall* – [14] **relief blanket** *Decke für Rettungshilfe, Katastrophen, usw.* – [15] **loom** *Webstuhl* – [16] **to thrive** to grow, develop or be successful – [17] **gap-toothed** *mit Zahnlücken* – [18] **to manoeuvre** [mə'nu:və(r)] to turn and direct an object – [19] **tedious** in a way that takes too long – [20] **to yield a profit** to make profit – [21] **shop steward** a worker elected by workers in a factory or business to represent them in discussions with the management, usually a member of a trade union – [22] **rand** the standard unit of money used in South Africa – [23] **to chop up** *kleinhacken* – [24] **margin** profit – [25] **apprehensive** feeling worried about something that you are going to do or that is going to happen

Copy the grid into your notebook and complete it.

potentials	lacking performance
• resources • cheap labour • …	• low output • … • …

2. Summarize the text in about 200 words, pointing out briefly the general problems African countries have to deals with which hinder economic growth and development.
→ Focus on Skills, Writing a Summary, p. 40

ANALYSIS

3. Team up with a partner and take a close look at the map on p. 231 depicting sub-Saharan Africa's Gross Domestic Product (GDP) and the development of its exports.

Step 1: Present the information given in the map to each other.

Step 2: Explain the increase and decrease of exports and relate it to the explanations given in the text.
→ Focus on Skills, Analysis of Statistical Data, p. 379

4. Identify the type of text* and analyse its features and their function. Particularly, focus on:
- linguistic devices (adjectives, positive/negative emotive words, etc.)
- stylistic devices (metaphors, adjectives, anaphora, etc.)
- rhetorical devices (appeals, personal remarks, comparisons, etc.)

Examples:
- (l. 3) Manufacturing in Africa is only for the brave. → personal remark, evaluation, statement
- (ll. 7 ff.) … down from … fell … has shrunk … → negative emotive words

→ Focus on Skills, Analysis of a Non-Fictional Text, p. 377
→ Focus on Facts, Basic Types of Non-Fictional Texts, p. 368

ACTIVITIES

5. "In the meantime, the best hope comes from locals, who know how the system works, and from products sold locally rather than across borders." (ll. 93 ff.)

"For people who source their own materials locally, now is a great time to grow." (ll. 107 f.)

Discuss these statements in class and assess whether local production and trade is the solution to Africa's economic problems.
Is the old slogan "Think globally, act locally" still valid in an era of increasing globalisation?
Which advantages/benefits and disadvantages/risks are connected with it?
→ Focus on Language, Conversation and Discussion, p. 385

GRAMMAR / LANGUAGE

6. The author has employed many technical terms which may not be understandable for everybody. Turn the words and phrases on the following page into everyday language using your own words as often as possible.
Tips: You may use a dictionary for help, but do not simply copy the explanations given there.
Example: manufacturing → the industrial production of large quantities of goods, i. e. products made in factories

• manufacturing • a developed country • a developing country • output • domestic consumption • infrastructure • currency • investment • facility • capacity • syndicate • inflation • assembly line • start-up • to source materials

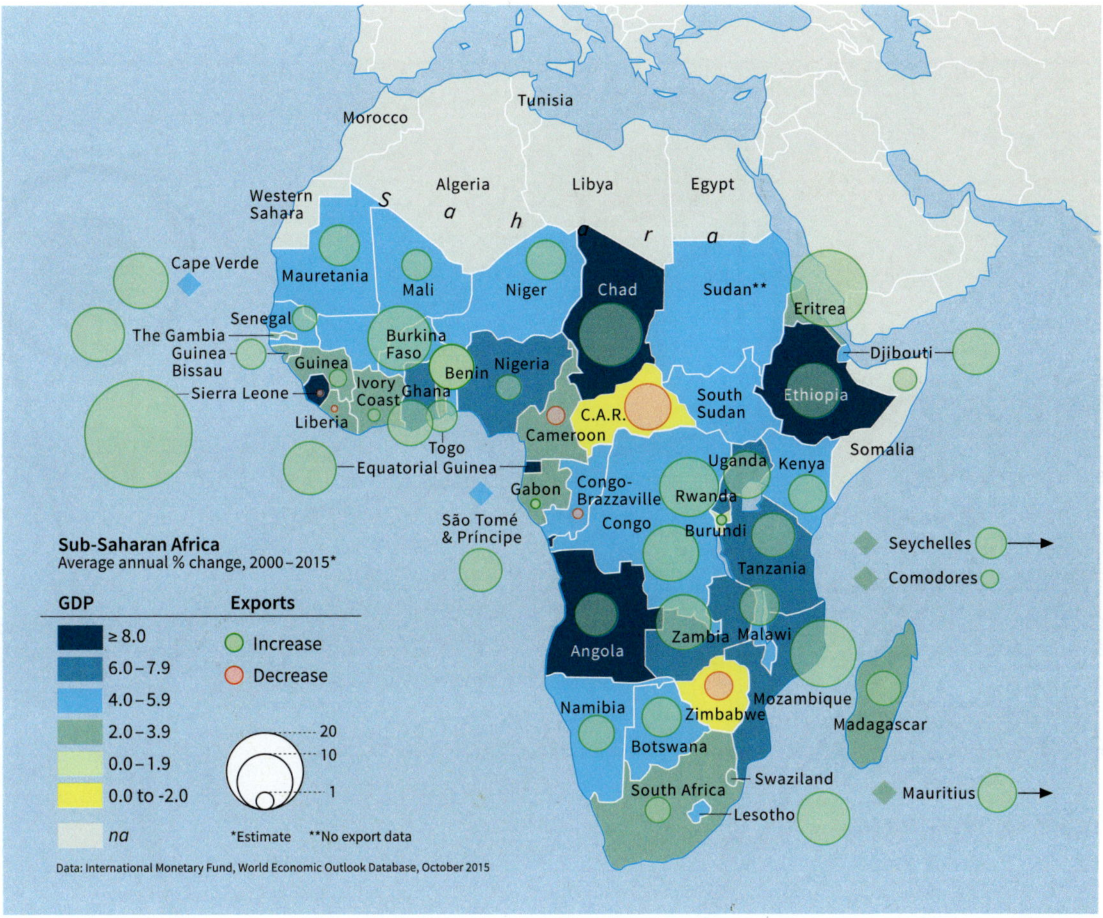

Baffour Ankomah

Solving the Great Conundrum – How Africa Can Own Its Natural Resources

AWARENESS

Step 1: In a group puzzle activity, mediate what is written about the three major gear wheels *(Getrieberäder)* of the looting machinery on the following page.

→ Focus on Skills, Mediation, p. 384

Step 2: Point out what types of natural and human resources are looted in Africa – and who/which country/region benefits from it.

Tips on vocab

from left to right: raw materials ■ university/college graduate ■ skilled worker ■ highly-qualified personnel ■ ore ■ art ■ development/humanitarian aid ■ IMF (International Monetary Fund) ■ pseudo democracy ■ structural adjustment ■ people fleeing poverty ■ debt ■ remittance/transferring money to one's home country ■ profiteer ■ agricultural area ■ crude oil ■ direct investments ■ industrial/manufactured goods/products ■ investment

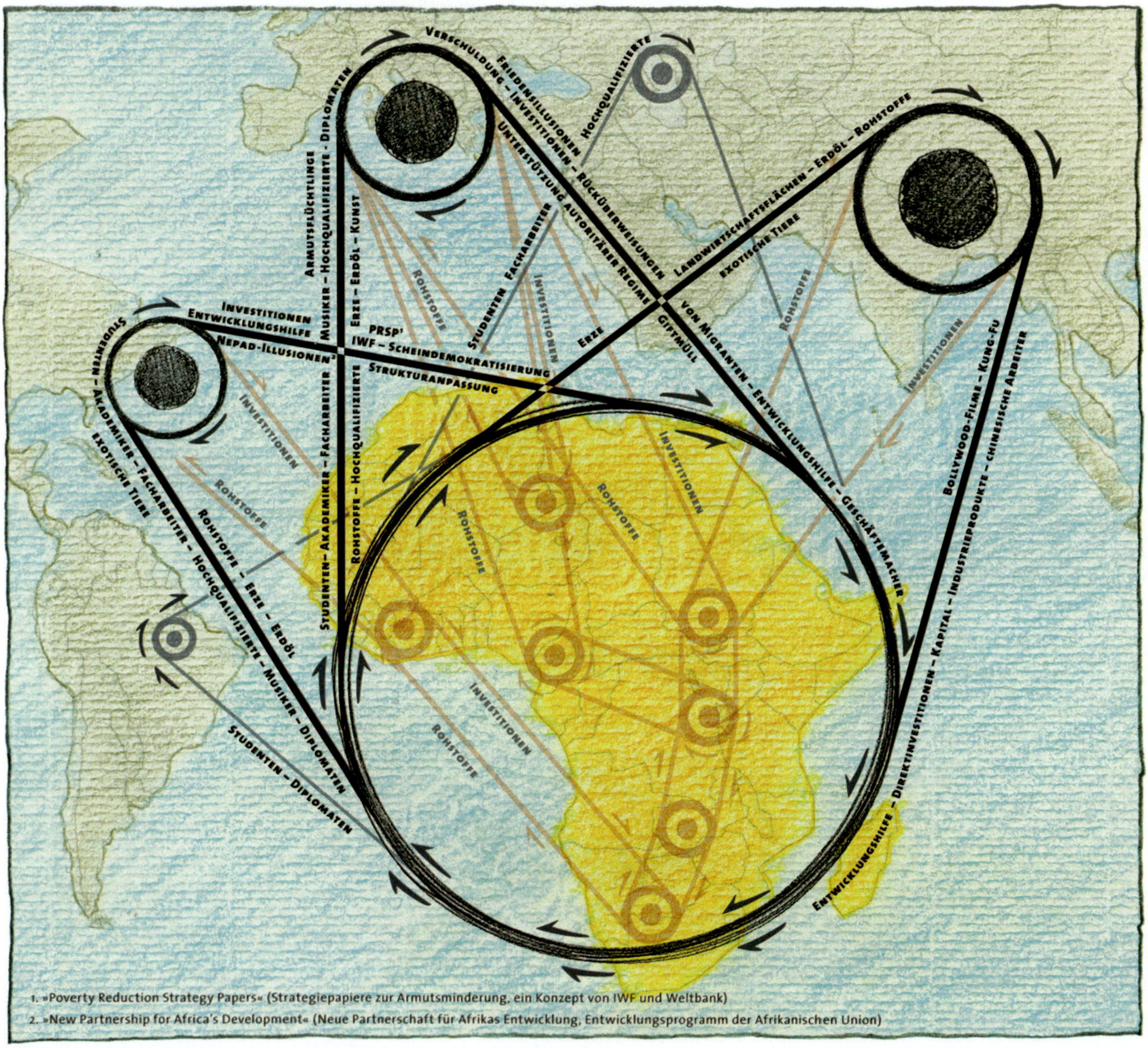

The Looting Machinery

Media and Modern Life: Making Dreams Come True

A Project on Africa

AWARENESS

Now that you have gained an overview of Africa's history/colonial past and its economic situation in general, this project focuses on two African states in particular: **Nigeria** and **Kenya**.

Webcode NG-40183-028

Step 1: Divide the class into two to four groups, with one or two groups doing research on either Kenya or Nigeria and using the links provided on the webcode.

Step 2: In your groups, compile mind maps using the example below and add further information/details.

Step 3: Display, explain and discuss your mind maps in class and evaluate your results.
→ Focus on Language, Conversation and Discussion, p. 385

Example:

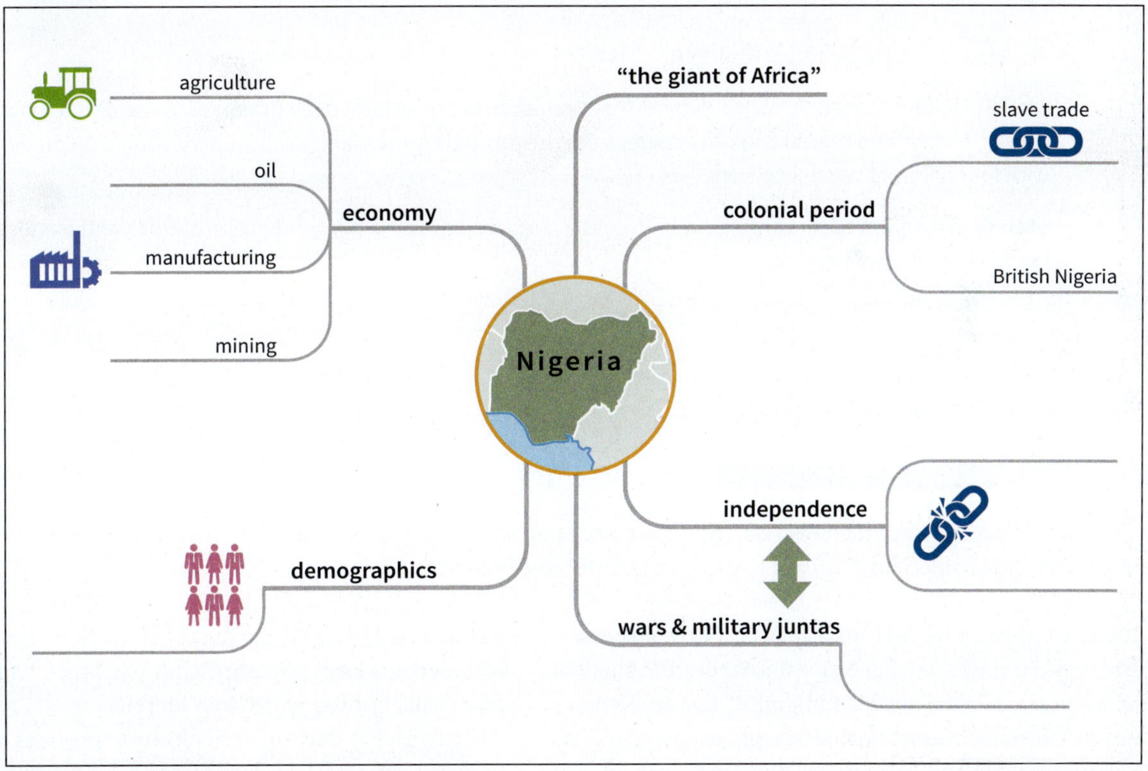

ACTIVITIES

This project requires you to work independently as well as together with your group. It is based on the idea of the division of labour.

The **different materials** on the following pages will provide you with information on
- different African countries (**Nigeria** and **Kenya**),
- different business concepts of modern African countries,
- different perspectives on Africa (British, German, American).

You can
a) improve your **viewing skills** and **watch the videos** provided on the webcode (p. 240),
or
b) improve your **reading skills** and read the **texts** (pp. 238 ff.)
or
c) improve your **mediation skills** and work with the German article (pp. 245 f.)

Now, here are a work plan and some tips:

Step 1: Form four expert groups, with each group focusing on one of the four materials.

Step 2: Work with the **material of your choice** and do the respective assignments.

Step 3: If necessary, do **further research** on the Internet to clarify questions and/or complete your notes. Each member of your group is the expert on his/her topic/material and should be prepared to present and explain it to the others.

Step 4: Prepare presentations about your chosen topic.

Tip: Compile posters and handouts for your classmates that visualize and illustrate your presentation.
→ Focus on Skills, Presentations, p. 391
→ Focus on Skills, Writing a Handout, p. 397

Step 5: Finally, after all the work is done, the groups remix and inform each other about their topics and results. Each group should contain experts from the previous groups and each student should be provided with four different handouts in the end.

Step 6: In a final step, the entire class discusses and evaluates the different presentations and clarifies further questions if necessary.

1 Coming up Roses

AWARENESS

In a round robin activity, first reflect on, then state what you associate with Mother's Day or Valentine's Day. What kind of gifts or "little somethings" do you like to give to or receive from others?

Kenya's flower-export business is a rare success

Around the edges of Lake Naivasha, under the shadow of a dormant[1] volcano, Mt Longonot, one of Kenya's most successful export businesses of recent years has become established. All around the lake, and off dirt roads that lead from it, are acres and acres of plastic tenting in which flowers of all sorts, but especially roses, are grown for export. At the biggest operators, thousands of workers go in each day to water, feed, pick and prepare the crop[2]. On average, 360 tonnes of flowers are flown out of Nairobi airport every day, mostly to Europe but also to Asia and the Middle East. Kenya is the world's third-largest producer of cut flowers; the crop is its second-largest export, after tea. Since 1988 the industry has grown more than tenfold[3].

Africa's global share of agricultural exports, as of manufactured exports, has declined in the decades since independence, from over 8% in the 1970s to just 2% in 2009. Nigeria used to be the world's biggest producer of palm oil; Ghana of cocoa; and Kenya and Ethiopia of coffee. All have now been overtaken by other regions. Yet the plastic-roofed greenhouses of Kenya's flower farms are the closest thing the country has to an Asian-style high-tech manufacturing cluster[4].

[1] **dormant** not active – [2] **crop** *Ernte* – [3] **tenfold** ten times as big or as much – [4] **cluster** a group of similar things that are close together

Growing flowers and vegetables is a competitive business, says Mark Low, the boss of Groove Flowers, one of the smaller outfits around Lake Naivasha. "The margins[5] are getting smaller and smaller." Colombia, Ecuador and Ethiopia are all chasing the same customers. But many of Kenya's growers are hoping to do better by running a highly sophisticated operation. Mr Low, an earthy white Kenyan, mostly grows roses, bouvardia[6] and delphiniums[7]. He does not sell to supermarket suppliers because the prices they pay do not give him a decent margin. Instead, he goes to a lot of trade fairs to find out what Russian oligarchs will order for their daughters' weddings.

Fashions keep changing, so Mr Low experiments a great deal. Walking through a greenhouse full of spray roses[8], with several flowers growing on one stem, he explains that these are much harder to grow than the single-flower variety but can fetch higher prices from florists. Sadly, so far they have not done as well as he had hoped because the drop in the rouble[9] is making for less lavish[10] wedding budgets. A lot of other factors also have to be taken into account. For example, if a flower is particularly heavy, it may not be worth growing even if it fetches good prices, because air freight is very expensive. Fragile flowers are no good either, because they will get shaken up on his rutted[11] dirt roads.

Flower farming, then, is a bit like fast-fashion manufacturing. To thrive[12], it needs an educated workforce; effective, but not onerous[13], regulation; good access; a decent airport nearby; and plenty of electricity. Indeed, after air freight and labour, power is the main cost: flowers need plenty of light and carefully controlled air and water supplies. The industry has settled around Naivasha because the area's volcanic terrain is home to several geothermal power stations, the lake provides water and the airport is not far away. Other parts of Kenya are not so well provided for.

Africa's agricultural productivity has improved immensely over the past decade. Between 2000 and 2013, output of cereals grew by 3.3 % a year, faster than in any other region. But turning farming into a thriving export business and a big employer providing well-paid jobs is harder. In Kenya, flowers may have bloomed, but production of coffee, a more traditional export, has collapsed, falling from almost 100,000 tonnes a year in 2000 to below 40,000 in 2013. Many coffee farms have succumbed[14] to foreign competition or been swallowed up by housing development[15]. The success of Kenya's flower farms will not easily be replicated[16] by other crops.

http://www.economist.com/news/special-report/21696791-kenyas-flower-export-business-rare-success-coming-up-roses, 16 April 2016 [19.05.2016]

COMPREHENSION

1. Present the importance of flower production and export to Kenya's economy.
2. Point out Mr Mow's business concept and experiments.
3. State what makes Kenya in general and the Naivasha region in particular perfect for flower farming.

ANALYSIS

4. Examine the author's choice of words and explain how it supports the message of the article.
   → Focus on Skills, Analysis of a Non-Fictional Text, p. 377
5. First, describe and explain the statistical data given in the graphics on the following page. In a second step, relate the data compiled by Kenya's Flower Council to the magazine article. Which similarities and differences can you detect?
   → Focus on Skills, Analysis of Statistical Data, p. 380

[5] **margin** the profit made on a product or service – [6] **bouvardia** *Bouvardie (eine Schnittblume)* – [7] **delphinum** *Rittersporn* – [8] **spray rose** *Rose mit verzweigten Blüten* – [9] **rouble** ['ru:bəl] *Rubel; russische Währung* – [10] **lavish** large, expensive or impressive – [11] **rutted** *ausgefahren, uneben* – [12] **to thrive** to grow, develop or be successful – [13] **onerous** difficult to do or needing a lot of effort – [14] **to succumb to sth.** to not be able to fight an attack, an illness, a temptation, etc. – [15] **housing development** *Wohnsiedlung* – [16] **to replicate** to make or do sth. again in exactly the same way

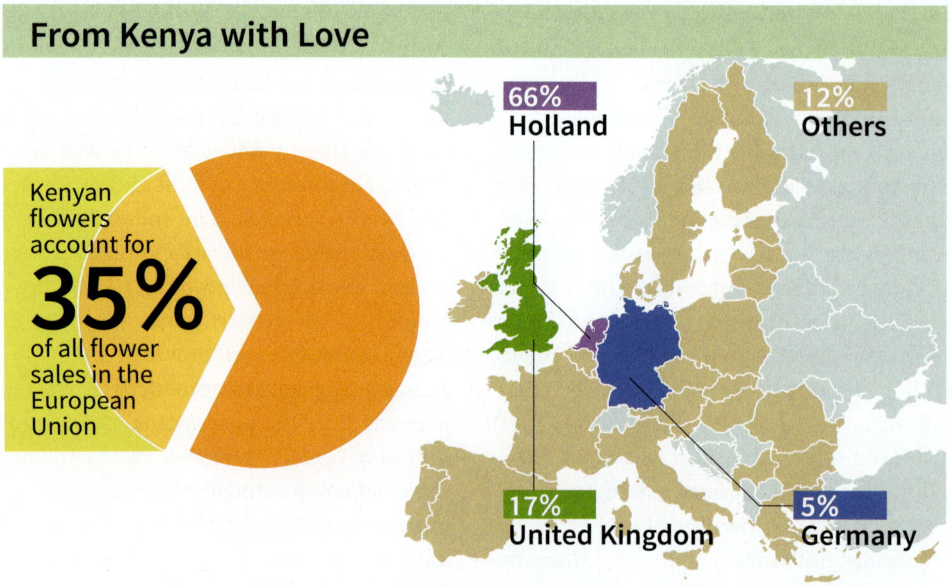

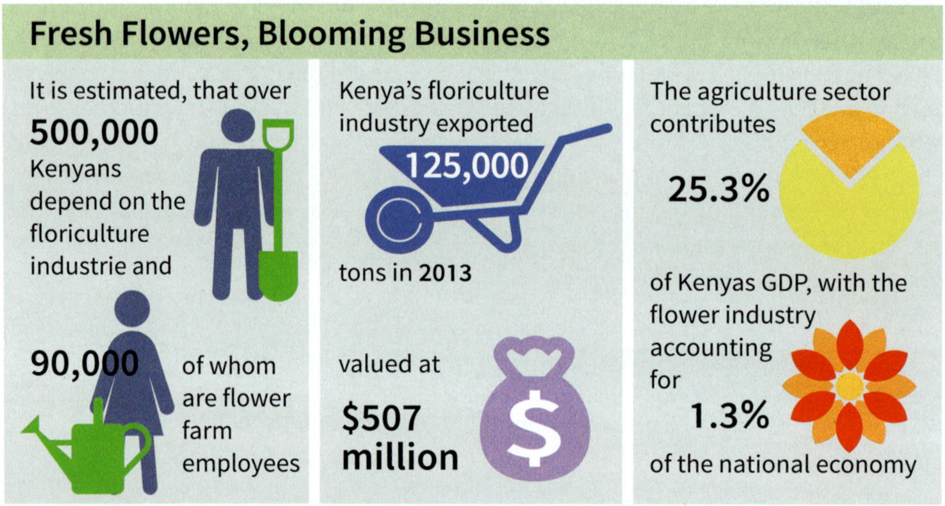

Data: Kenya Flower Council/Kenya National Bureau of Statistics

2 Felicity Lawrence: The True Cost of Mother's Day Flowers

Ramadhan Khamis: Dangerous Flowers: The Impact of the Cut Flower Industry in Kenya

AWARENESS

In a round robin activity, reflect on the titles of the documentaries: What might the "true cost" of the mass production of flowers be and why are they "dangerous"?

COMPREHENSION

Webcode SNG-40183-028 @ 1. Use the links provided on the webcode and **watch** the videos/documentaries **a first time**. Try to answer the following questions:

The True Cost of Mother's Day Flowers

- What are the major concerns about
  a) the environmental impact and
  b) the working conditions
  in the horticultural industry around Lake Naivasha?
- What are the benefits of Kenya's horticultural industries?
- Why is the water quality and condition of Lake Naivasha of vital importance to
  - the population,
  - the horticultural industry,
  - the flora and fauna?
- What measures has Flamingo Farm taken to avoid conflicts regarding the farm's water use?
- How does Enock Kiminta, a Masai pastoralist leader, view the situation/condition of Lake Naivasha?
- What is Enock Kiminta's opinion about the flower farms around the lake?
- What is Flamingo Farm's personnel policy?
- What has Flamingo Farm done in order to meet Fair Trade standards?
- What is the overall impact of the horticultural industry on the Naivasha region?
- What is the economic impact of Kenya's flower industry?
  - How much money of the generated revenue *(Gewinn)* actually stays in the community?
  - What is the multinational companies' monetary policy?
- What is Jane Ngige's (CEO of Kenya Flower Council) view of the flower business and its profits?
- What does Attiya Wari (lecturer in tax laws, University of Nairobi) criticize about the multinational flower companies?

Dangerous Flowers: The Impact of the Cut Flower Industry in Kenya

- What makes flowers important for different sectors?
- What is the business between the Netherlands and Kenya and how does it work?
- What is the impact of the flower industry on the financial situation and workers' health?
- Why is the flower industry so important to Kenyan women?
- What is a working day like?
- What problems incite workers/employees to go on strike?
- How do the local authorities react to demonstrations and unionists?
- What is the environmental impact of the horticultural industry?
- How do the Masai view the situation?
- What should European consumers learn about flower production in Kenya?

2. In a **second viewing**, complete your notes.

ANALYSIS

3. The first video ("The True Cost of Mother's Day Flower") was commissioned by the British quality newspaper *The Guardian* in a series of so-called "investigative documentaries".
   Watch the video again and find examples of the the documentary's investigative characteristics/qualities.
   → Focus on Skills, The Press, p. 370
   → Focus on Skills, Analysis of a Film Scene, p. 375

3 Rana Foroohar: Hooray for Nollywood

AWARENESS

Step 1: In a round robin activity, reflect on and state what you associate with the word "Hollywood".

Step 2: In a nod to that legendary name and place, Nigeria's film industry is called Nollywood. Against the background of your previous research results on Nigeria (Awareness task, p. 237), what do you expect this film industry to be like?

Nigeria's film industry struggles against red tape[1] and corruption, but like the country itself, it finds a way to grow

You have to go to Alaba market in the chaotic metropolis of Lagos. It's where the country's film industry, Nollywood, was born over two decades ago – not that most of its stars would set foot there today. You can't blame them. Getting to West Africa's largest consumer-electronics market requires a three-hour drive from Victoria Island, where many stars and producers live, to the mainland, in standstill traffic on a potholed[2] highway that varies between pavement and dirt. Once at the perimeter[3], it's another two hours' walk into the DVD section, so visitors in a hurry must hitch[4] life-threatening rides with boys on motorbikes, speeding along the narrow market streets through a sea of bodies selling anything and everything: extension cords[5], plantain chips[6], porn, cassava[7], washing machines – and black-market DVDs. Everyone is looking for an angle[8]. A woman hawks[9] used plastic bags to another woman who fills them with grain and resells them. Two young men stand guard over a 2-m-long board thrown over an open ditch and force people to pay a toll to cross their makeshift bridge.

Once inside, different layers of the Nollywood economy unfold, layers that mirror the complexity, corruption and entrepreneurial energy of Nigeria as a whole. There's a young man, one of many, who has traveled 80 minutes from his part of the city to buy locally made movies, sold on DVDs for 50 to 85 naira (about 30¢ to 50¢). He will sell them in a stall at home for 100 naira (about 60¢). But what's striking is that the pirated versions of foreign films, like 12 Years a Slave, sell for just 35 naira (20¢). That's considerably less than the local stuff, which is a tawdry[10] mix of action, romance, gospel, soft-core porn and horror, mixed in with the occasional tribal drama. Distributors, many of whom are local thugs[11] or the filmmakers themselves, take the movies, make copies of them (legitimate and otherwise) and sell them from warehouses behind the market stalls to buyers both big and small from all over – Ghana, Kenya, the Caribbean, the U.K., the U.S., everywhere.

To call Alaba a sharp-elbowed place is an understatement. (A few years ago, armed distributors chased out military police and filmmakers who'd come to complain about pirating.) But it's a place where an ambitious person can rise quickly – like 22-year-old Tochukwu James, who sits wrapping DVDs in cellophane in a market stall[12]. James had no money for college, so after secondary school, he took a series of odd jobs before ending up here, in Alaba. "I'm going to save my money, and one day I'll open my own stall and eventually make films like this," he says, pointing to the DVD he is wrapping, which features a low-budget drama about a family-inheritance squabble[13]. "You have to be tough here. But I'm going to make it. I'm going to be a Nollywood boss."

The story of Nollywood is the story of the Nigerian economy – and even of Africa itself. It's about sheer[14] entrepreneurial will overcoming an array[15] of obstacles[16], from inept[17] governance to corruption and crime, to the lack of basics like power, roads and even proper water and sewage. After years of treating the continent as a place of unending misery, the Western press has been touting[18] the optimistic story about Africa, with reason – six of the world's top 10 fastest-growing economies are here, and Nigeria is first among them. It's got just over 7% growth, huge oil and mineral resources, and a GDP that recently jumped by 89% thanks to a

[1] **red tape** bureaucracy – [2] **pothole** *Schlagloch* – [3] **perimeter** *Grenze* – [4] **to hitch a ride** *(infml.)* to get a free ride on sb. else's vehicle – [5] **extension cords** *Verlängerungskabel* – [6] **plantain chips** *Chips aus Kochbananen* – [7] **cassava** *Maniokmehl* – [8] **angle** here: a new way to make money – [9] **to hawk** to sell goods informally in public places – [10] **tawdry** *billig und von minderer Qualität* – [11] **thug** *(infml.) Schurke* – [12] **stall** *Marktstand* – [13] **squabble** an argument about sth. unimportant – [14] **sheer** pure; used to describe a great size, degree or amount of sth. – [15] **array** *Ansammlung* – [16] **obstacle** *Hürde, Hindernis* – [17] **inept** not skilled or effective – [18] **to tout** [taʊt] *etw. aufdringlich anpreisen*

recalculation by Nigerian authorities to better include sectors like telecom and entertainment, the latter dominated by Nollywood. The larger size of these areas reflects huge consumer-spending potential and a growing middle class.

It also has systemic corruption at every level. Forty-six percent of Nigeria's 173.6 million people live in poverty, 18 % of children are not in education, and life expectancy is just 52 years – the 11th lowest in the world. Then there is a total lack of security, as tragically evidenced by the number of fatal terrorist attacks doubling from June 2013 to June 2014 compared with the same period last year, and the kidnapping by Islamist terrorist group Boko Haram of over 200 girls. (Some of those girls are still being held, months after their capture, in a remote bush area in the north of the country, with almost no real effort on the part of the Nigerian government to rescue them.)

Nollywood films don't shy away from documenting many of the daily struggles of Nigerians – the violence, the poverty and the social disruption[19] as Africa urbanizes. But the movies also showcase their dreams – dreams that have a grounding in reality. Post–GDP "rebasing" (which means updating the way GDP is measured), filmed entertainment now represents 1.4 % of the economy, over $7 billion, which is a conservative estimate, given that it doesn't include the vast black market. That's huge for an emerging economy – all of America's creative industries put together represent just over 3 % of GDP. And it's likely to grow faster now, as a crop of returning expat[20] entrepreneurs prepares to transform the industry by taking it digital. [...]

But the high-volume, low-budget, straight-to-video industry that we think of as Nollywood began in another traditionally Nigerian way – through trade. Sometime in the 1980s, a group of Alaba market traders went to Europe to see what discarded[21] goods they could pick up and hawk back home. They came back with a bunch of discarded VHS tapes, which they soon figured out would sell for more if they put a bit of cheap local content on them. Since Nigeria had almost no stand-alone cinemas (even today, there are only 15 in a country of 173.6 million people) or mass-market content geared[22] at locals, the tapes quickly became gold. An industry was born.

Alaba market in Lagos is Nigeria's biggest hub for buying and selling movies.

It's easy to make fun of Nollywood movies, with titles like Occult Sacrifice and Educated Housemaids, which, of course, is the much awaited sequel to Authentic Housemaids. But there's a reason the industry has, until now, remained low end – it literally lacks power. Spotty electricity service is the biggest impediment[23] to doing business in Nigeria. It affects everyone – from Nigerian industrial magnate and Africa's richest man Aliko Dangote, who finally spent $1.2 billion to build his own grid system[24] to overcome repeated blackouts, to small filmmakers and producers of Nollywood. The government and private companies control a grid, which runs haphazardly[25] at best – sometimes because of poor infrastructure, other times because power gets diverted to choice areas. Either way, it means people have to buy generators and diesel to keep the lights on reliably. Most Nigerians spend around 40 % of their take-home pay creating their own power, while some supply their own water and repair their own roads. [...]

Despite the problems, the Nigerian film industry is nothing if not aspirational[26]. Nigerians have a phrase for keeping up with the Joneses[27]: "I better pass my neighbor." The term embodies the spirit of hustle[28], the striving energy that infuses the entire country and Lagos, its largest city, in particular. On Victoria Island, a growing ecosystem of stars, minders and hangers-on gather nightly at clubs, preening[29] for the paparazzi. At a recent Nollywood party in the Lekki district of Lagos, sponsored by MTV and Absolut Vodka, starlets arrive in their

[19] **disruption** *Unruhe* – [20] **expat** *(abbr.)* expatriate; immigrant – [21] **to discard** *wegwerfen* – [22] **gear at sb.** to be suitable for a particular group of people – [23] **impediment** *Hindernis* – [24] **grid system** *Rastersystem* – [25] **haphazard** [ˌhæpˈhæzəd] not having an obvious order or plan – [26] **aspirational** ambitious – [27] **keeping up with the Joneses** wanting to be as good as sb. else – [28] **hustle** energetic action – [29] **to preen** *sich herausputzen*

international uniform – platform heels, false eyelashes, skintight dresses and knockoff[30] designer handbags.

Lekki is an appropriate location for a Nollywood soirée[31], as it is in many ways the New Jersey of Lagos – a place for strivers. Indeed, there's even a hit Nollywood series called Lekki Wives, a takeoff on the Desperate Housewives theme. [...]

Indeed, there are now a spate[32] of Nigerian expats who have returned home with the aim of professionalizing, internationalizing and cashing in on the burgeoning[33] business of Nollywood. Chief among them is Jason Njoku, a British-Nigerian expat who has become the first in the industry to garner major Western venture-capital funding. His startup, iROKOtv, has become the largest digital platform for on-demand Nollywood content. Always entrepreneurial, Njoku had started a print-publishing venture[34] during his time as a student at the University of Manchester in England – just in time to see the world go online. In 2009 he was broke and had moved back to London to live with his mother, when he noticed a shift in her video-consumption patterns. "She'd always watched British soaps, like Coronation Street or EastEnders," he says. "But suddenly, she was watching these Nigerian videos all day." Around the same time, a Nigerian musical act sold out a major stadium in Britain. Njoku sensed an opportunity. He jumped on a plane, headed to Alaba and picked up hundreds of videos. "I paid about 200 naira for each, and the distributors thought they'd stolen from me. I thought it was gold."

While he could do a brisk[35] business in DVDs, Njoku realized that the future lay in digital content. He persuaded YouTube to give him a partnership, which allowed for 50 % revenue[36] sharing. The day after, he moved back to Lagos. Within six months, he had 1.3 million users and was making $50,000 a week in revenue. Soon after, he raised funding from the New York City–based hedge fund Tiger Global to build a worldwide video-on-demand platform, iROKOtv, which now has $5 million a year in revenue. [...] "We have more people watching in London than in Nigeria, which tells me that all of our growth is ahead of us," says Njoku. "It will take a long time, but as more consumers come online, it will force the system to change."

http://time.com/3153912/hooray-for-nollywood
Time, 1 September 2014, pp. 23 ff.

COMPREHENSION

1. Subdivide the text into thematic units and find an appropriate headline for each.
2. Describe Alaba market and how people do business there.
3. Present the genesis of Nollywood.
4. Point out Jason Njoku's success story.
5. What are Nollywood's biggest problems?

ANALYSIS

6. Try to identify the author's stance on the matter by examining
   - the structure of the article (e. g. the line of argument),
   - her references and examples,
   - her choice of words in connection with Nigeria's thriving film industry.

   → Focus on Skills, Analysis of a Non-Fictional Text, p. 377

7. The author remarks that the Nigerian film industry is trying to "keep [...] up with the Joneses". Explain that phrase in relation to the information in the article about Victoria Island and its inhabitants.

[30] **knockoff** *(infml.)* a cheaper copy of an expensive and popular product – [31] **soirée** an evening party – [32] **a spate** *Häufung* – [33] **burgeoning** [ˈbɜːdʒənɪŋ] developing quickly – [34] **venture** *Unternehmen* – [35] **brisk** quick, energetic, active – [36] **revenue** profit

4 Marc Goergen: Das neue Gesicht Afrikas

AWARENESS

Take a look at the photo below. What impression is revealed about "Africa's new face"? State your views in a round robin activity.

Models on the way to a fashion show in Cape Town, South Africa

Joan Okorodudu ist 56 und trägt ein schrill[1] gemustertes[2] Kleid, dazu Flipflops, beides Stücke aus ihrer eigenen Kollektion[3]. […]
Sie steht für all das, was wohl nur wenige mit Afrika verbinden: einen erstaunlichen Aufbruch[4] in Sachen Mode.
Viele Jahrzehnte lang hatte der Kontinent in der Branche die Rolle des Statisten[5] inne. Stammestrachten[6] endeten als billige Ethnomuster, in den Savannen wurde im „Safari"-Look fotografiert. Seit ein paar Jahren beginnen Afrikaner, sich ihren Platz in den Schaufenstern[7] und den Schauen[8] zu erkämpfen.
Noch sind die Umsatzzahlen[9] bescheiden[10]. Noch sind ihre Kleider in Europa nur schwer zu bekommen. Die Szene gleicht einem rebellischen Heranwachsenden: voll kreativer Ideen, aber auch chaotisch und improvisiert. Manchmal beginnen Modenschauen zwei Tage später als geplant, weil es gerade keinen Strom gibt. Manchmal, wie unlängst in Lagos, werden Schauen zwei Wochen vor Beginn einfach abgesagt.
Der Boom der Branche wurzelt im Aufbruch Afrikas. Die Wirtschaft des Kontinents wächst rasant[11] – und das nicht mehr nur aufgrund von Öl, Kupfer oder Zinn[12]. Nairobi hat sich als Zentrum für App-Entwicklungen etabliert, ein „Silicon Savannah". In Nigeria verzeichnet die dortige Variante des Online-Händlers Amazon, „Jumia" genannt, erstaunliche Wachstumsraten. Der so lange abgeschriebene[13] Kontinent Afrika ist dabei, eine Mittelklasse hervorzubringen[14]. Und die will auch: schick und schön sein. […]
Es gibt immer mehr Blogger, immer mehr Models, und bei immer mehr von alldem ist dabei: Joan Okorodudu. […] Nach dem Auslandsstudium in Boston vertrieb sie in einem Laden in Delaware Stoffe aus Nigeria. Richtig los ging's 2007, da besaß sie eine kleine Baufirma[15] in Lagos. „Ich wollte die Mode bei uns voranbringen", sagt sie. Das Vehikel[16] dazu: „Nigeria's Next Supermodel". Okorodudu suchte sich Sponsoren, organisierte Castings und quartierte die besten Mädchen in einem Ferienort[17] bei Lagos ein. Ihr besonderes Prinzip des Model-Camps hat sie bis heute beibehalten: „Wir müssen den Mädchen beibringen, in der Model-Welt zu überleben." Das bedeutet für Okorodudu: um sechs Uhr aufstehen, dann beten, putzen, abwaschen, joggen. Erst

[1] flamboyant – [2] patterned – [3] collection – [4] awakening – [5] extra – [6] ethnic clothing – [7] display window – [8] fashion show – [9] revenue – [10] small – [11] rapidly – [12] tin – [13] to depreciate – [14] to produce, to yield – [15] construction business – [16] vehicle – [17] holiday resort

am Ende werden die Mädchen auf einer Yacht durch die Lagune[18] von Lagos geschippert. Der Drill macht Quote[19]. Mittlerweile ist die nigerianische Model-Show sogar in England zu sehen. [...]

Lagos ist ein Moloch. Niemand weiß, wie viele Menschen hier wirklich leben, Vielleicht acht Millionen, vielleicht aber auch 15 oder 20. Das Klima in der Lagunenstadt[20] gleicht einer Sauna mit stinkendem Abwasseraufguss[21]. [...]

Menschen, Trubel, Hitze: All das ist Okorodudus Welt. Sie redet hier laut und schnell und geschäftsmäßig. Sagt Sätze wie: „Mode ist kein Selbstzweck[22], sondern ein Geschäft, das unser Land voranbringen kann." [...] Denn Lagos, bekannt eher für Slums und Crime, ist verrückt nach Mode. Für Frauen, aber auch für Männer, gilt: Ein möglichst schrilles Outfit dient dazu, sich von der Masse abzusetzen. Selbst wer sich keine Edelmarken[23] leisten kann[24], wird alles dransetzen, per Handarbeit[25] und Accessoire[26] aus einem einfachen Kleid oder Anzug etwas zu machen. [...]

In diesem November [2013] organisiert Okorodudu ihre erste eigene Modewoche. Sie hat die westafrikanische Wirtschaftsgemeinschaft „Ecowas" überzeugt, dass Mode die große Chance der Region sein kann. Mehrere Dutzend Designer und Investoren kommen dazu in Nigerias Wirtschaftszentrum Lagos zusammen. Dann beginnt Ende des Jahres das Finale der neuen Staffel[27] von „Nigeria's Next Supermodel", mittlerweile in siebter Auflage[28]. „Warum sollte nicht eines Tages Nigeria für Mode stehen so wie Deutschland für Autos?", sagt Okorodudu.

Stern, 21.11.2013, pp. 98 ff.

COMPREHENSION

1. Identify the key terms and phrases in the magazine article and organize them in topical order.

2. Following the topical order of the key terms/phrases, mediate the relevant information given in the text into English.
In doing so, consider these aspects:
- Nigeria's fashion industry in the past
- obstacles the industry has to cope with
- Africa's economic rise/emergence
- Joan Okorodudu's business concept
- Lagos' demand for fashion

→ Focus on Skills, Mediation, p. 384

ANALYSIS

Webcode SNG-40183-028 @

3. Step 1: Access the links provided on the webcode and examine the information given about
- the evolution of the Kenyan fashion industry,
- the state of Kenya's local fashion industry,
- challenges and opportunities Africa's fashion industry faces.

Step 2: Relate the information given in the online articles to the German text and add relevant further information to your presentation.

[18] lagoon – [19] to reach a high quota – [20] lagoon city – [21] waste water infusion – [22] an end in itself – [23] premuim labels – [24] to afford sth. – [25] by hand – [26] accessory – [27] season – [28] edition

historical development		
collapse of sth.	the end or failure of sth.	*Zusammenbruch*
(political) crisis **crises** (pl.)	a situaton in which people no longer believe that a government or an economic system is working properly	*(politische) Krise*
to defeat sb./sth.; defeat	to win a victory over sb. in a war, fight, etc.	*besiegen*
to found sth.; foundation	to build or establish sth.	*gründen; Gründung*
to invade	to enter a country/an area using military force in order to control it	*eindringen, einmaschieren*
to occupy; occupation	taking control of a group of people by military force	*belagern; Belagerung*
(leading) power	a country that is strong and important and can influence events, or that has a lot of military strength	*Führungsmacht*
to rebel [rɪ'bel] **rebellion**	to oppose or fight against an authority or an idea	*rebellieren/Rebellion*
tribe; tribal ['traɪbl]	a social group consisting of people of the same race who have the same beliefs, customs, language etc. and usually live in one particular area	*(Volks)Stamm, Stammes-*
colonization		
the acquisition of colonies	the act of getting land	*Übernahme von Kolonien*
to civilize sb.	to improve a society so that it is more organized and developed	*zivilisieren*
to claim a territory	being the owner of a certain area of land	*Land beanspruchen*
(colonial) policy	a way of doing sth. that has been officially agreed upon and chosen by a political party	*Grundsatz, Richtlinie*
to colonize; colonization; colonist	to establish political control over another country, and send your citizens there to settle	*besiedeln, kolonisieren; Kolonialisierung; Kolonist*
to gain control over sb.	to obtain or achieve something you want or need	*Kontrolle über jdn. erlangen*
to conquer ['kɒŋkə(r)] **conqueror**	to gain control of a country by fighting	*erobern/Eroberer*
to decolonize sb.	to make a former colony politically independent	*dekolonialisieren*
to invade; invasion [ɪn'veɪʒn]	to enter a country using military force in order to take control of it	*einmarschieren; Einmarsch, Übergriff*
trade		
(economic) supremacy [su':preməsi]	the position in which you are more powerful or advanced than anyone else	*(ökonomische) Übermacht, Überlegenheit*
to manufacture sth.	to produce sth.	*herstellen*
raw [rɔ:] **materials**	natural substances that are used in manufacturing goods	*Rohmaterial*
to run sth. for profit	to do sth. because you want to make money with it	*gewinnorientiert leiten*
to trade with	to buy and sell goods as your business	*handeln*
trading post/trading station	a place where people can buy and exchange goods in a country	*Handelsstätte*
trading company	a business that buys and sells goods, especially internationally	*Handelsgesellschaft*
transatlantic trade	trade/business involving countries on both sides of the Atlantic	*transatlantischer Handel*
transportation network	a system of roads/channels/railroads to transport goods	*Transportnetz (auch: Verkehrsnetz)*
triangular trade	trade involving three continents: Europe, Africa and America	*Dreieckshandel*

The World Going Global: Opportunities and Options

A Dangerous World – Modern Triangular Trade

Tips on vocab

chain reaction ■ state bankruptcy ■ real estate prices (*Immobilienpreise*) ■ share prices (*Aktienkurse*) ■ speculative bubbles ■ national economy ■ economic activity ■ domino effect ■ machine parts ■ grain(s) ■ crude oil ■ pharmaceuticals [ˌfaːməˈsuːtɪkəls] ■ plastics/toys ■ chemical products

Rana Foroohar

Globalization in Reverse

Globalization is often defined as the free movement of goods, people and money across borders. Lately, all of those have become under threat[1] – and not just because of sanctions limiting travel and the flow of money among Russia, the U.S. and Europe. Over the past two years, global trade growth has been lower than global GDP[2] growth. It's the first time that has happened since World War II, and it marks a turning point in the global economy, with sweeping[3] implications for countries, companies and consumers.

There are many reasons global trade is growing more slowly than it has in the past. Europe is still struggling to end its debt crisis, and emerging markets are expanding more slowly than they were. But one of the biggest factors is that the American economy is going through a profound shift: the U.S. is no longer the global consumer of last resort[4]. [...] After now five years of recovery, the U.S. trade deficit isn't growing but shrinking. [...] Part of the reason the deficit is shrinking is that the U.S. shale-oil[5] and gas boom means Americans are buying less foreign fossil fuel, and the nation's manufacturing sector is growing. But part of it is that wages haven't come up since the crisis, and consumer spending is still sluggish[6]. In order for the U.S. and the world economy to keep growing, somebody has to shell out[7] for the electronics, cars and other goods we used to buy more of. Unfortunately, no one is doing that. [...]

With global economic integration seemingly in reverse, at the least for the moment, many economists and trade experts are beginning to talk about a new era of deglobalization, during which countries turn inward. Some of the implications are worrisome. Complaints to the World Trade Organization about protectionism, intellectual-property theft and new trade barriers are rising. Trade talks themselves are no longer regional but local, threatening to create a destructive so-called spaghetti bowl of competing[8] economic alliances.

Time, 7 April 2014, p. 14

START-UP ACTIVITIES

1. In groups, take a look at the graphic *Modern Triangular Trade* and get an overview of its various elements:
- Mediate the comments and questions using the vocab box.
- What are the manifold tasks and challenges the countries worldwide are confronted with?
- Describe the flow and exchange of products.

→ Focus on Skills, Analysis of Statistical Data, p. 380

2. Compare "modern triangular trade" to its historic counterpart, the "transatlantic triangular trade" of the 18th century.
What striking similarities and differences can you detect? What changes have taken place over the last 250 years?

→ Focus on Facts, The British Empire, p. 49

3. In a group, collect photos and further material concerning the topic "the world going global" and design collages that reflect your understanding and opinion of globalisation.

4. Summarize Rana Foroohar's view of globalization and the reasons given for its slow-down.

5. What outlook does Foroohar give on the "new era of deglobalization"?

[1] **threat** [θret] *Bedrohung* – [2] **GDP** [ˌdʒiːdiːˈpiː] (*abbr.*) gross domestic product; the total value of goods and services produced by a country in a year – [3] **sweeping** affecting many things or people – [4] **of last resort** *als letzter Ausweg* – [5] **shale-oil** *Schieferöl* – [6] **sluggish** slow; *schleppend* – [7] **to shell sth. out** (*phr. v., infml.*) to pay or give money for sth., usually unwillingly; *für jdn./etw. Geld abdrücken* – [8] **to compete** to try to be more successful than sb./sth. else

Moving Heaven and Earth? – Global Migration and Modern-Day Slavery

The Abuse of Migrants – And Still They Come

AWARENESS

According to a 2013 OECD[1] study, there are about 232 million international migrants living in the world today trying to find a better life.

In groups, first collect information about possible reasons why people migrate to other countries, then sort your findings in a mind map and discuss your results in class.

COMPREHENSION

1. **Before reading:**
   The statements below are taken from the 2013 OECD study.

- During the period 2000 – 2010, the global migrant stock[2] grew twice as fast than during the previous decade.
- While the proportion of international migrants continues to rise in the North, it remains stable in the South.
- Women comprise about 48 % of all international migrants.
- In 2013, only 7 % of all international migrants were refugees seeking asylum[3].
- 34.9 million of the international migrants are below the age of 20.
- 37 million of the international migrants are aged 60 and above.
- Ca. 27.3 million of the international migrants are highly educated (tertiary education[4]).
- Ca. 30 % of the international migrants have limited education (less than secondary education).

Step 1: In a Think! Pair! Share! activity, choose two of the statements above and reflect on and discuss
- possible reasons for the trends mentioned,
- the impact of the depicted situation on

a) the migrants themselves, b) the countries the migrants are leaving (sending countries),
c) the countries the migrants are immigrating to (receiving countries).

Step 2: Take a look at the map on p. 251 and collect information on peak migration trends. Make a ranking of the countries with the highest and lowest numbers of migrants.

Step 3: Speculate on and exchange ideas about the information and data you have collected in steps 1 and 2.
- Why do you think that some countries have a comparatively high percentage of migrants (e. g. Qatar, Kuwait, United Arab Emirates, etc.)?
- Which of the countries shown in the map might be particularly attractive for the different migrant groups mentioned in steps 1 and 2?

[1] **OECD** (*abbr.*) Organization for Economic Co-Operation and Development; an international organization whose members are countries with advanced economies and whose aim is to encourage economic growth around the world – [2] **migrant stock** the total amount of migrant people – [3] **to seek asylum** [əˈsaɪləm] *Asyl suchen* – [4] **tertiary education** relating to education in colleges and universities

Balancing the interests of migrant workers and the countries they live in

What government would tolerate its citizens' passports being confiscated[1], their earnings being withheld[2] and their deaths being covered up? Nepal's, it seems. In September reports of the abuse of Nepalese migrants working on stadiums for the 2022 Football World Cup in Qatar, and the deaths of at least 44 of them, appeared in the Guardian, a British newspaper. The Nepalese government's first response was to recall its ambassador to Qatar: the Guardian had quoted her describing the Gulf state as an "open jail". Shortly afterwards, Nepalese and Qatari officials held a joint[3] press conference in Doha at which they insisted Nepalese workers were "safe and fully respected". Reports to the contrary were false and driven by "inappropriate targets and agendas".

According to Martin Ruhs of Oxford University, the Nepalese government's apparent lack of concern can be explained by looking at the interests of those involved. For all the mistreatment, Nepalese workers earn far more in Qatar than they could at home. Remittances[4] make up a quarter of Nepalese GDP[5]. If the Nepalese government were to insist that rules protecting migrant workers in Qatar should be enforced, Qatari employers might look for workers elsewhere.

Mr Ruhs has drawn up an index of migrant rights (see chart): he finds that countries with more rights for migrant workers tend to be less keen on[6] admitting new ones. In the Gulf states and Singapore, where migrants have few rights on paper, the foreign workforce is huge: 94% of workers in Qatar were born abroad. Sweden and Norway, where migrants can use public services, claim welfare benefits and bring in dependents[7], admit relatively few purely economic migrants.

This trade-off[8] is visible even within the European Union, where the recent accession[9] of 12 relatively poor eastern European countries has sparked[10] a debate about migrants' rights to welfare. In January David Cameron, Britain's prime minister, clashed with his Oxford contemporary[11], Radek Sikorski, Poland's foreign minister. Mr Cameron wants to be able to exclude recently arrived European immigrants from welfare and public housing[12]. "If Britain gets our taxpayers, shouldn't it also pay their benefits?" Mr Sikorski responded.

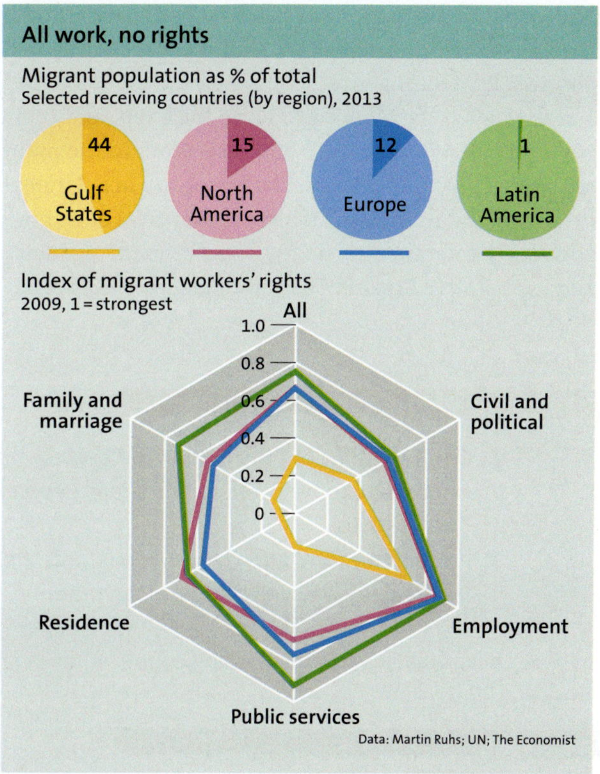

In Europe the debate is multilateral[13]; Mr Cameron intends to promote his point of view as part of a package to reform the EU's single labour market[14]. Elsewhere the movement of people is increasingly regulated by bilateral agreements and diplomacy. Since a diaspora[15] can help poor countries develop, sending states must try to protect the rights of migrant workers without making them such a burden as to be unwelcome, points out David McKenzie of the World Bank. Receiving countries weigh their national interests, real or perceived[16], against international obligations[17].

[1] **to confiscate sth.** *etw. einziehen, beschlagnahmen* – [2] **to withhold sth.** to refuse to give sth. to sb.; *etw. zurückhalten* – [3] **joint** belonging to or shared between two or more people – [4] **remittance** [rɪˈmɪtəns] (*fml.*) *Heimatüberweisung* – [5] **GDP** [ˌdʒiːdiːˈpiː] (*abbr.*) gross domestic product; the total value of goods and services produced by a country in one year – [6] **to be keen on sth.** to be very interested or wanting to do sth. very much – [6] **dependent** sb. who depends on your financial support, such as a child or family member who does not work – [7] **trade-off** a situation in which you accept sth. bad in order to have sth. good – [8] **accession** *Aufstieg* – [9] **to spark** *etw. entzünden* – [10] **contemporary** *Zeitgenosse* – [11] **public housing** *sozialer Wohnungsbau* – [12] **multilateral** involving more than two groups or countries – [13] **single labour market** *einheitlicher Arbeitsmarkt* – [14] **diaspora** [daɪˈæspərə] (*fml.*) the spreading of people from one original country to other countries – [15] **perceived** *vermeintlich* – [16] **obligation** sth. that you must do; *Verpflichtung* – [17] **envoy** [ˈenvɔɪ] sb. who is sent from one government or organization to another

The calculations vary from country to country. Some sending countries, such as the Philippines, come down on the side of stronger rights: Filipinos must be offered a high wage to be allowed to leave for a job, and their government sends envoys[18] and inspectors to the main receiving countries. Others, like Nepal, are lax. Amnesty International, an NGO, is almost as critical of its government's tolerance of dodgy[19] recruitment agencies and exploitative brokers[20] as it is of Qatari employers.

A UN convention on migrant workers' rights which came into force in 2003 has been ratified[21] by only 47 countries, most of which are net senders of migrants. It is largely unenforced. A weaker treaty covering just the basics might do more good, argues Mr Ruhs, since the rich countries most migrants move to might sign it, and help to crack down on the worst abuses in places such as Qatar.

The Economist, 19 April 2014, p. 52

COMPREHENSION

2. Give an outline of the situation of Nepalese migrants in Qatar and the Nepalese and Qatari governments' response to the allegations (*Vorwürfe, Beschuldigungen*).

3. Present the correlation between migrants' rights and the admittance policy in countries like the Gulf states, Sweden, Norway and the European Union.

4. In what way do the sending countries take care of the migrants?

ANALYSIS

5. Analyse the author's stance on the matter and examine
- his/her line of argument* as well as the structure of the article,
- his/her examples and citations.

→ Focus on Skills, Analysis of a Non-Fictional Text, p. 377

6. In groups, analyse the graphic on p. 253 and explain the different migrant workers' rights in the respective regions.
What do the comparatively low index numbers reveal about the receiving countries' migration and work policies?

→ Focus on Skills, Analysis of Statistical Data, p. 380

7. Compare the migrant workers' rights and their violations mentioned in the text to the *Universal Declaration of Human Rights* that was proclaimed by the United Nations (→ FoD, p. 284). Which further violations can you detect and which further rights should migrant workers be guaranteed, according to this document?

8. The concluding paragraph (ll. 66–73) of the article refers to a UN convention on migrant workers' rights and Mr Ruhs' suggestion to work out a "weaker treaty" that only covers the basic migrant workers' rights, assuming that this would "crack down the worst abuses".
Act out a pyramid discussion in which you discuss your view on the controversial matter.

[18] **dodgy** (*infml.*) dishonest – [19] **broker** *Zwischenhändler* – [20] **to ratify sth.** (*fml.*) to make an agreement official

ACTIVITIES

Webcode SNG-40183-029 @ **9.** Do a project on world migration using the links provided on the webcode.
Prepare a presentation in which you provide your class with

- the most relevant background information on the history and development of migration,
- relevant facts and data,
- maps and illustrations.

Tip: Your presentation should be no longer than 5 – 10 minutes and you should make a handout (1 – 2 pages) that contains the most important information.

→ Focus on Skills, Presentations, p. 391
→ Fokus on Skills, Writing a Handout, p. 397

Countries with Peak Migration Numbers

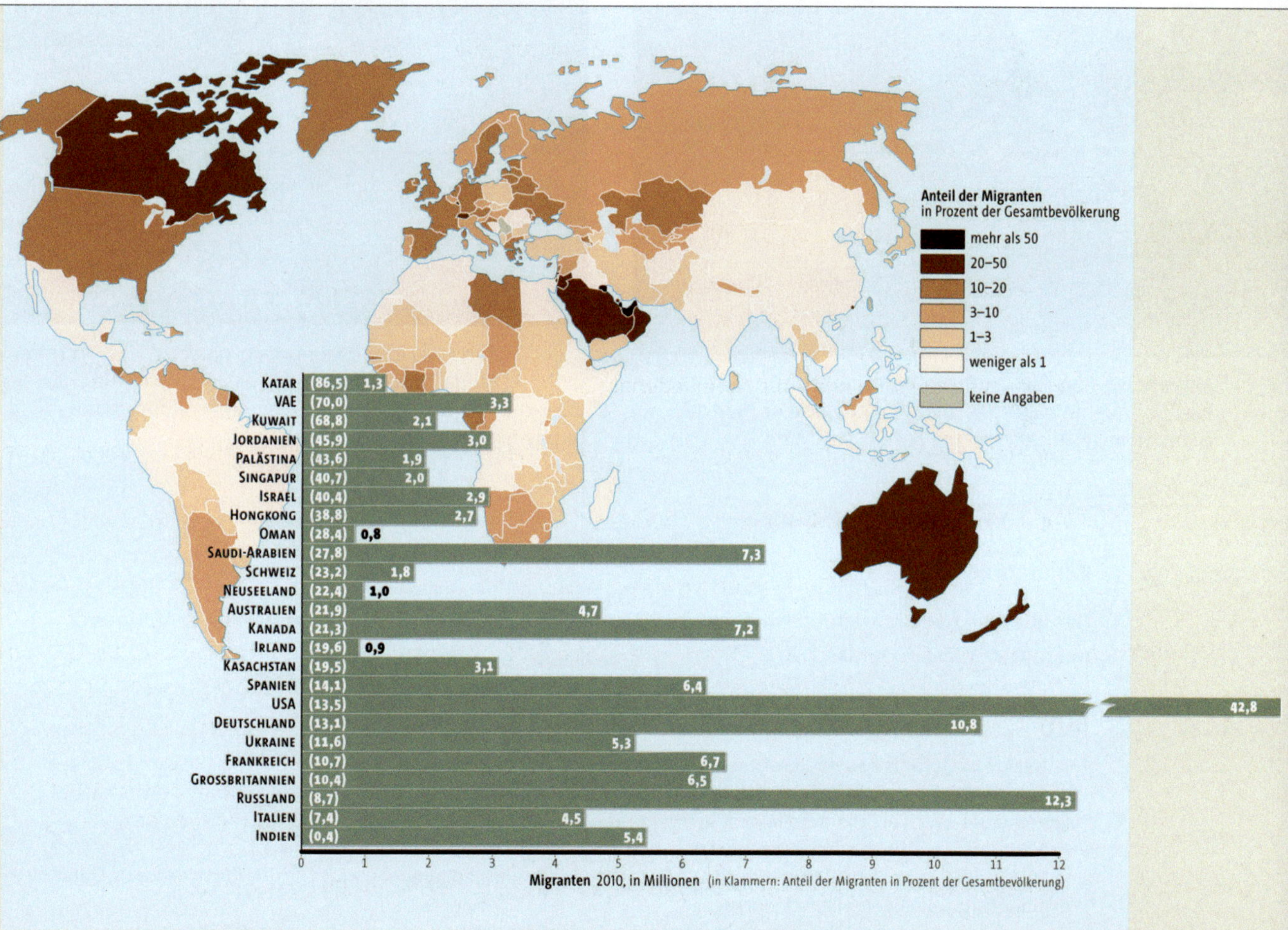

Die Länder mit den meisten Migranten

Quellen: »Trends in Total Migrant Stock: The 2008 Revision«, United Nations Department of Economic and Social Affairs, Population Division, http://esa.un.org/migration, Angaben für 2010.

Robert Booth, Pete Pattison

Modern-Day Slavery. Qatar World Cup: Migrants Wait a Year to Be Paid for Building Offices

AWARENESS

In a round robin activity, give short statements about what you associate with the terms
- modern-day slavery,
- labour camp.

Migrant workers from India in Doha, Qatar. The mistreatment of migrant workers, including the late or non-payment of wages, has attracted severe criticism

A worker formerly employed on a project to fit out offices in the Al Bidda Tower who now lives and works illegally after the company that employed him collapsed and failed to pay him for a year

COMPREHENSION

Webcode SNG-40183-030 @

Before reading:

1. Describe the two photographs above: What do they reveal about the working and living conditions of migrant workers in Qatar?

Info

The **state of Qatar** is a sovereign Arab country with a population of about 2 million people. It is the world's richest country with a per capita income of ca. $98,814 (2013) (cf. Germany: $44,000) and its wealth is based on its natural gas reserves which are the third largest in the world.
In 2022, Qatar will be the first Arab country to host the FIFA world cup.
In 2013, British journalists Robert Booth and Pete Pattison made a documentary for *The Guardian*, accusing Qatar of exploiting its 1.4 million migrant workers.

Webcode SNG-40183-030 @

2. Together with a partner, watch the two video clips provided on the webcode and take notes on the aspects listed below.

Tip: Be prepared to watch the video clips at least two times; do not focus on each detail but try to get a general understanding of the information given.

Here are the points you should **focus and take notes on**:

- the FIFA preparations at Aspire Academy and the Aspire Zone Foundation
- the living and working conditions of migrant workers in Qatar
- Qatar's labour system and its rules
- the position of the Qatari government
- the Qatari construction industry
- desert labour camps and accommodations
- recruitment and contracting practices
  - Lee Trading Company
  - Katara Projects Company
  - Capital International Manpower
  - IBEX Technical Trading and Contracting
- the "sudden death syndrome" and the death of Rishi Kandal in May 2014
- the construction of the Al Wakrah stadium and opportunities to reform the exploitative Qatari migrant worker system.

The article below is one in a series of Robert Booth and Pete Pattison's critical investigative articles about the appalling living and working conditions of migrant workers in Qatar.

1 Migrant workers who built luxury offices used by Qatar's 2022 Football World Cup organisers have told the Guardian they have not been paid for more than a year and are now working illegally from cockroach-infested[1] lodgings.

Officials in Qatar's Supreme Committee for Delivery and Legacy[2] have been using offices on the 38th and 39th floors of Doha's landmark al-Bidda skyscraper – known as the Tower of Football – which were fitted out by men from Nepal, Sri Lanka and India who say they have not been paid for up to 13 months' work.

The project, a Guardian investigation shows, was directly commissioned by the Qatar government and the workers' plight[3] is set to raise fresh doubts over the autocratic[4] emirate's commitment to labour rights as construction starts this year [2014] on five new stadiums for the World Cup.

The offices, which cost £2.5m to fit[5], feature[6] expensive etched glass[7], handmade Italian furniture, and even a heated executive[8] toilet, project sources said. Yet some of the workers have not been paid, despite complaining to the Qatari authorities months ago and being owed[9] wages as modest as £6 a day.

By the end of this year, several hundred thousand extra migrant workers from some of the world's poorest countries are scheduled to have travelled to Qatar to build World Cup facilities and infrastructure. The acceleration[10] in the building programme comes amid international concern over a rising death toll[11] among migrant workers and the use of forced labour.

"We don't know how much they are spending on the World Cup, but we just need our salary," said one worker who had lost a year's pay on the project. "We were working, but not getting the salary. The government, the company: just provide the money."

The migrants are squeezed seven to a room, sleeping on thin, dirty mattresses on the floor and on bunk beds[12], in breach[13] of Qatar's own labour standards. They live in constant fear of imprisonment because they have been left without paperwork after the contractor on the project, Lee Trading and Contracting, collapsed. They say they are now being exploited on wages as low as 50 p an hour.

Their case was raised with Qatar's prime minister by Amnesty International last November, but the workers have said 13 of them remain stranded in Qatar. Despite having done nothing wrong, five have even been arrested and imprisoned by Qatari police because they did not have ID papers. Legal claims[14] lodged against[15] the former employer at the labour court in November have proved fruitless. They are so poor they can no longer afford the taxi to court to pursue their cases, they say.

[1] **cockroach-infested** *mit Kakerlaken verseucht* – [2] **Supreme Committee for Delivery and Legacy** ['legəsi] *das oberste Planungs- und Veranstaltungskomitee* – [3] **plight** *Notlage, Zwangslage* – [4] **autocratic** related to a regime with unlimited power that demands obedience from its people – [5] **to fit sth.** *etw. einbauen* – [6] **to feature sth.** to include sth. as an important part – [7] **etched glass** *Glas mit Gravuren* – [8] **executive** [ɪg'zekjʊtɪv] here: expensive; for the use of sb. who is considered important – [9] **to owe sth. to sb.** *jdm. etw. schulden* – [10] **acceleration** *Beschleunigung* – [11] **death toll** the number of people who die in an accident, a war, a disaster, etc. – [12] **bunk bed** *Etagenbett* – [13] **to be in breach of sth.** (*fml.*) to be breaking a particular law or rule – [14] **legal claim** *Rechtsanspruch* – [15] **to lodge a claim against sb.** to make an official complaint about sb./sth.

A 35-year-old Nepalese worker and father of three who said he too had lost a year's pay: "If I had money to buy a ticket, I would go home."

2 Qatar's World Cup organising committee confirmed that it had been granted use of temporary offices on the floors fitted out by the unpaid workers. It said it was "heavily dismayed[16] to learn of the behaviour of Lee Trading with regard to the timely[17] payment of its workers". The committee stressed it did not commission[18] the firm. "We strongly disapprove and will continue to press for a speedy and fair conclusion to all cases," it said.

Jim Murphy, the shadow[19] international development secretary, said the revelation[20] added to the pressure on the World Cup organising committee. "They work out of this building, but so far they can't even deliver justice for the men who toiled[21] at their own HQ," he said.

Sharan Burrow, secretary general of the International Trade Union Confederation, said the workers' treatment was criminal. "It is an appalling abuse of fundamental rights, yet there is no concern from the Qatar government unless they are found out," she said. "In any other country you could prosecute this behaviour."

Contracts show the project was commissioned by Katara Projects, a Qatar government organisation under the auspices[22] of the office of the then heir apparent[23], Sheikh Tamim bin Hamad al-Thani, who is now the emir[24]. He also heads[25] the supreme committee, the World Cup organising body. The committee is spending at least £4bn building new stadiums for the tournament[26], which has become mired[27] in allegations[28] of bribery[29], while there is disbelief at the prospect of playing the tournament in Qatar's 50C summer heat.

Katara said it terminated[30] its agreement with Lee Trading when it discovered the mistreatment of workers and non-payment of wages, and made efforts to repatriate those affected or find them new jobs. It said several workers had been compensated after court settlements[31].

"If there are employees who were not repatriated, did not find employment or did not receive compensation, we would be happy to engage in any effort with the ministry of labour and ministry of interior to rectify[32] the situation," a spokesman said.

3 The problems at the Tower of Football workers are not isolated, despite Qatar's pledges to monitor salary payments and abolish the kafala sponsorship system, which stops migrant workers from changing job or leaving Qatar without their employer's consent. In 2012 and 2013, 70 labourers from India, Nepal and Sri Lanka died from falls or strikes[33] by objects, 144 died in traffic accidents and 56 killed themselves, the government's own figures show. Dozens more young migrant workers die mysteriously in their sleep from suspected heart attacks every summer.

The Guardian discovered more projects where salaries had not been paid. They included a desert camp of 65 workers who had not been paid for several months, were sleeping eight to a room, and were living with dirty drinking water, filthy, unplumbed[34] toilets and no showers.

Another group said they were being paid only sporadically, that there was sometimes no water in their housing and no electricity to power air conditioning.

This month, the Qatar Foundation, a state body, published a report examining trafficking[35], debt bondage[36] and forced labour among migrant workers. It identified practices that contravene[37] International Labour Organisation conventions on forced labour and UN anti-trafficking protocols, "widespread" non-payment of wages and bribery and extortion[38] among recruitment agents and employers.

From January to May this year 87 Nepalese workers died in Qatar, a death rate two-and-a-half times higher than that of British expats, new figures from the Nepal government reveal.

"We know there is much more to do," said Abdullah al-Khulaifi, Qatar's minister of labour and social affairs in a statement detailing progress on labour law reforms. "But we are making definite progress and are determined to build momentum[39]."

www.theguardian.com/global-development/2014/jul/28/qatar-world-cup-migrants-not-paid-building-office, 28 July 2014 [08.11.2014]

[16] **dismayed** unhappy and disappointed – [17] **timely** *rechtzeitig, zeitlich angemessen* – [18] **to commission sth.** to formally choose sb. to do a particular task – [19] **shadow secretary** used in the title of important politicians in the main opposition party; *Schattensekretär* – [20] **revelation** *Enthüllung* – [21] **to toil** to work hard – [22] **under the auspices of sb./sth.** [ˈɔːspɪsɪz] (*fml.*) with the protection and support of sb./sth., esp. an organization – [23] **heir** [eə] **apparent** *Thronanwärter, gesetzlicher Erbe* – [24] **emir** [emˈɪə] a ruler of particular Muslim countries in the Middle East – [25] **to head sth.** to be in charge of a group or organization – [26] **tournament** *Turnier, Meisterschaft* – [27] **to be mired in sth.** [maɪəd] to be involved in a difficult situation, especially for a long period of time – [28] **allegation** *Vorwurf, Beschuldigung* – [29] **bribery** *Bestechung* – [30] **to terminate** to end or stop sth. – [31] **court settlement** *gerichtlicher Vergleich* – [32] **to rectify** to correct sth. or make sth. right – [33] **strike** here: a sudden and powerful hit – [34] **unplumbed** *ohne Kanalanschluss* – [35] **trafficking** *Menschenhandel* – [36] **debt bondage** *Schuldknechtschaft* – [37] **to contravene** (*fml.*) to break a rule or law – [38] **extortion** *Erpressung* – [39] **to build momentum** *in Schwung kommen*

COMPREHENSION

3. In a **first reading**, **scan the text** and get a general understanding of what is said.

4. Divide the class into groups of three students each, with each student working with one section of the article.

   Step 1: In a **second reading**, extract the most relevant information given in your section of the text.

   Step 2: Clarify unknown words and expressions using a dictionary.

   Step 3: Summarize your section of the text in about 100 – 150 words and be sure to
   - leave out irrelevant details,
   - turn quotations into indirect speech,
   - use predominantly the simple present tense.

   → Focus on Skills, Writing a Summary, p. 401

   Step 4: In your groups, read the summaries of the respective sections to each other and clarify questions if necessary.
   Make sure that each student takes notes on the relevant aspects.

ANALYSIS

5. Explain Qatar's labour system and the *kafala* sponsorship system by referring to evidence given in the article.
   How are migrant workers lured (*ködern, locken*) into signing contracts and trapped in appalling and life-threatening working and living conditions?
   → Focus on Skills, Analysis of a Non-Fictional Text, p. 377

6. Explain how the author juxtaposes the "two worlds" that live side by side in Qatar: the world of luxury and the world of poverty.

luxury	poverty
• ll. 1 f. luxury offices • ll. … • …	• ll. 4 f. cockroach-infested lodgings • ll. … • …

7. Examine the style of the article and give evidence from the text that reveals its investigative character.
   Pay particular attention to
   - the choice of words and language register,
   - the use of rhetorical devices,
   - the author's line of argument*.

   → Focus on Skills, Analysis of a Non-Fictional Text, p. 377
   → Focus on Facts, Basic Types of Non-Fictional Texts, p. 368

ACTIVITIES

8. A group of migrant workers, supported by civil rights activists, have finally decided to file a lawsuit (*einen Prozess anstrengen*) at a Qatari court.
Choose one of the following persons/groups and write a statement that clarifies and emphasizes your position:
a) a prosecutor (*Ankläger*) accusing the recruitment agencies of enslaving and abusing migrant workers
b) a prosecutor accusing the Qatari government of supporting human trafficking, debt bondage and forced labour among migrant workers
c) a Qatari counsel for the defence (of the recruitment agencies and the government)
d) representatives of the Qatari and international FIFA committee
e) various immigrant workers laying out their situation
f) the British investigative journalists Robert Booth and Pete Pattison giving evidence to the court based on their research and investigations
g) representatives of civil and human rights organizations (e. g. Amnesty International, Human Rights Watch, etc.) who give evidence of the appalling violation of basic human and civil rights

In a role play, act out the trial and present the respective statements in class. Finally, the class should consider the evidence and find a verdict.

9. After the trial, which has gained international attention, journalists review and comment on the court's decision.
Choose a newspaper or magazine (e. g. *The Qatari Times*, *The Guardian*, *The Indian Times* or a publication for the FIFA World Cup Committee) and write an article that represents the respective point of view.
→ Focus on Skills, Writing a Newspaper Article, p. 399

GRAMMAR / LANGUAGE

10. Imagine you are a migrant worker who has been lured to work in Qatar; you are reflecting on your situation. Use **if-clauses (conditional sentences) of various types** to express what you/the recruitment agency/the Qatari government should have done differently.

Examples:
- If I had been more suspicious when they charged the recruitment fee, I could have avoided … (type III)
- If I were able to escape from … I would have to leave behind … (type II)

11. Turn the passages of direct speech in the article into **indirect speech**. Be sure to
- avoid the overuse of the verb "say" and find more appropriate introductory verbs and formulations (e.g. to explain, to utter, to mention, to criticize, etc.),
- backshift the tenses where necessary.

Example: One of the workers stated that he/they didn't know how much the Qatari government were spending on … but the workers just needed their salary …

Going Hot and Cold – Environment vs. Resources

Roger Howard

Is the U.S. Fracking Boom a Bubble?

AWARENESS

In a 4-corners activity, reflect on and discuss your views concerning energy consumption and how to deal with the shortage of resources. Here are some keywords to start with:

- fossil energy
- energy reserves
- hybrid cars
- reducing consumption
- energy efficiency
- insulation of houses
- energy-saving measures
- conventional energy sources (e. g. coal, oil, gas)
- renewable energy (e. g. solar energy, wind power, biogas)

What is fracking?

Hydraulic fracturing or fracking is a method of forcing natural gas or oil from rock layer deep below the earth's surface.

How fracking works …

1. A pressurized mixture of sand, water and chemicals is injected into a horizontally drilled well.
2. The mix cracks the shale and fills the cracks with sandy grit, allowing natural gas to flow up the well.
3. The recovered water is stored in lined pits or taken to a treatment plant.

… and why it's controversial

Much of the water used in fracking is collected from the well and processed, but some communities have raised concerns that potentially carcinogenic chemicals can escape into drinking water.

- Nearby water wells face a slight risk of contamination. (There's about a 1% chance of a hydraulic fracture extending beyond 1,150 feet of a fracture zone.[1])

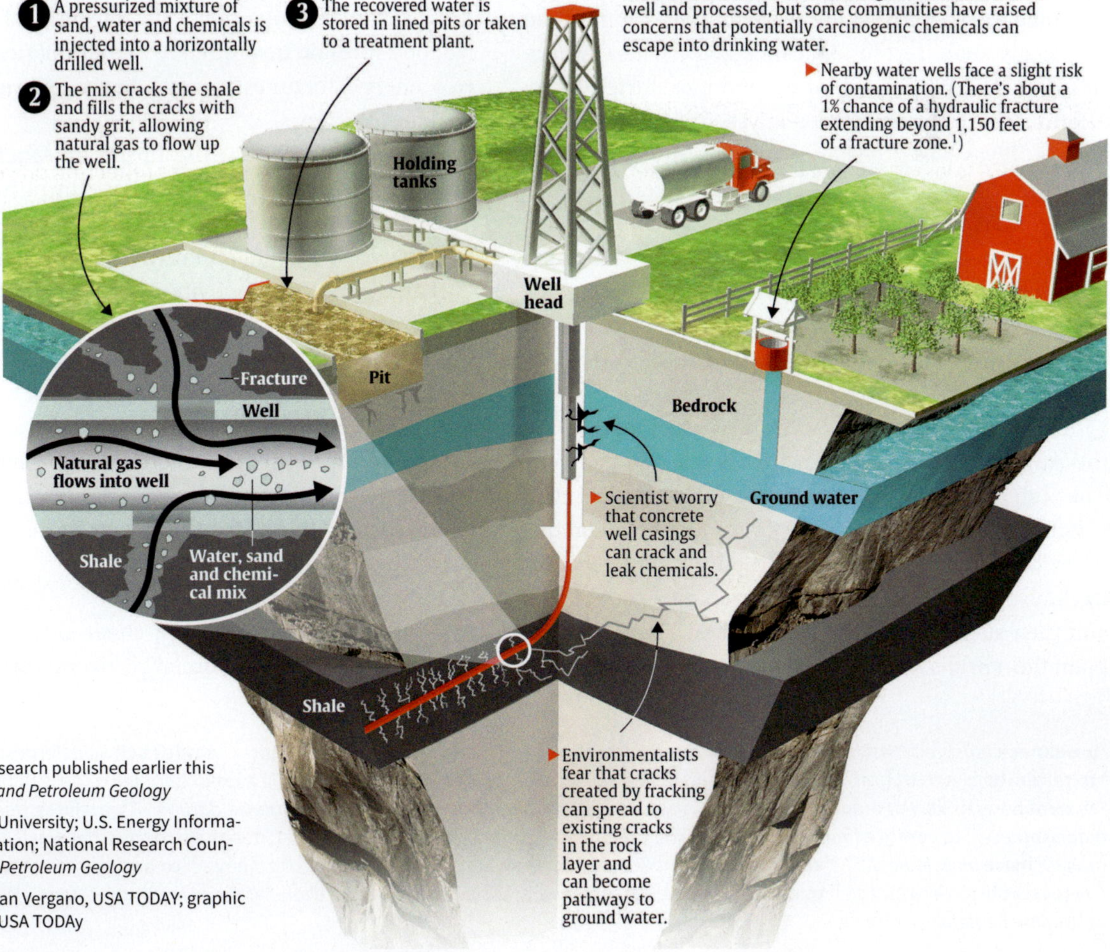

1 – Based on research published earlier this year in *Marine and Petroleum Geology*

Sources: Duke University; U.S. Energy Information Administration; National Research Council; *Marine and Petroleum Geology*

Reporting by Dan Vergano, USA TODAY; graphic by Karl Gelles, USA TODAy

COMPREHENSION

1. **Before reading:** By definition, **hydraulic fracturing** [haɪˈdrɒlɪk ˈfræktʃərɪŋ], commonly known as **fracking**, is the creation of fractures in rock formations in the earth using a pressurized mixture of water, sand and chemicals, for the purpose of releasing and extracting natural gas.

   Together with a partner, describe the visual on the previous page and prepare a short presentation in which you lay out the process of fracking to your class. Use everyday English as much as possible. Additionally, prepare a short handout for your listeners that illustrates the complex matter, e. g. by using a visual and giving the most relevant information.
   → Focus on Skills, Writing a Handout, p. 397

   Tip: In order to get a better understanding of the complex scientific matter, first clarify important technical terms and transform them into everyday English. Work together with a partner and use a dictionary for help.

1 America's oil boom, one of the most spectacular the world has witnessed, continues at breakneck[1] speed. Last week the Bank of America released figures showing that the US has now become the world's leading oil producer, overtaking both Saudi Arabia and Russia. Ways of extracting "tight[2]" oil and gas from shale rock[3] and other "unconventional" sources have revolutionized energy production and allowed the US to produce 11 million barrels of oil every day (mbd) in the first half of this year. Yet some experts are asking searching questions about America's shale revolution. Since 2009, when America's domestic production of oil and gas started to accelerate sharply, respected analysts like Arthur Berman, a Texas-based geologist and energy consultant, and David Hughes, a Canadian geoscientist, have claimed that the shale revolution is just a bubble. Now they are reiterating[4] their warnings that this shale bubble could burst with devastating[5] impact, forcing the US to rely, once again, on the Middle East while severely denting[6] the drive for greener fuels.

2 Through their sceptical eyes, it is the longevity[7] of the American shale bonanza[8] that is open to question. The International Energy Agency, an independent watchdog[9] based in Paris, ventures[10] some bold[11] predictions, claiming that American oil output will continue to climb over the next few years, reaching a high in 2019 and then stabilizing in the 2020s. The US will then remain the world's leading oil producer, continue the IEA experts, until the early 2030s when other countries will overtake it. But its critics point out that such claims are not really predictions at all but mere[12] conjecture[13].
It is true that the story of American shale neatly illustrates how hard it is to predict the future of energy in particular. As recently as 2008, America's dependency on foreign sources of oil was a very hot political topic in Washington. Our "addiction to oil," as President George W. Bush said in his 2006 State of the Union address, meant relying upon "unstable parts of the world". Nobody foresaw how quickly and dramatically America's energy fortunes[14] would be transformed by the shale revolution.
Sceptics point out that the future of America's shale industry is equally hard to predict – or rather to guess. The US undoubtedly has huge shale reserves but it is impossible to be sure about their size. For example, in 2011 the Department of Energy published its findings about one of America's Monterey Shale deposits in California – and claimed it harboured[15] 15 billion barrels of recoverable[16] oil reserves. But just a few weeks ago, the department released a radically revised figure, massively slashing[17] its earlier forecast. Now Monterey was said to hold something closer to 600 million. Some experts think that even this much more modest estimate hugely inflates[18] the true figure.

3 More important than the sheer size of resources, however, is their commercial recoverability[19]. The en-

[1] **breakneck** *halsbrecherisch* – [2] **tight** held or fixed in position firmly; difficult to move or undo – [3] **shale rock** *Schiefergestein* – [4] **to reiterate** [riˈɪtəreɪt] (*fml.*) to say sth. again, once or several times – [5] **devastating** causing a lot of damage or destruction – [6] **to dent** here: to slow or reduce sth. – [7] **longevity** [lɒnˈdʒevəti] (*fml.*) *Langlebigkeit* – [8] **bonanza** *Goldgrube* – [9] **watchdog** *Überwachungsorganisation* – [10] **to venture** (*fml.*) to risk saying sth. that might be criticized – [11] **bold** confident; not afraid to say what you feel or to take risks – [12] **mere** *bloß, lediglich* – [13] **conjecture** *Mutmaßung* – [14] **fortune** here: a large amount of money – [15] **to harbour** to contain – [16] **recoverable** *förderwürdig* – [17] **to slash** to reduce sth. drastically – [18] **in inflate** to make sth. larger or more important – [19] **recoverability** *Ausbeutefaktor*

ergy industry, not just shale in particular, is ultimately all about economics – at what point upfront[20] costs can be recouped[21], profits reaped[22] and risks rewarded. The shale revolution was born in 2008, when American oil production was a very modest 600,000 b/d. It was at this time that the technologies it depends upon became more affordable, and that the global price of oil was high enough to support the very high infrastructure and drilling costs involved. Fracking – the process of hydraulically fracturing shale rock to release oil and gas – is prohibitively[23] expensive, and operators reply upon clear commercial margins[24] to make it viable[25].

At the moment, the global price of oil lies close to the breakeven[26] cost that many American companies require[27]. But some industry experts argue that if the price does fall below $90 a barrel – it is currently just over $100 – then the impact will be huge.

"Much of the American shale industry could find itself in real trouble and shut down relatively quickly," argues Professor Jonathan Stern of the Oxford Institute of Energy Studies. Even at the $100 figure some producers are reported to be struggling financially.

The oil price could fall fast and perhaps far in all manner of circumstances[28]. A Washington-Tehran rapprochement[29] will bring, at some point, voluminous quantities of Iranian crude[30] onto the global market; the Iraqi government might not only placate[31] the country but also coax[32] foreign companies with more generous terms; or a downturn in China would dampen[33] demand.

4 Even in their best-case scenario – of a high and climbing oil price – America's shale producers will be pushed to maintain, or even imitate, the astonishing level of output of recent years.

This is because a shale well[34] has a very limited lifespan, of around seven or eight years on average. Its output plummets[35] drastically after the first three years and then deteriorates[36] steadily thereafter. By contrast a conventional oil field has a longevity that a shale well simply does not possess, producing crude at a level that wanes[37] slowly over years or decades: Saudi's massive Ghawar field, for example, began production in 1951 and is still pumping out around 5 million barrels every day.

The IEA itself points out that the US shale industry will need to bring 2,500 wells into service every year to sustain[38] the output – of one million barrels every day – from just one of its main reserves, located in North Dakota. Some of these wells may also require more investment than their predecessors: "a rising percentage of supplies require a higher breakeven price," as the IEA has said in a separate report, "may be in sight."

Critics like Berman and Hughes conclude that the US needs to hedge its bets[39] and ensure that it can cope when, as they claim it will, the shale phenomenon retreats and disappoints. If this happens, then America could continue to be afflicted[40], as before, by burgeoning[41] domestic demand for both oil and gas. Tens, perhaps hundreds, of thousands of jobs would be lost and the economy would be highly vulnerable to price spikes[42]. The US would, once again, become dependent on foreign suppliers, particularly the Middle Eastern exporters that offer long term, plentiful sources.

5 Such sceptics point to another adverse[43] consequence. Because the US is currently relying too much on shale, they argue, it is failing to address the fundamentals that underwrite the energy market – supply and demand.

Washington should be finding ways of sponsoring fuel efficiency in the United States – for example by subsidizing[44] the use of less gluttonous[45] cars: in 2013, the American public consumed only 6 % less gasoline than in 2007, when domestic intake[46] hit an all-time high.

Equally, they say that more emphasis needs to be placed upon developing a generation of greener, cleaner fuels – solar power and fuel cell technology for example – than both oil and natural gas. In their eyes, one danger of the shale revolution is that it makes this seem less of a priority – on economic as well as environmental grounds – than it should be. Shale, in other words, is

[20] **upfront** *im Voraus* – [21] **to recoup** [rɪ'ku:p] *ausgleichen* – [22] **to reap profit** *Gewinn erzielen, abschöpfen* – [23] **prohibitive** [prə'hɪbɪtɪv] *unerschwinglich* – [24] **margin** *Gewinnmarge* – [25] **viable** ['vaɪəbl] *realisierbar* – [26] **breakeven** *Rentabilitätsgrenze* – [27] **to require** to need – [28] **in all manner of circumstances** *unter allen möglichen Umständen* – [29] **rapprochement** [ræ'prɒʃmɒ̃] (*fml.*) *Wiederannäherung* – [30] **crude (oil)** *Rohöl* – [31] **to placate** *jdn. besänftigen* – [32] **to coax** *schmeicheln* – [33] **to dampen** to reduce – [34] **shale well** *Quellen im Schiefergestein* – [35] **to plummet** to suddenly fall – [36] **to deteriorate** to become worse – [37] **to wane** to become less – [38] **to sustain** *etw. aufrechterhalten* – [39] **to hedge one's bets** (*idm.*) *sich nach allen Seiten absichern* – [40] **afflicted** *betrübt, geplagt* – [41] **to burgeon** ['bɜ:dʒən] (*lit.*) to develop and grow quickly – [42] **spike** a sudden large increase – [43] **adverse** *nachteilig* – [44] **to subsidize** *subventionieren* – [45] **gluttonous** ['glʌtənəs] *gefräßig* – [46] **domestic intake** *heimischer Verbrauch*

making American complacent[47] about the need to find alternative fuels that can sustain the future, delaying the moment when they could be introduced.

Only time will tell if they are right and the shale revolution will end up in disaster.

www.newsweek.com/2014/07/18/how-long-will-americas-shale-gas-boom-last-260823.html, 18 July 2014 [03.10.2014]

COMPREHENSION

2. As the text contains a number of technical terms and elaborated vocabulary, it has already been subdivided into five thematic sections to help your reading and understanding.

   Step 1: In a **paired reading activity**, team up with a partner and help each other do the respective tasks.

   Step 2: Read the section individually first, trying to get a general understanding. Note down the most relevant information as well as questions that you have.

   Step 3: Now, team up with your partner and summarize each section of the text to each other. Clarify your questions and make corrections and/or additions to your notes.

3. **While reading**, concentrate and take notes on these aspects:

1
- the position of the U. S. amid the world's oil-producing nations
- questions raised by scientists and energy consultants
- possible impacts of the energy bubble

2
- predictions of America's (future) oil output
- the history of America's shale industry
- the incalculability of America's shale industry and possible reserves

3
- the (im-)balance of cost and production
- the correlation between oil production and fracking
- consequences of falling oil prices

4
- the lifespan of a shale well
- the lifespan of a conventional oil field
- means of sustaining the output of shale gas in the U. S.
- consequences of declining shale gas production and rising cost

5
- possible solutions to avoiding dependency
- the importance of renewable energies
- consequences of and lessons from the shale revolution

ANALYSIS

4. **Step 1:** Together with a partner, take a closer look at the visual on p. 259 and explain the possible risks of fracking depicted there.

   Step 2: Taking into consideration the information given in the visual as well as the magazine article, juxtapose the possible benefits and risks of fracking. Copy the grid and complete it.

benefits/advantages	**risks/disadvantages**
• independence from politically unstable oil producers • …	• contamination of drinking water • potentially carcinogenic chemicals

[47] **complacent** [kəm'pleisənt] *selbstgefällig*

5. Examine the author's line of argument* and state whether or not he is in favour of fracking. Give evidence from the text to support your findings.
→ Focus on Skills, Analysis of a Non-Fictional Text, p. 377

6. Identify the particular type of text by showing and explaining specific characteristics and features (e. g. neutral vs. biased information, topical order, means of persuasion, etc.).
→ Focus on Facts, Basic Types of Non-Fictional Texts, p. 368

Reinhard Kowalewsky, Thomas Reisener

Exxon verspricht harmloses Fracking

AWARENESS

Germany has been extremely critical about "hydraulic fracturing" or "fracking".
In a round robin activity, state and share your views on fracking and its potential opportunities and dangers.

Der US-Konzern setzt auf ein neues Chemie-Gemisch. NRW verlängert die Frist für die Abbaurechte[1] von Exxon.

Energiemultis wie Exxon und die deutsche BASF-Tochter Wintershall haben in NRW 20 Claims abgesteckt[2], wie die potenziellen Abbaugebiete[3] für Gas, Gold und Öl im Fachjargon heißen. Ihr Problem: NRW hat 2011 faktisch sogar Probebohrungen[4] verboten. Denn das Gas ist in tiefen Gesteinsschichten eingeschlossen[5] und müsste mit der umstrittenen Fracking-Technologie gefördert werden, bei der ein Chemie-Cocktail tief unter der Erdoberfläche das Gestein aufsprengt. Das gefährdet das Grundwasser. [...]

Der Claim, den Exxon sich nun für weitere drei Jahre hat sichern lassen, heißt „NRW-Nord" und reicht vom nördlichen Münsterland bis Unna und von der niederländischen bis zur niedersächsischen[6] Landesgrenze – es ist einer der größten in NRW. „Damit hat Exxon sich das Zugriffsrecht[7] für Probebohrungen und eine eventuelle Förderung gesichert, falls es irgendwann doch eine gesetzliche Grundlage für Fracking-Genehmigungen geben sollte", sagt [Andreas] Nörten [vom zuständigen Bergamt[8] bei der Bezirksregierung[9] Arnsberg]. [...]

Der Präsident des Bundesverbandes Groß- und Außenhandel, Anton Börner, sagt: „Die USA profitieren vom Boom mit Schiefergas. Wenn Europa ähnliche Vorkommen nutzen würde, könnte uns das unabhängiger von Gasimporten machen." Vor dem Hintergrund des Ukraine-Konfliktes mit Russland ein aktueller Hinweis: Deutschland bezieht 40 Prozent seines Gases aus Russland.

Wohl auch vor diesem Hintergrund startete Exxon gestern eine Imagekampagne. In Zeitungsanzeigen warb Exxon-Chef Gernot Kalkoffen: „Wir möchten in Deutschland für Schiefergas mit höchsten Umweltstandards, modernster Technologie und unter Beteiligung der kritischen Öffentlichkeit neue Maßstäbe setzen[10] – mit Fracking, aber giftfrei."

Auf Nachfrage erklärte ein Exxon-Sprecher, man habe einen neuen Cocktail erfunden, der neben Wasser und Sand mit nur noch zwei Chemikalien auskomme [...]. Beide machten zusammen nur noch 0,2 Prozent des neuen Gemisches aus. Ob das Fracking dann wirklich gefahrenlos wird, wurde von Fachleuten gestern kontrovers eingeschätzt[11].

Rheinische Post, 26 September 2014, p. B1

[1] mining/drilling rights – [2] to stake a claim – [3] mining areas – [4] test drilling – [5] embedded/encased – [6] Lower Saxony – [7] access right/authorization – [8] local mining authority – [9] District Council – [10] to set standards – [11] to assess sth.

COMPREHENSION

M

1. Your American pen pal does not understand why the German government refuses to approve the energy companies' requests to allow fracking in Germany.
   Mediate the relevant passages of the German newspaper article and inform your friend about
   - the reasons and explanations of the North Rhine-Westphalian government for not approving the energy companies' requests,
   - the argumentation of Anton Börger, the president of the association of wholesale and retail trade,
   - ExxonMobil's attempts to improve fracking and make it less dangerous.

   → Focus on Skills, Mediation, p. 384

ANALYSIS

M

2. Mediate and examine ExxonMobil's advertisement which was published in various German newspapers and magazines.
   - Explain ExxonMobil's line of argument*: Which aspects do they emphasize in favour of fracking?
   - Which linguistic and rhetorical devices* are used to address German consumers and win their confidence?
   - How does ExxonMobil allude (*auf etw. anspielen*) to Germany's decision to focus on renewable energies?

   → Focus on Skills, Mediation, p. 384
   → Focus on Skills, Analysis of a Non-Fictional Text, p. 377

ACTIVITIES

3. Write a letter to ExxonMobil Europe's CEO, Gernot Kalkoffen, in which you respond to his "open letter" and his invitation to "critically accompany" ExxonMobil's efforts and begin a dialogue with the company.

   → Focus on Skills, Writing a Formal Letter, p. 396
   → Focus on Language, Connectives and Adverbs, p. 404

4. **Step 1:** Reactivate your knowledge about the process of fracking and read Roger Howard's article (pp. 259 ff.).

   Step 2: Extract arguments for and against fracking from both texts and complete the grid below:

against fracking	in favour of fracking
• use of poisonous, potentially carcinogenic additives • possibility of groundwater contamination • …	• only two non-poisonous/non-toxic additives • additives are biodegradable • …

   Step 3: Based on your findings from steps 1 and 2, discuss whether the concerns expressed there are being met by ExxonMobil Europe and the invention of the "non-poisonous" fracking method.

   → Focus on Language, Conversation and Discussion, p. 385

ExxonMobil Central Europe Holding
Caffamacherreihe 5
20355 Hamburg

ExxonMobil

29. September 2014

Lassen Sie uns über Fracking reden.

Sehr geehrte Damen und Herren,

Deutschland hat sich für die Energiewende[1] entschieden. Dafür braucht unser Land verlässlich[2] und ausreichend Erdgas. Die gute Nachricht ist: Deutschland hat noch für viele Jahrzehnte eigenes Erdgas – insbesondere das heimische Schiefergas.

Wir von ExxonMobil wollen die Energiewende unterstützen und scheuen dabei keine unkonventionellen Wege. Wir möchten in Deutschland für Schiefergas mit höchsten Umweltstandards, modernster Technologie und unter Beteiligung der kritischen Öffentlichkeit neue Maßstäbe setzen – mit Fracking, aber giftfrei.

Es ist uns gelungen, eine Kernforderung[3] aus Öffentlichkeit und Politik zu erfüllen: Es werden nur noch zwei ungiftige und zudem biologisch leicht abbaubare[4] Zusätze zum Einsatz kommen. Schiefergas hat darüber hinaus weitere Vorteile: Der Flächenbedarf[5] ist gering, was gerade in einem dichtbesiedelten Land von zentraler Bedeutung ist. Und schließlich wird kein salziges Wasser aus dem Untergrund mitgefördert, das entsorgt[6] werden muss.

Wir laden Sie ein, uns dabei kritisch zu begleiten. Sprechen Sie uns gerne an.

Gernot Kalkoffen
Vorstandsvorsitzender

Telefon: 0511-641 641 0
E-Mail: dialog.fracking@exxonmobil.com
www.erdgassuche-in-deutschland.de

[1] shift to renewable energy – [2] reliable – [3] key demand – [4] biodegradable ['baɪəʊdɪ'greɪdəbl] – [5] land requirements – [6] to dispose of sth.

Shop Till You Drop ... Global Trade and Consumption

Joseph Stiglitz

Why Globalization Fails

AWARENESS

Joseph Stiglitz (*1943) is an American economist and professor at Columbia University in New York City. In 2001, he was awarded the Nobel Memorial Prize in Economic Sciences. His work focuses on global trade, corporate gover-nance and income distribution. He is known for his critical view of the free-market economy and the management of globalization.

Reactivate your knowledge of the relevant components, risks and opportunities of globalization and read the Focus on Facts page *Progress & Responsibility in a Global World* (p. 272).
In groups, make a ranking of the various aspects you think might be beneficial or dangerous to society.

COMPREHENSION

1. **Step 1:** In a shared listening activity, team up with a partner and be prepared to listen to the audio text at least twice.

4 CD3

Step 2: In a **first listening**, get a general understanding of the various aspects Stiglitz mentions about globalization and jot down some notes on what you consider to be relevant information.

Step 3: Exchange your notes with your partner and briefly summarize your notes to each other.

Step 4: Listen to Stiglitz' remarks and observations **a second time**, now paying attention to details and taking notes on the aspects listed below:

- globalization in the 1990s
- changed perceptions of globalization
- reasons for people's antipathy towards globalization
- the management of globalization in
  a) the advanced industrialized world,
  b) developing countries
- (possible benefits) of globalization
- how to manage globalization correctly
- further aspects of globalization
- environmental issues

Step 5: Compare and exchange your notes with your partner, making additions or corrections if necessary.
→ Focus on Skills, Listening Comprehension, p. 366

Tips on vocab

to generate sth. *etw. hervorbringen* ■ **psychiatry** [saɪˈkaɪətri] relating to mental or emotional disorders ■ **to be better off** to have more money; to be happier or more satisfied ■ **to make sb. worse off** to make sb. poorer or be in a worse situation than before ■ **gains** *Erträge, Gewinne* ■ **to proceed** to continue as planned ■ **subsidy** *Subvention* ■ **to reciprocate** (*fml.*) to behave in the same way as sb. else ■ **to constitute** to form or make sth. ■ **to live up to sth.** (*phr. v.*) *den Erwartungen gerecht werden* ■ **for instance** for example ■ **capital flow** *Kapitalbewegung, Kapitalstrom* ■ **foreign direct investment (FDI)** money that is invested in companies, property or other assets by people or organizations from other countries ■ **recipient** *Empfänger* ■ **to give sth. short shrift** to be treated without sympathy and with little attention ■ **to put sth. in jeopardy** [ˈdʒepədi] to put sth. at risk

Webcode SNG-40183-031 @

Tip: In order to get a deeper understanding and better impression of Joseph Stiglitz, you can also watch the video clip provided on the webcode.

ANALYSIS

2. **Listen** to Stiglitz' remarks **a third time**. Against the background of your notes taken in task no. 1, together with a partner, compile a mind map that illustrates the various components of globalization as depicted by Stiglitz.

Tip: Draw your mind map on posters or wallpaper, using different colours and pictures to visualize the interdependencies, effects and connections.

Example:

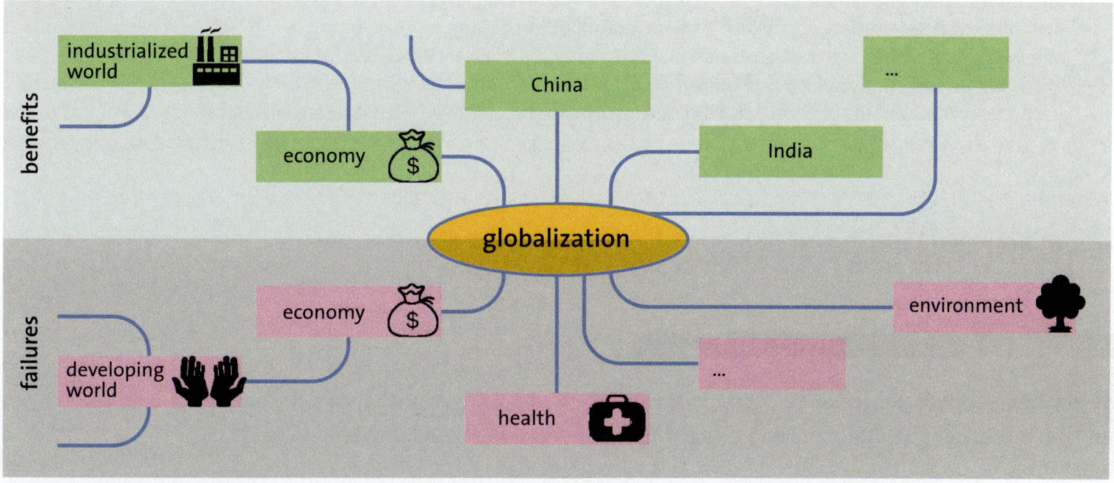

3. Examine and explain Stiglitz' statement that globalization "has put in jeopardy [...] values that have enormous consequences". Which values (and their loss) might he be referring to?

4. Describe and analyse the cartoon. To what extent can it be related to Joseph Stiglitz' observations on the failure of globalization?
→ Focus on Skills, Analysis of Visuals, p. 381

Credit: Jeff Danziger, NY Times Syndicate

Tips on vocab

to lean against sth. ■ sneakers ■ to have a grim facial expression ■ to have one's hands in one's pockets ■ to sweat ■ sewing machine ■ piles of (Nike) shoe cartons ■ old-fashioned equipment

ACTIVITIES

5. In class, discuss Joseph Stiglitz' rather negative view of globalization – is he being overly critical?
State whether or not you share his view.
→ Focus on Language, Conversation and Discussion, p. 385

GRAMMAR / LANGUAGE

6. Together with a partner, turn Joseph Stiglitz' statements and explanations into **indirect speech**. Be careful to use appropriate introductory verbs and be sure to backshift **tenses** if necessary.

Example: Stiglitz introduced himself, explaining that he had been involved in the global debates for ... He added that in the 1990s, there had been enormous support for ...

Info

Historical roots of globalization

- **Early "world economies"** like **Phoenicia** (1200 – 800 B. C.), the **Roman Empire** (510 B. C. – 500 A. D.), the **Silk Road** (1st century) and the **British East India Company** (founded in 1608) establish an international network of trading routes and commercial outposts.
- **Inventions and discoveries** of the late **Middle Ages** and **Renaissance** enable people **in Europe** to sail and **travel longer distances** and become less dependent on weather conditions (e. g. 13th cent.: magnetic compass, mechanical clock, spectacles/lenses, scales for weighing; 16th/17th cent.: pocket watch, thermometer, telescope).
→ International trading and exchange of goods is fostered.
- The **discovery of new continents** and their subsequent conquest in the 16th and 17th centuries gives European countries access to natural resources and labour.
- The **Industrial Revolution**, starting with the invention of James Watt's steam engine, enables the industrialized mass production of goods which is based on the constant input of resources, e. g. from overseas colonies.
- In the **19th century colonialism and imperialism** is at its peak, leading to the growth of Western economic power and dominance, but also dramatic and long-lasting social and economic problems in the colonized countries which linger to this day.

The Emporium[1] Strikes Back

AWARENESS

Describe the photo below and discuss its message. Do you think that demonstrations like this can make people aware of "the forces of consumerism" and make them reflect on their consumption habits?

The Blind Ones, photo by Nuno Guimaraes, 2013. Demonstration by students of the University of Sao Paulo, Brazil, in front of a shopping mall to make people aware of the forces of consumerism

Tips on vocab

to carry (bunches of) brown paper bags ■ to be blindfolded ■ to be covered with brown paint ■ anonymous ■ wheelchair ■ pavement/sidewalk ■ passers-by ■ to have a blank/dull facial expression

[1] **emporium** (*old-fashioned*) a large shop selling a large range of goods

Retailers in the rich world are suffering as people buy more things online. But they are finding ways to adapt

"The staff at Jessops would like to thank you for shopping with Amazon." With that parting shot[2] plastered to the front door of one of its shops, a company that had been selling cameras in Britain for 78 years shut down in January. The bitter note sums up the mood of many who work on high streets[3] and in shopping centres (malls) across Europe and America. As sales migrate to Amazon and other online vendors[4], shop after shop is closing down, chain after chain is cutting back. Borders, a chain of American bookshops, is gone. So is Comet, a British white-goods[5] and electronics retailer[6]. Virgin Megastores[7] have vanished from France, Tower Records[8] from America. In just two weeks in June and July, five retail chains with a total turnover of £600m ($900m) failed in Britain.

Watching the destruction, it is tempting to conclude that shops are to shopping what typewriters are to writing: an old technology doomed[9] by a better successor[10]. Seattle-based Amazon, nearing its 19th birthday, has lower costs than the vast majority of bricks-and-mortar[11] retailers. However, many shops, of whatever remarkable hypersize, a company builds in the attempt to offer vast[12] choice at low prices, the internet is vaster and cheaper. Prosperous Londoners and New Yorkers ask themselves when was the last time they went shopping; their shopping comes to them. "Retail guys are going to go out of business and e-commerce will become the place everyone buys," pronounces Marc Andreessen, a celebrity venture capitalist. "You are not going to have a choice."

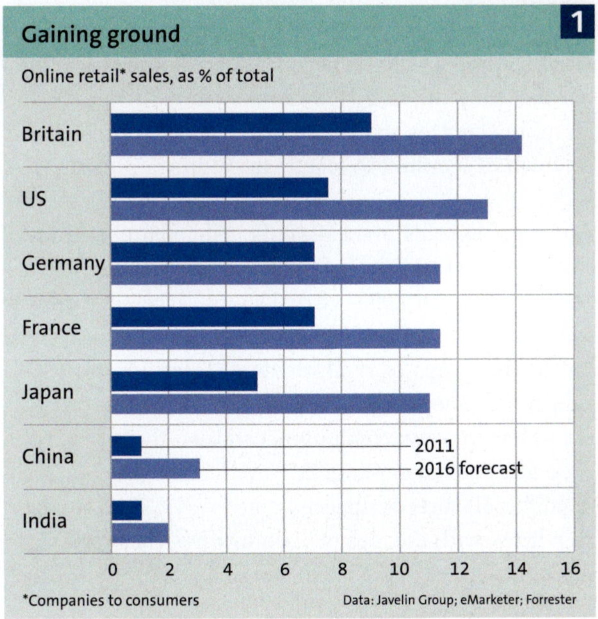

Online commerce has grown at different rates in different countries, but everywhere it is gaining fast (see chart 1). In Britain, Germany and France 90% of the rather modest growth in retail sales expected between now and 2016 will be online, predicts AXA Real Estate, a property-management company.

Old dog, meet new tricks

This would hurt less if shoppers were spending more; smaller slices are more acceptable when they come from bigger pies. But in many rich countries, especially in Europe, consumers are still smarting[13] from the bursting of the credit bubble and high unemployment. American consumers are perkier[14], but seem to be clinging to the bargain-hunting[15] habits of the recession. Services have been consuming a bigger share of their wallets[16] for decades, leaving less to spend on things (see chart 2). Ageing populations could shrink the pie further. Old people shop less.

When shoppers both know what they want and are willing to wait for it they will go online. And retail's simple moneymaking ways of yesteryear – find a catchy concept, fuel growth by opening new shops and attracting more shoppers to existing ones, use your growing size to squeeze suppliers for better margins – have run out of steam. But that does not mean that there are no new options for bricks and mortar.

Shopping is about entertainment as well as acquisition[17]. It allows people to build desires as well as fulfil them – if it did not, no one would ever window-shop[18]. It encom-

[2] **parting shot** a remark that you make when you are leaving, so that it has a stronger effect – [3] **high street** a street where the most important shops and businesses in a town are – [4] **vendor** sb. who is selling sth. – [5] **white-goods** large electrical goods for the house, such as cookers and washing machines – [6] **retailer** a person, shop or business that sells goods to the public – [7] **Virgin Records** a record label founded in 1972 – [8] **Tower Records** a US retail music chain (1950–2006) – [9] **doomed** certain to fail, die or be destroyed – [10] **successor** *Nachfolger* – [11] **bricks-and-mortar** businesses with buildings that customers go to (as opposed to online retailers) – [12] **vast** extremely large in amount – [13] **to smart from sth.** to feel upset because of failure or criticism; *von etw. schmerzen* – [14] **perky** happy and full of energy – [15] **bargain-hunting** *Schnäppchenjagd* – [16] **wallet** *Portemonnaie* – [17] **acquisition** the process of getting sth. – [18] **to window-shop** to spend time looking at the goods for sale in shop windows without intending to buy them

passes[19] exploration[20] and frivolity[21], not just necessity. It can be immersive[22], too. While computer screens can bewitch the eye, a good shop has four more senses to ensorcell[23]. No one makes the point better than Apple; in terms of sales per unit area its showrooms-slash-playrooms best[24] all other American retailers.

And shops make money. Bricks-and-mortar retail may be losing ground to online shopping, but it remains more profitable. The physical world is also increasingly capable of taking the fight to its online competitors. Last year online sales of shop-based American retailers grew by 29 %; those of online-only merchants grew by just 21 %. Apart from Amazon – which has long spurned[25] profits in favour of growth – most pure-play online retailers are losing market share, says Sucharita Mulpuru of Forrester Research. The bricks-and-mortar retrenchment[26] will be painful, but the survivors may make shopping a less formulaic, more satisfying and possibly even more profitable experience, both offline and on.

Many brands still think shops are the best way to attract customers. Inditex of Spain, owner of the ubiquitous[27] Zara fashion brand, opened 482 stores in 2012, bringing its total to 6,009 in 86 countries. Primark, a fast-growing vendor of nearly disposable[28] clothing, sells nothing on its website, relying on its 242 shops for almost all its sales. The same can hold at the luxury end, too – few will buy a $10,000 necklace online, or entrust it to the post. Space on the snazziest[29] streets in London, Paris and New York is in such demand that luxury retailers pay millions in "key money" to secure it, says Mark Burlton of Cushman & Wakefield, a property company.

Offline-only, though, is a shrinking category

[...] The future shopscape[30] will be emptier, but more attractive. Shoppers can expect new rewards for simply showing up. Shopkick, a mobile-phone app, gives American shoppers points that earn them goodies like iTunes songs just for stepping across the threshold of a participating store. Inspired by Apple, shops promise "experience" and hope that sales will follow. Germany's Kochhaus claims to be the first food store organised around recipes rather than grocery categories. The ingredients are strewn[31] across tables, not stacked on shelves. Some shops will opt[32] to sell nothing at all on the premises[33]. Desigual, a Spanish fashion merchant, has shops in Barcelona and Paris that carry only samples[34]. Shoppers are helped to assemble them into outfits that they then buy online.

Shopping centres are reallocating[35] space from the classic form of retailing to leisure and entertainment.

[...]

And new hybrids are emerging. Yihaodian, a Chinese company owned by Walmart, has used an app to let phone users visit 1,000 "virtual stores" accessible only at specific sites – many of which, rather cheekily[36], were on the doorsteps of rival retailers. Tesco's Korean subsidiary[37], Homeplus, puts up images of products on posters in the subway; commuters can scan them to get the products delivered. Tangible[38] and virtual retailing may meld[39] in all sorts of unaccustomed ways. Even Amazon has flirted with the idea of opening physical stores. Consumers have reason to cheer the survival of the sexiest.

The Economist, 13 July 2013, pp. 20 ff.

Dematerialising **2**

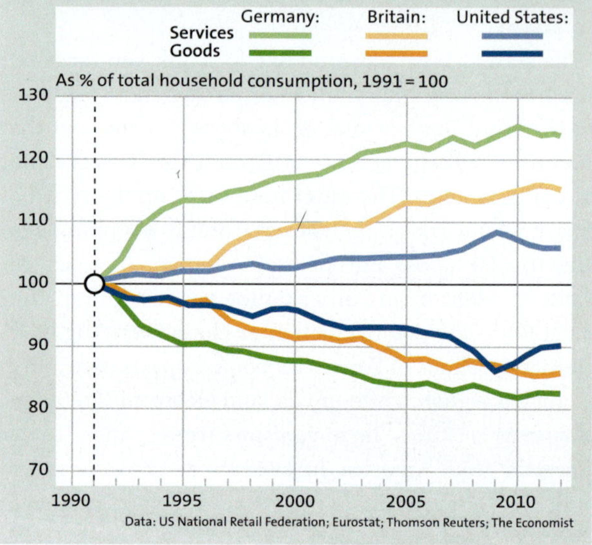

[19] **to encompass** (*fml.*) to include different types of things – [20] **exploration** *Erforschung, Erkundung* – [21] **frivolity** [frɪˈvɒləti] *Frivolität, Leichtsinnigkeit* – [22] **immersive** *eindringend* – [23] **to ensorcell** [ɪnˈsɔːsəl] *verhexen, verzaubern* – [24] **to best** (*fml.*) to defeat sb. in a fight or competition; *jdn. übertreffen* – [25] **to spurn** (*fml.*) *zurückweisen* – [26] **retrenchment** *Einschränkung, Einsparung* – [27] **ubiquitous** [juːˈbɪkwɪtəs] (*fml.*) seeming to be everywhere – [28] **disposable** *Wegwerf-* – [29] **snazzy** (*infml.*) modern and stylish in a way that attracts attention – [30] **shopscape** *Verkaufsraum* – [31] **to strew** (strewed, strewn) to spread things untidily over a surface – [32] **to opt** here: to choose – [33] **premises** *Geschäftsräume* – [34] **sample** *Muster, Probe* – [35] **to reallocate** *etw. umverteilen* – [36] **cheeky** *frech* – [37] **subsidiary** [səbˈsɪdiəri] *Filiale* – [38] **tangible** able to be shown, touched or experienced – [39] **to meld** *sich vermischen*

COMPREHENSION

1. Give an outline of the damage that online or e-commerce is doing to retailers.
2. Present the shopping habits of European and American consumers.
3. State why "bricks-and-mortar" retail shops are still attractive to consumers.
4. Describe the new strategies and shopping "hybrids" that have been created to motivate people to shop and consume.

ANALYSIS

5. Examine bar chart no. 1 and relate the presented trends and forecast to the new retail strategies depicted in the article.
   → Focus on Skills, Analysis of Statistical Data, p. 380
6. Analyse line graph no. 2 and explain what the peaks and lows reveal about shopping trends in the respective countries.
7. Explain the statement that "[w]hile computer screens can bewitch the eye, a good shop has four more senses to ensorcell" (ll. 64 ff.).
   What further senses – in addition to vision – do "physical stores" appeal to and in what way?
   Give examples.

ACTIVITIES

8. Team up with three other students and collect ideas about the "perfect shop" or shopping environment. Design a "shop", virtual or physical, that meets your desires and needs but is also profitable, competitive (*wettbewerbsfähig*) and environmentally friendly. Draw sketches on posters/wallpaper, then display them in class and discuss and evaluate your various ideas.
9. Annie Leonard is an American proponent (*Befürworter*) of sustainability and a critic of excessive consumerism. In 2008, she created the animated documentary *The Story of Stuff* in which she narrates the lifecycle of material goods and the impact of the materials economy.

   Webcode SNG-40183-032 @

   Step 1: Watch the video provided on the webcode and get an overview of the "materials economy".

   Step 2: Get information about and take notes on the "golden arrow of consumption".

   Step 3: Encouraged by the enormous success of *The Story of Stuff*, Annie Leonard and her team have produced further animated films to make people aware of environmental, economic and political grievances (*Missstände*).
   Divide your class into six groups, with each group working with one of Lennox' further films.
   - The Story of Bottled Water
   - The Story of Electronics
   - The Story of Cosmetics
   - The Story of Broke
   - The Story of Change
   - The Science of Persuasion

   Use the links provided on the webcode and prepare presentations on the various "stories".
   Additionally, you should provide your class with a 1–2 page handout that focuses on the most relevant information presented in each film.
   → Focus on Skills, Presentations, p. 391
   → Focus on Skills, Writing a Handout, p. 397

Progress & Responsibility in a Global World

The three historical periods of globalization

- **exploration (until 1500)**
  - founding and forming of villages, cities and infrastructure
- **colonization (1500 – 1900)**
  - development of writing and printing technologies (e. g. the Gutenberg printing press)
  - the Industrial Revolution (1750 – 1830)
  - advances in communications (e.g. telephone, telegraph)
- **internationalization (1900 – present)**
  - international trade and organizations (e. g. WTO (World Trade Organization), IMF (International Monetary Fund), World Bank, United Nations)
  - technology and global media (e. g. satellite, computers, Internet, WWW)
  - information revolution (e. g. personalization of communications → social networks, etc.)

Components of globalization

environment
- ecology
- global warming
- deforestation
- pollution
- efficient use vs. plunder of resources

culture/society
- education
- language
- shift of norms & values
- Westernization
- tourism
- change of lifestyles

economy
- production
- work
- trade
- markets
- consumption

technology
- scientific & technological advancement
- modernization
- information
- health care

population
- decline (rich countries) vs. expansion (poor countries)
- migration
- overpopulation
- outsourcing
- diseases (e. g. AIDS, HIV)
- ageing

media
- communication
- information
- surveillance

politics
- UN agencies
- NGOs
- NATO

Risks and opportunities

risks	opportunities	future tasks & requirements
• rising competition • increasing (inter-)dependencies • control by multinationals • uncontrolled money flow • growing inequalities • widening social gaps • environmental degradation • degradation of social standards • widening power imbalances • concentration of multinational companies	• diffusion of new ideas, technologies, products, services, lifestyles • new potential markets and customers • increase of communication • increasing coherence of politics in economy, society and employment due to international standards • global information network and exchange • cooperation through partnerships	• thinking globally → locally and globally • being prepared to venture into the unknown • developing intercultural competencies • being prepared for crosscultural encounters • being future-oriented → sustainability • developing production and service skills • developing flexibility • getting access to information

World Trade

World Economic Forum

The **World Economic Forum** (WEF), founded in 1971, is a Swiss non-profit foundation that meets annually in Davos, and **brings together international business and political leaders, intellectuals and journalists to discuss pressing global issues.**
Besides its economic focus, the annual meeting has become a neutral platform for political leaders to resolve political differences. In 2008, Microsoft founder Bill Gates gave a keynote speech on "creative capitalism", which combines generating profits and solving the world's inequities by using market forces to address the needs of the poor worldwide. The participants are considered a global elite – a think tank of internationally-oriented experts, including a group of "Young Global Leaders" consisting of under-forty-year-old leaders from all around the world and representing a wide range of disciplines and sectors.
WEF has also **launched several global initiatives**, e.g. the **Global Health Initiative**, the **Global Education Initiative** and the **Partnering Against Corruption Initiative**.
However, there is heavy criticism as well: WEF, along with the G8 and the World Trade Organisation, are viewed as a "mix of pomp and platitude" by anti-globalisation activists and many NGOs.

Further economic forums

- **The Group of Eight (G8):** France, Germany, Italy, Japan, the United Kingdom, the United States, Canada and Russia

This group has occasionally been expanded, e.g.:

- **Outreach Five (O5):** plus Brazil, China, India, Mexico and South Africa
- **Group of Twenty (G20):** the 20 major economies of Africa, North America, South America, East Asia, South Asia, Southeast Asia, Western Asia, Eurasia, Europe and Oceania; the group meets semi-annually, and the last meeting took place in Seoul in November 2010.

Global players – and the consequences

- **multinational companies** (or mega corporations) play an important role in the international economy: they often have powerful influence on local economies, international relations and even politics (→ lobbying)
- **many multinational companies are criticized** due to lax environmental standards, bad labour standards (e.g. sweatshops in developing countries, control of tariffs → unfair wages), marginalization of local businesses/markets
- many multinationals hold **patents** (e.g. Siemens, Adidas) in order to prevent the rise of competitors
- examples of **influential multinational corporations** are: ExxonMobil, Wal-Mart, McDonald's, General Electric, Boeing, Microsoft and British Petrol
- the United Nations declares **2005 the International Year of Microcredit**; microloans are designed to spur entrepreneurship in developing countries and gain acceptance in the mainstream finance industry as a source of future growth

Democracy Going Global: Peace, Stability and Human Rights

David Rovics

The Best Democracy Money Can Buy

AWARENESS

Step 1: Reflect on the title of the song: Can democracy (really) be bought? What is the price?

Step 2: How is democracy connected to "money", i.e. the economy of a country, industries or companies? Discuss in class.

COMPREHENSION

Before reading:

1. Bar codes are on every product we buy and we do not usually pay attention to them. Do you know what their function is? Collect ideas in class.
2. Now, have a look at the painting below and describe it in detail using the vocab box. Does the depiction of the bar code in the painting differ from the bar codes we know from everyday life?

Tips on vocab

square ■ metal platte ■ brass-coloured ■ barcode ■ engraving *(Gravur)* ■ indentation *(Vertiefung)* ■ metallic gleam/shimmer ■ blurry/stained *(fleckig, angelaufen)* ■ binary code (= using only 0 and 1 as a system of numbers)

The United Nations

The **United Nations Organization** (UNO, UN) was **founded in 1945 to replace the League of Nations** in order **to stop wars** between countries and as **a platform for international dialogue**. It contains multiple subsidiary organizations with diverse functions to carry out the UN's missions. Today, about 192 nations belong to the UN. When nations become a member of the UN, they agree to accept the obligations of **the UN Charter**, which states the **four basic purposes of the UN**:

- to maintain **international peace and security**
- to develop **friendly relations among nations**
- to be a centre for **harmonizing the actions of nations**
- to cooperate in **solving international problems** and promoting **respect for human rights**

The organization of the United Nations

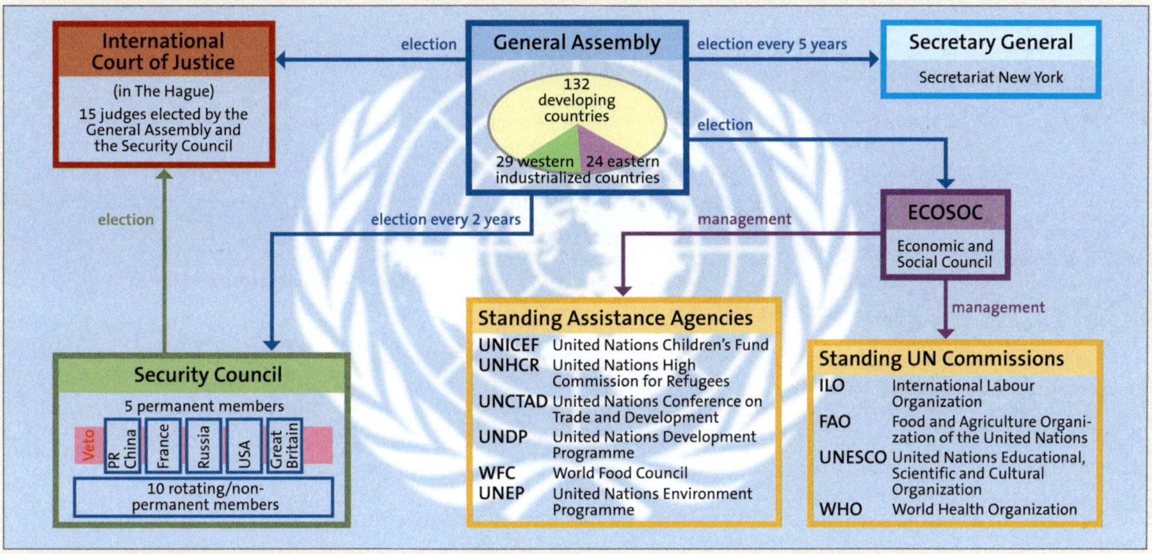

Global issues on the UN Agenda

- Africa
- Ageing
- Agriculture
- AIDS
- Atomic Energy
- Children
- Climate Change
- Culture
- Decolonization
- Demining
- Development Corporation
- Persons with Disabilities
- Disarmament
- Drugs and Crime
- Education
- Elections
- Energy
- Environment
- Family
- Food
- Governance
- Health
- Human Rights
- Human Settlements
- Humanitarian and Disaster Relief Assistance
- Indigenous People
- Information Communications Technology
- Intellectual Property
- International Finance
- Iraq
- Labour
- International Law
- Oceans and the Law of the Sea
- Least Developed Countries
- The Millenium UN General Assembly – The Goals
- Questions of Palestine
- Peace and Security
- Population
- Refugees
- Science and Technology
- Social Development
- Outer Space
- Statistics
- Sustainable Development
- Terrorism
- Trade and Development
- Volunteerism
- Water
- Women
- Youth

www.un.org/issues

The Universal Declaration of Human Rights

On **10 December 1948 the General Assembly of the United Nations** adopted and proclaimed the Universal Declaration of Human Rights. Although it is not a legally binding document it outlines a distinct understanding and view of human rights.

Article 1. All human beings are born free and equal in dignity and rights. They are endowed[1] with reason and conscience and should act towards one another in a spirit of brotherhood.

Article 2. Everyone is entitled to all the rights and freedoms set forth in this Declaration, without distinction of any kind, such as race, colour, sex, language, religion, political or other opinion, national or social origin, property, birth or other status. [...]

Article 3. Everyone has the right to life, liberty and security of person.

Article 4. No one shall be held in slavery or servitude; slavery and the slave trade shall be prohibited in all their forms.

Article 5. No one shall be subjected to torture or to cruel, inhuman or degrading treatment or punishment.

Article 6. Everyone has the right to recognition everywhere as a person before the law.

Article 7. All are equal before the law and are entitled without any discrimination to equal protection of the law. All are entitled to equal protection against any discrimination in violation of this Declaration and against any incitement[2] to such discrimination.

Article 8. Everyone has the right to an effective remedy[3] by the competent national tribunals for acts violating the fundamental rights granted him by the constitution or by law.

Article 9. No one shall be subjected to arbitrary[4] arrest, detention[5] or exile. [...]

Article 12. No one shall be subjected to arbitrary interference with his privacy, family, home or correspondence, nor to attacks upon his honor and reputation. Everyone has the right to the protection of the law against such interference or attacks. [...]

Article 16. (1) Men and women of full age, without any limitation due to race, nationality or religion, have the right to marry and to found a family. They are entitled to equal rights as to marriage, during marriage and at its dissolution. (2) Marriage shall be entered into only with the free and full consent of the intending spouses[6]. [...]

Article 17. (1) Everyone has the right to own property alone as well as in association with others. (2) No one shall be arbitrarily deprived[7] of his property. [...]

Article 19. Everyone has the right to freedom of opinion and expression; this right includes freedom to hold opinions without interference and to seek, receive and impart information and ideas through any media and regardless of frontiers. [...]

Article 26. (1) Everyone has the right to education. Education shall be free, at least in the elementary and fundamental stages. Elementary education shall be compulsory[8]. Technical and professional education shall be made generally available and higher education shall be equally accessible to all on the basis of merit[9]. [...]

Article 28. Everyone is entitled to a social and international order in which the rights and freedoms set forth in this Declaration can be fully realized.

www.un.org/en/documents/udhr/index.shtml#atop [03.12.2012]

[1] **to endow sb. with. sth.** [ɪn'daʊ] *jdn. mit etw. ausstatten* – [2] **incitement** *Anstiftung* – [3] **remedy** a successful way of curing an illness or dealing with a problem or difficulty – [4] **arbitrary** *willkürlich* – [5] **detention** *Haft, Internierung* – [6] **spouse** wife, husband – [7] **to deprive sb. of sth.** *jdm. etw. aberkennen* – [8] **compulsory** that has to done; *verpflichtend* – [9] **merit** (*fml.*) the quality of being good and deserving praise

The Plague of Global Terrorism

AWARENESS

Terrorism is not a new threat – there have been terrorist attacks and plots for centuries all over the world. One example is the Gunpowder Plot of 1605, when English Catholics attempted – and failed – to blow up the House of Lords during the State Opening ceremony and assassinate King James I of England and VI of Scotland. The night before the State Opening, one of the conspirators, Guy Fawkes, was discovered guarding 36 barrels of gunpowder and was arrested. At the trial, Guy Fawkes was sentenced to be hanged, drawn and quartered.
However, the 20th and 21st centuries have shown new shocking dimensions of terrorism worldwide.
In a placemat activity, share and discuss your knowledge of and thoughts about terrorism in general and certain terrorist acts in particular.

COMPREHENSION

Before reading:

Step 1: In groups, describe the cartoon below in detail, paying attention to these aspects:
- the depiction of the IS fighter
- how he sees the world
- the IS fighter's vision of Europe, European culture and Europe's religious orientation
- the overall atmosphere of the cartoon
- → Focus on Skills, Analysis of Visuals, p. 381

Step 2: Discuss the message of the cartoon.
- What is the cartoonist's view of the IS?
- What image of the IS in general does the cartoon convey?

Konkrete Vorstellung

Tips on vocab

the right side: a disguised (*vermummt*) man ■ a thin slit for the eyes ■ to wear an ammunition belt ■ the world is flat (like a disc) ■ a grid (*Raster*)
the left side: a thought bubble ■ a woman wearing a black niqab (= a dress covering the entire body, with a thin slit for the eyes) ■ allusion: Europa, a figure from Greek mythology, sitting on a bull – depicting the continent → personification ■ the bull: a grim facial expression ■ the half-moon as a symbol for Islam

The appalling attacks in Paris on November 13th [2015] are a brutal reminder of the danger of terrorism to the West, mainly from jihadist[1] groups such as Islamic State (IS). Yet terrorism is a threat everywhere. The day before the atrocities[2] in Paris, two bomb blasts killed 37 people in Beirut. On November 17th [2015] a suicide bomber blew up a market in northern Nigeria, leaving at least 36 people dead. Last year 32,700 people were killed in attacks worldwide, nearly twice as many as in 2013. And this year the toll[3] may turn out to be even higher.

Most of the deaths last year (and every year) are in the Middle East and Africa – not the West. Iraq, Nigeria, Syria, Pakistan and Afghanistan together account for three-quarters of the global total. Western countries suffered under 3 % of all deaths in the past 15 years. Boko Haram, a jihadist group that operates mainly in northern Nigeria and Cameroon (and recently pledged[4] affiliation[5] to Islamic State), was responsible for over 6,600 deaths according to the Institute for Economics and Peace (which excludes military targets). That is more than any other group in the world – even IS. Nigeria has also been plagued by a new outfit in the south, the Fulani militants, which did not even exist until 2013. The increased bloodiness of both groups contributed to a quadrupling[6] of deaths to 7,500 in 2014, the largest rise ever seen in one country. If deaths caused by war were counted, IS is far more deadly than any other organisation, even using the most conservative estimates.

The Paris attacks and the downing[7] of a Russian airliner in Egypt killed more than 100 people each. Such lethal[8] attacks are rare but are increasing. Last year, there were 26 compared with a handful in 2013. Most were carried out by IS, and most occurred in Iraq. And terrorism is spreading. 67 countries saw at least one death last year compared with 59 the year before. The number of plots by jihadist groups against Western countries has leaped[9], in particular since September 2014 when an IS spokesman called for its followers to attack those Western countries involved in military efforts in Syria and Iraq. Most plots[10] have failed, though a growing number have been successful. But the terrorists only need to carry out one big plot to succeed.

http://www.economist.com/blogs/graphicdetail/2015/11/daily-chart-12, 18 November 2015 [17.07.2016]

COMPREHENSION

1. Find evidence in the text that matches the following statements:
a) Terrorism cannot be reduced to local conspiracies.
b) The number of victims of terrorist attacks has risen dramatically.
c) Africa has suffered most from terrorist attacks.
d) The IS has become the most dangerous terrorist organization globally.
e) Terrorism is spreading significantly worldwide.
f) The number of terrorist attacks against the West is extremely low.
g) In general, terrorist attacks have been rather unsuccessful.

ANALYSIS

2. Find passages in the article that match the information and figures presented in the statistics on the following page.
Team up with a partner and explain the correlations to each other.
→ Focus on Skills, Analysis of Statistical Data, p. 380
→ Focus on Skills, Analysis of a Non-Fictional Text, p. 377

[1] **jihadist** [dʒəˈhædist] a Muslim who is fighting for Islam, esp. a radical, who believes in using violence to achieve religious and political aims – [2] **atrocity** an extremely cruel, violent or shocking act – [3] **toll** suffering, deaths or damage – [4] **to pledge** to make a serious or formal promise to make or do sth. – [5] **affiliation** a connection with a political party, religion or organization – [6] **to quadruple** to become four times as big – [7] **downing** *Abschuss* – [8] **lethal** [ˈliːθəl] able to cause or causing death – [9] **to leap** (leapt, leapt) to increase or grow very quickly – [10] **plot** conspiracy

1

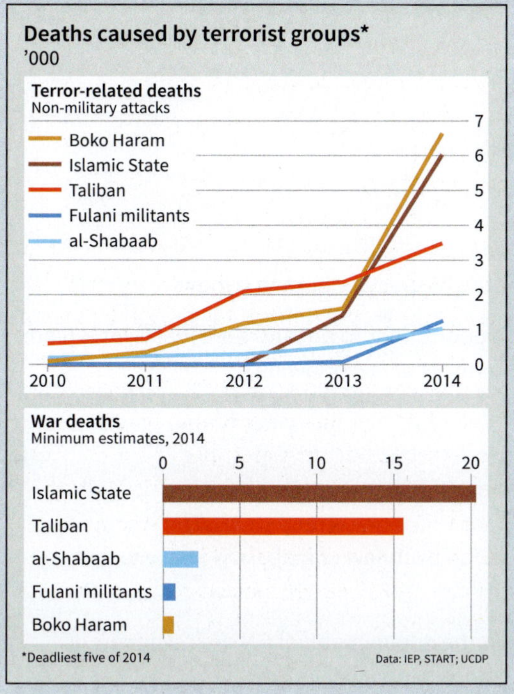

2

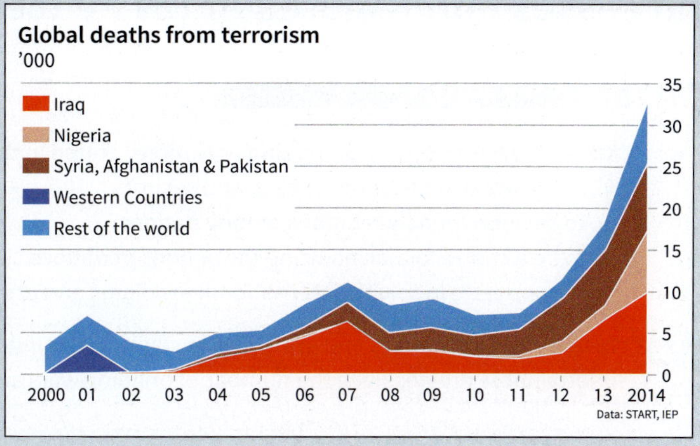

3

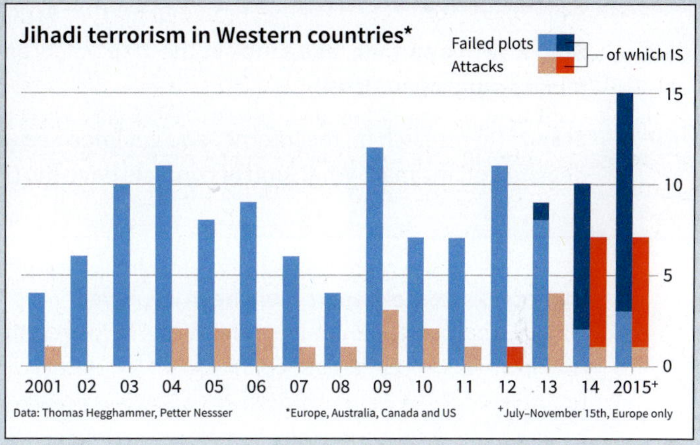

ACTIVITIES

3. Your class is planning the graduation/end-of-school trip, which has led to a very controversial discussion. In light of terrorist attacks in recent years (e.g. in France and Sweden), you want to choose a safe – but also affordable – destination for your trip.
Discuss the possible pros and cons of different travel destinations in class.
→ Focus on Language, Conversation and Discussion, p. 385

Barney Henderson

Successes and Failures of UN Peacekeeping Missions

AWARENESS

The four basic purposes of the United Nations, stated in the UN Charter, are:

- to maintain international peace and security
- to develop friendly relations among nations
- to be a centre for harmonizing the actions of nations
- to cooperate in solving international problems and promoting respect for human rights

Discuss these purposes and principles in class: Is the United Nations right to pursue these ideals, or is it an unattainable dream, given the number of ongoing wars and terrorist acts worldwide?

COMPREHENSION

1. **Before reading:**

Step 1: With a partner, take a look at the map below and get an overview of global UN peacekeeping missions and operations.

@ **Step 2:** Do research on the Internet and get informed about the deployment[1] of UN peacekeepers as depicted on the map. What kind of conflicts have the UN troops been involved in?

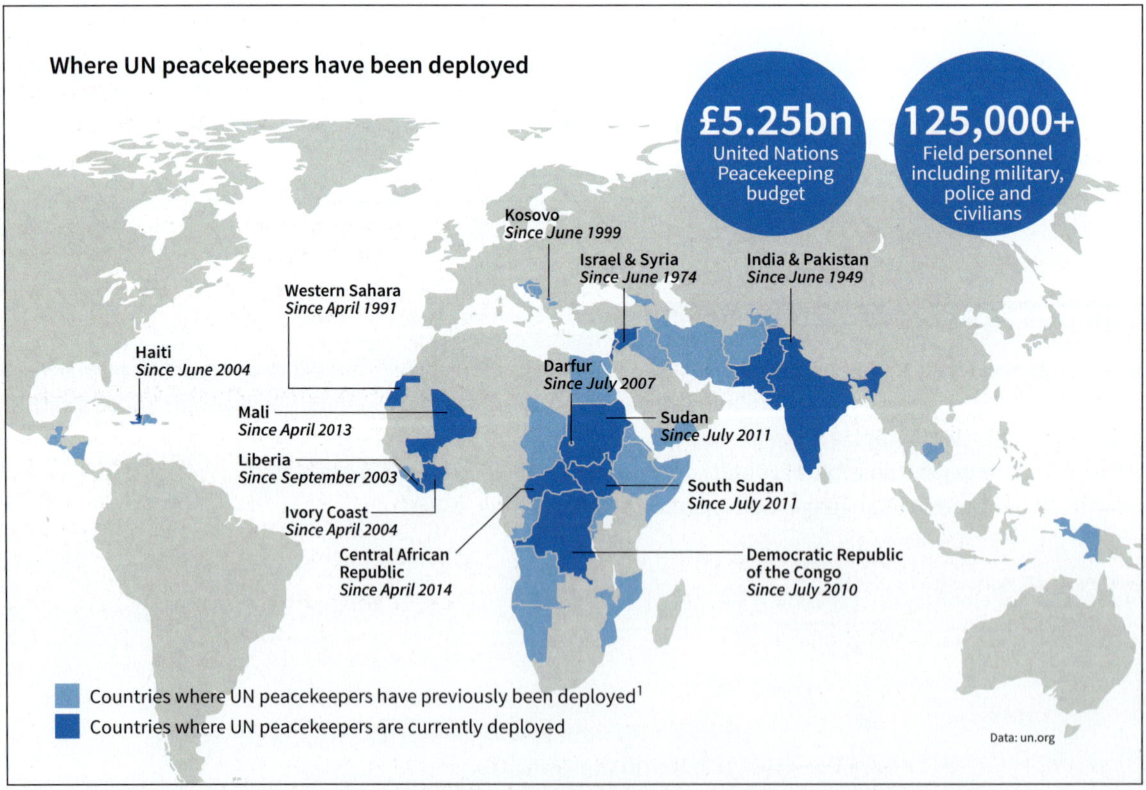

[1] **to deploy** to move soldiers and weapons into a position where they are ready for military action

The UN General Assembly session opened on September 15 [2015]. This year the organisation celebrates its 70th birthday but how has the UN had an impact on the world's conflicts?
United Nations peacekeeping operations began in 1948 and the light blue helmets and berets[1] have been deployed to many of the world's trouble spots from Papua New Guinea to Haiti ever since, with varying levels of effectiveness.
An internal UN study last year found that UN peacekeeping missions routinely avoid using force to protect civilians who are under attack, intervening in only 20 per cent of cases despite being authorised to do so by the UN Security Council.
While some peacekeeping missions perform adequately, others have failed to protect civilians – notably at Srebrenica[2], where Dutch peacekeepers watched on powerless as thousands of men were murdered.
Of the 69 UN peacekeeping missions over the past 68 years, there have been some notable failures – and cases of successful intervention.

Where peacekeepers have succeeded – and failed

Srebrenica

On July 11, 1995, towards the end of Bosnia's 1992–95 war, Bosnian Serb forces swept into the eastern Srebrenica enclave[3] and executed 8,000 Muslim men and boys in the days that followed, dumping[4] their bodies into pits[5]. It was the worst massacre in post-Second World War European history. The UN had previously declared the town one of the safe areas, to be "free from any armed attack or any other hostile act." 600 Dutch infantry[6] were supposed to be protecting thousands of civilians who had taken refuge from earlier Serb offensives in north-eastern Bosnia.
As Serb forces began shelling[7] Srebrenica, Bosnian Muslim fighters in the town asked for the return of weapons they had surrendered to the UN peacekeepers but their request was refused. The Dutch peacekeepers were obliged[8] to watch as the killings began. The failure led in part to the creation of the United Nations Peacebuilding Commission and set the West on a new course of 'liberal interventionism.'

Rwanda

Another major failing of the UN peacekeeping organisation was not doing more to prevent the 1994 Rwandan genocide[9] that left up to one million people dead. A 1999 inquiry found that the UN ignored evidence that the genocide was planned and refused to act once it had started. More than 2,500 UN peacekeepers were withdrawn after the murder of ten Belgian soldiers. In one case, the peacekeeping forces deserted a school where Tutsis were taking shelter – hundreds of people inside were immediately massacred.
Kofi Annan, who was then head of UN peacekeeping forces was accused of failing to pass on warnings of the massacre. UN soldiers did not return to Rwanda until June, by which time hundreds of thousands of people were dead. The UN was accused of "leaving Rwanda to its fate."

Somalia

The UN operation was the first time the peacekeeping force had been used for "humanitarian intervention." However, the peacekeepers were met with a hostile[10] reception in Mogadishu. Several of them were killed and the bodies of dead US soldiers were paraded through the streets on the orders of the Somali warlords.
When an American Black Hawk helicopter was shot down as part of the Battle of Mogadishu, the US withdrew its troops. In 1995 the UN withdrew all peacekeeping troops. It was described at the time by one UN official as "the greatest failure of the UN in our lifetime."

Sierra Leone

The UN peacekeeping force that operated in Sierra Leone from 1999 to 2005 is hailed as a success. It was created to help implement[11] a peace agreement after the country's devastating[12] civil war.
Mr Ban officially closed the UN offices in Freetown in 2014, declaring a "successful conclusion" to the organisations work in helping to bring peace to the country, calling it a "triumph for the people of Sierra Leone" after what had been a decade of warfare. "Our blue helmets disarmed more than 75,000 ex-fighters, including

[1] **beret** *Baskenmütze* – [2] **Srebrenica** a town in the eastern part of Bosnia, where, in the course of the civil war, more than 8,000 Muslim Bosniaks were killed in 1995 in a genocidal killing *(Völkermord)* – [3] **enclave** *Enklave, eingeschlossenes Gebiet* – [4] **to dump** to drop sth. in a careless way – [5] **pit** *Grube* – [6] **infantry** the part of an army that fights on foot – [7] **to shell sth.** *etw. bombardieren* – [8] **obliged** to be forced to do sth. – [9] **genocide** *Völkermord* – [10] **hostile** *feindlich* – [11] **to implement** to start using a plan or system – [12] **devastating** causing a lot of damage or destruction

hundreds of child soldiers. The UN destroyed more than 42,000 weapons and 1.2 million rounds of ammunition[13] – a potentially deadly arsenal that is now itself dead," Mr Ban declared.

Burundi

Burundi is also frequently cited as a success story for the UN peacekeeping operation, helping it recover from decades of ethnic war. Ban Ki-moon, UN secretary-general, hailed Burundi's "substantial progress, overcoming formidable[14] challenges since the end of the civil war." But in 2014 he extended the peacekeeping mission for a year to help the country through elections, that took place earlier in July, and cautioned[15] that the gains made under the UN's watch were not irreversible[16].

http://www.telegraph.co.uk/news/worldnews/europe/bosnia/11729436/Srebrenica-20-years-on-What-have-been-the-successes-and-failures-of-UN-peacekeeping-missions.html, 28 September 2015 [20.05.2016]

COMPREHENSION

2. Read the first part of the article and sum up the 70-year history of the UN peacekeeping operations.

3. Now, read the rest of the text and take notes on the failures and successes of the UN peacekeeping missions and the reasons behind them.
Copy the grid below into your notebook and complete it.

UN peacekeeping missions	
successes	**failures**
• Sierra Leone → reason: … •	• Srebrebica, Bosnia → reason: … •

ANALYSIS

4. The author points out that the massacre of Srebrenica has led to
a) the creation of the UN Peacebuilding Commission (ll. 39 f.) and
b) a new course of "liberal interventionism" (l. 42).

Try to find an explanation for this new policy. How can an international army/corps "intervene in a liberal way" when being confronted with massacres and extreme violence?
→ Focus on Skills, Analysis of a Non-Fictional Text, p. 377

5. Keeping in mind the frequent claims that UN peacekeeping operations are ineffective, take a close look at the cartoons below.
Describe them in detail and explain what they criticize in particular.
→ Focus on Skills, Analysis of Visuals, p. 381

[13] **round of ammunition** a bullet or single piece of ammunition – [14] **formidable** causing you to have fear or respect for sth. or someone because that thing or person is large, powerful, or difficult – [15] **to caution** to give sb. an official warning – [16] **irreversible** impossible to change

1

ACTIVITIES

6. Use the information given in the map on page 288 and do further research on the UN peacekeeping missions. Which of the operations depicted in the map have been successful and which ones have failed?

7. Now that you have dealt with the topic, take a look at the Awareness task on page 288 again. To put it in a nutshell, are the UN peacekeeping forces really worth £5.25bn (= ca. 6.22bn Euro), or are they merely a diplomatic "token" that gives the Western nations a good conscience? Discuss in class.
   → Focus on Language, Conversation and Discussion, p. 385

2

Science & Technology: Man Between Molecules and Machines

Monsanto Dominates the Global Seed Market

AWARENESS

Genetic engineering, **genetic modification (GM)** and **gene splicing** are terms for the process of manipulating genes; it is the direct alteration of specific genetic codes (inclusion, removal, etc.) in order to achieve a desired result.

Biotechnology refers to any technical application that uses biological systems, living organisms, or derivatives thereof, to make or modify products or processes for specific use. It also uses micro-organisms, such as bacteria, to perform specific industrial or manufacturing processes.

In groups, study the two definitions above:
What differences and similarities can you detect between the described genetic and biotechnological processes? What feelings do these definitions evoke? Give reasons for your assessment.

COMPREHENSION

6–7 CD 3

1. In a **first listening**, try to get **a general understanding** of
   a) Monsanto's company policy,
   b) Troy Roush's problems with Monsanto.

2. Then, **while listening** to the recording **a second time**, take notes on the following aspects:

6 CD 3

- Monsanto's objectives for the future
- the impact of agricultural technology
- Monsanto's role in biotechnology
- Monsanto's justification of its business tactics and company policy

7 CD 3

- Troy Roush's problems with Monsanto
- how Monsanto dictates the rules of farming
- how Roush views his situation as a farmer today
- attorney Adam Levitt's assessment of Monsanto's and the farmers' positions
- the future of farming

→ Focus on Skills, Listening Comprehension, p. 366

Webcode SNG-40183-034 @

Tip: In order to get a deeper understanding of the situation, you can also watch the video on Monsanto and Troy Roush provided on the webcode.

If necessary, listen to the recording **a third time** and complete your notes.

Tips on vocab

yield an amount of sth. positive, such as food or profit, that is produced or supplied ■ **bushel** a unit of measurement equal to ca. 35.2 litres in the U. S. ■ **fierce** strong, powerful and frightening ■ **stakeholder** *Interessengruppe* ■ **breach** an act of breaking a law or agreement ■ **to purchase** to buy sth. ■ **to allege** to state sth. as a fact but without giving proof ■ **to sue sb.** to take legal action against a person or organization; *jdn. gerichtlich verfolgen* ■ **legal bill** *Gerichtskosten* ■ **to mount** to increase ■ **to divulge** to make sth. secret known ■ **suit** *Prozess, Klage* ■ **bottom line** *Reingewinn* ■ **pawn** *Schachfigur* ■ **extended arm** *verlängerter Arm*

ANALYSIS

3. As depicted in the recording, the American biotech corporation Monsanto holds many patents on seeds and crops in the U. S., making it almost impossible for farmers to grow non-modified plants. Farmers like Troy Roush are trying to find ways out of the system that companies like Monsanto impose on them.

M Mediate relevant passages of the German magazine article below and write an English blog entry for the international Internet forum "No Patents on Seeds".
Explain how farmers in Europe are fighting against corporations like Monsanto and trying to prevent patents on plants, animals and seeds.
→ Focus on Skills, Mediation, p. 384

ACTIVITIES

4. Over time, Europeans, especially Germans, have become particularly critical towards GM food. Environmentalists and scientists have tried to save and re-establish old crops, e. g. certain cultivars (= *Sorten*) of historical potatoes that were planted in the past.
@ Do research on these "old-fashioned" crops (e. g. *Bamberger Hörnchen*, *La Ratte*, *Rosa Tannenzapfen*, *Sieglinde*, *Blauer Schwede*, *Ackersegen*, etc.), some of which date back to the early eighteenth century. What advantages do they have over modern GM seeds?

5. Monsanto is a U. S.-based multinational agricultural biotechnology corporation and the world's leading producer of GM seed. It provides the technology for 90 % of the world's GM seeds and holds many patents. One of its leading products, the so-called "Terminator" seed, is sterile, which means it does not flower or grow fruit after the initial planting.
@ Do research on the Monsanto corporation and prepare a short presentation in which you outline the company's philosophy and fields of research.
→ Focus on Skills, Presentations, p. 391

Philip Bethge: Der Brokkoli gehört uns allen

Dürfen Pflanzen und Tiere patentiert werden? In Europa ist das stark eingeschränkt[1]. Patente würden nicht erteilt für „Pflanzensorten[2] oder Tierrassen" sowie „im Wesentlichen biologische" Züchtungsverfahren[3], heißt es im Europäischen Patentabkommen. Doch das Europäische Patentamt (EPA) scheint die Regeln nicht ernst zu nehmen. Etwa 2400 Patente auf Pflanzen und 1400 Patente auf Tiere seien schon erteilt worden, kritisiert die Initiative No Patents on Seeds im Vorfeld[4] einer Anhörung[5] vor der Großen Beschwerdekammer[6] des EPA. Aktuell will sich die Firma Plant Bioscience konventionell gezüchteten Brokkoli als Erfindung schützen lassen, das israelische Landwirtschaftsministerium[7] Tomaten. Und es ist zu befürchten[8], dass die Patente am Ende bestätigt werden. Möglich ist dies, weil die Industrie Übung darin hat, auf geschickte Weise rechtliche Schlupflöcher[9] auszunutzen. Eine bestimmte Apfelsorte mit erhöhtem Vitamingehalt beispielsweise lässt sich in Europa nicht patentieren. Wenn indes in der Patentschrift[10] allgemein von vitaminangereicherten Pflanzen die Rede ist (also nicht von einer einzigen Sorte), lassen die EPA-Beamten oftmals mit sich reden. Die Patentierung hänge „in vielen Fällen" davon ab, „wie geschickt die Ansprüche formuliert werden", gibt die Technische Beschwerdekammer im EPA offen zu. Ein Armutszeugnis[11].

Dabei ist es brisant, wenn Lebewesen geistiges Eigentum von Firmen werden. Der Zugang zur genetischen Vielfalt muss öffentlich bleiben. Sonst können unabhängige Forscher und Züchter nicht mehr uneingeschränkt nach neuen Sorten fahnden[12], um die Nahrungsmittelversorgung für eine wachsende Weltbevölkerung sicherzustellen. Sonst geraten Bauern in Abhängigkeiten, die sie sich gerade in Entwicklungsländern nicht leisten können. Natürlich müssen Saatgutfirmen Geld verdienen können mit ihren Innovationen. Doch Patente sind dafür der falsche Weg – vor allem, wenn sie mithilfe juristischer Wortklauberei[13] zustande kommen.

Die Patentierung von Leben ist eine ethische Grundsatzfrage, die nicht in Hinterzimmern des EPA entschieden werden darf. Nur in einer offenen gesellschaftlichen Diskussion kann geklärt werden, wem die genetische Vielfalt gehört.

Der Spiegel, 44/2014, 27 November 2014, p. 127

[1] limited – [2] cultivar – [3] breeding techniques – [4] the forefront of – [5] hearing – [6] Board of Appeal – [7] ministry of agriculture – [8] to fear – [9] legal loophole – [10] patent specification – [11] a demonstration of the poor state of sth. – [12] to pursue sth. – [13] quibbling

Genetic Engineering

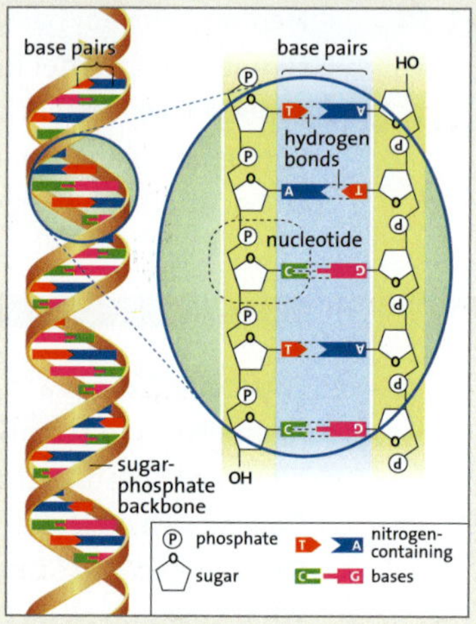

Genetic engineering (or genetic modification) is the **human manipulation of an organism's genetic material** to create **a genetically modified organism** that does not exist under natural conditions.

During this process, new genetic material (DNA) is inserted into the host genome (= the entirety of an organism's hereditary information). First the **genetic material of interest is isolated and copied**, thereby generating a construct that contains all the necessary genetic elements, which is then **inserted into a host organism** in a second step.

Thus, **genetic engineering changes the genetic design or genetic blueprint** (*Kopie*) **of an organism** and **forms new combinations** of heritable (= *erblich*) genetic material. Although **stem cell research** and **cloning** are not considered to be genetic engineering by definition, these areas of scientific research are closely connected to genetic engineering because they can be used together.

In **medicine** genetic engineering is used e. g. for **the mass production of insulin, human growth hormones, follitism (for treating infertility) and vaccines** (*Impfstoff*). Researchers are also working to genetically engineer humans and e. g. **replace defective humans genes with functional ones** and thus **cure genetic disorders and diseases** like Parkinson's disease, cancer, diabetes, heart diseases and arthritis.

Despite all the (possible) benefits of genetic engineering there are also **ethical concerns and criticism** that this technology is not only used for treatment but for enhancement, modification or alteration of a human being's character, behaviour, appearance, intelligence or adaptability.

Historical development

year	major scientific discovery or achievement
1856–1863	Austrian monk and scientist **Gregor Johann Mendel** (1822–1884) shows that the inheritance of certain traits follows particular laws (the **"Laws of Inheritance"**); he is considered to be the "father of modern genetics"
1953	American zoologist **James Watson** and British physicist **Francis Crick discover the double helix**, the chemical structure of DNA which makes up genes
1972	American biochemist **Paul Berg creates the first recombinant** (= altered, modified) **DNA**
1974	German biologist **Rudolf Jaenisch creates a transgenic mouse** by inserting foreign DNA into its embryo
1976	Genetic Engineering Technology Inc. (Genentech Inc.), **the first biotechnology company, is founded in California** by US businessman Robert A. Swanson and biochemist Dr. Herbert Boyer
1978	Genentech Inc. **produces genetically engineered human insulin**
1980	the **US Supreme Court rules that genetically altered life can be patented**
1986	first field trials in the **USA and France: genetically engineered tobacco plants** are resistant to herbicides (= *Unkrautvernichtungsmittel*)
1992	**China commercializes virus-resistant tobacco plants**
1994	the **first genetically-modified tomato**, designed to have a longer shell life, is released
June 2000	President Clinton announces **the completion of the first draft of the human genome**
Feb 2001	first analyses of the public and private genome projects are published; the big discovery: **Humans have about 30,000 to 40,000 genes, hardly more than a common weed or worm**
April 2003	the **human genome is declared a finished product**; the announcement coincides with the 50th anniversary of the discovery of the double helix
2008	Craig Venter announces first synthetic organism controlled by a **completely synthetic chromosome**
1996–2011	increasing **commercialization of biotech crops** at a growth rate of 8 % (1.7 mio hectares in 1996 – 160 mio hectares in 2011; corn, soybean, cotton)
2013	production of a **synthetic yeast** (*Hefe*) **cell with 16 artificial chromosomes**; creation of **genetically-engineered mice with artificial human chromosomes** in every cell of their bodies

Stephen Baxter

Into the Future ☒

AWARENESS

In a Think! Pair! Share! activity, describe the cartoons below and specify the different kinds of jobs and services the drones do.

a) Then, discuss whether you think this technology is positive and useful or threatening and unnecessary.

b) Finally, collect ideas about further (useful) services and jobs that could be done by drones.

1

2

Robots are increasingly doing jobs a human once did, but is it a path to utopia?

Henry Ford first started selling his famous black-only Model T Fords to the American public 100 years ago. Actually the cars had been in production since 1908, and it had been in 1909 that Ford told his management team "Any customer can have a car painted any colour that he wants so long as it is black" – but it was in 1914 that the black-only policy was finally implemented[1]. And by 1918, half of all the cars in the US were Ford's black Model Ts. Ford's success derived from[2] his innovations, most notably[3] assembly line production to replace individual hand-crafting[4] of the vehicles. All the Model Ts were exactly the same as each other, as symbolized by the "black-only" policy, which created cheapness and reliability.

This represented a huge transformation in the nature of work. New technologies had always destroyed old jobs, but created new ones. Craftsmen in the old horse-based economy could transfer their skills to the new industries – they could build the chassis[5] of a car, rather than the chassis of a horse-drawn trap[6].

But Ford's assembly lines were different, with the manufacture of a vehicle broken down into a series of simpler tasks, each performed by a single less skilled worker, over and over again.

At least, however, assembly-line jobs were still jobs. What of the future? Today we are going through another vast transformation of the workplace. What's striking for economists [...] is that in the US, for example, in the wake[7] of the 2008 banking crisis, the economy has never generated[8] fewer new jobs in any recovery since the records began. The reason is technological advance. Robots are making assembly-line workers unnecessary. High-tech corporations like Google and Facebook are becoming massive economic entities[9], but

[1] **to implement** to start using a plan or system – [2] **to derive from** (*phr. v.*) to come from sth. – [3] **notable** important and deserving attention – [4] **hand-crafting** a skilled activity in which sth. is made in a traditional way with the hands; *Handarbeit, Handwerk* – [5] **chassis** ['ʃæsi] the frame of a vehicle, including the wheels and the engine; *Fahrgestell* – [6] **trap** a light carriage with two wheels pulled by a horse, used esp. in the past – [7] **in the wake of sth.** (*idm.*) *als Folge von* – [8] **to generate** to create sth. – [9] **entity** ['entɪti] (*fml.*) *Gebilde, Einheit*

as much of what they create and distribute is pure data, they are not mass employers the way the old manufacturing industries were.

This trend is surely going to accelerate[10]. The military use of drone aircraft is demonstrating the growing capability of robots to do jobs once monopolized by humans. We can imagine robots replacing people in such services as waste disposal and parking lots; in shops automated tellers are already replacing human assistants. Thanks to driverless cars, as being developed by Google and others, jobs for drivers of all sorts will vanish[11].

We should not be too parochial[12] about this. Workers in some poorer nations, still laboring in primitive conditions, would not be impressed by our complaints about competition with robots and too much leisure[13] time. But given sufficient economic growth we may be seeing a challenge for all of us. Are we heading for a future in which the only meaningful jobs for humans will be at high intellectual levels – the designers of software that will control the new legions of robots?

Perhaps, but there are more positive visions. The elimination of drudgery[14] and danger, from housework to mining, must be a benefit. There will surely always be a role for people in fields like medical care and the raising of the very young. And perhaps we should celebrate the return of leisure. People could work at more personal and rewarding jobs: running micro-breweries[15], for example. Maybe we will see the final reversal of the trend pioneered by Henry Ford, of reducing human craftsmen to the role of robots.

The human race has only been working at its present levels of intensity since the invention of farming some ten thousand years ago. Perhaps, with the help of robots, we will be able to rediscover the rich cultural life enjoyed by our less pressured ancestors.

BBC Focus, Science and Technology, February 2014, p. 31

COMPREHENSION

1. Give evidence from the text that proves the following statements:
   - The automated production of goods was/is a blessing for the consumer but a curse for the workers.
   - The impact of technological advancement was more beneficial in the past than it is today.

2. Juxtapose the assumed positive and negative effects of robotized production and services as depicted in the last part of the text (ll. 57 – 71).

assumed benefits/advantages	assumed risks/disadvantages
• relief/support for workers in primitive working conditions • …	• the only meaningful jobs are at high intellectual levels • …

ANALYSIS

3. Explain Henry Ford's "black-only" policy: What was his production and marketing policy?

4. Examine and analyse the stylistic devices and show how they emphasize the author's stance on robots. Pay particular attention to
   - the use of rhetorical questions,
   - the thematic structure of the text,
   - the use of irony,
   - the use of contrast/antithesis,
   - the use of grammatical tenses.

   → Focus on Skills, Analysis of a Non-Fictional Text, p. 377

[10] **to accelerate** to start to go faster – [11] **to vanish** to disappear, esp. in a sudden, surprising way – [12] **parochial** [pəˈrəʊkiəl] *engstirnig* – [13] **leisure** [ˈleʒə(r)] *Freizeit* – [14] **drudgery** hard boring work – [15] **micro-brewery** [ˈmaɪkrəʊˈbruːəri] *Hausbrauerei*

ACTIVITIES

5. Discuss the author's introductory question (ll. 1 f.) in a pyramid discussion.
Are robots and automated production the way to utopia?
→ Focus on Language, Conversation and Discussion, p. 385

6. In groups, work out a future scenario in which the following have become reality:
- "designers of software … will control the new legions of robots" … **or**
- the reduction of "human craftsmen to the role of robots" … **or**
- the rediscovery of a "rich cultural life" …

Tip: Your scenarios can be utopian or dystopian; they can be written as dialogue, diary entries, a travel log, etc. Choose a literary genre of your liking and flesh it out with the corresponding stylistic devices.

Finally, read out/act out your scenarios in class and evaluate their content and style.

GRAMMAR / LANGUAGE

7. You work in a PR (Public Relations) team of a company that produces drones and various kinds of robots. In groups, think about campaigns to promote your products to companies and/or private households.
Pay attention to
- present the benefits and advantages of your company's robots,
- dispel people's fear of being replaced by robots at their workplace.

Use a dictionary and look up **adjectives and adverbials** that emphasize the robots' qualities.

8. Tess, the robot shown below, was one of the major attractions of the 2014 *CeBit*, the world's largest international industry trade fair focusing on office automation, information technology and telecommunication.
In class, first mediate the information given beside the photo. Second, discuss whether you consider a "female" robot stripper or table dancer to be an appropriate advertising gag to attract customers' attention and evoke their interest in robotics.

10.03.2014 – Wie eine Stripperin

Tess trägt hohe Schuhe, nimmt die Beine leicht auseinander, bewegt sich lasziv und umtanzt die Stange wie eine Stripperin in einem Bordell. Das macht den Roboter mit seinem 12-Volt-Motor zu einer Attraktion auf der CeBit in Hannover. Tess lässt sich von einem Android-Smartphone aus steuern. Die Firma Tobit Software in Ahaus modifizierte Tess und sagt: „Wir wollten ihn ein bisschen interessanter machen." Preis: 39 500 Dollar.

Der Spiegel, Chronik 2014, 4 December 2014, p. 51

trade		
(economic) supremacy [suːˈpreməsi]	the position in which a country/an economy is more powerful or advanced than others	*Übermacht, Überlegenheit*
industrialized country	a country that has a lot of factories, etc.	*Industrieland*
Industrial Revolution	the period in the 18th and 19th centuries in Europe and the US when machines began to be used to do work, and industry grew rapidly	*Industrielle Revolution*
secure markets	safe markets	*sichere Märkte*
shipping	the delivery of goods	*Lieferung, Zustellung*
trade embargo	trade boycott	*Handelsembargo, -sperre*
taxation	the system of charging taxes	*Besteuerung*
consumerism and consumption		
acquisition of sth.	the act of buying sth.	*Anschaffung, Erwerb*
availability [əˌveɪləˈbɪlɪti]	the fact that sb. is free to be contacted; the fact that sth. is there to be bought	*Verfügbarkeit*
consumer	sb. who buys and uses products and services	*Konsument*
customer	sb. who buys goods or services from a shop or company	*Kunde*
discount shopping	to go shopping at a store that sells goods cheaply	*Kauf von preisreduzierter Ware*
distribution of sth.	the act of giving or delivering sth. to a number of people	*Verteilung*
efficiency [ɪˈfɪʃənsi]	the quality of doing sth. well without wasting money or time	*Effizienz, Effektivität*
industrialized mass production	when products are made in large numbers by industrial machines so they can be sold cheaply	*industrielle Massenproduktion*
to instil a desire	to put the idea in sb.'s mind that they desire sth.	*in jdm. eine Begierde wecken*
Internet retailer	Internet shop	*Internet-Versandhandel*
to line the shelves	to offer sth. for sale in large amounts	*den Absatz steigern*
mounting consumer debt	strongly rising consumer debt	*steigende Konsumenten-verschuldung*
online shopping portal	a website where you can buy things	*Plattform für Online-Einkäufe*
purchasing power	the amount of money a person or group has available to spend	*Kaufkraft*
range of products	selection of products	*Produktauswahl, Produkt-palette*
retailer/retail store	a person or store that sells goods	*Händler, Einzelhändler*
trade unions and labour policy		
company board	a group of elected or appointed members who super-vise the activities of a company	*Aufsichtsrat*
company pension plan	an arrangement between a company and its employees (or a union representing the employees) to provide money for the employees' retirement	*betriebliche Altersvorsorge*
to dismiss	to officially remove sb. from their job	*jdn. entlassen*
employment legislation	laws that govern the employer-employee relations and rights of employees; labour legislation	*Arbeitsrecht*
freelancing	working independently (for different companies)	*freiberuflich arbeiten*
(to work) flexitime	system in which employees work a particular number of hours each week/month but can choose when they start and finish work	*flexible Arbeitszeiten*
(to work) full-time	for all the hours of a week/month which people nor-mally work	*Vollzeit-*
labour contract	contract between employee and employer	*Arbeitsvertrag*

labour market	the number of people who are available for work in relation to the number of jobs available	*Arbeitsmarkt*
to lay off (laid off, laid off)	to stop employing sb.	*entlassen*
(to work) overtime	working more hours than you have to according to your contract	*Überstunden, Mehrarbeit*
(to work) part-time	working for part of the day/week	*Teilzeit-, in Teilzeit*
paternity/maternity leave	time that a father/mother is allowed to spend away from work when they have a baby	*Erziehungsurlaub*
personnel [ˌpɜːsənˈel]	the people working in a firm, etc.; staff	*Personal*
salary	wage, pay; money that you receive for doing your job	*(Jahres-/Monats-)Gehalt*
to (go on) strike	to refuse to work in order to protest against sth.	*streiken*
unemployment benefit	money paid by the government to sb. who is unemployed	*Arbeitslosengeld*
(trade) union	organization of workers to protect their interests	*Gewerkschaft*
wages (*pl.*)	pay, salary; money that you receive for doing your job	*Lohn, Löhne*
works council	a group representing the employees of a company whose members are elected to negotiate working conditions, etc. with the company's management	*Betriebsrat*
	globalisation	
capital market	financial market	*Finanzmarkt, Kapitalmarkt*
cultural imperialism	the imposing of a foreign culture on sb.	*kultureller Imperialismus*
domestic demand	amount of money spent on goods and services by the people, companies and government within a particular country	*inländische Nachfrage*
domestic labour market	the number of workers and available jobs within a particular country	*inländischer Arbeitsmarkt*
entrepreneurship [ˌɒntrəprəˈnɜːʃɪp]	running one's own business	*Unternehmertum*
expatriate	a person living (and working) in a country that is not their own	*jd., der sein Heimatland verlässt, um Arbeit zu finden*
to generate capital	to yield/produce money	*Kapital erwirtschaften*
global labour market	global workforce	*globaler Arbeitsmarkt*
infrastructure	the basic systems and services, such as transport or power supplies, that a country or organization uses in order to work effectively	*Infrastruktur*
interdependency	a situation in which people or things depend on each other	*Korrelation, gegenseitige Abhängigkeit*
to internationalize	to make sth. become international	*etw. internationalisieren*
labour standards	the working conditions	*Arbeitsgesetzgebung*
liberalization of sth.	the act of making sth. less strict	*Liberalisierung von etw.*
logistics	the practical organization of sth.	*Logistik*
migrant worker	sb. who moves to a richer country in order to work there	*Wanderarbeiter, Gastarbeiter*
multinationals	large companies that operate in several countries	*multinationale Konzerne*
output	amount of sth. that a company produces	*Produktion, Leistung*
outsourcing of work	the act of arranging for sb. outside the company to do work for that company	*Ausgliederung/Auslagerung von Arbeit*
to promote international trade	to do sth. in order to increase international trade	*internationalen Handel fördern*
protectionism	when a government tries to help industries in its own country by taxing or restricting goods	*Protektionismus, Schutzpolitik*

to raise living standards	to improve the level of comfort and increase the amount of money that people have	*Lebensstandards erhöhen*
repatriate	a person who has lived and worked abroad and returns to his or her homeland	*jd., der in sein Heimatland zurückkehrt*
trade negotiation	discussion in order to reach an agreement on trade	*Wirtschaftsverhandlung(en)*
unskilled worker	sb. who works in a job that requires little or no training	*Hilfskraft, ungelernter Arbeiter*
	ecology and energy	
carbon emission	carbon dioxide that planes, cars, factories, etc. produce, which is harmful to the environment	*Kohlenstoffausstoß*
climate change	a permanent change in weather conditions	*Klimawandel*
crops	plants that are grown by farmers and used as food	*Getreide*
deforestation	the cutting or burning down of all the trees in an area	*Waldrodung*
exploitation	when sb. treats sb. else unfairly – esp. to make money from their work	*Ausbeutung*
fracking	a technique used to force oil and natural gas from rock by pumping pressurized fluid into the ground and creating new channels in the rock which makes oil, etc. more easily available	*Fracking*
fragility of sth.	the quality of being easily broken or damaged	*Zerbrechlichkeit*
fossil fuel	fuel (e.g. coal and oil), which were formed underground from plant and animal remains millions of years ago	*fossiler Brennstoff*
greenhouse effect	the gradual warming of the air surrounding the earth as a result of heat being trapped by pollution	*Treibhauseffekt*
to have an impact on sth.	to influence sth.	*etw. beeinflussen*
heatwave	a period of unusually hot weather	*Hitzewelle*
the incineration of trash	the act of burning trash in a facility	*Müllverbrennung*
to pose a threat for/to sb.	to create a threat, problem, etc. that has to be dealt with	*für jdn. eine Bedrohung darstellen*
renewable energies	types of energy such as wind or solar power that can be replaced as quickly as they are used	*erneuerbare Energien*
sustainability [səˌsteɪnəˈbɪlɪti]	able to continue for a long time without causing damage to the environment	*Nachhaltigkeit*
waste disposal	getting rid of garbage	*Müllentsorgung*
water supply	the water that is provided for a particular area	*Wasserversorgung*
	democracy	
amendment [əˈmendmənt]	an addition to a law or document	*Ergänzung, Gesetzesnovelle*
to cast one's ballot/vote	to vote in an election	*eine Stimme abgeben*
collective military action	military action that is carried out by more than one country, member state, etc.	*gemeinsame militärische Aktion*
to declare sth. unconstitutional	to declare that a law or rule is not allowed by the constitution of a country or organization	*etw. für nicht verfassungsgemäß erklären*
diplomacy [dɪˈpləʊməsi]	the job or activity of managing the relationships between countries	*Diplomatie*
electorate	the people in a country who have the right to vote	*Wähler, Wählerschaft*
General Assembly	representatives of all the member nations of the United Nations	*Vollversammlung*
to impose sanctions	to use official orders or laws as a way of forcing a leader of another country to make political changes	*Sanktionen verhängen*
inaugural address	the first speech of a new leader	*Amtsantrittsrede*
inauguration	the ceremony of putting sb. into an official position	*Amtseinführung*
legislation	a law or a set of laws	*Gesetzgebung*

to maintain peace	to make peace continue	*Frieden aufrechterhalten*
to mediate between	to try to end a disagreement between two or more people or groups by talking to them	*vermitteln (zwischen)*
oath of office	a formal promise sb. takes before undertaking the duties of an office	*Amtseid*
to run for president	to be a candidate in an election for president	*als Präsident(in) kandidieren*
separation of powers	the principle of dividing the political power of a government into an executive, a legislative and a judicial branch	*Gewaltentrennung*
to serve a term	to spend a fixed or limited period of time in a job	*eine Amtszeit lang dienen*
system of checks and balances	the principle of government (in the US) by which the President, Congress and the Supreme Court each have some control over the others	*Gewaltenteilung (gegenseitige Kontrolle der drei Gewalten)*
tribunal [traɪˈbjuːnl]	a type of court that is given official authority	*Tribunal, Gericht*
	political systems	
administration	the government of a country at a particular time	*Regierung*
to amend (a bill) [əˈmend] **amendment**	to correct or make changes to sth.; an addition to a law or document	*(ein Gesetz) ändern, ergänzen; Gesetzesänderung; Zusatzartikel*
to dissolve (parliament)	to officially end (parliament)	*auflösen*
domestic policy	laws and policies that apply within a particular nation's borders	*Innenpolitik*
to be eligible to vote	to be legally allowed to vote	*wahlberechtigt sein*
first-past-the-post system	a voting system in which the person who gets the most votes is elected; majority vote	*Mehrheitswahlrecht*
foreign policy	policy dealing with or involving other countries	*Außenpolitik*
proportional representation	a political system in which parties are represented in parliament according to the number of votes	*Verhältniswahlrecht*
universal suffrage [ˈsʌfrɪdʒ]	the right of all the people in the country to vote	*allgemeines Wahlrecht*
	science and technology	
artificial intelligence	the study of how to make computers copy intelligent human behaviour	*künstliche Intelligenz*
assembly line production	a system of making things in which the product moves past a line of workers who each make or check one part	*Fließbandproduktion*
to develop sth.	to think of or produce a new product; to design	*entwickeln*
drone	a vehicle, e. g. an aircraft or missile, that does not have a pilot but is remote-controlled	*unbemanntes (Luft-)Fahrzeug*
enhanced [ɪnˈhɑːnst]	improved, better	*erweitert, verbessert*
findings	results	*Ergebnisse*
to invent sth.; invention	to make, design or think of a new type of thing; a useful machine, tool, instrument, etc. that has been invented	*etw. erfinden; Erfindung*
microelectronics [ˌmaɪkrəʊˌɪlekˈtrɒnɪks]	the science and technology involved in the making and using of very small electronic parts	*Mikroelektronik*
progress; progressive	the process of improving or developing, or of getting closer to finishing or achieving sth.; in favour of new or modern ideas, methods and change	*Fortschritt; fortschrittlich*
research; researcher	the careful study of a subject; sb. who studies a subject in detail in order to discover new information	*Forschung, Recherche; Forscher*
to verify	to determine whether sth. is correct, to confirm	*überprüfen, bestätigen*

Communication or Confusion? – English Around the World

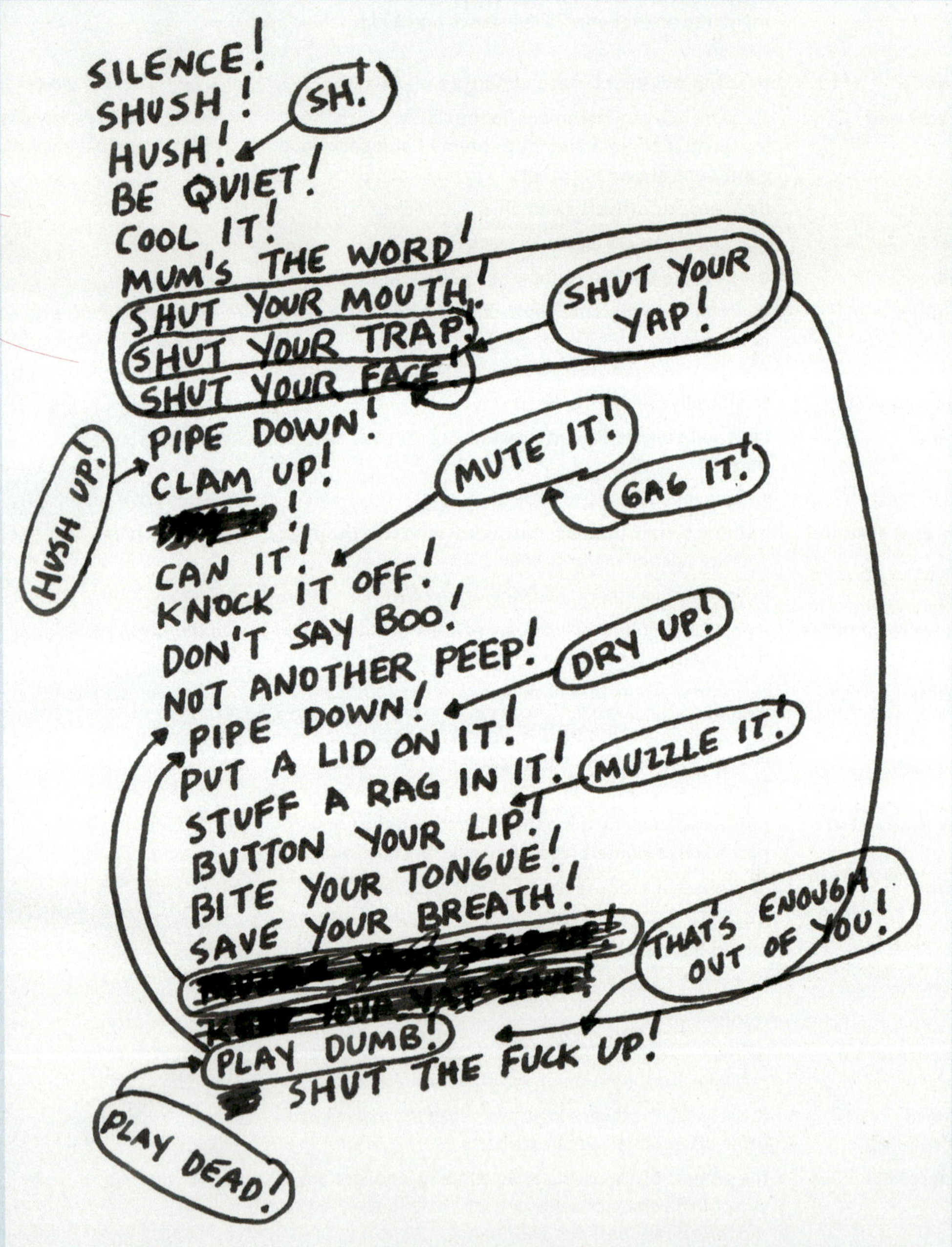

Mel Bochner, *Silence!*, ink on paper, 2008

Tips on vocab

scribbling (*das Gekritzel*) ■ capitalization, capital letters (*Großschreibung, Großbuchstaben*) ■ exclamation marks ■ synonymous language ■ (to) paraphrase ■ slang expressions ■ informal English ■ a list of words and phrases

Communication ... Hearing What Isn't Said ...

Of course, English is a powerful language, a colonizer's language and a gift to a writer. English has destroyed and sucked up[1] the language of other cultures – its cruelty and vitality.
Louise Erdrich

The price a world language must be prepared to pay is submission[2] to many different kinds of use.
Chinua Achebe

The two words "information" and "communication" are often used interchangeably, but they signify quite different things. Information is giving out; communication is getting through.
Sydney J. Harris

The more elaborate our means of communication, the less we communicate.
Joseph Priestley

Societies have always been shaped more by the nature of the media by which men communicate than by the content of the communication.
Marshall McLuhan

A man's character may be learned from the adjectives which he habitually[3] uses in conversation.
Mark Twain

We gave you a perfectly good language and you f***ed it up.
Stephen Fry about American English

Fainali, xen, aafte sam 2o iers ov orxogrefkl riform, wi wud hev a lojikl, Ingliy-spiking werld.
Mark Twain

If you have an important point to make, don't try to be subtle[4] or clever. Use a pile driver[5]. Hit the point once. Then come back and hit again. Then hit a third time – a tremendous[6] whack[7].
Winston Churchill

There is only one rule for being a good talker – learn to listen.
Christopher Morley

www.brainyquote.com/quotes/topics/topic_communication.html [23.01.2015]

START-UP ACTIVITIES

1. In his drawing *Silence!*, a so-called "Thesaurus[8] Painting", American artist Mel Bochner uses different figures of speech to express and describe a single idea or feeling.
a) In groups, first discuss what idea or message *Silence!* wants to convey.
b) Choose three or four expressions you like best and turn them into so-called pictograms. Be careful to illustrate exactly your chosen expression and look up its specific meaning in a dictionary if necessary. Display your pictograms in class and discuss whether or not they really match Mel Bochner's expressions.

2. In a pyramid discussion, choose one of the statements above that you agree with the most and give a short comment on it on a sheet of paper. Reflect on and discuss to what extent you agree with the statement and whether or not it matches your understanding of "communication" and the function of language.
→ Focus on Language, Conversation and Discussion, p. 385

3. Discuss the headline above: Is communication really about "hearing what isn't said"?

[1] **to suck sth. up** to absorb sth. – [2] **submission** here: *Duldung* – [3] **habitually** *gewohnheitsmäßig* – [4] **subtle** [ˈsʌtəl] not loud or noticeable – [5] **pile driver** *die Handramme* – [6] **tremendous** very great – [7] **whack** the action of hitting sb./sth. noisily; *Schlag* – [8] **thesaurus** [θɪˈsɔːrəs] (*fml.*) a type of dictionary in which words with similar meanings are arranged in groups; *Synonymwörterbuch*

It's English, Stupid! – English As a Changing Language

Peter Lavelle

CrossTalk: English vs. Globish

AWARENESS

You have been learning English for a number of years now. Looking back at your "biography" as an ESL[1] student, would you say that all the effort you put into learning and studying English vocabulary and grammar has been worth the effort so far?
In a round robin activity, state what you like or dislike about English as a foreign language and whether you are satisfied with your language acquisition so far.

COMPREHENSION

1. Before listening:
In groups, take a look at the FoF page *English Around the World* (p. 311) and the reasons listed there for the popularity and success of the English language worldwide.

- Discuss whether or not you identify with the explanations given there.
- Make a ranking: What do you consider to be the most/least important reasons?
- Evaluate your own stage and level of language learning and proficiency in English: Do you feel well-equipped with regard to the ranking you have just made? If not – which further language skills do you need to learn?

Tips on vocab

emeritus [ɪ'merɪtəs] no longer having a position, esp. in a college or university, but keeping the title of the position; *emeritiert* ■ **scholar** ['skɒlər] a person who studies a subject in great detail, esp. at a university ■ **for partly** *teilweise* ■ **derivative** [dɪ'rɪvɪtɪv] here: *Ableitung (von einem Wort)* ■ **to comprise** (*fml.*) to have as parts or members; *aus etw. bestehen* ■ **Gibberish** ['dʒɪbərɪʃ] spoken or written words that have no meaning ■ **to negotiate meaning** *darum ringen, die Bedeutung eines Begriffes zu erfassen* ■ **a quick fix** (*infml., disapproving*) sth. that seems to be a fast and easy solution to a problem but is in fact not very good ■ **guidance** ['gaɪdəns] *Anleitung, Beratung* ■ **to deploy** to use sth., esp. in an effective way; *etw. anwenden* ■ **to go in line with sb./sth.** to agree with sb./sth. ■ **to close a deal** *ein Geschäft abschließen* ■ **to be at ease with sb./sth.** to feel comfortable and relaxed ■ **to equip sb.** to give sb. the skills to do a particular thing; *jdn. mit etw. ausstatten* ■ **assumption** *Annahme, Vermutung* ■ **it's a different ballgame** (*infml.*) *es ist anders gelagert*

2. In 2004, Jean-Paul Nerrière, a former French IBM executive, published the book *Don't Speak English, Parlez Globish*, in which he introduces the international auxiliary language "Globish". He promotes Globish as a reduced set of English patterns with a vocabulary of about 1,500 words, which is based on a subset of English grammar. Globish is intended to serve as common ground that non-native speakers of English use to communicate in order to do international business.

[1] **ESL** (*abbr.*) English as a second language

The recordings you are going to listen to are two excerpts from a video conference in which RTS[2] News Channel host Peter Lavelle talks to Jean-Paul Nerrière as well as two experts on the matter, Robert Phillipson and David Graddol.

8–9 CD 3

Step 1: In a paired listening activity, team up with a partner and **listen** to the audio text **individually first** and try to get a **general understanding**.

Tip: Be prepared to listen to the text at least two times. Jean-Paul Nerrière has a very strong French accent and is difficult to understand at times.

Webcode SNG-40183-035 @

In order to get a better impression of the participants you can also watch the video conference using the link provided on the webcode.

Step 2: Take notes on the basic aspects you have understood as well as on questions you have concerning vocabulary or the content of the statements.

Step 3: After a first listening, tell each other what you have understood and try to clarify questions and vocabulary.

Step 4: Now listen to the text individually again and **take notes on the aspects** and questions listed below.

Step 5: Afterwards, compare your notes with your partner and make additions and corrections if necessary.
→ Focus on Skills, Listening Comprehension, p. 366

Take notes on these aspects and questions:

8 CD 3

- Who is taking part in the video conference and what is each participant's function and position?
- How does Jean-Paul Nerrière define Globish and what – according to him – is its foremost advantage and purpose?
- What makes Globish a form of "McDonaldization"?
- What concerns does Robert Phillipson express with regard to the wide range of purposes that "real English" has in the "real world"?
- What – according to Peter Lavelle – justifies the "McDonaldization" of English?
- How are native and non-native speakers of English involved when it comes to using and dealing with Globish?

9 CD 3

- What are the "two kinds of English" – according to Nerrière?
- What makes Globish particularly important and useful with regard to international business?
- What position should native speakers of English take when communicating with non-native speakers?
- What are Peter Lavelle's concerns about using Globish when doing business and making contracts?
- How does Phillipson view the position of English as a "world language/lingua franca"?
- What does he consider to be wrong about some Danish companies' explanation of failures in business?
- What is Phillipson's conclusion concerning the purpose and use of Globish in complex negotiations?

If necessary, listen to the text again and complete your notes.

3. Summarize both parts of the CrossTalk interview in about 150 – 200 words each.
→ Focus on Skills, Writing a Summary, p. 401

Tip: Be careful to use **indirect speech** when reporting what the participants said and to **backshift tenses** if necessary.

[2] **RTS** (*abbr.*) Royal Television Society, Britain's leading forum for television and related media

ANALYSIS

4. Using your notes from task 2,
a) compare the advantages and disadvantages of Globish,
b) explain whether Jean-Paul Nerrière's line of argument* is convincing.
→ Focus on Skills, Analysis of a Non-Fictional Text, p. 377

advantages	**disadvantages**
• limited/efficient list of vocabulary • everybody can participate • ...	• McDonaldization (= limitation, reduction) of meaning • lack of differentiation • ...

5. Explain Robert Phillipson's statement that Globish is "a bit like McDonaldization, [...] a packaged version ..." and a "quick fix", and that to in order to be able to "negotiate meaning" and to be "culturally sensitive", people need "real English".

6. Listen to Jean-Paul Nerrière speak again. Does his use of Globish help him to bring his message across to the audience or is there more to communicating in English successfully than just using a simplified version of English? Explain.

Webcode SNG-40183-035 @ **7.** Examine the "Globish lexicon" consisting of the 1,500 most relevant words using the link provided on the webcode and compare it to a "real dictionary of English". Is this "English light" or "Gibberish"? What differences can you detect?

8. Take a close look at the example of Globish given below and compare the Standard English formulations to the simplified Globish version.
a) Illustrate the differences.
b) Discuss whether the Globish version is really easier to comprehend and a convincing alternative.

Standard English with non-Globish vocabulary highlighted	**Globish**
• Globish is a subset of English words and grammar first codified by Jean-Paul Nerrière as documented by the Globish Foundation, and may include extension vocabularies.	• Globish uses some English words and ways first defined by Jean Paul Nerrière (documented by the Globish Foundation), and may include extra sets of words.
• Globish includes recommended behaviors for use in global communication.	• Globish includes useful movements for global communication.
• As a subset of English, Globish does not involve any invented words or grammars.	• As a part of English, Globish does not involve any invented words or word use.
• Globish has a core of only 1,500 words (1,500 is a recognized number for basic, general communication);	• Globish starts with only 1,500 words (1,500 is a recognized number for easy, general communication);
• the vocabulary is declared (people can use Globish words with confidence and add others by agreement, defining them in Globish);	• there is a list of words (people can use any Globish words and add others by agreement, defining them in Globish);

Standard English with non-Globish vocabulary highlighted	Globish
• typical behaviors are identified so everyone knows 'how' to communicate (e.g. watching a listener to see if they are following the conversation);	• good ways of acting are identified so everyone knows 'how' to communicate (by watching a listener to see if they are following the communication);
• Globish assumes the communicator is responsible for understanding (not the person receiving the communication);	• Globish makes the speaker responsible for understanding (not the person receiving the communication);
• Globish assumes the person receiving the communication will indicate any problems they are having (they are not responsible for their lack of understanding);	• Globish says the person receiving the communication must indicate any problems they are having (they are not responsible for their lack of understanding);
• Globish does not include exotic tenses and grammar (so it is easier to understand, learn and use);	• Globish does not include strange, difficult English (so it is easier to understand, learn and use);
• Globish does not include cultural references, idioms, etc. (so understanding is more broadly available);	• Globish does not include local ideas, images, (so understanding is more broadly available);
• Globish uses active voice, simple-tenses, shorter sentences (so it can be translated easily into other languages);	• Globish uses easy speech, simple-tenses, shorter sentences (so it can be changed easily into other languages);
• Globish assumes many accents and even spellings (Australian spelling is not the same as Thai spelling);	• Globish allows for many ways of speaking and spelling (Australian spelling is not the same as Thai spelling);
• having learned Globish, a person can grow their communication to speak and write English, if required;	• a person who knows Globish can learn to speak and write full English, if required;
• with technology, teachers who are non-native speakers of English can teach others to communicate in Globish;	• with computers, teachers who are not native speakers of English can teach others to communicate in Globish;
• with technology, people can learn Globish for themselves, by themselves;	• with computers, people can learn Globish without a teacher;
• people with difficulties with respect to unfettered English communication can use Globish to communicate (inclusive of people with intellectual disabilities, etc.) [...].	• people with difficulties with respect to full English communication can use Globish to communicate (including people with learning problems) [...].

http://globishfoundation.org/about-globish/57-globish-example-1.html [15.01.2015]

ACTIVITIES

9. Globish is a modern simplified version of English. You are learning English the traditional way, and sometimes English grammar can be complicated. What would you rather not learn? What do you think can be left out? Make suggestions, write them on a transparency and present them in class.

Varieties of English

Paul Roberts

Set Us Free from Standard English

AWARENESS

What view of the English language (and British culture) do these statements reveal? Discuss in class.

Even if you do learn to speak correct English, whom are you going to speak it to?
Clarence Darrow (1857–1938), American lawyer

When the English language gets in my way, I walk over it.
Billy Sunday (1862–1935), American athlete

To cultivate an English accent is already a departure away from what you are.
*Sir Sean Connery (*1930), Scottish actor*

Language is a token[1] of identity as well as a means of communication. It follows that language is part of a complex system allowing speakers to show they belong to a group from which they may exclude others. In this respect, English speakers are similar to speakers of any other language. [...]

The so-called native speakers of Standard English are those people who have somehow espoused[2] to a particular set of conventions that loosely have to do with the way English has been codified and prescribed in dictionaries, grammar books and guides to good speaking and writing. This group of people includes a large number of those who, having espoused the conventions, nevertheless do not consider themselves to be excellent users of those conventions.

For many of these so-called native speakers the English language is a unique entity[3] that exists outside or beyond its users. Rather than considering themselves owners of English, users often think of themselves as guardians of something precious: they wince[4] when they hear or read uses of English that they consider to be substandard, and they worry, in their letters to newspapers, that the language is becoming degraded. The degradation may be perceived to come from non-native speakers, but much more prevalent[5] is the notion[6] that it is native users of English themselves who are bringing about the decline. Indeed, a fairly commonly held notion claims that "foreigners", or non-native speakers, can, and do, use English better than the native speakers.

Turning things round the other way, I have met native speakers teaching English who have been upbraided[7] by their non-native-speaker employers for accepting their students' idiomatic, non-standard usages and not correcting their English according to standard English conventions.

Those who do feel they have rights and privileges, who have a sense of ownership of the English language and who can make pronouncements[8] about what is or is not acceptable, as well as those to whom these attributes are accorded[9] by others, do not necessarily belong to a speech community whose members learned English in infancy. Native speakers of non-standard varieties of English, in other words, the majority of native speakers of English, have never had any real authority over Standard English and have never "owned" it. The actual proprietors[10] may, after all, simply be those who have learned thoroughly how to use a Standard English to enjoy the sense of empowerment[11] that comes with it.

www.guardian.co.uk/education/2002/jan/24/tefl.wordsandlanguage, 24 January 2002 [04.02.2011]

[1] **token** here: expression – [2] **to espouse** [ɪˈspaʊz] (*fml.*) to give your support to a belief, policy, etc. – [3] **entity** (*fml.*) sth. that exists separately from other things and has its own identity – [4] **to wince** [wɪns] *zusammenzucken* – [5] **prevalent** [ˈprevalant] common, widespread – [6] **notion** an idea, a belief or an understanding of sth. – [7] **to upbraid** (*fml.*) *jdn. zurechtweisen* – [8] **pronouncement** (*fml.*) an official announcement; *Verkündigung* – [9] **to accord sth. to sb.** (*fml.*) to give sb./sth. authority, status or a particular type of treatment – [10] **proprietor** [prəˈpraɪətə(r)] (*fml.*) the owner – [11] **empowerment** [ɪmˈpaʊəmənt] *Ermächtigung*

COMPREHENSION

1. Explain the author's definition of a native speaker of Standard English.

2. What or whom do native speakers of English blame for the degradation of the English language?

3. Point out the author's view of "native" and "non-native speakers" of English and their "authority over Standard English".

ANALYSIS

4. Examine the rhetorical devices* and explain how they create the humorous and ironic tone of the article.

   Example: l. 7, l. 16: so-called native speakers → choice of words → calls into question the authority of native speakers

   → Focus on Skills, Analysis of a Non-Fictional Text, p. 377

5. The article is a prime example of Standard English and the use of an elaborated code. Find examples from the text that support this view.

   Example: l. 9: conventions → rules, habits

Varieties of English Around the World

1 10 CD 3

Leonardo DiCaprio
Speech at the 2014 UN Climate Change Summit

2 11 CD 3

Prince William
On Baby George and Fatherhood

3 12 CD 3

Australian Prime Minister Julia Gillard
Speech at U.S. Congress

4 13 CD 3

Malala Yousafzai
Nobel Peace Prize Speech

5 14 CD 3

Bishop Desmond Tutu
On Post-Apartheid South Africa

6 15 CD 3

Usain Bolt
About Training Sessions

Tips on vocab

1 **undeniable** *unleugbar, unstrittig* ■ **drought** *Dürre* ■ **methane plumes** *Methangasschwaden* ■ **unprecedented** *beispiellos* ■ **to vilify** (*fml.*) *jdn. verunglimpfen, verschmähen* ■ **large-scale** large in size ■ **to put a price tag on sth.** to say how much sth. costs ■ **scrutiny** *genaue Untersuchung/Überprüfung* ■ **partisan** belonging to or supporting a political party 2 **dauntingness** the feeling of being frightened or worried about your ability to achieve sth. ■ **heir** *Thronfolger* ■ **to curse sb.** *jdn. verfluchen* ■ **nerve-racking** *nervenzerreißend* ■ **fuss** unnecessary excitement, worry or activity ■ **to stall** *abwürgen* 3 **ultimate sacrifice** here: to die for sth. ■ **grief** *Gram* ■ **ally** *Verbündeter* ■ **resolve** strong determination ■ **safe haven** *Schutzbereich* ■ **prosperity** the state of being successful and having a lot of money ■ **corrosive** here: harmful and causing bad feelings ■ **aimlessness** *Ziellosigkeit* 4 **Nobel laureate** *Nobel Preisträger* 5 **to prevail** (*fml.*) to get control or influence ■ **presto** when sth. appears or happens so quickly and easily that it seems to be magic ■ **ANC** (*abbr.*) African National Congress; social democratic political party ■ **retribution** *Vergeltung, Strafe* ■ **nurse a grudge** *gegen jdn. einen Groll hegen* 6 **track and field** *Leichtathletik*

COMPREHENSION

10–15 CD 3

1. **Step 1:** Listen to the recordings **a first time**.
   - Try to get the gist of what is said.
   - Identify the topic and the general situation.
   - Describe the overall tone and say whether the situation is more formal or informal.

   Step 2: In a **second listening**, pay attention to the differences in the varieties of English concerning:
   - pronunciation
   - choice of words
   - sentence structure
   - accent
   - rhythm
   - speed

   → Focus on Skills, Listening Comprehension, p. 366

ANALYSIS

2. Now, choose a recording and work with its content and message **in detail**.
   Listen to the recordings once more, **paying attention to details** and taking notes on:

10 CD 3 — 1
- DiCaprio's motivation for giving the speech
- his observations of the effects of climate change
- the addressees of his speech
- DiCaprio's demands and his appeal to take action

11 CD 3 — 2
- Prince William's emotions as a father
- how Prince William views his obligations and duties as a member of the Royal Family
- Prince William's tightrope walk between personal independence and serving "the system"

12 CD 3 — 3
- the partnership and bonds between Australia and the U. S.
- shared sorrows and concerns
- shared goals and objectives

13 CD 3 — 4
- Malala's feelings about being awarded the Nobel Peace Prize
- the importance of the prize to herself and in a wider context
- her introduction of her co-awardee Kailash Satyarthi
- Malala's appeal to the people

14 CD 3 — 5
- the impact of segregation in South Africa
- gaining freedom and democracy
- the positive impact of forgiving

15 CD 3 — 6
- Usain Bolt's motivation to become an Olympic champion
- how he deals with pressure
- Bolt's view of winning and losing

Webcode SNG-40183-036 @

Tip: You can also watch the people speak using the links provided on the webcode.

English Around the World

English-speaking countries

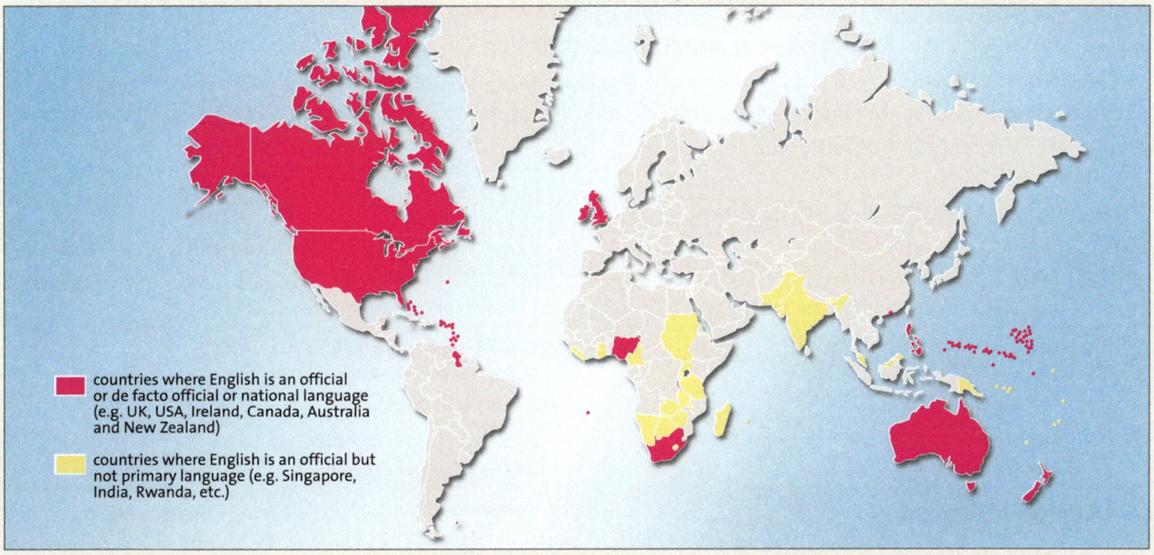

In addition, an increasing number of nations recognize the importance of English as an international language and e.g. teach English as a foreign language (e.g. China, Japan, Russia, Israel, etc.).

Why English?

Reasons for the spread and popularity of English:

- **Historical reasons:** as a result of British or American imperialism a country's main institutions may carry out their proceedings in English (e.g. parliament, educational system, the civil service, courts, the media, etc.)
- **Political reasons:** in a country where many different languages are spoken (e.g. India, Africa) English can serve as a means of communication between different ethnic groups and provide a neutral means of communication
- **Economic reasons:** English is the predominant language used to carry out international trade and business and to participate in global economic markets
- **Practical reasons:** English is the language of international communication (e.g. tourism, international traffic control, emergency services, academic conferences, etc.)
- **Intellectual reasons:** most scientific, technological and academic information is encoded in English and stored in English-based electronic retrieval systems
- **Entertainment reasons:** English is the main language of pop music, satellite broadcasting, home computers, advertising, etc.

History of the English language

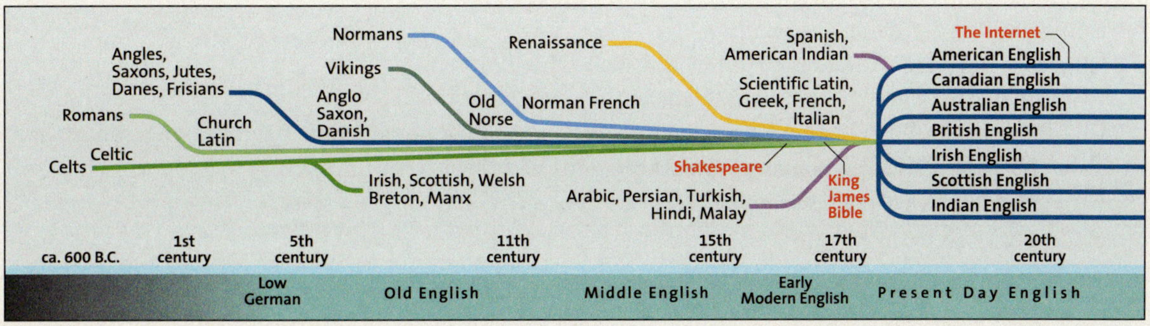

The Language Register of English

Many English words and phrases have similar meanings, and are, at first glance, synonyms. However, different contexts or situations typically require more or less formal wording. Some synonyms are more appropriate or more commonly used in **formal texts or situations** (e. g. *to proceed*), whereas in more informal, **everyday spoken English**, you would choose another phrase (e. g. *to go ahead*). Formal or *Standard English* is written in formal documents, e. g. essays, business letters, (traditional) literature; it is spoken in business negotiations, news broadcasts, official examinations, etc.

Different registers of English

everyday English	formal English
• I'm sorry/Sorry/Pardon me/Excuse me …	→ I (would like to) apologize …
• In my opinion/view, … The way I see it, … (*spoken*) If you ask me, … (*spoken*)	→ I am of the opinion that … I take the view that … It is my belief that …
• Is it all right/OK if I … Do you think I could …	→ I was wondering whether I could … Would it bother you if I …?
• Why don't we …? Let's … How about …?/What about …?	→ Maybe we could …/Perhaps we could … You might like/want to … Shall we …?
• Hi! What's up? How are you? How are you doing?	→ How do you do? (formal, only used when meeting sb. for the first time) Pleased/Lovely/Nice to meet you.
• Thanks. I can't thank you enough.	→ I appreciate … I am most grateful …

Colloquialisms

Colloquial language (i. e. informal, relaxed speech) is only appropriate for casual, familiar or informal conversation and is **not used in formal speech or writing**, except for artistic purposes, such as in novels or poetry. Some examples are: *gonna* (going to), *wanna* (want to), *ain't nothin'* (there is not anything), *not the sharpest knife in the drawer* (not very smart/intelligent).

Slang

Slang words are used in **very informal** situations, and usually only by a specific social group, e. g. teenagers, soldiers, etc. or in literature and song texts. Typically, slang words or phrases are **taboo words** and are often meant in a derogatory way (i. e. insulting, disapproving). Here is an example taken from literature:

> I'm trying to sleep when the other cons on my row are waking up. One of them hears me sigh, and tosses some words through his door. "Little? You a fuckin star!"
> "Yeah, right," I say. "Tell the prosecution."
> "Hell, youse'll get the *bestest* fuckin attorneys, hear what I'm sayin?"
> "My attorney can't even speak fuckin English."
> "Nah," says the con, "they dissed his ass, he history. I saw on TV he said he still workin on it, but that's bullshit, he ain't even hired no more. You get big guns now, hear what I'm sayin?"
> from *Vernon God Little* by DBC Pierre. Faber and Faber, London 2003, pp. 197 f.

language		
accent ['æksənt]	manner of pronunciation characteristic of a region	*Akzent*
acronym	a word formed from the first letters of the words that make up the name of sth., e. g. UN (United Nations)	*Akronym, Kurzwort*
antonym	a word that is opposite in meaning to another word	*Gegensatzwort*
bilingual [baˈlɪŋgwəl]	a person with a command of two languages	*zweisprachig*
colloquial; colloquialism	used in conversation but not in formal speech or writing; an informal expression or word	*umgangssprachlich; umgangssprachlicher Ausdruck*
communication	activity of exchanging information or meaning	*Kommunikation, Austausch*
communicative competence	a person's awareness of the rules governing the appropriate use of language in social situations	*kommunikative Fähigkeit/ Kompetenz*
communication strategies	strategies of expressing meaning (e. g. in a second language) without knowing the exact words for it	*kommunikative Strategien*
dialect	variety of language common among a group of speakers, usually defined by region	*Dialekt, lokale/regionale Sprachvariante*
ESL [ˌi:esˈel]	English as a Second Language	*Englisch als Zweitsprache*
four-letter words	swear/curse words	*Schimpfwort, Kraftausdruck*
Globish (Global English)	a simplified form of international English	*internationales Englisch*
idiom	combination of words in common use; an expression that cannot be translated word for word	*Redensart*
lingua franca	a medium of communication used by people who speak different first languages	*Verkehrssprache, Lingua franca*
literary freedom	personal variation of language as used by writers, poets, etc.	*dichterische Freiheit*
loanword/borrowing	a word from another language used in its original form	*Lehnwort*
mother tongue	the language that you first learn to speak as a child	*Muttersprache*
multilingual	a person with a command of several languages	*mehrsprachig*
native speaker	a speaker of a certain language as a first language	*Muttersprachler*
Netspeak	language used to communicate on the Internet	*Netzjargon*
non-Standard English	informal or slang vocabulary, grammar or pronunciation	*umgangssprachliches Englisch*
paraphrase	an alternate way of saying sth.	*Umschreibung*
phrase	a group of words that together have a particular meaning	*Wendung*
primary language	the language you learned first, or the one you use most often	*Primärsprache*
pronunciation	the way in which a word is spoken	*Aussprache*
Queen's English (*outdated*)	the standard accent of British English; sometimes also called Oxford English	*Standardenglisch, britisches Englisch*
register	language used in a particular social environment	*Sprachebene*
secondary language	a person's second language or one that is used less often	*Zweitsprache*
slang	informal, non-standard vocabulary	*Umgangssprache*
sociolect	variety of language common among the members of a specific social group	*Soziolekt, Gruppensprache*
synonym	a word that has the same meaning as another word	*sinnverwandtes Wort*
syntax	sentence structure	*Satzbau*
technical term	a word for a particular subject that is difficult to understand if you do not know about that subject	*Fachbegriff*
variety [vəˈraɪəti]	diversity, plurality; manner, kind, type	*Varietät; Vielfalt; Art*

Modern Media – Social, Smart and Spying?!

Walk the walk, don't talk the talk, Washington D.C.

START-UP ACTIVITIES

1. In groups, reflect on the title of this unit: What are "modern media"? What are the positive and negative sides of modern media? What opportunities and pitfalls (*Fallstricke*) are connected with them? Compile mind maps that include the various aspects and discuss them in class.

2. Look at the photo above showing a divided sidewalk for distracted pedestrians in Washington D. C. Do you think this a good idea? What are your experiences with phoning and walking – or other people who are distracted while texting or phoning?

16 CD 3

Webcode SNG-40183-037

3. Listen to and/or watch the Associated Press news coverage on "Distracted Walking" using the link on the webcode.
   - Why has this topic become a serious issue?
   - Discuss: Do you think that creating "e-lanes" or "distracted walking bills" are effective ways of handling the problem?

4. Read Michael Grunwald's article and compare the advantages and disadvantages of "Big Data".

5. In a pyramid discussion, discuss whether "Big Data" "optimize" or "overtax" (*überfordern*) most people. Have we lost "serendipity", and do people live in "online cocoons"?

COMPREHENSION

1. Read the introductory part (ll. 1–15) and the last part (ll. 86–95) of the text:
   - What is Mae's impression of the Circle?
   - What differences does she perceive between the Circle and "the rest of America"?

2. Now, read the main part of the excerpt (ll. 16–85) and describe how people used the Internet *before* and *after* the installation of the "unified operating system" TruYou.

before TruYou	after TruYou
• various passwords • different … • …	• combining and connecting everything online • … • …

ANALYSIS

3. Compare the concept of *TruYou* to Michael Grunwald's description of "The Second Age of Reason" and people's "Internet-optimizing" (p. 315). What similarities and disparities can you find?

4. Most parts of the excerpt could serve as a script for a commercial or advertising campaign promoting the Circle, its inventions and objectives.
   Find evidence from the text that supports this thesis, paying particular attention to stylistic, structural and rhetorical devices.
   → Focus on Skills, Analysis of a Fictional Text, p. 374

ACTIVITIES

5. The excerpt describes Mae Holland's first day at the Circle. As mentioned in the awareness task, Mae rapidly climbs the company ladder and has a successful career.
   In a group, use the clues given in the introduction and the excerpt and add a further (part of a) chapter. Think about other characters, inventions or a specific incident on the Circle campus. Imagine how the story might go on. Your texts can be utopian or dystopian.

   Finally, read/act out your texts in class and evaluate your continuations of the novel.
   → Focus on Skills, Continuation of a Fictional Text, p. 392

6. Do a project and watch the 2012 American drama film *Disconnect* which illustrates the negative sides of modern communication technologies such as social networking, cyber-bullying and identity theft. Prepare a presentation on the film's plot and related topics for your class.
   → Focus on Skills, Presentations, p. 391

Webcode SNG-40183-038 @

Tip: As a first step, watch the trailer of the film provided on the webcode.

7. Against the backdrop of global terrorism and terrorist threats, governments worldwide, in addition to companies and organizations, are also interested in collecting information about citizens.
   Do research on the Internet and collect information on these aspects:
   - the storage of
     – location data, – call detail records, – telephony, – Internet traffic and transaction data,
   - traffic analysis and surveillance,
   - data retention/data preservation (*Vorratsdatenspeicherung*).

   Prepare short presentations on the respective topics and exchange your findings in class.

Andreas Gruhn

Daten sind das Öl des 21. Jahrhunderts

AWARENESS

In a Think! Pair! Share! activity, reflect on and discuss the headline of this text.
What makes "Big Data" as important as or even more important than oil in the 21st century?

Ein Gespenst geht um in der digitalen Welt, und sein Name birgt Verheißung[1] und Verdammnis[2] zugleich. Big Data heißt es, und es macht möglich, wovon die Menschheit ziemlich lange geträumt hat: Der Blick in die Zukunft auf Grundlage der Analyse riesiger Datenmengen erlaubt die Optimierung der Welt, wie sie ein Unternehmen gerne hätte. Vereinfacht gesagt: Big Data macht das Wetter nicht besser, aber es sorgt dafür, dass die Menschen immer optimal ausgestattet sind für das Wetter in den nächsten Stunden. Und das ist vielen unheimlich wie ein Gespenst.

Aber: Was ist so schlimm daran, wenn ein Navigationsgerät[3] genau weiß, wo wie viele Autos auf welcher Strecke zu meinem Ziel unterwegs sind und wie schnell sie fahren? Warum soll die Verbreitung[4] einer Erkältung[5] nicht über die Häufung[6] von Foreneinträgen[7] im Netz zum Thema Halsschmerzen[8] vorhergesagt werden? Wo liegt das Problem, wenn der Supermarkt weiß, dass in einem Stadtteil viele Menschen im Internet nach Tipps zum Grillen suchen – und dann eben mehr Fleisch als sonst in der Kühltruhe bereit liegt? Bisher mussten das Marktforschungsunternehmen[9] aufwendig herausfinden, künftig reicht ein einziger Datenanalyst. Denn die Informationen hat die Masse ja bereitwillig zur Verfügung gestellt. Vor allem bei Gesundheit, Sicherheit und Verkehr sorgt eine kleine gelieferte Datenmenge des Einzelnen für eine Verbesserung für die Allgemeinheit.

Big Data ist aber Fluch und Segen zugleich. Ein hochrangiger Google-Vertreter bekannte[10] neulich, es werde für Nutzer künftig immer schwerer, Angebote zu erhalten, die nicht auf sie zugeschnitten[11] sind. Und Big-Data-Experte und Buchautor Viktor Mayer-Schönberger warnt: „Wir werden als Menschen immer vorhersehbarer[12]. Anhand der Daten lässt sich ablesen, wie wir denken und wie wir in der Zukunft handeln werden."

Für den Konsumenten wirken sich analysierte Daten so aus, als würde er mit Scheuklappen[13] durch ein Kaufhaus rennen. Zielgerichtet wird er aufmerksam gemacht auf das, was er gerade braucht und das, was ihn interessiert. Auf der anderen Seite sieht er kaum mehr das, was abseits seines Regals auf ihn wartet, wonach er bisher einfach nicht gesucht hat. Die ureigenste[14] Eigenschaft der Internetnutzung wandert aus der digitalen Welt in die Wirklichkeit: Der Mensch findet nichts mehr, er sucht nur noch. Das veranlasst einige Experten dazu, das Ende des Zufalls[15] über die Menschheit hereinbrechen[16] zu sehen. Die düsterste Vision: Algorithmen bestimmen die Lebenswelt des Konsumenten und entscheiden, was er erlebt und konsumiert und was nicht. Die Welt wird eine Suchmaschine, und Daten sind ihr Öl. Das Öl des 21. Jahrhunderts.

Der Unterschied ist: Die Daten sprudeln[17] unendlich[18], ihre Quellen sind unerschöpflich[19], aber sie liegen an allen Ecken und Enden des Internets. Nur wer sie geschickt zu verknüpfen versteht, der kann Zusammenhänge erkennen und nutzen, um sich einen Wettbewerbsvorteil zu verschaffen: Man ist der erste, der ein Produkt anbietet, das übermorgen gebraucht wird. Man produziert keine Überschüsse mehr, die schon morgen kein Mensch mehr haben will – und minimiert so finanzielle Einbußen[20]. Für Geschäftsführungen sind aus der Datenanalyse gewonnene Erkenntnisse eine riesige Entscheidungshilfe. „Der breite Einsatz von Big Data ist eine Frage der Wettbewerbsfähigkeit[21] der deutschen Wirtschaft", sagt Dieter Kempf, Präsident des IT-Branchenverbands Bitkom.

Digitale Wertschöpfung[22] heißt das – und steht in Deutschland erst am Anfang. Rund zehn Prozent aller Unternehmen in Deutschland setzen bisher Big-Data-

[1] promise – [2] perdition – [3] GPS device – [4] spread of sth. – [5] cold – [6] accumulation – [7] entries on forums – [8] a sore throat – [9] market research company – [10] to admit sth. – [11] to tailor sth. to sb./sth. – [12] predictable – [13] blinkers – [14] innate – [15] coincidence – [16] to befall sb. – [17] to gush – [18] endlessly – [19] inexhaustibe – [20] losses – [21] competitiveness – [22] creation of value/added value

Lösungen ein, berichtet Bitkom. Doch ihr Anteil wird weiter steigen: Fast 31 Prozent haben konkrete Pläne, dies künftig zu tun. Die Umsatz[23]-Vorhersagen[24] für den Markt überbieten sich im Jahresrhythmus. Nach einer Bitkom-Erhebung, die zur Computermesse Cebit im März veröffentlicht wurde, wird sich der Umsatz für Big-Data-Lösungen von 6,2 Milliarden Euro in diesem Jahr bis 2016 mehr als verdoppelt haben.

Dafür, dass es nicht noch schneller geht, haben die Unternehmen eine ganz einfache Erklärung: Es gibt nur zu wenig Spezialisten.

Rheinische Post, 10 August 2014, p. B3

COMPREHENSION

1. Mediate the German newspaper article into English for an international student forum on Internet security, focusing on these points:
- Big Data and the optimization of people's lives
- the practical use of Big Data
- risks and threats of Big Data for consumers
- how to use Big Data efficiently and productively
- plans of German companies to use Big Data

→ Focus on Skills, Mediation, p. 384

ANALYSIS

2. Additionally, mediate the bar chart on the following page and explain the expected potentials and business revenues (*Erträge*) in connection with Big Data.

→ Focus on Skills, Mediation, p. 384
→ Focus on Skills, Analysis of Statistical Data, p. 380

Step 1: Contrast the assumed advantages and benefits of collecting and using people's data to possible risks. Copy the grid below and complete it.

benefits	**risks**
• coordinating traffic and preventing traffic jams • preventing food shortages or waste of food • …	• manipulation of consumers' shopping habits • limitation of … • …

Step 2: Discuss in class:

a) Does the analysis and use of people's data really lead to the "optimization of the world"? (compare also: "the loss of serendipity", Students' Book, p. 315, ll. 66 ff.).

b) Do the assumed benefits of Big Data justify the risks and disadvantages?

→ Focus on Language, Conversation and Discussion, p. 385

3. Relate the list of examples and alleged advantages to the excerpt from Dave Egger's novel *The Circle* (pp. 319 f.) in which the benefits of *TruYou* are presented.
To what extent do the two "visions" match?

→ Focus on Skills, Analysis of a Non-Fictional Text, p. 377
→ Focus on Skills, Analysis of a Fictional Text, p. 374

[23] sales/turnover – [24] prediction/forecast

ACTIVITIES

4. Divide the class into groups and work creatively with the information you collected on Big Data and their possible (ab-)use.
Imagine scenarios in which, for example, consumers want to go shopping in a mall or supermarket for fun or relaxation but are constantly guided or lured into certain shops or to certain products based on the analysis of their personal data.

Write a short scene or story in which you include dialogues*, interior monologues*, etc.
Your texts can be funny, ironic or scary and threatening. Additionally, you can use props and details to flesh out the action.

Finally, read and/or act out your texts in class and discuss the different views taken.

GRAMMAR / LANGUAGE

5. Together with a partner, compile a flyer in which you promote the collection of "Big Data" and the potential value this adds to people's lives.
Use **future tenses** (will-future, going-to future) and **conditional sentences** to depict the advantages of "Big Data" for people's future lives.

Examples:
- Customers will not have to waste their precious time looking for bargains and special offers because …
- If retailers are able to predict customers' wishes and needs, they will …

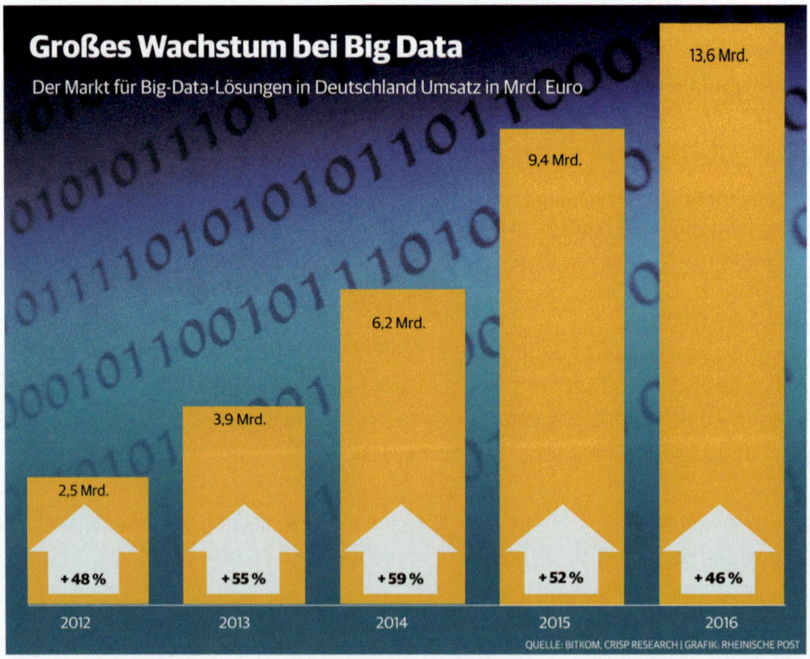

The Media

In the domain of communication, **media** are tools used to store or transmit information and/or data. The term **mass media** or **public media** is used to describe the sum of mass distributors of news and entertainment. These media include **print media**, **electronic media**, and **digital media**. Gutenberg, who perfected the printing press with movable types in 1454, is considered the inventor of "print media". Today, modern communication media facilitate so-called **"many-to-many communication"** (e.g. via e-mail or Internet forums), whereas more traditional media typically represent **"one-to-many communication"** (e.g. TV, radio, cinema). Generally, the purpose of mass media is to promote businesses and their products by providing entertainment, information and socially-relevant services.

Tools of media and types of communication

print media
- books
- newspapers
- magazines
- catalogues
- → from the late 15th century
- → physical distribution

digital media
- Internet (websites)
- e-mail
- mobile phone
- blogs (web logs)
- vlogs (video logs)
- RSS feeds
- podcasts
- QR code
- video games
- social networking
- → digital distribution

broadcast/electronic media
- radio (ca. 1910)
- recorded music (late 19th century)
- film/cinema (ca. 1900)
- TV (ca. 1950)
- discs (1908s), tapes (1920s)
- e-book (1990s)
- podcasts
- e-publishing
- → electronic distribution

public communication
- TV
- newspapers/magazines
- social networking
- → many-to-many communication

↔

personal communication
- telephony
- mail (post)
- mobile phones
- → person-to-person communication

Impact and influence of the media

advantages/positive effects	risks/dangers/negative effects
• effective and quick exchange of information • possibility of being interconnected supports people in authoritarian states, e.g. the Arab Spring of 2011 – "democratization" process • giving public access to hidden/withheld information • (almost) unlimited access to information even in remote places, e.g. developing countries • exchange of cultural and social values • achievement of social control (e.g. public polls, citizen journalism) • platforms for individual presentations and contributions	• influencing politics and public opinion • spying and surveillance (e.g. domestic wiretapping; *Telefonüberwachung*), datamining, etc. • publishing secret information (e.g. WikiLeaks) • influencing children and teenagers (e.g. exposure to violence, role models, advertising, etc.) • creation of an illusionary world (e.g. through soap operas – escapism) • imbalance of information (e.g. developed vs. developing world)

Gary Turk

Look Up

AWARENESS

Only ten days after its launch, the YouTube video *Look Up* had been clicked 11 billion times.
In his video, British music video filmmaker Gary Turk tells a love story and appeals to people to turn off their smartphones and "live the real way".

a) What is it about using a smartphone that can make people forget about and ignore "real life" and having "real social networks and face to face contacts"? Discuss in class.
b) Describe the Banksy painting *Mobile Lovers* and speculate about its intended message.

Banksy, *Mobile Lovers*, 2014

COMPREHENSION

1. **Step 1:**
   First, **get an overview of the whole poem**:
   Webcode SNG-40183-039 @
   a) watch the video clip using the link provided on the webcode and/or
   17 CD 3
   b) listen to the recording of the poem.
   → Focus on Skills, Listening Comprehension, p. 366

   Tip: In addition to listening to the recording of the poem, you can also read the lyrics which are provided on the webcode.

   Step 2:
   - Make sure that you have understood the content, i. e. the "message" of the poem.
   - Clarify unknown vocabulary and questions, if necessary.

ACTIVITIES

2. The poem-like text consists of 21 four-line stanzas and two stanzas consisting of just two lines. Divide the class into 6 – 7 groups, with each group working with 3 – 4 of the 4-line stanzas and all groups working with the two 2-lined stanzas.

   Work creatively with the stanzas you have chosen and prepare a recitation in class.
   - Create your own version, choosing a particular rhythm or style of reciting.
   - Be creative and recite the lines e. g. as a rap song. You may even use accompanying music. The two 2-line stanzas can serve as the refrain.
   - Present and perform your chosen stanzas in class, with all the groups reciting the 2-line stanzas.

3. Turn this version of *Look Up* into a different type of text, e. g. satire, fairy tale, drama, comedy, soap opera, etc. and prepare short performances, recitations, etc. of your texts in class.

4. The video clip *Look Up* triggered a controversial discussion and viewers' reactions to it were mixed. Some viewers were enthusiastic about it, saying it made them cry – some viewers condemned it as stupid and ignorant, claiming that it oversimplified the topic.
   What do *you* think about the video clip? Write a review for an Internet blog in about 200 words and evaluate the poem's/video's quality.
   → Focus on Skills, Writing a Comment and a Review, p. 393

	means of communication	
to access sth.; (to have) access to sth. [ˈækses]	to find information, esp. using a computer; to have a computer, a car, etc. that you can use	*auf etw. zugreifen; Zugang (zu etw. haben)*
blog; blogger	web log, a web page containing information or opinions from a particular person or about a particular subject, to which new information is added regularly; sb. who writes a blog	*Blog (das, der); Blogger*
to broadcast (broadcast, broadcast)	to send out radio or television programmes	*ausstrahlen, senden*
cell phone	mobile phone	*Handy*
to communicate with sb.	to exchange information, news, ideas, etc. with sb.	*kommunizieren*
to connect; connected (to)	to join two or more things together; to be joined to a large system or network	*verbinden; verbunden (mit)*
cyberbullying [ˈsaɪbəˌbʊliɪŋ]	the activity of sending Internet or text messages to insult or threaten sb.	*Cybermobbing*
to design a website	to create or develop a website	*eine Internetseite erstellen*
digital traffic	the number of people who have clicked or used a website	*Zahl der Besucher einer Website; Datenverkehr*
to distribute sth. via the Internet	to share things, e. g. news, among a group of people (using the Internet), esp. in a planned way	*etw. (über das Internet) ver-breiten*
podcast	a digital medium consisting of a series of audio files users can download or stream to a mobile device	*Podcast (der)*
to post sth. online	to put sth. on a website	*im Internet veröffentlichen*
on the net	on the Internet	*im Internet*
(online) privacy [ˈprɪvəsi, *BE*; ˈpraɪvəsi, *US*]	the state of being free from the attention of others (when using the Internet)	*Privatsphäre im Internet*
to reply (replied, replied); reply	to answer; an answer	*antworten; Antwort*
to revolutionize sth.	to completely change the way that sth. is done	*umwälzen, revolutionieren*
search engine	a computer programme that searches the Internet for information	*Suchmaschine*
search term	a term/word which you enter in a search engine	*Suchbegriff*
to share	to let sb. have/use sth. that belongs to you; to tell others about your ideas, opinions, etc.	*etw. teilen; mitteilen*
smart phone	a mobile phone with an operating system	*Smartphone*
social networking (service)	a platform people can use to share their ideas and opinions and to stay in contact	*soziales Netzwerk(en); soziales Vernetztsein*
source of information	the place where sb. finds information	*Informationsquelle*
to subscribe	to pay money regularly to become a member of an organization, or to use a service regularly	*sich bei etw. anmelden; etw. abonnieren*
to text (message)	to send someone a written message on a mobile device	*SMS schreiben*
wireless communication	a system of sending and receiving signals that does not use wires	*drahtlose Kommunikation*
	electronic and digital media	
(targeted) advertising	the activity of telling the public about a product or service in order to persuade them to buy it (aiming at a particular group of potential customers)	*(gezielte) Werbung*
app(lication)	a software designed to perform operations on comput-ers or mobile devices	*Anwendungssoftware*
audio file	a file on a computer in which sound data are stored	*Audiodatei*
to collect data	to gather information	*Daten sammeln*

compatibility [kəmˌpætəˈbɪlɪti]	the ability of computers and programmes to be used together	*Verträglichkeit, Kompatibilität*
computer-literate (*adj.*)	able to use a computer	*sich mit Computern auskennen; wissen, wie man einen Computer bedient*
data [ˈdeɪtə, ˈdɑːtə]	facts or information, esp. when examined and used to find out things or to make decisions	*Daten*
data preservation	the activity of storing data for later use or analysis	*Vorratsdatenspeicherung*
data protection	the act of guaranteeing that personally identifiable information is safe from being exposed	*Datenschutz*
data theft	the act of stealing data	*Datendiebstahl*
GPS	global positioning system	*Globales Positionsbestimmungssystem*
interactive media systems	media systems which allow information to be passed continuously and in both directions between the system/computer and the person using it	*interaktive Medien*
to invade sb.'s privacy	to affect sb.'s privacy in an unpleasant or annoying way	*in jds. Privatsphäre eindringen*
to spy	to secretly collect information	*spionieren, ausspähen*
to track	to search for sb. by following the marks they leave behind them	*jdn. verfolgen*
to transfer data	to move information from one place to another	*Daten übertragen*
virtual	made, done, seen on the Internet or on a computer, rather than in the real world; artificial	*virtuell, nicht real, künstlich*
virus [ˈvaɪrəs]	instructions hidden in a computer programme, designed to cause faults or destroy data	*Computervirus*
	online journalism	
24/7 news cycle (*infml.*)	when news stories are investigated and reported all day and all night long, at a very fast pace	*Nachrichten rund um die Uhr*
breaking news	a special report on an important topic, usually interrupting the regular programme	*Eilmeldung*
to comment on sth.	to express an opinion about sb. or sth.	*etw. kommentieren*
infographic	visual representation of data or information in the form of charts, maps, etc.	*Infografik*
news agency	an organization that collects news stories and supplies them to newspapers, radio stations, etc.	*Presseagentur*
newsfeed	a way of providing online readers with constantly updated news	*Nachrichteneinspeisung*
newsworthy	important or interesting enough to be reported	*berichtenswert*
paywall	a system asking readers to pay for content that is available online, e. g. on the website of a newspaper	*Bezahlschranke*
press coverage	when a subject or event is reported in the media	*Berichterstattung*
to quote; quotation	to repeat exactly what someone else has said or written; a sentence or phrase from a book, speech, etc. which you repeat e. g. in a piece of writing	*zitieren; Zitat*
short attention span	the period of time during which you continue to be interested in sth. is not very long	*kurze Aufmerksamkeitsspanne*
sound bite	a very short part of a speech or statement, esp. one made by a politician, that is broadcast on a news programme	*kurzes, prägnantes Zitat*

Find more vocabulary on Focus on Facts, The Press (p. 370) and Focus on Facts, The Media (p. 325).

Shakespeare: Such Stuff As Dreams Are Made On ...

Tips on vocab

pictogram ■ **to stab sb.** *jdn. erstechen* ■ **dagger** *Dolch* ■ **to drown** *ertrinken* ■ **to smother sb.** *jdn. ersticken* ■ **shame** here: *Schande* ■ **to drop dead** *tot umfallen* ■ **grief** *Gram, Kummer*

START-UP ACTIVITIES

1. When William Shakespeare "turned 450" in April 2014, he was celebrated all over the world. Despite his age, Shakespeare himself as well as his work are still an icon in popular culture. In a round robin activity,
   a) give short statements on what you know about Shakespeare and his work,
   b) speculate about possible reasons for his undiminished popularity.

2. Divide the class into seven groups and assign each group one of the tragedies in the pictogram.
   - In a first step, try to identify the clues given in the respective graphic and speculate about a) the characters and b) the plot of the tragedy.
   - Usually, each of Shakespeare's plays focuses on a specific topic (→ FoF, p. 335) in connection with certain leitmotifs.

   @ In your groups, do research on your chosen tragedy and get an overview of
   a) the constellation of the main characters, b) the plot and c) the topic and relevant leitmotifs.
   - Prepare short presentations using your research results and the visual in the Students' Book.
   - Additionally, you can compile handouts which provide the most relevant information.

   → Focus on Skills, Presentations, p. 391
   → Focus on Skills, Writing a Handout, p. 397

3. Take a look at the cartoon above. Against the background of your results from task no. 2, discuss the lady's complaint: Are Shakespeare's plays a lineup of "sex and violence"?

4. Thomas Platter, a Swiss tourist, described his impressions of amusements and spectacles which he witnessed in London in 1599 in his diary.
   18 CD 3
   Listen to Thomas Platter's description of Elizabethan London and take notes on these aspects:
   - playhouses and theatres
   - ale-houses and beer gardens

5. Speculate on what made London a magnet for tourists and people of all kinds.
   Discuss in class.

Mr. Shakespeare: On Stage, Please!

John Orloff

Anonymous[1]

AWARENESS

Shakespeare's authorship was first questioned in the 19th century, with critics claiming that Shakespeare's lack of education, his humble origin and obscure life appeared to be in strong contrast to the poetic and literary genius of his work. Sceptics argue that only a worldly and highly-educated aristocrat could have written these plays and poems.
Against this backdrop, the 2011 political thriller and historical drama film *Anonymous*, set in the late Elizabethan era, presents Edward de Vere, 17th Earl of Oxford, as the true author of Shakespeare's works. Allegedly, William Shakespeare, who is nearly illiterate, only serves as a front man to cover up a larger conspiracy against Elizabeth I and the succession of the throne.

In class, discuss whether or not you can understand the ongoing controversy over the true authorship of Shakespeare's works – especially after more than 400 years. Is this merely a debate among brainy scholars or is the true authorship of Shakespeare's works of eminent importance?

INT. BROADWAY THEATER – BACKSTAGE – DUSK[2]
We follow the Man in the Grey Suit as he rushes through narrow backstage hallways, passing several ACTORS dressing in Elizabethan costumes, applying their make-up, etc. ... [...]

A STAGE MANAGER takes a nervous peek[3] through the curtains to check the audience – it's a full house. He holds a prop[4] umbrella in one hand, anxiously checks his watch in the other.
He looks on both wings[5] of the stage – and then relief[6] floods his face as he sees the Man in the Grey Suit hurrying over to him. The Stage Manager wordlessly hands him the umbrella and signals to a stagehand[7] in the background.
The curtains start to OPEN and the MURMUR of the audience dies down.

INT. BROADWAY THEATER – THE STAGE – CONTINUOUS
The man with the umbrella stands on the empty stage, a single light on him. He is "PROLOGUE". [...]

PROLOGUE
Soul of the Age!
The applause, delight, the wonder of our stage!
Our Shakespeare, rise ...
(beat, repeating)
Our Shakespeare ... For he is all of ours[8], is he not? The most performed playwright of all time! The author of 37 plays, 154 sonnets, and several epic poems[9] that are collectively known as the ultimate expressions of humanity in the English language. And yet ... And yet ...
(beat)

[1] **anonymous** [əˈnɒnɪməs] – [2] **dusk** the time before night when it not yet dark – [3] **to take a peek** (*infml.*) to look at sth. for a short time – [4] **prop** (*abbr.*) property, an object used by the actors performing in a play or film – [5] **wing** the sides of the stage that cannot be seen by the audience – [6] **relief** *Erleichterung* – [7] **stagehand** *Bühnenarbeiter* – [8] **all of ours** belonging to all of us – [9] **epic poems** [ˈepɪk] long narrative poems written in verse

Not a single manuscript of any kind has ever been found written in Shakespeare's own hand. In four hundred years, not one document – be it poem, play, diary or even a simple letter.

(beat)

He was born the son of a glove-maker[10], and at some unknown time, armed with[11] but[12] an elementary school education, he went to London where, the story goes, he became an actor and eventually a playwright. [...]

He died at the age of 56, and was survived by his wife and two daughters who were, like Shakespeare's own father, irrefutably[13] illiterate[14].

OFF STAGE

In the rafters[15] a stagehand opens valves[16]. It starts to rain.

PROLOGUE (O.C.[17]) (CONT'D)

His will famously left his second best bed to his widow. But it made no mention of a single book or manuscript. [...]

Is it possible Shakespeare owned no books at his death because ... he could not read? That he wrote no letters because he, like his father before him and his children after him, could not write?

(lets that sink in, then)

Our Shakespeare is a cipher[18], a ghost; his biography made not by history ... but by conjecture[19]. His story not written with facts, but with ... imagination.

The rain has intensified. "Prologue" turns and the camera starts to leave him and the TITLES end ...

PROLOGUE (CONT'D)

(more energetic)

So! Let me offer you a different story. A darker story ... Of quills[20] and swords[21]. Of power and betrayal. Of a stage conquered, and a throne lost!

A FLASH OF LIGHTNING, and for a moment only sheets of RAIN are visible. No stage, no "Prologue". Then, through the rain, we see the form of a man ...

http://cbsla.files.wordpress.com/2012/01/anonymous-screenplay.pdf [12.09.2014], pp. 1 ff.

COMPREHENSION

1. **Step 1:** Read the technical instructions and describe the atmosphere that is created in the introductory part of the film (= the opening credits).

   Step 2: Now read the lines spoken by "Prologue" and take notes on these questions:
   - What is said about Shakespeare's professional life?
   - What does the audience learn about Shakespeare's personal background?

2. Specify the questions that result from the information given about Shakespeare's professional and private life by "Prologue".

3. In order to get a deeper impression of the opening scene and the central notion of the film,
   a) watch the video clip of the trailer and
   b) scroll through the film stills.

   Webcode SNG-40183-040 @

   Both are provided on the webcode.

   Next, work together with a partner and take notes on these aspects:
   - How is the atmosphere of the opening scene rendered?
   - What image of the theatrical world of Shakespeare's time is conveyed?
   - What is revealed about Elizabethan London and society?
   - What clues are given concerning a political conspiracy?

[10] **glove-maker** *Handschuhmacher* – [11] **to be armed with sth.** here: *mit etw. ausgerüstet sein* – [12] **but** (*fml.*) here: only, just – [13] **irrefutable** [ˌɪrɪˈfjuːtəbl] (*fml.*) impossible to prove wrong – [14] **illiterate** unable to read and write – [15] **rafters** *oberer Teil der Bühne unter dem Dach* – [16] **valve** *Ventil* – [17] **O. C.** (*abbr.*) original character – [18] **cipher** [ˈsaɪfər] (*fml., disapproving*) *Strohmann* – [19] **conjecture** *Mutmaßung* – [20] **quill** *Federkiel* – [21] **sword** [sɔːd] *Schwert*

ANALYSIS

4. The opening scene of a film, play, etc. is of utmost importance in order to attract the audience's attention and evoke their curiosity.
Together with a partner, examine the excerpt from the screenplay again and find examples of narrative and cinematic devices that entice (= *verlocken*) the viewer into watching the film.
→ Focus on Skills, Analysis of a Film Scene, p. 375

5. Describe and examine the cartoon:
- What does it say about Shakespeare's authorship?
- To what extent does this view match/differ from the notion of the screenplay?

→ Focus on Skills, Analysis of Visuals, p. 381

"I ASKED WILL IF HE WROTE IT. HE SAID HE WASN'T SURE."

ACTIVITIES

6. Team up with a partner and choose either the screenshot on p. 332 or one of the photos/film stills provided on the webcode.

Webcode SNG-40183-040

Step 1: Do further research on the film *Anonymous*, its characters and the conspiracy the film deals with.

Step 2: Write (interior) monologues* or dialogues for the characters in your screenshot and imagine what they might be talking and/or thinking about.

Step 3: Act out your monologues/dialogues in class and discuss and evaluate how they convey the motifs of the film and whether they pick up on the clues given in the screenplay excerpt.

7. In his final lines, "Prologue" offers the audience a "darker story" of "quills and swords", "power and betrayal" and a "throne lost" (ll. 65 ff.).
In groups, compile the front page of a gazette that informs the readership about the political snake pit of Elizabethan London and the "Shakespeare conspiracy". Flesh out your front page with photos, gossip, interviews – e.g. with Elizabeth I or Shakespeare himself – or famous lines from his poems or plays.
Display your front pages in class and evaluate their layout and information.
→ Focus on Skills, Writing a Newspaper Article, p. 399
→ Focus on Skills, Writing an Interview, p. 398

GRAMMAR / LANGUAGE

8. You are asked to write a review of *Anonymous* for your school's film club.

Webcode SNG-40183-040

Unfortunately, you do not have the time to watch the entire film but can only watch the trailer (cf. webcode) and read the excerpt from the screenplay at hand. However, you want to flesh out your review by **employing adjectives, adverbs and adverbials** to give your readers a more vivid impression of the film and its notion.

Example: The aerial view of New York City along with the outward appearance of … gives the expository scene a cosmopolitan and postmodern image of …

→ Focus on Skills, Writing a Comment and a Review, p. 393

Shakespeare's Stage

Reconstruction of the Globe in London, Southwark

Through the 1580s and 1590s London's Lord Mayors tried to **have plays banned** because **they were thought to be profane and ungodly**. Moreover, plays took apprentices and workmen away from their jobs, since they were performed in daylight each afternoon. As a consequence, the theatre companies began to move outside the city walls, and in **1594**, two new theatres were founded:

- the **Lord Chamberlain's Men** played at the **Theatre**, the company which Shakespeare joined as an actor and wrote plays for
- the **Lord Admiral's Company** played at the **Rose** and performed Christopher Marlowe's[1] plays.

In **1599**, the **Globe** was built on the south bank of the Thames, **in the suburb of Southwark**, which at that time was full of wayfarers'[2] inns for the many travellers who crossed London Bridge to get into or out of the city. During Shakespeare's time there were **ten open-air amphitheatres in London** with thousands of people going to see new plays every day. Until the **Globe** was destroyed in a fire in 1613, it was **the most successful and prosperous theatre** of the time.

Shakespeare's Globe, also called the **wooden O**, could hold around three thousand people. There was **no "theatre etiquette"** – people did not have to sit still or stand quietly; often theatres were drunken, rowdy places.
Some **ticket prices** of the time (a typical wage in 1594 was eight old pence a day):

- one penny: standing in the yard around the stage (→ for the "groundlings")
- twopence: a wooden seat in a covered gallery
- another penny: a cushion[3] for the seats
- sixpence: a seat in the "Lords' Gallery" – seats placed on either side of the balcony at the back of the stage

On the outside an Elizabethan playhouse had plain, white-plastered walls, but inside it was a blaze of colour. The first **Globe was described as "the glory of the Banke"**. The Globe had **a rectangular[4] stage**, projecting halfway into the yard. Above the stage was **a balcony** for musicians and actors. Its decorated ceiling was called the ***Heavens***. Beneath the stage lay ***Hell*** out of which ghosts and devils would emerge through a trap door.
The **demand for new plays was huge** and playwrights likely wrote several new plays every year. Of the thousands of plays which were written during that time, only **230 are still in existence – 39 are Shakespeare's plays** that have survived the last four centuries.
Some **topics and leitmotifs of Shakespeare's plays**:

- **Sex & crime vs. honour & virtue** (e. g. *Romeo and Juliet, Much Ado About Nothing, A Midsummer Night's Dream*)
- **Distant worlds vs. local colour** (e. g. *The Tempest, Much Ado About Nothing*)
- **Women's rights vs. patriarchal[5] structures** (*The Taming of the Shrew, Much Ado About Nothing*)
- **Racism** (e. g. *The Merchant of Venice, Othello*)
- **Language and social class** (verse vs. prose → e. g. *Romeo and Juliet* (Nurse), *Macbeth* (Porter), *A Midsummer Night's Dream* (craftsmen))
- **Crime (ocular proof[6])** (e. g. *Hamlet, Othello, Macbeth, Julius Cesar, Richard III*)
- **Sanity/madness ... order/disorder** (e. g. *King Lear, Hamlet, Macbeth*)
- **Social class → climbing the social ladder** (e. g. *Coriolanus, Romeo and Juliet, Much Ado About Nothing*)

[1] **Christopher Marlowe** (1564 – 1593) English playwright, poet and translator who influenced Shakespeare – [2] **wayfarer** (*old use*) *Wanderer, Reisender* – [3] **cushion** [ˈkʊʃən] pillow – [4] **rectangular** *rechteckig* – [5] **patriarchal** [ˌpeɪtriˈɑːkəl] ruled or controlled by men – [6] **ocular proof** sth. that can be seen with the eye

Drama and Theatre

Drama

A **drama or play** is written to be performed by **actors** in a theatre, in a film, on television or on the radio. Traditionally, a play is composed of **acts** (units that reflect main stages in the development of the action), which are further subdivided into **scenes** (= sequences of continuous, uninterrupted action). Modern plays may just present a sequence of scenes. More reduced forms are **one-act plays**. One of the basic elements of drama is a **conflict between opposing characters (= protagonist/antagonist)**, or contrasting ideas, attitudes and interests. Conflict creates tension and **dramatic action**, which unfolds in **dialogues** and/or **monologues**. Good dialogues or monologues must capture the personalities, social positions, attitudes, thoughts and emotions of the characters. **Stage directions** given by the **author/playwright** help the director and the actors perform the play on stage. Such directions may be rather short and leave room for individual interpretation, while others are very detailed and indicate the precise design and arrangement of the **setting** (= time and place), **scenery, props** (= properties, i. e. furniture, decoration, etc.), the characters' appearances, movements, gestures, ways of speaking, or the **sound and lighting** to be used.

Drama is the generic[1] term for the genre. The most important subclasses are:

- the **traditional tragedy**, which develops dramatic action like this:

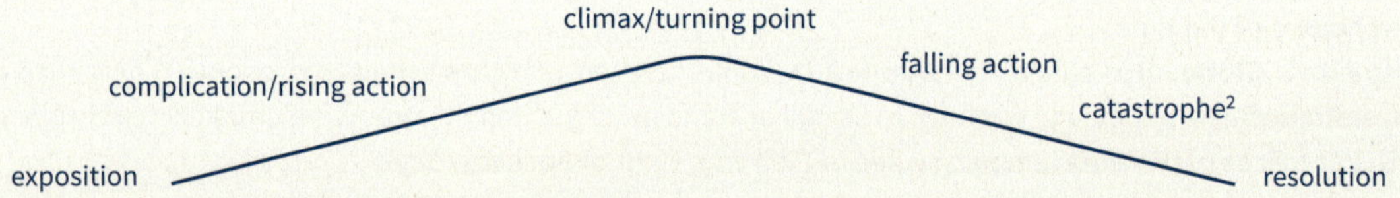

- the **traditional comedy**, which develops dramatic action like this:

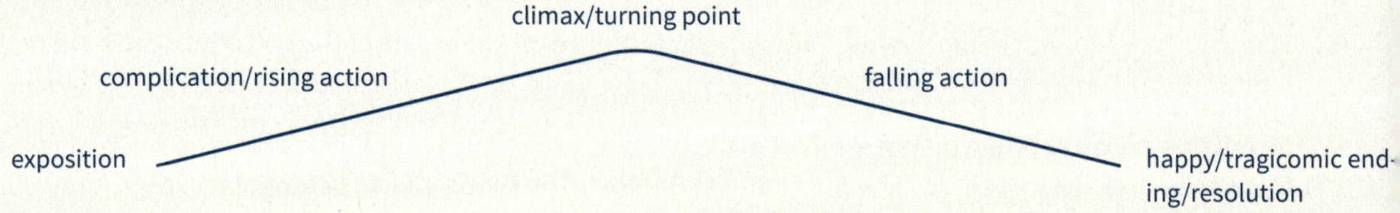

Theatre

Here are some of the important elements of a theatrical stage:

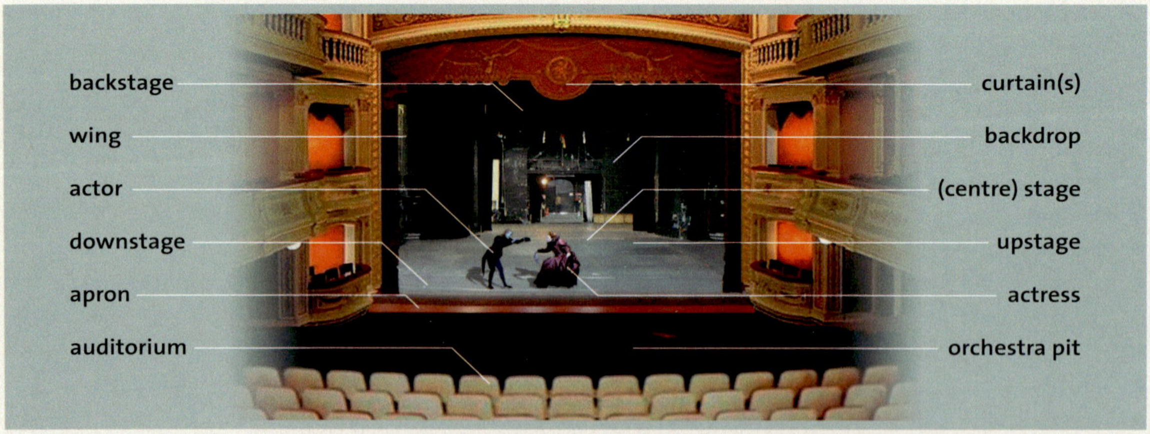

Note: Explanations of the respective technical terms can be found in the Literary Terms section, pp. 405 ff.

[1] **generic** shared by, including or typical of a whole group of things; not specific – [2] **catastophe** [kəˈtæstrəfi]

ACTIVITIES

Webcode SNG-40183-044

3. Do further research on the "Unhate" campaign using the links provided on the webcode.
In class, discuss and evaluate the campaign that was sponsored by Benetton. Do you consider this to be an appropriate way of making the public aware of youth unemployment and helping young people get jobs?

4. Take a look at the "employability skills" on p. 352 again.
Discuss whether having these skills or being "multi-skilled" is important – or will become even more important in the future – with regard to certain jobs or professions.
Think of examples: a teacher, a physician (*Arzt*), an engineer, etc.

From Application to Assessment Centre

Studies, Internships and Scholarships

AWARENESS

Choosing the right college or university or even the right course of study is very complicated and requires you to know a lot of new terms and abbreviations.
For a start, here is a selection of the most frequently used ones.

M.A.	B.A.	PhD	GCSE	SAT	NVQ
A-levels	M.Sc.	M.Eng.	B.Sc.	B.Eng.	MIB

Together with a partner, find out the meaning of these terms, abbreviations and acronyms. Use a dictionary and/or the vocab pages of your Students' Book for help.

Tips on vocab

to be split in two halves ▪ squares ▪ idiom/proverbial saying ▪ a leopard with square dots ▪ bright-coloured ▪ square bullet points ▪ eye-catching

[1] **vital** [ˈvaɪtl] necessary and extremely important – [2] **pack** a group of animals that hunt together or are kept for hunting; here: a group of similar people – [3] **bespoke** (*fml.*) specially made for a particular person

Tips on vocab

to be split in two halves ■ squares ■ details (*Ausschnitte*) ■ tin bowls/plates ■ rusty ■ the globe ■ Q & A (questions and answers) ■ eye-catching ■ complementary colours

COMPREHENSION

1. **Step 1:** Divide your class into two groups, with each group working with one of the adverts.

   Step 2: Study the adverts and identify the information that is given about:
   - the respective university and its background
   - the university's specific objectives
   - the courses and academic degrees (*Abschlüsse*) offered
   - the requirements concerning the students' qualifications
   - the application and formality
   - future perspectives (e. g. job/work opportunities, etc.)

2. Describe the layout of the advert in detail using the vocab boxes, paying particular attention to the relevant textual and visual elements.

[1] **graduate school** a college where students who already have a first degree are taught – [2] **MIB** (*abbr.*) Master of International Business – [3] **global forces** economic, social, political and cultural influences – [4] **geopolitics** the study of the effects of geography on international politics and international relations – [5] **consulting** the practice of helping companies or organizations to improve their performance, make development plans, etc. – [6] **MNC** (*abbr.*) multi-national corporation – [7] **NGO** (*abbr.*) non-governmental organization

ANALYSIS

3. Present the formal and stylistic devices employed in the advert and explain their function and effect with regard to the ad's specific target group.

4. Analyse the linguistic devices that are used and pay particular attention to
- the use of keywords,
- the use of humor, wit, irony,
- the use of expert language and technical terms,
- the use of references and allusions to certain topics of interest.

ACTIVITIES

5. Critically examine and evaluate: Are adverts that promote universities/colleges as a "product" the appropriate way to attract students? Shouldn't the reputation and quality of a university or college speak for itself?

6. Write an online application for a place at either the University of Warwick or the Fletcher School at Tufts University.

Webcode SNG-40183-045 @

Step 1: Do research on the university using the links provided on the webcode and try to get further information on
a) the student requirements,
b) possible scholarships offered.

Step 2: Write an email to the given address in which you
a) briefly introduce yourself,
b) ask for further application material,
c) ask for further information and requirements concerning students' grades and scholarships.

7. Imagine the university asks for a letter of recommendation from one of your teachers. Together with a partner, collect ideas about
a) which teachers should write a letter of recommendation with regard to the subject you want to study and the intended scholarship,
b) the information this/these letter(s) should contain about your qualifications as well as academic and personal skills.

Afterwards, compile a letter of recommendation that contains the most relevant information using a dictionary and/or the vocab box below.
Then, compare your letters in class and evaluate their wording and composition.

Tips on vocab

to act on one's own initiative ■ self-assured/self-confident ■ to fulfill sb.'s requirements ■ diligent (*gewissenhaft*) ■ loyal ■ cooperative ■ to recommend sb. ■ attentive/attentiveness ■ extracurricular activities ■ to be focused ■ to approach sth. skillfully/thoroughly ■ responsible ■ open-minded ■ competent ■ to do sth. in a profound way ■ to communicate fluently ■ to deal with sth. independently ■ in a differentiated/sophisticated way ■ to be capable of doing/managing/handling sth. ■ to be a valuable asset to … ■ to gain knowledge/experience in sth.

8. The University of Warwick/The Fletcher School is interested in having you as a student – but in order to decide whether you are eligible for a scholarship, the counselor's office requires you to submit information on
a) your coursework (*Facharbeit*) and its objectives or
b) your specific knowledge and focus in one of your advanced courses (*LKs*).

Take a close look at the adverts again and specify which information concerning your curricular activities is most relevant.

Examples:
- business school → focus on social sciences, math, statistics, etc.
- international affairs → focus on foreign languages, politics, etc.
- geopolitics → …

Finally, write a handout of 2 – 3 pages on your chosen subject/topic presenting your objectives and relevant qualifications.
→ Focus on Skills, Writing a Handout, p. 397

9. In order to get some practice before you apply to a university, do a role play in which you **apply for an internship first**.
In a group puzzle activity, prepare role cards using the **interview role cards on the following page**.

M
- Form four/six groups, of which two/three groups take the role of the German applicant (Susanne/Thomas Reichelt) while the others take the part of the American interviewer (Melissa/Sam Stone).
- Each group prepares the respective tasks/questions and takes notes. Use your dictionary and/or the vocab pages in your Students' Book to mediate the German applicant's tasks.
- Then the groups remix (see diagram below).
- Act out the interviews in class.
- During the interviews, the other students should listen and take notes on the performance of the interview partners.
- Finally, the class evaluates the job interviews and exchanges ideas for further improvement. You can use the evaluation form on the webcode.

Webcode SNG-40183-045 @

→ Focus on Skills, Job Interview, p. 387
→ Focus on Skills, Telephoning, p. 389
→ Focus on Skills, Mediation, p. 384

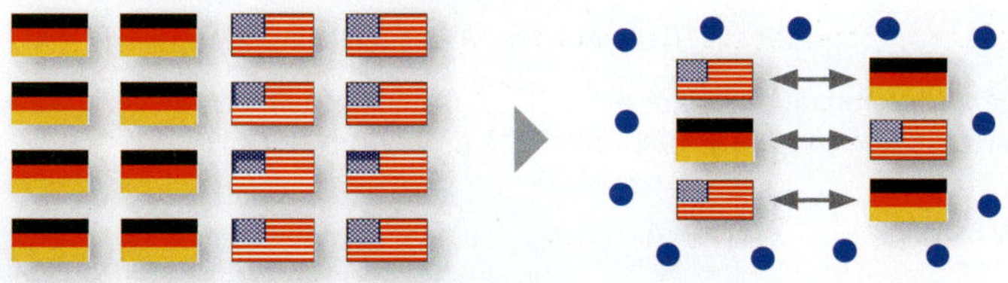

Tip: Before you start **writing interview role cards**, you should **collect information** about
a) Ellis Island National Monument,
b) Deutsches Auswandererhaus Bremerhaven.
Use the links provided on the webcode.

Webcode SNG-40183-045 @

Role A

Sie sind Susanne/Thomas Reichelt und haben gerade das Gymnasium mit dem Abitur absolviert. In einem Internetportal haben Sie die Ausschreibung von Praktikumsplätzen durch die *US Embassy* in Zusammenarbeit mit den amerikanischen *National Park Services* sowie den *National Parks of New York Harbor* gesehen. Die *National Parks of New York Harbor* sind u. a. für die Verwaltung und Organisation des *National Monuments Ellis Island* im Hafen von New York zuständig.

In einem bilateralen Projekt zwischen Deutschland und den USA werden speziell deutsche Praktikanten gesucht, die, in Zusammenarbeit mit dem *Deutschen Auswandererhaus* in Bremerhaven und dem *National Monument Ellis Island*, die Spuren deutscher Auswanderer in die USA recherchieren und eine geplante deutsch-amerikanische Sonderausstellung auf Ellis Island vorbereiten helfen.

Sie haben einen Termin für ein telefonisches *job interview* mit der amerikanischen Ausstellungsorganisatorin Ms Melissa Stone/dem Ausstellungsorganisator Mr Sam Stone, in dem Sie folgende Punkte berücksichtigen sollten:

- Beziehen Sie sich auf die o. g. Informationen.
- Beschreiben Sie Ihre Motivation für den Praktikumsplatz.
- Stellen Sie Ihre Auslandserfahrungen/Erfahrungen mit den USA dar.
- Sagen Sie, dass Sie Kenntnisse der deutsch-amerikanischen Auswanderergeschichte haben.
- Weisen Sie auf Ihre Leistungskurse/Facharbeit etc. mit diesem Themenbezug hin.
- Verweisen Sie auf Zertifkate wie z. B. das Cambridge Certificate.
- Weisen Sie auf Ihre PC-Kenntnisse hin (Windows, Word, Excel …).
- Betonen Sie, dass Sie flexibel sind und innerhalb von … Wochen/Monaten nach New York ziehen könnten.
- Sagen Sie, dass Sie auch bereit sind, zu reisen.
- Verweisen Sie auf weitere Praktika, z. B. … bei …
- Bitten Sie um Hilfe/Unterstützung bei der Wohnungssuche …
- Fragen Sie nach der zu erwartenden Bezahlung …
- Fragen Sie nach der geplanten Dauer des Projektes sowie nach den Chancen, nach einem erfolgreichen Praktikum übernommen zu werden … der Möglichkeit, in den USA zu studieren …

Role B

You are Melissa/Sam Stone and work for the National Parks of New York Harbor. In a two-year project, your team plans to organize the German-American exhibition in cooperation with the American Embassy, the German *Auswärtiges Amt* and the *Deutsches Auswandererhaus* in Bremerhaven as well as *Ellis Island National Monument*.
In your interview with Susanne/Thomas Reichelt from Germany, you should refer to the following points:

- Internship based in New York City
- Graduation from high school/secondary school
- Advanced courses in history, English and/or social sciences
- Interest in history, especially immigration/emigration/migration
- Reasons for wanting to do this internship
- Computer literacy
- Readiness to travel between the U. S. and Germany frequently
- Personal flexibility
- Fluency in English/bilingual …
- Offer of paying travel expenses and providing accommodation
- Necessity of submitting a written application/ CV/references …
- Projects/internships the applicant has participated in/done so far …
- Say he/she will hear from you within the next four weeks.

Ellis Island National Monument

Key Qualifications and Soft Skills

In today's working world, it has become increasingly important to **have certain essential key qualifications** (e. g. reading, writing, math, ICT skills, etc.) which are also described as **"profession-oriented skills"** as well as a variety of so-called **soft skills**.

Shell model[1] of the professional ability to perform: key competences and skills

All the four "shells" or sections of the model are "cross sectional" and intertwined, i. e. the skills, competences and qualifications correspond to skills, knowledge, capabilities and individual attitudes.

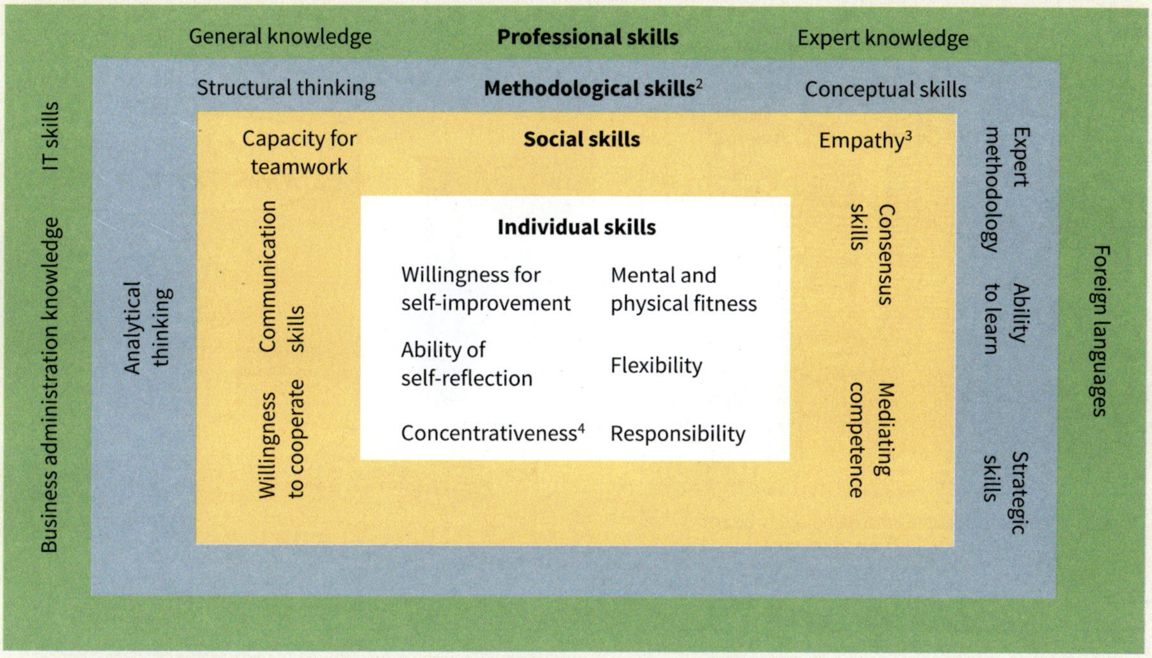

Further soft skills

- **Interpersonal skills**
  - the ability to lead, motivate and delegate (→ organizational responsibility)
- **Teamwork skills**
  - the process of teamwork itself; procedures to ensure the group works cohesively
- **Negotiation skills**
  - achieving desired outcomes; maintaining ongoing relationships; building relationships based on openness, trust, understanding, mutual respect
- **Intercultural competence**
  - experiences in dealing with different cultures; being unprejudiced; being open-minded
- **Problem-solving competence**
  - the ability to tackle problems systematically, learning from this process
  - dealing with a) diagnostic problems, b) design problems and c) contingency[5] problems
- **Time management**
  - controlling and using your time as effectively as possible
  - learning how to prioritize, categorizing responsibilities

[1] **shell model** *Schalenmodell* – [2] **methodological skill** *Methodenkompetenz* – [3] **empathy** *Einfühlungsvermögen* – [4] **concentrativeness** *Konzentrationsfähigkeit* – [5] **contingency** *unvorhergesehener Fall*

MAX Employment: The Top 10 Interview Questions

AWARENESS

Sometimes interviewers ask candidates to tell "something about themselves" as an opening question or "icebreaker".

In groups, think about appropriate answers to this question and collect ideas.
How much of their personal/private lives should candidates reveal in a job interview and what are the pitfalls (*Fallstricke*) of this kind of question?

1

"We look for people who can quickly adapt to changes in the workplace."

2

Tips on vocab

file (*Akte*) ■ pile/stack (*Stapel*) ■ moveable chair ■ height/vertically adjustable (*höhenverstellbar*) chair ■ to stockpile/stack/pile sth. ■ to hover (*in der Luft schweben*)

Tips on vocab

prefabricated components ■ leg of a chair ■ arm (rest) of a chair ■ back of a chair/chair-back ■ stabilizer bar (*Querstrebe*) ■ screwdriver ■ screw(s)

COMPREHENSION

Before listening:

1. Describe the cartoons and specify what each is making fun of.

Webcode SNG-40183-046

2. **Step 1:** Use the material provided on the webcode and identify the most memorable interview mistakes depicted in the online article.
Make a ranking: What do you consider to be more/less serious mistakes?

Step 2: In groups, examine how the article presents the mistakes and speculate on the intended function and message of the article.

Step 3: Based on your examination of the article and the cartoons, develop your own criteria and interview tips. In your groups, collect ideas and design a handout on how to have a successful job interview. Present your handouts in class and discuss your ideas.
→ Focus on Skills, Writing a Handout, p. 397

Tips on vocab

daunting *entmutigend, abschreckend* ■ **tongue-tied** *sprachlos* ■ **outlet** here: branch office ■ **role** here: position ■ **to expand on sth.** to give more detailed information on sth. ■ **work force** *erwerbstätige Bevölkerung* ■ **arena** here: a certain field of work ■ **to let sb. down** *jdn. im Stich lassen* ■ **suitability** [ˌsuːtəˈbɪlɪti] *Eignung, Befähigung* ■ **to commence** [kəˈmens] (*fml.*) to begin ■ **to finalize sth.** to make a final and certain decision about sth. ■ **fortnight** a period of two weeks – **to follow up on sth.** (*phr. v.*) *etw. weiterverfolgen*

3. *MAX Employment* is an Australian employment organization and the interview you are going to listen to was recorded and videotaped for promotional and educational purposes.

23 CD 3 **Listen** to the job interview **a first time** and try to get a general understanding of the topics mentioned.

4. In a **second listening**, take notes on what the interview partners say and reveal about:
- the candidate's qualifications, skills and work experience
- the applicant's personal background
- the applicant's motivation for applying for the job
- the candidate's strengths and weaknesses
- the candidate's aspirations
- the support the company offers to new employees

→ Focus on Skills, Listening Comprehension, p. 366

ANALYSIS

Webcode SNG-40183-046 @ **5.** For a more detailed analysis, use the link provide on the webcode and watch the interview.

Step 1: Examine the interviewer's technique:
- What kind of questions does he ask?
- How does he react to the applicant's explanations?
- What does his body language reveals about his attitude?

Step 2: Now, examine and analyse the applicant's performance:
- How does her choice of words emphasize her motivation and ambition?
- How precisely does she respond to the interviewer's questions?
- How does she convey her professionalism, competence and suitability?
- What does her body language reveal about her attitude?

→ Focus on Skills, Job Interview, p. 387

Webcode SNG-40183-046 @ **Tip:** For further background information on the matter, use the *Job Interviews* material provided on the webcode and do the respective tasks.

ACTIVITIES

6. In order to find out about the applicants' qualifications and eligibility, many organizations invite the candidates to a **personal interview** and/or an **assessment centre**.

Step 1: Study the Info Box on p. 362 on assessment centres and learn about their basic elements and what participants do there.

Webcode SNG-40183-046 @ **Tip:** The links provided on the webcode give you further information on assessment centres and the respective procedures.

Webcode SNG-40183-046 @ **Step 2:** For starters, use the link provided on the webcode and access the **online assessment centre test**. Try to answer the 40 questions on diverse topics as quickly and correctly as possible. Afterwards, compare and discuss your results and the test in general in class.

Step 3: Prepare and act out a **group discussion** on the "The Risks and Benefits of Globalisation".

- Choose six students to act out the discussion and reactivate their knowledge on the topic.
  → Focus on Facts, Progress & Responsibility in a Global World, p. 272
  → Focus on Facts, World Trade, p. 273
- Arrange the chairs as in a fishbowl discussion, i.e. the students who are speaking sit in an inner circle and the other students are seated in an outer circle, watching the discussion and talking notes on the performance.
- The students are asked to discuss the respective topic for about 15 to 20 minutes.
- Imagine what kind of qualities and/or behavioural patterns a possible employer might focus on. Develop an evaluation form of the most relevant aspects.
- Afterwards, the class evaluates the discussion as well as each participant's performance.

Info

The six most commonly practiced elements of assessment centres

1. Presentation
You may be asked to give an off-the-cuff (*Stegreif-*)presentation on a current topic (e.g. fracking, immigration to Europe, etc.). Alternatively, you might be asked to present an outline of your coursework (*Facharbeit*), a subject or topic you have specialized in, etc.

2. Group discussion
The group is given a topic for discussion and the participants are asked to discuss the matter and/or find a solution or compromise to the debated problem.

3. Role play
Usually the participants are asked to take on roles (e.g. boss and employee, sales manager and customer, etc.) and act out a dialogue dealing with a certain problem, e.g. a complaint.

4. Interview
The personnel manager and/or human resource manager conduct(s) a face-to-face interview with the applicant to find out about his/her qualifications, motivation, strengths and possible weaknesses – and, of course, to get a personal impression of the candidate.

5. Scenario
Applicants are given a selection of documents, files and papers dealing with a certain project and their task is to read up on the matter quickly, interpret data and present the most important and relevant information.

6. Test
These tests generally focus on:
a) the intelligence and b) the personal skills of the applicant.
The applicants are required to answer a variety of different questions within a limited amount of time.

7. Your team works in the human resources department of your company.
Watch the job interview again and critically evaluate the applicant's and the interviewer's performance. What parts of the interview are you satisfied with – and what needs to be improved?
Webcode SNG-40183-046 @
Use the material provided in your Students' Book as well as the evaluation form on the webcode and make suggestions for improvements for both sides.

Finally, write, act out and videotape an educational job interview yourselves that serves as a training guide for your school and provides tips and advice to students.
→ Focus on Skills, Job Interview, p. 387

learning and studying		
A-levels	an examination that British students usually take when they are 18 (Advanced Level), at the end of secondary education	*Abitur*
compulsory education	a period of education that is required (by law)	*allgemeine Schulpflicht*
course of studies	degree programme, programme of studies	*Studiengang*
(academic) degree	a qualification given to sb. when they successfully complete a course of studies (bachelor's degree, master's degree, etc.)	*akademischer Grad*
(high school) diploma	a document showing that you have completed (high) school	*Abschlusszeugnis, Diplom*
to drop out (of)	to leave school or university without having graduated/ without a degree	*abbrechen, aufhören (mit), aussteigen (aus)*
extra-curricular activities [kəˈrɪkjʊlər]	activities that are not part of one's usual studies	*Aktivitäten außerhalb des Stundenplans*
to graduate; graduation	to complete school/college/university with a diploma/ degree	*Schul-/akademische Ausbildung absolvieren; Schulabschluss/akademischer Abschluss*
higher education	education and training at a university or college	*Hochschulausbildung, akademische Ausbildung*
to pass an exam	to achieve the required standard (opposite: to fail an exam)	*eine Prüfung/Klausur bestehen*
(work) placement	a job, usually as part of a course of studies, which gives you the opportunity to gain experience in a particular field of work	*Praktikum, Praktikantenstelle*
SAT (Scholastic Assessment Test) (*US*)	a test taken in the U. S. by high school students who want to go to college or university	*Zulassungstest, Eignungstest*
secondary education	the teaching of children between the ages of 10/11 and 16 or 18	*höhere Schulbildung*
scholarship	an amount of money that is given to sb. by an organization to help pay for their education	*Stipendium*
tuition fees [tjuːˈɪʃən]	money you have to pay (at a university or college) to be taught	*Studiengebühren*
vocational education	the teaching needed to do a particular job	*Berufsausbildung*
working		
to adapt to; adaptable (*adj.*)	to gradually change your behaviour in order to be successful in a new situation; able to change in order to be successful in new situations	*sich an etw. anpassen; anpassungsfähig*
to apply (for a job)	to make a formal request for sth.	*sich (für eine Stelle) bewerben*
(letter of) application	a formal written request for a job	*Bewerbung(sschreiben)*
apprenticeship	the period of time in which a young person works for an employer to learn the specific skills needed for the job	*Ausbildung, Lehre*
assessment center	method used for selecting candidates for a job in a company; a series of tests used to decide which applicant is most suitable for a particular job	*Assessment Center (Personalauswahlverfahren)*
blind (unsolicited) application	enquiry about the possibility of a job even though it has not been advertised	*Initiativbewerbung; Bewerbung auf eine nicht ausgeschriebene Stelle*
career	a profession you have been trained for and which you do for a long period of your life	*Karriere, Laufbahn*
CEO (chief executive officer) [ˌsiː iːˈəʊ]	the person with the highest rank in a company	*Geschäftsführer*

competitive	ambitious, trying hard to be better than others	*konkurrenzbetont, ehrgeizig, wettbewerbsorientiert*
CV (Curriculum Vitae) (*BE*)	a short written document listing someone's education and work experience; résumé (US)	*Lebenslauf*
employee [ɪmˈplɔɪiː]	a person who is paid to work for sb., a company or an organization	*Arbeitnehmer*
employer [ɪmˈplɔɪər]	a person, company or organization that pays people to work for them	*Arbeitgeber*
to gain work experience	to acquire experience by working in a particular job	*Arbeitserfahrung sammeln*
human resources (department)	in a company, the department that deals with employing, training and helping people	*Personalabteilung*
job advert(isement) [ədˈvɜːtɪsmənt]	an offer/advertisement published by a company to find new employees; job posting	*Stellenausschreibung*
job interview	an interview conducted by a company to find out about applicants' qualifications and motivation	*Bewerbungs-/Vorstellungsgespräch*
job satisfaction [ˈdʒɒb sætɪsˌfækʃn]	the enjoyment sb. gets from their job	*Zufriedenheit mit der Arbeit*
job security	how permanent one's job is likely to be	*sicherer Arbeitsplatz, Arbeitsplatzsicherheit*
qualification	a skill or type of experience that you need for a particular job	*Qualifikation, Fähigkeit*
requirement	a quality or an ability you must have to be able to do sth. else	*Voraussetzung, Anforderung*
résumé (*US*) [ˈrezəmeɪ]	a short written document listing someone's education and work experience; CV (*BE*)	*Lebenslauf*
to retire; retirement	to stop working; when you stop working, usually because you have reached a certain age	*in Rente gehen; Rente*
salary	money that sb. receives as payment from the organization, company, etc. they work for, usually paid every month; pay	*Gehalt*
soft skills	social skills such as interaction and communication with others	*soziale Kompetenzen*
team work	when several employees work together in a group	*Arbeit im Team, Teamwork*
trainee	someone who is being trained for a job	*Auszubildender, Lehrling*
training	the process of teaching or being taught for a particular job	*Ausbildung, Lehre*
unemployed; unemployment	to have no job; when sb. does not have a job	*arbeitslos; Arbeitslosigkeit*
wage; wages (*pl.*)	money that sb. earns that is paid according to the numbers, days or weeks that they work; salary, pay	*Lohn; Löhne*
working environment	the situation in which you work; working conditions	*Arbeitsumfeld, Arbeitsbedingungen*
	going abroad	
to apply for a visa	to make a formal request for permission to enter a foreign country	*ein Visum beantragen*
exchange student	a student who pays a visit to another school or university to study there	*Austauschschüler/-student*
gap year	a year that a young person spends working or travelling, usually between leaving school and starting university or an apprenticeship	*Auszeit; auch: freiwilliges (soziales/ökologisches/…) Jahr*
to study/work abroad	to go to university/to take up a job in a foreign country	*im Ausland studieren/arbeiten*

Competences, Skills & Methods

Note: An overview of **all** Focus on pages in thematic and alphabetical order can be found in the front cover of the Students' Book.

Listening Comprehension

Language learning is dependent on good listening. Therefore, it is important to **learn to adjust one's listening to various situations** in order to be able to interact well in spoken communication. These situations can be listening to a song, an interview, (watching and) listening to a film, or listening to somebody in a conversation. Usually, you already have a lot of background knowledge, e.g. about the topic, the person, and of course, you already know a lot of the vocabulary used in the spoken text you are supposed to listen to. Before you start **taking notes**, make use of the following strategies that can help you to understand texts more easily.

"His Master's Voice"

Strategies that can help to understand

a) Listening for the main idea

- Try to understand the gist of the text by paying attention to key nouns, people's names, official place names, etc.
- Try to find answers to the W-questions (who? what? where? when? why?).

b) Predicting

This technique helps you to mentally prepare yourself for the text.

- Try to imagine what the text will be about by judging from the title/headline.
- Try to make predictions about the further text after the first sentence or the first part of the text.

c) Drawing inferences – intelligent guessing

- Make use of German words that are very similar to English words (e.g. mouse – *Maus*, mile – *Meile*, house – *Haus*, etc.). However, watch out for false friends (e.g. become ≠ *bekommen*, chef ≠ *Chef*, etc.).
- Make use of other foreign languages that you know and link them to anglicized words (e.g. French *la qualité* – quality, *la circonstance* – circumstance, etc.).
- Listen for internationally-used English words (e.g. *crew*, *team*, *display*, *design*, etc.) and relate them to the possible contents of the text.
- Connect (parts of) words that you already know to words in the text that sound similar (e.g. to teach – *teacher*, to grow – *growth*, etc.).
- Double-check your guessed meaning of the word by relating it to the context.

d) The given-new strategy

- Pay attention to certain keywords employed in the text that emphasize an additional aspect given in a sentence (e.g. *The weather was warm,* ***but*** *rainy.*). Further keywords or phrases are: ***before***, ***after***, ***although***, ***such as***, ***another***, ***as you know***, ***to sum up***, ***conclusion***, etc.

Strategies that can help to process and memorize the information

Note-taking – mind mapping – summarizing

- Use your notes taken while or after listening to order and (re-)arrange your understanding of the text.
- Relate your findings to other contexts.
- Draw a mind map of your notes and try to find further useful details from the text.
- Write a summary using your notes and try to explain the text you listened to in your own words.

→ Focus on Skills, Writing a Summary, p. 401

Basic Types of Fictional Texts

1. narrative texts	**a) Novels** ● are an extended and complex work of fiction written in prose. ● contain a variety of characters, action and a greater complication of plot. ● present a sustained exploration of the milieu, the characters, their motives. ● can vary greatly in form, style and content; one less complex form is the novella (e. g. John Steinbeck, *Of Mice and Men* or *Cannery Row*). ● have certain subclasses, e. g. the social novel (e. g. Harriet Beecher-Stowe, *Uncle Tom's Cabin*), the coming-of-age story (e. g. Mark Twain, *Tom Sawyer and Huckleberry Finn*; Paul Auster, *Moon Palace*). **b) Short stories** ● are written in prose and are shorter and less complex than a novel. ● are mostly confined to one setting, a limited number of characters and events. ● often employ an open plot with an abrupt opening and ending. ● do not put focus on the development of a character but on a significant incident or decisive moment that reveals strengths and weaknesses of characters, mostly presented as a snapshot of life. ● are told from the point of view of a narrator who is created by the author. ● place maximum significance on the few things mentioned, which are aimed at producing a certain effect in the reader's mind. ● emerged in the USA in the 19th century in response to the development of the newspapers, which required shorter forms of text; Edgar Allan Poe (1809 – 1849) is often regarded as the originator of the short story; other famous writers of short stories include Ernest Hemingway, Annie Proulx, and T. C. Boyle. **c) Fables** ● are a short text in which animals represent human types (→ the beast fable). ● are a form of allegory exemplifying an abstract moral thesis or principle of human behaviour. ● are didactic and are intended to teach the reader a moral lesson. ● Two famous writers of fables are James Thurber and George Orwell.
2. dramatic texts	**a) Dramas/plays** ● are any work designed for performance in a theatre. ● require actors/actresses who take on the roles of different characters, performing the actions and speaking the dialogue or monologue. ● usually contain stage directions included by the playwright, telling the actors how and where to move on stage as well as giving information about how to arrange the stage, what props, sound effects or lighting to use. → Focus on Facts, Drama and Theatre, p. 336 **b) Screenplays/scripts** ● are a written work, especially for a film or a television programme. ● consist of numbered scenes which show action and dialogue descriptions. ● have numbered slug lines telling the reader that the story has changed in location and time (e. g. INT. WAREHOUSE – NIGHT; EXT. STREET – DAY) → Focus on Facts, Screenplays and Storyboards, p. 369
3. poetry/ lyrics	**a) Poetry** ● is a type of literature that is not prose, in which ideas, experiences and feelings are expressed in compact, imaginative and often musical language. ● may be arranged in lines and may contain patterns of rhyme/rhythm. ● often contains figures of speech and imagery to appeal to the readers' and listeners' emotions and imagination. **b) Lyrics** ● are a set of words that accompany music, either spoken or sung. → Focus on Skills, Analysis of Poetry and Lyrics, p. 378

Note: Explanations of the respective technical terms can be found in the Literary Terms section, pp. 405 ff.

Basic Types of Non-Fictional Texts

The 4 basic types of non-fictional texts

1. **Descriptive texts:** the author wants to inform in a relatively balanced and neutral way (e. g. description of a landscape, a place, a person, an object …)

2. **Narrative texts:** the author wants to inform the reader about a development or a sequence of events; the report (objectively or subjectively) gives answers to the questions *who? what? where? when? why?* and *how?* and often presents further details. Reports* are often made livelier by fictional elements, e. g. a detailed description of people or the way people are affected by an event, etc. (e. g. travel report, report on the development of a situation …)

3. **Expository texts:** complicated and difficult facts are presented and explained in a matter-of-fact way; the structure/pattern of such texts is called **topical order** (= a sequence of points follows a statement of the topic at the beginning of the text) (e. g. explanatory notes, scientific reports, factual texts, descriptions of historical events …)

4. **Argumentative texts:** the author tries to influence the reader directly; this text type tends to be more critical and appellative, using persuasive arguments (e. g. commentary, criticism, review*, essay*, sermon*, pamphlet, political speech* …); these texts usually deal with controversial topics; reasons are given for and/or against the matter and are arranged in a well-planned order

Forms of argumentative texts

structure	type 1	type 2	type 3
introduction	Presenting a topic and giving opinions on the problem	Presenting a topic and giving opinions on the problem	Presenting a topic and giving opinions on the problem
↓	**arguments** ↓	**arguments** ↓	**arguments** ↓
main part	supporting facts	counter-arguments and refutation to stress the author's position	argument → counter-argument argument → counter-argument argument → counter-argument, etc. [mainly used in disputes and debates]
↓	↓	↓	↓
conclusion	conclusion	conclusion	conclusion

A non-fictional text* that puts forth a personal view has a **unity of thought**, and usually follows a clear **structure** (line of thought*, train of thought*, line of argument*).
Here are some of the most common **compositional patterns for structuring texts**:

listing structure:	**method:** Enumerating, numbering of facts, ideas, arguments **effect:** Clarity and coherence through parallel arrangement
progressive structure:	**method:** Using a clearly-defined starting point; developing on a cause-to-effect or problem-solution arrangement **effect:** Clarity through unity and logical coherence
antithetical structure:	**method:** Contrasting and juxtaposing of facts, ideas and arguments **effect:** Clarity and emphasis through comparison and contrast

Field size/camera distance

long shot (*Totale*): people/objects shown from a distance; usually to introduce a new setting (see establishing shot)

full shot: shot of the whole body/object and not much else; to emphasize action and the constellation of characters

medium shot: upper body/part of an object; usually to show one or two characters in action

close-up (*Nahaufnahme*): head, face and shoulders of a person are shown; focus is on the expression of the face *(Mimik)* e. g. to show emotions

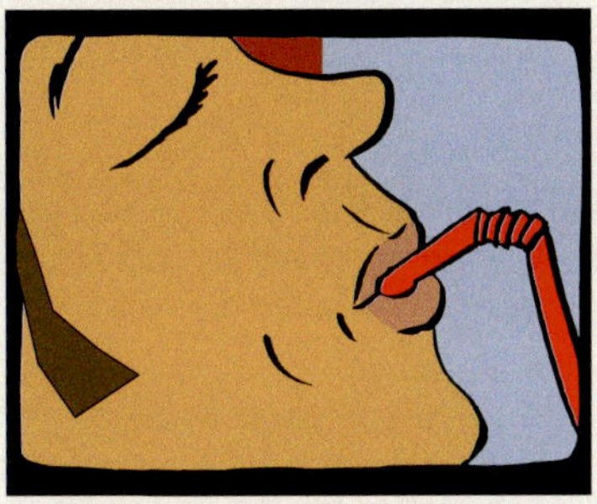

extreme close-up (*Detailaufnahme*): detailed shot of parts of the face/the object; often used to create suspense

point-of-view shot: a shot seen through a character's eyes; e. g. an establishing shot at the start of a scene

Camera angle

high-angle shot (bird's eye view, shot from above): used to make people seem smaller, weak, helpless, humiliated, less important

low-angle shot (worm's eye view, shot from below): used to make people seem bigger, stronger, superior, self-confident, powerful, threatening

eye-level shot (straight-on angle): relatively neutral and restrained

Analysis of a Fictional Text

The 3 basic types of fictional texts

a) Narrative texts (e.g. novel, short story, fable)
b) Dramatic texts (e.g. drama/play, screenplay/script)
c) Poetry/lyrics (e.g. poem, song, etc.)

Step 1: Analysis of the general meaning

- Identify and specify the type of text as well as the theme/topic/subject of the given text.
- Answer the W-questions: who, what, where, when, why?
- Write a summary of the given text of about 150 – 200 words at the most.
- Identify the narrator and specify what point of view is being used to tell the story.
- Develop a first (general) evaluation of the meaning and message of the text.

Step 2: Analysis of basic elements

a) Identify the structural and narrative/stylistic devices and show **what effect and function** they have. The following grid contains some terminology and tips for your analysis. The most relevant vocabulary can be found in the Literary Terms section.

narrator, narrative situation, point of view, mode of presentation	first-person narrator, witness/observer narrator, third-person narrator, objective/reliable narrator, subjective/unreliable narrator, limited point of view, unlimited/omniscient point of view, panoramic presentation, scenic presentation, relation of acting time and narrating time
structure	• (How) is the text structured? • What time span does the narration cover? • What is the relation between acting time and narrating time ? • Which conflict is the story based on? • How does the action develop – or stagnate? • Are there any leitmotifs?
characters	flat/round characters, protagonist vs. antagonist, minor character(s), hero(ine), anti-hero, outward appearance, behaviour, relationship to other characters, direct or indirect characterization
setting (= time and place)	scenery, mental climate, basic mood, social environment, atmosphere • Does the scenery/setting itself imply any symbolism? (e.g. thunderstorm = danger, large city = liveliness, anonymity, etc.) • What is the effect on the audience? • What intention might the author/playwright have had?
language/style	level of speech, manner of speaking, style, syntax, choice of words, inner monologue, chain of associations, stream of consciousness, register

b) Never forget to quote from the text to demonstrate the correctness and accuracy of your work.

Step 3: Comment on and evaluation of the text

- Classify and evaluate the text and its message.
- Relate the given text to other texts of the same epoch/time and compare it with other texts by the same author that you have dealt with. Pay attention to striking similarities and differences.
- Critically comment on the text and finish with a concluding sentence.

Note: Explanations of the respective technical terms can be found in the Literary Terms section, pp. 405 ff.

Analysis of a Film Scene

General tips on viewing and analysing a film

- Watch the film scene at least two times.
- Work systematically and concentrate on the devices employed in the scene in a certain order.
- Take notes while or immediately after each viewing of the film scene.
- Whenever you identify and specify a certain narrative technique and/or cinematic device used in a film scene, explain and illustrate its function and effect on the viewer.
- In order to explain the use and function of cinematic devices precisely and correctly, make use of technical terms.
  → Literary Terms section, pp. 405 ff., and Focus on Facts, Camera Operations, pp. 372 f.
- When viewing and analysing a film scene, it is not possible to explain and demonstrate every single detail; therefore, you should focus on the most striking and relevant devices employed in the scene.

Step 1: Focus on narrative techniques

guiding elements	function
• **setting**: What is the time and place of the action? What is the atmosphere like?	→ orientation for the viewer → general exposition
• **plot:** What happens and why?	→ drawing the viewers into the action, evoking and raising interest
• **suspense**: Which questions are raised and remain unanswered?	→ evoking the viewers' curiosity and keeping them interested
• **appearance of characters**: What do(es) the character(s) look like?	→ evoking interest, sympathy, antipathy, etc.
• **body language**: What is/are the character(s)' movements, gestures, postures, facial expressions?	→ revealing character traits, quirks, etc.
• **language/communication**: What choice of words and tone do(es) the character(s) use? How do they interact?	→ exposition of the intellectual background, demonstration of the characters' relationship(s)

Step 2: Focus on cinematic devices

cinematic device	function
• **camera operations**: Which field sizes, camera angles, camera positions, camera movements, etc. are employed?	→ transferring narration into film/images/pictures
• **visual symbols**: Which visual symbols (e. g. cross, blood, tombstone, eagle) are employed?	→ visual leitmotifs serve as links and help to express/ to intensify a deeper contextual meaning
• **film music/sound**: What kind of music/what (background) sounds are employed?	→ to show/emphasize a mood, to create suspense, to foreshadow, etc.
• **(special) effects**: What further effects (e. g. slow motion, voice-over narration) are employed?	→ to intensify the action, to reveal thoughts, to suggest speed, etc.

Step 3: Explanation of the function of the scene (in the context of the film)

- Place the scene in the context of the film.
- Explain and give examples of how the scene
  a) moves the action forward and creates suspense,
  b) presents an unexpected turning-point in the action,
  c) reveals a new character trait of the protagonist,
  d) introduces (a) new character(s),
  e) defines (a) relationship(s) between characters.

Analysis of a Screenplay

"Whatta you mean 'minor script changes?' It's supposed to be a western."

A screenplay or film script is a written work for a film or TV programme. Basically, a film script depicts the **movement, actions, expressions and dialogues of characters** and gives **technical directions and instructions**, e.g. concerning the camera operations. The "action" is always written in the present tense. Here are further characteristic features of film scripts that you should consider in your analysis.

Format and style

- A screenplay **focuses on what is audible and visible** on screen.
- Screenplays have a **specific layout and codified**[1] **notations**[2] of technical or dramatic elements, e.g. scene transitions[3], changes in the narrative perspective, sound effects, emphasis on dramatically relevant objects, emphasis on characters speaking from outside a scene. These notations are always **written in capital letters**.
- **Different scene elements** are visualized by **tab settings**[4], e.g. dialogue, scene headings, transitions or parentheticals[5].
- The **beginning** of a scene is usually marked with "FADE IN:", the **ending** with "FADE TO BLACK."

Slug lines[6]

One of the **most relevant and unique features** of screenplays are slug lines; they are always written in **capital letters** and are usually divided into three parts.
Part 1 … determines the **general setting** of a scene, e.g. inside (interior = INT.) or outside (exterior = EXT.).
Part 2 … determines the **location** of the scene, e.g. SUSAN'S APARTMENT – KITCHEN, JIMMY'S CAR, etc.
Part 3 … determines the **time** of the scene, e.g. DAY, NIGHT, DAWN, LATE NIGHT, etc.
If a character starts inside and then walks outside during a scene, a new slug line is needed which begins with CONTINUOUS[7].

Examples:
- INT. ALICE'S HOME – BATHROOM – NIGHT
- EXT. PARK – DAY/MORNING

Further characteristics:
- each slug line begins a new scene
- slug lines are numbered consecutively[8]
- any change of time or location requires a new slug line
- slug lines are on their own lines, flush with the left margin[9] and are completely typed in capital letters.

Common abbreviations used in scripts

ELS	extreme long shot	**2-S or 3-S**	two-shot or three shot	**VO**	voice-over
MLS	medium long shot	**INT**	interior	**OSV**	offscreen voice
LS	long shot	**EXT**	exterior	**DIS**	dissolve[10]
MS	medium shot	**BG**	background	**MIC**	microphone
MCU	medium close-up	**POV**	point of view shot	**VTR**	videotape
CU	close-up	**ZI or ZO**	zoom in or zoom out	**ANNCR**	announcer
ECU	extreme close-up	**SOT or SOF**	sound on tape or sound on film	**SUPER**	superimposition[11]
OS	over-the-shoulder-shot	**SFX or F/X**	special effects (sound or visual)	**Q**	cue[12]

→ Focus on Facts, Screenplays and Storyboards, p. 369

[1] **to codify** *festschreiben* – [2] **notation** *Bezeichnung* – [3] **transition** *Übergang* – [4] **tab setting** *Tabellator* – [5] **parenthetical** *Einschub* – [6] **slug line** a line of abbreviated text; master scene heading – [7] **continuous** *andauernd* – [8] **consecutive** *fortlaufend* – [9] **flush with left margin** *linksbündig* – [10] **to dissolve** *sich auflösen, verschwinden* – [11] **superimposition** *Einblendung, Überlagerung* – [12] **cue** *Stichwort, Regiesignal*

Analysis of a Non-Fictional Text

Step 1: Analysis of structure and content

- Identify and specify the theme/topic/subject* of the given text.
- Identify the characteristics of the heading* (e.g. provocative, ironic, funny, etc.).
- Divide the text into parts and relate these parts to the heading and the whole text.
- Write a summary of 150 words at most.
- Determine the message of the text. Predict the basic characteristics of the text (type).
- Clarify the line of argument, the train of thought* (general structure of the text).

Step 2: Analysis of stylistic devices/use of language

a) **Identify the stylistic devices** and show what effect and function they have.
The following grid contains some vocabulary for your analysis. The most relevant vocabulary is marked with * and can be found in the Literary Terms section (pp. 405 ff.).

register (= *Sprachebene*)	slang, colloquial, everyday English, written language, (in)formal, poetic, sophisticated, familiar, technical terms, scientific, religious, metaphorical
choice of words	denotations*, connotations*, keywords, figurative*/literal meaning of words, emphatic/negative function of words, euphemisms*, synonyms*, abstractions
style	plain, sober, natural, matter-of-fact, clear, precise, concise, vigorous, fluent, passionate, elegant, artificial, stilted, wordy, colourless, cliché-ridden, snappy, lengthy, clumsy, spontaneous, trite, expressing doubt/certainty
tone	humorous, playful, colloquial, conciliatory, depressive, serious, solemn, ironic, satirical, sarcastic, warm-hearted, aggressive, whining, reproachful
rhetorical devices	alliteration*, anaphora*, allusion*, reference*, antithesis*, ellipsis, hyperbole*, irony*, metaphor*, paradox*, personification*, simile*, symbol*, understatement, exaggeration*, parallelism*, employment of leitmotifs*, repetitions*, juxtapositions, (rhetorical) questions*, quotations, enumerations, appeals, comparisons, digressions from the main topic, grammatical tenses, illustrations, superlatives, personal pronouns/grammatical persons (we – they, I – you, our – their, us – them)

b) **Do not forget to include quotes** to demonstrate the correctness and accuracy of your work. This is how to do it:

- When **referring** to an important part of the text without quoting the words, give the page(s) and/or line(s): e.g. *Obama tells the audience about his jogging with foreign students (ll. 10 – 15).*
- You can **integrate the quotation** into your sentence: e.g. *Obama is determined to establish "an environment of lifelong learning" (l. 74), which means that …*
- You can **use a full quotation**: e.g. *Obama starts with the most important point: "First, to help every child begin school healthy and ready to learn." (l. 10).*
- Note the abbreviations:
  - one page or line: p. 17 / l. 12
  - more pages or lines: pp. 10 – 14 / ll. 25 – 30
  - the following page(s), line(s): f. / ff. (e.g. pp. 12 f. or pp. 10 ff.)
- **Omissions** of any kind are indicated by square brackets and three dots: […]. Remarks or **changes from the original text** are indicated by square brackets: *He* [Obama] *says* …

Step 3: Evaluation of the text

- State whether (or not) the text is well-structured/convincing/effective/appropriate …
- Discuss whether/to what extent the text/author is able to address the reader(ship).
- Critically comment on the text, and refer to similar texts that you have dealt with.
- Finish with a concluding sentence.

Analysis of Poetry and Lyrics

Poetry (from the Greek "poiesis" = making, creating) is a type of literature in which **ideas, experiences and feelings are expressed** in compact, imaginative, and often musical language. Poets arrange words in ways designed to touch readers' senses, emotions and minds. Lyrics are a set of words that accompany music, either by speaking or singing. The word *lyric* derives from the Greek word "lyrikos" (= a song sung by the lyre). Most poems and lyrics are written in lines that may contain patterns of rhyme and rhythm to help convey their meaning. They often use **figures of speech and imagery to appeal to the readers' and listeners' emotions and imagination**. The poet or songwriter usually invents a speaker from whose point of view the feelings, ideas, experiences, etc. are expressed. Poems and songs may be divided into stanzas (groups of lines) or sections and can greatly vary in structure, theme and atmosphere.

general meaning/ content	• What situation/topic is presented? • What is the theme; are there any (striking) leitmotifs? • What is the author's/singer's intention; what is the message of the poem/song? • What kind of register of English has been chosen (poetic, colloquial, archaic, slang, etc.)? • What is the melody like (harmonious, rhythmical, tuneful, staccato, etc.)?
formal analysis: **a) structural devices**	• Examine – the structure of the poem/song (stanzas, lines, (lack of) punctuation, refrain(s), break(s), enjambements, chorus, etc.), – the use of repetitions and/or enumerations/parallelisms, – the use of contrast(s)/antithesis, – the use of an illustration (= an example to make an idea clear), – the rhyme scheme (e. g. pair rhyme aa bb cc; cross rhyme abab; enclosed rhyme abba), – the use of free verse.
b) sense devices	– (How) are objects and ideas/thoughts brought together? – What type(s) of sentence(s) is/are used (hypotactical/paratactical sentences, questions, commands, etc.)? – Are there allusions/references to a certain topic (e. g. nature, city, love, etc.)? – Check on the use of simile (a direct comparison: "like, as"), metaphor (an implied comparison without a connective word: "an ocean of tears"), personifications (something non-human is given human characteristics: "the frosty cliffs were asleep"), or symbols (an object that also stands for some abstract idea: a red rose → symbol of love, beauty). – the use of grammatical tenses – the speaker's point of view – the use of hyperbole/exaggeration
c) sound devices	• Examine – the use of alliteration/anaphora, – the use of rhymes and/or assonances (= imperfect rhymes), – the use of a particular rhythm, beat, – the use of onomatopoeia (= words that imitate a sound: buzz, cuckoo, etc.), – the instrumentation, beat, vocal/instrumental type of music, vocals, etc. **→ Show how these devices support, stress/emphasize the meaning/content of the poem/song (→ function/effect).** **→ Show how style and content are connected.** **→ Show how sound and lyrics match and support each other.**
d) final comment and evaluation	Try to classify the given poem/song (refer to other poems/songs by the same author or authors of the same background). Evaluate the poem/song (Is the poem/song convincing? Has the author/singer succeeded in conveying his/her message? etc.). What do you consider to be the final message of the poem/song? What do you consider to be the effect on the reader/listener?

Note: Explanations of the respective technical terms can be found in the Literary Terms section, pp. 405 ff.

Analysis of a Political Speech

General aspects of political rhetoric

The purpose of most political speeches is persuasion rather than information. There is always a (hidden, underlying) message involved, often related to certain attitudes and values of the speaker. A political statement intends to affect the listeners by making use of diverse structural and rhetorical devices. In order to understand and evaluate a political speech, one should consider the following aspects:

first (general) impression:	• topic, subject matter, general tone, issues and purpose of the speech
contents and structure:	• salient and striking topics, important aspects • organization of the text, arrangement of parts (e. g. introduction, main part or body, conclusion) • train of thought, composition, line of argument
circumstances of the speech/ political context:	• time and place/medium (e. g. TV, radio, face-to-face, Internet) • position of the speaker (president, leader of a political party, leader of a protest movement, etc.) • audience (mass audience, a limited group of people) • occasion (election campaign, protest demonstration, political debate, informal gathering) • genre and type (presidential address to the nation, sermon, speech at a demonstration, campus speech, testimony)
formal and stylistic devices: **a) language**	• keywords and phrases • word groups/clusters related to a certain topic • different registers for different addressees (e. g. sophisticated language to address wealthy and/or educated people, use of dialect, etc.) • choice of words (colloquialisms, slang expressions, poetic expressions)
b) grammar	• sentence structure/syntax (use of main/sub-clauses) • use of grammatical tenses (indirect references to history, future, etc.)
c) rhetoric	• use of rhetorical questions • use of contrast and oppositions (positive/negative, familiar/alien, near/distant, etc.) • use of key symbols, slogans, stereotypes • abstractions and generalizations • use of grammatical persons (I, us, we – you, they: patterns of identification and solidarity or vice versa) • metaphors, personifications • allusions and references to history (American Dream, important political/historical issues, good/bad times, tradition, future, etc.); quotations • repetitions (alliterations, anaphora); parallelisms • comparisons, numbers, factual information • irony, exaggerations, simplifications • imperatives, emotionally-loaded words • concentration on essential points vs. wordy elaboration • insertions
d) manner of speaking/voice	• volume, tempo, stress, intonation, abrupt changes, pauses, rhythm
evaluation:	→ Comment on the personal integrity of the speaker, the general political circumstances, the impact on the listeners. → Compare the speech/speaker to other political speeches/speakers. Was he/she convincing?

Note: Explanations of the respective technical terms can be found in the Literary Terms section, pp. 405 ff.

Analysis of Statistical Data

different types

	1992	2001	2020
USA	230 mn	260 mn	300 mn
China	800 mn	1,000 mn	1,300 mn
India	600 mn	800 mn	1,100 mn

A table gives raw data as the basis for analysis and consists of a grid with numbers arranged in lines and columns. Typically, it aims to present data in an ordered way, thus making the information easy to understand.

general aspects

- How reliable/trustworthy is the source?
- Are the numbers up-to-date?
- Consider why a chart/graph/table has been chosen as the means of visual representation.
- Are the figures absolute numbers or percentage figures – and what is the function of this presentation?
- What do the numbers/data suggest?
- Turn the percentage figures/data into words and compare them.
- Relate the data to the given context.

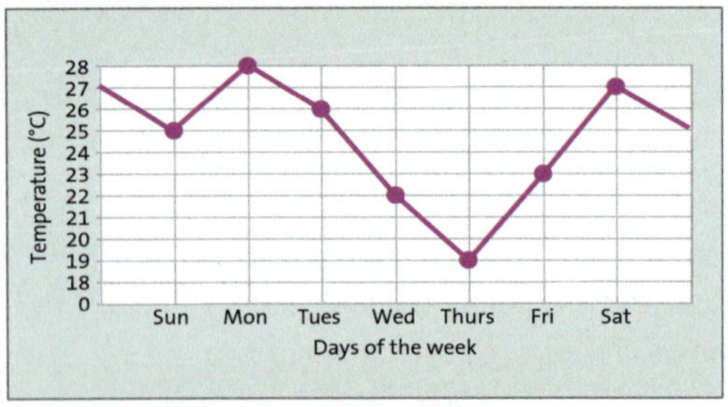

A (line) graph presents one or more lines in a system of coordinates/axes – a horizontal and a vertical axis. It shows the development of figures/variables over a period of time (trends, tendencies).

useful terms and phrases

■ to reach a peak/a low point/an all-time high/low of … ■ to remain constant/stable ■ to go through a period of growth ■ to increase/rise/grow/go up ■ to decrease/fall/drop/go down ■ a fall/decline/drop/decrease ■ an increase/a rise/growth ■ to grow … by 10 %/at a certain rate ■ a rise of 8 %/in temperature/to €25 ■ steep/strong/rapid … growth ■ a gradual/steady/continual … fall ■ a slight/barely noticeable … rise

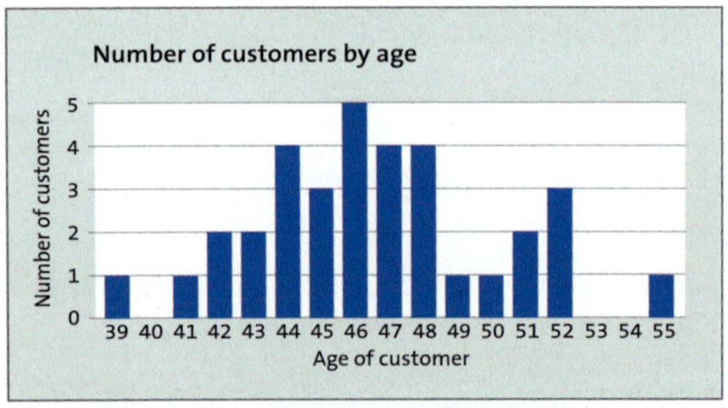

A bar chart shows differences between various things. It presents boxes/bars of different heights in a system of coordinates. The bars can be arranged horizontally or vertically.

useful terms and phrases

■ in comparison with/compared with ■ in contrast to ■ to achieve an average/below-average/above-average figure ■ to be at the top/bottom of the ranking ■ to rank first/second … last ■ the highest/lowest figure/score ■ no/little/a big difference between A and B (… with regards to … last year …) ■ the figures are identical/similar to … ■ the vast majority of/only a minority … ■ to experience a sudden rise/drop ■ after a brief recovery …

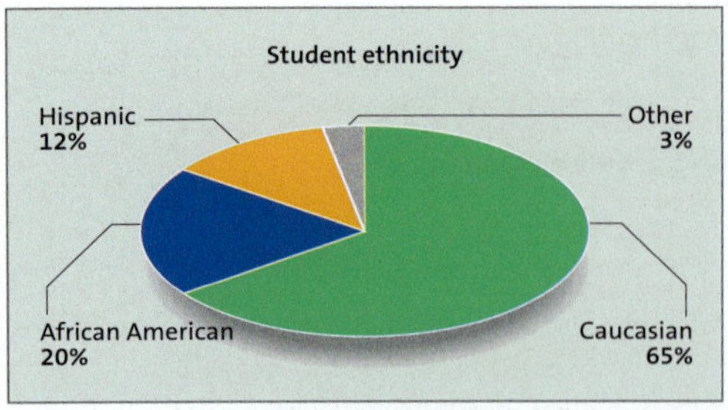

A pie chart shows percentages of a whole. It consists of a circle/pie divided into different sections/segments.

useful terms and phrases

■ the pie chart is divided into … ■ segments/sections ■ each segment represents … ■ the share of 5 % of the total amount is about 2 million euro … ■ the biggest/the smallest section ■ the whole circle represents/stands for … ■ the chart reveals the share of … ■ percentage-wise ■ a marginal percentage of … ■ an infinitely small amount of …

Analysis of Visuals

Visuals or images can be all kinds of graphical material, e. g. photos, film stills, adverts, paintings, etc.

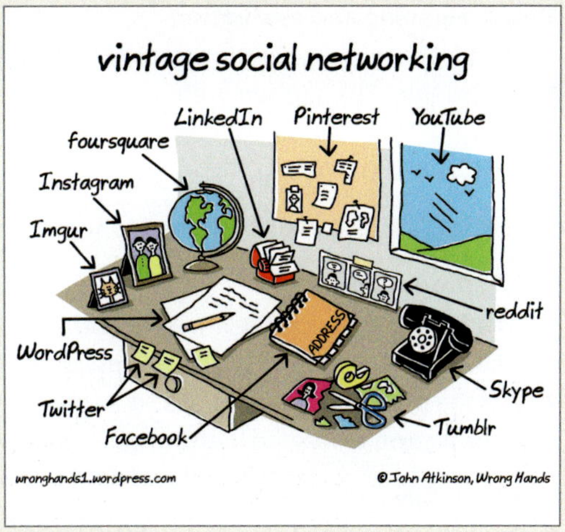

Analysis of cartoons

A **cartoon** is a **comic or satirical drawing** in a newspaper, a magazine or on the Internet that aims at humorously criticizing current, and especially political, events. It usually consists of a drawing (**pictorial part**) and speech balloons and a comment or a caption (= a short title), which is most frequently placed underneath (**textual part**). However, all the elements are not necessarily used in each cartoon.

Step 1: Author and source
- What is the title or caption of the cartoon?
- Which artist drew the cartoon (if known)?
- Where was the cartoon published (newspaper, magazine, Internet, etc.)?

Step 2: Descriptive level
- Describe the people, objects and the setting in the cartoon in detail. What action is taking place?
  Tip: Structure your description: What do you see e. g. in the foreground, centre, background, etc.?
- Which visual elements are employed, e. g. colours (black-white contrast), which visual metaphors?
- Which (political, historical, social) events or issues may have inspired the cartoon?

Step 3: Symbolic/figurative level
Cartoonists (often) employ pictures and words to express their personal opinions.
- What tools are used to convey a certain message?
- What do the symbols used stand for?
- Which person/group does the cartoon focus on?

irony	The recognition of the difference between reality and appearance. In **verbal irony**, there is a contrast between what is said and what is actually meant. **Situational irony** refers to a situation in which the opposite of what you expect to happen actually does happen.
parody	In literature, a text that imitates and slightly changes another well-known text in order to ridicule it, comment on it or trivialize it.
caricature	In literature, for example a character whose traits have been exaggerated to create a comic effect.
sarcasm	A bitter or aggressive remark used to express mockery or disapproval; often this is a statement which conveys the opposite of its literal meaning. In contrast to irony, which is gentle and more subtle, sarcasm is bitter and usually openly expressed.
pun	An expression involving a play on words, in which one word has two different meanings, so that a sentence can be understood in two different ways.
allusion/reference	An allusion or reference to for example a well-known (historical) person or event, politics, popular culture, the arts or a statement from a famous work of literature.
stereotype/ labeling	A word or phrase that describes a person in a way that is too general and often not true (*jdn. abstempeln*); cf. cliché
hyperbole	A figure of speech that contains an exaggeration.
symbol	An element of imagery in which a concrete object stands not only for itself but for some abstract idea or larger concept as well (e. g. rose → love).
visual/pictorial metaphor	The representation of a person, thing or idea by a visual image, e. g. Uncle Sam for the United States, an elephant for India, an orange for sunshine, etc.
black humour	Humorous effects resulting rather from grotesque, morbid or macabre situations. Black humour aims to shock and disorient readers, making them laugh in the face of anxiety, suffering or death.

Step 4: Meaning and evaluation

- What is the message of the cartoon?
- Do you think the cartoon is effective in conveying its message? Is the pictorial presentation convincing?

Analysis of photos

To help you analyse visuals or images, here are some steps for you to follow:

Step 1: Production

- When and where was the image taken?
- Who created the image (e. g. a professional photographer, a private person, an advertising agency, etc.)?
- Was the picture arranged or was it a snapshot?
- Is the picture presented in the original version or has it e.g. been photoshopped or blue-pencilled?

Step 2: Image

- **Describe the visual elements of the image and how they are arranged.**
  - What is being shown? (e. g. surroundings, people, facial expressions, gestures, posture, clothing, accessories, etc.)
  - What are the main visual components and how are they arranged?

    Tip: In order to get a better overview of the various elements, their arrangement and relationship to each other, make a rough draft before you start to describe them.
  - Where is the viewer's eye drawn to the picture – and why? (eye-catching/visually-dominant elements)
  - What use is made of colour?
- **Explain the function and effect of visual elements and symbols.**
  - What medium is the image taken from (e. g. film, advert, photo campaign, Internet, etc.)?
  - Is the image contradictory?
  - What visual symbols are employed – and what is their function and effect?
  - State whether they imply a deeper, symbolic meaning.
  - Point out whether they appeal to the viewer/the target audience/the addressee(s).

Step 3: Addressing the audience

- **Identify and explain the message of the photo/picture.**
  - Who does the image address?
  - Is there a particular target group (e. g. a snapshot of a demonstration, etc.)?
  - What relationship is created between the image and the viewer?
  - Is more than one interpretation possible?
  - How might different viewers interpret the image and its message?
  - What emotions does the image appeal to?
  - Is there a strategy behind the image? If so, which one?
  - Are there any political/cultural/social implications?
  - Are there any historical/political/religious references?
- **State whether the visual/image/picture is effective and convincing in its message.**

visual elements:
- dancing children → motion/vitality
- a street scene → everyday life
- b/w photo → focus on contrast

visual metaphor: black and white child playing together → overcoming racism

surroundings: street in New York City

snapshot: a glimpse of reality

use of contrast: black and white

function: emotional appeal to the viewer and (indirect) political message

Helen Levitt. New York, 1940s

Characterization of a Figure in Literature

Fictional characters can be presented in a number of ways. In general, a character in a fictional text is developed through action, description, language and ways of speaking.

Types of characters

relevance within the text and characteristics	
• **protagonist** (the main character around whom most of the work revolves)	• **major characters** (main characters who dominate the story)
• **antagonist** (the person who the protagonist is against; often the villain)	• **minor characters** (less important persons who support the main character(s) by letting them interact or reveal their personalities, etc.)
• **the modern hero** (the average man/woman)	• **dynamic character** (changing and developing, with different traits)
• **the anti-hero** (often dishonest, graceless or inept person who struggles in life; the loser)	• **static characters** (unchanging, often stereotypical)
• **the tragic hero** (e. g. *Macbeth*; person who ends tragically as a result of personal flaws)	• **round character** (three-dimensional, with different and changing facets to the personality)
• **romantic hero** (a character with a strong will and personality who goes against established norms; often this figure experiences melancholy, isolation and unfulfilled and unhappy love)	• **flat character** (one-dimensional, viewed only from one side, often stereotypical)
• **the Hemingway hero** (a character who has been at war, drinks too much, the loner, "cowboy")	

Types of characterization in literature

- In a **direct characterization of a character** the narrator or one of the other characters **tells** the readers/audience what the character's personality is like.
- In an **indirect characterization** the writer **shows/presents** the character talking and acting, which reveals the character's personality. Indirect characterization can be achieved through:
  a) **Speech** (What does the character say, how does he/she communicate and interact with others?)
  b) **Thoughts** (What is revealed through the person's private thoughts, e. g. in a monologue, soliloquy, a diary entry, etc.?)
  c) **Effect on others/on the character** (How does the person react/respond to others? Does he/she have any relationships? How do others react to the person?)
  d) **Actions** (What does the person do, how does he/she behave?)
  e) **Looks** (appearance, body language, gestures, facial expression, etc.)

How to write a literary characterization

Step 1: Collect the facts and clues given in the text and move from the outward features and characteristics to the inward nature of the character:

- **personal data** (name, age, sex, nationality)
- **attitudes/views** (thoughts, dreams, emotions)
- **relationships** (social background, family, friends)
- **outward appearance** (body, face, clothes, etc.)
- **behaviour** (toward other characters, actions)

Step 2: Draw your conclusions about the person's character and relate your findings to the text by referring to specific lines. Use the simple present for your characterization.

Step 3: Follow the "introduction – main part – conclusion" pattern in your characterization. Write an introductory sentence that answers the w-questions.

→ Focus on Language, Literary Terms, pp. 405 ff.

Mediation

Mediating a text means translating a written or recorded text from one language into another (e.g. German → English, English → German). In general, the person who is mediating must **consider the addressee(s), the meaning of the text/message, as well as cultural and situational aspects**.

When you are in a foreign country, you are constantly confronted with information/facts that you have to read or listen to: road signs, brochures, maps, (radio) announcements, advertisements, commercials, films, flight/train schedules, websites, letters, instructions, prescriptions, people talking to you, etc.

In a written examination you must consider the following aspects when asked to mediate a text:

How to mediate a text in a written examination

- **Select the most relevant information** from the text you are asked to mediate. Leave out less important details.
- **Focus** on the information **your communication partner** needs to know or what is important for the **topic**.
- Give an **analogous rendition** (*sinngemäße Wiedergabe*) of the text, not a literal translation.
- **Consider** the **addressee** (e.g. his/her cultural background).
- Take **situational aspects** into account (e.g. private, professional, etc.).
- Give **additional information** and explanations if necessary (e.g. on geography, culture, politics, etc.).
- **Consider** the **type of text you are required to write** (*Zieltextformat*) (e.g. a blog, a formal/informal letter, etc.).
- **Use compensation strategies** (i.e. paraphrasing, synonyms, etc.)

Criteria for evaluation

- Has the **purpose and intention** of the text been conveyed?
- Has the **addressee** been considered appropriately?
- Have the **assignments and standardized formulations** (*Operatoren*) been taken into consideration?
- Have the **characteristics of the type of text** (*Zieltextformat*) been considered?
- Is the **formulation self-directed** (*eigenständig*) and independent?
- Do the **style and choice of words** match the intention of the text?
- Does the **construction of sentences** vary (e.g. use of linking words and connectives)?
- Is the text **grammatically correct** (grammar, spelling, punctuation, word order)?

10 tips to help mediate a written or recorded text

1. Do not translate the text word for word.
2. Listen to/watch out for keywords and the most relevant/useful/appropriate information.
3. Leave out minor details and irrelevant information (→ summarizing).
4. Try to understand the gist of the text and put it into your own words (but do not change the facts!).
5. Sometimes there are words that cannot be translated into German/English because they imply cultural differences (e.g. homecoming, gap year, cheerleading or *Schützenfest*, *Abigag*, etc.). In such cases, give examples to illustrate the situation, or add information on the cultural background if necessary.
6. Do not interpret or evaluate the text, just mediate it.
7. Express difficult passages more simply; technical terms should be replaced by everyday language.
8. Make use of paraphrases (e.g. a cheerleader is a girl who …).
9. If you do not know a word, use a synonym (= word or expression that has the same or nearly the same meaning as another in the same language).
10. If you cannot think of the right word, try simply using the opposite.

→ Proverbs can reveal a great deal of cultural background. Try to find the equivalent proverb rather than trying to translate literally (e.g. *vom Regen in die Traufe* → out of the frying pan and into the fire).

→ Beware of false friends, i.e. English words that sound or look like German ones but **differ** in meaning (e.g. become, actual, sensible, etc.).

Writing a Comment and a Review

Comment

A written comment expresses your personal opinion on a certain topic or issue. It is a common means used in print media in order to present one's opinion to the readership in a more or less critical way.

Take some notes first, and structure your thoughts systematically before starting to write.

1. **Introduction**
   - Make some introductory remarks in which you raise a question, refer to a current problem, etc.
   - The introduction should clarify your topic/concern.
2. **Main part – arguments**
   - State, demonstrate and describe the positive and negative effects of a topic/situation.
   - Support your view of the situation by giving examples. You can, for example, refer to or quote famous people or experts on this matter, or relate your view to other comparable issues.
   - Emphasize the argument by referring to further/future consequences.
3. **Conclusion**
   - Conclude your comment by giving your personal view of the situation/problem.
   - Strategically, it is smart to relate your final remarks to your introduction in order to finally "wrap up" the topic and make your point.

→ Focus on Language, Conversation and Discussion, p. 385

Review of a fiction book or film

Step 1: Plot*/characters*/theme*
- Briefly summarize the plot of the book/film (approx. 150 words). ("Who/where/when/what/why"-questions should be answered.)
- Include the type of film (e. g. feature film*, western)/book (e. g. historical novel), title, author/director, publishing/release year, edition, special features.
- Briefly describe the main characters* and how they are related.
- Briefly outline the basic theme(s) and leitmotif(s)*.
- Describe the overall atmosphere.

Step 2: Narrative/cinematic aspects
- Point out striking narrative qualities (e. g. point of view*, metaphorical language, structure of the plot*).
- Refer to any striking cinematic devices that create/reinforce the atmosphere of the film.
- Mention which actors were chosen for the respective roles.
- Explain what the book's/film's message and the author's/director's intention may be.

Step 3: Evaluation
- Say what you like or dislike about: the plot, structure, directing, camera work, sound, special effects, casting and performance of the actors.
- Explain whether the book/film has successfully conveyed any/its core message.
- Comment on the actors: Have they successfully personified and typified the characters?
- Consider and quantify shortcomings/weaknesses and strengths of the book/film.
- If the film is a literary adaptation: How well has the story been adapted? – Is there anything missing (in comparison to the novel or in comparison to other books/films by the same author/director)?

Step 4: Conclusion
- Is the film worth viewing?/Is the book worth reading?
- Would you recommend the book/film? – What was your favourite part of the book/film?

Writing an Analysis

Writing a text analysis usually follows a standardized pattern, regardless of what kind of text or material you are required to analyse, e. g. a fictional or non-fictional text, a political speech, an excerpt from a play or a cartoon.

General aspects

Before writing:

- **Read the assignment carefully** and make sure that you have understood what exactly you are required to do. Pay particular attention to the **standardized terminology** (*Operatoren*) which tell you what to focus on. (→ Standardized Terminology for Tasks, pp. 12–15)
- Pay attention to **additional keywords** given in the assignment, e. g. which (stylistic) aspects of the text or which features of a character you are expected to analyse in particular.
- Read the text as often as necessary to **understand it thoroughly**. Underline and/or highlight the parts that are significant and important with regard to the assignment. Note down your observations and make notes in the margin of the text. Use your dictionary to crosscheck that you have understood expressions and formulations in the text correctly.
- Find the **main issue or message** that the text addresses and the **writer's position** in this regard.

While writing:

- Check for **features/references to lines to support your findings**, e. g. arguments, line of argument, choice of words, facts and numbers given, quotes from further experts, etc.
- Prepare a **draft outline** (*Entwurf, Konzeption*) of the text you want to write. Do not write every single sentence line-by-line but take notes on
  a) how you want to structure your composition, b) which textual references and quotes you want to use and c) what background knowledge you want to use and refer to.
- Pay attention to details: do not cover everything but focus on the most relevant/striking aspects.
- **Avoid wordy and generalized explanations** and repetitions but be **specific and precise**.
- Do not include your personal opinion or beliefs on the matter but be **factual and neutral**.

After writing:

- **Proofread** your analysis and crosscheck that you have not forgotten anything from your draft outline. Check for grammatical correctness, punctuation, spelling and that your composition is written in the **present tense**.

Your composition

Introduction

- Formulate a **connecting sentence at the beginning** in which you refer to a relevant aspect from your comprehension. Briefly state that the writer for example uses a specific line of argument to underline his ideas.
  Example: *As I have pointed out in the first part of my composition, the writer XY aims at persuading the reader of his critical view of the USA. In order to emphasize his position he uses several persuasive techniques which will be explained in the following.*
- Give a **concise** (*kurzgefasst*) **outline of the structure** of the text, referring to the writer's train of thought and/or line of argument and the general message of the text.
- **Do not repeat** the introductory part from your first assignment (w-questions).

Main part

- Use the **three-step method** for your analysis:

Step 1: Quote from the text	Step 2: Use the correct technical term	Step 3: Explain the function
(ll. 10 f.) "... some citizens, many people, the whole world ..."	→ climax, parallelism	→ emphasis on numbers and amounts involved

- Do not just follow the chronological order of the text but also **focus on relevant aspects, stylistic devices, characters**.
- Be careful to **quote correctly**. (→ Focus on Facts, Basic Types of Non-Fictional Texts, p. 368)

Conclusion

- End your text by **referring to your introduction** and formulating a **concluding sentence** in which you for example refer to the message or the type of the text (again).
- **Do not evaluate** the text. Stay factual and concise.

A newspaper commentary/an editorial

In contrast to a newspaper report, **a commentary or an editorial presents the newspaper's opinion on an issue**. Editorial writers build on an argument and try to influence the reader's opinion, **criticize** a certain issue or try to **clarify a complicated or controversial** matter. Sometimes they ask people to take action. In a nutshell, editorials are **opinionated news stories** which are **personalized** and which **evaluate** issues or events.

Structure

- **headline**
- **introduction, body, paragraphs, conclusion**
- **an objective explanation of the issue**
- **opinions from the opposing viewpoint**
- **opinions of the writer**
- **alternative solutions to the problem or issue being criticized**
- **a solid and concise conclusion**

"Sleaze, please."

How to write a newspaper commentary/an editorial

Step 1: Choose a significant topic that would interest readers.

Step 2: Do research and collect information, facts, statistical data, interview people, etc.

Step 3: In an introduction, state your opinion briefly, e. g. *Have you ever thought about … ? Taking into account that … Looking at the latest results of … one should … I think that …*

Step 4: Explain the topic/issue objectively and explain why this topic is important, e. g. *Looking at the facts/ numbers we do have to realize that … therefore it is our responsibility to …*

Step 5: Give the opposing viewpoint first with its quotations and facts, e. g. *On the contrary one might think that … the numbers suggest that … on the surface the situation appears to be …*

Step 6: Refute the opposing viewpoint and develop your case:
- present at least three arguments
- the strongest argument should come last
- back up your arguments by facts, e. g. statistics, quotations, expert information, etc.
- if you comment on a text, refer to the text with quotes to substantiate your arguments

Step 7: Repeat key phrases to reinforce an idea, e. g. *Let us get back to … Let us take a closer look at … This situation requires a clear judgment … We have no option but to …*

Step 8: Employ rhetorical devices to make your article more convincing (e. g. comparison, antithesis, metaphorical expressions, etc.).

Step 9: Give a (realistic) solution to the problem and encourage constructive criticism and pro-active reaction.

Step 10: Sum up the information and recapture important points and solutions. Refer back to your introductory remarks and statement. Your conclusion should have some punch, e. g. *If we do not take action against dangerous and poisonous food, who will?*

Writing a Formal Letter

Business letter/letter of complaint – layout

Tel: +49(0)221 123456
Fax: +49(0)221 1234567
tobymueller@web.de

Gartenweg 20
54327 Köln
Germany

> letterhead with post-code, telephone and fax numbers and e-mail

15 May 2016

> date

> reference initials

Your ref: TBS/1234

> inside address, including street, ZIP code, country

Digital World Inc.
8607 Main Street
Cornerstone, NJ 23657
USA

> attention line

Attention: Ms Goldwell, Customer Services

> salutation
> - *Dear Sir or Madam* → used if name is unknown
> - *Miss* → unmarried woman (old use)
> - *Mrs* → married woman
> - *Ms* → unclear if the woman is married or not
> - *Mr* → man
> - no comma at the end of the salutation

Dear Ms Goldwell

> subject line (optional)
> - after salutation in the UK
> - before salutation in the USA
> - in bold type
> - capitalized

My Order No. CF-23405 – Smartphone "Stay Connected", black, dated 4 March 2016

> body of the letter
> - begin with a capital letter
> - paragraphs are separated by a free line

The above-mentioned smartphone was delivered to me today and on opening the package I found that

- the touchscreen is badly scratched
- the GPS navigation does not work properly
- applications cannot be downloaded
- the headset is missing

Obviously the smartphone was poorly packed and roughly handled in transit and something must have gone wrong in production and while packaging the phone.

Needless to say, I cannot use the phone and thus would like to return it at your expense.

I am looking forward to hearing what you have to say about the matter and would welcome an immediate replacement of the damaged article.

> complimentary close
> - *Yours sincerely* → most common use
> - *Yours faithfully* → formal, only used if the name of the addressee is unknown
> - *(Best) Regards, Best wishes* → friendly
> - signature, name, position of the signatory

Yours sincerely

Tobias Müller
Tobias Müller

> enclosure (*Anlagen*)
> - Enc (singular), e.g. *order form*
> - Encs (plural), e.g. *cheque, folder*

Enc.: Copy of the packaging slip and invoice

Basic types of business letters

- **Enquiry:** a request for or question about information about sth. (*Anfrage*)
- **Offer:** a voluntary but conditional promise given by a buyer or seller to another for acceptance (*Angebot*)
- **Order:** a request to make or supply goods (*Bestellung*)
- **Reminder:** a request for an overdue payment that should have been paid by an earlier date (*Mahnung*)
- **Letter of complaint:** a request to deal with and solve a problem, e.g. delay in delivery, unsatisfactory or defective goods, wrong goods, etc. (*Beschwerdebrief, Reklamation*)

Writing a Handout

A handout is a useful tool that serves as a memory aid (= *Gedächtnisstütze*) for the listeners of a presentation and helps them to follow the presenter's line of argument or train of thought.
It should provide a short overview of the presentation, the most relevant facts, keywords and data, and may include some interesting or provocative statements for the audience to consider.

Structure

1. Heading
- name of school/college/university
- subject/course
- name of teacher/lecturer/professor
- name of student

2. Main part/body

a) title/topic of the presentation
b) introduction of the topic, e.g. main ideas, the central theme (= *roter Faden*)
c) depiction of the most relevant aspects in keywords; structuring elements such as bullet points, subheadings, etc.
d) conclusion and results of the project/coursework/presentation

3. List of references/indication of sources
- bibliographical references (e.g. books, essays, etc.)
- references of Internet websites, links, etc.

→ Focus on Skills, Research, p. 414

Example

Karl Kraus Gymnasium
Subject: English
Teacher: Mr/Ms …
Student: Katharina Müller 10 May 2016

The British Empire

Outline/overview:
1. Introduction/definition
2. Historical background
3. The Raj
4. The Impact on India
5. Gandhi
6. Conclusion

1. Introduction/definition
- British expansion …
- …

2. Historical background
- Queen Elizabeth I …
- …

3. …

List of references
Bibliographical references:
Darwin, John, Unfinished Empire: *The Global Expansion of Britain*, Penguin, London 2013, pp. xy

Internet:
www.bbc.co.uk/history/british/modern/endofempire_overview_01.shtml [03.04.2015]

Writing an Interview

In a written examination you might be required to **write an interview as a creative writing task** in addition to the comprehension and the analysis tasks. Your written interview text should be written in such a way that it can serve as a script or draft (*Vorlage*) for an interview you are asked to conduct. In general, an interview is a conversation between two (or more) people, (an) **interviewer(s)** and an **interviewee**, where (usually pre-formulated) questions are asked by the interviewer(s) to obtain information, facts or statements on a certain topic. In journalism, interviews are used to collect information, or present views and assessments to viewers or listeners. Interviews are also important in qualitative research, e. g. when interviewing an expert in some field.

Types of interviews

- **informal, conversational interview**
  No pre-formulated questions are asked; the interviewer stays as open and adaptable to the interviewee's nature, response and priorities as possible.
- **general interview**
  The focus is on collecting more general information from the interviewee; the interviewer pre-formulates questions but stays open to the interviewee's focus and priorities on a certain matter.
- **standardized, open-ended interview**
  The same, standardized and pre-formulated questions are asked to different interviewees. This method allows for rather fast interviews that can be easily analysed and compared.
- **closed, fixed response interview**
  All interviewees are asked the same pre-formulated questions and are asked to choose questions from the same set of alternatives.

The interviewer

Although the general aim of an interview is to elicit (*hervorlocken*) information from an interviewee by strategically and skilfully posing questions, the interviewer should follow certain rules. He/She should be **neutral**, **unemotional** and **unbiased**.

Technique and structure

- **introduction of the topic**; the reason for the interview/the occasion; introduction of the **interviewee(s)**, their background, position and reason for being interviewed on the matter, e. g. *Good evening … today our topic is … I would like to welcome our special guest … who is an expert in …*
- asking a **well-structured** sequence of (pre-formulated) questions
- **listening and reacting** to the interviewee(s) in order to achieve more focus and attention to detail
- asking **follow-up questions** throughout the interview to
  a) enable the interviewee to elaborate on certain topics and to gain more comprehensive information
  b) to clarify complicated or confusing aspects, e. g. *What do you mean by saying …? Could you elaborate on … and give us some more details on …?*
- asking **precise and respectful questions** in order not to offend the interviewee or make him/her become defensive or unwilling to share
- making the interviewee(s) feel comfortable and respected by **avoiding interrupting** him/them whenever possible
- **ending the interview** by
  a) summarizing the result of the discussion or the views taken by the participants
  b) thanking the participants, e. g. *I am sorry to say that our time is up. Thank you, … it has been most comprehensive … informative … It has been a pleasure to have you with us.*
- using **spoken English** (not formal, but avoiding colloquial English or slang)

Writing a Newspaper Article

In general, newspaper reports aim **at informing their readership** about events that have happened in their local area, or about national and international news. Newspaper reports usually **provide answers** to questions (who, what, where, when, why, how). They should be **easy to read, objective and present reliable, unbiased facts and information** and should be written in a snappy and concise style. However, the style of an article and the language register (formal, informal) depends on the type of newspaper the article is published in, e. g. a quality paper, a popular paper, etc. (→ Focus on Facts, The Press, p. 370).

Types of newspaper articles

- **local news** (focussing on the neighbourhood/the region)
- **national news** (focussing on one's country)
- **international news** (world news)
- **a feature article** ("soft news", e. g. about a celebrity; a person who does volunteer work in the community; a movie review, etc.; it is **not** considered a news story)
- **editorial** (an article that contains the writer's, publisher's or editor's opinion on an issue)
- **a column** (an article written by the same person on a regular basis, about for example subjects of interest to him/her, current events or community happenings; it is not considered a news story)

General structure/layout

- **headline** (catching the reader's attention)
- **sub-headlines** (structuring the article)
- **columns/paragraphs** (structuring the article; all paragraphs relate to the main idea/topic)
- **pictures, photos, graphics, visuals,** etc. (illustration, proof)
- **first paragraph** (introduces the main point of the story (who?); introduces the main idea (what?))
- **following paragraphs** (provide answers to the other questions (where, when, why, how); develop the main idea)
- **paragraphs** (short, punchy, not too long)
- **information** (clear, concise, factual)
- **language** (precise, clear sentence structure, explanation of technical terms)
- **grammatical tense** (usually past tense – when an event has already taken place)
- **references** to a) what people said (quotations/direct speech; reported speech),
  b) sources, further/former articles on the topic, etc.

How to write a newspaper report

Step 1: Select your target group (e. g. students, readers in a small town, a neighbourhood, etc.).

Step 2: Find a subject of interest (e. g. the expenses of schoolbooks or field trips; the quality of clothes, etc.).

Step 3: Do research on the matter (e. g. interviewing people, Internet research, etc.).

Step 4: List your potential sources. They shoud be reliable and credible (e. g. authority, expert, celebrity, hero, witness, ordinary people, etc.).

Step 5: Write your lead-in (the introductory paragraph).

Step 6: Write the rest of your article and
- structure it into paragraphs of 4–5 lines,
- develop a clear train of thought and line of argument,
- employ references to prove the reliability of your information.

Step 7: Find a suitable title for your report. It should be vivid and catchy and announce the topic in a short and concise way. Try to evoke your reader's interest by asking a question (*Why is ethical fashion so expensive?*) or using an exclamation mark (*No Boring Lessons Any Longer!*).

Note: The information given in a newspaper article should be true, objective and original.

Writing a Speech Script

In your written examination, you might be asked to write a speech in response to a text you analysed or on an issue related to the text at hand. A good speech always has a clear and distinct structure and follows clear-cut lines of argumentation and trains of thought.

Structure

Introduction

In order to **win your audience's attention** and **attract their interest** you can start by

- saying sth. thought-provoking,
- citing an interesting quotation or
- saying sth. controversial,
- telling a joke.

After having gained their attention, you should **introduce yourself** and **the subject** you are going to talk about. Additionally, you can make a positive remark/pay a compliment to the place where you are speaking, the audience, etc. – this will help you to bond with your audience.

Tips on vocab

Good evening, ladies and gentlemen. ■ Dear friends … ■ I feel deeply honoured to speak to such an illustrious audience. ■ Let me thank you for inviting me to this impressive meeting. ■ It is a great pleasure to be here and to talk to you. ■ As … said, it is never too late to take action. ■ Wouldn't it be wonderful if we managed to … ■ Let me assure you …

Main part/body of the speech

This is the longest part of your speech and should therefore have a clear structure, following a topical order, a line of argumentation or a train of thought.

- Start with a **thought-provoking** and **important thought** or argument.
- Decide on which pattern you want to choose for the **body of your speech**:
  a) **progressive structure** (developing on a cause-to-effect or problem-solution arrangement)
  → effect: clarity, unity and logical coherence
  b) **antithetical structure** (contrasting and juxtaposing of facts, ideas, arguments)
  → effect: clarity and emphasis through comparison and contrast
- **Support your arguments** with
  a) information (e.g. statistical data, facts),
  b) examples,
  c) quotations (e.g. of experts, political authorities, etc.),
  d) references to similar situations.
- **Work in some rhetorical devices**, e.g. alliterations, repetitions of relevant phrases/words/numbers, contrast, comparison, climax, rhetorical questions.
- **Use linkers and connectives** to vary the beginning of your sentences and to connect your thoughts and arguments.

Conclusion

This part of your speech is very important because it gives you the opportunity to end with a punch and/or an appeal that will stay in your audience's mind.

- Give a **concise summary of the most relevant points** of your speech.
- Finish with a **punchy remark, a call for action** or sth. personal to **reinforce your line of argument**.
- Relate your finishing remarks to the beginning of your speech in order to **round off your speech**.

Tips on vocab

Let me quote … again, … ■ (to put it) in a nutshell … ■ to put it bluntly … ■ Let us be honest, shouldn't we … ■ Now that you have realized the importance of … ■ I put my trust in you to … ■ I have absolutely no doubt that you will make the right decision. ■ Let us roll up our sleeves and get to work.

→ Focus on Skills, Giving a Speech, p. 390
→ Focus on Skills, Presentations, p. 391
→ Focus on Skills, Analysis of a Political Speech, p. 379

Writing a Summary

A **summary or an abstract** (*Zusammenfassung, Inhaltsangabe*) is common in all forms of writing and is aimed at **highlighting the major points** of a piece of writing and outlining the most important facts. Furthermore, it helps you to obtain a better **orientation and understanding of the structure and contents of a text** which you need for additional analysis and evaluation.

General aspects

A summary ...

- gives the **most relevant facts** and the overall meaning of a text,
- must not contain your own thoughts and opinions,
- begins with an **introductory sentence,**
- is about 150 – 200 words long, depending on the length of the text that is to be summed up,
- **must not contain direct speech or quotations,**
- should be **factual,**
- leaves out irrelevant details,
- should usually be written in the **present tense,**
- should present the events in **chronological order** (→ no suspense),
- closes with a sentence that **sums up the main message of the text and its intention,**
- prepares the analysis part of your composition – it must not analyse the text but **strictly focuses on depicting** *(wiedergeben)* **the text** in your own words.

Your composition

Before writing:

- **Underline** the most relevant aspects and facts given in the text.
- **Divide the text into paragraphs**/thematic units and **find a suitable headline** for each paragraph.
- Make sure that you understand everything – if necessary, **crosscheck the meaning of words** or expressions in your dictionary.
- Do not underline every detail but focus on the **most important information/striking keywords.**

While writing:

- **Use the present tense** for your text.
- Write an **introductory sentence** which answers the **w-questions** and informs about the **source** of the text: author, title of the text, type of text, topic, place and year of publication, information about whether the text is an excerpt or was abbreviated.
- Do not copy the words and expressions used in the text but **use your own words and/or try to find synonyms to paraphrase** the main aspects. Use your dictionary to find alternative formulations.
- **Do not quote** from the text and **do not use direct speech** (!).
- **Do not refer to any specific lines** in the text.
- **Use formulations** to state what the text/author writes about or wants to express.
  Example: *The author makes remarks on ...; The author expresses his/her concerns about ...*
- Be careful to not just follow the chronology of the text, but **restructure it and focus on key aspects/focal points** (*Schwerpunkte*).
- **Do not use short forms.**
- **Use standard English** for your summary even though the text you are to summarize may be written in informal English or in verse, etc.

After writing:

- **Proofread your text** and check for grammatical correctness, punctuation and spelling. Make sure that you have used the **present tense.**

Writing a CV and a Letter of Application

your own address in the top right-hand corner

Tel: +49 (0)221 123456

Gartenweg 20
54327 Köln
Germany

date of writing

15 May 2016

reference number or keywords related to the position

Your ref: TBS/1234

address in full, as on envelope

Roots & Shoots
The Jane Goodall Institute
1595 Spring Hill Road
Vienna, VA 22182
USA

Use "Madam or Sir" if you do not know the name of the person.

Dear Madam or Sir,

introductory paragraph; reason for your letter; start with a capital letter

I am writing to apply for an internship at your institute.
Please find enclosed a copy of my CV.

body of letter; your qualifications; reason(s) why you want the job

Since graduating from St. Thomas Grammar School, I have gained experience in working with various environmental groups as well as in a zoo. I have also had the opportunity of working in an animal shelter and have experienced the importance of giving more to these animals than just medical treatment.

I would welcome the opportunity to work in one of your camps and look forward to your response.

If you started with "Dear Madam or Sir," end with "Yours faithfully".
If you know the surname, e.g. "Dear Ms. Brown," end with "Yours sincerely".

Yours faithfully

Sign your name and print it in full afterwards.

T. Müller

Tobias Müller

Enc. CV

Curriculum Vitae

Name	Tobias Müller
Address	Gartenweg 20 54327 Köln (Cologne)
Telephone No.	+49(0)221 123456
Mobile	+49(0)1723456789
Email	tobymueller@web.de
Nationality	German
Date/place of birth	25 July 1999, Cologne
Profile	a highly motivated and creative Graduate from a Grammar School with experience in animal care
Education	
2009 – 2017	Grammar School (A-Level)
2005 – 2009	Elementary School
Employment/	practical work as animal caretaker/ keeper in a zoo and at an animal shelter
Interests	judo, tennis, music

- only refer to your most relevant qualifications or skills
- if possible, you can include references (= people that can be contacted in order to give a judgment of your qualifications, experience, character, etc.)
- enclose photocopies of relevant certificates
- begin with the most recent employment/qualification and work backwards

Tips on vocab

I noted with interest … ■ I am writing in response to … ■ With reference to your advertisement in … ■ As you can see from my CV, … ■ I am currently studying at … ■ Having gained a degree in …, ■ This position interests me because … ■ I would be grateful for the opportunity to … ■ I have extensive experience in … ■ I am available for an interview … ■ If you consider my qualifications to be suitable …

Writing a Letter to the Editor

A letter to the editor is a **formal letter** that has **different functions**:
A reader …
… **responds to an article** in a newspaper/magazine/on the Internet he/she has read and **states his/her opinion on the matter**.
… **expresses his/her criticism or support** of a stance taken by the publication.
… responds to **another reader's letter** to the editor.
… **comments on a current issue** or a problem of public interest.
… **remarks on materials** that have appeared in a (previous) publication.
… **corrects** a perceived **error or misinterpretation**.

Tips for writing

- **Read the publication thoroughly** and underline/highlight key phrases and the most relevant parts.
- Pay attention to the **focus and the standardized terminology** used in **your assignment**, e.g. *Write a letter to the editor and assess the author's view of immigration to Great Britain.*
- **Name the article** you are responding to in the first sentence of the body of your letter or in a subject line.
- Include your **name, address and e-mail address (phone number)** at the top of your letter to give the editor the opportunity to verify your identity.
- Since your letter may be edited, **get to the point and be concise** (*knapp und präzise*) and focused. Do not write a lengthy argument.
- Limit your letter to **two or three paragraphs**:
  a) **Introduce** the subject matter and briefly state your opinion/objection (*Einwand*).
  b) Include a few sentences (**arguments, examples**) to support your view.
  c) End with a **concluding remark** and a clever, punchy (*ausdrucksstark*) line.
  Keep in mind that a letter to the editor is a formal letter. Use **Standard English** and write in **a matter-of-fact style**, using clearly structured arguments. Avoid informal and insulting (*beleidigend*) or offensive language and do not be overly emotional.
  Start your letter like this:
  Dear Editor/Sir/Madam,
  I am writing in response to the article …
- **If you do not want your name published**, state so clearly, e.g. in the last paragraph.
  Example: *Please note, I do not want my (full) name published with this letter.*
- **Proofread** your letter to check for poor grammar and spelling errors.
- **Submit** your letter by e-mail (if possible) to enable the editor to cut and paste your letter.

Tips on vocab

to have a good/positive opinion about sb./sth. ■ to (strongly) (dis-)agree with sb. about sth. ■ to approve of sb./sth. (*billigen*) ■ to advise sb. to do sth. (*raten, beraten*) ■ to acknowledge that … (*anerkennen*) ■ to show one's solidarity with … ■ to argue in support of sb./sth. (*sich aussprechen für …*) ■ to take a negative view of sb./sth. ■ to refute sb.'s arguments (*entkräften, widerlegen*) ■ to express criticism of … ■ to call sth. into question ■ to express doubts about sb./sth. (*jdn./etw. anzweifeln*) ■ to protest against ■ to have reservations about (*Vorbehalte haben*) ■ to disassociate oneself from sb./sth. (*sich distanzieren von*) ■ to make remarks on ■ to make observations about ■ to maintain/claim that … (*behaupten*)

→ Focus on Skills, Writing a Comment and a Review, p. 393
→ Focus on Skills, Writing a Formal Letter, p. 396

Connectives and Adverbs

In order to improve your style and speak and write more fluently, you should employ connectives and adverbs. **Try to vary the beginnings of your sentences** and use sub-clauses to express your opinion and thoughts in a more diversified way.

listing/order first, second, third; firstly, secondly, thirdly; for one thing ... (and) for another (thing); to begin with; to start with; initially/in the first place; then; finally; to conclude[1]; last but not least	**adding/reinforcing**[11] also; as well; too; furthermore; moreover; then; in addition to; above all; what is more; again; equally; generally speaking
comparison/similarity[2] equally; likewise; similarly; in the same way; compared to ...; both; but while the first ...; although; though	**summary/conclusion/consequence** then; all in all; to sum up; in conclusion; accordingly; as a result; briefly; consequently; generally speaking; hence; it follows that; taking everything into account; thus; therefore
exemplification[3] namely; for example (e. g.); for instance; that is (i. e.); that is to say	**reformulation** or rather; to put it another way; in other words
alternative alternatively; on the other hand	**contrast** on the contrary; in contrast; by contrast; on the one hand ... on the other hand; compared to; although; likewise
concession[4] besides; however; nevertheless; still; though; in spite of that; on the other hand; despite this; admittedly[5]	**reason and purpose** as; because of; consequently; for this/that reason; hence; in order to; on account of; since; so; that explains why; this is why; therefore
emphasis[6] as a matter of fact; at any rate; clearly; evidently[7]; ideally; undoubtedly[8]	**condition** as long as; even if; if; in any case; on the condition that; provided that; unless
your own opinion from my point of view; in my opinion; in my view; the way I see it; to my mind; to my way of thinking	**an opposite point of view** alternatively; but; despite/in spite of (the fact); except for; however; in contrast to; instead of; nonetheless; on the contrary
reference[9] **to something/someone** according to; as for; the former; the latter; with reference to; referring to; with regard to; concerning	**assumption**[12] assuming that; given that; presumably; probably; granted that; allegedly[13]; seemingly; on the face of it; supposedly[14]
toning down[10] **arguments** a little (worrying); almost; fairly; hardly; more or less; somewhat; on second thought; at first sight	**emphasizing arguments** actually; absolutely; (not ...) at all; badly (needed); completely; extremely; entirely; indeed; not in the least; perfectly; really; seriously; thoroughly; totally; utterly[15]; very

[1] **to conclude sth. from sth.** *schlussfolgern* – [2] **similarity** the state of being like sth./sb. but not exactly the same – [3] **exemplification** illustration, giving an example – [4] **concession** *Zugeständnis* – [5] **admittedly** accepting that sth. is true – [6] **to put emphasis on sth.** to stress sth. – [7] **evidently** clearly, obviously – [8] **undoubtedly** *zweifellos* – [9] **reference** sth. that you connect or relate to sth. else – [10] **to tone down sth.** to express an opinion in a less extreme or offensive way – [11] **to reinforce sth.** to make a feeling/an idea stronger – [12] **assumption** *Annahme, Vermutung* – [13] **allegedly** *angeblich* – [14] **supposedly** *angeblich, vermutlich* – [15] **utterly** totally, very much

Literary Terms

This glossary of literary terms is designed to help you understand the meaning of terms used in connection with literature or the analysis of literary texts.
Important terms marked with the asterisk symbol (*) throughout the Students' Book can be found here in thematic order.

Fiction/fictional texts

a) narrative texts (e. g. novel, short story, fable)

- **structure and plot**

allegory [ˈæləgəri]	a text that may be understood on a superficial or factual level and a deeper, more philosophical level; the characters are often personifications of abstract ideas (e. g. evil, love, etc.)
climax	the moment when the conflict is most intense
conflict	a struggle between different forces which produces suspense
dénouement [ˌdeɪˈnuːmɑ̃ː] (resolution)	the final outcome, when the conflict is resolved
epigram	a short, witty statement which may be written in prose or verse
exposition	the very beginning of a fictional text which introduces the main character(s), the theme, the setting and the atmosphere
falling action	a reduction of suspense
flashback	an episode/event which interrupts the chronological order of a text and goes back in time to show what happened earlier
foreshadowing	hinting at later events
internal conflict	a struggle between two opposing views/values which takes place in a character's mind
(leit)motif [ˈlaɪtməʊtiːf]	a theme/expression/object which recurs throughout the text and which refers to a certain person, situation or atmosphere
open ending	the conflict remains unresolved → the reader is left to reflect on possible resolutions
plot	the author's selection and structure of action as a set of events connected by cause and effect that are meant to create suspense
rising action	an increase in suspense
setting	place and time of a story/play
surprise ending	a sudden and unexpected turn of fortune/action
suspense	a feeling of tension/expectation
tension	the emotional strain caused by a conflict

- **narration**

acting time	the time from the beginning to the end of an episode in a text, this is usually longer than the narrating time because the writer can describe the passing of years in just a sentence; *erzählte Zeit*
interior monologue	a technique used within the stream of consciousness; a special kind of scenic presentation, often not in chronological order
mode of presentation – panoramic presentation – scenic presentation	the way the writer narrates events; *Darstellungsart* – the narrator tells the story as a condensed series of events, summarizing in a few sentences what happens over a longer period of time – the narrator shows an event in detail as it occurs, using dialogue, depicting thoughts and emotions, describing a scene, etc.

narrating time (= reading time)	the time it takes to relate an episode in a text (= reading time); it depends on the mode of presentation; *Erzählzeit*
narrator – omniscient [ɒmˈnɪsiənt] narrator – third-person narrator – first-person narrator – witness/observer narrator – objective/reliable – subjective/unreliable	person who tells the story (*not* the author!) – a narrator who seems to know everything – a narrator who stands outside the story and describes events in the third person – a narrator who is a character in a story; this is a limited point of view – a narrator who is a character in a story (protagonist or minor character) – a narrator who the reader can trust – a narrator who the reader is critical of
point of view/viewpoint – unlimited point of view – limited point of view	the perspective from which the characters, topics and events are presented (*not* the author!) – the reader can examine the action/characters from various angles – e. g. a first-person narrator who only has limited insight into the action/characters
stream of consciousness [ˈkɒnʃəsnəs]	the presentation of experience through the mind of one character in a text

b) drama (any work meant to be performed on stage or as a film)

act	the major division of a drama; an act consists of scenes
comedy	a drama which deals with a (light) topic in a more amusing way; it always has a happy ending
comic relief	a comic episode in a serious drama which aims at relieving tension by amusing the audience
dialogue	two or more people speaking to each other in a text
monologue	an extended speech by one character in a text; it might address other characters or the audience
one-act play	a short drama consisting of only one act
play	any dramatic work intended to be presented on stage, in film or on TV
scene	a subdivision in a drama
setting	the place and/or time in which an action takes place
short play	a short drama which takes about 30 minutes to perform
soliloquy [səˈlɪləkwi]	a speech delivered by a character alone on stage (used to reveal the character's thoughts, feelings or motives to the audience)
stage directions	a playwright's notes about how the drama is to be performed
tragedy	a drama in which the protagonist undergoes a series of misfortunes until he or she finally falls; the hero(ine) has to experience a reversal of fortune, i. e. from happiness to misery

- **characters**

antagonist	the opponent of the protagonist
anti-hero(ine)	a protagonist who does not have the qualities of a typical hero, and is either more like an ordinary person or is morally bad and does not fit into society
characterization – direct characterization – indirect characterization	the way of presenting a character in a text – the narrator or another character describes the character; alternatively, the character may describe him- or herself – the reader/audience learns about the character through action and dialogue
flat character	a minor character who does not develop in the course of the action
hero(ine) [ˈhɪərəʊ; ˈherəʊɪn]	the principal male or female character in a drama; he/she is usually in conflict with another character, fate and/or society
minor character	a character of less importance for the course of the action

protagonist (= main character)	the main character in a drama/play
round character	a character who develops in the course of action and therefore has the ability to change

c) poetry (literature that has a certain pattern, such as rhyme, rhythm, sentence structure)

anapaest ['ænəpi:st]	metrical foot of three syllables (unstressed – unstressed – stressed): e. g. *underneath* – –'–
concrete poem	a type of poem in which the words form a shape or picture
connotation	additional meaning of a word beyond its dictionary definition, for example, due to the associations that are formed through personal experience
dactyl ['dæktɪl]	metrical foot of three syllables (stressed – unstressed – unstressed): e. g. *merrily* '– – –
denotation	the actual definition of a word (its dictionary definition)
end rhyme	a rhyme at the end of two lines
enjambement [ɪn'dʒæmbmənt] (= run-on line)	a sentence which runs from one line to another without a pause/break
foot	a group of stressed and unstressed syllables within a line of poetry which forms a metrical unit
free verse	a poem written without a particular rhyme scheme or regular metre
iamb ['aɪæm(b)]	metrical foot of two syllables (unstressed – stressed) e. g. *become* –'–
imagery ['ɪmɪdʒəri]	term for the use of images created by words that are used to appeal to the reader's imagination → often metaphors and/or similes
line	a structural unit in a poem; it is usually classified by a certain number of feet
metre	the regular rhythmic patterns of a poem/the arrangement of words according to stressed and unstressed syllables
poem	a composition which contains a structured line sequence and a special arrangement of words, a special rhythm, the use of imagery
rhyme	using words that repeat syllable sounds
rhyme scheme [ski:m] – rhyming couplets – alternate rhyme – embracing rhyme	the arrangement of rhymes in a poem – two consecutive lines with the same rhyme: aa bb – lines with the rhyme scheme: ab ab – lines with the rhyme scheme: abba
rhythm	the arrangement of stressed or unstressed syllables in writing
sonnet ['sɒnɪt] – quatrain – couplet	poem consisting of 14 lines, usually written in iambic pentameter; e. g. the Shakespearean sonnet consists of three quatrains and a couplet with the rhyme scheme abab cdcd efef gg – a stanza of four lines (e. g. in a sonnet) – two successive rhyming lines (e. g. at the end of a sonnet)
speaker	the fictional person who is imagined as saying the text of a poem (*not* identical with the poet!)
stanza	a major division in a poem consisting of several lines
trochee ['trəʊki:]	metrical foot of two syllables (stressed – unstressed) e. g. *happen* '– –
verse	a stanza in a poem or song; poetry written in metre

d) lyrics/songs (in addition to the aspects mentioned under *poetry*, also consider these devices)

genre of music	a particular type or style of music, e. g. Jazz, Rap, Funk, Heavy Metal, Protest Song, etc.
instrumentation	selection and combination of the musical instruments that are used in a song, e. g. electronic instruments, percussion, violin, etc.
onomatopoeia [ˌɒnəˌmætəˈpiːə]	words that imitate a sound associated with the thing being named, e. g. buzz, cuckoo, hum, etc.
registers of English	the words, style and grammar used, e. g. poetic, formal, slang, non-standard, in order to express a certain message or set of values
rhythm, beat	the regular pattern of long and short notes in music
vocals	the part of a piece of music that is sung, for example, by a lead singer, a choir, etc.

Non-fiction/non-fictional texts

- **text type**

argumentation	an argumentative text deals with ideas and/or controversy; it expresses a clear opinion and gives reasons/arguments to support it
description	a descriptive text aims at describing things/developments, etc.
exposition	in an expository text, the writer explains a rather complex problem in a precise and objective way
instruction	an instructive text gives advice about a particular matter; it typically includes commands and recommendations

- **text form**

comment	a kind of argumentation in which the writer/speaker gives his or her opinion on a certain topic
editorial	a comment, usually written by the chief editor, that gives his or her opinion on a certain topic of common interest
essay (= literary appreciation)	a text in which the writer expresses his or her personal views on a certain topic; it usually follows a certain compositional pattern, i. e. the use of unity and balance (= statement – development – conclusion)
feature story	a report written to arouse human interest, typically by concentrating on an individual case that many readers can identify with
interview	a dialogue in which someone, usually a journalist, asks another person questions on a topic of common interest; may appear in a newspaper, on TV, etc.
leader/leading article	the most important or prominent news story in a magazine/newspaper
letter to the editor	a letter written by a reader to the editor of a magazine/newspaper in order to express a personal opinion on some topic (→ comment)
news story	a report based on facts and background information that deals with a topical event that the public is interested in
report	a text that aims at answering the "five w's": who?, what?, when?, where? and why?, which can be checked and verified by the reader
review	a short critical evaluation of a work of art (literature, film, etc.)
scientific report	a text written for scientific purposes, usually containing many technical terms (→ report)
sermon	a religious discourse delivered as part of a church service
speech – political speech – laudatory [ˈlɔːdətəri] speech	a formal talk or an address delivered to an audience – an address delivered for a political purpose, e. g. the inaugural address of a president or a crisis speech – a speech delivered in order to express praise, e. g. when sb. is awarded a prize

- **structural devices**

column [ˈkɒləm]	*Textspalte*; mostly used in newspapers and magazines
conclusion	the main idea is often re-stated here or the main aspects of the text may be recapped (*kurz zusammenfassen*) in summary
heading/headline	a caption that is written above a text to arouse the reader's interest
introduction	lead-in to the topic, often by referring to the "five w's" in order to attract the reader's interest and lure him or her into the story
line of argument(ation)	the way different reasons are gradually developed and structured to convince a reader of a particular point of view (→ train of thought)
main part	the part of the text in which the writer demonstrates a topic/explains his or her intention/discusses a topic or problem, etc.
paragraph	a division of a text dealing with a particular idea that begins on a new line
passage	a short extract from a text that may consist of several paragraphs
subheading	a caption that subdivides a text into logical sections
theme/topic/subject	a central idea in a text which binds all of its elements together
train of thought	the way a series of ideas is gradually developed and structured

- **rhetorical/stylistic devices**

alliteration	the repetition of a sound, usually a consonant, at the beginning of neighbouring words
allusion	indirect reference to a famous event, person or piece of literature
anaphora [əˈnæfərə]	successive sentences starting with the same word
antithesis [ænˈtɪθəsɪs]	contrast; opposing words, phrases, views, characters, etc.
choice of words	the decision to use a particular word based on such aspects as style, register, connotation, etc.
euphemism [ˈjuːfəmɪzəm]	using polite expressions for sth. unpleasant
exaggeration/hyperbole [haɪˈpɜːbəli]	making sth./sb. sound better, more exciting, dangerous, etc. than in reality
image	a word intended to appeal to the reader's imagination and to bring a new perception to an object (→ figurative language, e. g. metaphors, similes)
irony	saying the opposite of what you mean
(leit)motif	a theme, expression or object which recurs throughout a text and which refers to a certain person, situation or atmosphere
manner of speaking	a style that is typical of a particular person, e. g. politician or worker, etc.
metaphor [ˈmetəfə(r)]	poetic comparison without using *like* or *as* (e. g. an ocean of love)
paradox	seeming impossible at first glance but recognized as true on second thought
parallelism	repeating similar or identical words/phrases in neighbouring lines/sentences/paragraphs
personification	presenting ideas/objects/animals as persons (e. g. a smiling moon)
pun	a play on words
reference	a connection to sth. else (→ allusion)
register/level of speech	the words, style and grammar used, e. g. formal/informal English, colloquialisms, slang, non-standard English, etc.; such aspects are typically adjusted according to the addressees
repetition	deliberately using a word/phrase more than once
rhetorical question	question to which the answer is obvious or to which no answer is possible/expected
simile [ˈsɪməli]	comparison using *like* or *as*

symbol	sth. concrete (object, character, event) standing for sth. abstract (cross – Christianity; horseshoe – luck)
syntax ['sɪntæks] – hypotactical structure – paratactical structure	arrangement of words in a phrase/sentence/text – rather complicated and long sentences, involving sub-clauses – a rather simple sentence structure, mostly consisting of main clauses, sometimes connected with the conjunctions *and, or*
tone	the manner or mood, e. g. macabre, optimistic, etc.

The media

agony aunt/uncle	a person who writes for a newspaper or magazine giving advice in reply to people's letters about their personal problems
feature story/human interest	a story or part of a story in a newspaper that people find interesting because it describes the feelings, experiences, etc. of the people involved
front page – cover story – special feature – leading article/editorial	the first page of a newspaper where the most important news is printed – the main story in a magazine that goes with the picture shown on the front cover – a special article or report on sb./sth. (*Sonderbeitrag*) – an important article in a newspaper that expresses the editor's opinion about a news item or a particular issue
headline	the title of a newspaper article printed in large letters, especially at the top of the front page
Internet – blog – chatroom – website – web forum	an international computer network connecting other networks and computers – a personal record that sb. puts on their website giving an account of their activities and their opinions, and discussing other sites on the Internet, events, etc. – a site on the Internet where people can communicate with each other in real time – a set of interconnected webpages, generally located on the same server, and prepared and maintained by a person, group or organization – a site on the Internet where people can exchange opinions and ideas on a particular issue
letter to the editor	a (mostly critical) letter written by the reader of a newspaper/magazine in response to an article or a story
masthead ['ma:sthed]	– the name of the newspaper at the top of the front page – the part of a newspaper or a news website which gives details about the people who work on it or other information about it
television/radio – broadcasting company/ corporation – channel – programme – commercial (break) – documentary [ˌdɒkju'mentri] – factual report – feature film – live coverage – soap (opera)	 – a company whose business is to make and transmit radio and TV programmes – a television station (*Programm*) – sth. that you watch on TV or listen to on the radio (*Sendung*) – an advertisement on the radio or on television – a film, radio or television programme giving facts about something – a report based on facts (*Tatsachenbericht*) – *Spielfilm* – sth. broadcast/sent while the event is actually happening, not pre-recorded (*Direktübertragung*) – a story about the life and problems of a group of fictional people that is broadcast every day or several times a week on TV or radio
the press – quality newspapers/ broadsheets – tabloids/popular newspapers – magazines/periodicals	 – usually larger formats that have in-depth articles and present facts that are based on serious research – usually smaller formats that are more sensationalist – periodical publications financed by advertising; printed in colour on quality paper

Films/movies

documentary (film)	a film, television or radio programme that gives detailed factual information about a particular subject
docusoap	a supposedly unscripted television programme that shows what happens in the daily life of real people (= reality TV)
feature film	a full-length film that has a story, which is acted out by professional actors, and is usually shown in a cinema (*Spielfilm*)
screenplay/script – shooting script	the words that are written down for actors to say in a film, and the instructions that tell them what they should do – a script with additional information/details given by the director (e. g. drafts, technical details, arrows to indicate how to move the camera, etc.)
slug lines	numbered lines between the dialogue lines that indicate a change in location and time (e. g. INT, EXT); each slug line begins a new scene
storyboard	a graphic organizer that displays images in sequence (like a picture story) in order to help the film crew to know where the cameras are to be positioned or where/how a character has to stand/move, etc.

Vocabulary and Phrases for Text Analysis

When you are asked to analyse and interpret a text, you should express yourself precisely and appropriately. Therefore, it is important to use a specific terminology that employs **technical terms** (e. g. stylistic devices) and a variety of formulations that make your text more fluent and less repetitive.

The following words and phrases are related to the most relevant aspects.

introduction	**the author**
• The text deals with/is about … • The theme of the text is … • The text is composed of/consists of … • Three/two … different parts can be distinguished … • The first part runs from line … to line … • At the beginning of the text, … • The author begins by saying … • At the end of the text,/Finally,/Lastly, … • The first part forms the introduction … • The main/central/principal idea is … • In the conclusion, the author states that … • In the final part, the author …	• The author thinks/says/believes that … • According to the author, …/In his/her view … • The author illustrates his/her point of view with … • The author makes a comment on … • The author is convinced that … • The author's judgments are (un)realistic/not objective/unfounded/well-founded … • The reader can sympathize with the author's view on … • The author expresses doubts/questions … • The author makes remarks on … • The intention/aim/objective of the author is … • The author portrays believable characters. • The author gives a detailed/vague description of …
the text/plot/story	**the characters**
• The story is told from the perspective of … • The plot is set in … • The text is written in an ironic tone. • The text contains comical elements. • The setting of the action is unreal/imaginary. • The action becomes more/less intense … • The situation seems quite absurd… • Suspense is created because/by … • The ending of the story is believable …	• The main/principal character in the story is … • The author characterizes him/her as … • He has many positive traits … • His behaviour is marked by … • Another essential quality is … • She shows her superiority by saying that … • He is characterized as … • The protagonist lacks … • As far as his outward appearance is concerned, … • She plays an important/a secondary role …
the structure	**the action**
• The exposition gives information about … • The first scene introduces … • The starting point for the action is … • The conflict reaches its climax in … • The turning point is indicated by … • The crisis is in scene … • In the last scene, … • This play/story has a happy/tragic ending.	• The action takes place in … • The action develops in … stages … • The action progresses fast … • The scene contains a flashback. • The action is interrupted by … • This is one of the central scenes … • The development of the action is slowed down by …

Note: Explanations of the respective technical terms can be found in the Literary Terms section, pp. 405 ff.

purpose (of texts)	vocabulary
• The author wants to arouse the reader's interest. • The text appeals to … • He/She tries to manipulate … • He/She wants the reader to become aware of … • The text addresses young/poor/… people … • It is the author's objective to create a feeling of … • The author attempts to influence the reader by … • The advert suggests to the reader that …	• The vocabulary contains many colloquial expressions/ technical terms … • This word/term expresses fear … • This word has a negative meaning/negative associations … • This phrase suggests … • These phrases are examples of spoken language. • The choice of words gives the text its romantic/ technical/… character. • These expressions are typical of …
criticizing the author	**further useful expressions**
• I (dis-)agree with the author on … • I do not understand why he/she … • I consider it to be wrong/difficult to … • This … cannot be taken seriously … • I would like to comment on … • It must be pointed out that … • This statement contradicts his/her view of … • There is a contradiction in … • It goes without saying that … • It is essential that … • This raises the question as to why he/she … • What really matters is … • This problem has nothing to do with … • This is of no importance/significance for … • As far as … is concerned, … • From this point of view, … • Generally speaking, … • As a matter of fact, … • In theory, …, but in reality, …	• To give an explanation for … • The author pretends to know … • The author describes the characteristics of … • The article is based on … • The author makes an allusion to … • This sentence reveals the true character of … • He/She appeals to emotions rather than … • He/She quotes some experts as an example of … • The article relates … to … • The text conveys the impression that … • The writer establishes a relationship between … • The author's theses are … • He supports his thesis with … • Her outlook on life is … • He/She takes a positive/negative view of … • The author generalizes about … • This is a great simplification of …

➔ When you analyse or interpret a text, you should use **Standard English**.

➔ You should generally use the **present tense** when you describe, explain or analyse specific aspects of the text.

➔ Be careful not to imitate the tone or the language of the text – when you write about a text written in colloquial English, you should still use Standard English in order to appear **impersonal and objective**.

➔ Try to **vary the beginnings of your sentences** by employing different connectives.

➔ Even when you express your personal opinion about a text/the author, etc., your choice of words should be appropriate and respectful. It can be helpful *not* to begin sentences with "I …" or "I think …" but to **focus on the text, the author**, etc. (e.g. *The article gives the impression that …, The author seems to intend to …*). This appears much more impersonal and academic.

➔ **Do not overdo it by being too formal** or stilted – your text should reflect your view and stance on the matter.

➔ Be careful **not to use short forms** (e.g. don't, doesn't, there's, haven't, you're, etc.) in the tasks that are related to the **comprehension, analysis and comment/evaluation** of texts. They should only be used in creative writing tasks, e.g. in an informal conversation, diary entry, or interior monologue, when you are asked to express your thoughts in a rather informal way. However, when you write e.g. a letter to the editor, you should use formal English.

Note: Explanations of the respective technical terms can be found in the Literary Terms section, pp. 405 ff.

Research

Before you start your research, you should check these aspects:

1. Read the assignment carefully – make sure that you understand what *exactly* your research task is.
2. Start a file in which you collect all your findings and research results.
3. Formulate research questions and aims.
4. Collect keywords and topics that can be used for your research.

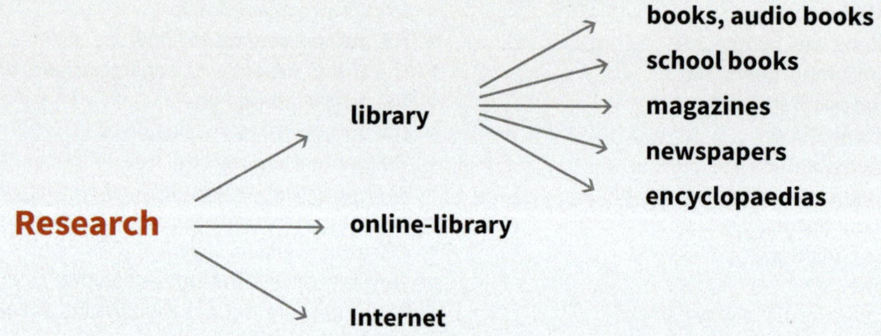

Indicators to check the quality/validity/reliability of the websites used

- The website has an author.
- The website has an impressum/copyright.
- The author is an expert in the respective subject matter/the author is recommended by other experts.
- The website is published by or related to a well-known organization, university, public institution, etc.
- The information provided on the website is relevant and up-to-date.
- The intention of the website is obvious; there is no hidden advertising or links to commercial websites (→ integrity, respectability).
- If there is any advertising, it is clearly distinguishable from the factual content of the website.
- The text is written in Standard English (few or no orthographic mistakes, colloquialisms, etc.).
- The author refers to his/her sources.
- There is more than *one* opinion.
- The views/opinions of others are respected.
- Statistical data and/or visuals are related to the text and are relevant (not just decorative elements).
- There are further links to other trustworthy websites/suggested reading.
- The website is designed appropriately for teenagers/children (in terms of contents, colours, graphics, animation etc.); it displays appropriate and functional pictures, videos, audio samples, etc.
- The website has a clear structure.
- The content of the website and the information given can be double-checked on other websites; there are references/links to other authors and/or other websites.
- The target group and the purpose of the website (e. g. commercial, educational, etc.) can be clearly identified.

Citing sources

In order to demonstrate the quality and credibility of your work, you need to name the sources that you have used. There are different citation styles. Here are some examples of how to cite different sources correctly:

Books

title of the book in italics

publishing company

page(s) where the quotation can be found

***Americanah* by Chimamanda Ngozi Adichie. Alfred A. Knopf, New York 2014, pp. 21 f.**

first name of author or editor (ed.)

surname

place and year of publiction

Articles from magazines/newspapers

title of the article in quotation marks

name of magazine or newspaper in italics

"Globalization in Reverse" by Rana Foroohar. *Time*, 7 April 2014, p. 9

first name of the author

surname

date of publication

page(s) where the article can be found

Internet

title of the article in quotation marks

URL[1] (name of the website)

"Huge Survey Reveals Seven Social Classes in UK". www.bbc.com/news/uk-22007058, 3 April 2013 [17.12.2014]

publication date of the article

date when you printed/used/quoted the website (*Abrufdatum*) in square brackets

Films

title of the film in italics

film company

***The Butler*. Directed by Lee Daniels. The Weinstein Company, USA 2014**

director of the film

place and year of release

[1] **URL** (*abbr.*) uniform/universal resource locator (the address of a World Wide Web page)

Acknowledgements

Images

|action press, Hamburg: Landmark Media Press and Picture 4…
images, Abingdon/Oxfordshire: Alex, Aaron 148 u.; Barritt, Peter…
torical Picture Archive 136; Green, Leigh 201; grzegorz knec 213 o.l., …
Pearson, David 309; Pictorial Press Ltd 39 m.; PRISMA ARCHIVO 145 …
Nick 21; Science History Images 39 o., 157; Stocktrek Images, Inc. 39 o…
lishing, Kansas City: AUTH © 2006 The Philadelphia Inquirer. Reprinte…
TION. All rights reserved 179. |Art Explosion, Calabasas, CA: 117, 173, 219, 2…
357, 357, 357, 357, 357, 357, 358, 393, 393, 393; ./. 309, 309. |Avenue Images…
|beck*cartoons, Leipzig: 60, 176. |Berghahn, Matthias, Bielefeld: 1, 369, 403. |B…
|Bochner, Mel, New York: Silence! 2008 ink on paper 11 x 8,5 inches 302. |Böthling, Jörg, Hamburg: visualindia.de 121. |Bulls Pressedienst GmbH, Frankfurt am Main: © Mike Peters 331. |Cagle Cartoons, Santa Barbara, CA: 2011 Daryl Cagle, msnbc.com, and PoliticalCartoons.com 132; Copyright 2008 Jeff Parker - All Rights Reserved. 138; Steve Sack 171; © 2010 Bob Englehart - All Rights Reserved 325; © 2014 Keith Knight 183; © Copyright 2003 Angel Boligan - All Rights Reserved. 180; © Randy Bish 295. |Canary Pete Images, Opglabbeek: 360. |Cartagena, Alejandro, Monterrey, Nuevo Leon: 175, 175. |Cartoon Movement, Amsterdam: © Miguel Villalba Sánchez (Elchicotriste) 80. |CartoonStock.com, Bath: 178, 291, 291, 334, 360, 376, 387, 395; Ralph Hagen 391. |Courtesy of Pest Control Office - Banksy, London: 128. |Danziger, Jeff, New York: 267. |David Lynch Interview Project: 130, 130, 130, 130, 130, 130, 130, 130, 130, 130. |ddp images GmbH, Hamburg: CAMERA PRESS/Norrington, Nigel 337; Capital Pictures/FB 165; interTOPICS /Evening Standard 83. |Deutsches Museum, München: Archiv, BN38583 39. |DIE ZEIT, Hamburg: Nora Coenenberg: Grafik "Eine gefährliche Welt" in: DIE ZEIT 29/2011 248; Wieslaw Smetek: Illustration "OH MY GOD!" / DIE ZEIT 47/2016 208. |Domke, Franz-Josef, Hannover: 27, 27, 27, 49, 50, 55, 62, 62, 65, 65, 66, 66, 73, 81, 91, 92, 114, 116, 118, 122, 131, 151, 152, 164, 180, 185, 188, 195, 198, 212, 228, 231, 236, 237, 240, 251, 267, 269, 270, 283, 287, 287, 287, 288, 294, 311, 311, 346, 348, 380, 380, 380, 424. |Ebert, Nik, Mönchengladbach: 88, 285. |Edelbrock, Iris, Viersen: 16, 16, 28, 136, 345. |Evans, Malcom, Auckland: 64. |ExxonMobil Central Europe Holding GmbH, Hannover: 265. |Focus Photo- u. Presseagentur GmbH, Hamburg: elliott erwitt/Magnum Photos 167; Jonas Bendiksen/MagnumPhotos 119, 120; Tinka und Frank Dietz 191. |Fotofinder GmbH, Berlin: The Art Archive 117. |fotolia.com, New York: Bob Rannells 358; jpegwiz 390; kraska 389; Lim, Cecilia 177; niroworld 325; Pixel Embargo 401; sguk 172; wwwebmeister 172. |Getty Images, München: AFP/MacDougall, John 297; Bettmann/CORBIS 160, 166, 168; Burt G. Phillips/Museum of the City of New York 169; DIBYANGSHU SARKAR/AFP 96; INDRANIL MUKHERJEE/AFP 124; Irving Browning/The New York Historical Society 48; VINCENZO PINTO/AFP 52. |Granlund, Dave, Waconia MN: www.davegranlund.com 187, 221, 295. |Hands, Phil, Wisconsin: 207. |HEART AGENCY, London: © Tom Gauld 392. |HUD Exchange, Washington, DC 20410: 192, 192. |Imago, Berlin: Xinhua 309. |Jennings, Ben: 36. |KAL/Kevin Kallaugher, Glyndon, MD: 170, 276. |Kassing, Reinhild, Kassel: 372, 372, 372, 372, 372, 372, 372, 372, 372, 373, 373, 373, 373, 373, 373, 373, 373, 373, 379, 394, 414. |laif, Köln: Casper Hedberg/Kontinent 243; Per-Anders Pettersson 245; Polaris 309. |Laux, Hans-Dieter, Bonn / Thieme, Günter, Köln: Die USA auf dem Weg in eine multiethnische Gesellschaft: Ergebnisse des Zensus 2010. In: Geographische Rundschau 63 (2), 2011, S. 64 173. |Lemay, Yannick, Quebec: 207. |Lörscher, Sebastian, Berlin: aus: Making Friends in Bangalore. Mit dem Skizzenbuch durch Indien (S. 70) Copyright © 2014 Büchergilde Gutenberg 110. |Marshall, Helen, London: TopFoto.co.uk / Mike O'Keefe Custodian of the Official Royal Image Library of HM The Queen and HRH The Duke of Edinburgh www.royalimages.co.uk 32. |Mester, Gerhard, Wiesbaden: 76, 205. |News Syndication, London: The Sun, 10 November 2016 208. |PA Photos Limited, London: Ben Birchall/PA Archive/PA Images 326. |PARS International, New York, NY 10001: "From USA Today - (Academic Permission), 5/29/2012 © 2012 Gannett-USAToday. All rights reserved. Used by permission and protected by the Copyright Laws of the United States. The printing, copying, redistribution, or retransmission of this Content without express written permission is prohibited." 259. |Pattisson, Pete, London, SE6 2NA: 254, 254. |Picture Press Bild- und Textagentur GmbH, Hamburg: Stern, 13.11.2014, S. 29 316. |Picture-Alliance GmbH, Frankfurt/M.: akg-images 217; AP Images/Kurihara, Reiri 213; AP Images/Minchillo, John 201; AP Images/Owen, Cliff 314; AP Photo 146; dpa 266; dpa-Bildarchiv 148; dpa/Downing, Larry 186; dpa/Filaktou, Evi 338; dpa/Fotoreport/Platt, Getty 148; dpa/Levitt, Helen 382; dpa/Melzer, Chris 154; dpa/Reynolds, Michael 309; dpa/Sony Pictures Releasing GmbH (Rafe Spall in: Anonymous, Regie Roland Emmerich, Columbia Pictures/Relativity Media/Centropolis Entertainment Studio Babelsberg/Anonymous Pic-

tures/Vierzehnte Babelsberg Film/Siebente Babelsberg Film/Achte Babelsberg Film,
Jane 82; empics/Findler, Rick 73 u.; empics/Jackson, Chris 309; empics/Parsons, St
Foto 37, 98; landov/Xiaolei, Niu 309; Newscom/Mayhew, Keith/Landmark Media
chives 17; zumapress.com/Brems, Louis 204. |PM Hoffmann, Leipzig: www.pmhoff
on Avon: Phillips, Duncan 57. |REUTERS, Berlin: Bensch, Fabrizio 16; Guimares, N
Post Verlagsgesellschaft mbH, Düsseldorf: aus: Rheinische Post, 18.08.2014 324
|Shutterstock.com, New York: Balazik, Robert F. 272; Legrand, Frederic-COMEO 3
London W5 4UJ: 113, 183. |SPIEGEL-Verlag Rudolf Augstein GmbH & Co. KG, Ham
46/2016 208. |stock.adobe.com, Dublin: amecold 290; Argus 378; Destina 91 o.
pixmatu 55 o.; takranik 335. |Taz Entwicklungs GmbH & Co. Medien KG, Berlin:
Paris, Berlin: Le Monde Diplomatique/taz 2011, S. 53 253; Le Monde diplomat
verstehen, was die Welt bewegt 232. |The Economist Group, London: © Th
24th, 2010) 161. |The Washington Post, New York: Nick Anderson/© 2018, The Washington Post 171. |The W
- TWC, New York City: (Forest Whitaker, Lenny Kravitz, Cuba Gooding Jr., Terrence Howard in: The Butler, Regie Lee D
Follow Through Productions/Salamander Pictures/Laura Ziskin Productions/Lee Daniels Entertainment/Pam Williams Productions/Windy Hill Pictures, USA 2013) 162; (n.n., Lenny Kravitz, Terrence Howard, Forest Whitaker in: The Butler, Regie Lee Daniels, Follow Through Productions/Salamander Pictures/Laura Ziskin Productions/Lee Daniels Entertainment/Pam Williams Productions/Windy Hill Pictures, USA 2013) 163; (The Butler, Regie Lee Daniels, Follow Through Productions/Salamander Pictures/Laura Ziskin Productions/Lee Daniels Entertainment/Pam Williams Productions/Windy Hill Pictures, USA 2013) 163, 163. |toonclipart - toonaday: 177; © Ron Leishman 399. |toonpool.com, Berlin, Castrop-Rauxel: Mark Lynch 24; Martin Erl 67; Martin Guhl 235; Rex May 345; sinann 54. |Trinity Mirror, London, E14 5AP: Daily Mirror, 10 November 2016, © Gee Vaucher 208. |ullstein bild, Berlin: 366; TopFoto 99. |VG BILD-KUNST, Bonn: 2015 142; 2017, © The Estate of Jean-Michel Basquiat 155. |Warwick Business School (WBS) - University of Warwick, Coventry: 354. |WeBritish.com: 18. |Wrong Hands / John Atkinson, Ottawa ON: "Vintage Social Networking" by John Atkinson (By granting the use of the cartoon titled "Vintage Social Networking" for one-time publication use in this textbook , I (John Atkinson) am in no way relinquishing the copyright, reproduction rights or intellectual property on this cartoon or on any other cartoon/artwork on the Wrong Hands site.) 381.

Wir arbeiten sehr sorgfältig daran, für alle verwendeten Abbildungen die Rechteinhaberinnen und Rechteinhaber zu ermitteln. Sollte uns dies im Einzelfall nicht vollständig gelungen sein, werden berechtigte Ansprüche selbstverständlich im Rahmen der üblichen Vereinbarungen abgegolten.

Texts

pp. 21 ff.: From The New York Times, May 7, 2016 © 2016 The New York Times. All rights reserved. Used by permission and protected by the Copyright Laws of the United States. The printing, copying, redistribution, or retransmission of this content without express written permission is prohibited.; p. 129: American Land Text (OT): Springsteen, Bruce Copyright: Bruce Springsteen Music Rondor Musikverlag GmbH, Berlin; pp. 132 ff.: from AMERICA AND AMERICANS AND SELECTED NONFICTION by John Steinbeck, edited by Susan Shillinglaw and Jackson J. Benson, copyright © 2002 by Elaine Steinbeck and Thomas Steinbeck. Used by permission of Viking Books, an imprint of Penguin Publishing Group, a division of Penguin Random House LLC.; pp. 142 f.: From The Essential Bogosian by Eric Bogosian. Copyright © 1994 by Eric Bogosian. Published by Theatre Communications Group. Used by permission of Theatre Communications Group.; p. 160: from A Documentary History of the United States, ed. by Richard D. Heffner, New York, Mentor, 51991, pp. 333 – 341, © Estate of Dr. Martin Luther King Jr., Atlanta; p. 174: "So Mexicans Are Taking Jobs from Americans" by Jimmy Santiago Baca, from IMMIGRANTS IN OUR OWN LAND, copyright © 1979 by Jimmy Santiago Baca. Reprinted by permission of New Directions Publishing Corp.; pp. 195 f.: From Newsweek, June 6, 2013 © 2013 IBT Media. All rights reserved. Used by permission and protected by the Copyright Laws of the United States. The printing, copying, redistribution, or retransmission of this Content without express written permission is prohibited.; p. 210 f.: From The New York Times, 11 November 2016 © 2016 The New York Times. All rights reserved. Used by permission and protected by the Copyright Laws of the United States. The printing, copying, redistribution, or retransmission of this Content without express written permission is prohibited.; pp. 274 f.: © David Rovics;

pp. 319 f.: Excerpt(s) from THE CIRCLE by Dave Eggers, copyright © 2013 by Dave Eggers. Used by permission of Alfred A. Knopf, an imprint of the Knopf Doubleday Publishing Group, a division of Penguin Random House LLC. All rights reserved.; pp. 351 f.: This information was provided by Career Centre: http://careercentre.dtwd.wa.gov.au
All other sources can be found bellow the texts.

Index